Contents

core JAVA™ 2

Volume I - Fundamentals

CAY S. HORSTMANN • GARY CORNELL

Sun Microsystems Press
A Prentice Hall Title

The publisher offers discounts on this book when ordered in bulk quantities.
For more information, contact Corporate Sales Department, Prentice Hall PTR ,
One Lake Street, Upper Saddle River, NJ 07458. Phone: 800-382-3419; FAX: 201- 236-7141.
E-mail: corpsales@prenhall.com.

Editorial/production supervision: *Navta Associates*
Project coordinator: *Anne Trowbridge*
Cover design director: *Jerry Votta*
Cover designer: *Nina Scuderi*
Cover illustration: *Karen Strelecki*
Manufacturing manager: *Alexis R. Heydt*
Marketing manager: *Debby van Dijk*
Acquisitions editor: *Gregory G. Doench*

Sun Microsystems Press:
Marketing manager: *Michael Llwyd Alread*
Publisher: *Rachel Borden*

10   9   8   7   6   5   4   3   2   1

ISBN 0-13-089468-0

Sun Microsystems Press
A Prentice Hall Title

Chapter 4

Objects and Classes, 111

Chapter 9

User Interface Components With Swing, 417

List of Tables, Code Examples, and Figures

Tables

Code Examples

Figures

Preface

To the Reader

In late 1995, the Java programming language burst onto the Internet scene and gained instant celebrity status. The promise of Java is that it will become the *universal glue* that connects users with information, whether that information comes from Web servers, databases, information providers, and any other imaginable source. Indeed Java is in a unique position to fulfill this promise. It is an extremely solidly engineered language that has gained acceptance by all major vendors, except for Microsoft. Its built-in security and safety features are reassuring both to programmers and to the users of Java programs. Java even has built-in support that makes advanced programming tasks, such as network programming, database connectivity, and multithreading, straightforward.

Since then, Sun Microsystems has released four major revisions of the Java Software Development Kit. Version 1.02, released in 1996, supported database connectivity and distributed objects. Version 1.1, released in 1997, added a robust event model, internationalization, and the Java Beans component model. Version 1.2, released at the end of 1998, has numerous enhancements, but one major improvement stands out: the "Swing" user interface toolkit that finally allows programmers to write truly portable GUI applications. Version 1.3, released in the spring of 2000, delivered many incremental improvements.

The book you have in your hand is the first volume of the fifth edition of the *Core Java* book. Each time, the book followed the release of the Java development kit as quickly as possible, and each time, we rewrote the book to take advantage of the newest Java features.

As with the previous editions of this book, we *still target serious programmers who want to put Java to work on real projects*. We still guarantee no nervous text or dancing tooth-shaped characters. We think of you, our reader, as a programmer with a solid background in a programming language. *But you do not need to know C++ or object-oriented programming*. Based on the responses we have received to the earlier editions of this book, we remain confident that experienced Visual Basic, C, or COBOL programmers will have no trouble with this book. (You don't even need any experience in building graphical user interfaces in Windows, Unix, or the Macintosh.)

What we do is assume you want to:

- Write real code to solve real problems

and

- Don't like books filled with toy examples (such as kitchen appliances or fruit trees).

You will find lots of sample code on the accompanying CD that demonstrates almost every language and library feature that we discuss. We kept the sample programs purposefully simple to focus on the major points, but, for the most part, they aren't fake and they don't cut corners. They should make good starting points for your own code.

We assume you are willing, even eager, to learn about all the advanced features that Java puts at your disposal. For example, we give you a detailed treatment of:

- Object-oriented programming

- Reflection and proxies

- Interfaces and inner classes

- The event listener model

- Graphical user interface design with the Swing UI toolkit

- Exception handling

- Stream input/output and object serialization

We *still* don't spend much time on the fun but less serious kind of Java programs whose sole purpose is to liven up your Web page. There are quite a few sources for this kind of material already—we recommend John Pew's book *Instant Java*, also published by Sun Microsystems Press/Prentice Hall.

Finally, with the explosive growth of the Java class library, a one-volume treatment of all the features of Java that serious programmers need to know is no longer possible. Hence, we decided to break the book up into two volumes. The first volume, which you hold in your hands, concentrates on the fundamental concepts of the Java language, along with the basics of user-interface programming. The second volume goes further into the enterprise features and advanced user-interface programming. It includes detailed discussions of:

- Multithreading
- Network programming
- Distributed objects
- Collection classes
- Databases
- Advanced graphics
- Advanced GUI components
- Internationalization
- Native methods
- JavaBeans

When writing a book, errors and inaccuracies are inevitable. We'd very much like to know about them. But, of course, we'd prefer to learn about each of them only once. We have put up a list of frequently asked questions, bugs fixes, and workarounds in a Web page at `http://www.horstmann.com/core-java.html`. Strategically placed at the end of the FAQ (to encourage you to read through it first) is a form you can use to report bugs and suggest improvements. Please don't be disappointed if we don't answer every query or if we don't get back to you immediately. We do read all e-mail and appreciate your input to make future editions of this book clearer and more informative.

We hope that you find this book enjoyable and helpful in your Java programming.

About This Book

Chapter 1 gives an overview of the capabilities of Java that set it apart from other programming languages. We explain what the designers of the language set out to do and to what extent they succeeded. Then, we give a short history of how Java came into being and how it has evolved.

In Chapter 2, we tell you how to install Java and the companion software for this book from the CD-ROM onto your computer. Then we guide you through compiling and running three typical Java programs, a console application, a graphical application, and an applet.

Chapter 3 starts the discussion of the Java language. In this chapter, we cover the basics: variables, loops, and simple functions. If you are a C or C++ programmer, this is smooth sailing because the syntax for these language features is essentially the same as in C. If you come from a non-C background such as Visual Basic or COBOL, you will want to read this chapter carefully.

Object-oriented programming (OOP) is now in the mainstream of programming practice, and Java is completely object oriented. Chapter 4 introduces encapsulation, the first of two fundamental building blocks of object orientation, and the Java language mechanism to implement it, that is, classes and methods. In addition to the rules of the Java language, we also give advice on sound OOP design. Finally, we cover the marvelous `javadoc` tool that formats your code comments as a set of hyperlinked web pages. If you are familiar with C++, then you can browse through this chapter quickly. Programmers coming from a non-object-oriented background should expect to spend some time mastering OOP concepts before going further with Java.

Classes and encapsulation are only one part of the OOP story, and Chapter 5 introduces the other, namely, *inheritance*. Inheritance lets you take an existing class and modify it according to your needs. This is a fundamental technique for programming in Java. The inheritance mechanism in Java is quite similar to that in C++. Once again, C++ programmers can focus on the differences between the languages.

Chapter 6 shows you how to use Java's notion of an *interface*. Interfaces let you go beyond the simple inheritance model of Chapter 5. Mastering interfaces allows you full access to the power of Java's completely object-oriented approach to programming. We also cover a useful technical feature of Java here. These are called *inner classes*. Inner classes help make your code cleaner and more concise.

In Chapter 7, we begin application programming in earnest. We show how you can make windows, how to paint on them, how to draw with geometric shapes, how to format text in multiple fonts, and how to display images.

Chapter 8 is a detailed discussion of the event model of the AWT, the *abstract windows toolkit*. (We discuss the event model that was added to Java 1.1, not the obsolete and simplistic 1.0 event model.) You'll see how to write the code that responds to events like mouse clicks or key presses. Along the way you'll see how to handle basic GUI elements like buttons and panels.

Chapter 9 discusses the Swing GUI toolkit in great detail. The Swing toolkit is how you can use Java to build a cross-platform graphical user interface. You'll learn all about the various kinds of buttons, text components, borders, sliders, list boxes, menus, and dialog boxes. However, some of the more advanced components are discussed in Volume 2.

After you finish Chapter 9, you finally have all mechanisms in place to write *applets*, those mini-programs that can live inside a Web page, and so applets are the topic of Chapter 10. We show you a number of useful and fun applets, but more importantly, we show you what goes on behind the scenes. And we show you how to use the Java Plug-in that enables you to roll out applets that take advantage of all the newest Java features, even if your users use old browsers or browsers made by hostile vendors.

Chapter 11 discusses *exception handling*, Java's robust mechanism to deal with the fact that bad things can happen to good programs. For example, a network connection can become unavailable in the middle of a file download, a disk can fill up, and so on. Exceptions give you an efficient way of separating the normal processing code from the error handling. Of course, even after hardening your program by handling all exceptional conditions, it still might fail to work as expected. In the second half of this chapter, we give you a large number of useful debugging tips. Finally, we guide you through sample sessions with various tools: the JDB debugger, the debugger of the Forte development environment, a profiler, a code coverage testing tool and the AWT robot.

We finish the book with input and output handling. In Java, all I/O is handled through so-called *streams*. Streams let you deal in a uniform manner with communicating with any source of data, such as files, network connections, or memory blocks. We include detailed coverage of the reader and writer classes, which make it easy to deal with Unicode; and we show you what goes on under the hood when you use object serialization mechanism, which makes saving and loading objects easy and convenient.

An appendix lists the Java language keywords.

Conventions

As is common in many computer books, we use `courier type` to represent computer code.

There are many C++ notes that explain the difference between Java and C++. You can skip over them if you don't have a background in C++ or if you consider your experience with that language a bad dream of which you'd rather not be reminded.

Notes and tips are tagged with "note" and "tip" icons that look like these.

When there is danger ahead, we warn you with a "Caution" icon.

Java comes with a large programming library or Application Programming Interface (API). When using an API call for the first time, we add a short summary description tagged with an API icon at the end of the section. These descriptions are a bit more informal, but we hope also a little more informative than those in the official on-line API documentation.

Programs whose source code is on the CD-ROM are listed as examples, for instance **Example 2–4: WelcomeApplet.java.**

CD-ROM

The CD-ROM on the back of the book contains the latest version of the Java Software Development Kit. At the time we are writing this, these materials are available only for Windows 95/NT or Solaris 2.

Of course, the CD-ROM contains all sample code from the book, in compressed form. You can expand the file either with one of the familiar unzipping programs or simply with the `jar` utility that is part of the Java Software Development Kit.

The CD-ROM also contains a small selection of "best of breed" programs that you may find helpful for your development. Generally, these programs require that you pay the vendors some amount of money if you use them beyond a trial period. We have no connection with the vendors, except as satisfied users of their products. Please contact the vendors directly with any questions you may have about the programs.

NOTE: People have often asked what the licensing requirements for using the sample code in a commercial situation are. You can freely use any code from this book for non-commercial use. However, if you do want to use the code as a basis for a commercial product, we simply require that every Java programmer on the development team for that project own a copy of *Core Java.*

Acknowledgments

Writing a book is always a monumental effort, and rewriting doesn't seem to be much easier, especially with continuous change in Java technology. Making a book a reality takes many dedicated people, and it is my great pleasure to acknowledge the contributions of the entire Core Java team.

A large number of individuals at Prentice-Hall PTR, Sun Microsystems Press and Navta Inc. provided valuable assistance, but they managed to stay behind the scenes. I'd like them all to know how much I appreciate their efforts. As always, my warm thanks go to my editor, Greg Doench of Prentice-Hall PTR, and his assistant, Mary Treacy, for steering the book through the writing and production process, and for allowing me to be blissfully unaware of the existence of all those folks behind the scenes. My thanks also to my co-author of earlier editions, Gary Cornell, who has since moved on to other ventures.

Thanks to the many readers of earlier editions who reported many embarrassing errors and made lots of thoughtful suggestions for improvement. I am particularly grateful to the excellent reviewing team that went over the manuscript with an amazing eye for detail and saved me from many more embarrassing errors. The reviewers are: Bob Lynch, Bradley A. Smith, Paul E. Sevinc from Teamup AG, Mark Morrissey from the Oregon Graduate Institute, Peter Sander from ESSI University, Nice, France, and Chuck Allison, Contributing Editor, *C/C++ Users Journal*.

Most importantly, my love, gratitude, and apologies go to my wife Hui-Chen and my children Thomas and Nina for their continuing support of this never-ending project.

Cay Horstmann

Cupertino, November 2000

Chapter *1*

An Introduction to Java

- ▼ JAVA AS A PROGRAMMING TOOL
- ▼ ADVANTAGES OF JAVA
- ▼ THE JAVA "WHITE PAPER" BUZZWORDS
- ▼ JAVA AND THE INTERNET
- ▼ A SHORT HISTORY OF JAVA
- ▼ COMMON MISCONCEPTIONS ABOUT JAVA

For a long time, to open a computer magazine that did not have a feature article on Java seemed impossible. Even mainstream newspapers and magazines like *The New York Times, The Washington Post,* and *Business Week* have run numerous articles on Java. It gets better (or worse, depending on your perspective): can you remember the last time National Public Radio ran a 10-minute story on a computer language? Or a $100,000,000 venture capital fund was set up solely for products produced using a *specific* computer language? CNN, CNBC, you name the mass medium, it seems everyone was, and to a certain extent still is, talking about how Java will do this or Java will do that.

However, we decided to write this book for serious programmers, and because Java is a serious programming language, there's a lot to tell. So, rather than immediately getting caught up in an analysis of the Java hype and trying to deal with the limited (if still interesting) truth behind the hype, we will write in some detail

1

about Java as a programming language (including, of course, the features added for its use on the Internet that started the hype). After that, we will try to separate current fact from fancy by explaining what Java can and cannot do.

In the early days of Java, there was a huge disconnect between the hype and the actual abilities of Java. As Java is maturing, the technology is becoming a lot more stable and reliable, and expectations are coming down to reasonable levels. As we write this, Java is being increasingly used for "middleware" to communicate between clients and server resources such as databases. While not glitzy, this is an important area where Java, primarily due to its portability and multithreading and networking capabilities, can add real value. Java is making great inroads in embedded systems, where it is well positioned to become a standard for hand-held devices, Internet kiosks, car computers, and so on. However, early attempts to rewrite familiar PC programs in Java were not encouraging—the applications were underpowered and slow. With the current version of Java, some of these problems have been overcome, but still, users don't generally care what programming language was used to write their applications. We think that the benefits of Java will come from new kinds of devices and applications, not from rewriting existing ones.

Java as a Programming Tool

As a computer language, Java's hype is overdone: Java is certainly a *good* programming language. There is no doubt that it is one of the better languages available to serious programmers. We think it could *potentially* have been a great programming language, but it is probably too late for that. Once a language is out in the field, the ugly reality of compatibility with existing code sets in. Moreover, even in cases where changes are possible without breaking existing code, it is hard for the creators of a language as acclaimed as Java to sit back and say, "Well, maybe we were wrong about X, and Y would be better." In sum, while we expect there to be some improvements over time, basically, the structure of the Java language tomorrow will be much the same as it is today.

Having said that, the obvious question is, Where did the dramatic improvements of Java come from? The answer is that they didn't come from changes to the underlying Java programming language, they came from *major changes in the Java libraries*. Over time, Sun Microsystems changed everything from the names of many of the library functions (to make them more consistent), to how graphics works (by changing the event handling model and rewriting parts from scratch), to adding important features like printing that were not part of Java 1.0. The result is a far more useful programming platform that has become enormously more capable and useful than early versions of Java.

NOTE: Microsoft has released a product called J++ that shares a family relationship with Java. Like Java, J++ is interpreted by a virtual machine that is compatible with the Java Virtual Machine for executing Java bytecodes, but there are substantial differences when interfacing with external code. The basic language syntax is almost identical to Java. However, Microsoft added language constructs that are of doubtful utility except for interfacing with the Windows API. In addition to Java and J++ sharing a common syntax, their foundational libraries (strings, utilities, networking, multithreading, math, and so on) are essentially identical. However, the libraries for graphics, user interfaces, and remote object access are completely different. At this point, Microsoft is no longer supporting J++ but has instead introduced another language called C# that also has many similarities with Java but uses a different virtual machine. We do not cover J++ or C# in this book.

Advantages of Java

One obvious advantage is a runtime environment that provides platform independence: you can use the same code on Windows, Solaris, Linux, Macintosh, and so on. This is certainly necessary when programs are downloaded over the Internet to run on a variety of platforms.

Another programming advantage is that Java has a syntax similar to that of C++, making it easy for C and C++ programmers to learn. Then again, Visual Basic programmers will probably find the syntax annoying.

NOTE: If you are coming from a language other than C++, some of the terms used in this section will be less familiar—just skip those sections. You will be comfortable with all of these terms by the end of Chapter 6.

Java is also fully object oriented—even more so than C++. Everything in Java, except for a few basic types like numbers, is an object. (Object-oriented programming has replaced earlier structured techniques because it has many advantages for dealing with sophisticated projects. If you are not familiar with Object-oriented programming, Chapters 3 through 6 provide what you need to know.)

However, having yet another, somewhat improved, dialect of C++ would not be enough. The key point is this: *It is far easier to turn out bug-free code using Java than using C++.*

Why? The designers of Java thought hard about what makes C++ code so buggy. They added features to Java that *eliminate the possibility* of creating code with the most common kinds of bugs.

- The Java designers eliminated manual memory allocation and deallocation.

  Memory in Java is automatically garbage collected. You *never* have to worry about memory corruption.

- They introduced true arrays and eliminated pointer arithmetic.

  You *never* have to worry about overwriting an area of memory because of an off-by-one error when working with a pointer.

- They eliminated the possibility of confusing an assignment with a test for equality in a conditional statement.

  You cannot even compile `if (ntries = 3)` . . . . (Visual Basic programmers may not see the problem, but, trust us, this is a common source of confusion in C/C++ code.)

- They eliminated multiple inheritance, replacing it with a new notion of *interface* that they derived from Objective C.

  Interfaces give you most of what you want from multiple inheritance, without the complexity that comes with managing multiple inheritance hierarchies. (If inheritance is a new concept for you, Chapter 5 will explain it.)

NOTE: The Java language specification is public. You can find it on the Web at `http://java.sun.com/docs/books/jls/html/index.html`.

The Java "White Paper" Buzzwords

The authors of Java have written an influential White Paper that explains their design goals and accomplishments. Their paper is organized along the following eleven buzzwords:

Simple	Portable
Object Oriented	Interpreted
Distributed	High Performance
Robust	Multithreaded
Secure	Dynamic
Architecture Neutral	

We touched on some of these points in the last section. In this section, we will:

- Summarize via excerpts from the White Paper what the Java designers say about each buzzword, and

- Tell you what we think of that particular buzzword, based on our experiences with the current version of Java.

NOTE: As we write this, the White Paper can be found at `http://java.sun.com/doc/language_environment`.

Simple

We wanted to build a system that could be programmed easily without a lot of esoteric training and which leveraged today's standard practice. So even though we found that C++ was unsuitable, we designed Java as closely to C++ as possible in order to make the system more comprehensible. Java omits many rarely used, poorly understood, confusing features of C++ that, in our experience, bring more grief than benefit.

The syntax for Java is, indeed, a cleaned-up version of the syntax for C++. There is no need for header files, pointer arithmetic (or even a pointer syntax), structures, unions, operator overloading, virtual base classes, and so on. (See the C++ notes interspersed throughout the text for more on the differences between Java and C++.) The designers did not, however, attempt to fix all of the clumsy features of C++. For example, the syntax of the `switch` statement is unchanged in Java. If you know C++, you will find the transition to the Java syntax easy.

If you are used to a visual programming environment (such as Visual Basic), you will not find Java simple. There is much strange syntax (though it does not take long to get the hang of it). More importantly, you must do a lot more programming in Java. The beauty of Visual Basic is that its visual design environment provides a lot of the infrastructure for an application almost automatically. The equivalent functionality must be programmed manually, usually with a fair bit of code, in Java. There are, however, third-party development environments that provide "drag-and-drop" style program development.

Another aspect of being simple is being small. One of the goals of Java is to enable the construction of software that can run stand-alone in small machines. The size of the basic interpreter and class support is about 40K bytes; adding the basic standard libraries and thread support (essentially a self-contained microkernel) adds an additional 175K.

This is a great achievement. Note, however, that the graphical user interface (GUI) libraries are significantly larger.

Object Oriented

Simply stated, object-oriented design is a technique for programming that focuses on the data (= objects) and on the interfaces to that object. To make an analogy with carpentry, an "object-oriented" carpenter would be mostly concerned with the chair he was building, and secondarily with the tools used to make it; a "non-object-oriented" carpenter would think primarily of his tools. The object-oriented facilities of Java are essentially those of C++.

Object orientation has proven its worth in the last 30 years, and it is inconceivable that a modern programming language would not use it. Indeed, the object-oriented features of Java are comparable to C++. The major difference between

Java and C++ lies in multiple inheritance, for which Java has found a better solution, and in the Java metaclass model. The reflection mechanism (see Chapter 5) and object serialization feature (see Chapter 12) make it much easier to implement persistent objects and GUI builders that can integrate off-the-shelf components.

> NOTE: If you do not have any experience with object-oriented programming languages, you will want to carefully read Chapters 4 through 6. These chapters explain what object-oriented programming is and why it is more useful for programming sophisticated projects than traditional, procedure-oriented languages like C or Basic.

Distributed

> *Java has an extensive library of routines for coping with TCP/IP protocols like HTTP and FTP. Java applications can open and access objects across the Net via URLs with the same ease as when accessing a local file system.*

We have found the networking capabilities of Java to be both strong and easy to use. Anyone who has tried to do Internet programming using another language will revel in how simple Java makes onerous tasks like opening a socket connection. An elegant mechanism, called servlets, makes server-side processing in Java extremely efficient. Many popular web servers support servlets. (We will cover networking in Volume 2 of this book.) The remote method invocation mechanism enables communication between distributed objects (also covered in Volume 2).

Robust

> *Java is intended for writing programs that must be reliable in a variety of ways. Java puts a lot of emphasis on early checking for possible problems, later dynamic (run-time) checking, and eliminating situations that are error-prone. . . . The single biggest difference between Java and C/C++ is that Java has a pointer model that eliminates the possibility of overwriting memory and corrupting data.*

This feature is also very useful. The Java compiler detects many problems that, in other languages, would show up only at run time. As for the second point, anyone who has spent hours chasing memory corruption caused by a pointer bug will be very happy with this feature of Java.

If you are coming from a language like Visual Basic or Cobol that doesn't explicitly use pointers, you are probably wondering why this is so important. C programmers are not so lucky. They need pointers to access strings, arrays, objects, even files. In Visual Basic, you do not use pointers for any of these entities, nor do you need to worry about memory allocation for them. On the other hand, there are many data structures that are difficult to implement in a pointerless language. Java gives you the best of both worlds. You do not need pointers for everyday constructs like strings and arrays. You have the power of pointers if you need it, for example, for linked lists. And you always have complete safety, since you can never access a bad pointer, make memory allocation errors, or have to protect against memory leaking away.

Secure

Java is intended to be used in networked/distributed environments. Toward that end, a lot of emphasis has been placed on security. Java enables the construction of virus-free, tamper-free systems.

In the first edition of *Core Java* we said: "Well, one should 'never say never again,'" and we turned out to be right. A group of security experts at Princeton University found the first bugs in the security features of Java 1.0—not long after the first version of the Java Development Kit was shipped. Moreover, they and various other people have continued to find other bugs in the security mechanisms of all subsequent versions of Java. For opinions from outside experts on the current status of Java's security mechanisms, you may want to check the URL for the Princeton group (`http://www.cs.princeton.edu/sip/`) and the `comp.risks` newsgroup. The good side is that the Java team has said that they will have a "zero tolerance" for security bugs and will immediately go to work on fixing any bugs found in the applet security mechanism. In particular, by making public the internal specifications of how the Java interpreter works, Sun is making it far easier for people to find any bugs in Java's security features—essentially enlisting the outside community in the ever-so-subtle security bug detection. This makes one more confident that security bugs will be found as soon as possible. In any case, Java makes it extremely difficult to outwit its security mechanisms. The bugs found so far have been very subtle and (relatively) few in number.

NOTE: Sun's URL for security-related issues is currently at
`http://java.sun.com/sfaq/`

Here is a sample of what Java's security features are supposed to keep a Java program from doing:

1. Overrunning the runtime stack, like the infamous Internet worm did
2. Corrupting memory outside its own process space
3. Reading or writing local files when invoked through a security-conscious class loader, like a Web browser that has been programmed to forbid this kind of access

All of these features are in place and for the most part seem to work as intended. Java is certainly the most secure programming language to date. But, caution is always in order. Though the bugs found in the security mechanism to date were not trivial to find and full details are often kept secret, still it may be impossible to *prove* that Java is secure.

A number of security features have been added to Java over time. Since version 1.1, Java has the notion of digitally signed classes (see Volume 2). With a signed class, you can be sure of who wrote it. Any time you trust the author of the class, the class can be allowed more privileges on your machine.

NOTE: A competing code delivery mechanism from Microsoft based on its ActiveX technology relies on digital signatures alone for security. Clearly this is not sufficient—as any user of Microsoft's own products can confirm, programs from well-known vendors do crash and in so doing, create damage. Java has a far stronger security model than ActiveX since it controls the application as it runs and stops it from wreaking havoc.

Architecture Neutral

The compiler generates an architecture-neutral object file format—the compiled code is executable on many processors, given the presence of the Java run time system. The Java compiler does this by generating bytecode instructions which have nothing to do with a particular computer architecture. Rather, they are designed to be both easy to interpret on any machine and easily translated into native machine code on the fly.

This is not a new idea. More than twenty years ago, both Niklaus Wirth's original implementation of Pascal and the UCSD Pascal system used the same technique. With the use of bytecodes, performance takes a major hit (but just-in-time compilation mitigates this in many cases). The designers of Java did an excellent job developing a bytecode instruction set that works well on today's most common computer architectures. And the codes have been designed to translate easily into actual machine instructions.

Portable

Unlike C and C++, there are no "implementation-dependent" aspects of the specification. The sizes of the primitive data types are specified, as is the behavior of arithmetic on them.

For example, an `int` in Java is always a 32-bit integer. In C/C++, `int` can mean a 16-bit integer, a 32-bit integer, or any other size that the compiler vendor likes. The only restriction is that the `int` type must have at least as many bytes as a `short int` and cannot have more bytes than a `long int`. Having a fixed size for number types eliminates a major porting headache. Binary data is stored and transmitted in a fixed format, eliminating the "big endian/little endian" confusion. Strings are saved in a standard Unicode format.

The libraries that are a part of the system define portable interfaces. For example, there is an abstract Window class and implementations of it for UNIX, Windows, and the Macintosh.

As anyone who has ever tried knows, it is an effort of heroic proportions to write a program that looks good on Windows, the Macintosh, and 10 flavors of UNIX. Java 1.0 made the heroic effort, delivering a simple toolkit that mapped common user-interface elements to a number of platforms. Unfortunately, the result was a library that, with a lot of work, could give barely acceptable results on different systems. (And there were often *different* bugs on the different platform graphics implementations.) But it was a start. There are many applications in which portability is more important than user interface slickness, and these applications did benefit from early versions of Java. By now, the user interface toolkit has been completely rewritten so that it no longer relies on the host user interface. The result is far more consistent and, we think, more attractive than in earlier versions of Java.

Interpreted

> *The Java interpreter can execute Java bytecodes directly on any machine to which the interpreter has been ported. Since linking is a more incremental and light-weight process, the development process can be much more rapid and exploratory.*

Perhaps this is an advantage while developing an application, but it is clearly overstated. In any case, we have found the Java compiler that comes with the Java Software Development Kit (SDK) to be quite slow. (Some third party compilers, for example those by IBM, are quite a bit faster.) And recompilation speed is only one of the ingredients of a development environment with fast turnaround. If you are used to the speed of the development cycle of Visual Basic, you will likely be disappointed with the performance of Java development environments.

High Performance

> *While the performance of interpreted bytecodes is usually more than adequate, there are situations where higher performance is required. The bytecodes can be translated on the fly (at run time) into machine code for the particular CPU the application is running on.*

If you use an interpreter to execute the bytecodes, "high performance" is not the term that we would use. However, on many platforms, there is also another form of compilation, the *just-in-time* (JIT) compilers. These work by compiling the byte-codes into native code once, caching the results, and then calling them again if needed. This approach speeds up commonly used code tremendously since one has to do the interpretation only once. Although still slightly slower than a true native code compiler, a just-in-time compiler can give you a 10- or even 20-fold speedup for some programs and will almost always be significantly faster than the Java interpreter. This technology is being improved continuously and may eventually yield results that cannot be matched by traditional compilation systems. For example, a just-in-time compiler can monitor which code is executed frequently and optimize just that code for speed.

Multithreaded

> *[The] benefits of multithreading are better interactive responsiveness and real-time behavior.*

If you have ever tried to do multithreading in another language, you will be pleasantly surprised at how easy it is in Java. Threads in Java also have the capacity to take advantage of multiprocessor systems if the base operating system does so. On the downside, thread implementations on the major platforms differ widely, and Java makes no effort to be platform independent in this regard. Only the code for calling multithreading remains the same across machines; Java offloads the implementation of multithreading to the underlying operating system or a thread library. (Threading will be covered in volume 2.) Nonetheless, the ease of multithreading is one of the main reasons why Java is such an appealing language for server-side development.

Dynamic

> *In a number of ways, Java is a more dynamic language than C or C++. It was designed to adapt to an evolving environment. Libraries can freely add new methods and instance variables without any effect on their clients. In Java, finding out run time type information is straightforward.*

This is an important feature in those situations where code needs to be added to a running program. A prime example is code that is downloaded from the Internet to run in a browser. In Java 1.0, finding out runtime type information was anything but straightforward, but current versions of Java give the programmer full insight into both the structure and behavior of its objects. This is extremely useful for systems that need to analyze objects at run time such as Java GUI builders, smart debuggers, pluggable components, and object databases.

Java and the Internet

The idea here is simple: users will download Java bytecodes from the Internet and run them on their own machines. Java programs that work on Web pages are called *applets*. To use an applet, you need a Java-enabled Web browser, which will interpret the bytecodes for you. Because Sun is licensing the Java source code and insisting that there be no changes in the language and basic library structure, you can be sure that a Java applet will run on any browser that is advertised as Java enabled. Note that Netscape 2.x and Netscape 3.x are only *Java 1.02 enabled*, as is Internet Explorer 3.0. Netscape 4 and Internet Explorer 4 run different subsets of Java 1.1. This sorry situation made it increasingly difficult to develop applets that take advantage of the most current Java version. To remedy this problem, Sun has developed the *Java Plug-in*, a tool that makes the newest Java runtime environment available to both Netscape and Internet Explorer (see Chapter 10).

We suspect that most of the initial hype around Java stemmed from the lure of making money from special-purpose applet software. You have a nifty "Will Writer" program. Convert it to an applet, and charge people per use—presumably, most people would be using this kind of program infrequently. Some people predict a time when everyone downloads software from the Net on a per-use basis. This might be great for software companies, but we think it is absurd, for example, to expect people to download and pay for a spell-checker applet each time they send an e-mail message.

Another early suggested use for applets was for so-called content and protocol handlers that allow a Java-enabled Web browser to deal with new types of information dynamically. Suppose you invent a new fractal compression algorithm for dealing with humongous graphics files and want to let someone sample your technology before you charge them big bucks for it. Write a Java content handler that does the decompression and send it along with the compressed files. The HotJava browser by Sun Microsystems supports this feature, but neither Netscape nor Internet Explorer ever did.

Applets can also be used to add buttons and input fields to a Web page. But downloading those applets over a dialup line is slow, and you can do much of the same with Dynamic HTML, HTML forms, and a scripting language such as JavaScript. And, of course, early applets were used for animation: the familiar spinning globes, dancing cartoon characters, nervous text, and so on. But animated GIFs can do much of this, and Dynamic HTML combined with scripting can do even more of what Java applets were first used for.

As a result of the browser incompatibilities and the inconvenience of downloading applet code through slow net connections, applets on Internet Web pages have not become a huge success. The situation is entirely different on *intranets*. There are typically no bandwidth problems, so the download time for applets is no issue. And in an intranet, it is possible to control which browser is being used or to use the Java Plug-in consistently. Employees can't misplace or misconfigure programs that are delivered through the Web with each use, and the system administrator never needs to walk around and upgrade code on client machines. Many corporations have rolled out programs such as inventory checking, vacation planning, travel reimbursement, and so on, as applets that use the browser as the delivery platform.

Applets at Work

This book includes a few sample applets; ultimately, the best source for applets is the Web itself. Some applets on the Web can only be seen at work; many others include the source code. When you become more familiar with Java, these applets can be a great way to learn more about Java. A good Web site to check for Java applets is Gamelan—it is now hosted as part of the `developer.com` site, but you can still reach it through the URL `http://www.gamelan.com`. (By the way, *gamelan* also stands for a special type of Javanese musical orchestra. Attend a gamelan performance if you have a chance—it is gorgeous music.)

When the user downloads an applet, it works much like embedding an image in a Web page. (For those who know HTML, we mean one set with an IMG tag.) The applet becomes a part of the page, and the text flows around the space used for the applet. The point is, the image is *alive*. It reacts to user commands, changes its appearance, and sends data between the computer viewing the applet and the computer serving it.

Figure 1–1 shows a good example of a dynamic web page that carries out sophisticated calculations, an applet to view molecules. By using the mouse, you can rotate and zoom each molecule to better understand its structure. This kind of direct manipulation is not achievable with static web pages, but applets make it possible. (You can find the applet at `http://www.openscience.org/jmol/JmolApplet.html`.)

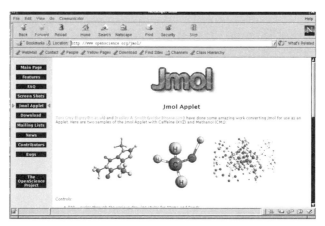

Figure 1–1: The Jmol applet

Server-side Java

At the time of this writing, the pendulum has swung back from client-focused programs to *server-side programming*. In particular, *application servers* can use the monitoring capabilities of the Java virtual machine to perform automatic load balancing, database connection pooling, object synchronization, safe shutdown and restart, and other services that are needed for scalable server applications but are notoriously difficult to implement correctly. Thus, application programmers can buy rather than build these sophisticated mechanisms. This increases programmer productivity—programmers focus on their core competency, the business logic of their programs, and not on tweaking server performance.

A Short History of Java

This section gives a short history of Java's evolution. It is based on various published sources (most importantly, on an interview with Java's creators in the July 1995 issue of *SunWorld's* on-line magazine).

Java goes back to 1991, when a group of Sun engineers, led by Patrick Naughton and Sun Fellow (and all-around computer wizard) James Gosling, wanted to design a small computer language that could be used for consumer devices like cable TV switchboxes. Since these devices do not have a lot of power or memory, the language had to be small and generate very tight code. Also, because different manufacturers may choose different central processing units (CPUs), it was important not to be tied down to any single architecture. The project got the code name "Green."

The requirements for small, tight, and platform-neutral code led the team to resurrect the model that some Pascal implementations tried in the early days of PCs. What Niklaus Wirth, the inventor of Pascal, had pioneered, and UCSD Pascal did commercially, was to design a portable language that generated intermediate code for a hypothetical machine. (These are often called *virtual machines*—hence, the Java Virtual Machine or JVM.) This intermediate code could then be used on any machine that had the correct interpreter. The Green project engineers used a virtual machine as well, so this solved their main problem.

The Sun people, however, come from a UNIX background, so they based their language on C++ rather than Pascal. In particular, they made the language object oriented rather than procedure oriented. But, as Gosling says in the interview, "All along, the language was a tool, not the end." Gosling decided to call his language "Oak." (Presumably because he liked the look of an oak tree that was right outside his window at Sun.) The people at Sun later realized that Oak was the name of an existing computer language, so they changed the name to Java.

In 1992, the Green project delivered its first product, called "*7." It was an extremely intelligent remote control. (It had the power of a SPARCstation in a box that was 6 inches by 4 inches by 4 inches.) Unfortunately, no one was interested in producing this at Sun, and the Green people had to find other ways to market their technology. However, none of the standard consumer electronics companies were interested. The group then bid on a project to design a cable TV box that could deal with new cable services such as video on demand. They did not get the contract. (Amusingly, the company that did was led by the same Jim Clark who started Netscape—a company that did much to make Java successful.)

The Green project (with a new name of "First Person, Inc.") spent all of 1993 and half of 1994 looking for people to buy its technology—no one was found. (Patrick Naughton, one of the founders of the group and the person who ended up doing most of the marketing, claims to have accumulated 300,000 air miles in trying to sell the technology.) First Person was dissolved in 1994.

While all of this was going on at Sun, the World Wide Web part of the Internet was growing bigger and bigger. The key to the Web is the browser that translates the hypertext page to the screen. In 1994, most people were using Mosaic, a noncommercial Web browser that came out of the supercomputing center at the University of Illinois in 1993. (Mosaic was partially written by Marc Andreessen for $6.85 an hour as an undergraduate student on a work-study project. He moved on to fame and fortune as one of the cofounders and the chief of technology at Netscape.)

In the *SunWorld* interview, Gosling says that in mid-1994, the language developers realized that "We could build a real cool browser. It was one of the few things in the client/server mainstream that needed some of the weird things we'd done: architecture neutral, real-time, reliable, secure—issues that weren't terribly important in the workstation world. So we built a browser."

The actual browser was built by Patrick Naughton and Jonathan Payne and evolved into the HotJava browser that we have today. The HotJava browser was written in Java to show off the power of Java. But the builders also had in mind the power of what are now called applets, so they made the browser capable of executing code inside web pages. This "proof of technology" was shown at SunWorld '95 on May 23, 1995, and inspired the Java craze that continues unabated today.

The big breakthrough for widespread Java use came in the fall of 1995, when Netscape decided to make the Navigator browser Java enabled in January 1996. Other licensees include IBM, Symantec, Inprise, and many others. Even Microsoft has licensed Java. Internet Explorer is Java enabled, and Windows ships with a Java virtual machine. (Note that Microsoft does not support the most current version of Java, however, and that its implementation differs from the Java standard.)

Sun released the first version of Java in early 1996. It was followed by Java 1.02 a couple of months later. People quickly realized that Java 1.02 was not going to cut it for serious application development. Sure, you could use Java 1.02 to make a nervous text applet that moves text randomly around in a canvas. But you couldn't even *print* in Java 1.02. To be blunt, Java 1.02 was not ready for prime time.

The big announcements about Java's future features trickled out over the first few months of 1996. Only at the JavaOne conference held in San Francisco in May of 1996 did the bigger picture of where Java was going become clearer. At JavaOne the people at Sun Microsystems outlined their vision of the future of Java with a seemingly endless stream of improvements and new libraries.

The big news of the 1998 JavaOne conference was the upcoming release of Java 1.2, which replaces the early toy-like GUI and graphics toolkits with sophisticated and scalable versions that come a lot closer to the promise of "Write Once, Run

Anywhere"™ than their predecessors. Three days after (!) its release in December 1998, the name was changed to Java 2.

Since then, the core Java platform has stabilized. The current release, with the catchy name *Java 2 Software Development Kit, Standard Edition version 1.3*, is an incremental improvement over the initial Java 2 release, with a small number of new features, increased performance and, of course, quite a few bug fixes. Now that a stable foundation exists, innovation has shifted to advanced Java libraries such as the Java 2 Enterprise Edition and the Java 2 Micro Edition.

Common Misconceptions About Java

In summary, what follows is a list of some common misconceptions about Java, along with commentary.

Java is an extension of HTML.

Java is a programming language; HTML is a way to describe the structure of a Web page. They have nothing in common except that there are HTML extensions for placing Java applets on a Web page.

Java is an easy programming language to learn.

No programming language as powerful as Java is easy. You always have to distinguish between how easy it is to write toy programs and how hard it is to do serious work. Also, consider that only four chapters in this book discuss the Java language. The remaining chapters of both volumes show how to put the language to work, using the Java *libraries*. The Java libraries contain thousands of classes and interfaces, and tens of thousands of functions. Luckily, you do not need to know every one of them, but you do need to know surprisingly many to use Java for anything realistic.

Java is an easy environment in which to program.

The Java SDK is not an easy environment to use—except for people who are accustomed to command-line tools. There are integrated development environments that feature integrated editors, compilers, drag-and-drop form designers combined with decent debugging facilities, but they can be somewhat complex and daunting for the newcomer. They also work by generating what is often hundreds of lines of code. We don't think you are well served when first learning Java by starting with hundreds of lines of computer-generated UI code filled with comments that say DO NOT MODIFY or the equivalent. We have found in teaching Java that using your favorite text editor is still the best way to learn Java, and that is what we will do.

Java will become a universal programming language for all platforms.

This is possible, in theory, and it is certainly the case that every vendor but Microsoft seems to want this to happen. However, there are many applications, already working perfectly well on desktops, that would not work well on other devices or inside a browser. Also, these applications have been written to take advantage of the speed of the processor and the native user-interface library and have been ported to all of the important platforms anyway. Among these kinds of applications are word processors, photo editors, and web browsers. They are typically written in C or C++, and we see no benefit to the end user in rewriting them in Java. And, at least in the short run, there would be significant disadvantages since the Java version is likely to be slower and less powerful.

Java is just another programming language.

Java is a nice programming language; most programmers prefer it over C or C++. But there have been hundreds of nice programming languages that never gained widespread popularity, whereas languages with obvious flaws, such as C++ and Visual Basic, have been wildly successful.

Why? The success of a programming language is determined far more by the utility of the *support system* surrounding it than by the elegance of its syntax. Are there useful, convenient, and standard libraries for the features that you need to implement? Are there tool vendors that build great programming and debugging environments? Does the language and the tool set integrate with the rest of the computing infrastructure? Java is successful on the server because its class libraries let you easily do things that were hard before, such as networking and multithreading. The fact that Java reduces pointer errors is a bonus and so programmers seem to be more productive with Java, but these are not the source of its success.

This is an important point that one vendor in particular—who sees portable libraries as a threat—tries to ignore, by labeling Java "just a programming language" and by supplying a system that uses a derivative of Java and a proprietary and nonportable library. The result may well be a very nice language that is a direct competitor to Visual Basic but has little to do with Java.

Java is interpreted, so it is too slow for serious applications on a specific platform.

Many programs spend most of their time on things like user-interface interactions or waiting for data from a network connection. All programs, no matter what language they are written in, will detect a mouse click in adequate time. It is true that we would not do CPU-intensive tasks with the interpreter supplied with the Java SDK. However, on platforms where a just-in-time compiler is available, all you need to do is run the bytecodes through it and most performance issues simply go away. Finally, Java is great for network-bound programs. Experience has shown that Java can comfortably keep up with the data rate of a network connection, even when doing computationally intensive work such as encryption. As long as Java is faster than the data that it processes, it does not matter that C++ might be faster still. Java is easier to program, and it is portable. This makes Java a great language for implementing network services.

All Java programs run inside a Web page.

All Java *applets* run inside a Web browser. That is the definition of an applet—a Java program running inside a browser. But it is entirely possible, and quite useful, to write stand-alone Java programs that run independently of a Web browser. These programs (usually called *applications*) are completely portable. Just take the code and run it on another machine! And because Java is more convenient and less error-prone than raw C++, it is a good choice for writing programs. It is an even more compelling choice when it is combined with database access tools like Java Database Connectivity (see Volume 2). It is certainly the obvious choice for a first language in which to learn programming.

Most of the programs in this book are stand-alone programs. Sure, applets are fun. But stand-alone Java programs are more important and more useful in practice.

Java applets are a major security risk.

There have been some well-publicized reports of failures in the Java security system. Most have been in the implementation of Java in a specific browser. Researchers viewed it as a challenge to try to find chinks in the Java armor and to defy the strength and sophistication of the applet security model. The technical failures that they found have all been quickly corrected, and to our knowledge, no actual systems were ever compromised. To keep this in perspective, consider the literally millions of virus attacks in Windows executable files and Word macros that cause real grief but surprisingly little criticism of the weaknesses of the attacked platform. Also, the ActiveX mechanism in Internet Explorer would be a fertile ground for abuse, but it is so boringly obvious how to circumvent it that few have bothered to publicize their findings.

Some system administrators have even deactivated Java in company browsers, while continuing to permit their users to download executable files, ActiveX controls, and Word documents. That is pretty ridiculous—currently, the risk of being attacked by hostile Java applets is perhaps comparable to the risk of dying from a plane crash; the risk of being infected by opening Word documents is comparable to the risk of dying while crossing a busy freeway on foot.

JavaScript is a simpler version of Java.

JavaScript, a scripting language that can be used inside Web pages, was invented by Netscape and originally called LiveScript. JavaScript has a syntax that is reminiscent of Java, but otherwise there are no relationships (except for the name, of course). A subset of JavaScript is standardized as ECMA-262, but the extensions that you need for real work have not been standardized, and as a result, writing JavaScript code that runs both in Netscape and Internet Explorer is an exercise in frustration.

You should use Java instead of Perl for CGI scripting.

This is half right. Not only should you no longer use Perl, you should also not use CGI scripts for server-side processing. Java servlets are a superior solution. Servlets execute much more efficiently than CGI scripts, and you can use Java— a real programming language—to implement them.

Java will revolutionize client-server computing.

This is possible and it is where much of the best work in Java is being done. There are quite a few application servers such as BEA Weblogic that are built entirely in Java. The JDBC discussed in Volume 2 certainly makes using Java for client-server development easier. As third-party tools continue to be developed, we expect database development with Java to be as easy as the Net library makes network programming. Accessing remote objects is significantly easier in Java than in C++ (see Volume 2).

Java will allow the component-based model of computing to take off.

No two people mean the same thing when they talk about components. Regarding visual controls, like ActiveX components that can be dropped into a GUI program, Java 1.1 includes the JavaBeans initiative (see Volume 2). Java beans can do the same sorts of things as ActiveX components *except* they are *automatically* cross-platform. On the server side, reusable *enterprise beans* can potentially be deployed in a wide variety of application servers. It is possible that a market for these components will materialize, similar to the market of ActiveX components in the Wintel world.

With Java, I can replace my computer with a $500 "Internet appliance."

Some people are betting big that this is going to happen. We believe it is pretty absurd to think that home users are going to give up a powerful and convenient desktop for a limited machine with no local storage. However, a Java-powered network computer is a viable option for a "zero administration initiative" to cut the costs of computer ownership in a business.

We also see an Internet appliance as a portable *adjunct* to a desktop. Provided the price is right, wouldn't you rather have an Internet-enabled *device* with a screen on which to read your e-mail or see the news? Because the Java kernel is so small, Java is the obvious choice for such a telephone or other Internet "appliance."

Chapter 2

The Java Programming Environment

▼ INSTALLING THE JAVA SOFTWARE DEVELOPMENT KIT
▼ DEVELOPMENT ENVIRONMENTS
▼ USING THE COMMAND LINE TOOLS
▼ USING AN INTEGRATED DEVELOPMENT ENVIRONMENT
▼ COMPILING AND RUNNING PROGRAMS FROM A TEXT EDITOR
▼ GRAPHICAL APPLICATIONS
▼ APPLETS

In this chapter, you will learn how to install the Java Software Development Kit (SDK) and how to compile and run various types of programs: console programs, graphical applications, and applets. You run the SDK tools by typing commands in a shell window. However, many programmers prefer the comfort of an integrated development environment. We show you how to use the freely available Forte environment to compile and run Java programs. There are many other environments for developing Java applications with similar user interfaces. While easier to learn and use, integrated development environments take a long time to load and require heavy resources. As a middle ground, you may want to use a text editor that can call the Java compiler and interpreter. We show you a couple of text editors with Java integration. Once you have mastered the techniques in this chapter and picked your development tools, you are ready to move on to Chapter 3, where you will begin exploring the Java programming language.

NOTE: A good, general source of information on Java can be found via the links on the Java frequently asked questions (FAQ) page: `http://java.sun.com/people/linden/intro.html`.

Installing the Java Software Development Kit

The most complete versions of Java are available for Sun's Solaris 2.x, Windows NT/2000, or Windows 95/98. (We will refer to these platforms collectively as "Windows." Note that this does not include Windows 3.1.) Versions of Java in various states of development exist for Linux, OS/2, Macintosh, Windows 3.1, and many other platforms.

The CD that accompanies this book contains a version of the Java SDK for Windows and Solaris. You can also download versions of the Java SDK for other platforms. Installation directions differ on each platform.

NOTE: Only the installation and compilation instructions for Java are system dependent. Once you get Java up and running, everything else in this book should apply to you. System independence is a major benefit of Java.

On Windows, simply run the self-installing executable file. On Solaris, look inside the compressed tar file for a README file. For other platforms, you'll need to consult the platform-specific installation instructions.

NOTE: The setup procedure offers a default for the installation directory that contains the Java SDK version number, such as `jdk1.2.3`. If you prefer, you can change the installation directory to `jdk`. However, if you are a Java enthusiast who enjoys collecting different versions of the Java SDK, go ahead and accept the default. In this book, we will refer to the installation directory as `jdk`. For example, when we refer to the `jdk/bin` directory, we mean the directory named `bin` under the Java SDK installation directory. Also note that we use UNIX style directory names. Under Windows, you'll have to use backslashes and drive letters such as `c:\jdk\bin`.

Setting the Execution Path

After you are done installing the Java SDK, you need to carry out one additional step: add the `jdk/bin` directory to the execution path, the list of directories that the operating system traverses to locate executable files. Directions for this step also vary among operating systems.

- In UNIX (including Solaris or Linux), the procedure for editing the execution path depends on the *shell* that you are using. If you use the

C shell (which is the Solaris default), then add a line such as the following to the end of your ~/.cshrc file:

```
set path=(/usr/local/jdk/bin $path)
```

If you use the Bourne Again shell (which is the Linux default), then add a line such as the following to the end of your ~/.bashrc or ~/.bash_profile file:

```
export PATH=/usr/local/jdk/bin:$PATH
```

For other UNIX shells, you'll need to find out how to carry out the analogous procedure.

- Under Windows 95/98, place a line such as the following at the end of your AUTOEXEC.BAT file:

```
SET PATH=c:\jdk\bin;%PATH%
```

Note that there are *no spaces* around the =. You must reboot your computer for this setting to take effect.

- Under Windows NT/2000, start the control panel, select System, then Environment. Scroll through the User Variables window until you find a variable named PATH. Add the jdk\bin directory to the beginning of the path, using a semicolon to separate the new entry, like this:

```
c:\jdk\bin;other stuff
```

Save your settings. Any new console windows that you start have the correct path.

Here is how you test whether you did it right:

Start a shell window. How you do this depends on your operating system. Type the line

```
java -version
```

and press the ENTER key. You should get a display such as this one:

```
java version "1.3.0"
Java(TM) 2 Runtime Environment, Standard Edition
Java HotSpot(TM) Client VM
```

If instead you get a message such as "java: command not found," "Bad command or file name," or "The name specified is not recognized as an internal or external command, operable program or batch file," then you need to go back and double-check your installation.

Installing the Library Source and Documentation

The library source files are delivered in the Java SDK as a compressed file src.jar , and you must unpack that file to get access to the source code. We highly recommend that you do that. Simply do the following:

1. Make sure the Java SDK is installed and the jdk/bin directory is on the execution path.

2. Open a command shell.

3. Change to the `jdk` directory (e.g. `/usr/local/jdk` or `C:\jdk`).

4. Execute the command:

   ```
   jar xvf src.jar
   ```

> **TIP:** The `src.jar` file contains the source code for all public libraries. To get even more source (for the compiler, the virtual machine, the native methods, and the private helper classes), go to `http://www.sun.com/software/communitysource/java2`.

The documentation is contained in a compressed file that is separate from the Java SDK. Several formats (.zip, .gz, and .Z) are available. Uncompress the format that works best for you. If in doubt, use the zip file because you can uncompress it with the `jar` program that is a part of the Java SDK. If you decide to use `jar`, follow these steps:

1. Make sure the Java SDK is installed and the `jdk/bin` directory is on the execution path.

2. Copy the documentation zip file into the directory that contains the `jdk` directory (such as `/usr/local` or `C:\`). The file is called `jdkversion-doc.zip`, where *version* is something like `1_2_3`.

3. Open a command shell.

4. Change to the directory that contains the `jdk` directory and the compressed documentation file.

5. Execute the command:

   ```
   jar xvf jdkversion-doc.zip
   ```

   where *version* is the appropriate version number.

Installing the Core Java Program Examples

You also want to install the Core Java program examples. You can find them on the CD-ROM or download them from `http://www.phptr.com/corejava`. The programs are packaged into a zip file `corejava.zip`. You should unzip them into a separate directory—we recommend you call it `CoreJavaBook`. You can use any zip file utility such as WinZip (on the CD ROM and at `http://www.winzip.com`), or you can simply use the `jar` utility that is part of the Java SDK. If you use `jar`, do the following:

1. Make sure the Java SDK is installed and the `jdk/bin` directory is on the execution path.

2. Make a directory `CoreJavaBook`.

3. Copy the `corejava.zip` file to that directory.

4. Open a command shell.

5. Change to the `CoreJavaBook` directory.

6. Execute the command:
   `jar xvf corejava.zip`

Navigating the Java Directories

In your explorations of Java, you will occasionally want to peek inside the Java source files. And, of course, you will need to work extensively with the library documentation. Table 2–1 shows the Java directory tree. The layout will be different if you have an integrated development environment, and the root will be different depending on the Java SDK version that you installed.

Table 2–1: Java directory tree

`jdk`	(the name may be different, for example, `jdk1.2`)	
	`docs`	library documentation in HTML format is here
	`bin`	the compiler and tools are here
	`demo`	look here for demos
	`include`	files for native methods (see volume 2)
	`lib`	library files
	`src`	look in the various subdirectories for the library source (after expanding `src.jar`)
	`jre`	Java runtime environment files

The two most important subdirectories in this tree are `docs` and `src`. The `docs` directory contains the Java library documentation in HTML format. You can view it with any web browser, such as Netscape.

TIP: Set a bookmark in your browser to the local version of `docs\api\index.html`. You will be referring to this page a lot as you explore the Java platform.

The `src` directory contains the source code for the public part of the Java libraries. As you become more comfortable with Java, you may find yourself in situations for which this book and the on-line information do not provide what you need to know. At this point, the source code for Java is a good place to begin digging. It is occasionally reassuring to know that you can always dig into the source to find out what a library function really does. For example, if you are curious about the inner workings of the `System` class, you can look inside `src/java/lang/System.java`.

Development Environments

If your programming experience comes from Visual Basic or Visual C++, you are accustomed to a development environment with a built-in text editor and menus to compile and launch a program along with an integrated debugger. The basic Java SDK contains nothing even remotely similar. *Everything* is done by typing in commands in a shell window. We tell you how to install and use the basic Java SDK, because we have found that the full-fledged development environments don't necessarily make it easy to learn Java—they can be complex and they hide some of the interesting and important details from the programmer.

Integrated development environments tend to be more cumbersome to use for a simple program since they are slower, require more powerful computers, and often require a somewhat tedious project setup for each program you write. These environments have the edge if you write larger Java programs consisting of many source files. And these environments also supply debuggers, which are certainly necessary for serious development—the command-line debugger that comes for free with the Java SDK is extremely awkward to use. We will show you how to get started with Forte Community Edition, a freely available development environment that is itself written in Java. Of course, if you already have a development environment such as JBuilder, Kawa, CodeWarrior or Café that supports the current version of Java, then you can certainly use it with this book.

For simple programs, a good middle ground between command-line tools and an integrated development environment is an editor that integrates with the Java SDK. On Linux, our preferred choice is Emacs. On Windows, we also like Text-Pad, an excellent shareware programming editor for Windows with good Java integration. Many other editors have similar features. Using a text editor with Java SDK integration can make developing Java programs easy and fast. We used that approach for developing and testing most of the programs in this book. Since you can compile and execute source code from within the editor, it can become your de facto development environment as you work through this book.

In sum, you have three choices for a development environment:

- Use the Java SDK and your favorite text editor. Compile and launch programs in a command shell.

- Use the Java SDK and a text editor that is integrated with the Java SDK. Emacs and TextPad have this capability, and there are many others. Compile and launch programs inside the editor.

- Use an integrated development environment such as the free Forte Community Edition, or one of many other freely or commercially available environments.

Using the Command Line Tools

There are two methods for compiling and launching a Java program: from the command line, or from another program, such as an integrated development environment or a text editor. Let us do it the hard way first: from the command line.

Open a shell or terminal window. Go to the `CoreJavaBook/v1ch2/Welcome` directory. Then enter the following commands:

```
javac Welcome.java
java Welcome
```

You should see the message shown in Figure 2–1 on the screen.

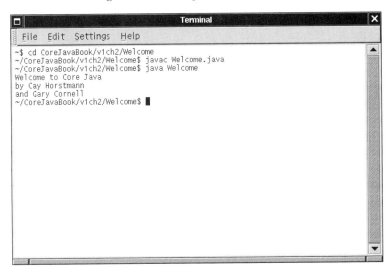

Figure 2–1: **Compiling and running Welcome.java**

Congratulations! You have just compiled and run your first Java program.

What happened? The `javac` program is the Java compiler. It compiles the file `Welcome.java` into the file `Welcome.class`. The `java` program is the Java interpreter. It interprets the bytecodes that the compiler placed in the class file.

TIP: If you use the MS-DOS shell in Windows, you should use the DOSKEY program. The DOSKEY utility keeps a *command history.* Type the up and down arrow keys to cycle through the previously typed commands. Use the left and right arrow keys to edit the current command.

To install DOSKEY automatically, simply add the line

```
DOSKEY /INSERT
```

into your `AUTOEXEC.BAT` file and reboot.

If you use the `bash` or `tcsh` shell under UNIX, you have the same benefits.

The `Welcome` program is extremely simple. It merely prints a message to the console. You may enjoy looking inside the program shown in Example 2–1—we will explain how it works in the next chapter.

Example 2–1: Welcome.java

```
1. public class Welcome
2. {
3.    public static void main(String[] args)
4.    {
5.       String[] greeting = new String[3];
6.       greeting[0] = "Welcome to Core Java";
7.       greeting[1] = "by Cay Horstmann";
8.       greeting[2] = "and Gary Cornell";
9.
10.      for (int i = 0; i < greeting.length; i++)
11.          System.out.println(greeting[i]);
12.   }
13. }
```

Troubleshooting Hints

In the age of visual development environments, many programmers are unfamiliar with running programs in a shell window. There are any number of things that can go wrong and lead to frustrating results.

Pay attention to the following points:

*   If you type in the program by hand, make sure you pay attention to uppercase and lowercase letters. In particular, the class name is `Welcome` and not `welcome` or WELCOME.

*   The compiler requires a *file name* `Welcome.`**java**. The interpreter requires a *class name* `Welcome` without a `.java` or `.class` extension.

*   If you get a message such as "Bad command or file name" or "javac: command not found," then you need to go back and double-check your installation, in particular the execution path setting.

*   If `javac` reports an error "cannot read: Welcome.java," then you should check whether that file is present in the directory.

    Under UNIX, check that you used the correct capitalization for `Welcome.java`.

    Under Windows, use the `dir` shell command, *not* the graphical Explorer tool. Some text editors (in particular Notepad) insist on adding an extension `.txt` after every file. If you use Notepad to edit `Welcome.java`, then it actually saves it as `Welcome.java.txt`. Under the default Windows settings, Explorer conspires with Notepad and hides the `.txt` extension because it belongs to a "known file type." In that case, you need to rename the file, using the `ren` shell command.

- If `java` reports an error message complaining about a `java.lang.NoClassDefFoundError`, then carefully check the name of the offending class.

  If the interpreter complains about `welcome` (with a lowercase `w`), then you should reissue the `java Welcome` command with an uppercase `W`. As always, case matters in Java.

  If the interpreter complains about `Welcome/java`, then you accidentally typed `java Welcome.java`. Reissue the command as `java Welcome`.

  If the interpreter complains about `Welcome`, then someone has set the *class path* on your system. You need to either remove the setting of that environment variable, or add the current directory (symbolized as a period) to the class path. See Chapter 4 for more details.

- If you have too many errors in your program, then all the error messages fly by very quickly. The `java` interpreter sends the error messages to the standard error stream which makes it a bit tricky to capture them if they fill more than one screen.

  On a UNIX or Windows NT/2000 system, this is not a big problem. You can use the `2>` shell operator to redirect the errors to a file:

  ```
  javac MyProg.java 2> errors.txt
  ```

  Under Windows 95/98, you cannot redirect the standard error stream from the command shell. You can download the `errout` program from `http://www.horstmann.com/corejava/faq.html` and run

  ```
  errout javac MyProg.java > errors.txt
  ```

TIP: There is an excellent tutorial at `http://java.sun.com/docs/books/tutorial/getStarted/cupojava/` that goes into much greater detail about the "gotchas" that beginners can run into.

Using an Integrated Development Environment

In this section, we show you how to compile a program with Forte Community Edition, a free integrated development environment from Sun Microsystems. You can download your copy from `http://www.sun.com/forte/ffj/ce/`. Forte is written in Java and should run under any platform that has a Java 2 runtime environment. Preconfigured versions exist for Solaris, Linux, and Windows.

After starting Forte, various toolbars and windows are loaded (see Figure 2–2).

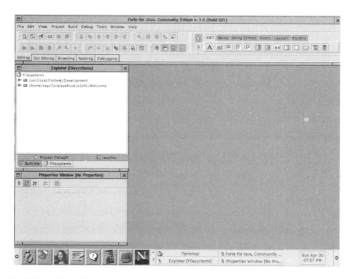

Figure 2–2: Starting Forte

Select File -> Open File from the menu, then load `CoreJavaBook/v1ch2/Welcome/Welcome.java`. You will be asked if this file should be in the "default package." Click Accept. (See Chapter 4 for more information on packages. For now, all our programs are in the default package.) You should now see a window with the program code (see Figure 2–3).

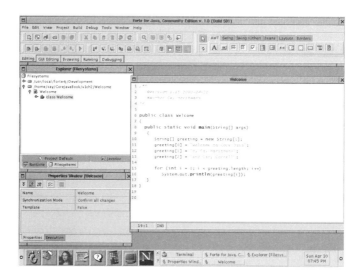

Figure 2–3: The edit window of Forte

Select Build -> Compile from the menu. Your program is compiled. If it compiles correctly, select Build -> Execute from the menu. The edit window goes away, and an output window appears at the bottom of the screen. The program output is displayed in the output window (see Figure 2–4).

Figure 2–4: The output window of Forte

To return to the edit window after the program is finished, click on the "Editing" tab at the top of the screen.

Locating Compilation Errors

Presumably, this program did not have typos or bugs. (It was only a few lines of code, after all.) Let us suppose, for the sake of argument, that you occasionally have a typo (perhaps even a bug) in your code. Try it out—ruin our file, for example, by changing the capitalization of `String` as follows:

```
string[] greeting = new String[3];
```

Now, run the compiler again. You will get error messages (see Figure 2–5). The first one complains about an unknown `string` type. Simply click on the error message. The cursor moves to the matching line in the edit window, and you can correct your error. This allows you to fix your errors quickly.

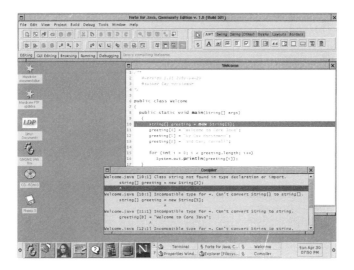

Figure 2–5: Error messages in Forte

To start a new program with Forte, select File -> New from Template from the menu. In the resulting dialog, open up the "doorlatch" labeled Classes by clicking on the icon. Then select Empty and click the Next button (see Figure 2–6).

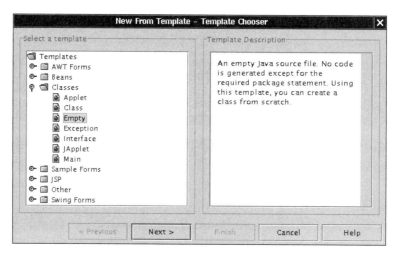

Figure 2–6: Starting a new program in Forte

You will be asked if you want to add this file to the current project. Until you use projects in earnest, there is no harm in answering either Yes or No. Now you are ready to edit your new file, compile it, and run it.

We will discuss the Forte debugger in Chapter 11.

Compiling and Running Programs from a Text Editor

An integrated development environment such as Forte offers many comforts, but there are also some drawbacks. In particular, for simple programs that are not distributed over multiple source files, an environment with its long startup time and many bells and whistles can seem like overkill. Also, many programmers have become accustomed to their favorite text editor and can be reluctant to use the generally wimpy editors that are part of the integrated development environments. Fortunately, many text editors have the ability to launch the Java compiler and interpreter and to capture error messages and program output. In this section, we look at two text editors, Emacs and TextPad, as typical examples.

NOTE: GNU Emacs is available from `http://www.gnu.org/software/emacs/`. For the Windows port of GNU Emacs, see `http://www.gnu.org/software/emacs/windows/ntemacs.html`. XEmacs is a version of Emacs with a slightly more modern

For example, Figure 2–7 shows XEmacs, a version of the Emacs editor that is popular among UNIX programmers, compiling a Java program. (Choose JDE -> Compile from the menu to run the compiler.)

The error messages show up in the lower half of the screen. When you move the cursor on an error message and press the ENTER key, then the cursor moves to the corresponding source line.

Once all errors are fixed, you can run the program by choosing JDE -> Run App from the menu. The output shows up inside an editor window (see Figure 2–8).

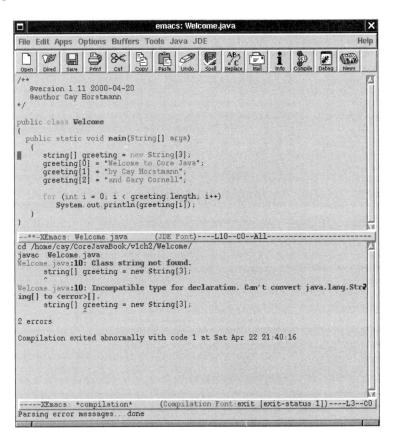

Figure 2–7: Compiling a program with XEmacs

Figure 2–8: Running a program from within XEmacs

Emacs is a splendid text editor that is freely available for UNIX and Windows. However, many Windows programmers find the learning curve rather steep. For those programmers, we can recommend TextPad. Unlike Emacs, TextPad conforms to standard Windows conventions. TextPad is available on this book's CD-ROM and at `http://www.textpad.com`. Note that TextPad is shareware. You are expected to pay for it if you use it beyond a trial period. (We have no relationship with the vendor, except as satisfied users of the program.)

To compile a program in TextPad, choose Tools -> Compile Java from the menu, or use the CTRL+1 keyboard shortcut.

NOTE: If there is no such menu option, select Configure -> Preferences, then select Tools from the tree on the left. On the right hand side, click the button labeled Add until it drops down and reveals a setting JDK commands. Select that setting, then click Ok. The JDK commands are now added to the Tools menu.

Compilation errors are displayed in a separate window (see Figure 2–9).

Move the cursor onto the first line of an error message and press ENTER to move to the matching location in the file. Use the Search -> Jump Next command (or the F4 key) to walk through the remaining error messages.

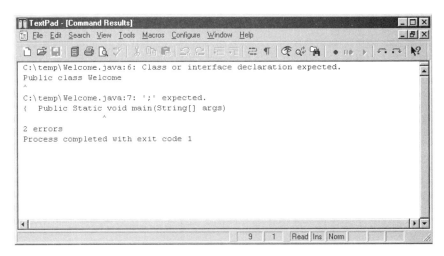

Figure 2–9: Locating compilation errors in TextPad

To run a program, select Tools -> Run Java Application from the menu, or use the CTRL+2 keyboard shortcut. The program runs in a separate shell window. Figure 2–10 shows a Java program launched from TextPad.

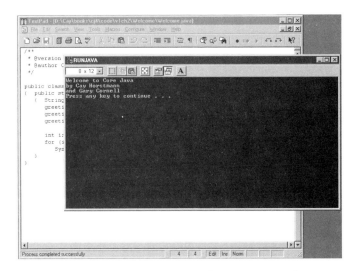

Figure 2–10: Running a Java program from TextPad

When the program is completed, you need to press a key to continue and then close the shell window.

Graphical Applications

The `Welcome` program was not terribly exciting. Next, let us run a graphical application. This program is a very simple GIF file viewer. It simply loads and displays a GIF file. Again, let us first compile and run it from the command line.

1. Open a shell window.
2. Change to the directory `CoreJavaBook/v1ch2/ImageViewer`.
3. Enter:
```
javac ImageViewer.java
java ImageViewer
```

A new program window pops up with our ImageViewer application. (See Figure 2–11.)

Now select File -> Open and look for a GIF file to open. (We supplied a couple of sample files in the same directory.)

Figure 2–11: Running the ImageViewer application

To close the program, click on the Close box in the title bar or pull down the system menu and close the program. (To compile and run this program inside a text editor or an integrated development environment, do the same as before. For example, for Emacs, choose JDE -> Compile, then choose JDE -> Run App.)

We hope that you find this program interesting and useful. Have a quick look at the source code. The program is substantially longer than the first program, but it is not terribly complex if you consider how much code it would take in C or C++ to write a similar application. In Visual Basic, of course, it is easy to write or, rather, drag and drop, such a program—you need only add a couple of lines of code to make it functional. The JDK does not have a visual interface builder, so you need to write code for everything, as shown in Example 2–2. You will learn how to write graphical programs like this in Chapters 7–9.

CAUTION: If you run this program with a version of the Java SDK prior to 1.3, then you will get a compile-time error at the line

```
frame.setDefaultCloseOperation(JFrame.EXIT_ON_CLOSE);
```

In that case, comment out the line and recompile. Then the program won't exit when you close the frame. Instead, choose the File -> Exit menu option. See Chapter 7 for more information on this issue.

Example 2–2: ImageViewer.java

```
1. import java.awt.*;
2. import java.awt.event.*;
3. import java.awt.image.*;
4. import java.io.*;
5. import javax.swing.*;
6.
7. public class ImageViewer
8. {
9.    public static void main(String[] args)
10.    {
11.       JFrame frame = new ImageViewerFrame();
12.       frame.setTitle("ImageViewer");
13.       frame.setSize(300, 400);
14.       frame.setDefaultCloseOperation(JFrame.EXIT_ON_CLOSE);
15.       frame.show();
16.    }
17. }
18.
19. class ImageViewerFrame extends JFrame
20. {
21.    public ImageViewerFrame()
22.    {
23.       // set up menu bar
24.       JMenuBar menuBar = new JMenuBar();
25.       setJMenuBar(menuBar);
26.
27.       JMenu menu = new JMenu("File");
28.       menuBar.add(menu);
29.
30.       JMenuItem openItem = new JMenuItem("Open");
31.       menu.add(openItem);
```

```
32.      openItem.addActionListener(new FileOpenListener());
33.
34.      JMenuItem exitItem = new JMenuItem("Exit");
35.      menu.add(exitItem);
36.      exitItem.addActionListener(new
37.         ActionListener()
38.         {
39.            public void actionPerformed(ActionEvent event)
40.            {
41.               System.exit(0);
42.            }
43.         });
44.
45.      // use a label to display the images
46.      label = new JLabel();
47.      Container contentPane = getContentPane();
48.      contentPane.add(label, "Center");
49.   }
50.
51.   private class FileOpenListener implements ActionListener
52.   {
53.      public void actionPerformed(ActionEvent evt)
54.      {
55.         // set up file chooser
56.         JFileChooser chooser = new JFileChooser();
57.         chooser.setCurrentDirectory(new File("."));
58.
59.         // accept all files ending with .gif
60.         chooser.setFileFilter(new
61.            javax.swing.filechooser.FileFilter()
62.            {
63.               public boolean accept(File f)
64.               {
65.                  return f.getName().toLowerCase()
66.                     .endsWith(".gif")
67.                     || f.isDirectory();
68.               }
69.               public String getDescription()
70.               {
71.                  return "GIF Images";
72.               }
73.            });
74.
75.         // show file chooser dialog
76.         int r = chooser.showOpenDialog(ImageViewerFrame.this);
77.
78.         // if image file accepted, set it as icon of the label
79.         if(r == JFileChooser.APPROVE_OPTION)
```

```
80.            {
81.               String name
82.                  = chooser.getSelectedFile().getPath();
83.               label.setIcon(new ImageIcon(name));
84.            }
85.         }
86.      }
87.
88.      private JLabel label;
89. }
```

Applets

The first two programs presented in this book are Java *applications,* stand-alone programs like any native programs. On the other hand, as we mentioned in the last chapter, most of the hype about Java comes from its ability to run *applets* inside a web browser. We want to show you how to build and run an applet from the command line. Then we will load the applet into the applet viewer that comes with the JDK. Finally, we will display it in a web browser.

First, go to the directory CoreJavaBook/v1ch2/WelcomeApplet, then enter the following commands:

```
javac WelcomeApplet.java
appletviewer WelcomeApplet.html
```

Figure 2–12 shows what you see in the applet viewer window.

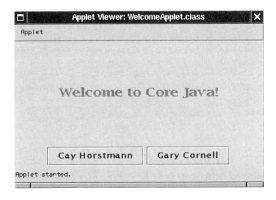

Figure 2–12: The WelcomeApplet applet as viewed by the applet viewer

The first command is the now-familiar command to invoke the Java compiler. This compiles the WelcomeApplet.java source into the bytecode file WelcomeApplet.class.

This time, however, we do not run the Java interpreter. We invoke the appletviewer program instead. This program is a special tool included with the Java SDK that lets you quickly test an applet. You need to give it an HTML file, rather than the name of a Java class file. The contents of the `WelcomeApplet.html` file are shown below in Example 2–3.

Example 2–3: WelcomeApplet.html

```
1. <HTML>
2. <TITLE>WelcomeApplet</TITLE>
3. <BODY>
4. <HR>
5. <P>
6. This applet is from the book
7. <A HREF="http://www.horstmann.com/corejava.html">
8. Core Java</A> by <I>Cay Horstmann</I> and <I>Gary Cornell</I>,
9. published by Sun Microsystems Press.
10. </P>
11. <APPLET CODE=WelcomeApplet.class WIDTH=400 HEIGHT=200>
12. <PARAM NAME=greeting VALUE="Welcome to Core Java!">
13. </APPLET>
14. <HR>
15. <P><A href="WelcomeApplet.java">The source.</A></P>
16. </BODY>
17. </HTML>
```

If you are familiar with HTML, you will notice some standard HTML instructions and the `APPLET` tag, telling the applet viewer to load the applet whose code is stored in `WelcomeApplet.class`. The applet viewer ignores all HTML tags except for the `APPLET` tag.

The other HTML tags show up if you view the HTML file in a browser. However, there is a problem. The applet uses features of the Java 2 platform, whereas at the time of this writing, the most commonly used browsers (Netscape 4 and Microsoft Internet Explorer 5) only support version 1.1. Thus, you cannot simply load the HTML file into these browsers. You have two options:

1. Install the Java Plug-in into your Netscape 4 or Internet Explorer 5 browser. You can download the plug-in from `http://java.sun.com/plugin`. You then need to use a different HTML page that loads the plug-in and tells the plug-in to load the applet code. Unfortunately, this requires rather messy HTML tags—see Example 2–4. (This code has been automatically generated by the Java Plug-in HTML converter—see Chapter 10 for details.)

2. Use a browser that supports the Java 2 platform, such as Netscape 6 or Opera (`http://www.opera.com`). You can then use the same simple HTML file that works with the applet viewer.

Provided you have a browser with Java 2 platform support, you can try loading the applet inside the browser.

1.   Start your browser.

2.   Select File -> Open File (or the equivalent).

3.   Go to the `CoreJavaBook/v1ch2/WelcomeApplet` directory.

You should see the `WelcomeApplet.html` and `WelcomeAppletPlugin.html` files in the file dialog. Load the file that is appropriate for your setup. Your browser now loads the applet, including the surrounding text. It will look something like Figure 2–13.

You can see that this application is actually alive and willing to interact with the Internet. Click on the Cay Horstmann button. The applet directs the browser to display Cay's web page. Click on the Gary Cornell button. The applet directs the browser to pop up a mail window, with Gary's e-mail address already filled in.

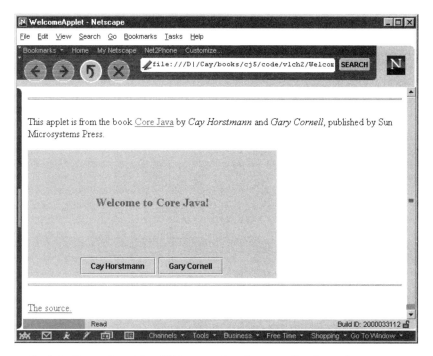

Figure 2–13: Running the WelcomeApplet applet in a browser

Notice that neither of these two buttons works in the applet viewer. The applet viewer has no capabilities to send mail or display a web page, so it ignores your requests. The applet viewer is good for testing applets in isolation, but you need to put applets inside a browser to see how they interact with the browser and the Internet.

TIP: You can also run applets from inside your editor or integrated development environment. In Emacs, select JDE -> Run Applet from the menu. In TextPad, choose Tools -> Run Java Applet or use the CTRL+3 keyboard shortcut. You will be presented with a dialog that lists all HTML files in the current directory. If you press ESC, TextPad automatically creates a minimal HTML file for you. In Forte, you simply load the HTML page with the applet tags. Forte contains a simple browser that shows the applet running inside the web page. Alternatively, you can right-click on the source file and set the value of the "Executor" property in the Execution tab to "Applet Execution."

Finally, the code for the Welcome applet is shown in Example 2–5. At this point, do not give it more than a glance. We will come back to writing applets in Chapter 10.

In this chapter, you learned about the mechanics of compiling and running Java programs. You are now ready to move on to Chapter 3 where you will start learning the Java language.

Example 2–4: WelcomeAppletPlugin.html

```
1. <HTML>
2. <TITLE>WelcomeApplet</TITLE>
3. <BODY>
4. <HR>
5. <P>
6. This applet is from the book
7. <A HREF="http://www.horstmann.com/corejava.html">
8. Core Java</A> by <I>Cay Horstmann</I> and <I>Gary Cornell</I>,
9. published by Sun Microsystems Press.
10. </P>
11. <!--"CONVERTED_APPLET"-->
12. <!-- CONVERTER VERSION 1.0 -->
13. <OBJECT classid="clsid:8AD9C840-044E-11D1-B3E9-00805F499D93"
14. WIDTH = 400 HEIGHT = 200  codebase="http://java.sun.com/products/
    plugin/1.2/jinstall-12-win32.cab#Version=1,2,0,0">
15. <PARAM NAME = CODE VALUE = WelcomeApplet.class >
16.
17. <PARAM NAME="type" VALUE="application/x-java-applet;version=1.2">
18.
19. <PARAM NAME = greeting VALUE  ="Welcome to Core Java!">
20. <COMMENT>
21. <EMBED type="application/x-java-applet;version=1.2" java_CODE =
    WelcomeApplet.class WIDTH = 400 HEIGHT = 200  greeting = "Welcome
    to Core Java!"  pluginspage="http://java.sun.com/products/
    plugin/1.2/plugin-install.html"><NOEMBED></COMMENT>
22.
```

```
23. </NOEMBED></EMBED>
24. </OBJECT>
25.
26. <!--
27. <APPLET  CODE = WelcomeApplet.class WIDTH = 400 HEIGHT = 200 >
28. <PARAM NAME = greeting VALUE  ="Welcome to Core Java!">
29.
30.
31. </APPLET>
32. -->
33. <!--"END_CONVERTED_APPLET"-->
34.
35. <HR>
36. <P><A href="WelcomeApplet.java">The source.</A></P>
37. </BODY>
38. </HTML>
```

Example 2–5: WelcomeApplet.java

```
1. import javax.swing.*;
2. import java.awt.*;
3. import java.awt.event.*;
4. import java.net.*;
5.
6. public class WelcomeApplet extends JApplet
7. {
8.    public void init()
9.    {
10.      Container contentPane = getContentPane();
11.      contentPane.setLayout(new BorderLayout());
12.
13.      JLabel label = new JLabel(getParameter("greeting"),
14.         SwingConstants.CENTER);
15.      label.setFont(new Font("TimesRoman", Font.BOLD, 18));
16.      contentPane.add(label, "Center");
17.
18.      JPanel panel = new JPanel();
19.
20.      JButton cayButton = new JButton("Cay Horstmann");
21.      cayButton.addActionListener(getURLActionListener
22.         ("http://www.horstmann.com"));
23.      panel.add(cayButton);
24.
25.      JButton garyButton = new JButton("Gary Cornell");
26.      garyButton.addActionListener(getURLActionListener
27.         ("mailto:gary@thecornells.com"));
28.      panel.add(garyButton);
29.
30.      contentPane.add(panel, "South");
```

```
31.     }
32.
33.     public ActionListener getURLActionListener(final String
34.         urlString)
35.     {
36.         return new
37.             ActionListener()
38.             {
39.                 public void actionPerformed(ActionEvent evt)
40.                 {
41.                     try
42.                     {
43.                         URL u = new URL(urlString);
44.                         getAppletContext().showDocument(u);
45.                     }
46.                     catch(Exception e) { e.printStackTrace(); }
47.                 }
48.             };
49.     }
50. }
```

Chapter 3

Fundamental Programming Structures in Java

At this point, we are assuming that you successfully installed Java and were able to run the sample programs that we showed you in Chapter 2. It's time to start programming. This chapter shows you how the basic programming concepts such as data types, branches, and loops are implemented in Java.

Unfortunately, in Java you can't easily write a program that uses a graphical user interface—you need to learn a fair amount of machinery to put up windows, add text boxes and buttons that respond to them, and so on. Since introducing the techniques needed to write GUI-based Java programs would take us too far away from our goal of introducing the basic programming concepts, the sample programs in this chapter will be "toy" programs, designed to illustrate a concept. All these examples will simply send output to the console. (For example, if you are using Windows, the console is an MS-DOS window.) When it comes to getting user input, we will stick to reading the information from a pop-up window. In particular, we will be writing *applications* rather than *applets* in this chapter.

Finally, if you are an experienced C++ programmer, you can get away with just skimming this chapter: concentrate on the C/C++ notes that are interspersed throughout the text. Programmers coming from another background, such as Visual Basic, will find most of the concepts familiar and all of the syntax very different—you will want to read this chapter very carefully.

A Simple Java Program

Let's look more closely at about the simplest Java program you can have—one that simply prints a message to the console window:

```java
public class FirstSample
{
   public static void main(String[] args)
   {
      System.out.println("We will not use 'Hello, World!'");
   }
}
```

It is worth spending all the time that you need in order to become comfortable with the framework of this sample; the pieces will recur in all applications. First and foremost, *Java is case sensitive*. If you made any mistakes in capitalization (such as typing `Main` instead of `main`), the program will not run.

Now let's look at this source code line by line. The keyword `public` is called an *access modifier;* these modifiers control what other parts of a program can use this code. We will have more to say about access modifiers in Chapter 5. The keyword `class` is there to remind you that everything in a Java program lives inside a class. Although we will spend a lot more time on classes in the next chapter, for now think of a class as a container for the program logic that defines the behavior of an application. As mentioned in Chapter 1, classes are the building blocks with which all Java applications and applets are built. *Everything* in a Java program must be inside a class.

Following the keyword `class` is the name of the class. The rules for class names in Java are quite generous. Names must begin with a letter, and after that, they can have any combination of letters and digits. The length is essentially unlimited. You cannot use a Java reserved word (such as `public` or `if`) for a class name. (See Appendix I for a list of reserved words.)

As you can see in the name `FirstSample`, the convention is that class names are nouns that start with an uppercase letter.

You need to make the file name for the source code the same as the name of the public class, with the extension `.java` appended. Thus, we must store this code in a file called `FirstSample.java`. (Again, case is important—don't use `firstsample.java`.) If you don't do this, you'll get a pretty obvious error message when you try to run this source code through a Java compiler ("Public class FirstSample must be defined in a file called 'FirstSample.java'").

If you have named the file correctly and not made any typos in the source code, then when you compile this source code, you end up with a file containing the bytecodes for this class. The Java compiler automatically names the bytecode file `FirstSample.class` and stores it in the same directory as the source file. Finally, run the bytecode file through the Java interpreter by issuing the command:

```
java FirstSample
```

(Remember to leave off the `.class` extension.) When the program executes, it simply displays the string `We will not use 'Hello, World'!` on the console.

NOTE: Applets have a different structure—see Chapter 10 for information on applets.

When you use

```
java NameOfClass
```

to run a compiled program, the Java interpreter always starts execution with the code in the `main` method in the class you indicate. Thus, you *must* have a `main` method in the source file for your class in order for your code to execute. You can, of course, add your own methods to a class and call them from the `main` method. (We cover writing your own methods in the next chapter.)

Next, notice the braces in the source code. In Java, as in C/C++, braces are used to delineate the parts (usually called *blocks*) in your program. In Java, the code for any method must be started by an opening brace { and ended by a closing brace }.

Brace styles have inspired an inordinate amount of useless controversy. We use a style that lines up matching braces. Since white space is irrelevant to the Java compiler, you can use whatever brace style you like. We will have more to say about the use of braces when we talk about the various kinds of loops.

For now, don't worry about the keywords `static void`—just think of them as part of what you need to get a Java program to compile. By the end of Chapter 4, you will understand this incantation completely. The point to remember for now is that every Java application must have a `main` method whose header is identical to the one shown here.

```
public class ClassName
{
   public static void main(String[] args)
   {
      program instructions
   }
}
```

> **C++ NOTE:** You know what a class is. Java classes are similar to C++ classes, but there are a few differences that can trap you. For example, in Java *all* functions are methods of some class. (The standard terminology refers to them as methods, not member functions.) Thus, in Java you must have a shell class for the `main` method. You may also be familiar with the idea of *static member functions* in C++. These are member functions defined inside a class that do not operate on objects. The `main` method in Java is always static. Finally, as in C/C++, the `void` keyword indicates that this method does not return a value. Unlike C/C++, the `main` method does not return an "exit code" to the operating system. If the `main` method exits normally, the Java program has the exit code 0, indicating successful completion. To terminate the program with a different exit code, use the `System.exit` method.

Next, turn your attention to this fragment.

```
{
    System.out.println("We will not use 'Hello world!'");
}
```

Braces mark the beginning and end of the *body* of the method. This method has only one statement in it. As with most programming languages, you can think of Java statements as being the sentences of the language. In Java, every statement must end with a semicolon. In particular, carriage returns do not mark the end of a statement, so statements can span multiple lines if need be.

The body of the `main` method contains a statement that outputs a single line of text to the console.

Here, we are using the `System.out` object and calling its `println` method. Notice the periods used to invoke a method. Java uses the general syntax

```
object.method(parameters)
```

for its equivalent of function calls.

In this case, we are calling the `println` method and passing it a string parameter. The method displays the string parameter on the console. It then terminates the output line so that each call to `println` displays its output on a new line. Notice that Java, like C/C++, uses double quotes to delimit strings. (You will find more information about strings later in this chapter.)

Methods in Java, like functions in any programming languages, can use zero, one, or more *parameters* (some languages call them *arguments*). Even if a method takes zero parameters, you must still use empty parentheses. For example, there is a variant of the `println` method with no parameters that just prints a blank line. You invoke it with the call

```
System.out.println();
```

> CAUTION: There also is a `print` method in `System.out` that doesn't add a new line character to the output. For example, `System.out.print("Hello")` prints `"Hello"` without a new line. The next output appears immediately after the `"o"`.

Comments

Comments in Java, like comments in most programming languages, do not show up in the executable program. Thus, you can add as many comments as needed without fear of bloating the code. Java has three ways of showing comments. The most common method is a `//`. You use this for a comment that will run from the `//` to the end of the line.

```
System.out.println("We will not use 'Hello world!'");
// is this too cute?
```

When longer comments are needed, you can mark each line with a `//`. Or you can use the `/*` and `*/` comment delimiters that let you block off a longer comment. This is shown in Example 3–1.

Example 3–1: FirstSample.java

```
1. /*
2.    This is the first sample program in Core Java Chapter 3
3.    Copyright (C) 1996...2000 Cay Horstmann and Gary Cornell
4. */
5.
6. public class FirstSample
7. {
8.    public static void main(String[] args)
9.    {
10.       System.out.println("We will not use 'Hello, World!'");
11.    }
12. }
```

Finally, there is a third kind of comment that can be used to generate documentation automatically. This comment uses a `/**` to start and a `*/` to end. For more on this type of comment and on automatic documentation generation, please see Chapter 4.

> CAUTION: `/* */` comments do not nest in Java. That is, you cannot deactivate code simply by surrounding it with `/*` and `*/` since the code that you want to deactivate might itself contain a `*/` delimiter.

Data Types

Java is a *strongly typed language*. This means that every variable must have a declared type. There are eight *primitive types* in Java. Four of them are integer types; two are floating-point number types; one is the character type `char`, used for characters in the Unicode encoding (see the section on the `char` type), and one is a `boolean` type for truth values.

> NOTE: Java has an arbitrary precision arithmetic package. However, "Big numbers," as they are called, are Java *objects* and not a new Java type. You will see how to use them later in this chapter.

Integers

The integer types are for numbers without fractional parts. Negative values are allowed. Java provides the four integer types shown in Table 3–1.

Table 3–1: Java integer types

Type	Storage Requirement	Range (inclusive)
int	4 bytes	–2,147,483,648 to 2,147,483, 647 (just over 2 billion)
short	2 bytes	–32,768 to 32,767
long	8 bytes	–9,223,372,036,854,775,808L to 9,223,372,036,854,775,807L
byte	1 byte	–128 to 127

In most situations, the `int` type is the most practical. If you want to represent the number of inhabitants of our planet, you'll need to resort to a `long`. The `byte` and `short` types are mainly intended for specialized applications, such as low-level file handling, or for large arrays when storage space is at a premium.

Under Java, the ranges of the integer types do not depend on the machine on which you will be running the Java code. This alleviates a major pain for the programmer who wants to move software from one platform to another, or even between operating systems on the same platform. In contrast, C and C++ programs use the most efficient integer type for each processor. As a result, a C program that runs well on a 32-bit processor may exhibit integer overflow on a 16-bit system. Since Java programs must run with the same results on all machines, the ranges for the various types are fixed.

Long integer numbers have a suffix L (for example, `4000000000L`). Hexadecimal numbers have a prefix `0x` (for example, `0xCAFE`). Octal numbers have a prefix `0`.

For example, `010` is 8. Naturally, this can be confusing, and we recommend against the use of octal constants.

C++ NOTE: In C and C++, `int` denotes the integer type that depends on the target machine. On a 16-bit processor, like the 8086, integers are 2 bytes. On a 32-bit processor like the Sun SPARC, they are 4-byte quantities. On an Intel Pentium, the integer type of C and C++ depends on the operating system: for DOS and Windows 3.1, integers are 2 bytes. When using 32-bit mode for Windows programs, integers are 4 bytes. In Java, the sizes of all numeric types are platform independent.

Note that Java does not have any `unsigned` types.

Floating-Point Types

The floating-point types denote numbers with fractional parts. There are two floating-point types, as shown in Table 3–2.

Table 3–2: Floating-point types

Type	Storage Requirement	Range
`float`	4 bytes	approximately ±3.40282347E+38F (6–7 significant decimal digits)
`double`	8 bytes	approximately ±1.79769313486231570E+308 (15 significant decimal digits)

The name `double` refers to the fact that these numbers have twice the precision of the `float` type. (Some people call these *double-precision* numbers.) Here, the type to choose in most applications is `double`. The limited precision of `float` is simply not sufficient for many situations. Seven significant (decimal) digits may be enough to precisely express your annual salary in dollars and cents, but it won't be enough for your company president's salary. The only reason to use `float` is in the rare situations in which the slightly faster processing of single-precision numbers is important, or when you need to store a large number of them.

Numbers of type `float` have a suffix F, for example, `3.402F`. Floating-point numbers without an F suffix (such as `3.402`) are always considered to be of type `double`. You can optionally supply the D suffix such as `3.402D`.

All floating-point computations follow the IEEE 754 specification. In particular, there are three special floating-point values:

- positive infinity
- negative infinity
- NaN (not a number)

to denote overflows and errors. For example, the result of dividing a positive number by 0 is positive infinity. Computing 0/0 or the square root of a negative number yields NaN.

> NOTE: There are constants `Double.POSITIVE_INFINITY`, `Double.NEGATIVE_INFINITY` and `Double.NaN` (as well as corresponding `Float` constants) to represent these special values. But they are rarely used in practice. In particular, you cannot test
>
> ```
>     if (x == Double.NaN) // is never true
> ```
>
> to check whether a particular result equals `Double.NaN`. All "not a number" values are considered distinct. However, you can use the `Double.isNaN` method:
>
> ```
>     if (Double.isNaN(x)) // check whether x is "not a number"
> ```

The Character Type

First, single quotes are used to denote `char` constants. For example, `'H'` is a character. It is different from `"H"`, a string containing a single character. Second, the `char` type denotes characters in the Unicode encoding scheme. You may not be familiar with Unicode, and, fortunately, you don't need to worry much about it if you don't program international applications. (Even if you do, you still won't have to worry about it too much because Unicode was designed to make the use of non-Roman characters easy to handle.) Because Unicode was designed to handle essentially all characters in all written languages in the world, it is a 2-byte code. This allows 65,536 characters, of which about 35,000 are currently in use. This is far richer than the ASCII codeset, which is a 1-byte code with 128 characters, or the commonly used ISO 8859-1 extension with 256 characters. That character set (which some programmers call the "Latin-1" character set) is a subset of Unicode. More precisely, it is the first 256 characters in the Unicode coding scheme. Thus, character codes like `'a'`, `'1'`, `'['` and `'ä'` are valid Unicode characters with character codes < 256. Unicode characters have codes between 0 and 65535, but they are usually expressed as hexadecimal values that run from `'\u0000'` to `'\uFFFF'` (with `'\u0000'` to `'\u00FF'` being the ordinary ISO 8859-1 characters). The `\u` prefix indicates a Unicode value, and the four hexadecimal digits tell you what Unicode character. For example, `\u2122` is the trademark symbol (™). For more information on Unicode, you might want to check out the Web site at `http://www.unicode.org`.

Besides the `\u` escape character that indicates the encoding of a Unicode character, there are several escape sequences for special characters shown in Table 3–3.

Table 3–3: Special characters

Escape Sequence	Name	Unicode Value
\b	backspace	\u0008
\t	tab	\u0009
\n	linefeed	\u000a
\r	carriage return	\u000d
\"	double quote	\u0022
\'	single quote	\u0027
\\	backslash	\u005c

NOTE: Although you can theoretically use any Unicode character in a Java application or applet, whether you can actually see it displayed depends on your browser (for applets) and (ultimately) on your operating system for both. For example, you cannot use Java to output Kanji on a machine running the U.S. version of Windows. For more on internationalization issues, please see Chapter 12 of Volume 2.

The `boolean` *Type*

The `boolean` type has two values, `false` and `true`. It is used for evaluating logical conditions. You cannot convert between integers and `boolean` values.

C++ NOTE: In C++, numbers and even pointers can be used in place of `boolean` values. The value 0 is equivalent to the `bool` value `false`, and a non-zero value is equivalent to `true`. This is *not* the case in Java. Thus, Java programmers are shielded from accidents such as

```
if (x = 0) // oops...meant x == 0
```

In C++, this test compiles and runs, always evaluating to `false`. In Java, the test does not compile because the integer expression `x = 0` cannot be converted to a `boolean` value.

Variables

In Java, every variable has a *type*. You declare a variable by placing the type first, followed by the name of the variable. Here are some examples:

```
double salary;
int vacationDays;
long earthPopulation;
char yesChar;
boolean done;
```

Notice the semicolon at the end of each declaration. The semicolon is necessary because a declaration is a complete Java statement.

The rules for a variable name are as follows:

A variable name must begin with a letter, and must be a sequence of letters or digits. Note that the terms "letter" and "digit" are much broader in Java than in most languages. A letter is defined as `'A'-'Z'`, `'a'-'z'`, `'_'`, or *any* Unicode character that denotes a letter in a language. For example, German users can use umlauts such as `'ä'` in variable names; Greek speakers could use a π. Similarly, digits are `'0'-'9'` and *any* Unicode characters that denote a digit in a language. Symbols like `'+'` or `'©'` cannot be used inside variable names, nor can spaces. *All* characters in the name of a variable are significant and *case is also significant*. The length of a variable name is essentially unlimited.

TIP: If you are really curious as to what Unicode characters are "letters" as far as Java is concerned, you can use the `isJavaIdentifierStart` and `isJavaIdentifierPart` methods in the `Character` class to check.

You also cannot use a Java reserved word for a variable name. (See Appendix I for a list of reserved words.)

You can have multiple declarations on a single line

```
int i, j; // both are integers
```

However, we don't recommend this style. If you define each variable separately, your programs are easier to read.

NOTE: As you saw, names are case-sensitive, for example `hireday` and `hireDay` are two separate names. In general, you should not have two names that only differ in their letter case. However, sometimes it is difficult to come up with a good name for a variable. Many programmers then give the variable the same name of the type, such as

```
Box box; // ok--Box is the type and box is the variable name
```

However, a better solution is to use an "a" prefix for the variable:

```
Box aBox;
```

Assignments and Initializations

After you declare a variable, you must explicitly initialize it by means of an assignment statement—you can never use the values of uninitialized variables. You assign to a previously declared variable using the variable name on the left, an equal sign (=), and then some Java expression that has an appropriate value on the right.

```
int vacationDays; // this is a declaration
vacationDays = 12; // this is an assignment
```

Here's an example of an assignment to a character variable:

```
char yesChar;
yesChar = 'Y';
```

One nice feature of Java is the ability to both declare and initialize a variable on the same line. For example:

```
int vacationDays = 12; // this is an initialization
```

Finally, in Java you can put declarations anywhere in your code. For example, the following is valid code in Java:

```
double salary = 65000.0;
System.out.println(salary);
int vacationDays = 12; // ok to declare variable here
```

Of course, you cannot declare two variables with the same name in the same scope.

C++ NOTE: C and C++ distinguish between the *declaration* and *definition* of variables. For example,

```
        int i = 10;
```

is a definition, whereas

```
        extern int i;
```

is a declaration. In Java, there are no declarations that are separate from definitions.

Constants

In Java, you use the keyword `final` to denote a constant. For example,

```
public class Constants
{
   public static void main(String[] args)
   {
      final double CM_PER_INCH = 2.54;
      double paperWidth = 8.5;
      double paperHeight = 11;
      System.out.println("Paper size in centimeter: "
         + paperWidth * CM_PER_INCH + " by "
         + paperHeight * CM_PER_INCH);
   }
}
```

The keyword `final` indicates that you can assign to the variable once, then its value is set once and for all. It is customary to name constants in all upper case.

It is probably more common in Java to want a constant that is available to multiple methods inside a single class. These are usually called *class constants*. You set up a class constant with the keywords `static final`. Here is an example of using a class constant:

```
public class Constants2
{
   public static final double CM_PER_INCH = 2.54;;

   public static void main(String[] args)
   {
      double paperWidth = 8.5;
      double paperHeight = 11;
      System.out.println("Paper size in centimeter: "
         + paperWidth * CM_PER_INCH + " by "
         + paperHeight * CM_PER_INCH);
   }
}
```

Note that the definition of the class constant appears *outside* the `main` method. Thus, the constant can also be used in other methods of the same class. Furthermore, if (as in our example) the constant is declared `public`, methods of other classes can also use the constant—in our example, as `Constants2.CM_PER_INCH`.

 C++ NOTE: `const` is a reserved Java keyword, but it is not currently used for anything. You must use `final` for a constant.

Operators

The usual arithmetic operators + − * / are used in Java for addition, subtraction, multiplication, and division. The / operator denotes integer division if both arguments are integers, and floating-point division otherwise. Integer remainder (that is, the mod function) is denoted by %. For example, 15 / 2 is 7, 15 % 2 is 1, and 15.0 / 2 is 7.5.

Note that integer division by 0 raises an exception, whereas floating-point division by 0 yields an infinite or NaN result.

You can use the arithmetic operators in your variable initializations:

```
int n = 5;
int a = 2 * n; // a is 10
```

There is a convenient shortcut for using binary arithmetic operators in an assignment. For example,

```
x += 4;
```

is equivalent to

```
x = x + 4;
```

(In general, place the operator to the left of the = sign, such as *= or %=.)

NOTE: One of the stated goals of the Java programming language is portability. A computation should yield the same results no matter on which virtual machine it executes. For arithmetic computations with floating-point numbers, it is surprisingly difficult to achieve this portability. The `double` type uses 64 bits to store a numeric value, but some processors use 80 bit floating-point registers. These registers yield added precision in intermediate steps of a computation. For example, consider the computation:

```
double w = x * y / z;
```

Many Intel processors compute `x * y` and leave the result in an 80-bit register, then divide by `z` and finally truncate the result back to 64 bits. That can yield a more accurate result, and it can avoid exponent overflow. But the result may be *different* from a computation that uses 64 bits throughout. For that reason, the initial specification of the Java virtual machine mandated that all intermediate computations must be truncated. The numeric community hated it. Not only can the truncated computations cause overflow, they are actually *slower* than the more precise computations because the truncation operations take time. For that reason, the Java programming language was updated to recognize the conflicting demands for optimum performance and perfect reproducibility. By default, virtual machine designers are now permitted to use extended precision for intermediate computations. However, methods tagged with the `strictfp` keyword must use strict floating-point operations that yield reproducible results. For example, you can tag `main` as

```
public static strictfp void main(String[] args)
```

Then all instructions inside the `main` method use strict floating-point computations. If you tag a class as `strictfp`, then all of its methods use strict floating-point computations.

The gory details are very much tied to the behavior of the Intel processors. In default mode, intermediate results are allowed to use an extended exponent, but not an extended mantissa. (The Intel chips support truncation of the mantissa without loss of performance.) Therefore, the only difference between default and strict mode is that strict computations may overflow when default computations don't.

If your eyes glazed over when reading this note, don't worry. For most programmers, this issue is not important. Floating-point overflow isn't a problem that one encounters for most common programs. We don't use the `strictfp` keyword in this book.

Increment and Decrement Operators

Programmers, of course, know that one of the most common operations with a numeric variable is to add or subtract 1. Java, following in the footsteps of C and C++, has both increment and decrement operators: x++ adds 1 to the current value of the variable x, and x-- subtracts 1 from it. For example, the code

```
int n = 12;
n++;
```

changes n to 13. Because these operators change the value of a variable, they cannot be applied to numbers themselves. For example, 4++ is not a legal statement.

There are actually two forms of these operators; you have seen the "postfix" form of the operator that is placed after the operand. There is also a prefix form, ++n. Both change the value of the variable by 1. The difference between the two only appears when they are used inside expressions. The prefix form does the addition first; the postfix form evaluates to the old value of the variable.

```
int m = 7;
int n = 7;
int a = 2 * ++m; // now a is 16, m is 8
int b = 2 * n++; // now b is 14, n is 8
```

We recommend against using ++ inside other expressions as this often leads to confusing code and annoying bugs.

(Of course, while it is true that the ++ operator gives the C++ language its name, it also led to the first joke about the language. C++ haters point out that even the name of the language contains a bug: "After all, it should really be called ++C, since we only want to use a language after it has been improved.")

Relational and boolean Operators

Java has the full complement of relational operators. To test for equality you use a double equal sign, ==. For example, the value of

```
3 == 7
```

is false.

Use a != for inequality. For example, the value of

```
3 != 7
```

is true.

Finally, you have the usual < (less than), > (greater than), <= (less than or equal), and >= (greater than or equal) operators.

Java, following C++, uses && for the logical "and" operator and || for the logical "or" operator. As you can easily remember from the != operator, the exclamation point ! is the logical negation operator. The && and || operators are evaluated in "short circuit" fashion. This means that when you have an expression like:

```
A && B
```

once the truth value of the expression `A` has been determined to be `false`, the value for the expression `B` is *not* calculated. For example, in the expression

```
x != 0 && 1 / x > x + y // no division by 0
```

the second part is never evaluated if `x` equals zero. Thus, `1 / x` is not computed if `x` is zero, and no divide-by-zero error can occur.

Similarly, if `A` evaluates to be `true`, then the value of `A || B` is automatically `true`, without evaluating `B`.

Finally, Java supports the ternary `?:` operator that is occasionally useful. The expression

```
condition ? e1 : e2
```

evaluates to `e1` if the `condition` is `true`, to `e2` otherwise. For example,

```
x < y ? x : y
```

gives the smaller of `x` and `y`.

Bitwise Operators

When working with any of the integer types, you have operators that can work directly with the bits that make up the integers. This means that you can use masking techniques to get at individual bits in a number. The bitwise operators are:

    `&` ("and")   `|` ("or")   `^` ("xor")   `~` ("not")

These operators work on bit patterns. For example, if `n` is an integer variable, then

```
int fourthBitFromRight = (n & 8) / 8;
```

gives you a one if the fourth bit from the right in the binary representation of `n` is one, and a zero if not. Using `&` with the appropriate power of two lets you mask out all but a single bit.

NOTE: When applied to `boolean` values, the `&` and `|` operators yield a `boolean` value. These operators are similar to the `&&` and `||` operators, except that the `&` and `|` operators are not evaluated in "short-circuit" fashion. That is, both arguments are first evaluated before computing the result.

There are also `>>` and `<<` operators, which shift a bit pattern to the right or left. These operators are often convenient when you need to build up bit patterns to do bit masking:

```
int fourthBitFromRight = (n & (1 << 3)) >> 3;
```

Finally, there is even a `>>>` operator that fills the top bits with zero, whereas `>>` extends the sign bit into the top bits. There is no `<<<` operator.

CAUTION: The right hand side argument of the shift operators is reduced modulo 32 (unless the left hand side is a `long` in which case the right hand side is reduced modulo 64). For example, the value of `1 << 35` is the same as `1 << 3` or 8.

C++ NOTE: In C/C++, there is no guarantee as to whether >> performs an arithmetic shift (extending the sign bit) or a logical shift (filling in with zeroes). Implementors are free to choose whatever is more efficient. That means the C/C++ >> operator is really only defined for non-negative numbers. Java removes that ambiguity.

Mathematical Functions and Constants

The `Math` class contains an assortment of mathematical functions that you may occasionally need, depending on the kind of programming that you do.

To take the square root of a number, you use the `sqrt` method:

```
double x = 4;
double y = Math.sqrt(x);
System.out.println(y); // prints 2.0
```

NOTE: There is a subtle difference between the `println` method and the `sqrt` method. The `println` method operates on an object, `System.out`, and has a second parameter, namely `y`, the value to be printed. (Recall that `out` is an object defined in the `System` class that represents the standard output device.) But the `sqrt` method in the `Math` class does not operate on any object. It has a single parameter, `x`, the number of which to extract the square root. Such a method is called a *static* method. You will learn more about static methods in Chapter 4.

The Java programming language has no operator for raising a quantity to a power: you must use the `pow` method in the `Math` class. The statement

```
double y = Math.pow(x, a);
```

sets y to be x raised to the power a (x^a). The `pow` method has parameters that are both of type `double`, and it returns a `double` as well.

The `Math` class supplies the usual trigonometric functions

```
Math.sin
Math.cos
Math.tan
Math.atan
Math.atan2
```

and the exponential function and its inverse, the natural log:

```
Math.exp
Math.log
```

Finally, there are two constants

```
Math.PI
Math.E
```

that denote the closest possible approximations to the mathematical constants π and e.

NOTE: The functions in the `Math` class use the routines in the computer's floating-point unit for fastest performance. If completely predictable results are more important than fast performance, use the `StrictMath` class instead. It implements the algorithms from the "Freely Distributable Math Library" `fdlibm`, guaranteeing identical results on all platforms. See `http://www.netlib.org/fdlibm/index.html` for the source of these algorithms. (Where `fdlibm` provides more than one definition for a function, the `StrictMath` class follows the IEEE 754 version whose name starts with an "e".)

Conversions Between Numeric Types

It is often necessary to convert from one numeric type to another. Figure 3–1 shows the legal conversions:

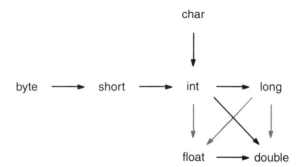

Figure 3–1: Legal conversions between numeric types

The six black arrows in Figure 3–1 denote conversions without information loss. The three grey arrows denote conversions that may lose precision. For example, a large integer such as 123456789 has more digits than the `float` type can represent. When converting it to a `float`, the resulting value has the correct magnitude, but it loses some precision.

```
int n = 123456789;
float f = n; // f is 1.23456792E8
```

When combining two values with a binary operator (such as n + f where n is an integer and f is a floating-point value), both operands are converted to a common type before the operation is carried out.

- If any of the operands is of type double, the other one will be converted to a double.
- Otherwise, if any of the operands is of type float, the other one will be converted to a float.
- Otherwise, if any of the operands is of type long, the other one will be converted to a long.
- Otherwise, both operands will be converted to an int.

Casts

In the preceding section, you saw that int values are automatically converted to double values when necessary. On the other hand, there are obviously times when you want to consider a double as an integer. Numeric conversions are possible in Java, but of course information may be lost. Conversions where loss of information is possible are done by means of *casts*. The syntax for casting is to give the target type in parentheses, followed by the variable name. For example:

```
double x = 9.997;
int nx = (int)x;
```

Then, the variable nx has the value 9, as casting a floating-point value to an integer discards the fractional part.

If you want to *round* a floating-point number to the *nearest* integer (which is the more useful operation in most cases), use the Math.round method:

```
double x = 9.997;
int nx = (int)Math.round(x);
```

Now the variable nx has the value 10. You still need to use the cast (int) when you call round. The reason is that the return value of the round method is a long, and a long can only be assigned to an int with an explicit cast since there is the possibility of information loss.

NOTE: If you try to cast a number of one type to another that is out of the range for the target type, the result will be a truncated number that has a different value. For example, (byte)300 is actually 44. It is, therefore, a good idea to explicitly test that the value is in the correct range before you perform a cast.

C++ NOTE: You cannot cast between `boolean` values and any numeric type. This prevents common errors. In the rare case that you want to convert a `boolean` value to a number, you can use a conditional expression such as `b ? 1 : 0`.

Parentheses and Operator Hierarchy

As in all programming languages, you are best off using parentheses to indicate the order in which you want operations to be carried out. However, in Java the hierarchy of operations is as shown in Table 3–4.

Table 3–4: **Operator precedence**

Operators	Associativity
`[]` `.` `()` (method call)	left to right
`!` `~` `++` `--` `+` (unary) `–` (unary) `()` (cast) `new`	right to left
`*` `/` `%`	left to right
`+` `-`	left to right
`<<` `>>` `>>>`	left to right
`<` `<=` `>` `>=` `instanceof`	left to right
`==` `!=`	left to right
`&`	left to right
`^`	left to right
`|`	left to right
`&&`	left to right
`||`	left to right
`?:`	left to right
`=` `+=` `-=` `*=` `/=` `%=` `&=` `|=` `^=` `<<=` `>>=` `>>>=`	right to left

If no parentheses are used, operations are performed in the hierarchical order indicated. Operators on the same level are processed from left to right, except for those that are right associative, as indicated in the table.

C++ NOTE: Unlike C or C++, Java does not have a comma operator. However, you can use a *comma-separated list of expressions* in the first and third slot of a `for` statement.

Strings

Strings are sequences of characters, such as `"Hello"`. Java does not have a built-in string type. Instead, the standard Java library contains a predefined class called, naturally enough, `String`. Each quoted string is an instance of the `String` class:

```
String e = ""; // an empty string
String greeting = "Hello";
```

Concatenation

Java, like most programming languages, allows you to use the + sign to join (concatenate) two strings together.

```
String expletive = "Expletive";
String PG13 = "deleted";
String message = expletive + PG13;
```

The above code makes the value of the string variable `message` `"Expletivedeleted"`. (Note the lack of a space between the words: the + sign joins two strings together in the order received, *exactly* as they are given.)

When you concatenate a string with a value that is not a string, the latter is converted to a string. (As you will see in Chapter 5, every Java object can be converted to a string.) For example:

```
int age = 13;
String rating = "PG" + age;
```

sets `rating` to the string `"PG13"`.

This feature is commonly used in output statements; for example,

```
System.out.println("The answer is " + answer);
```

is perfectly acceptable and will print what one would want (and with the correct spacing because of the space after the word `is`).

Substrings

You extract a substring from a larger string with the `substring` method of the `String` class. For example,

```
String greeting = "Hello";
String s = greeting.substring(0, 4);
```

creates a string consisting of the characters `"Hell"`. Java counts the characters in strings in a peculiar fashion: the first character in a string has position 0, just as in C and C++. (In C, there was a technical reason for counting positions starting at 0, but that reason has long gone away, and only the nuisance remains.)

For example, the character `'H'` has position 0 in the string `"Hello"`, and the character `'o'` has position 4. The second parameter of `substring` is the first position that you *do not* want to copy. In our case, we want to copy the characters in positions 0, 1, 2, and 3 (from position 0 to position 3 inclusive). As `substring` counts it, this means from position 0 inclusive to position 4 *exclusive*.

There is one advantage to the way `substring` works: it is easy to compute the length of the substring. The string `s.substring(a, b)` always has `b - a` characters. For example, the substring `"Hell"` has length 4 – 0 = 4.

String Editing

To find out the length of a string, use the `length` method. For example:

```
String greeting = "Hello";
int n = greeting.length(); // is 5.
```

Just as `char` denotes a Unicode character, `String` denotes a sequence of Unicode characters. It is possible to get at individual characters of a string. For example, `s.charAt(n)` returns the Unicode character at position n, where n is between 0 and `s.length() – 1`. For example,

```
char last = greeting.charAt(4); // fourth is 'o'
```

However, the `String` class gives no methods that let you *change* a character in an existing string. If you want to turn `greeting` into `"Hell!"`, you cannot directly change the last position of `greeting` into a `'!'`. If you are a C programmer, this will make you feel pretty helpless. How are you going to modify the string? In Java, it is quite easy: take the substring that you want to keep, and then concatenate it with the characters that you want to replace.

```
greeting = greeting.substring(0, 4) + "!";
```

This changes the current value of the `greeting` variable to `"Hell!"`.

Since you cannot change the individual characters in a Java string, the documentation refers to the objects of the `String` class as being *immutable*. Just as the number 3 is always 3, the string `"Hello"` will always contain the character sequence `'H'`, `'e'`, `'l'`, `'l'`, `'o'`. You cannot change these values. You can, as you just saw however, change the contents of the string *variable* `greeting` and make it refer to a different string, just as you can make a numeric variable currently holding the value 3 hold the value 4.

Isn't that a lot less efficient? It would seem simpler to change the characters than to build up a whole new string from scratch. Well, yes and no. Indeed, it isn't efficient to generate a new string that holds the concatenation of `"Hell"` and `"!"`. But immutable strings have one great advantage: The compiler can arrange that strings are *shared*.

To understand how this works, think of the various strings as sitting in a common pool. String variables then point to locations in the pool. If you copy a string variable, both the original and the copy share the same characters. Overall, the designers of Java decided that the efficiency of sharing outweighs the inefficiency of string editing by extracting substrings and concatenating.

Look at your own programs; we suspect that most of the time, you don't change strings—you just compare them. Of course, there are some cases in which direct manipulation of strings is more efficient. (One example is when assembling strings from individual characters that come from a file or the keyboard.) For these situations, Java provides a separate `StringBuffer` class that we describe in Chapter 12. If you are not concerned with the efficiency of string handling (which is not a bottleneck in many Java applications anyway), you can ignore `StringBuffer` and just use `String`.

C++ NOTE: C programmers generally are bewildered when they see Java strings for the first time, because they think of strings as arrays of characters:

```
char greeting[] = "Hello";
```

That is the wrong analogy: a Java string is roughly analogous to a `char*` pointer,

```
char* greeting = "Hello";
```

When you replace `greeting` with another string, the Java code does roughly the following:

```
char* temp = malloc(6);
strncpy(temp, greeting, 4);
strncpy(temp + 4, "!", 2);
greeting = temp;
```

Sure, now `greeting` points to the string `"Hell!"`. And even the most hardened C programmer must admit that the Java syntax is more pleasant than a sequence of `strncpy` calls. But what if we make another assignment to `greeting`?

```
greeting = "Howdy";
```

Don't we have a memory leak? After all, the original string was allocated on the heap. Fortunately, Java does automatic garbage collection. If a block of memory is no longer needed, it will eventually be recycled.

If you are a C++ programmer and use the `string` class defined by ANSI C++, you will be much more comfortable with the Java `String` type. C++ `string` objects also perform automatic allocation and deallocation of memory. The memory management is performed explicitly by constructors, assignment operators, and destructors. However, C++ strings are mutable—you can modify individual characters in a string.

Testing Strings for Equality

To test whether or not two strings are equal, use the `equals` method; the expression

```
s.equals(t)
```

returns `true` if the strings `s` and `t` are equal, `false` otherwise. Note that `s` and `t` can be string variables or string constants. For example,

```
"Hello".equals(command)
```

is perfectly legal. To test if two strings are identical except for the upper/lower-case letter distinction, use the `equalsIgnoreCase` method.

```
"Hello".equalsIgnoreCase("hello")
```

Do *not* use the `==` operator to test if two strings are equal! It only determines whether or not the strings are stored in the same location. Sure, if strings are in the same location, they must be equal. But it is entirely possible to store multiple copies of identical strings in different places.

```
String greeting = "Hello"; //initialize greeting to a string
if (greeting == "Hello") . . .
   // probably true
if (greeting.substring(0, 4) == "Hell") . . .
   // probably false
```

If the virtual machine would always arrange for equal strings to be shared, then you could use `==` for testing equality. But only string *constants* are shared, not strings that are the result of operations like `+` or `substring`. Therefore, *never* use `==` to compare strings or you will have a program with the worst kind of bug—an intermittent one that seems to occur randomly.

C++ NOTE: If you are used to the C++ `string` class, you have to be particularly careful about equality testing. The C++ `string` class does overload the `==` operator to test for equality of the string contents. It is perhaps unfortunate that Java goes out of its way to give strings the same "look and feel" as numeric values but then makes strings behave like pointers for equality testing. The language designers could have redefined `==` for strings, just as they made a special arrangement for `+`. Oh well, every language has its share of inconsistencies.

C programmers never use `==` to compare strings but use `strcmp` instead. The Java method `compareTo` is the exact analog to `strcmp`. You can use

```
if (greeting.compareTo("Help") == 0) . . .
```

but it seems clearer to use `equals` instead.

The `String` class in Java contains more than 50 methods. A surprisingly large number of them are sufficiently useful so that we can imagine using them frequently. The following API note summarizes the ones we found most useful.

NOTE: You will find these API notes throughout the book to help you understand the Java Application Programming Interface (API). Each API note starts with the name of a class such as `java.lang.String`—the significance of the so-called *package* name `java.lang` will be explained in Chapter 5. The class name is followed by the names, explanations, and parameter descriptions of one or more methods.

We typically do not list all methods of a particular class but instead select those that are most commonly used, and describe them in a concise form. For a full listing, consult the on-line documentation.

java.lang.String

- `char charAt(int index)`
  returns the character at the specified location.

- `int compareTo(String other)`
  returns a negative value if the string comes before `other` in dictionary order, a positive value if the string comes after `other` in dictionary order, or 0 if the strings are equal.

- `boolean endsWith(String suffix)`
  returns `true` if the string ends with `suffix`.

- `boolean equals(Object other)`
  returns `true` if the string equals `other`.

- `boolean equalsIgnoreCase(String other)`
  returns `true` if the string equals `other`, except for upper/lowercase distinction.

- `int indexOf(String str)`
- `int indexOf(String str, int fromIndex)`
  return the start of the first substring equal to `str`, starting at index 0 or at `fromIndex`.

- `int lastIndexOf(String str)`
- `int lastIndexOf(String str, int fromIndex)`
  return the start of the last substring equal to `str`, starting at index 0 or at `fromIndex`.

- `int length()`
  returns the length of the string.

- `String replace(char oldChar, char newChar)`
  returns a new string that is obtained by replacing all characters `oldChar` in the string with `newChar`.

- `boolean startsWith(String prefix)`
  returns `true` if the string begins with `prefix`.

- `String substring(int beginIndex)`
- `String substring(int beginIndex, int endIndex)`

    return a new string consisting of all characters from `beginIndex` until the end of the string or until `endIndex` (exclusive).

- `String toLowerCase()`

    returns a new string containing all characters in the original string, with uppercase characters converted to lower case.

- `String toUpperCase()`

    returns a new string containing all characters in the original string, with lowercase characters converted to upper case.

- `String trim()`

    returns a new string by eliminating all leading and trailing spaces in the original string.

Reading the On-line API Documentation

As you just saw, the `String` class has lots of methods. Furthermore, there are hundreds of classes in the standard libraries, with many more methods. It is plainly impossible to remember all useful classes and methods. Therefore, it is essential that you become familiar with the on-line API documentation that lets you look up all classes and methods in the standard library. The API documentation is part of the Java SDK. It is in HTML format. Point your web browser to the `docs/api/index.html` subdirectory of your Java SDK installation. You will see a screen as in Figure 3–2.

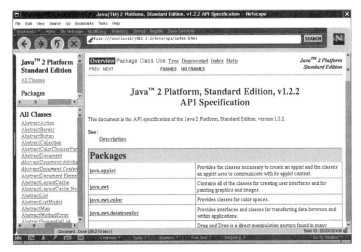

Figure 3–2: The three panes of the API documentation

The screen is organized into three windows. A small window on the top left shows all available packages. Below it, a larger window lists all classes. Click on any class name, and the API documentation for the class is displayed in the large window to the right (see Figure 3–3). For example, to get more information on the methods of the `String` class, scroll the second window until you see the String link, then click on it.

Figure 3–3: Class description for the `String` class

Then scroll the window on the right until you reach a summary of all methods, sorted in alphabetical order (see Figure 3–4). Click on any method name for a detailed description of the method (see Figure 3–5). For example, if you click on the compareToIgnoreCase link, you get the description of the compareToIgnoreCase method.

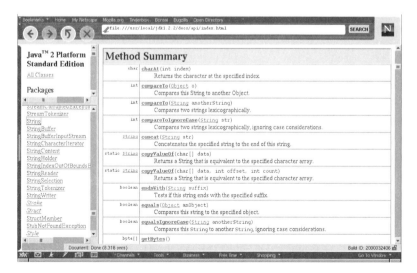

Figure 3–4: Method summary of the `String` class

Figure 3–5: Detailed description of a `String` **method**

TIP: Bookmark the `docs/api/index.html` page in your browser right now.

Reading Input

You saw that it is easy to print output to the "standard output device" (that is, the console window) just by calling `System.out.println`. Unfortunately, it is quite a bit more complex to read keyboard input from the "standard input device."

However, it is easy to supply a dialog box for keyboard input. The method call

```
JOptionPane.showInputDialog(promptString)
```

puts up a dialog box that prompts the user for input (see Figure 3–6). The return value is the string that the user typed.

Figure 3–6: An input dialog

For example, here is how you can query the name of the user of your program:

```
String name = JOptionPane.showInputDialog("What is your name?");
```

To read in a number, you have to work a little harder. The `JOptionPane.showInputDialog` method returns a string, not a number. You use the

`Integer.parseInt` or `Double.parseDouble` method to convert the string to its numeric value. For example,

```
String input = JOptionPane.showInputDialog("How old are you?");
int age = Integer.parseInt(input);
```

If the user types `40`, then the string variable `input` is set to the string `"40"`. The `Integer.parseInt` method converts the string to its numeric value, the number 40.

> NOTE: If the parameter of the `parseInt` method contains non-digits, then the method *throws an exception*. Unless your program "catches" the exception, the virtual machine terminates the program and prints an error message to the console. You will see in Chapter 11 how to catch exceptions.

The program in Example 3–2 asks for the user's name and age and then prints out a message like

```
Hello, Cay. Next year, you'll be 41
```

When you run the program, you will see that a first dialog appears to prompt for the name. The dialog goes away, and a second dialog asks for the age. Finally, the reply is displayed in the console window, not in a dialog window. This is not very elegant, of course. You will see in later chapters how to program much more pleasant user interfaces. For now, we'll stick to `JOptionPane.showInput-Dialog` and `System.out.println` because they are easy to use.

Note that the program ends with the method call:

```
System.exit(0);
```

Whenever your program calls `JOptionPane.showInputDialog`, you need to end it with a call to `System.exit(0)`. The reason is a bit technical. Showing a dialog box starts a new thread of control. When the `main` method exits, the new thread does not automatically terminate. To end all threads, you need to call the `System.exit` method. (For more information on threads, see Chapter 1 of Volume 2.)

The `System.exit` method receives an integer parameter, the "exit code" of the program. By convention, a program exits with exit code 0 if it completed successfully, and with a non-zero exit code otherwise. You can use different exit codes to indicate different error conditions. The exiting program communicates the exit code to the operating system. Shell scripts and batch files can then test the exit code.

Finally, note the line

```
import javax.swing.*;
```

at the beginning of the program. The `JOptionPane` class is defined in the `javax.swing` package. Whenever you use a class that is not defined in the basic java.lang package, you need to use an import directive. We will look at packages and import directives in more detail in Chapter 5.

Example 3–2: InputTest.java

```
1. import javax.swing.*;
2.
3. public class InputTest
4. {
5.    public static void main(String[] args)
6.    {
7.        // get first input
8.        String name = JOptionPane.showInputDialog
9.            ("What is your name?");
10.
11.        // get second input
12.        String input = JOptionPane.showInputDialog
13.            ("How old are you?");
14.
15.        // convert string to integer value
16.        int age = Integer.parseInt(input);
17.
18.        // display output on console
19.        System.out.println("Hello, " + name +
20.            ". Next year, you'll be " + (age + 1));
21.
22.        System.exit(0);
23.    }
24. }
```

---

javax.swing.JOptionPane

• static String showInputDialog(Object message)
  displays a dialog box with a message prompt, an input field, and "Ok" and "Cancel" buttons. The method returns the string that the user typed.

java.lang.System

• static void exit(int status)
  terminates the virtual machine and passes the status code to the operating system. By convention, a non-zero status code indicates an error.

Formatting Output

You can print a number x to the console with the statement System.out.print(x). That command will print x with the maximum number of non-zero digits for that type. For example,

```
x = 10000.0 / 3.0;
System.out.print(x);
```

prints

```
3333.3333333333335
```

That is a problem if you want to display, for example, dollars and cents.

You can control the display format to arrange your output neatly. The `NumberFormat` class in the `java.text` package has three methods that yield standard *formatters* for

- numbers
- currency values
- percentage values

Suppose that the United States locale is your default locale. (A *locale* is a set of specifications for country-specific properties of strings and numbers, such as collation order, currency symbol, and so on. Locales are an important concept for writing *internationalized* applications—programs that are acceptable to users from countries around the world. We will discuss internationalization in Volume 2.) Then, the value `10000.0 / 3.0` will print as

```
3,333.333
$3,333.33
333,333%
```

in these three formats. As you can see, the formatter adds the commas that separate the thousands, currency symbols ($), and percent signs.

To obtain a formatter for the default locale, use one of the three methods:

```
NumberFormat.getNumberInstance()
NumberFormat.getCurrencyInstance()
NumberFormat.getPercentInstance()
```

Each of these methods returns an object of type `NumberFormat`. You can use that object to format one or more numbers. You then apply the `format` method to the `NumberFormat` object to get a string that contains the formatted number. Once you have the formatted string, you will probably simply display the newly formatted number by printing the string:

```
double x = 10000.0 / 3.0;
NumberFormat formatter = NumberFormat.getNumberInstance();
String s = formatter.format(x); // the string "3,333.33"
System.out.println(s);
```

You also may want to set the minimum and maximum number of integer digits or fractional digits to display. You can do this with the `setMinimumIntegerDigits`, `setMinimumFractionDigits`, `setMaximumIntegerDigits`, and `setMaximumFractionDigits` methods in the `NumberFormat` class. For example,

```
double x = 10000.0 / 3.0;
NumberFormat formatter = NumberFormat.getNumberInstance();
```

```
formatter.setMaximumFractionDigits(4);
formatter.setMinimumIntegerDigits(6);
String s = formatter.format(x); // the string "003,333.3333"
```

Setting the maximum number of fractional digits is often useful. The last displayed digit is rounded up if the first discarded digit is 5 or above. If you want to show trailing zeroes, set the minimum number of fractional digits to the same value as the maximum. Otherwise, you should leave the minimum number of fractional digits at the default value, 0.

Setting the number of integer digits is much less common. By specifying a minimum number, you force leading zeroes for smaller values. Specifying a maximum number is downright dangerous—the displayed value is silently truncated, yielding a nicely formatted but very wrong result.

NOTE: If you are familiar with the C `printf` function and are longing for its simplicity, check out the `Format` class at `http://www.horstmann.com/core-java.html`. It is a Java class that faithfully replicates the behavior of `printf`. For example, `Format.printf("%8.2f", 10000.0 / 3.0)` prints the string `" 3333.33"` (with a leading space to yield a field width of 8 digits, and 2 digits after the decimal point).

You can also obtain number formats that are appropriate for different locales. For example, let us look up the number formats that are used by the German locale and use them to print our test output. There is a predefined object named `Locale.GERMANY` of a type called `Locale` that knows about German number formatting rules. When we pass that `Locale` object to the `getNumberInstance` method, we obtain a formatter that follows those German rules.

```
double x = 10000.0 / 3.0;
NumberFormat formatter
    = NumberFormat.getNumberInstance(Locale.GERMANY);
System.out.println(formatter.format(x));
formatter = NumberFormat.getCurrencyInstance(Locale.GERMANY);
System.out.println(formatter.format(x));
```

This code prints the numbers:

```
3.333,333
3.333,33 DM
```

Note that the German convention for periods and commas in numbers is the exact opposite of the U.S. convention: a comma is used as the decimal separator, and a period is used to separate thousands. Also, the formatter knows that the currency symbol (DM) is placed *after* the number.

java.text.NumberFormat

- static NumberFormat getCurrencyInstance()

  returns a NumberFormat object to convert currency values to strings using the conventions of the current locale.

- static NumberFormat getNumberInstance()

  returns a NumberFormat object to format numbers using the conventions of the current locale.

- static NumberFormat getPercentInstance()

  returns a NumberFormat object to convert percentages to strings.

- void setMaximumFractionDigits(int digits)

  Parameters: digits   the number of digits to display

  sets the maximum number of digits after the decimal point for the format object. The last displayed digit is rounded.

- void setMaximumIntegerDigits(int digits)

  Parameters: digits   the number of digits to display

  sets the maximum number of digits before the decimal point for the format object. *Use this method with extreme caution.* If you specify too few digits, then the number is simply truncated, displaying a dramatically wrong result!

- void setMinimumFractionDigits(int digits)

  Parameters: digits   the number of digits to display

  sets the minimum number of digits after the decimal point for the format object. If the number has fewer fractional digits than the minimum, then trailing zeroes are supplied.

- void setMinimumIntegerDigits(int digits)

  Parameters: digits   the number of digits to display

  sets the minimum number of digits before the decimal point for the format object. If the number has fewer digits than the minimum, then leading zeroes are supplied.

Control Flow

Java, like any programming language, supports both conditional statements and loops to determine control flow. We start with the conditional statements and then move on to loops. We end with the somewhat cumbersome switch statement that you can use when you have to test for many values of a single expression.

C++ NOTE: The Java control flow constructs are identical to those in C and C++, with two exceptions. There is no `goto`, but there is a "labeled" version of `break` that you can use to break out of a nested loop (where you perhaps would have used a `goto` in C).

Block Scope

Before we get into the actual control structures, you need to know more about *blocks.*

A block or compound statement is any number of simple Java statements that are surrounded by a pair of braces. Blocks define the scope of your variables. Blocks can be *nested* inside another. Here is a block that is nested inside the block of the `main` method.

```
public static void main(String[] args)
{
   int n;
   . . .
   {
      int k;
      . . .
   } // k is only defined up to here
}
```

However, it is not possible to declare identically named variables in two nested blocks. For example, the following is an error and will not compile:

```
public static void main(String[] args)
{
   int n;
   . . .
   {
      int k;
      int n; // error--can't redefine n in inner block
      . . .
   }
}
```

C++ NOTE: In C++, it is possible to redefine a variable inside a nested block. The inner definition then shadows the outer one. This can be a source of programming errors; hence Java does not allow it.

Conditional Statements

The conditional statement in Java has the form

```
if (condition) statement
```

The condition must be surrounded by parentheses.

In Java, as in most programming languages, you will often want to execute multiple statements when a single condition is true. In this case, you use a *block statement* that takes the form:

```
{
    statement₁
    statement₂
    . . .
}
```

For example:

```
if (yourSales >= target)
{
    performance = "Satisfactory";
    bonus = 100;
}
```

In this code all the statements surrounded by the braces will be executed when `yourSales` is greater than or equal to `target`. (See Figure 3–7.)

Figure 3–7: Flowchart for the `if` statement

> **NOTE:** A block (sometimes called a *compound statement*) allows you to have more than one (simple) statement in any Java programming structure that might otherwise have a single (simple) statement.

The more general conditional in Java looks like this (see Figure 3–8):

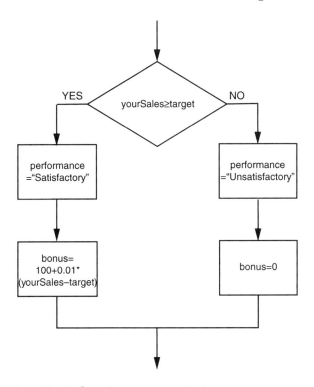

Figure 3–8: Flowchart for the `if/else` statement

```java
if (condition) statement₁ else statement₂;
```

For example:

```java
if (yourSales >= target)
{
   performance = "Satisfactory";
   bonus = 100 + 0.01 * (yourSales - target);
}
else
```

```
{
    performance = "Unsatisfactory";
    bonus = 0;
}
```

The `else` part is always optional. An `else` groups with the closest `if`. Thus, in the statement

```
if (x <= 0) if (x == 0) sign = 0; else sign = -1;
```

the `else` belongs to the second `if`.

Repeated `if . . . else if . . .` alternatives are very common (see Figure 3–9). For example:

```
if (yourSales >= 2 * target)
{
    performance = "Excellent";
    bonus = 1000;
}
else if {yourSales >= 1.5 * target)
{
    performance = "Fine";
    bonus = 500;
}
else if (yourSales >= target)
{
    performance = "Satisfactory";
    bonus = 100;
}
else
{
    System.out.println("You're fired");
}
```

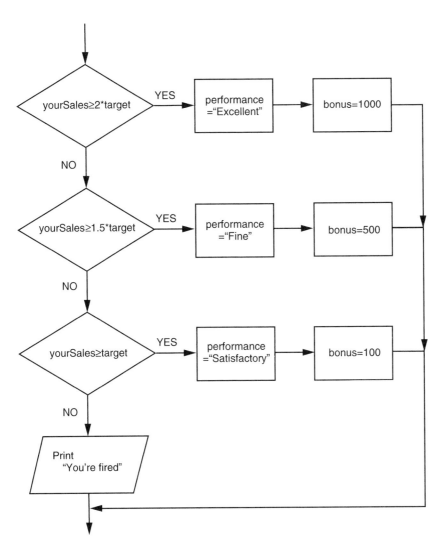

Figure 3–9: Flowchart for the `if/else if` (multiple branches)

Indeterminate Loops

In Java, as in all programming languages, there are control structures that let you repeat statements. There are two forms for repeating loops that are best when you do not know how many times a loop should be processed (these are "indeterminate loops").

First, there is the `while` loop that only executes the body of the loop while a condition is `true`. The general form is:

```
while (condition) statement
```

The `while` loop will never execute if the condition is `false` at the outset (see Figure 3–10).

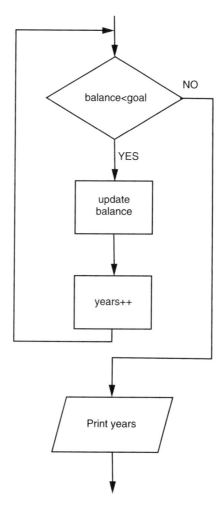

Figure 3–10: Flowchart for the `while` statement

In Example 3–3, we write a program to determine how long it will take to save a specific amount of money for your well-earned retirement, assuming that you deposit the same amount of money per year and the money earns a specified interest rate.

In the example, we are incrementing a counter and updating the amount currently accumulated in the body of the loop until the total exceeds the targeted amount.

```java
while (balance < goal)
{
   balance += payment;
   double interest = balance * interestRate / 100;
   balance += interest;
   years++;
}
```

(Don't rely on this program to plan for your retirement. We left out a few niceties such as inflation and your life expectancy.)

A `while` loop tests at the top. Therefore, the code in the block may never be executed. If you want to make sure a block is executed at least once, you will need to move the test to the bottom. This is done with the `do`/`while` loop. Its syntax looks like this:

```java
do statement while (condition);
```

This statement executes the block and only then tests the condition. It then repeats the block and retests the condition, and so on. For instance, the code in Example 3–4 computes the new balance in your retirement account and then asks you if you are ready to retire:

```java
do
{
   balance += payment;
   double interest = balance * interestRate / 100;
   balance += interest;
   year++;
   // print current balance
   . . .
   // ask if ready to retire and get input
   . . .
}
while (input.equals("N"));
```

As long as the user answers `"N"`, the loop is repeated (see Figure 3–11). This program is a good example of a loop that needs to be entered at least once, because the user needs to see the balance before deciding whether it is sufficient for retirement.

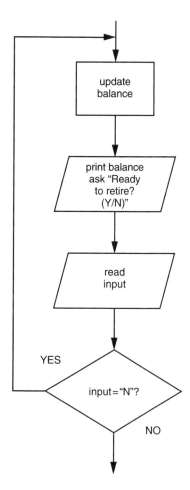

Figure 3–11: Flowchart for the `do/while` **statement**

Example 3–3: Retirement.java

```
1. import javax.swing.*;
2.
3. public class Retirement
4. {
5.    public static void main(String[] args)
6.    {
7.       // read inputs
8.       String input = JOptionPane.showInputDialog
9.          ("How much money do you need to retire?");
```

```
10.      double goal = Double.parseDouble(input);
11.
12.      input = JOptionPane.showInputDialog
13.         ("How much money will you contribute every year?");
14.      double payment =  Double.parseDouble(input);
15.
16.      input = JOptionPane.showInputDialog
17.         ("Interest rate in %:");
18.      double interestRate =  Double.parseDouble(input);
19.
20.      double balance = 0;
21.      int years = 0;
22.
23.      // update account balance while goal isn't reached
24.      while (balance < goal)
25.      {  // add this year's payment and interest
26.
27.         balance += payment;
28.         double interest = balance * interestRate / 100;
29.         balance += interest;
30.
31.         years++;
32.      }
33.
34.      System.out.println
35.         ("Your can retire in " + years + " years.");
36.      System.exit(0);
37.   }
38. }
```

Example 3–4: Retirement2.java

```
1. import java.text.*;
2. import javax.swing.*;
3.
4. public class Retirement2
5. {
6.    public static void main(String[] args)
7.    {
8.       String input = JOptionPane.showInputDialog
9.          ("How much money will you contribute every year?");
10.      double payment =  Double.parseDouble(input);
11.
12.      input = JOptionPane.showInputDialog
```

```
13.           ("Interest rate in %:");
14.       double interestRate =  Double.parseDouble(input);
15.
16.       double balance = 0;
17.       int year = 0;
18.
19.       NumberFormat formatter
20.           = NumberFormat.getCurrencyInstance();
21.
22.       // update account balance while user isn't ready to retire
23.       do
24.       {
25.           // add this year's payment and interest
26.           balance += payment;
27.           double interest = balance * interestRate / 100;
28.           balance += interest;
29.
30.           year++;
31.
32.           // print current balance
33.           System.out.println("After year " + year
34.               + ", your balance is "
35.               + formatter.format(balance));
36.
37.           // ask if ready to retire and get input
38.           input = JOptionPane.showInputDialog
39.               ("Ready to retire? (Y/N)");
40.           input = input.toUpperCase();
41.       }
42.       while (input.equals("N"));
43.
44.       System.exit(0);
45.   }
46. }
```

Determinate Loops

The `for` loop is a very general construct to support iteration that is controlled by a counter or similar variable that is updated after every iteration. As Figure 3–12 shows, the following loop prints the numbers from 1 to 10 on the screen.

```
for (int i = 1; i <= 10; i++)
    System.out.println(i);
```

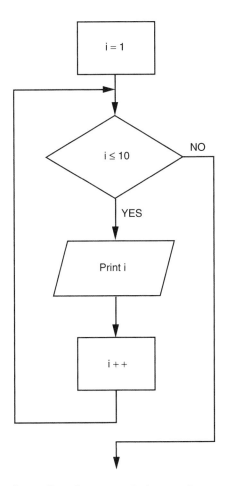

Figure 3–12: Flowchart for the `for` statement

The first slot of the `for` statement usually holds the counter initialization. The second slot gives the condition which will be tested before each new pass through the loop, and the third slot explains how to update the counter.

Although Java, like C++, allows almost any expression in the various slots of a `for` loop, it is an unwritten rule of good taste that the three slots of a `for` statement should only initialize, test, and update the same counter variable. One can write very obscure loops by disregarding this rule.

Even within the bounds of good taste, much is possible. For example, you can have loops that count down:

```
for (int i = 10; i > 0; i--)
    System.out.println("Counting down . . . " + i);
System.out.println("Blastoff!");
```

NOTE: Be careful about testing for equality of floating-point numbers in loops. A `for` loop that looks like this:

```
for (double x = 0; x != 10; x += 0.1) . . .
```

may never end. Due to roundoff errors, the final value may not be reached exactly. For example, in the loop above, x jumps from 9.99999999999998 to 10.09999999999998, because there is no exact binary representation for 0.1.

When you declare a variable in the first slot of the `for` statement, the scope of that variable extends until the end of the body of the `for` loop.

```
for (int i = 1; i <= 10; i++)
{
    . . .
}
// i no longer defined here
```

In particular, if you define a variable inside a `for` statement, you cannot use the value of that variable outside the loop. Therefore, if you wish to use the final value of a loop counter outside the `for` loop, be sure to declare it outside the header for the loop!

```
int i;
for (i = 1; i <= 10; i++)
{
    . . .
}
// i still defined here
```

On the other hand, you can define variables with the same name in separate `for` loops:

```
for (int i = 1; i <= 10; i++)
{
    . . .
}
. . .
for (int i = 11; i <= 20; i++) // ok to redefine i
{
    . . .
}
```

Of course, a `for` loop is equivalent to a `while` loop. More precisely,

```
for (statement₁; expression₁; expression₂) statement₂;
```

is completely equivalent to:

```
{
    statement₁;
    while (expression₁)
    {
        statement₂;
        expression₂;
    }
}
```

Example 3–5 shows a typical example of a `for` loop.

The program computes the odds on winning a lottery. For example, if you must pick 6 numbers from the numbers 1 to 50 to win, then there are $(50 \times 49 \times 48 \times 47 \times 46 \times 45)/(1 \times 2 \times 3 \times 4 \times 5 \times 6)$ possible outcomes, so your chance is 1 in 15,890,700. Good luck!

In general, if you pick k numbers out of n, there are

$$\frac{n \times (n-1) \times (n-1) \times \ldots \times (n-k)}{1 \times 2 \times 3 \times \ldots \times k}$$

possible outcomes. The following `for` loop computes this value:

```
int lotteryOdds = 1;
for (int i = 1; i <= k; i++)
    lotteryOdds = lotteryOdds * (n - i + 1) / i;
```

Example 3–5: LotteryOdds.java

```
1. import javax.swing.*;
2.
3. public class LotteryOdds
4. {
5.    public static void main(String[] args)
6.    {
7.       String input = JOptionPane.showInputDialog
8.          ("How many numbers do you need to draw?");
9.       int k = Integer.parseInt(input);
10.
11.      input = JOptionPane.showInputDialog
12.         ("What is the highest number you can draw?");
13.      int n = Integer.parseInt(input);
14.
15.      /*
16.         compute binomial coefficient
17.         n * (n - 1) * (n - 2) * . . . * (n - k + 1)
18.         -------------------------------------------
```

```
19.          1 * 2 * 3 * . . . * k
20.       */
21.
22.       int lotteryOdds = 1;
23.       for (int i = 1; i <= k; i++)
24.          lotteryOdds = lotteryOdds * (n - i + 1) / i;
25.
26.       System.out.println
27.          ("Your odds are 1 in " + lotteryOdds + ". Good luck!");
28.
29.       System.exit(0);
30.    }
31. }
```

Multiple Selections—the switch *Statement*

The if/else construct can be cumbersome when you have to deal with multiple selections with many alternatives. Java has a switch statement that is exactly like the switch statement in C and C++, warts and all.

For example, if you set up a menuing system with four alternatives like that in Figure 3–13, you could use code that looks like this:

```
String input = JOptionPane.showInputDialog
   ("Select an option (1, 2, 3, 4)");
int choice = Integer.parseInt(input);
switch (choice)
{
   case 1:
      . . .
      break;
   case 2:
      . . .
      break;
   case 3:
      . . .
      break;
   case 4:
      . . .
      break;
   default:
      // bad input
      . . .
      break;
}
```

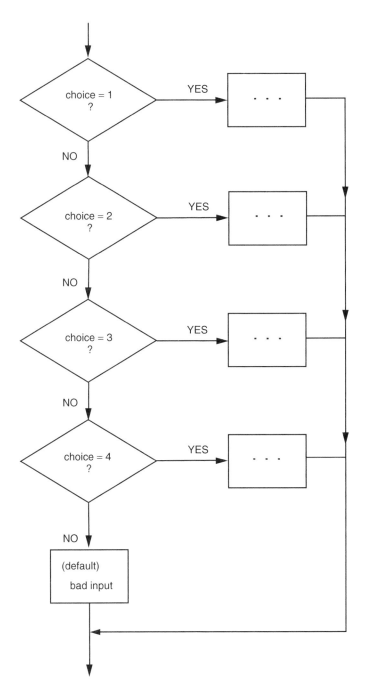

Figure 3–13: Flowchart for the `switch` **statement**

Execution starts at the `case` label that matches the value on which the selection is performed and continues until the next `break` or the end of the switch. If none of the case labels matches, then the `default` clause is executed, if it is present.

Note that the `case` labels must be integers. You cannot test strings. For example, the following is an error:

```
String input = . . .;
switch (input) // ERROR
{
   case "A": // ERROR
      . . .
      break;
   . . .
}
```

CAUTION: It is possible for multiple cases to be triggered. If you forget to add a `break` at the end of a case, then execution falls through to the next case! This behavior is plainly dangerous and a common cause for errors. For that reason, we never use the `switch` statement in our programs.

Breaking Control Flow

Although the designers of Java kept the `goto` as a reserved word, they decided not to include it in the language. In general, `goto` statements are considered poor style. Some programmers feel the anti-`goto` forces have gone too far (see, for example, the famous article of Donald Knuth called "Structured Programming with goto's"). They argue that unrestricted use of `goto` is error-prone, but that an occasional jump *out of a loop* is beneficial. The Java designers agreed and even added a new statement to support this programming style, the labeled break.

Let us first look at the unlabeled `break` statement. The same `break` statement that you use to exit a `switch` can also be used to break out of a loop. For example,

```
while (years <= 100)
{
   balance += payment;
   double interest = balance * interestRate / 100;
   balance += interest;
   if (balance >= goal) break;
   years++;
}
```

Now the loop is exited if either `years > 100` occurs on the top of the loop or `balance >= goal` occurs in the middle of the loop. Of course, you could have computed the same value for `years` without a `break`, like this:

```
while (years <= 100 && balance < goal)
{
   balance += payment;
   double interest = balance * interestRate / 100;
   balance += interest;
   if (balance < goal)
      years++;
}
```

But note that the test `balance < goal` is repeated twice in this version. To avoid this repeated test, some programmers prefer the `break` statement.

Unlike C++, Java also offers a *labeled break* statement that lets you break out of multiple nested loops. Occasionally something weird happens inside a deeply nested loop. In that case, you may want to break completely out of all the nested loops. It is inconvenient to program that simply by adding extra conditions to the various loop tests.

Here's an example that shows this at work. Notice that the label must precede the outermost loop out of which you want to break. It also must be followed by a colon.

```
int n;
read_data:
while (. . .) // this loop statement is tagged with the label
{
   . . .
   for (. . .) // this inner loop is not labeled
   {
      String input
         = JOptionPane.showInputDialog("Enter a number >= 0");
      n = Integer.parseInt(input);
      if (n < 0) // should never happen—can't go on
         break read_data;
         // break out of read_data loop
      . . .
   }
}
// this statement is executed immediately after the break
if (n < 0) // check for bad situation
{
   // deal with bad situation
```

```
   }
   else
   {
      // carry out normal processing
   }
```

If there was a bad input, the labeled break moves past the end of the labeled block. As with any use of the `break` statement, you then need to test if the loop exited normally or as a result of a break.

> **NOTE:** Curiously, you can apply a label to any statement, even an `if` statement or a block statement, like this:
>
> ```
> label:
> {
>       . . .
>    if (condition) break label; // exits block
>       . . .
> }
> // jumps here when the break statement executes
> ```
>
> Thus, if you are lusting after a `goto`, and if you can place a block that ends just before the place to which you want to jump, you can use a `break` statement! Naturally, we don't recommend this approach. Note, however, that you can only jump out of a block, never into a block.

Finally, there is a `continue` statement that, like the `break` statement, breaks the regular flow of control. The `continue` statement transfers control to the header of the innermost enclosing loop. Here is an example:

```
while (sum < goal)
{
   String input = JOptionPane.showInputDialog("Enter a number");
   n = Integer.parseInt(input);
   if (n < 0) continue;
   sum += n; // not executed if n < 0
}
```

If $n < 0$, then the `continue` statement jumps immediately to the loop header, skipping the remainder of the current iteration.

If the `continue` statement is used in a `for` loop, it jumps to the "update" part of the `for` loop. For example, consider this loop.

```
for (count = 0; count < 100; count++)
{
   String input = JOptionPane.showInputDialog("Enter a number");
   n = Integer.parseInt(input);
```

```
    if (n < 0) continue;
    sum += n; // not executed if n < 0
}
```

If n < 0, then the continue statement jumps to the count++ statement.

There is also a labeled form of the continue statement that jumps to the header of the loop with the matching label.

TIP: Many programmers find the break and continue statements confusing. These statements are entirely optional—you can always express the same logic without them. In this book, we never use break or continue.

Big Numbers

If the precision of the basic integer and floating-point types is not sufficient, you can turn to a couple of handy classes in the java.math package, called BigInteger and BigDecimal. These are classes for manipulating numbers with an arbitrarily long sequence of digits. The BigInteger class implements arbitrary precision integer arithmetic, and BigDecimal does the same for floating-point numbers.

Use the static valueOf method to turn an ordinary number into a big number:

```
BigInteger a = BigInteger.valueOf(100);
```

Unfortunately, you cannot use the familiar mathematical operators such as + and * to combine big numbers. Instead, you must use methods such as add and multiply in the big number classes.

```
BigInteger c = a.add(b); // c = a + b
BigInteger d = c.multiply(b.add(BigInteger.valueOf(2)));
    // d = c * (b + 2)
```

C++ NOTE: Unlike C++, Java has no programmable operator overloading. There was no way for the programmer of the BigInteger class to redefine the + and * operators to give the add and multiply operations of the BigInteger classes. The language designers did overload the + operator to denote concatenation of strings. They chose not to overload other operators, and they did not give Java programmers the opportunity to overload operators themselves.

Example 3–6 shows a modification of the lottery odds program of Example 3–5, updated to work with big numbers. For example, if you are invited to participate in a lottery in which you need to pick 60 numbers out of a possible 490 numbers, then this program will tell you that your odds are 1 in 716395843461995557415116 22254009293341171761278926349349335101345948110466 8848. Good luck!

The program in Example 3–5 computed the following statement:

```
lotteryOdds = lotteryOdds * (n - i + 1) / i;
```

When using big numbers, the equivalent statement becomes:

```
lotteryOdds = lotteryOdds.multiply(BigInteger.valueOf(n - i + 1))
    .divide(BigInteger.valueOf(i));
```

Example 3–6: BigIntegerTest.java

```
1. import javax.swing.*;
2. import java.math.*;
3.
4. public class BigIntegerTest
5. {
6.    public static void main(String[] args)
7.    {
8.       String input = JOptionPane.showInputDialog
9.          ("How many numbers do you need to draw?");
10.       int k = Integer.parseInt(input);
11.
12.       input = JOptionPane.showInputDialog
13.          ("What is the highest number you can draw?");
14.       int n = Integer.parseInt(input);
15.
16.       /*
17.          compute binomial coefficient
18.          n * (n - 1) * (n - 2) * . . . * (n - k + 1)
19.          -----------------------------------------
20.          1 * 2 * 3 * . . . * k
21.       */
22.
23.       BigInteger lotteryOdds = BigInteger.valueOf(1);
24.
25.       for (int i = 1; i <= k; i++)
26.          lotteryOdds = lotteryOdds
27.             .multiply(BigInteger.valueOf(n - i + 1))
28.             .divide(BigInteger.valueOf(i));
29.
30.       System.out.println("Your odds are 1 in " + lotteryOdds +
31.          ". Good luck!");
32.
33.       System.exit(0);
34.    }
35. }
```

java.math.BigInteger

- BigInteger add(BigInteger other)
- BigInteger subtract(BigInteger other)
- BigInteger multiply(BigInteger other)
- BigInteger divide(BigInteger other)
- BigInteger mod(BigInteger other)

  Return the sum, difference, product, quotient, and remainder of this big integer and other.

- int compareTo(BigInteger other)

  Returns 0 if this big integer equals other, a negative result if this big integer is less than other, and a positive result otherwise.

- static BigInteger valueOf(long x)

  Returns a big integer whose value equals x.

java.math.BigDecimal

- BigDecimal add(BigDecimal other)
- BigDecimal subtract(BigDecimal other)
- BigDecimal multiply(BigDecimal other)
- BigDecimal divide(BigDecimal other, int roundingMode)

  Return the sum, difference, product, or quotient of this big decimal and other. To compute the quotient, you need to supply a *rounding mode*. The mode BigDecimal.ROUND_HALF_UP is the rounding mode that you learned in school (i.e. round down digits 0 . . . 4, round up digits 5 . . . 9). It is appropriate for routine calculations. See the API documentation for other rounding modes.

- int compareTo(BigDecimal other)

  Returns 0 if this big Decimal equals other, a negative result if this big decimal is less than other, and a positive result otherwise.

- static BigDecimal valueOf(long x)
- static BigDecimal valueOf(long x, int scale)

  Return a big decimal whose value equals x or $x\ /\ 10^{scale}$.

Arrays

An array is a data structure that stores a collection of values of the same type. You access each individual value through an integer *index*. For example, if a is an array of integers, then a[i] is the ith integer in the array.

You declare an array variable by specifying the array type—which is the element type followed by `[]`—and the array variable name. For example, here is the declaration of an array `a` of integers:

```
int[] a;
```

However, this statement only declares the variable `a`. It does not yet initialize `a` with an actual array. You use the `new` operator to create the array.

```
int[] a = new int[100];
```

This statement sets up an array that can hold 100 integers. The array entries are *numbered from 0 to 99* (and not 1 to 100). Once the array is created, you can fill the entries in an array, for example, by using a loop:

```
int[] a = new int[100];
for (int i = 0; i < 100; i++)
    a[i] = i;  // fills the array with 0 to 99
```

> CAUTION: If you construct an array with 100 element and then try to access the element `a[100]` (or any other index outside the range 0 . . . 99), then your program will terminate with an "array index out of bounds" exception.

To find the number of elements of an array, use *arrayName*`.length`. For example,

```
for (int i = 0; i < a.length; i++)
    System.out.println(a[i]);
```

Once you create an array, you cannot change its size (although you can, of course, change an individual array element). If you frequently need to expand the size of an array while a program is running, you should use a different data structure called an *array list*. (See Chapter 5 for more on array lists.)

> NOTE: You can define an array variable either as
> ```
> int[] a;
> ```
> or as
> ```
> int a[];
> ```
> Most Java programmers prefer the former style because it neatly separates the type `int[]` (integer array) from the variable name.

Array Initializers and Anonymous Arrays

Java has a shorthand to create an array object and supply initial values at the same time. Here's an example of the syntax at work:

```
int[] smallPrimes = { 2, 3, 5, 7, 11, 13 };
```

Notice that you do not use a call to `new` when you use this syntax.

You can even initialize an *anonymous array:*

```
new int[] { 17, 19, 23, 29, 31, 37 }
```

This expression allocates a new array and fills it with the values inside the braces. It counts the number of initial values and sets the array size accordingly. You can use this syntax to reinitialize an array without creating a new variable. For example,

```
smallPrimes = new int[] { 17, 19, 23, 29, 31, 37 };
```

is a shorthand for

```
int[] anonymous = { 17, 19, 23, 29, 31, 37 };
smallPrimes = anonymous;
```

NOTE: It is legal to have arrays of length 0. Such an array can be useful if you write a method that computes an array result, and the result happens to be empty. You construct an array of length 0 as

```
new elementType[0]
```

Note that an array of length 0 is not the same as `null`. (See Chapter 4 for more information about `null`.)

Copying Arrays

You can copy one array variable into another, but then *both variables refer to the same array:*

```
int[] luckyNumbers = smallPrimes;
luckyNumbers[5] = 12; // now smallPrimes[5] is also 12
```

Figure 3–14 shows the result. If you actually want to copy all values of one array into another, you have to use the `arraycopy` method in the `System` class. The syntax for this call is

```
System.arraycopy(from, fromIndex, to, toIndex, count);
```

The `to` array must have sufficient space to hold the copied elements.

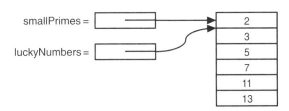

Figure 3–14: Copying an array variable

For example, the following statements, whose result is illustrated in Figure 3–15, set up two arrays and then copy the last four entries of the first array to the second array. The copy starts at position 2 in the source array and copies 4 entries, starting at position 3 of the target.

```java
int[] smallPrimes = {2, 3, 5, 7, 11, 13};
int[] luckyNumbers = {1001, 1002, 1003, 1004, 1005, 1006, 1007};
System.arraycopy(smallPrimes, 2, luckyNumbers, 3, 4);
for (int i = 0; i < luckyNumbers.length; i++)
    System.out.println(i + ": " + luckyNumbers[i]);
```

The output is:

```
0: 1001
1: 1002
2: 1003
3: 5
4: 7
5: 11
6: 13
```

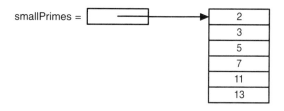

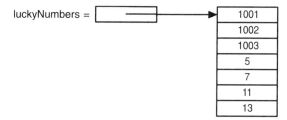

Figure 3–15: Copying values between arrays

C++ NOTE: A Java array is quite different from a C++ array on the stack. It is, however, essentially the same as a pointer to an array allocated on the *heap*. That is,

```java
int[] a = new int[100]; // Java
```

is not the same as

```cpp
int a[100]; // C++
```

but rather

```
int* a = new int[100]; // C++
```
In Java, the `[]` operator is predefined to perform *bounds checking.* Furthermore, there is no pointer arithmetic—you can't increment `a` to point to the next element in the array.

Command Line Parameters

You have already seen one example of Java arrays repeated quite a few times. Every Java program has a `main` method with a `String[] args` parameter. This parameter indicates that the `main` method receives an array of strings, namely, the arguments specified on the command line.

For example, consider this program:

```java
public class Message
{
   public static void main(String[] args)
   {
      if (args[0].equals("-h"))
         System.out.print("Hello,");
      else if (args[0].equals("-g"))
         System.out.print("Goodbye,");
      // print the other command line arguments
      for (int i = 1; i < args.length; i++)
         System.out.print(" " + args[i]);
      System.out.println("!");
   }
}
```

If the program is called as

```
java Message -g cruel world
```

then the `args` array has the following contents:

```
args[0]: "-g"
args[1]: "cruel"
args[2]: "world"
```

The program prints the message

```
Goodbye, cruel world!
```

C++ NOTE: In the `main` method of a Java program, the name of the program is not stored in the `args` array. For example, when you start up a program as

```
java Message -h world
```

from the command line, then `args[0]` will be `"-h"` and not `"Message"` or `"java"`.

Sorting an Array

If you want to sort an array of numbers, you can use one of the `sort` methods in the `Arrays` class:

```
int[] a = new int[10000];
. . .
Arrays.sort(a)
```

This method uses a tuned version of the QuickSort algorithm that is claimed to be very efficient on most data sets. The `Arrays` class provides several other convenience methods for arrays that are included in the API notes at the end of this section.

The program in Example 3–7 puts arrays to work. This program draws a random combination of numbers for a lottery game. For example, if you play a "choose 6 numbers from 49" lottery, then the program might print:

```
Bet the following combination. It'll make you rich!
   4
   7
   8
   19
   30
   44
```

To select such a random set of numbers, we first fill an array `numbers` with the values 1, 2, . . ., n:

```
int[] numbers = new int[n];
for (int i = 0; i < numbers.length; i++)
   numbers[i] = i + 1;
```

A second array holds the numbers to be drawn:

```
int[] result = new int[k];
```

Now we draw k numbers. The `Math.random` method returns a random floating point number that is between 0 (inclusive) and 1 (exclusive). By multiplying the result with n, we obtain a random number between 0 and n - 1.

```
int r = (int)(Math.random() * n);
```

We set the `i`th result to be the number at that index. Initially, that is just `r` itself, but as you'll see presently, the contents of the `numbers` array is changed after each draw.

```
result[i] = numbers[r];
```

Now we must be sure never to draw that number again—all lottery numbers must be distinct. Therefore, we overwrite `numbers[r]` with the *last* number in the array and reduce n by 1.

```
numbers[r] = numbers[n - 1];
n--;
```

The point is that in each draw we pick an *index*, not the actual value. The index points into an array that contains the values that have not yet been drawn.

After drawing k lottery numbers, we sort the `result` array for a more pleasing output:

```
Arrays.sort(result);
for (int i = 0; i < result.length; i++)
    System.out.println(result[i]);
```

Example 3–7: LotteryDrawing.java

```
1. import java.util.*;
2. import javax.swing.*;
3.
4. public class LotteryDrawing
5. {
6.    public static void main(String[] args)
7.    {
8.       String input = JOptionPane.showInputDialog
9.          ("How many numbers do you need to draw?");
10.       int k = Integer.parseInt(input);
11.
12.       input = JOptionPane.showInputDialog
13.          ("What is the highest number you can draw?");
14.       int n = Integer.parseInt(input);
15.
16.       // fill an array with numbers 1 2 3 . . . n
17.       int[] numbers = new int[n];
18.       for (int i = 0; i < numbers.length; i++)
19.          numbers[i] = i + 1;
20.
21.       // draw k numbers and put them into a second array
22.
23.       int[] result = new int[k];
24.       for (int i = 0; i < result.length; i++)
25.       {
26.          // make a random index between 0 and n - 1
27.          int r = (int)(Math.random() * n);
28.
29.          // pick the element at the random location
30.          result[i] = numbers[r];
31.
32.          // move the last element into the random location
33.          numbers[r] = numbers[n - 1];
34.          n--;
35.       }
36.
```

```
37.        // print the sorted array
38.
39.        Arrays.sort(result);
40.        System.out.println
41.          ("Bet the following combination. It'll make you rich!");
42.        for (int i = 0; i < result.length; i++)
43.            System.out.println(result[i]);
44.
45.        System.exit(0);
46.     }
47. }
```

java.lang.System

- static void arraycopy(Object from, int fromIndex, Object to, int toIndex, int count)

Parameters:	from	an array of any type (Chapter 5 explains why this is a parameter of type Object)
	fromIndex	the starting index from which to copy elements
	to	an array of the same type as from
	toIndex	the starting index to which to copy elements
	count	the number of elements to copy

copies elements from the first array to the second array.

java.util.Arrays

- static void sort(*Xxx*[] a)

Parameters:	a	an array of type int, long, short, char, byte, boolean, float or double

sorts the array, using a tuned QuickSort algorithm.

- static int binarySearch(*Xxx*[] a, *Xxx* v)

Parameters:	a	a *sorted* array of type int, long, short, char, byte, boolean, float or double
	v	a value of the same type as the elements of a

uses the BinarySearch algorithm to search for the value v. If it is found, its index is returned. Otherwise, a negative value r is returned; -r - 1 is the spot at which v should be inserted to keep a sorted.

- `static void fill(Xxx[] a, Xxx v)`

  Parameters: a   an array of type `int`, `long`, `short`, `char`, `byte`,
                      `boolean`, `float` or `double`

                   v   a value of the same type as the elements of `a`

  sets all elements of the array to `v`.

- `static boolean equals(Xxx[] a, Object other)`

  Parameters: a   an array of type `int`, `long`, `short`, `char`, `byte`,
                      `boolean`, `float` or `double`

                   other   an object

  returns `true` if `other` is an array of the same type, if it has the same length, and if the elements in corresponding indexes match.

Multidimensional Arrays

Multidimensional arrays use more than one index to access array elements. They are used for tables and other more complex arrangements. You can safely skip this section until you have a need for this storage mechanism.

Suppose you want to make a table of numbers that shows how much an investment of $10,000 will grow under different interest rate scenarios in which interest is paid annually and reinvested. Table 3–5 illustrates this scenario.

Table 3–5: Growth of an investment at different interest rates

10%	11%	12%	13%	14%	15%
$10,000.00	$10,000.00	$10,000.00	$10,000.00	$10,000.00	$10,000.00
$11,000.00	$11,100.00	$11,200.00	$11,300.00	$11,400.00	$11,500.00
$12,100.00	$12,321.00	$12,544.00	$12,769.00	$12,996.00	$13,225.00
$13,310.00	$13,676.31	$14,049.28	$14,428.97	$14,815.44	$15,208.75
$14,641.00	$15,180.70	$15,735.19	$16,304.74	$16,889.60	$17,490.06
$16,105.10	$16,850.58	$17,623.42	$18,424.35	$19,254.15	$20,113.57
$17,715.61	$18,704.15	$19,738.23	$20,819.52	$21,949.73	$23,130.61
$19,487.17	$20,761.60	$22,106.81	$23,526.05	$25,022.69	$26,600.20
$21,435.89	$23,045.38	$24,759.63	$26,584.44	$28,525.86	$30,590.23
$23,579.48	$25,580.37	$27,730.79	$30,040.42	$32,519.49	$35,178.76

The obvious way to store this information is in a two-dimensional array (or matrix), which we will call `balance`.

Declaring a matrix in Java is simple enough. For example:

```
double[][] balance;
```

As always, you cannot use the array until you initialize it with a call to `new`. In this case, you can do the initialization as follows:

```
balance = new double[NYEARS][NRATES];
```

In other cases, if you know the array elements, you can use a shorthand notion for initializing multidimensional arrays without needing a call to `new`. For example;

```
int[][] magicSquare =
   {
      {16, 3, 2, 13},
      {5, 10, 11, 8},
      {9, 6, 7, 12},
      {4, 15, 14, 1}
   };
```

Once the array is initialized, you can access individual elements, by supplying two brackets, for example `balance[i][j]`.

The example program stores a one-dimensional array `interest` of interest rates and a two-dimensional array `balance` of account balances, one for each year and interest rate. We initialize the first row of the array with the initial balance:

```
for (int j = 0; j < balance[0].length; j++)
   balance[0][j] = 10000;
```

Then we compute the other rows, as follows:

```
for (int i = 1; i < balance.length; i++)
{
   for (int j = 0; j < balance[i].length; j++)
   {
      double oldBalance = balance[i - 1][j];
      double interest = . . .;
      balance[i][j] = oldBalance + interest;
   }
}
```

Example 3–8 shows the full program.

Example 3–8: CompoundInterest.java

```
1. import java.text.*;
2. import javax.swing.*;
3.
4. public class CompoundInterest
5. {
6.    public static void main(String[] args)
```

```
7.      {
8.         final int STARTRATE = 10;
9.         final int NRATES = 6;
10.        final int NYEARS = 10;
11.
12.        // set interest rates to 10 . . . 15%
13.        double[] interestRate = new double[NRATES];
14.        for (int j = 0; j < interestRate.length; j++)
15.           interestRate[j] = (STARTRATE + j) / 100.0;
16.
17.        double[][] balance = new double[NYEARS][NRATES];
18.
19.        // set initial balances to 10000
20.        for (int j = 0; j < balance[0].length; j++)
21.           balance[0][j] = 10000;
22.
23.        // compute interest for future years
24.
25.        for (int i = 1; i < balance.length; i++)
26.        {
27.           for (int j = 0; j < balance[i].length; j++)
28.           {
29.              // get last year's balance from previous row
30.              double oldBalance = balance[i - 1][j];
31.
32.              // compute interest
33.              double interest = oldBalance * interestRate[j];
34.
35.              // compute this year's balance
36.              balance[i][j] = oldBalance + interest;
37.           }
38.        }
39.
40.        // print one row of interest rates
41.
42.        NumberFormat formatter = NumberFormat.getPercentInstance();
43.
44.        for (int j = 0; j < interestRate.length; j++)
45.        {
46.           System.out.print("          ");
47.           System.out.print(formatter.format(interestRate[j]));
48.        }
49.        System.out.println();
50.
51.        // print balance table
52.
53.        formatter = NumberFormat.getCurrencyInstance();
54.
55.        for (int i = 0; i < balance.length; i++)
```

```
56.        {
57.           // print table row
58.           for (int j = 0; j < balance[i].length; j++)
59.           {
60.              System.out.print(" ");
61.              System.out.print(formatter.format(balance[i][j]));
62.           }
63.           System.out.println();
64.        }
65.     }
66. }
```

Ragged Arrays

So far, what you have seen is not too different from other programming languages. But there is actually something subtle going on behind the scenes that you can sometimes turn to your advantage: Java has *no* multidimensional arrays at all, only one-dimensional arrays. Multidimensional arrays are faked as "arrays of arrays."

For example, the `balance` array in the preceding example is actually an array that contains ten elements, each of which is an array of six floating-point numbers (see Figure 3–16).

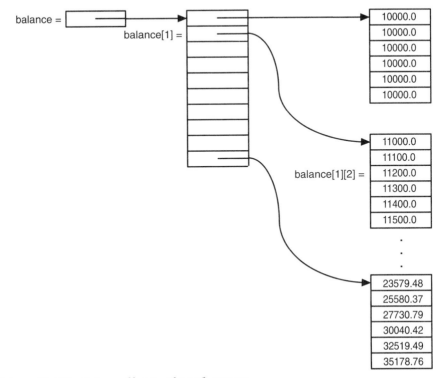

Figure 3–16: A two-dimensional array

The expression `balance[i]` refers to the `i`th subarray, that is, the `i`th row of the table. It is, itself, an array, and `balance[i][j]` refers to the `j`th entry of that array.

Because rows of arrays are individually accessible, you can actually swap them!

```
double[] temp = balance[i];
balance[i] = balance[i + 1];
balance[i + 1] = temp;
```

It is also easy to make "ragged" arrays, that is, arrays in which different rows have different lengths. Here is the standard example. Let us make an array in which the entry at row `i` and column `j` equals the number of possible outcomes of a "choose `j` numbers from `i` numbers" lottery.

```
1
1    1
1    2    1
1    3    3    1
1    4    6    4    1
1    5    10   10   5    1
1    6    15   20   15   6    1
```

Because `j` can never be larger than `i`, the matrix is triangular. The `i`th row has `i + 1` elements. (We allow choosing 0 elements; there is one way to make such a choice.) To build this ragged array, first allocate the array holding the rows.

```
int[][] odds = new int[NMAX + 1][];
```

Next, allocate the rows.

```
for (n = 0; n <= NMAX; n++)
   odds[n] = new int[n + 1];
```

Now that the array is allocated, we can access the elements in the normal way, provided we do not overstep the bounds.

```
for (n = 0; n < odds.length; n++)
   for (k = 0; k < odds[n].length; k++)
   {
      // compute lotteryOdds
      . . .
      odds[n][k] = lotteryOdds;
   }
```

Example 3–9 gives the complete program.

C++ NOTE: The Java declaration

```
double[][] balance = new double[10][6]; // Java
```
is not the same as
```
double balance[10][6]; // C++
```
or even
```
double (*balance)[6] = new double[10][6]; // C++
```
in C++. Instead, an array of five pointers is allocated:
```
double** balance = new double*[10]; // C++
```
Then, each element in the pointer array is filled with an array of 6 numbers:
```
for (i = 0; i < 10; i++)
    balance[i] = new double[6];
```
Mercifully, this loop is automatic when you ask for a `new double[10][6]`. When you want ragged arrays, you allocate the row arrays separately.

Example 3–9: LotteryArray.java

```
1. public class LotteryArray
2. {
3.    public static void main(String[] args)
4.    {
5.       final int NMAX = 10;
6.
7.       // allocate triangular array
8.       int[][] odds = new int[NMAX + 1][];
9.       for (int n = 0; n <= NMAX; n++)
10.         odds[n] = new int[n + 1];
11.
12.      // fill triangular array
13.      for (int n = 0; n < odds.length; n++)
14.         for (int k = 0; k < odds[n].length; k++)
15.         {
16.            /*
17.               compute binomial coefficient
18.               n * (n - 1) * (n - 2) * . . . * (n - k + 1)
19.               -------------------------------------------
20.               1 * 2 * 3 * . . . * k
21.            */
22.            int lotteryOdds = 1;
23.            for (int i = 1; i <= k; i++)
24.               lotteryOdds = lotteryOdds * (n - i + 1) / i;
25.
```

```
26.                    odds[n][k] = lotteryOdds;
27.                }
28.
29.        // print triangular array
30.        for (int n = 0; n < odds.length; n++)
31.        {
32.            for (int k = 0; k < odds[n].length; k++)
33.            {
34.                // pad output with spaces
35.                String output = "    " + odds[n][k];
36.                // make output field 4 characters wide
37.                output = output.substring(output.length() - 4);
38.                System.out.print(output);
39.            }
40.            System.out.println();
41.        }
42.    }
43. }
44.
```

Chapter 4

Objects and Classes

This chapter will:

- Introduce you to object-oriented programming
- Show you how you can create objects that belong to classes in the standard Java library
- Show you how to write your own classes

If you do not have a background in object-oriented programming, you will want to read this chapter carefully. Object-oriented programming requires a different way of thinking than for procedure-oriented languages. The transition is not always easy, but you do need some familiarity with object concepts to go further with Java.

For experienced C++ programmers, this chapter, like the previous chapter, will present familiar information; however, there are enough differences between the two languages that you should read the later sections of this chapter carefully. You'll find the C++ notes helpful for making the transition.

Introduction to Object-Oriented Programming

Object-oriented programming (or OOP for short) is the dominant programming paradigm these days, having replaced the "structured," procedure-based programming techniques that were developed in the early '70s. Java is totally object oriented, and it is impossible to program it in the procedural style that you may be most comfortable with. We hope this section—especially when combined with the example code supplied in the text and on the CD—will give you enough information about OOP to become productive with Java.

Let's begin with a question that, on the surface, seems to have nothing to do with programming: How did companies like Compaq, Dell, Gateway, and the other major personal computer manufacturers get so big, so fast? Most people would probably say they made generally good computers and sold them at rock-bottom prices in an era when computer demand was skyrocketing. But go further—how were they able to manufacture so many models so fast and respond to the changes that were happening so quickly?

Well, a big part of the answer is that these companies farmed out a lot of the work. They bought components from reputable vendors and then assembled them. They often didn't invest time and money in designing and building power supplies, disk drives, motherboards, and other components. This made it possible for the companies to produce a product and make changes quickly for less money than if they had done the engineering themselves.

What the personal computer manufacturers were buying was "prepackaged functionality." For example, when they bought a power supply, they were buying something with certain properties (size, shape, and so on) and a certain functionality (smooth power output, amount of power available, and so on). Compaq provides a good example of how effective this operating procedure is. When Compaq moved from engineering most of the parts in their machines to buying many of the parts, they dramatically improved their bottom line.

OOP springs from the same idea. Your program is made of objects, with certain properties and operations that the objects can perform. Whether you build an object or buy it might depend on your budget or on time. But, basically, as long as objects satisfy your specifications, you don't care how the functionality was implemented. In OOP, you only care about what the objects *expose*. So, just as computer manufacturers don't care about the internals of a power supply as long as it does what they want, most Java programmers don't care how an object is implemented as long as it does what *they* want.

Traditional structured programming consists of designing a set of functions (or *algorithms*) to solve a problem. After the functions were determined, the traditional next step was to find appropriate ways to store the data. This is why the designer of the Pascal language, Niklaus Wirth, called his famous book on programming *Algorithms + Data Structures = Programs* (Prentice Hall, 1975). Notice that in Wirth's title, algorithms come first, and data structures come second. This mimics the way programmers worked at that time. First, you decided how to manipulate the data; then, you decided what structure to impose on the data to make the manipulations easier. OOP reverses the order and puts data first, then looks at the algorithms that operate on the data.

The key to being most productive in OOP is to make each object responsible for carrying out a set of related tasks. If an object relies on a task that isn't its responsibility, it needs to have access to another object whose responsibilities include that task. The first object then asks the second object to carry out the task. This is done with a more generalized version of the function call that you are familiar with in procedural programming. (Recall that in Java these function calls are usually called *method calls*.)

In particular, an object should never directly manipulate the internal data of another object, nor should it expose data for other objects to access directly. All communication should be via method calls. By *encapsulating* object data, you maximize reusability, reduce data dependency and minimize debugging time.

Of course, just as with modules in a procedure-oriented language, you will not want an individual object to do *too* much. Both design and debugging are simplified when you build small objects that perform a few tasks, rather than humongous objects with internal data that are extremely complex, with hundreds of functions to manipulate the data.

The Vocabulary of OOP

You need to understand some of the terminology of OOP to go further. The most important term is the *class*, which you have already seen in the code examples of Chapter 3. A class is the template or blueprint from which objects are actually made. This leads to the standard way of thinking about classes: as cookie cutters. Objects are the cookies themselves. When you *construct* an object from a class, you are said to have created an *instance* of the class.

As you have seen, all code that you write in Java is inside a class. The standard Java library supplies several thousand classes for such diverse purposes as user interface design, dates and calendars, and network programming. Nonetheless, you still have to create your own classes in Java, to describe the objects of the problem domains of your applications, and to adapt the classes that are supplied by the standard library to your own purposes.

Encapsulation (sometimes called data hiding) is a key concept in working with objects. Formally, encapsulation is nothing more than combining data and behavior in one package and hiding the implementation of the data from the user of the object. The data in an object are called its *instance fields*, and the functions and procedures that operate on the data are called its *methods*. A specific object that is an instance of a class will have specific values for its instance fields. The set of those values is the current *state* of the object. Whenever you apply a method to an object, its state may change.

It cannot be stressed enough that the key to making encapsulation work is to have methods *never* directly access instance fields in a class other than their own. Programs should interact with object data *only* through the object's methods. Encapsulation is the way to give the object its "black box" behavior, which is the key to reuse and reliability. This means a class may totally change how it stores its data, but as long as it continues to use the same methods to manipulate the data, no other object will know or care.

When you do start writing your own classes in Java, another tenet of OOP makes this easier: classes can be built on other classes. We say that a class that builds on another class *extends* it. Java, in fact, comes with a "cosmic superclass" called, naturally enough, `Object`, because it is the factory for all objects. All other classes extend this class. You will see more about the `Object` class in the next chapter.

When you extend an existing class, the new class has all the properties and methods of the class that you extend. You supply new methods and data fields that apply to your new class only. The concept of extending a class to obtain another class is called *inheritance*. See the next chapter for details on inheritance.

Objects

To work with OOP, you should be able to identify three key characteristics of objects. The three key characteristics are:

- The object's *behavior*—what can you do with this object, or what methods can you apply to it?
- The object's *state*—how does the object react when you apply those methods?
- The object's *identity*—how is the object distinguished from others that may have the same behavior and state?

All objects that are instances of the same class share a family resemblance by supporting the same *behavior*. The behavior of an object is defined by the methods that you can call.

Next, each object stores information about what it currently looks like. This is the object's *state*. An object's state may change over time, but not spontaneously.

A change in the state of an object must be a consequence of method calls. (If the object state changed without a method call on that object, someone broke encapsulation.)

However, the state of an object does not completely describe it, since each object has a distinct *identity*. For example, in an order-processing system, two orders are distinct even if they request identical items. Notice that the individual objects that are instances of a class *always* differ in their identity and *usually* differ in their state.

These key characteristics can influence each other. For example, the state of an object can influence its behavior. (If an order is "shipped" or "paid," it may reject a method call that asks it to add or remove items. Conversely, if an order is "empty," that is, no items have yet been ordered, it should not allow itself to be shipped.)

In a traditional procedure-oriented program, you start the process at the top, with the `main` function. When designing an object-oriented system, there is no "top," and newcomers to OOP often wonder where to begin. The answer is: You first find classes and then you add methods to each class.

TIP: A simple rule of thumb in identifying classes is to look for nouns in the problem analysis. Methods, on the other hand, correspond to verbs.

For example, in an order-processing system, some of these nouns are:

* Item
* Order
* Shipping address
* Payment
* Account

These nouns may lead to the classes `Item`, `Order`, and so on.

Next, one looks for verbs. Items are *added* to orders. Orders are *shipped* or *canceled*. Payments are *applied* to orders. With each verb, such as "add," "ship," "cancel," and "apply," you have to identify the one object that has the major responsibility for carrying it out. For example, when a new item is added to an order, the order object should be the one in charge since it knows how it stores and sorts items. That is, `add` should be a method of the `Order` class that takes an `Item` object as a parameter.

Of course, the "noun and verb" rule is only a rule of thumb, and only experience can help you decide which nouns and verbs are the important ones when building your classes.

Relationships Between Classes

The most common relationships between classes are:

- *Dependence* ("uses–a")
- *Aggregation* ("has–a")
- *Inheritance* ("is–a")

The *dependence* or "uses–a" relationship is the most obvious and also the most general. For example, the Order class uses the Account class, since Order objects need to access Account objects to check for credit status. But the Item class does not depend on the Account class, since Item objects never need to worry about customer accounts. Thus, a class depends on another class if its methods manipulate objects of that class.

TIP: Try to minimize the number of classes that depend on each other. The point is, if a class A is unaware of the existence of a class B, it is also unconcerned about any changes to B! (And this means that changes to B do not introduce bugs into A.) In software engineering terminology, you want to minimize the *coupling* between classes.

The *aggregation* or "has-a" relationship is easy to understand because it is concrete; for example, an Order object contains Item objects. Containment means that objects of class A contain objects of class B.

NOTE: Some methodologists view the concept of aggregation with disdain and prefer to use a more general "association" relationship. From the point of view of modeling, that is understandable. But for programmers, the "has-a" relationship makes a lot of sense. We like to use aggregation for a second reason—the standard notation for associations is less clear. See Table 4–1.

The *inheritance* or "is-a" relationship expresses a relationship between a more special and a more general class. For example, a RushOrder class inherits from an Order class. The specialized RushOrder class has special methods for priority handling and a different method for computing shipping charges, but its other methods, such as adding items and billing, are inherited from the Order class. In general, if class A extends class B, class A inherits methods from class B but has more capabilities. (We will describe inheritance more fully in the next chapter, in which we discuss this important notion at some length.)

Many programmers use the UML (Unified Modeling Language) notation to draw *class diagrams* that describe the relationships between classes. You can see an example of such a diagram in Figure 4–1. You draw classes as rectangles, and relationships as arrows with various adornments. Table 4–1 shows the most common UML arrow styles:

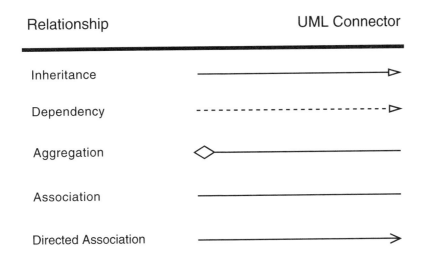

Relationship	UML Connector
Inheritance	
Dependency	
Aggregation	
Association	
Directed Association	

Table 4–1: UML notation for class relationships

Figure 4–1 shows an example of a class diagram.

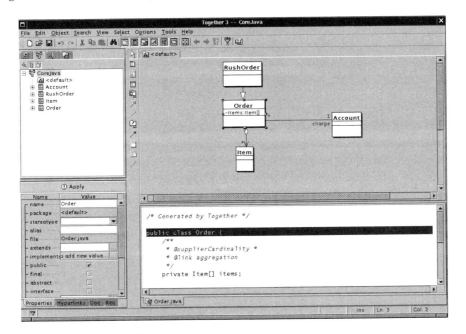

Figure 4–1: A class diagram

NOTE: The diagram in Figure 4–1 was created using the whiteboard edition of Together/J, a Java application to keep design diagrams and Java code synchronized. You can find the program on the book's CD-ROM or download it from
`http://www.togethersoft.com.`

Contrasting OOP with Traditional Procedural Programming Techniques

We want to end this short introduction to OOP by contrasting OOP with the procedural model that you may be more familiar with. In procedure-oriented programming, you identify the tasks to be performed and then:

- By a stepwise refinement process, break the task to be performed into subtasks, and these into smaller subtasks, until the subtasks are simple enough to be implemented directly (this is the top-down approach).
- Write procedures to solve simple tasks and combine them into more sophisticated procedures, until you have the functionality you want (this is the bottom-up approach).

Most programmers, of course, use a mixture of the top-down and bottom-up strategies to solve a programming problem. The rule of thumb for discovering procedures is the same as the rule for finding methods in OOP: look for verbs, or actions, in the problem description. The important difference is that in OOP, you *first* isolate the classes in the project. Only then do you look for the methods of the class. And there is another important difference between traditional procedures and OOP methods: each method is associated with the class that is responsible for carrying out the operation.

For small problems, the breakdown into procedures works very well. But for larger problems, classes and methods have two advantages. Classes provide a convenient clustering mechanism for methods. A simple Web browser may require 2,000 functions for its implementation, or it may require 100 classes with an average of 20 methods per class. The latter structure is much easier to grasp by a programmer. It is also much easier to distribute over a team of programmers. The encapsulation built into classes helps you here as well: classes hide their data representations from all code except their own methods. As Figure 4–2 shows, this means that if a programming bug messes up data, it is easier to search for the culprit among the 20 methods that had access to that data item than among 2,000 procedures.

You may say that this doesn't sound much different than *modularization*. You have certainly written programs by breaking the program up into modules that communicate with each other through procedure calls only, not by sharing data. This (if well done) goes far in accomplishing encapsulation. However, in many programming languages, the slightest sloppiness in programming allows you to get at the data in another module—encapsulation is easy to defeat.

There is a more serious problem: while classes are factories for multiple objects with the same behavior, you cannot get multiple copies of a useful module. Suppose you have a module encapsulating a collection of orders, together with a spiffy balanced binary tree module to access them quickly. Now it turns out that you actually need *two* such collections, one for the pending orders and one for the completed orders. You cannot simply link the order tree module twice. And you don't really want to make a copy and rename all procedures for the linker to work! Classes do not have this limitation. Once a class has been defined, it is easy to construct any number of instances of that class type (whereas a module can have only one instance).

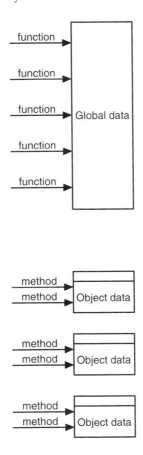

Figure 4–2: Procedural vs. OO programming

We have only scratched a very large surface. The end of this chapter has a short section on "Class Design Hints," but for more information on understanding the OO design process, see the following note for some book recommendations.

NOTE: There are many books on UML. We like *The Unified Modeling Language User Guide* by Grady Booch, Ivar Jacobson, and James Rumbaugh (Addison-Wesley 1999).

You can also check out Rational's Web site for lots of free information about UML (http://www.rational.com/uml). You can find a lighter version of the methodology adapted to both C++ and Java in *Practical Object-Oriented Development in C++ and Java*, by Cay S. Horstmann (John Wiley & Sons, 1997).

Using Existing Classes

Since you can't do anything in Java without classes, you have already seen several classes at work. Unfortunately, many of these are quite anomalous in the Java scheme of things. A good example of this is the Math class. You have seen that you can use methods of the Math class, such as Math.random, without needing to know how they are implemented—all you need to know is the name and parameters (if any). That is the point of encapsulation and will certainly be true of all classes. Unfortunately, the Math class *only* encapsulates functionality; it neither needs nor hides data. Since there is no data, you do not need to worry about making objects and initializing their instance fields—there aren't any!

In the next section, we will look at a more typical class, the Date class. You will see how to construct objects and call methods of this class.

Objects and Object Variables

To work with objects, you first construct them and specify their initial state. Then you apply methods to the objects.

In the Java programming language, you use *constructors* to construct new instances. A constructor is a special method whose purpose is to construct and initialize objects. Let us look at an example. The standard Java library contains a Date class. Its objects describe points in time, such as "December 31, 1999, 23:59:59 GMT."

NOTE: You may be wondering: Why use classes to represent dates rather than (as in some languages) a built-in type? For example, Visual Basic has a built-in date type and programmers can specify dates in the format #6/1/1995#. On the surface, this sounds convenient—programmers can simply use the built-in date type rather than worrying about classes. But actually, how suitable is the Visual Basic design? In some locales, dates are specified as month/day/year, in others as day/month/year. Are the language designers really equipped to foresee these kinds of issues? If they do a poor job, the language becomes an unpleasant muddle, but unhappy programmers are powerless to do anything about it. By using classes, the design task is offloaded to a library designer. If the class is not perfect, other programmers can easily write their own classes to enhance or replace the system classes.

Constructors always have the same name as the class name. Thus, the constructor for the `Date` class is called `Date`. To construct a `Date` object, you combine the constructor with the `new` operator, as follows:

```
new Date()
```

This expression constructs a new object. The object is initialized to the current date and time.

If you like, you can pass the object to a method:

```
System.out.println(new Date());
```

Alternatively, you can apply a method to the object that you just constructed. One of the methods of the `Date` class is the `toString` method. That method yields a string representation of the date. Here is how you would apply the `toString` method to a newly constructed `Date` object.

```
String s = new Date().toString();
```

In these two examples, the constructed object is used only once. Usually, you will want to hang on to the objects that you construct so you can keep using them. Simply store the object in a variable:

```
Date birthday = new Date();
```

Figure 4–3 shows the object variable `birthday` which refers to the newly constructed object.

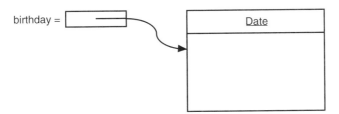

Figure 4–3: Creating a new object

There is an important difference between objects and object variables. For example, the statement

```
Date deadline; // deadline doesn't refer to any object
```

defines an object variable, `deadline`, that can refer to objects of type `Date`. It is important to realize that the variable `deadline` *is not an object* and, in fact, does not yet even refer to an object. You cannot use any `Date` methods on this variable at this time. The statement

```
s = deadline.toString(); // not yet
```

would cause a compile-time error.

You must first initialize the `deadline` variable. You have two choices. Of course, you can initialize the variable with a newly constructed object:

```
deadline = new Date();
```

Or you can set the variable to refer to an existing object:

```
deadline = birthday;
```

Now both variables refer to the *same* object. (See Figure 4–4.)

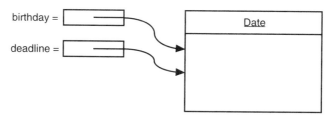

Figure 4–4: Object variables that refer to the same object

It is important to realize that an object variable doesn't actually contain an object. It only *refers* to an object.

In Java, the value of any object variable is a reference to an object that is stored else-where. The return value of the `new` operator is also a reference. A statement such as

```
Date deadline = new Date();
```

has two parts. The expression `new Date()` makes an object of type `Date`, and its value is a reference to that newly created object. That reference is then stored in the `deadline` variable.

You can explicitly set an object variable to `null` to indicate that it currently refers to no object.

```
deadline = null;
. . .
if (deadline != null)
   System.out.println(deadline);
```

If you apply a method to a variable that holds `null`, then a run-time error occurs.

```
birthday = null;
String s = birthday.toString(); // runtime error!
```

Local object variables are not automatically initialized to `null`. You must initialize them, either by calling `new` or by setting them to `null`.

C++ NOTE: Many people mistakenly believe that Java object variables behave like C++ references. But in C++ there are no null references, and references cannot be assigned. You should think of Java object variables as analogous to *object pointers* in C++. For example,

```
Date birthday; // Java
```

is really the same as

```
Date* birthday; // C++
```

Once you make this association, everything falls into place. Of course, a `Date*` pointer isn't initialized until you initialize it with a call to `new`. The syntax is almost the same in C++ and Java.

```
Date* birthday = new Date(); // C++
```

If you copy one variable to another, then both variables refer to the same date—they are pointers to the same object. The equivalent of the Java `null` reference is the C++ `NULL` pointer.

All Java objects live on the heap. When an object contains another object variable, that variable still contains just a pointer to yet another heap object.

In C++, pointers make you nervous because they are so error-prone. It is easy to create bad pointers or to mess up memory management. In Java, these problems simply go away. If you use an uninitialized pointer, the run-time system will reliably generate a run-time error, instead of producing random results. You don't worry about memory management because the garbage collector takes care of it.

C++ makes quite an effort, with its support for copy constructors and assignment operators, to allow the implementation of objects that copy themselves automatically. For example, a copy of a linked list is a new linked list with the same contents but with an independent set of links. This makes it possible to design classes with the same copy behavior as the built-in types. In Java, you must use the `clone` method to get a complete copy of an object.

The `GregorianCalendar` *Class of the Java Library*

In the preceding examples, we used the `Date` class that is a part of the standard Java library. An instance of the `Date` class has a state, namely *a particular point in time*.

Although you don't need to know this when you use the `Date` class, the time is represented by the number of milliseconds (positive or negative) from a fixed point, the so-called *epoch,* which is 00:00:00 UTC, January 1, 1970. UTC is the Coordinated Universal Time, the scientific time standard that is, for practical purposes, the same as the more familiar GMT or Greenwich Mean Time.

But as it turns out, the `Date` class is not very useful for manipulating dates. The designers of the Java library take the point of view that a date description such as "December 31, 1999, 23:59:59" is an arbitrary convention, governed by a *calendar.* This particular description follows the Gregorian calendar, which is the calendar used in most places of the world. The same point in time would be described quite differently in the Chinese or Hebrew lunar calendars, not to mention the calendar used by your customers from Mars.

NOTE: Throughout human history, civilizations grappled with the design of calendars that attached names to dates and brought order to the solar and lunar cycles. For a fascinating explanation of calendars around the world, from the French revolutionary calendar to the Mayan long count, see *Calendrical Calculations* by Nachum Dershowitz and Edward M. Reingold (Cambridge University Press, 1997).

The library designers decided to separate the concerns of keeping time and attaching names to points in time. Therefore, the standard Java library contains two separate classes: the `Date` class which represents a point in time, and the `GregorianCalendar` class which expresses dates in the familiar calendar notation. In fact, the `GregorianCalendar` class extends a more generic `Calendar` class that describes the properties of calendars in general. In theory, you can extend the `Calendar` class and implement the Chinese lunar calendar or a Martian calendar. However, the standard library does not contain any calendar implementations besides the Gregorian calendar.

Separating time measurement from calendars is good object-oriented design. In general, it is a good idea to use separate classes to express different concepts.

The `Date` class has only a small number of methods that allow you to compare two points in time. For example, the `before` and `after` methods tell you if one point in time comes before or after another.

```
if (today.before(birthday))
   System.out.println("Still time to shop for a gift.");
```

NOTE: Actually, the `Date` class has methods such as `getDay`, `getMonth`, and `getYear`, but these methods are *deprecated*. A method is deprecated when a library designer realizes that the method should have never been introduced in the first place.

These methods were a part of the `Date` class before the library designers realized that it makes more sense to supply separate calendar classes. When the calendar classes were introduced, the `Date` methods were tagged as deprecated. You can still use them in your programs, but you will get unsightly compiler warnings if you do. It is a good idea to stay away from using deprecated methods because they may be removed in a future version of the library.

The `GregorianCalendar` class has many more methods than the `Date` class. In particular, it has several useful constructors. The expression

```
new GregorianCalendar()
```

constructs a new object that represents the date and time at which the object was constructed.

You can construct a calendar object for midnight on a specific date by supplying year, month and day:

```
new GregorianCalendar(1999, 11, 31)
```

Somewhat curiously, the months are counted from 0. Therefore, 11 is December. For greater clarity, there are constants like `Calendar.DECEMBER`.

```
new GregorianCalendar(1999, Calendar.DECEMBER, 31)
```

You can also set the time:

```
new GregorianCalendar(1999, Calendar.DECEMBER, 31, 23, 59, 59)
```

Of course, you will usually want to store the constructed object in an object variable:

```
GregorianCalendar deadline = new GregorianCalendar(. . ,);
```

The `GregorianCalendar` has encapsulated instance fields to maintain the date to which it is set. Without looking at the source code, it is impossible to know the representation that the class uses internally. But, of course, the whole point is that this doesn't matter. What matters are the methods that a class exposes.

Mutator and accessor methods

At this point, you are probably asking yourself: How do I get at the current day or month or year for the date encapsulated in a specific `GregorianCalendar` object? And how do I change the values if I am unhappy with them? You can find out how to carry out these tasks by looking at the online documentation or the API notes at the end of this section. We will go over the most important methods in this section.

The job of a calendar is to compute attributes, such as the date, weekday, month, or year, of a certain point in time. To query one of these settings you use the `get` method of the `GregorianCalendar` class. To select the item that you want to get, you pass a constant defined in the `Calendar` class, such as `Calendar.MONTH` or `Calendar.DAY_OF_WEEK`:

```
GregorianCalendar now = new GregorianCalendar();
int month = now.get(Calendar.MONTH);
int day = now.get(Calendar.DAY_OF_WEEK);
```

The API notes list all the constants that you can use.

You change the state with a call to the `set` method:

```
deadline.set(Calendar.YEAR, 2001);
deadline.set(Calendar.MONTH, Calendar.APRIL);
deadline.set(Calendar.DAY, 15);
```

There is also a convenience method to set the year, month, and day with a single call:

```
deadline.set(2001, Calendar.APRIL, 15);
```

Finally, you can add a number of days, weeks, months, etc., to a given date.

```
deadline.add(Calendar.MONTH, 3); // move deadline by 3 months
```

If you add a negative number, then the calendar is moved backwards.

There is a conceptual difference between the `get` method on the one hand and the `set` and `add` methods on the other hand. The `get` method only looks up the state of the object and reports on it. The `set` and `add` methods modify the state of the object. Methods that change instance fields are called *mutator methods* and those that only access instance fields without modifying them are called *accessor methods*.

C++ NOTE: In C++, the `const` suffix is used to denote accessor methods. A method that is not declared as `const` is assumed to be a mutator. However, in the Java programming language there is no special syntax to distinguish between accessors and mutators.

A common convention is to prefix accessor methods with the prefix `get` and mutator methods with the prefix `set`. For example, the `GregorianCalendar` class has methods `getTime` and `setTime` that get and set the point in time that a calendar object represents.

```
Date time = calendar.getTime();
calendar.setTime(time);
```

These methods are particularly useful to convert between the `GregorianCalendar` and `Date` classes. Here is an example. Suppose you know the year, month, and day and you want to make a `Date` object with those settings. Since the `Date` class knows nothing about calendars, first construct a `GregorianCalendar` object and then call the `getTime` method to obtain a date:

```
GregorianCalendar calendar
    = new GregorianCalendar(year, month, day);
Date hireDay = calendar.getTime();
```

Conversely, if you want to find the year, month, or day of a `Date` object, you construct a `GregorianCalendar` object, set the time, and then call the `get` method:

```
GregorianCalendar calendar = new GregorianCalendar()
calendar.setTime(hireDay);
int year = calendar.get(Calendar.YEAR);
```

We will finish this section with a program that puts the `GregorianCalendar` class to work. The program displays a calendar for the current month, like this:

```
Sun Mon Tue Wed Thu Fri Sat
                          1
  2   3   4   5   6   7   8
  9  10  11  12  13  14  15
 16  17  18  19* 20  21  22
 23  24  25  26  27  28  29
 30  31
```

The current day is marked with an *, and the program knows how to compute the days of the week.

Let us go through the key steps of the program. First, we construct a calendar object that is initialized with the current date and time. (We don't actually care about the time for this application.)

```
GregorianCalendar d = new GregorianCalendar();
```

We capture the current day and month by calling the `get` method twice.

```
int today = d.get(Calendar.DAY_OF_MONTH);
int month = d.get(Calendar.MONTH);
```

Then we set `d` to the first of the month and get the weekday of that date.

```
d.set(Calendar.DAY_OF_MONTH, 1);
int weekday = d.get(Calendar.DAY_OF_WEEK);
```

The variable `weekday` is set to 0 if the first day of the month is a Sunday, to 1 if it is a Monday, and so on.

Next, we print the header and the spaces for indenting the first line of the calendar.

For each day, we print a space if the day is < 10, then the day, and then a * if the day equals the current day. Each Saturday, we print a new line.

Then we advance `d` to the next day:

```
d.add(Calendar.DAY_OF_MONTH, 1);
```

When do we stop? We don't know whether the month has 31, 30, 29 or 28 days. Instead, we keep iterating while `d` is still in the current month.

```
do
{
    . . .
}
while (d.get(Calendar.MONTH) == month);
```

Once `d` has moved into the next month, the program terminates.

Example 4–1 shows the complete program.

As you can see, the `GregorianCalendar` class makes it is simple to write a calendar program that takes care of complexities such as weekdays and the varying month lengths. You don't need to know *how* the `GregorianCalendar` class computes months and weekdays. You just use the *interface* of the class—the `get`, `set`, and `add` methods.

The point of this example program is to show you how you can use the interface of a class to carry out fairly sophisticated tasks, without ever having to know the implementation details.

Example 4–1: CalendarTest.java

```
 1. import java.util.*;
 2.
```

```
3. public class CalendarTest
4. {
5.    public static void main(String[] args)
6.    {
7.       // construct d as current date
8.       GregorianCalendar d = new GregorianCalendar();
9.
10.       int today = d.get(Calendar.DAY_OF_MONTH);
11.       int month = d.get(Calendar.MONTH);
12.
13.       // set d to start date of the month
14.       d.set(Calendar.DAY_OF_MONTH, 1);
15.
16.       int weekday = d.get(Calendar.DAY_OF_WEEK);
17.
18.       // print heading
19.       System.out.println("Sun Mon Tue Wed Thu Fri Sat");
20.
21.       // indent first line of calendar
22.       for (int i = Calendar.SUNDAY; i < weekday; i++ )
23.          System.out.print("    ");
24.
25.       do
26.       {
27.          // print day
28.          int day = d.get(Calendar.DAY_OF_MONTH);
29.          if (day < 10) System.out.print(" ");
30.          System.out.print(day);
31.
32.          // mark current day with *
33.          if (day == today)
34.             System.out.print("* ");
35.          else
36.             System.out.print("  ");
37.
38.          // start a new line after every Saturday
39.          if (weekday == Calendar.SATURDAY)
40.             System.out.println();
41.
42.          // advance d to the next day
43.          d.add(Calendar.DAY_OF_MONTH, 1);
44.          weekday = d.get(Calendar.DAY_OF_WEEK);
45.       }
46.       while (d.get(Calendar.MONTH) == month);
47.       // the loop exits when d is day 1 of the next month
48.
49.       // print final end of line if necessary
50.       if (weekday != Calendar.SUNDAY)
51.          System.out.println();
52.    }
53. }
```

java.util.GregorianCalendar

- `GregorianCalendar()`
  constructs a calendar object that represents the current time in the default time zone with the default locale.

- `GregorianCalendar(int year, int month, int date)`
  constructs a Gregorian calendar with the given date.

Parameters:	year	the year of the date
	month	the month of the date. This value is 0-based; for example, 0 for January
	date	the day of the month

- `GregorianCalendar(int year, int month, int date, int hour, int minutes, int seconds)`
  constructs a Gregorian calendar with the given date and time.

Parameters:	year	the year of the date
	month	the month of the date. This value is 0-based; for example, 0 for January
	date	the day of the month
	hour	the hour (between 0 and 23)
	minutes	the minutes (between 0 and 59)
	seconds	the seconds (between 0 and 59)

- `boolean equals(Object when)`
  compares this calendar object with when and returns true if the objects represent the same point in time.

- `boolean before(Object when)`
  compares this calendar object with when and returns true if it comes before when.

- `boolean after(Object when)`
  compares this calendar object with when and returns true if it comes after when.

- `int get(int field)`
  gets the value of a particular field.

Parameters:	field	one of `Calendar.ERA`, `Calendar.YEAR`, `Calendar.MONTH`, `Calendar.WEEK_OF_YEAR`, `Calendar.WEEK_OF_MONTH`, `Calendar.DAY_OF_MONTH`, `Calendar.DAY_OF_YEAR`, `Calendar.DAY_OF_WEEK`, `Calendar.DAY_OF_WEEK_IN_MONTH`,

```
Calendar.AM_PM, Calendar.HOUR,
Calendar.HOUR_OF_DAY, Calendar.MINUTE,
Calendar.SECOND, Calendar.MILLISECOND,
Calendar.ZONE_OFFSET, Calendar.DST_OFFSET
```

- `void set(int field, int value)`
  sets the value of a particular field.

  Parameters: `field`   one of the constants accepted by get

  `value`   the new value

- `void set(int year, int month, int day)`
  sets the date fields to a new date.

  Parameters: `year`   the year of the date

  `month`   the month of the date. This value is 0-based; for example, 0 for January

  `day`   the day of the month

- `void set(int year, int month, int day, int hour, int minutes, int seconds)`
  sets the date and time fields to new values.

  Parameters: `year`   the year of the date

  `month`   the month of the date. This value is 0-based; for example, 0 for January

  `day`   the day of the month

  `hour`   the hour (between 0 and 23)

  `minutes` the minutes (between 0 and 59)

  `seconds` the seconds (between 0 and 59)

- `void add(int field, int amount)`
  is a date arithmetic method. Adds the specified amount of time to the given time field. For example, to add 7 days to the current calendar date, call `c.add(Calendar.DAY_OF_MONTH, 7)`.

  Parameters: `field`   the field to modify (using one of the constants documented in the `get` method)

  `amount` the amount by which the field should be changed (can be negative)

- `void setTime(Date time)`
  sets this calendar to the given point in time.

  Parameters: `time`   a point in time

- `Date getTime()`
  gets the point in time that is represented by the current value of this calendar object.

Building Your Own Classes

In Chapter 3, you started writing simple classes. However, all those classes had just a single `main` method. Now the time has come to show you how to write the kind of "workhorse classes" that are needed for more sophisticated applications. These classes typically do not have a `main` method. Instead, they have their own instance fields and methods. To build a complete program, you combine several classes, one of which has a `main` method.

An `Employee` Class

The simplest form for a class definition in Java is:

```
class NameOfClass
{
    constructor₁
    constructor₂
    . . .
    method₁
    method₂
    . . .
    field₁
    field₂
    . . .
}
```

> NOTE: We adopt the style that the methods for the class come first and the fields come at the end. Perhaps this, in a small way, encourages the notion of looking at the interface first and paying less attention to the implementation.

Consider the following, very simplified version of an `Employee` class that might be used by a business in writing a payroll system.

```
class Employee
{
    // constructor
    public Employee(String n, double s,
        int year, int month, int day)
    {
        name = n;
        salary = s;
        hireDay = new GregorianCalendar(year, month - 1, day);
    }

    // method 1
    public String getName()
    {
        return name;
    }
```

```
    // more methods
    . . .

    // instance fields

    private String name;
    private double salary;
    private Date hireDay;
}
```

We will break down the implementation of this class in some detail in the sections that follow. First, though, Example 4–2 shows a program code that shows the `Employee` class in action.

In the program, we construct an `Employee` array and fill it with three employee objects:

```
Employee[] staff = new Employee[3];

staff[0] = new Employee("Carl Cracker", . . .);
staff[1] = new Employee("Harry Hacker", . . .);
staff[2] = new Employee("Tony Tester", . . .);
```

Next, we use the `raiseSalary` method of the `Employee` class to raise every employee's salary by 5%:

```
for (i = 0; i < staff.length; i++)
   staff[i].raiseSalary(5);
```

Finally, we print out information about each employee, by calling the `getName`, `getSalary` and `getHireDay` methods:

```
for (int i = 0; i < staff.length; i++)
{
   Employee e = staff[i];
   System.out.println("name=" + e.getName()
      + ",salary=" + e.getSalary()
      + ",hireDay=" + e.getHireDay());
}
```

Note that the example program consists of *two* classes: the `Employee` class and a class `EmployeeTest` with the `public` access specifier. The `main` method with the instructions that we just described is contained in the `EmployeeTest` class.

The name of the source file is `EmployeeTest.java` since the name of the file must match the name of the `public` class. You can only have one public class in a source file, but you can have any number of non-public classes.

Next, when you compile this source code, the compiler creates two class files in the directory: `EmployeeTest.class` and `Employee.class`.

You start the program by giving the bytecode interpreter the name of the class that contains the `main` method of your program:

```
java EmployeeTest
```

The bytecode interpreter starts running the code in the `main` method in the `EmployeeTest` class. This code in turn constructs three new `Employee` objects and shows you their state.

Example 4–2: EmployeeTest.java

```
1. import java.util.*;
2.
3. public class EmployeeTest
4. {
5.    public static void main(String[] args)
6.    {
7.       // fill the staff array with three Employee objects
8.       Employee[] staff = new Employee[3];
9.
10.      staff[0] = new Employee("Carl Cracker", 75000,
11.         1987, 12, 15);
12.      staff[1] = new Employee("Harry Hacker", 50000,
13.         1989, 10, 1);
14.      staff[2] = new Employee("Tony Tester", 40000,
15.         1990, 3, 15);
16.
17.      // raise everyone's salary by 5%
18.      for (int i = 0; i < staff.length; i++)
19.         staff[i].raiseSalary(5);
20.
21.      // print out information about all Employee objects
22.      for (int i = 0; i < staff.length; i++)
23.      {
24.         Employee e = staff[i];
25.         System.out.println("name=" + e.getName()
26.            + ",salary=" + e.getSalary()
27.            + ",hireDay=" + e.getHireDay());
28.      }
29.   }
30. }
31.
32. class Employee
33. {
34.    public Employee(String n, double s,
35.       int year, int month, int day)
36.    {
37.       name = n;
38.       salary = s;
39.       GregorianCalendar calendar
40.          = new GregorianCalendar(year, month - 1, day);
41.          // GregorianCalendar uses 0 for January
42.       hireDay = calendar.getTime();
43.    }
44.
```

```
45.    public String getName()
46.    {
47.       return name;
48.    }
49.
50.    public double getSalary()
51.    {
52.       return salary;
53.    }
54.
55.    public Date getHireDay()
56.    {
57.       return hireDay;
58.    }
59.
60.    public void raiseSalary(double byPercent)
61.    {
62.       double raise = salary * byPercent / 100;
63.       salary += raise;
64.    }
65.
66.    private String name;
67.    private double salary;
68.    private Date hireDay;
69. }
```

Using Multiple Source Files

The program in Example 4–2 has two classes in a single source file. Many programmers prefer to put each class into its own source file. For example, you can place the class `Employee` into a file `Employee.java` and `EmployeeTest` into `EmployeeTest.java`.

If you like this arrangement, then you have two choices for compiling the program/ You can invoke the Java compiler with a wildcard:

```
javac Employee*.java
```

Then, all source files matching the wildcard will be compiled into class files. Or, you can simply type:

```
javac EmployeeTest.java
```

You may find it surprising that the second choice works since the `Employee.java` file is never explicitly compiled. However, when the Java compiler sees the `Employee` class being used inside `EmployeeTest.java`, it will look for a `Employee.class` file. If it does not find that file, it automatically searches for `Employee.java` and then compiles it. Even more is true: if the time stamp of the version of `Employee.java` that it finds is newer than that of the existing `Employee.class` file, the Java compiler will *automatically* recompile the file.

NOTE: If you are familiar with the "make" facility of UNIX (or one of its Windows cousins such as "nmake"), then you can think of the Java compiler as having the "make" functionality already built in.

Analyzing the Employee Class

In the sections that follow, we want to dissect the Employee class. Let's start with the methods in this class. As you can see by examining the source code, this class has one constructor and four methods:

```
public Employee(String n, double s, int year, int month, int day)
public String getName()
public double getSalary()
public Date getHireDay()
public void raiseSalary(double byPercent)
```

All methods of this class are all tagged as public. The keyword public means that any method in any class can call the method. (There are four possible access levels; they are covered in this and the next chapter.)

Next, notice that there are three instance fields that will hold the data we will manipulate inside an instance of the Employee class.

```
private String name;
private double salary;
private Date hireDay;
```

The private keyword makes sure that the *only* methods that can access these instance fields are the methods of the Employee class itself. No outside method can read or write to these fields.

NOTE: It is possible to use the public keyword with your instance fields, but it would be a very bad idea. Having public data fields would allow any part of the program to read and modify the instance fields. That completely ruins encapsulation. We strongly recommend that you always make your instance fields private.

Finally, notice that two of the instance fields are themselves objects: The name and hireDay fields are refererences to String and Date objects. This is quite usual: classes will often contain instance fields of class type.

First Steps with Constructors

Let's look at the constructor listed in our Employee class.

```
public Employee(String n, double s, int year, int month, int day)
{
   name = n;
   salary = s;
```

```
GregorianCalendar calendar
    = new GregorianCalendar(year, month - 1, day);
hireDay = calendar.getTime();
}
```

As you can see, the name of the constructor is the same as the name of the class. This constructor runs when you construct objects of the `Employee` class—giving the instance fields the initial state you want them to have.

For example, when you create an instance of the `Employee` class with code like this:

```
new Employee("James Bond", 100000, 1950, 1, 1);
```

you have set the instance fields as follows:

```
name = "James Bond";
salary = 100000;
hireDay = January 1, 1950;
```

There is an important difference between constructors and other methods: A constructor can only be called in conjunction with the `new` operator. You can't apply a constructor to an existing object to reset the instance fields. For example,

```
james.Employee("James Bond", 250000, 1950, 1, 1); // ERROR
```

is a compile-time error.

We will have more to say about constructors later in this chapter. For now, keep the following in mind:

- A constructor has the same name as the class.
- A class can have more than one constructor.
- A constructor may take zero, one, or more parameters.
- A constructor has no return value.
- A constructor is always called with the `new` operator.

C++ NOTE: Constructors work the same way in Java as they do in C++. But keep in mind that all Java objects are constructed on the heap and that a constructor must be combined with `new`. It is a common C++ programmer error to forget the `new` operator:

```
Employee number007("James Bond", 100000, 1950, 1, 1);
    // C++, not Java
```

That works in C++ but does not work in Java.

CAUTION: Be careful not to introduce local variables with the same names as the instance fields. For example, the following constructor will not set the salary.

```
public Employee(String n, double s, . . .)
{
    String name = n; // ERROR
    double salary = s; // ERROR
    . . .
}
```

The constructor declares *local* variables `name` and `salary`. These variables are only accessible inside the constructor. They *shadow* the instance fields with the same name. Some programmers—such as the authors of this book—write this kind of code when they type faster than they think, because their fingers are used to adding the data type. This is a nasty error that can be hard to track down. You just have to be careful in all of your methods that you don't use variable names that equal the names of instance fields.

The Methods of the `Employee` Class

The methods in our `Employee` class are quite simple. Notice that all of these methods can access the private instance fields by name. This is a key point: instance fields are always accessible by the methods of their own class.

For example,

```
public void raiseSalary(double byPercent)
{
   double raise = salary * byPercent / 100;
   salary += raise;
}
```

sets a new value for the `salary` instance field in the object that executes this method. (This particular method does not return a value.) For example, the call

```
number007.raiseSalary(5);
```

raises `number007`'s salary by increasing the `number007.salary` variable by 5%. More specifically, the call executes the following instructions:

```
double raise = number007.salary * 5 / 100;
number007.salary += raise;
```

The `raiseSalary` method has two parameters. The first parameter, called the *implicit* parameter, is the object of type `Employee` that appears before the method name. The second parameter, the number inside the parentheses after the method name, is an *explicit* parameter.

As you can see, the explicit parameters are explicitly listed in the method declaration, for example, `double byPercent`. The implicit parameter does not appear in the method declaration.

In every method, the keyword `this` refers to the implicit parameter. If you like, you can write the `raiseSalary` method as follows:

```
public void raiseSalary(double byPercent)
{
   double raise = this.salary * byPercent / 100;
   this.salary += raise;
}
```

Some programmers prefer that style because it clearly distinguishes between instance fields and local variables.

C++ NOTE: In C++, you generally define methods outside the class:

```
void Employee::raiseSalary(double byPercent) // C++, not Java
{
    . . .
}
```

If you define a method inside a class, then it is automatically an inline method.

```
class Employee
{
    . . .
    int getName() { return name; } // inline in C++
}
```

In the Java programming language, all methods are defined inside the class itself. This does not make them inline.

Finally, let's look more closely at the rather simple `getName`, `getSalary`, and `getHireDay` methods.

```
public String getName()
{
    return name;
}

public double getSalary()
{
    return salary;
}

public Date getHireDay()
{
    return hireDay;
}
```

These are obvious examples of accessor methods. Because they simply return the values of instance fields, they are sometimes called *field accessors*.

Wouldn't it be easier to simply make the `name`, `salary`, and `hireDay` fields public, instead of having separate accessor methods?

The point is that the `name` field is a "read only" field. Once you set it in the constructor, there is no method to change it. Thus, we have a guarantee that the `name` field will never be corrupted.

The `salary` field is not read-only, but it can only be changed by the `raise-Salary` method. In particular, should the value ever be wrong, only that method needs to be debugged. Had the `salary` field been public, the culprit for messing up the value could have been anywhere.

Sometimes, it happens that you want to get and set the value of an instance field. Then you need to supply *three* items:

*   A private data field
*   A public field accessor method
*   A public field mutator method

This is a lot more tedious than supplying a single public data field, but there are considerable benefits:

1. The internal implementation can be changed without affecting any code other than the methods of the class.

    For example, if the storage of the name is changed to

    ```
    String firstName;
    String lastName;
    ```

    then the `getName` method can be changed to return

    ```
    firstName + " " + lastName
    ```

    This change is completely invisible to the remainder of the program.

Of course, the accessor and mutator methods may need to do a lot of work and convert between the old and the new data representation. But that leads us to our second benefit.

2. Mutator methods can perform error-checking, whereas code that simply assigns to a field may not go through the trouble.

    For example, a `setSalary` method might check that the salary is never less than 0.

CAUTION: Be careful not to write accessor methods that return references to mutable objects. Consider the following example where we store the `hireDay` field as a `GregorianCalendar` object instead of a `Date` object.

```
class Employee
{
   . . .
   public GregorianCalendar getHireDay()
   {
      return hireDay;
   }
   . . .
   private GregorianCalendar hireDay;
}
```

This breaks the encapsulation! Consider the following rogue code:

```
Employee harry = . . . .;
GregorianCalendar d = harry.getHireDay();
d.add(Calendar.YEAR, -10);
// let's give Harry ten years added seniority
```

The reason is subtle. Both d and `harry.hireDay` refer to the same object (see Figure 4–5). Applying mutator methods to d automatically changes the private state of the employee object!

Why didn't the `Date` class in our original implementation suffer from the same problem? Couldn't someone get the date and change it? No. The `Date` class is *immutable*. There is no method that can change a `Date` object. In contrast, `GregorianCalendar` objects are mutable.

If you need to return a reference to a mutable object, you should *clone* it first. A clone is an exact copy of an object that is stored in a new location. We will discuss cloning in detail in Chapter 6. Here is the corrected code:

```
class Employee
{
    . . .
    public GregorianCalendar getHireDay()
    {
        return (GregorianCalendar)hireDay.clone();
    }
    . . .
}
```

As a rule of thumb, always use `clone` whenever you need to return a copy of a mutable data field.

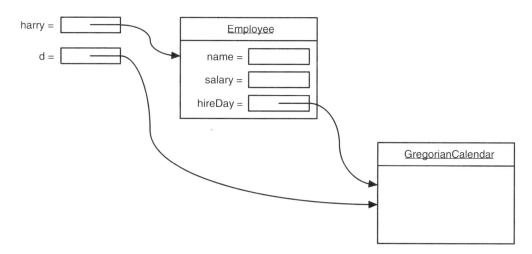

Figure 4–5: Returning a reference to a mutable data field

Method Access to Private Data

You know that a method can access the private data of the object on which it is invoked. What many people find surprising is that a method can access the private data of *all objects of its class*. For example, consider a method `equals` that compares two employees.

```
class Employee
{
   . . .
   boolean equals(Employee other)
   {
      return name.equals(other.name);
   }
}
```

A typical call is

```
if (harry.equals(boss)) . . .
```

This method accesses the private fields of `harry`, which is not surprising. It also accesses the private fields of `boss`. This is legal because `boss` is an object of type `Employee`, and a method of the `Employee` class is permitted to access the private fields of *any* object of type `Employee`.

C++ NOTE: C++ has the same rule. A method can access the private features of any object of its class, not just of the implicit parameter.

Private Methods

When implementing a class, we make all data fields private, since `public` data are dangerous. But what about the methods? While most methods are `public`, `private` methods occur quite frequently. These methods can be called only from other methods of the same class. The reason is simple: to implement certain methods, you may wish to break up the code into many separate methods. Some of these internal methods may not be particularly useful to the public. (For example, they may be too close to the current implementation or require a special protocol or calling order.) Such methods are best implemented as `private`.

To implement a private method in Java, simply change the `public` keyword to `private`.

By making a method private, you are under no obligation to keep it available if you change to another implementation. The method may well be *harder* to implement or *unnecessary* if the data representation changes: this is irrelevant. The point is that as long as the method is private, the designers of the class can be assured that it is never used outside the other class operations and can simply drop it. If a method is public, you cannot simply drop it because other code might rely on it.

In sum, choose private methods:

- For those methods that are of no concern to the class user
- For those methods that could not easily be supported if the class implementation were to change

Final Instance Fields

You can define an instance field as `final`. Such a field must be initialized when the object is constructed. That is, it must be guaranteed that the field value is set after the end of every constructor. Afterwards, the field may not be modified again. For example, the `name` field of the `Employee` class may be declared as `final` since it never changes after the object is constructed—there is no `setName` method.

```
class Employee
{
   . . .
   private final String name;
}
```

TIP: It is a good idea to tag fields that don't change during an object's lifetime as `final`. If all fields of a class are final, then the class is *immutable*—its objects never change after they are constructed. For example, the `String` and `Date` classes are immutable. Immutable classes have one important advantage—you don't have to worry about sharing references.

Static Fields and Methods

In all sample programs that you have seen, the `main` method is tagged with the `static` modifier. We are now ready to discuss the meaning of this modifier.

Static Fields

If you define a field as `static`, then there is only one such field per class. In contrast, each object has its own copy of all instance fields. For example, let's suppose we want to assign a unique identification number to each employee. We add an instance field `id` and a static field `nextId` to the `Employee` class:

```
class Employee
{
   . . .
   private int id;
   private static int nextId = 1;
}
```

Now, every employee object has its own `id` field, but there is only one `nextId` field that is shared among all instances of the class. Let's put it another way. If there are one thousand objects of the `Employee` class, then there are one thousand instance fields `id`, one for each object. But there is a single static field `nextId`. Even if there are no employee objects, the static field `nextId` is present. It belongs to the class, not to any individual object.

Let's implement a simple method:

```
public void setId()
{
    id = nextId;
    nextId++;
}
```

Suppose you set the employee identification number for `harry`:

```
harry.setId();
```

Then the `id` field of `harry` is set, and the value of the static field `nextId` is incremented:

```
harry.id = . . .;
Employee.nextId++;
```

Constants

Static variables are quite rare. However, static constants are more common. For example, the `Math` class defines a static constant:

```
public class Math
{
    . . .
    public static final double PI = 3.14159265358979323846;
    . . .
}
```

You can access this constant in your programs as `Math.PI`.

If the keyword `static` had been omitted, then `PI` would have been an instance field of the `Math` class. That is, you would need an object of the `Math` class to access `PI`, and every object would have its own copy of `PI`.

Another static constant that you have used many times is `System.out`. It is declared in the `System` class as:

```
public class System
{
    . . .
    public static final PrintStream out = . . .;
    . . .
}
```

As we mentioned several times, it is never a good idea to have public fields because everyone can modify them. However, public constants (that is, `final` fields) are ok. Since `out` has been declared as `final`, you cannot reassign another print stream to it:

```
out = new PrintStream(. . .); // ERROR--out is final
```

NOTE: If you look at the System class, you will notice a method setOut that lets you set System.out to a different stream. You may wonder how that method can change the value of a final variable. However, the setOut method is a *native* method, not implemented in the Java programming language. Native methods can bypass the access control mechanisms of the Java language. This is a very unusual workaround that you should not emulate in your own programs.

Static Methods

Static methods are methods that do not operate on objects. For example, the pow method of the Math class is a static method. The expression:

```
Math.pow(x, y)
```

computes the power x^y. It does not use any Math object to carry out its task. In other words, it has no implicit parameter.

In other words, you can think of static methods as methods that don't have a this parameter.

Because static methods don't operate on objects, you cannot access instance fields from a static method. But static methods can access the static fields in their class. Here is an example of such a static method:

```
public static int getNextId()
{
    return nextId; // returns static field
}
```

To call this method, you supply the name of the class:

```
int n = Employee.getNextId();
```

Could you have omitted the keyword static for this method? Yes, but then you would need to have an object reference of type Employee to invoke the method.

NOTE: It is legal to use an object to call a static method. For example, if harry is an Employee object, then you can call harry.getNextId() instead of Employee.getnextId(). However, we find that notation confusing. The getNextId method doesn't look at harry at all to compute the result. We recommend that you use class names, not objects, to invoke static methods.

You use static methods in two situations:

1. When a method doesn't need to access the object state because all needed parameters are supplied as explicit parameters (example: Math.pow)

2. When a method only needs to access static fields of the class (example: `Employee.getNextId`)

C++ NOTE: Static fields and methods have the same functionality in Java and C++. However, the syntax is slightly different. In C++, you use the `::` operator to access a static field or method outside its scope, such as `Math::PI`.

The term "static" has a curious history. At first, the keyword `static` was introduced in C to denote local variables that don't go away when exiting a block. In that context, the term "static" makes sense: the variable stays around and is still there when the block is entered again. Then `static` got a second meaning in C, to denote global variables and functions that cannot be accessed from other files. The keyword `static` was simply reused, to avoid introducing a new keyword. Finally, C++ reused the keyword for a third, unrelated interpretation, to denote variables and functions that belong to a class but not to any particular object of the class. That is the same meaning that the keyword has in Java.

Factory Methods

Here is another common use for static methods. Consider the methods

```
NumberFormat.getNumberInstance()
NumberFormat.getCurrencyInstance()
```

that we discussed in Chapter 3. Each of these methods returns an object of type `NumberFormat`. For example,

```
NumberFormat formatter = NumberFormat.getCurrencyInstance();
System.out.println(formatter.format(salary));
   // prints salary with currency symbol
```

As you now know, these are static methods—you call them on a class, not an object. However, their purpose is to generate an object of the same class. Such a method is called a *factory method*.

Why don't we use a constructor instead? There are two reasons. You can't give names to constructors. The constructor name is always the same as the class name. In the `NumberFormat` example, it makes sense to have two separate names for getting number and currency formatter objects. Furthermore, the factory method can return an object of the type `NumberFormat`, or an object of a subclass that inherits from `NumberFormat`. (See Chapter 5 for more on inheritance.) A constructor does not have that flexibility.

The `main` Method

Note that you can call static methods without having any objects. For example, you never construct any objects of the `Math` class to call `Math.pow`.

For the same reason, the `main` method is a static method.

```
public class Application
{
    public static void main(String[] args)
    {
        // construct objects here
        . . .
    }
}
```

The `main` method does not operate on any objects. In fact, when a program starts, there aren't any objects yet. The static `main` method executes, and constructs the objects that the program needs.

TIP: Every class can have a `main` method. That is a handy trick for unit testing of classes. For example, you can add a `main` method to the `Employee` class:

```
class Employee
{
    public Employee(String n, double s,
        int year, int month, int day)
    {
        name = n;
        salary = s;
        GregorianCalendar calendar
            = new GregorianCalendar(year, month - 1, day);
        hireDay = calendar.getTime();
    }
    . . .
    public static void main(String[] args) // unit test
    {
        Employee e = new Employee("Romeo", 50000);
        e.raiseSalary(10);
        System.out.println(e.getName() + " " + e.getSalary());
    }
    . . .
}
```

If you want to test the `Employee` class in isolation, you simply execute

```
java Employee
```

If the employee class is a part of a larger application, then you start the application with

```
java Application
```

and the `main` method of the `Employee` class is never executed.

The program in Example 4–3 contains a simple version of the `Employee` class with a static field `count` and a static method `getCount`. We fill an array with three `Employee` objects and then print the employee information. Finally, we print the number of identification numbers assigned.

Note that the `Employee` class also has a static `main` method for unit testing. Try running both

```
java Employee
```

and

```
java StaticTest
```

to execute both `main` methods.

Example 4–3: StaticTest.java

```
1. public class StaticTest
2. {
3.    public static void main(String[] args)
4.    {
5.       // fill the staff array with three Employee objects
6.       Employee[] staff = new Employee[3];
7.
8.       staff[0] = new Employee("Tom", 40000);
9.       staff[1] = new Employee("Dick", 60000);
10.      staff[2] = new Employee("Harry", 65000);
11.
12.      // print out information about all Employee objects
13.      for (int i = 0; i < staff.length; i++)
14.      {
15.         Employee e = staff[i];
16.         e.setId();
17.         System.out.println("name=" + e.getName()
18.            + ",id=" + e.getId()
19.            + ",salary=" + e.getSalary());
20.      }
21.
22.      int n = Employee.getNextId(); // calls static method
23.      System.out.println("Next available id=" + n);
24.   }
25. }
26.
27. class Employee
28. {
29.    public Employee(String n, double s)
30.    {
31.       name = n;
32.       salary = s;
33.       id = 0;
34.    }
35.
36.    public String getName()
37.    {
```

```
38.        return name;
39.    }
40.
41.    public double getSalary()
42.    {
43.        return salary;
44.    }
45.
46.    public int getId()
47.    {
48.        return id;
49.    }
50.
51.    public void setId()
52.    {
53.        id = nextId; // set id to next available id
54.        nextId++;
55.    }
56.
57.    public static int getNextId()
58.    {
59.        return nextId; // returns static field
60.    }
61.
62.    public static void main(String[] args) // unit test
63.    {
64.        Employee e = new Employee("Harry", 50000);
65.        System.out.println(e.getName() + " " + e.getSalary());
66.    }
67.
68.    private String name;
69.    private double salary;
70.    private int id;
71.    private static int nextId = 1;
72. }
```

Method Parameters

Let us review the computer science terms that describe how parameters can
be passed to a method (or a function) in a programming language. The term
call by value means that the method gets just the value that the caller provides.
In contrast, *call by reference* means that the method gets the *location* of the variable that the caller provides. Thus, a method can *modify* the value stored in a
variable that is passed by reference but not in one that is passed by value.
These "call by . . . " terms are standard computer science terminology that
describe the behavior of method parameters in various programming languages, not just Java. (In fact, there is also a *call by name* that is mainly of
historical interest, being employed in the Algol programming language, one
of the oldest high-level languages.)

The Java programming language *always* uses call by value. That means, the method gets a copy of all parameter values. In particular, the method cannot modify the contents of any parameter variables that are passed to it.

For example, consider the following call:

```
double percent = 10;
harry.raiseSalary(percent);
```

No matter how the method is implemented, we know that after the method call, the value of `percent` is still 10.

Let us look a little more closely at this situation. Suppose a method tried to triple the value of a method parameter:

```
public static void tripleValue(double x) // doesn't work
{
    x = 3 * x;
}
```

Let's call this method:

```
double percent = 10;
tripleValue(percent);
```

However, this does not work. After the method call, the value of `percent` is still 10. Here is what happens:

1. `x` is initialized with a copy of the value of `percent` (that is, 10).
2. `x` is tripled—it is now 30. But `percent` is still 10 (see Figure 4–6).
3. The method ends, and the parameter variable `x` is no longer in use.

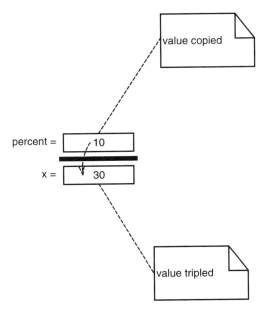

percent = 10

x = 30

Figure 4–6: Modifying a numeric parameter has no lasting effect

There are, however, two kinds of method parameters:

- Primitive types (numbers, Boolean values)
- Object references

You have seen that it is impossible for a method to change a primitive type parameter. The situation is different for object parameters. You can easily implement a method that triples the salary of an employee:

```
public static void tripleSalary(Employee x) // works
{
   x.raiseSalary(200);
}
```

When you call

```
harry = new Employee(. . .);
tripleSalary(harry);
```

then the following happens:

1. x is initialized with a copy of the value of `harry`, that is, an object reference.

2. The `raiseSalary` method is applied to that object reference. The `Employee` object to which both x and `harry` refer gets its salary raised by 200%.

3. The method ends, and the parameter variable x is no longer in use. Of course, the object variable `harry` continues to refer to the object whose salary was tripled (see Figure 4–7).

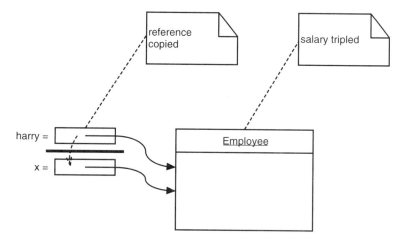

Figure 4–7: Modifying an object parameter has a lasting effect

As you have seen, it is easily possible—and in fact very common—to implement methods that change the state of an object parameter. The reason is simple. The method gets a copy of the object reference, and both the original and the copy refer to the same object.

Many programming languages (in particular, C++ and Pascal) have two methods for parameter passing: call by value and call by reference. Some programmers (and unfortunately even some book authors) claim that the Java programming language uses call by reference for objects. However, that is false. Because this is such a common misunderstanding, it is worth examining a counterexample in detail.

Let's try to write a method that swaps two employee objects:

```
public static void swap(Employee x, Employee y) // doesn't work
{
    Employee temp = x;
    x = y;
    y = temp;
}
```

If the Java programming language used call by reference for objects, this method would work:

```
Employee a = new Employee("Alice", . . .);
Employee b = new Employee("Bob", . . .);
swap(a, b);
// does a now refer to Bob, b to Alice?
```

However, the method does not actually change the object references that are stored in the variables a and b. The x and y parameters of the swap method are initialized with *copies* of these references. The method then proceeds to swap these copies.

```
// x refers to Alice, y to Bob
Employee temp = x;
x = y;
y = temp;
// now x refers to Bob, y to Alice
```

But ultimately, this is a wasted effort. When the method ends, the parameter variables x and y are abandoned. The original variables a and b still refer to the same objects as they did before the method call.

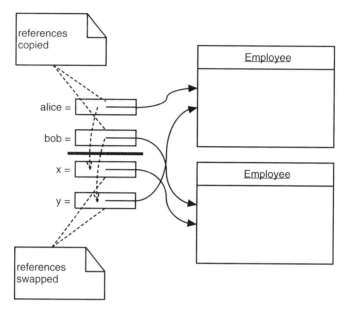

Figure 4–8: Swapping object parameters has no lasting effect

This discussion demonstrates that the Java programming language does not use call by reference for objects. Instead, *object references are passed by value.*

Here is a summary of what you can and cannot do with method parameters in the Java programming language:

- A method cannot modify a parameter of primitive type (that is, numbers or Boolean values).
- A method can change the *state* of an object parameter.
- A method cannot make an object parameter refer to a new object.

The program in Example 4–4 demonstrates these facts. The program first tries to triple a value of a number parameter and does not succeed:

```
Testing tripleValue:
Before: percent=10.0
End of method: x=30.0
After: percent=10.0
```

It then successfully triples the salary of an employee:

```
Testing tripleSalary:
Before: salary=50000.0
End of method: salary=150000.0
After: salary=150000.0
```

After the method, the state of the object to which `harry` refers has changed. This is possible because the method modified the state through a copy of the object reference.

Finally, the program demonstrates the failure of the swap method:

```
Testing swap:
Before: a=Alice
Before: b=Bob
End of method: x=Bob
End of method: y=Alice
After: a=Alice
After: b=Bob
```

As you can see, the parameter variables x and y are swapped, but the variables a and b are not affected.

C++ NOTE: C++ has both call by value and call by reference. You tag reference parameters with &. For example, you can easily implement methods
`void tripleValue(double& x)` or `void swap(Employee& x, Employee& y)`
that modify their reference parameters.

Example 4–4: ParamTest.java

```
1. public class ParamTest
2. {
3.    public static void main(String[] args)
4.    {
5.       /*
6.          Test 1: Methods can't modify numeric parameters
7.       */
8.       System.out.println("Testing tripleValue:");
9.       double percent = 10;
10.      System.out.println("Before: percent=" + percent);
11.      tripleValue(percent);
12.      System.out.println("After: percent=" + percent);
13.
14.      /*
15.         Test 2: Methods can change the state of object
16.         parameters
17.      */
18.      System.out.println("\nTesting tripleSalary:");
19.      Employee harry = new Employee("Harry", 50000);
20.      System.out.println("Before: salary=" + harry.getSalary());
21.      tripleSalary(harry);
22.      System.out.println("After: salary=" + harry.getSalary());
23.
24.      /*
25.         Test 3: Methods can't attach new objects to
26.         object parameters
27.      */
28.      System.out.println("\nTesting swap:");
29.      Employee a = new Employee("Alice", 70000);
```

```
30.        Employee b = new Employee("Bob", 60000);
31.        System.out.println("Before: a=" + a.getName());
32.        System.out.println("Before: b=" + b.getName());
33.        swap(a, b);
34.        System.out.println("After: a=" + a.getName());
35.        System.out.println("After: b=" + b.getName());
36.     }
37.
38.    public static void tripleValue(double x) // doesn't work
39.    {
40.       x = 3 * x;
41.       System.out.println("End of method: x=" + x);
42.    }
43.
44.    public static void tripleSalary(Employee x) // works
45.    {
46.       x.raiseSalary(200);
47.       System.out.println("End of method: salary="
48.          + x.getSalary());
49.    }
50.
51.    public static void swap(Employee x, Employee y)
52.    {
53.       Employee temp = x;
54.       x = y;
55.       y = temp;
56.       System.out.println("End of method: x=" + x.getName());
57.       System.out.println("End of method: y=" + y.getName());
58.    }
59. }
60.
61. class Employee // simplified Employee class
62. {
63.    public Employee(String n, double s)
64.    {
65.       name = n;
66.       salary = s;
67.    }
68.
69.    public String getName()
70.    {
71.       return name;
72.    }
73.
74.    public double getSalary()
75.    {
76.       return salary;
77.    }
78.
```

```
79.    public void raiseSalary(double byPercent)
80.    {
81.       double raise = salary * byPercent / 100;
82.       salary += raise;
83.    }
84.
85.    private String name;
86.    private double salary;
87. }
```

Object Construction

You have seen how to write simple constructors that define the initial state of your objects. However, because object construction is so important, Java offers quite a variety of mechanisms for writing constructors. We will go over these mechanisms in the sections that follow.

Overloading

Recall that the GregorianCalendar class had more than one constructor. We could use:

```
GregorianCalendar today = new GregorianCalendar();
```

or:

```
GregorianCalendar deadline
    = new GregorianCalendar(2099, Calendar.DECEMBER, 31);
```

This capability is called *overloading*. Overloading occurs if several methods have the same name (in this case, the GregorianCalendar constructor method) but different parameters. The compiler must sort out which method to call. It picks the correct method by matching the parameter types in the headers of the various methods with the types of the values used in the specific method call. A compile-time error occurs if the compiler cannot match the parameters or if more than one match is possible. (This process is called *overloading resolution*.)

NOTE: Java allows you to overload any method—not just constructor methods. Thus, to completely describe a method, you need to specify the name of the method together with its parameter types. This is called the *signature* of the method. For example, the String class has four methods called indexOf. They have signatures

```
indexOf(int)
indexOf(int, int)
indexOf(String)
indexOf(String, int)
```

The return type is not part of the method signature. That is, you cannot have two methods with the same names and parameter types but different return types.

Default Field Initialization

If you don't set a field explicitly in a constructor, it is automatically set to a default value: numbers to zero, Booleans to `false`, and object references to `null`. But it is considered poor programming practice to rely on this. Certainly, it makes it harder for someone to understand your code if fields are being initialized invisibly.

> NOTE: This is an important difference between fields and local variables. You must always explicitly initialize local variables in a method. But if you don't initialize a field in a class, it is automatically initialized to a default (zero, `false` or `null`).

For example, consider the `Employee` class. Suppose you don't specify how to initialize some of the fields in a constructor. By default, the `salary` field would be initialized with 0 and the `name` and `hireDay` fields would be initialized with `null`.

However, that would not be a good idea. If anyone called the `getName` or `getHireDay` method, then they would get a `null` reference that they probably don't expect:

```
Date h = harry.getHireDay();
calendar.setTime(h); // throws exception if h is null
```

Default Constructors

A *default constructor* is a constructor with no parameters. (This constructor is sometimes called a *no-arg* constructor.) For example, here is a default constructor for the `Employee` class:

```
public Employee()
{
   name = "";
   salary = 0;
   hireDay = new Date();
}
```

If you write a class with no constructors whatsoever, then a default constructor is provided for you. This default constructor sets *all* the instance fields to their default values. So, all numeric data contained in the instance fields would be `zero`, all Booleans would be `false`, and all object variables would be set to `null`.

If a class supplies at least one constructor but does not supply a default constructor, it is illegal to construct objects without construction parameters. For example, our original `Employee` class in Example 4–2 provided a single constructor:

```
Employee(String name, double salary, int y, int m, int d)
```

With that class, it was not legal to construct default employees. That is, the call

```
e = new Employee();
```

would have been an error.

CAUTION: Please keep in mind that you get a free default constructor *only* when your class has no other constructors. If you write your class with even a single constructor of your own, and you want the users of your class to have the ability to create an instance via a call to

```
new ClassName()
```

then you must provide a default constructor (with no parameters). Of course, if you are happy with the default values for all fields, you can simply supply:

```
public ClassName()
{
}
```

Explicit Field Initialization

Since you can overload the constructor methods in a class, you can obviously build in many ways to set the initial state of the instance fields of your classes. It is always a good idea to make sure that, regardless of the constructor call, every instance field is set to something meaningful.

You can simply assign a value to any field in the class definition. For example,

```
class Employee
{
   . . .
   private String name = "";
}
```

This assignment is carried out before the constructor executes. This syntax is particularly useful if all constructors of a class need to set a particular instance field to the same value.

The initialization value doesn't have to be a constant value. Here is an example where a field is initialized with a method call. Consider an Employee class where each employee has an id field. You can initialize it as follows:

```
class Employee
{
   . . .
   static int assignId()
   {  int r = nextId;
      nextId++;
      return r;
   }
   . . .
   private int id = assignId();
}
```

C++ NOTE: In C++, you cannot directly initialize instance fields of a class. All fields must be set in a constructor. However, C++ has a special initializer list syntax, such as:

```
Employee::Employee(String n, double s,
    int y, int m, int d) // C++
: name(n),
  salary(s),
  hireDay(y, m, d)
{
}
```

C++ uses this special syntax to call field constructors. In Java, there is no need for it because objects have no subobjects, only pointers to other objects.

Parameter Names

When you write very trivial constructors (and you'll write a lot of them), then it can be somewhat frustrating to come up with parameter names.

We have generally opted for single-letter parameter names:

```
public Employee(String n, double s)
{
    name = n;
    salary = s;
}
```

However, the drawback is that you need to read the code to tell what the n and s parameters mean.

Some programmers prefix each parameter with an "a":

```
public Employee(String aName, double aSalary)
{
    name = aName;
    salary = aSalary;
}
```

That is quite neat. Any reader can immediately figure out the meaning of the parameters.

There is another commonly used trick. It relies on the fact that parameter variables *shadow* instance fields with the same name. For example, if you call a parameter salary, then salary refers to the parameter, not the instance field. But you can still access the instance field as this.salary. Recall that this denotes the implicit parameter, that is, the object that is being constructed. Here is an example:

```
public Employee(String name, double salary)
{
    this.name = name;
    this.salary = salary;
}
```

> C++ NOTE: In C++, it is common to prefix instance fields with an underscore or a fixed letter. (The letters "m" and "x" are common choices.) For example, the salary field might be called `_salary` or `mSalary`. Programmers don't usually do that in the Java programming language.

Calling Another Constructor

The keyword `this` refers to the implicit parameter of a method. However, there is a second meaning for the keyword.

If *the first statement of a constructor* has the form `this(. . .)`, then the constructor calls another constructor of the same class. Here is a typical example:

```
public Employee(double s)
{
    // calls Employee(String, double)
    this("Employee #" + nextId, s);
    nextId++;
}
```

When you call `new Employee(60000)`, then the `Employee(double)` constructor calls the `Employee(String, double)` constructor.

Using the `this` keyword in this manner is useful—you only need to write common construction code once.

> C++ NOTE: The `this` object in Java is identical to the `this` pointer in C++. However, in C++ it is not possible for one constructor to call another. If you want to factor out common initialization code in C++, you must write a separate method.

Initialization Blocks

You have already seen two ways to initialize a data field:

* By setting a value in a constructor
* By assigning a value in the declaration

There is a actually a *third* mechanism in Java; it's called an *initialization block*. Class declarations can contain arbitrary blocks of code. These blocks are executed whenever an object of that class is constructed. For example,

```
class Employee
{
    public Employee(String n, double s)
    {
        name = n;
        salary = s;
    }

    public Employee()
```

```
   {
      name = "";
      salary = 0;
   }
   . . .
   // object initialization block
   {
      id = nextId;
      nextId++;
   }
   . . .
   private String name;
   private double salary
   private int id;
   private static int nextId;
}
```

In this example, the `id` field is initialized in the object initialization block, no matter which constructor is used to construct an object. The initialization block runs first, and then the body of the constructor is executed.

This mechanism is never necessary and is not common. It usually is more straightforward to place the initialization code inside a constructor.

With so many ways of initializing data fields, it can be quite confusing to give all possible pathways for the construction process. Here is what happens in detail when a constructor is called.

1. All data fields are initialized to their default value (0, `false`, or `null`)

2. If the first line of the constructor calls another constructor, then that constructor is executed. Otherwise, all field initializers and initialization blocks are executed, in the order in which they occur in the class declaration.

3. The body of the constructor is executed.

Naturally, it is always a good idea to organize your initialization code so that it is easy to understand without having to be a language lawyer. For example, it would be quite strange and somewhat error-prone to have a class whose constructors depend on the order in which the data fields are declared.

You initialize a static field either by supplying an initial value or by using a static initialization block. You have already seen the first mechanism:

```
static int nextId = 1;
```

If the static fields of your class require complex initialization code, use a static initialization block.

Place the code inside a block and tag it with the keyword `static`. Here is an example. We want the employee ID numbers to start at a random integer less than 10,000:

```
// static initialization block
static
```

```
   {
      Random generator = new Random();
      nextId = generator.nextInt(10000);
   }
```

Static initialization occurs when the class is first loaded. Like instance fields, static fields are 0, `false` or `null` unless you explicitly set them to another value. All static field initializers and static initialization blocks are executed in the order in which they occur in the class declaration.

NOTE: Here is a Java trivia fact to amaze your fellow Java coders: You can write a "Hello, World" program in Java without ever writing a `main` method.

```
public class Hello
{
   static
   {
      System.out.println("Hello, World");
   }
}
```

When you invoke the class with `java Hello`, the class is loaded, the static initialization block prints "Hello, World", and only then do you get an ugly error message that `main` is not defined. You can avoid that blemish by calling `System.exit(0)` at the end of the static initialization block.

The program in Example 4–5 shows many of the features that we discussed in this section:

- Overloaded constructors
- Calling another constructor with `this(...)`
- A default constructor
- An object initialization block
- A static initialization block
- An instance field initialization

Example 4–5: ConstructorTest.java

```
1. import java.util.*;
2.
3. public class ConstructorTest
4. {
5.    public static void main(String[] args)
6.    {
7.       // fill the staff array with three Employee objects
8.       Employee[] staff = new Employee[3];
9.
10.      staff[0] = new Employee("Harry", 40000);
```

```
11.        staff[1] = new Employee(60000);
12.        staff[2] = new Employee();
13.
14.        // print out information about all Employee objects
15.        for (int i = 0; i < staff.length; i++)
16.        {
17.           Employee e = staff[i];
18.           System.out.println("name=" + e.getName()
19.              + ",id=" + e.getId()
20.              + ",salary=" + e.getSalary());
21.        }
22.     }
23. }
24.
25. class Employee
26. {
27.    // three overloaded constructors
28.    public Employee(String n, double s)
29.    {
30.       name = n;
31.       salary = s;
32.    }
33.
34.    public Employee(double s)
35.    {
36.       // calls the Employee(String, double) constructor
37.       this("Employee #" + nextId, s);
38.    }
39.
40.    // the default constructor
41.    public Employee()
42.    {
43.       // name initialized to ""--see below
44.       // salary not explicitly set--initialized to 0
45.       // id initialized in initialization block
46.    }
47.
48.    public String getName()
49.    {
50.       return name;
51.    }
52.
53.    public double getSalary()
54.    {
55.       return salary;
56.    }
57.
58.    public int getId()
59.    {
60.       return id;
61.    }
```

```
62.
63.    // object initialization block
64.    {
65.       id = nextId;
66.       nextId++;
67.    }
68.
69.    // static initialization block
70.    static
71.    {
72.       Random generator = new Random();
73.       // set nextId to a random number between 0 and 9999
74.       nextId = generator.nextInt(10000);
75.    }
76.
77.    private String name = ""; // instance variable initialization
78.    private double salary;
79.    private int id;
80.    private static int nextId;
81. }
```

java.util.Random

- `Random()`

  constructs a new random number generator

- `int nextInt(int n)`

  returns a random number between 0 and n - 1

Object Destruction and the `finalize` Method

Some object-oriented programming languages, notably C++, have explicit destructor methods for any cleanup code that may be needed when an object is no longer used. The most common activity in a destructor is reclaiming the memory set aside for objects. Since Java does automatic garbage collection, manual memory reclamation is not needed, and Java does not support destructors.

Of course, some objects utilize a resource other than memory, such as a file or a handle to another object that uses system resources. In this case, it is important that the resource be reclaimed and recycled when it is no longer needed.

You can add a `finalize` method to any class. The `finalize` method will be called before the garbage collector sweeps away the object. In practice, *do not rely on the* `finalize` *method* for recycling any resources that are in short supply—you simply cannot know when this method will be called.

NOTE: There is a method call `System.runFinalizersOnExit(true)` to guarantee that finalizer methods are called before Java shuts down. However, this method is inherently unsafe and has been deprecated.

If a resource needs to be closed as soon as you have finished using it, you need to manage it manually. Add a `dispose` method that *you* call to clean up what needs cleaning. Just as importantly, if a class you use has a `dispose` method, you will want to call it when you are done with the object. In particular, if your class has an instance field that has a `dispose` method, provide a `dispose` method that disposes of the instance fields.

Packages

Java allows you to group classes in a collection called a *package*. Packages are convenient for organizing your work and for separating your work from code libraries provided by others.

The standard Java library is distributed over a number of packages, including `java.lang`, `java.util`, `java.net`, and so on. The standard Java packages are examples of hierarchical packages. Just as you have nested subdirectories on your hard disk, you can organize packages by using levels of nesting. All standard Java packages are inside the `java` and `javax` package hierarchies.

The main reason for using packages is to guarantee the uniqueness of class names. Suppose two programmers come up with the bright idea of supplying an `Employee` class. As long as both of them place their class into different packages, then there is no conflict. In fact, to absolutely guarantee a unique package name, Sun recommends that you use your company's Internet domain name (which is known to be unique) written in reverse. You then use subpackages for different projects. For example, `horstmann.com` is a domain that one of the authors registered. Written in reverse order, it turns into the package `com.horstmann`. That package can then be further subdivided into subpackages such as `com.horstmann.corejava`.

The sole purpose of package nesting is to manage unique names. From the point of view of the compiler, there is absolutely no relationship between nested packages. For example, the packages `java.util` and `java.util.jar` have nothing to do with each other. Each is its own independent collection of classes.

Using Packages

A class can use all classes from its own package and all *public* classes from other packages.

You can access the public classes in another package in two ways. The first is simply to add the full package name in front of *every* classname. For example:

```
java.util.Date today = new java.util.Date();
```

That is obviously tedious. The simpler, and more common, approach is to use the `import` keyword. The point of the `import` statement is simply to give you a shorthand to refer to the classes in the package. Once you use `import`, you no longer have to give the classes their full names.

You can import a specific class or the whole package. You place `import` statements at the top of your source files (but below any `package` statements). For example, you can import all classes in the `java.util` package with the statement:

```
import java.util.*;
```

Then you can use

```
Date today = new Date();
```

without a package prefix. You can also import a specific class inside a package.

```
import java.util.Date;
```

Importing all classes in a package is simpler. It has no negative effect on code size, so there is generally no reason not to do it.

However, note that you can only use the * notation to import a single package. You cannot use `import java.*` or `import java.*.*` to import all packages with the `java` prefix.

NOTE: You can only import classes, not objects. For example, you would never import `System.out`.

Most of the time, you just import the packages that you need, without worrying too much about them. The only time that you need to pay attention to packages is when you have a name conflict. For example, both the `java.util` and `java.sql` packages have a `Date` class. Suppose you write a program that imports both packages.

```
import java.util.*;
import java.sql.*;
```

If you now use the `Date` class, then you get a compile-time error:

```
Date today; // ERROR--java.util.Date or java.sql.Date?
```

The compiler cannot figure out which `Date` class you want. You can solve this problem by adding a specific `import` statement:

```
import java.util.*;
import java.sql.*;
import java.util.Date;
```

What if you really need both `Date` classes? Then you need to use the full package name with every class name.

```
java.util.Date deadline = new java.util.Date();
java.sql.Date today = new java.sql.Date();
```

Locating classes in packages is an activity of the *compiler*. The bytecodes in class files always use full package names to refer to other classes.

C++ NOTE: C++ programmers usually confuse `import` with `#include`. The two have nothing in common. In C++, you must use `#include` to include the declarations of external features because the C++ compiler does not look inside any files except the one that it is compiling and explicitly included header files. The Java compiler will happily look inside other files provided you tell it where to look.

In Java, you can entirely avoid the `import` mechanism by explicitly naming all packages, such as `java.util.Date`. In C++, you cannot avoid the `#include` directives.

The only benefit of the `import` statement is convenience. You can refer to a class by a name shorter than the full package name. For example, after an `import java.util.*` (or `import java.util.Date`) statement, you can refer to the `java.util.Date` class simply as `Date`.

The analogous construction to the package mechanism in C++ is the namespace feature. Think of the `package` and `import` keywords in Java as the analogs of the `namespace` and `using` directives in C++.

Adding a class into a package

To place classes inside a package, you must put the name of the package at the top of your source file, *before* the code that defines the classes in the package. For example, the file `Employee.java` in Example 4–7 starts out like this:

```
package com.horstmann.corejava;

public class Employee
{
    . . .
}
```

If you don't put a `package` statement in the source file, then the classes in that source file belong to the *default package*. The default package has no package name. Up to now, all our example classes were located in the default package.

You place files in a package into a subdirectory that matches the full package name. For example, all class files in the package `com.horstmann.corejava` package must be in subdirectory `com/horstmann/corejava` (`com\horstmann\corejava` on Windows). This is the simplest setup—you'll see a couple of other options later in this chapter.

The program in Examples 4–6 and 4–7 is distributed over two packages: the `PackageTest` class belongs to the default package and the `Employee` class belongs to the `com.horstmann.corejava` package. Therefore, the `Employee.class` file must be contained in a subdirectory `com/horstmann/corejava`. In other words, the directory structure is as follows:

```
. (current directory)
   PackageTest.java
   PackageTest.class
```

```
com/
    horstmann/
        corejava/
            Employee.java
            Employee.class
```

To compile this program, simply change to the directory containing `PackageTest.java` and run the command:

```
javac PackageTest.java
```

The compiler automatically finds the file `com/horstmann/corejava/Employee.java` and compiles it.

CAUTION: The compiler does *not* check directories when it compiles source files. For example, suppose you have a source file that starts with a directive:

```
package com.mycompany;
```

You can compile the file even if it is not contained in a subdirectory `com/mycompany`. The source file will compile without errors, but the *virtual machine* won't find the resulting classes when you try to run the program. Therefore, you should use the same hierarchy for source files as for class files.

Example 4–6: PackageTest.java

```
1. import com.horstmann.corejava.*;
2.    // the Employee class is defined in that package
3.
4. public class PackageTest
5. {
6.    public static void main(String[] args)
7.    {
8.       // because of the import statement, we don't have to
9.       // use com.horstmann.corejava.Employee here
10.      Employee harry = new Employee("Harry Hacker", 50000,
11.         1989, 10, 1);
12.
13.      // raise salary by 5%
14.      harry.raiseSalary(5);
15.
16.      // print out information about harry
17.      System.out.println("name=" + harry.getName()
18.         + ",salary=" + harry.getSalary());
19.   }
20. }
```

Example 4–7: Employee.java

```
1. package com.horstmann.corejava;
2.    // the classes in this file are part of this package
3.
4. import java.util.*;
```

```
5.     // import statements come after the package statement
6.
7. public class Employee
8. {
9.     public Employee(String n, double s,
10.        int year, int month, int day)
11.    {  name = n;
12.       salary = s;
13.       GregorianCalendar calendar
14.          = new GregorianCalendar(year, month - 1, day);
15.          // GregorianCalendar uses 0 for January
16.       hireDay = calendar.getTime();
17.    }
18.
19.    public String getName()
20.    {
21.       return name;
22.    }
23.
24.    public double getSalary()
25.    {
26.       return salary;
27.    }
28.
29.    public Date getHireDay()
30.    {
31.       return hireDay;
32.    }
33.
34.    public void raiseSalary(double byPercent)
35.    {
36.       double raise = salary * byPercent / 100;
37.       salary += raise;
38.    }
39.
40.    private String name;
41.    private double salary;
42.    private Date hireDay;
43. }
```

How the virtual machine locates classes

As you have seen, classes are stored in subdirectories of the file system. The path to the class must match the package name. You can also use the JAR utility to add class files to an *archive*. An archive contains multiple class files and subdirectories inside a single file, saving space and reducing access time. (We will discuss JAR files in greater detail in Chapter 10.)

For example, the thousands of classes of the runtime library are all contained in the runtime library file rt.jar. You can find that file in the jre/lib subdirectory of the Java SDK.

TIP: JAR files use the ZIP format to organize files and subdirectories. You can use any ZIP utility to peek inside `rt.jar` and other JAR files.

In the preceding example program, the package directory `com/horstmann/corejava` was a subdirectory of the program directory. However, that arrangement is not very flexible. Generally, multiple programs need to access package files. To share your packages among programs, you need to do the following:

1. Place your classes inside one or more special directories, say `/home/user/classdir`. Note that this directory is the *base* directory for the package tree. If you add the class `com.horstmann.corejava.Employee`, then the class file must be located in the subdirectory `/home/user/classdir/com/horstmann/corejava`.

2. Set the *class path.* The class path is the collection of all base directories whose subdirectories can contain class files.

How to set the class path depends on your compilation environment. If you use the Java SDK, then you have two choices: Specify the `-classpath` option for the compiler and bytecode interpreter, or set the CLASSPATH environment variable.

Details depend on your operating system. On UNIX, the elements on the class path are separated by colons.

    /home/user/classes:.:/home/user/archives/archive.jar

On Windows, they are separated by semicolons.

    c:\classes;.;c:\archives\archive.jar

In both cases, the period denotes the current directory.

This class path contains:

*   The base directory `/home/user/classes` or `c:\classes`
*   The current directory (`.`)
*   The JAR file `/home/user/archives/archive.jar` or `c:\archives\archive.jar`

The runtime library files (`rt.jar` and the other JAR files in the `jre/lib` and `jre/lib/ext` directories) are always searched for classes; you don't include them explicitly in the class path.

NOTE: This is a change from version 1.0 and 1.1 of the Java Software Development Kit. In those versions, the system classes were stored in a file `classes.zip` which had to be part of the class path.

For example, here is how you set the class path for the compiler:

```
javac -classpath /home/user/classes:.:/home/user/archives/
archive.jar MyProg.java
```

(All instructions should be typed onto a single line. In Windows, use semicolons to separate the items of the class path.)

> NOTE: With the `java` bytecode interpreter (but not with the `javac` compiler), you can use `-cp` instead of `-classpath`.

The class path lists all directories and archive files that are *starting points* for locating classes. Let's consider a sample class path:

```
/home/user/classes:.:/home/user/archives/archive.jar
```

Suppose the interpreter searches for the class file of the `com.horstmann.corejava.Employee` class. It first looks in the system class files which are stored in archives in the `jre/lib` and `jre/lib/ext` directories. It won't find the class file there, so it turns to the class path. It then looks for the following files:

- `/home/user/classes/com/horstmann/corejava/Employee.class`
- `com/horstmann/corejava/Employee.class` starting from the current directory
- `com/horstmann/corejava/Employee.class` inside `/home/user/archives/archive.jar`.

> NOTE: The compiler has a harder time locating files than the virtual machine. If you refer to a class without specifying its package, the compiler first needs to find out the package that contains the class. It consults all `import` directives as possible sources for the class. For example, suppose the source file contains directives
>
> ```
> import java.util.*;
> import com.horstmann.corejava.*;
> ```
>
> and the source code refers to a class `Employee`. Then the compiler tries to find `java.lang.Employee` (because the `java.lang` package is always imported by default), `java.util.Employee`, `com.horstmann.corejava.Employee`, and `Employee` in the current package. It searches for *each* of these classes in all of the locations of the class path. It is a compile-time error if more than one class is found. (Because classes must be unique, the order of the `import` statements doesn't matter.)
>
> The compiler goes one step further. It looks at the *source files* to see if the source is newer than the class file. If so, the source file is recompiled automatically. Recall that you can only import public classes from other packages. A source file can only contain one public class, and the names of the file and the public class must match. Therefore, the compiler can easily locate source files for public classes. However, you can import non-public classes from the current packages. These classes may be defined in source files with different names. If you import a class from the current package, the compiler searches *all* source files of the current package to see which one defines the class.

CAUTION: The `javac` compiler always looks for files in the current directory, but the `java` interpreter only looks into the current directory if the " . " directory is on the class path. If you have no class path set, this is not a problem—the default class path consists of the " . " directory. But if you have set the class path and forgot to include the " . " directory, then your programs will compile without error, but they won't run.

Setting the class path

You can set the class path with the `-classpath` option for the `javac` and `java` programs. However, that can get tedious. Alternatively, you can set the CLASSPATH environment variable. Here are some tips for setting the CLASSPATH environment variable on UNIX/Linux and Windows.

* On UNIX/Linux, edit your shell's startup file.
  If you use the C shell, add a line such as the following to the `.cshrc` file in your home directory.
  ```
  setenv CLASSPATH /home/user/classdir:.
  ```
  If you use the Bourne Again shell or `bash`, add the following line to the `.bashrc` or `.bash_profile` file in your home directory.
  ```
  export CLASSPATH=/home/user/classdir:.
  ```
* On Windows 95/98, edit the `autoexec.bat` file in the boot drive (usually the C: drive). Add a line:
  ```
  SET CLASSPATH=c:\user\classdir;.
  ```
  Make sure not to put any spaces around the =.
* On Windows NT/2000, open the control panel. Then open the System icon and select the Environment tab. In the Variable field, type CLASSPATH. In the value field, type the desired class path such as `c:\user\classdir;.`

Package scope

You have already encountered the access modifiers `public` and `private`. Features tagged as `public` can be used by any class. Private features can only be used by the class that defines them. If you don't specify either `public` or `private`, then the feature (that is, the class, method, or variable) can be accessed by all methods in the same *package*.

Consider the program in Example 4–2. The `Employee` class was not defined as a public class. Therefore, only other classes in the same package—the default package in this case—such as `EmployeeTest` can access it. For classes, this is a reasonable default. However, for variables, this default was an unfortunate choice. Variables now must explicitly be marked private or they will default to being package-visible. This, of course, breaks encapsulation. The problem is that it is awfully easy to forget to type the `private` keyword. Here is an example from the `Window` class in the `java.awt` package, which is part of the source code supplied with the SDK:

```
public class Window extends Container
{
```

```
String warningString;
    . . .
}
```

Note that the `warningString` variable is not `private`! That means, the methods of all classes in the `java.awt` package can access this variable and set it to whatever they like (such as `"Trust me!"`). Actually, the only methods that access this variable are in the `Window` class, so it would have been entirely appropriate to make the variable private. We suspect that the programmer typed the code in a hurry and simply forgot the `private` modifier. (We won't mention the programmer's name to protect the guilty—you can look into the source file yourself.)

 NOTE: Amazingly enough, this problem has never been fixed, even though we have pointed it out in four editions of this book—apparently the library implementors don't read *Core Java*. Not only that—new fields have been added to the class over time, and about half of them aren't private either.

Is this really a problem? It depends. By default, packages are not closed entities. That is, anyone can add more classes to a package. Of course, hostile or clueless programmers can then add code that modifies variables with package visibility. For example, in earlier versions of the Java programming language, it was an easy matter to smuggle in another class into the `java.awt` package—simply start out the class with

```
package java.awt;
```

Then place the resulting class file inside a subdirectory `java\awt` somewhere on the class path, and you have gained access to the internals of the `java.awt` package. Through this subterfuge, it was possible to set the warning border (see Figure 4–9).

Figure 4–9: Changing the warning string in an applet window

Starting with version 1.2, the SDK implementors rigged the class loader to explicitly disallow loading of user-defined classes whose package name starts with `"java."`! Of course, your own classes won't benefit from that protection. Instead, you can use another mechanism, *package sealing*, to address the issue of promiscuous package access. If you seal a package, no further classes can be added to it. You will see in Chapter 10 how you can produce a JAR file that contains sealed packages.

Documentation Comments

The Java SDK contains a very useful tool, called `javadoc`, that generates HTML documentation from your source files. In fact, the online API documentation that we described in Chapter 3 is simply the result of running `javadoc` on the source code of the standard Java library.

If you add comments that start with the special delimiter /** to your source code, you too can produce professional-looking documentation easily. This is a very nice scheme because it lets you keep your code and documentation in one place. If you put your documentation into a separate file, then you probably know that the code and comments tend to diverge over time. But since the documentation comments are in the same file as the source code, it is an easy matter to update both and run `javadoc` again.

How to Insert Comments

The `javadoc` utility extracts information for the following items:

- Packages
- Public classes and interfaces
- Public and protected methods
- Public and protected fields

Protected features are introduced in Chapter 5, interfaces in Chapter 6.

You can (and should) supply a comment for each of these features. Each comment is placed immediately *above* the feature it describes. A comment starts with a /** and ends with a */.

Each /** . . . */ documentation comment contains *free-form text* followed by *tags*. A tag starts with an @, such as `@author` or `@param`.

The *first sentence* of the free-form text should be a *summary statement*. The `javadoc` utility automatically generates summary pages that extract these sentences.

In the free-form text, you can use HTML modifiers such as `<em>...</em>` for emphasis, `<code>...</code>` for a monospaced "typewriter" font, `<strong>...</strong>` for strong emphasis, and even `<img ...>` to include an image. You should, however, stay away from heading `<h1>` or rules `<hr>` since they can interfere with the formatting of the document.

NOTE: If your comments contain links to other files such as images (for example, diagrams or images of user interface components), place those files into subdirectories named `doc-files`. The `javadoc` utility will copy these directories, and the files in them, from the source directory to the documentation directory.

Class Comments

The class comment must be placed *after* any `import` statements, directly before the `class` definition.

Here is an example of a class comment:

```
/**
   A <code>Card</code> object represents a playing card, such
   as "Queen of Hearts". A card has a suit (Diamond, Heart,
   Spade or Club) and a value (1 = Ace, 2 . . . 10, 11 = Jack,
   12 = Queen, 13 = King).
*/
public class Card
{
   . . .
}
```

NOTE: Many programmers start each line of a documentation with an asterisk, like this:
```
/**
 * A <code>Card</code> object represent a playing card, such
 * as "Queen of Hearts". A card has a suit (Diamond, Heart,
 * Spade or Club) and a value (1 = Ace, 2 . . . 10, 11 = Jack,
 * 12 = Queen, 13 = King)
 */
```
We don't do this because it *discourages* programmers from updating the comments. Nobody likes rearranging the * when the line breaks change. However, some text editors have a mode that takes care of this drudgery. If you know that all future maintainers of your code will use such a text editor, you may want to add the border to make the comment stand out.

Method Comments

Each method comment must immediately precede the method that it describes. In addition to the general-purpose tags, you can use the following tags:

`@param variable description`

This tag adds an entry to the "parameters" section of the current method. The description can span multiple lines and can use HTML tags. All `@param` tags for one method must be kept together.

`@return description`

This tag adds a "returns" section to the current method. The description can span multiple lines and can use HTML tags.

`@throws class description`

This tag adds a note that this method may throw an exception. Exceptions are the topic of Chapter 11.

Here is an example of a method comment:

```
/**
   Raises the salary of an employee.
   @param byPercent the percentage by which to raise the salary
      (e.g. 10 = 10%)
   @return the amount of the raise
*/
public double raiseSalary(double byPercent)
{
   double raise = salary * byPercent / 100;
   salary += raise;
   return raise;
}
```

Field Comments

You only need to document public fields—generally that means static constants. For example,

```
/**
   The "Hearts" card suit
*/
public static final int HEARTS = 1;
```

General Comments

The following tags can be used in class documentation comments.

`@author` *name*

This tag makes an "author" entry. You can have multiple `@author` tags, one for each author.

`@version` *text*

This tag makes a "version" entry. The *text* can be any description of the current version.

The following tags can be used in all documentation comments.

`@since` *text*

This tag makes a "since" entry. The *text* can be any description of the version that introduced this feature. For example, `@since version 1.7.1`

`@deprecated` *text*

This tag adds a comment that the class, method, or variable should no longer be used. The *text* should suggest a replacement. For example,

`@deprecated Use <code>setVisible(true)</code> instead`

You can use hyperlinks to other relevant parts of the `javadoc` documentation, or to external documents, with the `@see` and `@link` tags.

`@see` *link*

This tag adds a hyperlink in the "see also" section. It can be used with both classes and methods. Here, `link` can be one of the following:

- `package.class#feature  label`
- `<a href="...">label</a>`
- `"text"`

The first case is the most useful. You supply the name of a class, method, or variable, and `javadoc` inserts a hyperlink to the documentation. For example,

```
@see com.horstmann.corejava.Employee#raiseSalary(double)
```

makes a link to the `raiseSalary(double)` method in the `com.horstmann.corejava.Employee` class. You can omit the name of the package or both the package and class name. Then, the feature will be located in the current package or class.

Note that you must use a `#`, not a period, to separate the class from the method or variable name. The Java compiler itself is highly skilled in guessing the various meanings of the period character, as separator between packages, subpackages, classes, inner classes, and methods and variables. But, the `javadoc` utility isn't quite as clever, and you have to help it along.

If the `@see` tag is followed by a `<` character, then you need to specify a hyperlink. You can link to any URL you like. For example,

```
@see <a href="www.horstmann.com/corejava.html">The Core Java
home page</a>
```

In each of these cases, you can specify an optional `label` that will appear as the link anchor. If you omit the label, then the user will see the target code name or URL as the anchor.

If the `@see` tag is followed by a `"` character, then the text is displayed in the "see also" section. For example,

```
@see "Core Java 2 volume 2"
```

You can add multiple `@see` tags for one feature, but you must keep them all together.

If you like, you can place hyperlinks to other classes or methods anywhere in any of your comments. You insert a special tag of the form `{@link package.class#feature  label}` anywhere in a comment. The feature description follows the same rules as for the `@see` tag.

Package and Overview Comments

You place class, method, and variable comments directly into the Java source files, delimited by `/** . . . */` documentation comments. However, to generate package comments, you need to add a file named `package.html` in each package directory. All text between the tags `<BODY>...</BODY>` is extracted.

You can also supply an overview comment for all source files. Place it in a file called `overview.html`, located in the parent directory that contains all the source files. All text between the tags `<BODY>...</BODY>` is extracted. This comment is displayed when the user selects "Overview" from the navigation bar.

How to Extract Comments

Here, `docDirectory` is the name of the directory where you want the HTML files to go. Follow these steps:

1. Change to the directory that contains the source files you want to document. If you have nested packages to document, such as `com.horstmann.corejava`, you must be in the directory that contains the subdirectory `com`. (This is the directory that contains the `overview.html` file, if you supplied one.)

2. Run the command

    ```
    javadoc -d docDirectory nameOfPackage
    ```

    for a single package. Or run

    ```
    javadoc -d docDirectory nameOfPackage1 nameOfPackage2...
    ```

    to document multiple packages. If your files are in the default package, then run

    ```
    javadoc -d docDirectory *.java
    ```

    instead.

If you omit the `-d docDirectory` option, then the HTML files are extracted to the current directory. That can get messy, and we don't recommend it.

The `javadoc` program can be fine-tuned by numerous command-line options. For example, you can use the `-author` and `-version` options to include the `@author` and `@version` tags in the documentation. (By default, they are omitted.) We refer you to the online documentation of the `javadoc` utility at `http://java.sun.com/products/jdk/javadoc/index.html`.

NOTE: If you require further customization, for example, to produce documentation in a format other than HTML, then you can supply your own *doclet* to generate the output in any form you desire. Clearly, this is a specialized need, and we refer you to the online documentation for details on doclets at `http://java.sun.com/products/jdk/1.3/docs/tooldocs/javadoc/overview.html`.

Class Design Hints

Without trying to be comprehensive or tedious, we want to end this chapter with some hints that may make your classes more acceptable in well-mannered OOP circles.

1. *Always keep data private.*

   This is first and foremost: doing anything else violates encapsulation. You may need to write an accessor or mutator method occasionally, but you are still better off keeping the instance fields private. Bitter experience has shown that how the data are represented may change, but how they are used will change much less frequently. When data are kept private, changes in their representation do not affect the user of the class, and bugs are easier to detect.

2. *Always initialize data.*

   Java won't initialize local variables for you, but it will initialize instance fields of objects. Don't rely on the defaults, but initialize the variables explicitly, either by supplying a default or by setting defaults in all constructors.

3. *Don't use too many basic types in a class.*

   The idea is to replace multiple *related* uses of basic types with other classes. This keeps your classes easier to understand and to change. For example, replace the following instance fields in a `Customer` class

   ```
   private String street;
   private String city;
   private String state;
   private int zip;
   ```

   with a new class called `Address`. This way, you can easily cope with changes to addresses, such as the need to deal with international addresses.

4. *Not all fields need individual field accessors and mutators.*

   You may need to get and set an employee's salary. You certainly won't need to change the hiring date once the object is constructed. And, quite often, objects have instance fields that you don't want others to get or set, for example, an array of state abbreviations in an `Address` class.

5. *Use a standard form for class definitions.*

   We always list the contents of classes in the following order:

   > public features
   > package scope features
   > private features

   Within each section, we list:

   > instance methods
   > static methods
   > instance fields
   > static fields

After all, the users of your class are more interested in the public interface than in the details of the private implementation. And they are more interested in methods than in data.

However, there is no universal agreement on what is the best style. The Sun coding style guide for the Java programming language recommends listing fields first and then methods.

Whatever style you use, the most important thing is to be consistent.

6. *Break up classes with too many responsibilities.*

This hint is, of course, vague: "too many" is obviously in the eye of the beholder. However, if there is an obvious way to make one complicated class into two classes that are conceptually simpler, seize the opportunity. (On the other hand, don't go overboard; 10 classes, each with only one method, is usually overkill.)

Here is an example of a bad design.

```
class CardDeck // bad design
{
   public CardDeck() { . . . }
   public void shuffle() { . . . }
   public int getTopValue() { . . . }
   public int getTopSuit() { . . . }
   public void draw() { . . . }

   private int[] value;
   private int[] suit;
}
```

This class really implements two separate concepts: a *deck of cards*, with its shuffle and draw methods, and a *card*, with the methods to inspect the value and suit of a card. It makes sense to introduce a Card class that represents an individual card. Now you have two classes, each with its own responsibilities:

```
class CardDeck
{
   public CardDeck() { . . . }
   public void shuffle() { . . . }
   public Card getTop() { . . . }
   public void draw() { . . . }

   private Card[] cards;
}

class Card
{
```

```
      public Card(int aValue, int aSuit) { . . . }
      public int getValue() { . . . }
      public int getSuit() { . . . }

      private int value;
      private int suit;
}
```

7. *Make the names of your classes and methods reflect their responsibilities.*

    Just as variables should have meaningful names that reflect what they represent, so should classes. (The standard library certainly contains some dubious examples, such as the `Date` class that describes time.)

    A good convention is that a class name should be a noun (`Order`) or a noun preceded by an adjective (`RushOrder`) or a gerund (an "-ing" word, like `BillingAddress`). As for methods, follow the standard convention that accessor methods begin with a lowercase `get` (`getSalary`), and mutator methods use a lowercase `set` (`setSalary`).

Chapter **5**

Inheritance

▼ Extending Classes
▼ Object: The Cosmic Superclass
▼ The Class Class
▼ Reflection
▼ Design Hints for Inheritance

Chapter 4 introduced you to classes and objects. In this chapter, you will learn about *inheritance*, another fundamental concept of object-oriented programming. The idea behind inheritance is that you can create new classes that are built upon existing classes. When you inherit from an existing class, you reuse (or inherit) methods and fields, and you add new methods and fields to adapt your new class to new situations. This technique is essential in Java programming.

As with the previous chapter, if you are coming from a procedure-oriented language like C, Visual Basic, or COBOL, you will want to read this chapter carefully. For experienced C++ programmers or those coming from another object-oriented language like Smalltalk, this chapter will seem largely familiar, but there are many differences between how inheritance is implemented in Java and how it is done in C++ or in other object-oriented languages.

The latter part of this chapter covers *reflection*, the ability to find out more about classes and their properties in a running program. Reflection is a powerful feature, but it is undeniably complex. Since reflection is of greater interest to tools builders than to application programmers, you can probably glance over that part of the chapter upon first reading and come back to it later.

Extending Classes

Let's return to the `Employee` class that we discussed in the previous chapter. Suppose (alas) you work for a company at which managers are treated differently than other employees. Managers are, of course, just like employees in many respects. Both employees and managers are paid a salary. However, while employees are expected to complete their assigned tasks in return for receiving their salary, managers get *bonuses* if they actually achieve what they are supposed to do. This is the kind of situation that cries out for inheritance. Why? Well, you need to define a new class, `Manager`, and add functionality. But you can retain some of what you have already programmed in the `Employee` class, and *all* the fields of the original class can be preserved. More abstractly, there is an obvious "is–a" relationship between `Manager` and `Employee`. Every manager *is an* employee: this "is–a" relationship is the hallmark of inheritance.

Here is how you define a `Manager` class that inherits from the `Employee` class. You use the Java keyword `extends` to denote inheritance.

```
class Manager extends Employee
{
    added methods and fields
}
```

C++ NOTE: Inheritance is similar in Java and C++. Java uses the `extends` keyword instead of the : token. All inheritance in Java is public inheritance; there is no analog to the C++ features of private and protected inheritance.

The keyword `extends` indicates that you are making a new class that derives from an existing class. The existing class is called the *superclass, base class,* or *parent class*. The new class is called the *subclass, derived class,* or *child class*. The terms superclass and subclass are those most commonly used by Java programmers, although some programmers prefer the parent/child analogy, which also ties in nicely with the "inheritance" theme.

The `Employee` class is a superclass, but not because it is superior to its subclass or contains more functionality. *In fact, the opposite is true*: subclasses have *more* functionality than their superclasses. For example, as you will see when we go over the rest of the `Manager` class code, the `Manager` class encapsulates more data and has more functionality than its superclass `Employee`.

NOTE: The prefixes *super* and *sub* come from the language of sets used in theoretical computer science and mathematics. The set of all employees contains the set of all managers, and this is described by saying it is a *superset* of the set of managers. Or, put it another way, the set of all managers is a *subset* of the set of all employees.

Our `Manager` class has a new field to store the bonus, and a new method to set it:

```
class Manager extends Employee
{
    . . .

    public void setBonus(double b)
    {
        bonus = b;
    }

    private double bonus;
}
```

There is nothing special about these methods and fields. If you have a manager object, you can simply apply the `setBonus` method.

```
Manager boss = . . .;
boss.setBonus(5000);
```

Of course, if you have an `Employee` object, you cannot apply the `setBonus` method—it is not among the methods that are defined in the `Employee` class.

However, you *can* use methods such as `getName` and `getHireDay` with Manager objects. Even though these methods are not explicitly defined in the `Manager` class, they are automatically inherited from the `Employee` superclass.

Similarly, the fields `name`, `salary`, and `hireDay` are inherited from the superclass. Every `Manager` object has four fields: `name`, `salary`, `hireDay` and `bonus`.

When defining a subclass by extending its superclass, you only need to indicate the *differences* between the subclass and the superclass. When designing classes, you place the most general methods into the superclass, and more specialized methods in the subclass. Factoring out common functionality by moving it to a superclass is very common in object-oriented programming.

However, some of the superclass methods are not appropriate for the `Manager` subclass. In particular, the `getSalary` method should return the sum of the base salary and the bonus. You need to supply a new method to *override* the superclass method:

```
class Manager extends Employee
{
    . . .
    public double getSalary()
```

```
    {
        . . .
    }
    . . .
}
```

How can you implement this method? At first glance, it appears to be simple: Just return the sum of the `salary` and `bonus` fields:

```
public double getSalary()
{
    return salary + bonus; // won't work
}
```

However, that won't work. The `getSalary` method of the `Manager` class *has no direct access to the private fields of the superclass*. This means that the `getSalary` method of the `Manager` class cannot directly access the `salary` field, even though every `Manager` object has a field called `salary`. Only the methods of the `Employee` class have access to the private fields. If the `Manager` methods want to access those private fields, they have to do what every other method does—use the public interface, in this case, the public `getSalary` method of the `Employee` class.

So, let's try this again. You need to call `getSalary` instead of simply accessing the `salary` field.

```
public double getSalary()
{
    double baseSalary = getSalary(); // still won't work
    return baseSalary + bonus;
}
```

The problem is that the call to `getSalary` simply calls *itself*, because the `Manager` class has a `getSalary` method (namely the method we are trying to implement). The consequence is an infinite set of calls to the same method, which leads to a program crash.

We need to indicate that we want to call the `getSalary` method of the `Employee` superclass, not the current class. You use the special keyword `super` for this purpose: The call

```
super.getSalary()
```

calls the `getSalary` method of the `Employee` class. Here is the correct version of the `getSalary` method for the `Manager` class:

```
public double getSalary()
{
    double baseSalary = super.getSalary();
    return baseSalary + bonus;
}
```

> NOTE: Some people think of `super` as being analogous to the `this` reference. However, that analogy is not quite accurate—`super` is not a reference to an object. For example, you cannot assign the value `super` to another object variable. Instead, `super` is a special keyword that directs the compiler to invoke the superclass method.

As you saw, a subclass can *add* fields, and it can *add* or *override* methods of the superclass. However, inheritance can never take away any fields or methods.

> C++ NOTE: Java uses the keyword `super` to call a superclass method. In C++, you would use the name of the superclass with the `::` operator instead. For example, the `getSalary` method of the `Manager` class would call `Employee::getSalary` instead of `super.getSalary`.

Finally, let us supply a constructor.

```
public Manager(String n, double s, int year, int month, int day)
{
    super(n, s, year, month, day);
    bonus = 0;
}
```

Here, the keyword `super` has a different meaning. The instruction

```
super(n, s, year, month, day);
```

is shorthand for "call the constructor of the `Employee` superclass with n, s, year, month, and day as parameters."

Since the `Manager` constructor cannot access the private fields of the `Employee` class, it must initialize them through a constructor. The constructor is invoked with the special `super` syntax. The call using `super` must be the first statement in the constructor for the subclass.

If the subclass constructor does not call a superclass constructor explicitly, then the superclass uses its default (no-parameter) constructor. If the superclass has no default constructor and the subclass constructor does not call another superclass constructor explicitly, then the Java compiler reports an error.

> NOTE: Recall that the `this` keyword has two meanings: to denote a reference to the implicit parameter, and to call another constructor of the same class. Likewise, the `super` keyword has two meanings: to invoke a superclass method, and to invoke a superclass constructor. When used to invoke constructors, the `this` and `super` keywords are closely related. The constructor calls can only occur as the first statement in another constructor. The construction parameters are either passed to another constructor of the same class (`this`) or a constructor of the superclass (`super`).

C++ NOTE: In a C++ constructor, you do not call `super`, but you use the initializer list syntax to construct the superclass. The `Manager` constructor looks like this in C++:

```
Manager::Manager(String n, double s, int year, int month,
    int day) // C++
: Employee(n, s, year, month, day)
{
    bonus = 0;
}
```

Having redefined the `getSalary` method for `Manager` objects, managers will *automatically* have the bonus added to their salaries.

Here's an example of this at work: we make a new manager and set the manager's bonus:

```
Manager boss = new Manager("Carl Cracker", 80000,
    1987, 12, 15);
boss.setBonus(5000);
```

We make an array of three employees:

```
Employee[] staff = new Employee[3];
```

We populate the array with a mix of managers and employees:

```
staff[0] = boss;
staff[1] = new Employee("Harry Hacker", 50000,
    1989, 10, 1);
staff[2] = new Employee("Tony Tester", 40000,
    1990, 3, 15);
```

We print out everyone's salary:

```
for (int i = 0; i < staff.length; i++)
{
    Employee e = staff[i];
    System.out.println(e.getName() + " "
        + e.getSalary());;
}
```

This loop prints the following data:

```
Carl Cracker 85000.0
Harry Hacker 50000.0
Tommy Tester 40000.0
```

Now `staff[1]` and `staff[2]` each print their base salary because they are `Employee` objects. However, `staff[0]` is a `Manager` object and its `getSalary` method adds the bonus to the base salary.

What is remarkable is that the call

```
e.getSalary()
```

picks out the *correct* getSalary method. Note that the *declared* type of e is
Employee, but the *actual* type of the object to which e refers can be either
Employee (that is, when i is 1 or 2) or Manager (when i is 0).

When e refers to an Employee object, then the call e.getSalary() calls the
getSalary method of the Employee class. However, when e refers to a
Manager object, then the getSalary method of the Manager class is called
instead. The virtual machine knows about the actual type of the object to which e
refers, and therefore can invoke the correct method.

The fact that an object variable (such as the variable e) can refer to multiple actual types
is called *polymorphism*. Automatically selecting the appropriate method at runtime is
called *dynamic binding*. We will discuss both topics in more detail in this chapter.

C++ NOTE: In Java, you do not need to declare a method as virtual. Dynamic binding
is the default behavior. If you do *not* want a method to be virtual, you tag it as final.
(We discuss the final keyword later in this chapter.)

Example 5–1 contains a program that shows how the salary computation differs
for Employee and Manager objects.

Example 5–1: ManagerTest.java

```
1. import java.util.*;
2.
3. public class ManagerTest
4. {
5.    public static void main(String[] args)
6.    {
7.       // construct a Manager object
8.       Manager boss = new Manager("Carl Cracker", 80000,
9.          1987, 12, 15);
10.      boss.setBonus(5000);
11.
12.      Employee[] staff = new Employee[3];
13.
14.      // fill the staff array with Manager and Employee objects
15.
16.      staff[0] = boss;
17.      staff[1] = new Employee("Harry Hacker", 50000,
18.         1989, 10, 1);
19.      staff[2] = new Employee("Tommy Tester", 40000,
20.         1990, 3, 15);
21.
22.      // print out information about all Employee objects
23.      for (int i = 0; i < staff.length; i++)
```

```
24.        {
25.            Employee e = staff[i];
26.            System.out.println("name=" + e.getName()
27.                + ",salary=" + e.getSalary());
28.        }
29.    }
30. }
31.
32. class Employee
33. {
34.    public Employee(String n, double s,
35.        int year, int month, int day)
36.    {
37.        name = n;
38.        salary = s;
39.        GregorianCalendar calendar
40.            = new GregorianCalendar(year, month - 1, day);
41.            // GregorianCalendar uses 0 for January
42.        hireDay = calendar.getTime();
43.    }
44.
45.    public String getName()
46.    {
47.        return name;
48.    }
49.
50.    public double getSalary()
51.    {
52.        return salary;
53.    }
54.
55.    public Date getHireDay()
56.    {
57.        return hireDay;
58.    }
59.
60.    public void raiseSalary(double byPercent)
61.    {
62.        double raise = salary * byPercent / 100;
63.        salary += raise;
64.    }
65.
66.    private String name;
67.    private double salary;
68.    private Date hireDay;
69. }
70.
71. class Manager extends Employee
72. {
73.    /**
74.        @param n the employee's name
75.        @param s the salary
76.        @param year the hire year
```

```
77.       @param month the hire month
78.       @param day the hire day
79.    */
80.    public Manager(String n, double s,
81.       int year, int month, int day)
82.    {
83.       super(n, s, year, month, day);
84.       bonus = 0;
85.    }
86.
87.    public double getSalary()
88.    {
89.       double baseSalary = super.getSalary();
90.       return baseSalary + bonus;
91.    }
92.
93.    public void setBonus(double b)
94.    {
95.       bonus = b;
96.    }
97.
98.    private double bonus;
99. }
```

Inheritance Hierarchies

Inheritance need not stop at deriving one layer of classes. We could have an `Executive` class that derives from `Manager`, for example. The collection of all classes extending from a common superclass is called an *inheritance hierarchy,* as shown in Figure 5–1. The path from a particular class to its ancestors in the inheritance hierarchy is its *inheritance chain.*

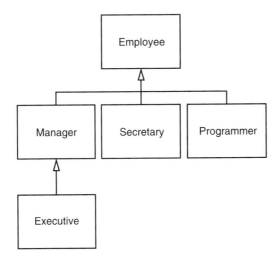

Figure 5–1: Employee inheritance hierarchy

There is usually more than one chain of descent from a distant ancestor class. You could derive a `Programmer` class from `Employee` class or a `Secretary` class from `Employee`, and they would have nothing to do with the `Manager` class (or with each other). This process can continue as long as is necessary.

Polymorphism

There is a simple rule to know whether or not inheritance is the right design for your data. The "is-a" rule states that every object of the subclass is an object of the superclass. For example, every manager is an employee. Thus, it makes sense for the `Manager` class to be a subclass of the `Employee` class. Naturally, the opposite is not true—not every employee is a manager.

Another way of formulating the "is-a" rule is the *substitution principle*. That principle states that you can use a subclass object whenever the program expects a superclass object.

For example, you can assign a subclass object to a superclass variable.

```
Employee e;
e = new Employee(. . .);  // Employee object expected
e = new Manager(. . .); // OK, Manager can be used as well
```

In the Java programming language, object variables are *polymorphic*. A variable of type `Employee` can refer to an object of type `Employee` or an object of any subclass of the `Employee` class (such as `Manager`, `Executive`, `Secretary`, and so on).

We took advantage of this principle in Example 5–1:

```
Employee[] staff = new Employee[3];
Manager boss = new Manager(. . .);
staff[0] = boss;
```

In this case, the variables `staff[0]` and `boss` refer to the same object. However, `staff[0]` is considered to be only an `Employee` object by the compiler.

That means, you can call

```
boss.setBonus(5000); // OK
```

but you can't call

```
staff[0].setBonus(5000); // ERROR
```

The declared type of `staff[0]` is `Employee`, and the `setBonus` method is not a method of the `Employee` class.

However, you cannot assign a superclass reference to a subclass variable. For example, it is not legal to make the assignment:

```
Manager m = staff[i]; // ERROR
```

The reason is clear: Not all employees are managers. If this assignment were to succeed and m were to refer to an `Employee` object that is not a manager, then it would later be possible to call `m.setBonus(...)`, and a runtime error would occur.

C++ NOTE: Java does not support multiple inheritance. (For ways to recover much of the functionality of multiple inheritance, see the section on Interfaces in the next chapter.)

Dynamic Binding

It is important to understand what happens when a method call is applied to an object. Here are the details:

1. The compiler looks at the declared type of the object and the method name. Let's say we call `x.f(args)`, and the implicit parameter `x` is declared to be an object of class `C`. Note that there may be multiple methods, all with the same name `f`, but with different parameter types. For example, there may be a method `f(int)` and a method `f(String)`. The compiler enumerates all methods called `f` in the class `C` and all `public` methods called `f` in the superclasses of `C`.

   Now the compiler knows all possible candidates for the method to be called.

2. Next, the compiler determines the types of the parameters that are supplied in the method call. If among all the methods called `f` there is a unique method whose parameter types are a best match for the supplied parameters, then that method is chosen to be called. This process is called *overloading resolution*. For example, in a call `x.f("Hello")`, the compiler picks `f(String)` and not `f(int)`. The situation can get complex because of type conversions (`int` to `double`, `Manager` to `Employee`, and so on). If the compiler cannot find any method with matching parameter types, or if there are multiple methods that all match after applying conversions, then the compiler reports an error.

   Now the compiler knows the name and parameter types of the method that needs to be called.

NOTE: Recall that the name and parameter type list for a method is called the method's *signature*. For example, `f(int)` and `f(String)` are two methods with the same name but different signatures. If you define a method in a subclass that has the same signature as a superclass method, then you override that method. However, the return type is not part of the signature. Therefore, you cannot define a method **int** `f(String)` in a superclass and a method **void** `f(String)` in a subclass.

---

3. If the method is `private`, `static`, `final`, or a constructor, then the compiler knows exactly which method to call. (The `final` modifier is explained in the next section.) This is called *static binding*. Otherwise, the method to be called depends on the actual type of the implicit parameter, and dynamic

binding must be used at run time. In our example, the compiler would generate an instruction to call f(String) with dynamic binding.

4. When the program runs and uses dynamic binding to call a method, then the virtual machine must call the version of the method that is appropriate for the *actual* type of the object to which x refers. Let's say the actual type is D, a subclass of C. If the class D defines a method f(String), that method is called. If not, D's superclass is searched for a method f(String), and so on.

It would be time-consuming to carry out this search every time a method is called. Therefore, the virtual machine precomputes a *method table* for each class that lists all method signatures and the actual methods to be called. When a method is actually called, the virtual machine simply makes a table lookup. In our example, the virtual machine consults the method table for the class D and looks up the method to call for f(String). That method may be D.f(String) or X.f(String), where X is some superclass of D.

There is one twist to this scenario. If the call is super.f(args), then the compiler consults the method table of the superclass of the implicit parameter.

Let's look at this process in detail in the call e.getSalary() in Example 5–1. The declared type of e is Employee. The Employee class has a single method called getSalary, and there are no method parameters. Therefore, in this case, we don't worry about overloading resolution.

Since the getSalary method is not private, static, or final, it is dynamically bound. The compiler produces method tables for the Employee and Manager classes. The Employee table shows that all methods are defined in the Employee class itself:

```
Employee:
    getName() -> Employee.getName()
    getSalary() -> Employee.getSalary()
    getHireDay() -> Employee.getHireDay()
    raiseSalary(double) -> Employee.raiseSalary(double)
```

Actually, that isn't quite true—as you will see later in this chapter, the Employee class has a superclass Object from which it inherits a number of methods. We ignore the Object methods for now.

The Manager method table is slightly different. Three methods are inherited, one method is redefined and one method is added.

```
Manager:
    getName() -> Employee.getName()
    getSalary() -> Manager.getSalary()
    getHireDay() -> Employee.getHireDay()
    raiseSalary(double) -> Employee.raiseSalary(double)
    setBonus(double) -> Manager.setBonus(double)
```

At run time, the call `e.getSalary()` is resolved as follows.

1. First, the virtual machine fetches the method table for the actual type of `e`. That may be the table for `Employee`, `Manager`, or another subclass of `Employee`.
2. Then, the virtual machine looks up the defining class for the `getSalary()` signature. Now it knows which method to call.
3. Finally, the virtual machine calls the method.

Dynamic binding has a very important property: it makes programs *extensible* without the need for recompiling existing code. Suppose a new class `Executive` is added, and there is the possibility that the variable `e` refers to an object of that class. The code containing the call `e.getSalary()` need not be recompiled. The `Executive.getSalary()` method is called automatically if `e` happens to refer to an object of type `Executive`.

CAUTION: When you override a method, the subclass method must be *at least as visible* as the superclass method. In particular, if the superclass method is `public`, then the subclass method must also be declared as `public`. It is a common error to accidentally omit the `public` specifier for the subclass method. Then the compiler complains that you try to supply a weaker access privilege.

Preventing Inheritance: Final Classes and Methods

Occasionally, you want to prevent someone from deriving a class from one of your classes. Classes that cannot be extended are called *final* classes, and you use the `final` modifier in the definition of the class to indicate this. For example, let us suppose we want to prevent others from subclassing the `Executive` class. Then, we simply declare the class using the `final` modifier as follows:

```
final class Executive extends Manager
{
    . . .
}
```

You can also make a specific method in a class `final`. If you do this, then no subclass can override that method. (All methods in a `final` class are automatically `final`.) For example,

```
class Employee
{
    . . .
    public final String getName()
    {
        return name;
    }
    . . .
}
```

NOTE: Recall that fields can also be declared as `final`. A final field cannot be changed after the object has been constructed. However, if a class is declared as `final`, only the methods, not the fields, are automatically `final`.

You will want to make a class or method `final` for one of two reasons:

1. *Efficiency*

    Dynamic binding has more overhead than static binding—thus, programs with dynamic calls run slower. More importantly, the compiler cannot replace a trivial method with inline code because it is possible that a subclass would override that trivial code. The compiler can put `final` methods inline. For example, if `e.getName()` is `final`, the compiler can replace it with `e.name`.

    CPUs hate procedure calls because procedure calls interfere with their strategy of getting and decoding the next instructions while processing the current one. Replacing calls to trivial procedures with inline code is a big win. Naturally, this is an issue for a compiler, not for a bytecode interpreter.

2. *Safety*

    The flexibility of the dynamic dispatch mechanism means that you have no control over what happens when you call a method. When you send a message, such as `e.getName()`, it is possible that `e` is an object of a subclass that redefined the `getName` method to return an entirely different string. By making the method `final`, you avoid this possible ambiguity.

For example, the `String` class is a `final` class. That means, nobody can define a subclass of `String`, and the compiler and virtual machine can optimize calls to `String` methods.

C++ NOTE: In C++, a method is not dynamically bound by default, and you can tag it as `inline` to have method calls replaced with the method source code. However, there is no mechanism that would prevent a subclass from overriding a superclass method. In C++, it is possible to write classes from which no other class can derive, but it requires an obscure trick, and there are few reasons to do so. (The obscure trick is left as an exercise to the reader. Hint: Use a virtual base class.)

Casting

Recall from Chapter 3 that the process of forcing a conversion from one type to another is called casting. The Java programming language has a special notation for casts. For example:

```
double x = 3.405;
int nx = (int)x;
```

converts the value of the expression x into an integer, discarding the fractional part.

Just as you occasionally need to convert a floating-point number to an integer, you also need to convert an object reference from one class to another. To actually make a cast of an object reference, you use a syntax similar to what you use for casting a numeric expression. Surround the target class name with parentheses and place it before the object reference you want to cast. For example:

```
Manager boss = (Manager)staff[0];
```

There is only one reason why you would want to make a cast—to use an object in its full capacity after its actual type has been temporarily forgotten. For example, in the Manager class, the staff array had to be an array of Employee objects since *some* of its entries were regular employees. We would need to cast the managerial elements of the array back to Manager to access any of its new variables. (Note that in the sample code for the first section, we made a special effort to avoid the cast. We initialized the boss variable with a Manager object before storing it in the array. We needed the correct type to set the bonus of the manager.)

As you know, in Java, every object variable has a type. The type describes the kind of object the variable refers to and what it can do. For example, staff[i] refers to an Employee object (so it can also refer to a Manager object).

You rely on these descriptions in your code, and the compiler checks that you do not promise too much when you describe a variable. If you assign a subclass object to a superclass variable, you are promising less, and the compiler will simply let you do it. If you assign a superclass object to a subclass variable, you are promising more, and you must confirm that you mean what you say to the compiler with the (*Subclass*) cast notation.

What happens if you try to cast down an inheritance chain and you are "lying" about what an object contains?

```
Manager boss = (Manager)staff[1]; // ERROR
```

When the program runs, the Java runtime system notices the broken promise, and generates an exception. If you do not catch the exception, your program terminates. Thus, it is good programming practice to find out whether a cast will succeed before attempting it. Simply use the instanceof operator. For example:

```
if (staff[1] instanceof Manager)
{
   boss = (Manager)staff[1];
   . . .
}
```

Finally, the compiler will not let you make a cast if there is no chance for the cast to succeed. For example, the cast

```
Date c = (Date)staff[1];
```

is a compile-time error because `Date` is not a subclass of `Employee`.

To sum up:

- You can cast only within an inheritance hierarchy.
- Use `instanceof` to check before casting from a superclass to a subclass.

> NOTE: The test
>
> ```
> x instanceof C
> ```
>
> does not generate an exception if `x` is `null`. It simply returns `false`. That makes sense. Since `null` refers to no object, it certainly doesn't refer to an object of type `C`.

Actually, converting the type of an object by performing a cast is not usually a good idea. In our example, you do not need to cast an `Employee` object to a `Manager` object for most purposes. The `getSalary` method will work correctly on both types because the dynamic binding that makes polymorphism work locates the correct method automatically.

The only reason to make the cast is to use a method that is unique to managers, such as `setBonus`. If you for some reason find yourself wanting to call `setBonus` on `Employee` objects, ask yourself whether this is an indication of a design flaw in the superclass. It may make sense to redesign the superclass and add a `setBonus` method. Remember, it takes only one bad cast to terminate your program. In general, it is best to minimize the use of casts and the `instanceof` operator.

Casts are commonly used with generic containers such as the `ArrayList` class, which will be introduced later in this chapter. When retrieving a value from a container, its type is known only as the generic type `Object`, and you must use a cast to cast it back to the type of the object that you inserted into the container.

> C++ NOTE: Java uses the cast syntax from the "bad old days" of C, but it works like the safe dynamic_cast operation of C++. For example,
>
> ```
> Manager boss = (Manager)staff[1]; // Java
> ```
>
> is the same as

```
    Manager* boss = dynamic_cast<Manager*>(staff[1]); // C++
```
with one important difference. If the cast fails, it does not yield a null object, but throws an exception. In this sense, it is like a C++ cast of *references*. This is a pain in the neck. In C++, you can take care of the type test and type conversion in one operation.

```
    Manager* boss = dynamic_cast<Manager*>(staff[1]); // C++
    if (boss != NULL) . . .
```
In Java, you use a combination of the instanceof operator and a cast.

```
    if (staff[1] instanceof Manager)
    {
        Manager boss = (Manager)staff[1];
        . . .
    }
```

Abstract Classes

As you move up the inheritance hierarchy, classes become more general and probably more abstract. At some point, the ancestor class becomes *so* general that you think of it more as a basis for other classes than as a class with specific instances you want to use. Consider, for example, an extension of our `Employee` class hierarchy. An employee is a person, and so is a student. Let us extend our class hierarchy to include classes `Person` and `Student`. Figure 5–2 shows the inheritance relationships between these classes.

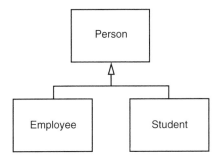

Figure 5–2: Inheritance diagram for `Person` and its subclasses

Why bother with so high a level of abstraction? There are some attributes that make sense for every person, such as the name. Both students and employees have names, and introducing a common superclass lets us factor out the `getName` method to a higher level in the inheritance hierarchy.

Now let's add another method, `getDescription`, whose purpose is to return a brief description of the person, such as:

```
    an employee with a salary of $50,000.00
    a student majoring in computer science
```

It is easy to implement this method for the `Employee` and `Student` classes. But what information can you provide in the `Person` class? The `Person` class knows nothing about the person except for the name. Of course, you could implement `Person.getDescription()` to return an empty string. But there is a better way. If you use the `abstract` keyword, you do not need to implement the method at all.

```
public abstract String getDescription();
   // no implementation required
```

For added clarity, a class with one or more abstract methods must itself be declared abstract.

```
abstract class Person
{   . . .
   public abstract String getDescription();
}
```

In addition to abstract methods, abstract classes can have concrete data and methods. For example, the `Person` class stores the name of the person and has a concrete method that returns it.

```
abstract class Person
{
   public Person(String n)
   {
      name = n;
   }

   public abstract String getDescription();

   public String getName()
   {
      return name;
   }

   private String name;
}
```

TIP: Many programmers think that abstract classes should have only abstract methods. However, this is not true. It always makes sense to move as much functionality as possible into a superclass, whether or not it is abstract. In particular, move common fields and *nonabstract* methods to the abstract superclass.

Abstract methods act as placeholder methods that are implemented in the subclasses. When you extend an abstract class, you have two choices. You can leave some or all of the abstract methods undefined. Then you must tag the subclass as abstract as well. Or you can define all methods. Then the subclass is no longer abstract.

For example, we will define a `Student` class that extends the abstract `Person` class and implements the `getDescription` method. Because none of the methods of the `Student` class are abstract, it does not need to be declared as an abstract class.

A class can even be declared as `abstract` even though it has no abstract methods.

Abstract classes cannot be instantiated. That is, if a class is declared as `abstract`, no objects of that class can be created. For example, the expression

```
new Person("Vince Vu")
```

is an error. However, you can create objects of concrete subclasses.

Note that you can still create *object variables* of an abstract class, but such a variable must refer to an object of a nonabstract subclass. For example,

```
Person p = new Student("Vince Vu", "Economics");
```

Here p is a variable of the abstract type `Person` that refers to an instance of the nonabstract subclass `Student`.

C++ NOTE: In C++, an abstract method is called a *pure virtual function* and is tagged with a trailing = 0 , such as in

```
class Person // C++
{
public:
    virtual string getDescription() = 0;
    . . .
};
```

A C++ class is abstract if it has at least one pure virtual function. In C++, there is no special keyword to denote abstract classes.

Let us define a concrete subclass `Student` that extends the abstract `Person` class:

```
class Student extends Person
{
    public Student(String n, String m)
    {
        super(n);
        major = m;
    }

    public String getDescription()
    {
        return "a student majoring in " + major;
    }

    private String major;
}
```

The `Student` class defines the `getDescription` method. Therefore, all methods in the `Student` class are concrete, and the class is no longer an abstract class.

The program shown in Example 5–2 defines the abstract superclass `Person` and two concrete subclasses `Employee` and `Student`. We fill an array of `Person` references with employee and student objects.

```
Person[] people = new Person[2];
people[0] = new Employee(. . .);
people[1] = new Student(. . .);
```

We then print the names and descriptions of these objects:

```
for (int i = 0; i < people.length; i++)
{
   Person p = people[i];
   System.out.println(p.getName() + ", " + p.getDescription());
}
```

Some people are baffled by the call:

```
p.getDescription()
```

Isn't this a call an undefined method? Keep in mind that the variable p never refers to a `Person` object since it is impossible to construct a `Person` object. The variable p always refers to an object of a concrete subclass such as `Employee` or `Student`. For these objects, the `getDescription` method is defined.

Could you have omitted the abstract method altogether from the `Person` superclass and simply defined the `getDescription` methods in the `Employee` and `Student` subclasses? Then you wouldn't have been able to invoke the `getDescription` method on the variable p. The compiler ensures that you only invoke methods that are declared in the class.

Abstract methods are an important concept in the Java programming language. You will encounter them most commonly inside *interfaces*. For more information about interfaces, please turn to Chapter 6.

Example 5–2: PersonTest.java

```
1. import java.text.*;
2.
3. public class PersonTest
4. {
5.    public static void main(String[] args)
6.    {
7.       Person[] people = new Person[2];
8.
9.       // fill the people array with Student and Employee objects
10.      people[0]
11.         = new Employee("Harry Hacker", 50000);
12.      people[1]
```

```
13.            = new Student("Maria Morris", "computer science");
14.
15.        // print out names and descriptions of all Person objects
16.        for (int i = 0; i < people.length; i++)
17.        {
18.           Person p = people[i];
19.           System.out.println(p.getName() + ", "
20.              + p.getDescription());
21.        }
22.     }
23. }
24.
25. abstract class Person
26. {
27.     public Person(String n)
28.     {
29.        name = n;
30.     }
31.
32.     public abstract String getDescription();
33.
34.     public String getName()
35.     {
36.        return name;
37.     }
38.
39.     private String name;
40. }
41.
42. class Employee extends Person
43. {
44.     public Employee(String n, double s)
45.     {
46.        // pass name to superclass constructor
47.        super(n);
48.        salary = s;
49.     }
50.
51.     public double getSalary()
52.     {
53.        return salary;
54.     }
55.
56.     public String getDescription()
57.     {
58.        NumberFormat formatter
59.           = NumberFormat.getCurrencyInstance();
60.        return "an employee with a salary of "
61.           + formatter.format(salary);
62.     }
63.
64.     public void raiseSalary(double byPercent)
65.     {
```

```
66.        double raise = salary * byPercent / 100;
67.        salary += raise;
68.    }
69.
70.    private double salary;
71. }
72.
73. class Student extends Person
74. {
75.    /**
76.        @param n the student's name
77.        @param m the student's major
78.    */
79.    public Student(String n, String m)
80.    {
81.        // pass n to superclass constructor
82.        super(n);
83.        major = m;
84.    }
85.
86.    public String getDescription()
87.    {
88.        return "a student majoring in " + major;
89.    }
90.
91.    private String major;
92. }
```

Protected Access

As you know, fields in a class are best tagged as `private`, and methods are usually tagged as `public`. Any features declared `private` won't be visible to other
classes. As we said at the beginning of this chapter, this is also true for subclasses:
a subclass cannot access the private fields of its superclass.

There are times, however, when you want to restrict a method to subclasses only,
or, less commonly, to allow subclass methods to access a superclass field. In that
case, you declare a class feature as `protected`. For example, if the superclass
`Employee` declares the `hireDay` field as `protected` instead of private, then the
`Manager` methods can access it directly.

However, the `Manager` class methods can only peek inside the `hireDay` field of
`Manager` objects, not of other `Employee` objects. This restriction is made so that
you can't abuse the protected mechanism and form subclasses just to gain access
to the protected fields.

In practice, use the `protected` attribute with caution. Suppose your class is
used by other programmers and you designed it with protected fields. Unbe-
knownst to you, other programmers may inherit classes from your class and
then start accessing your protected fields. In this case, you can no longer

change the implementation of your class without upsetting the other programmers. That is against the spirit of OOP, which encourages data encapsulation.

Protected methods make more sense. A class may declare a method as `protected` if it is tricky to use. This indicates that the subclasses (which, presumably, know their ancestors well) can be trusted to use the method correctly, but other classes cannot.

A good example of this kind of method is the `clone` method of the `Object` class—see Chapter 6 for more details.

C++ NOTE: As it happens, protected features in Java are visible to all subclasses as well as all other classes in the same package. This is slightly different from the C++ meaning of protected, and it makes the notion of `protected` in Java even less safe than in C++.

Here is a summary of the four access modifiers in Java that control visibility:

1. Visible to the class only (`private`).
2. Visible to the world (`public`).
3. Visible to the package and all subclasses (`protected`).
4. Visible to the package—the (unfortunate) default. No modifiers are needed.

`Object`: **The Cosmic Superclass**

The `Object` class is the ultimate ancestor—every class in Java extends `Object`. However, you never have to write:

```
class Employee extends Object
```

The ultimate superclass `Object` is taken for granted if no superclass is explicitly mentioned. Because *every* class in Java extends `Object`, it is important to be familiar with the services provided by the `Object` class. We will go over the basic ones in this chapter and refer you to later chapters or to the on-line documentation for what is not covered here. (Several methods of `Object` come up only when dealing with threads—see Volume 2 for more on threads.)

You can use a variable of type `Object` to refer to objects of any type:

```
Object obj = new Employee("Harry Hacker", 35000);
```

Of course, a variable of type `Object` is only useful as a generic holder for arbitrary values. To do anything specific with the value, you need to have some knowledge about the original type and then apply a cast:

```
Employee e = (Employee)obj;
```

> C++ NOTE: In C++, there is no cosmic root class. Of course, in C++, every pointer can be converted to a `void*` pointer. Java programmers often use `Object` references for generic programming, to implement data structures and algorithms that support a variety of data types. In C++, templates are commonly used for generic programming. But Java has no templates, so Java programmers often have to give up compile-time typing and make do with code that manipulates `Object` references.

The `equals` and `toString` methods

The `equals` method in the `Object` class tests whether or not one object is equal to another. The `equals` method, as implemented in the `Object` class, determines whether or not two objects point to the same area of memory. This is not a useful test. If you want to test objects for equality, you will need to override `equals` for a more meaningful comparison. For example,

```java
class Employee
{  // . . .
   public boolean equals(Object otherObject)
   {
      // a quick test to see if the objects are identical
      if (this == otherObject) return true;

      // must return false if the explicit parameter is null
      if (otherObject == null) return false;

      // if the classes don't match, they can't be equal
      if (getClass() != otherObject.getClass())
         return false;

      // now we know otherObject is a non-null Employee
      Employee other = (Employee)otherObject;

      // test whether the fields have identical values
      return name.equals(other.name)
         && salary == other.salary
         && hireDay.equals(other.hireDay);
   }
}
```

The `getClass` method returns the class of an object—we will discuss this method in detail later in this chapter. For two objects to be equal, they must first be objects of the same class.

NOTE: How should the `equals` method behave if the implicit and explicit parameters don't belong to the same class? Unfortunately, different programmers take different actions in this case. We recommend that `equals` should return `false` if the classes don't match exactly. But many programmers use a test:

```
if (!(otherObject instanceof Employee)) return false;
```

This leaves open the possibility that `otherObject` can belong to a subclass. Other programmers use no test at all. Then the `equals` method throws an exception if `otherObject` cannot be cast to an `Employee` object. Technically speaking, both of these approaches are wrong. Here is why. The Java Language Specification requires that the `equals` method has the following properties:

1. It is *reflexive*: for any non-null reference x, x.equals(x) should return `true`.
2. It is *symmetric*: for any references x and y, x.equals(y) should return `true` if and only if y.equals(x) returns `true`.
3. It is *transitive*: for any references x, y, and z, if x.equals(y) returns true and y.equals(z) returns `true`, then x.equals(z) should return `true`.
4. It is *consistent*: If the objects to which x and y refer haven't changed, then repeated calls to x.equals(y) return the same value.
5. For any non-null reference x, x.equals(null) should return `false`.

Rule 5 mandates that you include the test

```
if (otherObject == null) return false;
```

in your `equals` method. What is less obvious is that Rule 2 requires you to test for class equality. Consider a call

```
e.equals(m)
```

where e is an `Employee` object and m is a `Manager` object, both of which happen to have the same name, salary, and hire date. If you don't check that the class of m is the same as the class of e, this call returns `true`. But that means that the reverse call

```
m.equals(e)
```

also needs to return `true`—Rule 2 does not allow it to return `false`, or to throw an exception.

Unfortunately, the Java Language Specification does a poor job of explaining this consequence, and the majority of programmers seem to be unaware of it. The standard Java library contains over 150 implementations of `equals` methods, with a mishmash of using `instanceof`, calling `getClass`, catching a `ClassCastException`, or doing nothing at all. Only a tiny minority of implementations fulfills Rule 2. You can do better, by following our recipe for the perfect `equals` method.

Here is a recipe for writing the perfect `equals` method:

1. Call the explicit parameter `otherObject`—later, you need to cast it to another variable that you should call `other`.

2. Test whether `this` happens to be identical to `otherObject`:

```
if (this == otherObject) return true;
```

This is just an optimization. In practice, this is a common case. It is much cheaper to check for identity than to compare the fields.

3. Test whether `otherObject` is `null` and return `false` if it is. This test is required.

```
if (otherObject == null) return false;
```

4. Test whether `this` and `otherObject` belong to the *same class*. This test is required by the "symmetry rule".

```
if (getClass() != otherObject.getClass()) return false;
```

5. Cast `otherObject` to a variable of your class type:

```
ClassName other = (ClassName)otherObject
```

6. Now compare all fields. Use `==` for primitive type fields, `equals` for object fields. Return `true` if all fields match, `false` otherwise.

```
return field1 == other.field1
   && field2.equals(other.field2)
   && . . .;
```

In a subclass, first call `equals` on the superclass. If that test doesn't pass, then the objects can't be equal. If it does, then you are ready to compare the instance fields of the subclass.

```
class Manager extends Employee
{
   . . .
   public boolean equals(Object otherObject)
   {
      if (!super.equals(otherObject)) return false;
      Manager other = (Manager)otherObject;
      // super.equals checked that this and otherObject
      // belong to the same class
      return bonus == other.bonus;
   }
}
```

Another important method in `Object` is the `toString` method that returns a string that represents the value of this object. Almost any class will override this method to give you a printed representation of the object's current state. Here is a typical example. The `toString` method of the `Point` class returns a string like this:

```
java.awt.Point[x=10,y=20]
```

Most (but not all) `toString` methods follow this format: the name of the class, followed by the field values enclosed in square brackets. Here is an implementation of the `toString` method for the `Employee` class:

```
public String toString()
{
   return "Employee[name=" + name
      + ",salary=" + salary
      + ",hireDay=" + hireDay
      + "]";
}
```

Actually, you can do a little better. Rather than hardwiring the class name into the `toString` method, call `getClass().getName()` to obtain a string with the class name.

```
public String toString()
{
   return getClass().getName()
      + "[name=" + name
      + ",salary=" + salary
      + ",hireDay=" + hireDay
      + "]";
}
```

Then the `toString` method also works for subclasses.

Of course, the subclass programmer should define its own `toString` method and add the subclass fields. If the superclass uses `getClass().getName()`, then the subclass can simply call `super.toString()`. For example, here is a `toString` method for the `Manager` class:

```
class Manager extends Employee
{
   . . .
   public String toString()
   {
      return super.toString()
         + "[bonus=" + bonus
         + "]";
   }
}
```

Now a `Manager` object is printed as:

```
Manager[name=...,salary=...,hireDay=...][bonus=...]
```

The `toString` method is ubiquitous for an important reason: whenever an object is concatenated with a string, using the "+" operator, the Java compiler automatically invokes the `toString` method to obtain a string representation of the object. For example,

```
Point p = new Point(10, 20);
String message = "The current position is " + p;
   // automatically invokes p.toString()
```

TIP: Instead of writing `x.toString()`, you can write `"" + x`. This concatenates the empty string with the string representation of `x` that is exactly `x.toString()`.

If `x` is any object and you call

```
System.out.println(x);
```

then the `println` method simply calls `x.toString()` and prints the resulting string.

The `Object` class defines the `toString` method to print the class name and the memory location of the object. For example, the call

```
System.out.println(System.out)
```

produces an output that looks like this:

```
java.io.PrintStream@2f6684
```

The reason is that the implementor of the `PrintStream` class didn't bother to override the `toString` method.

The `toString` method is a great debugging tool. Many classes in the standard class library define the `toString` method so that you can get useful debugging information. Some debuggers let you invoke the `toString` method to display objects. And you can always insert trace messages like this:

```
System.out.println("Current position = " + position);
```

TIP: We strongly recommend that you add a `toString` method to each class that you write. You, as well as other programmers who use your classes, will be grateful for the debugging support.

The program in Example 5–3 implements the `equals` and `toString` methods for the `Employee` and `Manager` classes.

Example 5–3: EqualsTest.java

```
1. import java.util.*;
2.
3. public class EqualsTest
4. {
5.    public static void main(String[] args)
6.    {
7.       Employee alice1 = new Employee("Alice Adams", 75000,
8.          1987, 12, 15);
9.       Employee alice2 = alice1;
10.      Employee alice3 = new Employee("Alice Adams", 75000,
11.         1987, 12, 15);
12.      Employee bob = new Employee("Bob Brandson", 50000,
13.         1989, 10, 1);
14.
15.      System.out.println("alice1 == alice2: "
```

```
16.              + (alice1 == alice2));
17.
18.        System.out.println("alice1 == alice3: "
19.              + (alice1 == alice3));
20.
21.        System.out.println("alice1.equals(alice3): "
22.              + alice1.equals(alice3));
23.
24.        System.out.println("alice1.equals(bob): "
25.              + alice1.equals(bob));
26.
27.        System.out.println("bob.toString(): " + bob);
28.
29.        Manager carl = new Manager("Carl Cracker", 80000,
30.              1987, 12, 15);
31.        Manager boss = new Manager("Carl Cracker", 80000,
32.              1987, 12, 15);
33.        boss.setBonus(5000);
34.        System.out.println("boss.toString(): " + boss);
35.        System.out.println("carl.equals(boss): "
36.              + carl.equals(boss));
37.     }
38. }
39.
40. class Employee
41. {
42.    public Employee(String n, double s,
43.         int year, int month, int day)
44.    {
45.       name = n;
46.       salary = s;
47.       GregorianCalendar calendar
48.          = new GregorianCalendar(year, month - 1, day);
49.       hireDay = calendar.getTime();
50.    }
51.
52.    public String getName()
53.    {
54.       return name;
55.    }
56.
57.    public double getSalary()
58.    {
59.       return salary;
60.    }
61.
62.    public Date getHireDay()
63.    {
64.       return hireDay;
65.    }
66.
67.    public void raiseSalary(double byPercent)
68.    {
69.       double raise = salary * byPercent / 100;
```

```
70.        salary += raise;
71.     }
72.
73.     public boolean equals(Object otherObject)
74.     {
75.        // a quick test to see if the objects are identical
76.        if (this == otherObject) return true;
77.
78.        // must return false if the explicit parameter is null
79.        if (otherObject == null) return false;
80.
81.        // if the classes don't match, they can't be equal
82.        if (getClass() != otherObject.getClass())
83.           return false;
84.
85.        // now we know otherObject is a non-null Employee
86.        Employee other = (Employee)otherObject;
87.
88.        // test whether the fields have identical values
89.        return name.equals(other.name)
90.           && salary == other.salary
91.           && hireDay.equals(other.hireDay);
92.     }
93.
94.     public String toString()
95.     {
96.        return getClass().getName()
97.           + "[name=" + name
98.           + ",salary=" + salary
99.           + ",hireDay=" + hireDay
100.          + "]";
101.    }
102.
103.    private String name;
104.    private double salary;
105.    private Date hireDay;
106. }
107.
108. class Manager extends Employee
109. {
110.    public Manager(String n, double s,
111.       int year, int month, int day)
112.    {
113.       super(n, s, year, month, day);
114.       bonus = 0;
115.    }
116.
117.    public double getSalary()
118.    {
119.       double baseSalary = super.getSalary();
120.       return baseSalary + bonus;
121.    }
122.
123.    public void setBonus(double b)
```

```
124.     {
125.         bonus = b;
126.     }
127.
128.     public boolean equals(Object otherObject)
129.     {
130.         if (!super.equals(otherObject)) return false;
131.         Manager other = (Manager)otherObject;
132.         // super.equals checked that this and other belong to the
133.         // same class
134.         return bonus == other.bonus;
135.     }
136.
137.     public String toString()
138.     {
139.         return super.toString()
140.             + "[bonus=" + bonus
141.             + "]";
142.     }
143.
144.     private double bonus;
145. }
```

Generic Programming

All values of any class type can be held in variables of type `Object`. In particular, `String` values are objects:

```
Object obj = "Hello"; // OK
```

However, numbers, characters, and `boolean` values are not objects.

```
obj = 5; // ERROR
obj = false; // ERROR
```

You will see later in this chapter how you can turn these types into objects by using *wrapper classes* such as `Integer` and `Boolean`.

Furthermore, all array types, no matter whether they are arrays of objects or arrays of primitive types, are class types that derive from `Object`.

```
Employee[] staff = new Employee[10];
Object arr = staff; // OK
arr = new int[10]; // OK
```

An array of objects of class type can be converted to an array of objects. For example, an `Employee[]` array can be passed to a method that expects an `Object[]` array. That conversion is useful for *generic programming*.

Here is a simple example that illustrates the concept of generic programming. Suppose you want to find the index of an element in an array. This is a generic situation, and by writing the code for objects, you can reuse it for employees, dates, or whatever.

```
static int find(Object[] a, Object key)
{
    int i;
    for (i = 0; i < a.length; i++)
```

```
      if (a[i].equals(key)) return i;
   return -1; // not found
}
```

For example,

```
Employee[] staff = new Employee[10];
Employee harry;
. . .
int n = find(staff, harry);
```

Note that you can only convert an array of objects into an `Object[]` array. You cannot convert an `int[]` array into an `Object[]` array. (However, as previously pointed out, both arrays can be converted to `Object`.)

If you convert an array of objects to an `Object[]` array, the generic array still remembers its original type at run time. You cannot store a foreign object into the array.

```
Employee[] staff = new Employee[10];
. . . // fill with Employee objects
Object[] arr = staff;
arr[0] = new Date();
   // not legal, but suppose it was
for (i = 0; i < n; i++) staff[i].raiseSalary(3);
   // ouch, now the date gets a raise!
```

Of course, this must be checked at run time. The code above compiles without error—it is legal to store a `Date` value in `arr[0]`, which has type `Object`. But when the code executes, the array remembers its original type and monitors the type of all objects that are stored in it. If you store an incompatible type into an array, an exception is thrown.

C++ NOTE: C++ programmers may be surprised that the cast from `Employee[]` to `Object[]` is legal. Even if `Object` was a superclass of `Employee` in C++, the equivalent cast from `Employee**` to `Object**` would not be legal. (Of course, the cast from `Employee*` to `Object*` is legal in C++.)

There is a security reason behind this restriction. If the cast "`Subclass** → Superclass**`" were permitted, you could corrupt the contents of an array. Consider this code:

```
Employee** staff; // C++
Object** arr = staff;
   // not legal, but suppose it was
arr[0] = new Date();
   // legal, Date also inherits from Object
for (i = 0; i < n; i++) staff[i]->raiseSalary(3);
   // ouch, now the date gets a raise!
```

In Java, this problem is averted by remembering the original type of all arrays and by monitoring all array stores for type compatibility at run time.

java.lang.Object

- Class getClass()

  returns a class object that contains information about the object. As you will see later in this chapter, Java has a runtime representation for classes that is encapsulated in the Class class that you can often use to your advantage.

- boolean equals(Object otherObject)

  compares two objects for equality; returns true if the objects point to the same area of memory, and false otherwise. You should override this method in your own classes.

- Object clone()

  creates a clone of the object. The Java runtime system allocates memory for the new instance and copies the memory allocated for the current object.

NOTE: Cloning an object is important, but it also turns out to be a fairly subtle process filled with potential pitfalls for the unwary. We will have a lot more to say about the clone method in Chapter 6.

- String toString()

  returns a string that represents the value of this object. You should override this method in your own classes.

java.lang.Class

- String getName()

  returns the name of this class.

- Class getSuperclass()

  returns the superclass of this class as a Class object.

Array Lists

In many programming languages—in particular in C—you have to fix the sizes of all arrays at compile time. Programmers hate this because it forces them into uncomfortable trade-offs. How many employees will be in a department? Surely no more than 100. What if there is a humongous department with 150 employees? Do we want to waste 90 entries for every department with just 10 employees?

In Java, the situation is much better. You can set the size of an array at run time.

```
int actualSize = . . .;
Employee[] staff = new Employee[actualSize];
```

Of course, this code does not completely solve the problem of dynamically modifying arrays at run time. Once you set the array size, you cannot change it easily. Instead, the easiest way in Java to deal with this common situation is to use another Java class that works much like an array that will shrink and grow automatically. This class is called `ArrayList`. Thus, in Java, array lists are arraylike objects that can grow and shrink automatically without you needing to write any code.

> NOTE: In older versions of the Java programming language, programmers used the `Vector` class for automatically resizing arrays. However, the `ArrayList` class is more efficient, and you should generally use it instead of vectors. See Chapter 2 of Volume 2 for more information about vectors.

There is an important difference between an array and an array list. Arrays are a feature of the Java language, and there is an array type `T[]` for each element type `T`. However, the `ArrayList` class is a library class, defined in the `java.util` package. This is a single "one size fits all" type which holds elements of type `Object`. In particular, you will need a cast whenever you want to take an item out of an array list.

Use the `add` method to add new elements to an array list. For example, here is how you create an array list and populate it with employee objects:

```
ArrayList staff = new ArrayList();
staff.add(new Employee(. . .));
staff.add(new Employee(. . .));
```

The `ArrayList` class manages an internal array of `Object` references. Eventually, that array will run out of space. This is where array lists work their magic: If you call `add` and the internal array is full, the array list automatically creates a bigger array, and automatically copies all the objects from the smaller to the bigger array.

If you already know, or have a good guess, how many elements you want to store, then call the `ensureCapacity` method before filling the array list:

```
staff.ensureCapacity(100);
```

That call allocates an internal array of `100` objects. Then you can keep calling `add`, and no costly relocation takes place.

You can also pass an initial capacity to the `ArrayList` constructor:

```
ArrayList staff = new ArrayList(100);
```

> CAUTION: Allocating an array list as
> ```
> new ArrayList(100) // capacity is 100
> ```
> is *not* the same as allocating a new array as
> ```
> new Employee[100] // size is 100
> ```
> There is an important distinction between the capacity of an array list and the size of an array. If you allocate an array with 100 entries, then the array has 100 slots, ready for use. An array list with a capacity of 100 elements has the *potential* of holding 100 elements (and, in fact, more than 100, at the cost of additional relocations), but at the beginning, even after its initial construction, an array list holds no elements at all.

The `size` method returns the actual number of elements in the array list. For example,

```
staff.size()
```

returns the current number of elements in the `staff` array list. This is the equivalent of

```
a.length
```

for an array `a`.

Once you are reasonably sure that the array list is at its permanent size, you can call the `trimToSize` method. This method adjusts the size of the memory block to use exactly as much storage space as is required to hold the current number of elements. The garbage collector will reclaim any excess memory.

NOTE: Once you trim the size of an array list, adding new elements will move the block again, which takes time. You should only use `trimToSize` when you are sure you won't add any more elements to the array list.

C++ NOTE: The `ArrayList` class differs in a number of important ways from the C++ `vector` template. Most noticeably, since `vector` is a template, only elements of the correct type can be inserted, and no casting is required to retrieve elements from the vector. For example, the compiler will simply refuse to insert a `Date` object into a `vector<Employee>`. The C++ vector template overloads the `[]` operator for convenient element access. Since Java does not have operator overloading, it must use explicit method calls instead. C++ vectors are copied by value. If `a` and `b` are two vectors, then the assignment `a = b;` makes `a` into a new vector with the same length as `b`, and all elements are copied from `b` to `a`. The same assignment in Java makes both `a` and `b` refer to the same array list.

java.util.ArrayList

- `ArrayList()`
  constructs an empty array list.
- `ArrayList(int initialCapacity)`
  constructs an empty array list with the specified capacity.

  Parameters: `initialCapacity` the initial storage capacity of the array list

- `boolean add(Object obj)`
  appends an element at the end of the array list. Always returns `true`.

  Parameters: `obj`   the element to be added

- `int size()`
  returns the number of elements currently stored in the array list. (This is different from, and, of course, never larger than, the array list's capacity.)

- `void ensureCapacity(int capacity)`
  ensures that the array list has the capacity to store the given number of elements without relocating its internal storage array.

  Parameters: `capacity`   the desired storage capacity

- `void trimToSize()`
  reduces the storage capacity of the array list to its current size.

Accessing array list elements

Unfortunately, nothing comes for free; the automatic growth convenience that array lists give requires a more complicated syntax for accessing the elements. The reason is that the `ArrayList` class is not a part of the Java language; it is just a utility class programmed by someone and supplied in the standard library.

Instead of using the pleasant `[]` syntax to access or change the element of an array, you must use the `get` and `set` methods.

For example, to set the `i`th element, you use:

```
staff.set(i, harry);
```

This is equivalent to

```
a[i] = harry;
```

for an array `a`.

Getting an array list element is more complex because the return type of the `get` method is `Object`. You need to cast it to the desired type:

```
Employee e = (Employee)staff.get(i);
```

This is equivalent to, but much more cumbersome than,

```
Employee e = a[i];
```

NOTE: Array lists, like arrays, are zero-based.

TIP: You can sometimes get the best of both worlds—flexible growth and convenient element access—with the following trick. First, make an array list and add all the elements.

```
ArrayList list = new ArrayList();
while (. . .)
{
   x = . . .;
   list.add(x);
}
```

When you are done, use the `toArray` method to copy the elements into an array.

```
X[] a = new X[list.size()];
list.toArray(a);
```

CAUTION: Do not call `list.set(i, x)` until the *size* of the array list is larger than `i`. For example, the following code is wrong:

```
ArrayList list = new ArrayList(100); // capacity 100, size 0
list.set(0, x); // no element 0 yet
```

Use the `add` method instead of `set` to fill up an array, and use `set` only to replace a previously added element.

Array lists are inherently somewhat *unsafe*. It is possible to accidentally add an element of the wrong type to an array list.

```
Date birthday = . . .;
staff.set(i, birthday);
```

The compiler won't complain. It is perfectly willing to convert a `Date` to an `Object`, but when the accidental date is later retrieved out of the array list, it will probably be cast into an `Employee`. This is an invalid cast that will cause the program to abort. That *is* a problem! The problem arises because array lists store values of type `Object`. Had `staff` been an array of `Employee` references, then the compiler would not have allowed a calendar inside it.

```
Employee[] a = new Employee[100];
a[i] = calendar; // ERROR
```

On very rare occasions, array lists are useful for *heterogeneous collections*. Objects of completely unrelated classes are added on purpose. When an entry is retrieved, the type of every retrieved object must be tested, as in the following code:

```
ArrayList list;
list.add(new Employee(. . .));
list.add(new Date(. . .));
. . .
Object obj = list.get(n);
if (obj instanceof Employee)
{
    Employee e = (Employee)obj;
    . . .
}
```

However, this is generally considered a poor way to write code. It is not a good idea to throw away type information and laboriously try to retrieve it later.

java.util.ArrayList

- void set(int index, Object obj)

  puts a value in the array list at the specified index, overwriting the previous contents.

  Parameters: index   the position (must be between 0 and size() - 1)

                  obj   the new value

- Object get(int index)

  gets the value stored at a specified index.

  Parameters: index   the index of the element to get (must be between 0 and size() - 1)

Inserting and removing elements in the middle of an array list

Instead of appending elements at the end of an array list, you can also insert them in the middle.

```
int n = staff.size() / 2;
staff.add(n, e);
```

The elements at locations n and above are shifted up to make room for the new entry. If the new size of the array list after the insertion exceeds the capacity, then the array list reallocates its storage array.

Similarly, you can remove an element from the middle of an array list.

```
Employee e = (Employee)staff.remove(n);
```

The elements located above it are copied down, and the size of the array is reduced by one.

Inserting and removing elements is not terribly efficient. It is probably not worth worrying about for small array lists. But if you store many elements and frequently insert and remove in the middle of the sequence, consider using a linked list instead. We will explain how to program with linked lists in Volume 2.

Example 5–4 is a modification of the EmployeeTest program of Chapter 4. The Employee[] array is replaced by an ArrayList. Note the following changes:

- You don't have to specify the array size.
- You use add to add as many elements as you like.
- You use size() instead of length to count the number of elements.
- You use (Employee)a.get(i) instead of a[i] to access an element.

Example 5–4: ArrayListTest.java

```
1. import java.util.*;
2.
3. public class ArrayListTest
4. {
5.    public static void main(String[] args)
6.    {
7.       // fill the staff array list with three Employee objects
8.       ArrayList staff = new ArrayList();
9.
10.      staff.add(new Employee("Carl Cracker", 75000,
11.         1987, 12, 15));
12.      staff.add(new Employee("Harry Hacker", 50000,
13.         1989, 10, 1));
14.      staff.add(new Employee("Tony Tester", 40000,
15.         1990, 3, 15));
16.
17.      // raise everyone's salary by 5%
18.      for (int i = 0; i < staff.size(); i++)
19.      {
20.         Employee e = (Employee)staff.get(i);
21.         e.raiseSalary(5);
22.      }
23.
24.      // print out information about all Employee objects
25.      for (int i = 0; i < staff.size(); i++)
26.      {
27.         Employee e = (Employee)staff.get(i);
28.         System.out.println("name=" + e.getName()
29.            + ",salary=" + e.getSalary()
30.            + ",hireDay=" + e.getHireDay());
31.      }
32.   }
33. }
34.
35. class Employee
36. {
37.    public Employee(String n, double s,
38.       int year, int month, int day)
39.    {
40.       name = n;
41.       salary = s;
42.       GregorianCalendar calendar
43.          = new GregorianCalendar(year, month - 1, day);
44.          // GregorianCalendar uses 0 for January
45.       hireDay = calendar.getTime();
46.    }
47.
```

```
48.    public String getName()
49.    {
50.       return name;
51.    }
52.
53.    public double getSalary()
54.    {
55.       return salary;
56.    }
57.
58.    public Date getHireDay()
59.    {
60.       return hireDay;
61.    }
62.
63.    public void raiseSalary(double byPercent)
64.    {
65.       double raise = salary * byPercent / 100;
66.       salary += raise;
67.    }
68.
69.    private String name;
70.    private double salary;
71.    private Date hireDay;
72. }
```

java.util.ArrayList

- `void add(int index, Object obj)`

  shifts up elements to insert an element.

  Parameters: `index`   the insertion position (must be between 0 and `size()`)

                      `obj`   the new element

- `void remove(int index)`

  removes an element and shifts down all elements above it.

  Parameters: `index`   the position of the element to be removed (must be between 0 and `size() - 1`)

Object Wrappers

Occasionally, you need to convert a basic type like `int` to an object. All basic types have class counterparts. For example, there is a class `Integer` corresponding to the basic type `int`. These kinds of classes are usually called *object wrappers*. The wrapper classes have obvious names: `Integer`, `Long`, `Float`, `Double`, `Short`, `Byte`, `Character`, `Void`, and `Boolean`. (The first six inherit from the common wrapper `Number`.) The wrapper classes are `final`.

(So you can't override the `toString` method in `Integer` to display numbers using Roman numerals, sorry.) You also cannot change the values you store in the object wrapper.

Suppose we want an array list of floating-point numbers. As mentioned previously, simply adding numbers won't work.

```
ArrayList list = new ArrayList();
list.add(3.14); // ERROR
```

The floating-point number 3.14 is not an `Object`. Here, the `Double` wrapper class comes in. An instance of `Double` is an object that wraps the `double` type.

```
list.add(new Double(3.14));
```

Of course, to retrieve a number from an array list of `Double` objects, we need to extract the actual value from the wrapper by using the `doubleValue()` method in `Double`.

```
double x = ((Double)list.get(n)).doubleValue();
```

Ugh. Here it really pays off to define a class we will call `DoubleArrayList` that hides all this ugliness once and for all.

```
class DoubleArrayList
{
    public DoubleArrayList()
    {
        list = new ArrayList();
    }

    public void set(int n, double x)
    {
        list.set(n, new Double(x));
    }

    public void add(double x)
    {
        list.add(new Double(x));
    }

    public double get(int n)
    {
        return ((Double)list.get(n)).doubleValue();
    }

    public int size()
    {
        return list.size();
    }

    private ArrayList list;
}
```

CAUTION: Some people think that the wrapper classes can be used to implement methods that can modify numeric parameters. However, that is not correct. Recall from Chapter 4 that it is impossible to write a Java method that increments an integer because parameters to Java methods are always passed by value.

```
public static void increment(int x) // won't work
{
   x++; // increments local copy
}

public static void main(String[] args)
{
   int a = 3;
   increment(a);
   . . .

}
```

Changing x has no effect on a. Could we overcome this by using an Integer instead of an int?

```
public static void increment(Integer x) // won't work
{
   . . .
}

public static void main(String[] args)
{
   Integer a = new Integer(3);
   increment(a);
   . . .
}
```

After all, now a and x are references to the same object. If we managed to update x, then a would also be updated. The problem is that Integer objects are *immutable*: the information contained inside the wrapper can't change. In particular, there is no analog to the statement x++ for Integer objects. Thus, you cannot use these wrapper classes to create a method that modifies numeric parameters.

NOTE: If you do want to write a method to change numeric parameters, you can use one of the *holder* types defined in the org.omg.CORBA package. There are types IntHolder, BooleanHolder, and so on. Each holder type has a public (!) field value through which you can access the stored value.

```
public static void increment(IntegerHolder x)
{
   x.value++;
}

public static void main(String[] args)
{
   IntegerHolder a = new IntegerHolder(3);
```

```
        increment(a);
        int result = a.value;
        . . .
    }
```

You will often see the number wrappers for another reason. The designers of Java found the wrappers a convenient place to put certain basic methods, like the ones for converting strings of digits to numbers.

To convert a string to an integer, you need to use the following statement:

```
int x = Integer.parseInt(s);
```

This has nothing to do with Integer objects—`parseInt` is a static method. But the `Integer` class was a good place to put it.

Similarly, you can use the `Double.parseDouble` method to parse floating-point numbers.

NOTE: Until Java 2, there was no `parseDouble` method in the `Double` class. Instead, programmers had to use the cumbersome

```
double x = new Double(s).doubleValue();
```

or

```
double x = Double.valueOf(s).doubleValue();
```

This statement constructs a `Double` object from the string s and then extracts its value. The static `Double.parseDouble` method is more efficient because no object is created.

NOTE: There is another method for parsing numbers, although it isn't any simpler. You can use the `parse` method of the `NumberFormat` class. When s is a string and `formatter` is an object of type `NumberFormat`, then the method call `formatter.parse(s)` returns an object of type `Number`.

```
NumberFormat formatter = NumberFormat.getNumberInstance();
Number n = formatter.parse(s);
```

Actually, `Number` is an abstract class, and the returned object is an object of either type `Long` or `Double`, depending on the contents of the string s. You can use the `instanceof` operator to find out the return type of the object:

```
if (n instanceof Double) Double d = (Double)n;
```

But in practice, you don't usually care about the return type. The `doubleValue` method is defined for the `Number` class, and it returns the floating-point equivalent of the number object, whether it is a `Long` or a `Double`. That is, you can use the following code:

```
x = formatter.parse(s.trim()).doubleValue();
```

Using the `NumberFormat` has one advantage: the string can contain group separators for thousands such as `"12,301.4"`.

The API notes show some of the more important methods of the `Integer` class. The other number classes implement corresponding methods.

java.lang.Integer

- `int intValue()`
  returns the value of this `Integer` object as an `int` (overrides the `intValue` method in the Number class).
- `static String toString(int i)`
  returns a new `String` object representing the specified integer in base 10.
- `static String toString(int i, int radix)`
  lets you return a representation of the number `i` in the base specified by the `radix` parameter.
- `static int parseInt(String s)`
  returns the integer's value, assuming the specified `String` represents an integer in base 10.
- `static int parseInt(String s, int radix)`
  returns the integer's value, assuming the specified `String` represents an integer in the base specified by the `radix` parameter.
- `static Integer valueOf(String s)`
  returns a new `Integer` object initialized to the integer's value, assuming the specified `String` represents an integer in base 10.
- `static Integer valueOf(String s, int radix)`
  returns a new `Integer` object initialized to the integer's value, assuming the specified `String` represents an integer in the base specified by the `radix` parameter.

java.text.NumberFormat

- `Number parse(String s)`
  returns the numeric value, assuming the specified `String` represents a number.

The `Class` **Class**

While your program is running, the Java runtime system always maintains what is called runtime type identification on all objects. This information keeps track of the class to which each object belongs. Runtime type information is used by the virtual machine to select the correct methods to execute.

However, you can also access this information by working with a special Java class. The class that holds this information is called, somewhat confusingly, `Class`. The `getClass()` method in the `Object` class returns an instance of `Class` type.

```
Employee e;
. . .
Class cl = e.getClass();
```

Just like an `Employee` object describes the properties of a particular employee, a `Class` object describes the properties of a particular class. Probably the most commonly used method of `Class` is `getName`. This returns the name of the class. For example, the statement

```
System.out.println(e.getClass().getName() + " " + e.getName());
```

prints

```
Employee Harry Hacker
```

if `e` is an employee, or

```
Manager Harry Hacker
```

if `e` is a manager.

You can also obtain a `Class` object corresponding to a string by using the static `forName` method.

```
String className = "Manager";
Class cl = Class.forName(className);
```

You would use this method if the class name is stored in a string that varies at run time. This works if `className` is the name of a class or interface. Otherwise, the `forName` method throws a *checked exception*. See the sidebar on exceptions to see how you need to supply an *exception handler* whenever you use this method.

TIP: At startup, the class containing your `main` method is loaded. It loads all classes that it needs. Each of those loaded classes loads the classes that they need, and so on. That can take a long time for a big application, frustrating the user. You can give users of your program the illusion of a faster start, with the following trick. Make sure that the class containing the `main` method does not explicitly refer to other classes. First display a splash screen. Then manually force the loading of other classes by calling `Class.forName`.

A third method for obtaining an object of type `Class` is a convenient shorthand. If `T` is any Java type, then `T.class` is the matching class object. For example:

```
Class cl1 = Manager.class;
Class cl2 = int.class;
Class cl3 = Double[].class;
```

Note that a `Class` object really describes a *type*, which may or may not be a class. For example, `int` is not a class, but `int.class` is nevertheless an object of type `Class`.

NOTE: For historical reasons, the `getName` method returns somewhat strange names for array types:

```
System.out.println(Double[].class.getName());
   // prints [Ljava.lang.Double;
System.out.println(int[].class.getName());
   // prints [I
```

Catching Exceptions

We will cover exception handling fully in Chapter 11, but in the meantime you will occasionally encounter methods that threaten to throw exceptions.

When an error occurs at run time, a program can "throw an exception." Throwing an exception is more flexible than terminating the program because you can provide a *handler* that "catches" the exception and deals with it.

If you don't provide a handler, the program still terminates and prints a message to the console, giving the type of the exception. You may already have seen exception reports when you accidentally used a `null` reference or overstepped the bounds of an array.

There are two kinds of exceptions: *unchecked* exceptions and *checked* exceptions. With checked exceptions, the compiler checks that you provide a handler. However, many common exceptions, such as accessing a `null` reference, are unchecked. The compiler does not check whether you provide a handler for these errors—after all, you should spend your mental energy on avoiding these mistakes rather than coding handlers for them.

But not all errors are avoidable. If an exception can occur despite your best efforts, then the compiler insists that you provide a handler. The `Class.forName` method is an example of a method that throws a checked exception. In Chapter 11, you will see several exception handling strategies. For now, we'll just show you the simplest handler implementation.

Place one or more methods that might throw checked exceptions inside a `try` block. Then provide the handler code in the `catch` clause.

```
try
{
    statements that might throw exceptions
}
catch(Exception e)
{
    handler action
}
```

Here is an example:

```
try
{   String name = . . .; // get class name
    Class cl = Class.forName(name); // might throw exception
    . . . // do something with cl
}
catch(Exception e)
{
    e.printStackTrace();
}
```

If the class name doesn't exist, the remainder of the code in the `try` block is skipped, and the program enters the `catch` clause. (Here, we print a stack trace by using the `print-StackTrace` method of the `Throwable` class. `Throwable` is the superclass of the `Exception` class.) If none of the methods in the `try` block throw an exception, then the handler code in the `catch` clause is skipped.

You only need to supply an exception handler for checked exceptions. It is easy to find out which methods throw checked exceptions—the compiler will complain whenever you call a method that threatens to throw a checked exception and you don't supply a handler.

The virtual machine manages a unique `Class` object for each type. Therefore, you can use the `==` operator to compare class objects, for example:

```
if (e.getClass() == Employee.class) . . .
```

Another example of a useful method is one that lets you create an instance of a class on the fly. This method is called, naturally enough, `newInstance()`. For example,

```
e.getClass().newInstance();
```

creates a new instance of the same class type as `e`. The `newInstance` method calls the default constructor (the one that takes no parameters) to initialize the newly created object.

Using a combination of `forName` and `newInstance` lets you create an object from a class name stored in a string.

```
String s = "Manager";
Object m = Class.forName(s).newInstance();
```

NOTE: If you need to provide parameters for the constructor of a class you want to create by name in this manner, then you can't use statements like the above. Instead, you must use the `newInstance` method in the `Constructor` class. (This is one of several classes in the `java.lang.reflect` package. We will discuss reflection in the next section.)

C++ NOTE: The `newInstance` method corresponds to the idiom of a *virtual constructor* in C++. However, virtual constructors in C++ are not a language feature but just an idiom that needs to be supported by a specialized library. The `Class` class is similar to the `type_info` class in C++, and the `getClass` method is equivalent to the `typeid` operator. The Java `Class` is quite a bit more versatile than `type_info`, though. The C++ `type_info` can only reveal a string with the name of the type, not create new objects of that type.

`java.lang.Class`

- `static Class forName(String className)`
  returns the `Class` object representing the class with name `className`.

- `Object newInstance()`
  returns a new instance of this class.

`java.lang.reflect.Constructor`

- `Object newInstance(Object[] args)`
  constructs a new instance of the constructor's declaring class.

  Parameters: args the parameters supplied to the constructor. See the section on reflection for more information on how to supply parameters.

java.lang.Throwable

* void printStackTrace()

  prints the Throwable object and the stack trace to the standard error stream.

Reflection

The class Class gives you a very rich and elaborate toolset to write programs that manipulate Java code dynamically. This feature is heavily used in *JavaBeans*, the component architecture for Java (see Volume 2 for more on JavaBeans). Using reflection, Java is able to support tools like the ones users of Visual Basic have grown accustomed to. In particular, when new classes are added at design or run time, rapid application development tools that are JavaBeans enabled need to be able to inquire about the capabilities of the classes that were added. (This is equivalent to the process that occurs when you add controls in Visual Basic to the toolbox.)

A program that can analyze the capabilities of classes is called *reflective*. The package that brings this functionality to Java is therefore called, naturally enough, java.lang.reflect. The reflection mechanism is extremely powerful. As the next four sections show, you can use it to:

* Analyze the capabilities of classes at run time
* Inspect objects at run time, for example, to write a single toString method that works for *all* classes
* Implement generic array manipulation code
* Take advantage of Method objects that work just like function pointers in languages such as C++

Reflection is a powerful and complex mechanism; however, it is of interest mainly to tool builders, not application programmers. If you are interested in programming applications rather than tools for other Java programmers, you can safely skip the remainder of this chapter and return to it at a later time.

Using Reflection to Analyze the Capabilities of Classes

Here is a brief overview of the most important parts of the reflection mechanism for letting you examine the structure of a class.

The three classes Field, Method, and Constructor in the java.lang.reflect package describe the fields, methods, and constructors of a class, respectively. All three classes have a method called getName that returns the name of the item. The Field class has a method getType that returns an object, again of type Class, that describes the field type. The Method and Constructor classes have methods to report the return type and the types of the parameters used for these methods. All three of these classes also have a method called `getModifiers` that returns an integer, with various bits turned on and off, that describe the modifiers used, such as `public` and `static`. You can then use the static methods in the `Modifier` class in the `java.lang.reflect` package to analyze the integer that `getModifiers` returns. For example, there are methods like `isPublic`, `isPrivate`, or `isFinal` in the `Modifier` class that you could use to tell whether a method or constructor was `public`, `private`, or `final`. All you have to do is have the appropriate method in the `Modifier` class work on the integer that `getModifiers` returns. You can also use the `Modifier.toString` method to print the modifiers.

The `getFields`, `getMethods`, and `getConstructors` methods of the `Class` class return arrays of the *public* fields, operations, and constructors that the class supports. This includes public members of superclasses. The `getDeclaredFields`, `getDeclaredMethods`, and `getDeclaredConstructors` methods of the `Class` class return arrays consisting of all fields, operations, and constructors that are declared in the class. This includes private and protected members, but not members of superclasses.

Example 5–5 shows you how to print out all information about a class. The program prompts you for the name of a class and then writes out the signatures of all methods and constructors as well as the names of all data fields of a class. For example, if you enter

```
java.lang.Double
```

then the program prints:

```
class java.lang.Double extends java.lang.Number
{
    public java.lang.Double(java.lang.String);
    public java.lang.Double(double);

    public int hashCode();
    public int compareTo(java.lang.Object);
    public int compareTo(java.lang.Double);
    public boolean equals(java.lang.Object);
    public java.lang.String toString();
    public static java.lang.String toString(double);
    public static java.lang.Double valueOf(java.lang.String);
    public static boolean isNaN(double);
    public boolean isNaN();
    public static boolean isInfinite(double);
    public boolean isInfinite();
    public byte byteValue();
    public short shortValue();
    public int intValue();
    public long longValue();
    public float floatValue();
    public double doubleValue();
    public static double parseDouble(java.lang.String);
```

```
        public static native long doubleToLongBits(double);
        public static native long doubleToRawLongBits(double);
        public static native double longBitsToDouble(long);

        public static final double POSITIVE_INFINITY;
        public static final double NEGATIVE_INFINITY;
        public static final double NaN;
        public static final double MAX_VALUE;
        public static final double MIN_VALUE;
        public static final java.lang.Class TYPE;
        private double value;
        private static final long serialVersionUID;
   }
```

What is remarkable about this program is that it can analyze any class that the
Java interpreter can load, not just the classes that were available when the program was compiled. We will use this program in the next chapter to peek inside
the inner classes that the Java compiler generates automatically.

Example 5–5: ReflectionTest.java

```java
1. import java.lang.reflect.*;
2. import javax.swing.*;
3.
4. public class ReflectionTest
5. {
6.    public static void main(String[] args)
7.    {
8.       // read class name from command line args or user input
9.       String name;
10.      if (args.length > 0)
11.         name = args[0];
12.      else
13.         name = JOptionPane.showInputDialog
14.            ("Class name (e.g. java.util.Date): ");
15.
16.      try
17.      {
18.         // print class name and superclass name (if != Object)
19.         Class cl = Class.forName(name);
20.         Class supercl = cl.getSuperclass();
21.         System.out.print("class " + name);
22.         if (supercl != null && supercl != Object.class)
23.            System.out.print(" extends " + supercl.getName());
24.
25.         System.out.print("\n{\n");
26.         printConstructors(cl);
27.         System.out.println();
28.         printMethods(cl);
29.         System.out.println();
30.         printFields(cl);
31.         System.out.println("}");
```

```
32.          }
33.       catch(ClassNotFoundException e) { e.printStackTrace(); }
34.       System.exit(0);
35.    }
36.
37.    /**
38.       Prints all constructors of a class
39.       @param cl a class
40.     */
41.    public static void printConstructors(Class cl)
42.    {
43.       Constructor[] constructors = cl.getDeclaredConstructors();
44.
45.       for (int i = 0; i < constructors.length; i++)
46.       {
47.          Constructor c = constructors[i];
48.          String name = c.getName();
49.          System.out.print(Modifier.toString(c.getModifiers()));
50.          System.out.print("   " + name + "(");
51.
52.          // print parameter types
53.          Class[] paramTypes = c.getParameterTypes();
54.          for (int j = 0; j < paramTypes.length; j++)
55.          {
56.             if (j > 0) System.out.print(", ");
57.             System.out.print(paramTypes[j].getName());
58.          }
59.          System.out.println(");");
60.       }
61.    }
62.
63.    /**
64.       Prints all methods of a class
65.       @param cl a class
66.     */
67.    public static void printMethods(Class cl)
68.    {
69.       Method[] methods = cl.getDeclaredMethods();
70.
71.       for (int i = 0; i < methods.length; i++)
72.       {
73.          Method m = methods[i];
74.          Class retType = m.getReturnType();
75.          String name = m.getName();
76.
77.          // print modifiers, return type and method name
78.          System.out.print(Modifier.toString(m.getModifiers()));
79.          System.out.print("   " + retType.getName() + " " + name
80.             + "(");
81.
82.          // print parameter types
83.          Class[] paramTypes = m.getParameterTypes();
84.          for (int j = 0; j < paramTypes.length; j++)
```

```
85.            {
86.               if (j > 0) System.out.print(", ");
87.               System.out.print(paramTypes[j].getName());
88.            }
89.            System.out.println(");");
90.         }
91.   }
92.
93.   /**
94.      Prints all fields of a class
95.      @param cl a class
96.   */
97.   public static void printFields(Class cl)
98.   {
99.      Field[] fields = cl.getDeclaredFields();
100.
101.      for (int i = 0; i < fields.length; i++)
102.      {
103.         Field f = fields[i];
104.         Class type = f.getType();
105.         String name = f.getName();
106.         System.out.print(Modifier.toString(f.getModifiers()));
107.         System.out.println("   " + type.getName() + " " + name
108.            + ";");
109.      }
110.   }
111. }
```

java.lang.Class

- `Field[] getFields()`
- `Field[] getDeclaredFields()`

  The `getFields` method returns an array containing `Field` objects for the public fields. The `getDeclaredField` method returns an array of `Field` objects for all fields. The methods return an array of length 0 if there are no such fields, or if the `Class` object represents a primitive or array type.

- `Method[] getMethods()`
- `Method[] getDeclaredMethods()`

  return an array containing `Method` objects that give you all the public methods (for `getMethods`) or all methods (for `getDeclaredMethods`) of the class or interface. This includes those inherited from classes or interfaces above it in the inheritance chain.

- `Constructor[] getConstructors()`
- `Constructor[] getDeclaredConstructors()`

  return an array containing `Constructor` objects that give you all the public constructors (for `getConstructors`) or all constructors (for `getDeclaredConstructors`) of the class represented by this Class object.

java.lang.reflect.Field

java.lang.reflect.Method

java.lang.reflect.Constructor

- `Class getDeclaringClass()`
  returns the `Class` object for the class that defines this constructor, method, or field.
- `Class[] getExceptionTypes()` (in `Constructor` and `Method` classes)
  returns an array of `Class` objects that represent the types of the exceptions thrown by the method.
- `int getModifiers()`
  returns an integer that describes the modifiers of this constructor, method, or field. Use the methods in the `Modifier` class to analyze the return value.
- `String getName()`
  returns a string that is the name of the constructor, method, or field.
- `Class[] getParameterTypes()` (in `Constructor` and `Method` classes)
  returns an array of `Class` objects that represent the types of the parameters.

java.lang.reflect.Modifier

- `static String toString(int modifiers)`
  returns a string with the modifiers that correspond to the bits set in `modifiers`.

Using Reflection to Analyze Objects at Run Time

In the preceding section, we saw how we can find out the *names* and *types* of the data fields of any object:

- Get the corresponding `Class` object.
- Call `getDeclaredFields` on the `Class` object.

In this section, we go one step further and actually look at the *contents* of the data fields. Of course, it is easy to look at the contents of a specific field of an object whose name and type are known when you write a program. But reflection lets you look at fields of objects that were not known at compile time.

The key method to achieve this is the `get` method in the `Field` class. If `f` is an object of type `Field` (for example, one obtained from `getDeclaredFields`) and `obj` is an object of the class of which `f` is a field, then `f.get(obj)` returns an object whose value is the current value of the field of obj. This is all a bit abstract, so let's run through an example.

```
Employee harry = new Employee("Harry Hacker", 35000,
    10, 1, 1989);
Class cl = harry.getClass();
    // the class object representing Employee
Field f = cl.getField("name");
    // the name field of the Employee class
Object v = f.get(harry);
    // the value of the name field of the harry object
    // i.e. the String object "Harry Hacker"
```

Actually, there is a problem with this code. Since the name field is a private field, the get method will throw an IllegalAccessException. You can only use the get method to get the values of accessible fields. The security mechanism of Java lets you find out what fields any object has, but it won't let you read the values of those fields unless you have access permission.

The default behavior of the reflection mechanism is to respect Java access control. However, if a Java program is not controlled by a security manager that disallows it, it is possible to override access control. To do this, invoke the setAccessible method on a Field, Method, or Constructor object, for example:

```
f.setAccessible(true);
    // now OK to call f.get(harry);
```

The setAccessible method is a method of the AccessibleObject class, the common superclass of the Field, Method, and Constructor. This feature is provided for debuggers, persistent storage, and similar mechanisms. We will use it for a generic toString method later in this section.

There is another issue with the get method that we need to deal with. The name field is a String, and so it is not a problem to return the value as an Object. But suppose we want to look at the salary field. That is a double, and in Java, number types are not objects. To handle this, you can either use the getDouble method of the Field class, or you can call get, where the reflection mechanism automatically wraps the field value into the appropriate wrapper class, in this case, Double.

Of course, you can also set the values that you can get. The call f.set(obj, value) sets the field represented by f of the object obj to the new value.

Example 5–6 shows how to write a generic toString method that works for *any* class. It uses getDeclaredFields to obtain all data fields. It then uses the setAccessible convenience method to make all fields accessible. For each field, it obtains the name and the value. Each value is turned into a string by invoking *its* toString method. The toString method examines all superclass fields until it reaches the Object class.

```
class ObjectAnalyzer
{
  public static String toString(Object obj)
    {
      Class cl = obj.getClass();
      String r = cl.getName();

      // inspect the fields of this class and all superclasses
      do
      {
        r += "[";
        Field[] fields = cl.getDeclaredFields();
        AccessibleObject.setAccessible(fields, true);

        // get the names and values of all fields
        for (int i = 0; i < fields.length; i++)
        {
          Field f = fields[i];
          r += f.getName() + "=";
          try
          {
            Object val = f.get(obj);
            r += val.toString();
          }
          catch (Exception e) { e.printStackTrace(); }
          if (i < fields.length - 1)
            r += ",";
        }
        r += "]";
        cl = cl.getSuperclass();
      }
      while (cl != Object.class);

      return r;
    }
    . . .
}
```

You can use this `toString` method to peek inside any object. For example, here is what you get when you look inside the `System.out` object:

```
java.io.PrintStream[autoFlush=true,trouble=false,
textOut=java.io.BufferedWriter@8786b,
charOut=java.io.OutputStreamWriter@19c082,
closing=false][out=java.io.BufferedOutputStream@2dd2dd][]
```

In Example 5–6, the generic `toString` method is used to implement the `toString` of the `Employee` class:

```
public String toString()
{
```

```
      return ObjectAnalyzer.toString(this);
   }
```

This is a hassle-free method for supplying a `toString` method, and it is highly recommended, especially for debugging. The same recursive approach can also be used to define a generic `equals` method. See the code in the example program Example 5–6 for details.

Example 5–6: ObjectAnalyzerTest.java

```
1. import java.lang.reflect.*;
2. import java.util.*;
3.
4. public class ObjectAnalyzerTest
5. {
6.    public static void main(String[] args)
7.    {
8.       // test toString method of Employee
9.       Employee harry  = new Employee("Harry Hacker", 35000,
10.          1996, 12, 1);
11.       System.out.println("harry=" + harry);
12.
13.       // test equals method of Employee
14.       Employee coder  = new Employee("Harry Hacker", 35000,
15.          1996, 12, 1);
16.       System.out.println(
17.          "Before raise, harry.equals(coder) returns "
18.          + harry.equals(coder));
19.       harry.raiseSalary(5);
20.       System.out.println(
21.          "After raise, harry.equals(coder) returns "
22.          + harry.equals(coder));
23.
24.       Manager carl = new Manager("Carl Cracker", 80000,
25.          1987, 12, 15);
26.       Manager boss = new Manager("Carl Cracker", 80000,
27.          1987, 12, 15);
28.       boss.setBonus(5000);
29.       System.out.println("boss=" + boss);
30.       System.out.println(
31.          "carl.equals(boss) returns " + carl.equals(boss));
32.    }
33. }
34.
35. class ObjectAnalyzer
36. {
37.    /**
38.       Converts an object to a string representation that lists
39.       all fields.
40.       @param obj an object
41.       @return a string with the object's class name and all
42.       field names and values
43.    */
```

```
44.   public static String toString(Object obj)
45.   {
46.      Class cl = obj.getClass();
47.      String r = cl.getName();
48.
49.      // inspect the fields of this class and all superclasses
50.      do
51.      {
52.         r += "[";
53.         Field[] fields = cl.getDeclaredFields();
54.         AccessibleObject.setAccessible(fields, true);
55.
56.         // get the names and values of all fields
57.         for (int i = 0; i < fields.length; i++)
58.         {
59.            Field f = fields[i];
60.            r += f.getName() + "=";
61.            try
62.            {
63.               Object val = f.get(obj);
64.               r += val.toString();
65.            }
66.            catch (Exception e) { e.printStackTrace(); }
67.            if (i < fields.length - 1)
68.               r += ",";
69.         }
70.         r += "]";
71.         cl = cl.getSuperclass();
72.      }
73.      while (cl != Object.class);
74.
75.      return r;
76.   }
77.
78.   /**
79.      Tests whether two objects are equal by checking if all
80.      field values are equal
81.      @param a an object
82.      @param b another object
83.      @return true if a and b are equal
84.   */
85.   public static boolean equals(Object a, Object b)
86.   {
87.      if (a == b) return true;
88.      if (a == null || b == null) return false;
89.      Class cl = a.getClass();
90.      if (cl != b.getClass()) return false;
91.
92.      // inspect the fields of this class and all superclasses
93.      do
94.      {
95.         Field[] fields = cl.getDeclaredFields();
96.         AccessibleObject.setAccessible(fields, true);
97.         for (int i = 0; i < fields.length; i++)
```

```
98.              {
99.                 Field f = fields[i];
100.                // if field values don't match, objects aren't equal
101.                try
102.                {
103.                   if (!f.get(a).equals(f.get(b)))
104.                      return false;
105.                }
106.                catch (Exception e) { e.printStackTrace(); }
107.             }
108.          cl = cl.getSuperclass();
109.          }
110.       while (cl != Object.class);
111.
112.       return true;
113.    }
114. }
115.
116. class Employee
117. {
118.    public Employee(String n, double s,
119.       int year, int month, int day)
120.    {
121.       name = n;
122.       salary = s;
123.       GregorianCalendar calendar
124.          = new GregorianCalendar(year, month - 1, day);
125.          // GregorianCalendar uses 0 for January
126.       hireDay = calendar.getTime();
127.    }
128.
129.    public String getName()
130.    {
131.       return name;
132.    }
133.
134.    public double getSalary()
135.    {
136.       return salary;
137.    }
138.
139.    public Date getHireDay()
140.    {
141.       return hireDay;
142.    }
143.
144.    public void raiseSalary(double byPercent)
145.    {
146.       double raise = salary * byPercent / 100;
147.       salary += raise;
148.    }
149.
150.    public String toString()
151.    {
```

```
152.       return ObjectAnalyzer.toString(this);
153.    }
154.
155.    public boolean equals(Object b)
156.    {
157.       return ObjectAnalyzer.equals(this, b);
158.    }
159.
160.    private String name;
161.    private double salary;
162.    private Date hireDay;
163. }
164.
165. class Manager extends Employee
166. {
167.    public Manager(String n, double s,
168.       int year, int month, int day)
169.    {
170.       super(n, s, year, month, day);
171.       bonus = 0;
172.    }
173.
174.    public double getSalary()
175.    {
176.       double baseSalary = super.getSalary();
177.       return baseSalary + bonus;
178.    }
179.
180.    public void setBonus(double b)
181.    {
182.       bonus = b;
183.    }
184.
185.    private double bonus;
186. }
```

java.lang.reflect.AccessibleObject

- `void setAccessible(boolean flag)`
  sets the accessibility flag for this reflection object. A value of `true` indicates that Java language access checking is suppressed, and that the private properties of the object can be queried and set.

- `boolean isAccessible()`
  gets the value of the accessibility flag for this reflection object.

- `static void setAccessible(AccessibleObject[] array, boolean flag)`
  is a convenience method to set the accessibility flag for an array of objects.

Using Reflection to Write Generic Array Code

The `Array` class in the `java.lang.reflect` package allows you to create arrays dynamically. For example, when you use this feature with the `arrayCopy` method from Chapter 3, you can dynamically expand an existing array while preserving the current contents.

The problem we want to solve is pretty typical. Suppose you have an array of some type that is full and you want to grow it. And suppose you are sick of writing the grow-and-copy code by hand. You want to write a generic method to grow an array.

```
Employee[] a = new Employee[100];
. . .
// array is full
a = (Employee[])arrayGrow(a);
```

How can we write such a generic method? It helps that an `Employee[]` array can be converted to an `Object[]` array. That sounds promising. Here is a first attempt to write a generic method. We simply grow the array by 10% + 10 elements (since the 10% growth is not substantial enough for small arrays).

```
static Object[] arrayGrow(Object[] a) // not useful
{
   int newLength = a.length * 11 / 10 + 10;
   Object[] newArray = new Object[newLength];
   System.arraycopy(a, 0, newArray, 0, a.length);
   return newArray;
}
```

However, there is a problem with actually *using* the resulting array. The type of array that this code returns is an array of *objects* (`Object[]`) because we created the array using the line of code:

```
new Object[newLength]
```

An array of objects *cannot* be cast to an array of employees (`Employee[]`). Java would generate a `ClassCast` exception at run time. The point is, as we mentioned earlier, that a Java array remembers the type of its entries, that is, the element type used in the `new` expression that created it. It is legal to cast an `Employee[]` temporarily to an `Object[]` array and then cast it back, but an array that started its life as an `Object[]` array can never be cast into an `Employee[]` array. To write this kind of generic array code, we need to be able to make a new array of the *same* type as the original array. For this, we need the methods of the `Array` class in the `java.lang.reflect` package. The key is the static `newInstance` method of the `Array` class that constructs a new array. You must supply the type for the entries and the desired length as parameters to this method.

```
Object newArray = Array.newInstance(componentType, newLength);
```

To actually carry this out, we need to get the length and component type of the new array.

The length is obtained by calling `Array.getLength(a)`. The static `getLength` method of the `Array` class returns the length of any array. To get the component type of the new array:

1.   First, get the class object of `a`.

2.   Confirm that it is indeed an array.

3.   Use the `getComponentType` method of the `Class` class (which is defined only for class objects that represent arrays) to find the right type for the array.

Why is `getLength` a method of `Array` but `getComponentType` a method of `Class`? We don't know—the distribution of the reflection methods seems a bit ad hoc at times.

Here's the code:

```
static Object arrayGrow(Object a) // useful
{
    Class cl = a.getClass();
    if (!cl.isArray()) return null;
    Class componentType = cl.getComponentType();
    int length = Array.getLength(a);
    int newLength = length * 11 / 10 + 10;
    Object newArray = Array.newInstance(componentType,
        newLength);
    System.arraycopy(a, 0, newArray, 0, length);
    return newArray;
}
```

Note that this `arrayGrow` method can be used to grow arrays of any type, not just arrays of objects.

```
int[] ia = { 1, 2, 3, 4 };
ia = (int[])arrayGrow(ia);
```

To make this possible, the parameter of `arrayGrow` is declared to be of type `Object`, *not an array of objects* (`Object[]`). The integer array type `int[]` can be converted to an `Object`, but not to an array of objects!

Example 5–7 shows both array grow methods in action. Note that the cast of the return value of `badArrayGrow` will throw an exception.

Example 5–7: ArrayGrowTest.java

```
1. import java.lang.reflect.*;
2. import java.util.*;
3.
4. public class ArrayGrowTest
5. {
```

```
6.    public static void main(String[] args)
7.    {
8.       int[] a = { 1, 2, 3 };
9.       a = (int[])goodArrayGrow(a);
10.      arrayPrint(a);
11.
12.      String[] b = { "Tom", "Dick", "Harry" };
13.      b = (String[])goodArrayGrow(b);
14.      arrayPrint(b);
15.
16.      System.out.println
17.         ("The following call will generate an exception.");
18.      b = (String[])badArrayGrow(b);
19.   }
20.
21.   /**
22.      This method attempts to grow an array by allocating a
23.      new array and copying all elements.
24.      @param a the array to grow
25.      @return a larger array that contains all elements of a.
26.      However, the returned array has type Object[], not
27.      the same type as a
28.   */
29.   static Object[] badArrayGrow(Object[] a)
30.   {
31.      int newLength = a.length * 11 / 10 + 10;
32.      Object[] newArray = new Object[newLength];
33.      System.arraycopy(a, 0, newArray, 0, a.length);
34.      return newArray;
35.   }
36.
37.   /**
38.      This method grows an array by allocating a
39.      new array of the same type and copying all elements.
40.      @param a the array to grow. This can be an object array
41.      or a fundamental type array
42.      @return a larger array that contains all elements of a.
43.
44.   */
45.   static Object goodArrayGrow(Object a)
46.   {
47.      Class cl = a.getClass();
48.      if (!cl.isArray()) return null;
49.      Class componentType = cl.getComponentType();
50.      int length = Array.getLength(a);
51.      int newLength = length * 11 / 10 + 10;
52.
53.      Object newArray = Array.newInstance(componentType,
54.         newLength);
55.      System.arraycopy(a, 0, newArray, 0, length);
56.      return newArray;
57.   }
58.
59.   /**
```

```
60.        A convenience method to print all elements in an array
61.        @param a the array to print. can be an object array
62.        or a fundamental type array
63.     */
64.     static void arrayPrint(Object a)
65.     {
66.        Class cl = a.getClass();
67.        if (!cl.isArray()) return;
68.        Class componentType = cl.getComponentType();
69.        int length = Array.getLength(a);
70.        System.out.print(componentType.getName()
71.           + "[" + length + "] = { ");
72.        for (int i = 0; i < Array.getLength(a); i++)
73.           System.out.print(Array.get(a, i)+ " ");
74.        System.out.println("}");
75.     }
76. }
```

Method Pointers!

On the surface, Java does not have method pointers—ways of giving the location of a method to another method so that the second method can invoke it later. In fact, the designers of Java have said that method pointers are dangerous and error-prone and that Java *interfaces* (discussed in the next chapter) are a superior solution. However, it turns out that Java now does have method pointers, as a (perhaps accidental) byproduct of the reflection package.

NOTE: Among the nonstandard language extensions that Microsoft added to its Java derivative J++ (and its successor, C#) is another method pointer type that is different from the Method class that we discuss in this section. However, as you will see in chapter 6, inner classes are a more useful and general mechanism.

To see method pointers at work, recall that you can inspect a field of an object with the get method of the Field class. Similarly, the Method class has an invoke method that lets you call the method that is wrapped in the current Method object. The signature for the invoke method is:

```
Object invoke(Object obj, Object[] args)
```

The first parameter is the implicit parameter, and the array of objects provides the explicit parameters. For a static method, the first parameter is ignored—you can set it to null. If the method has no explicit parameters, you can pass null or an array of length 0 for the args parameter. For example, if m1 represents the getName method of the Employee class, the following code shows how you can call it:

```
String n = (String)m1.invoke(harry, null);
```

As with the get and set methods of the Field type, there's a problem if the parameter or return type is not a class but a basic type. You must wrap any of the basic types into their corresponding wrappers before inserting them into the `args` array. Conversely, the `invoke` method will return the wrapped type and not the basic type. For example, suppose that `m2` represents the `raiseSalary` method of the `Employee` class. Then, you need to wrap the `double` parameter into a `Double` object.

```
Object[] args = { new Double(5.5) };
m2.invoke(harry, args);
```

How do you obtain a `Method` object? You can, of course, call `getDeclaredMethods` and search through the returned array of `Method` objects until you find the method that you want. Or, you can call the `getMethod` method of the `Class` class. This is similar to the `getField` method that takes a string with the field name and returns a `Field` object. However, there may be several methods with the same name, so you need to be careful that you get the right one. For that reason, you must also supply an array that gives the correct parameter types. For example, here is how you can get method pointers to the `getName` and `raiseSalary` methods of the `Employee` class.

```
Method m1 = Employee.class.getMethod("getName", null);
Method m2 = Employee.class.getMethod("raiseSalary",
    new Class[] { double.class } );
```

The second parameter of the `getMethod` method is an array of `Class` objects. Since the `raiseSalary` method has one parameter of type `double`, we must supply an array with a single element, `double.class`. It is usually easiest to make that array on the fly, as we did in the example above. The expression

```
new Class[] { double.class }
```

denotes an array of `Class` objects, filled with one element, namely, the class object `double.class`.

Now that you have seen the syntax of `Method` objects, let's put them to work. Example 5–8 is a program that prints a table of values for a mathematical function such as `Math.sqrt` or `Math.sin`. The printout looks like this:

```
public static native double java.lang.Math.sqrt(double)
       1.0000 |      1.0000
       2.0000 |      1.4142
       3.0000 |      1.7321
       4.0000 |      2.0000
       5.0000 |      2.2361
       6.0000 |      2.4495
       7.0000 |      2.6458
       8.0000 |      2.8284
       9.0000 |      3.0000
      10.0000 |      3.1623
```

The code for printing a table is, of course, independent of the actual function that is being tabulated.

```
double dx = (to - from) / (n - 1);
for (double x = from; x <= to; x += dx)
{
   double y = f(x);
      // where f is the function to be tabulated
      // not the actual syntax--see below
   System.out.println(x + " | " + y);
}
```

We want to write a generic `printTable` method that can tabulate any function. We will pass the function as a parameter of type `Method`.

```
static void printTable(double from, double to, int n, Method f)
```

Of course, `f` is an object and not a function, so we cannot simply write `f(x)` to evaluate it. Instead, we must supply `x` in the parameter array (suitably wrapped as a `Double`), use the `invoke` method, and unwrap the return value.

```
Object[] args = { new Double(x) };
Double d = (Double)f.invoke(null, args);
double y = d.doubleValue();
```

The first parameter of `invoke` is `null` because we are calling a static method.

Here is a sample call to `printTable` that tabulates the square root function.

```
printTable(1, 10, 10,
   java.lang.Math.class.getMethod("sqrt",
   new Class[] { double.class }));
```

The hardest part is to get the method object. Here, we get the method of the `java.lang.Math` class that has the name `sqrt` and whose parameter list contains just one type, `double`.

Example 5–8 shows the complete code of the `printTable` method and a couple of test runs.

Example 5–8: MethodPointerTest.java

```
1. import java.lang.reflect.*;
2. import java.text.*;
3.
4. public class MethodPointerTest
5. {
6.    public static void main(String[] args) throws Exception
7.    {
8.       // get method pointers to the square and sqrt methods
9.       Method square = MethodPointerTest.class.getMethod("square",
10.         new Class[] { double.class });
11.       Method sqrt = java.lang.Math.class.getMethod("sqrt",
12.         new Class[] { double.class });
13.
```

```
14.        // print tables of x- and y-values
15.
16.        printTable(1, 10, 10, square);
17.        printTable(1, 10, 10, sqrt);
18.    }
19.
20.    /**
21.       Returns the square of a number
22.       @param x a number
23.       @return x squared
24.    */
25.    public static double square(double x)
26.    {
27.       return x * x;
28.    }
29.
30.    /**
31.       Prints a table with x- and y-values for a method
32.       @param from the lower bound for the x-values
33.       @param to the upper bound for the x-values
34.       @param n the number of rows in the table
35.       @param f a method with a double parameter and double
36.          return value
37.    */
38.    public static void printTable(double from, double to,
39.       int n, Method f)
40.    {
41.       // print out the method as table header
42.       System.out.println(f);
43.
44.       // construct formatter to print with 4 digits precision
45.
46.       NumberFormat formatter = NumberFormat.getNumberInstance();
47.       formatter.setMinimumFractionDigits(4);
48.       formatter.setMaximumFractionDigits(4);
49.       double dx = (to - from) / (n - 1);
50.
51.       for (double x = from; x <= to; x += dx)
52.       {
53.          // print x-value
54.          String output = formatter.format(x);
55.          // pad with spaces to field width of 10
56.          for (int i = 10 - output.length(); i > 0; i--)
57.             System.out.print(' ');
58.          System.out.print(output + " |");
59.
60.          try
61.          {
62.             // invoke method and print y-value
63.             Object[] args = { new Double(x) };
64.             Double d = (Double)f.invoke(null, args);
```

```
65.            double y = d.doubleValue();
66.
67.            output = formatter.format(y);
68.            // pad with spaces to field width of 10
69.            for (int i = 10 - output.length(); i > 0; i--)
70.                System.out.print(' ');
71.
72.            System.out.println(output);
73.         }
74.      catch (Exception e) {  e.printStackTrace(); }
75.      }
76.   }
77. }
```

As this example shows clearly, you can do anything with `Method` objects that you can do with function pointers in C. Just as in C, this style of programming is usually quite inconvenient and always error-prone. What happens if you invoke a method with the wrong parameters? The `invoke` method throws an exception.

Also, the parameters and return values of `invoke` are necessarily of type `Object`. That means you must cast back and forth a lot. As a result, the compiler is deprived of the chance to check your code. Therefore, errors surface only during testing, when they are more tedious to find and fix. Moreover, code that uses reflection to get at method pointers is significantly slower than simply calling methods directly.

For that reason, we suggest that you use `Method` objects in your own programs only when absolutely necessary. Using interfaces and inner classes (the subject of the next chapter) is almost always a better idea. In particular, we echo the developers of Java and suggest not using `Method` objects for callback functions. Using interfaces for the callbacks (see the next chapter as well) leads to code that runs faster and is a lot more maintainable.

Design Hints for Inheritance

We want to end this chapter with some hints for using inheritance that we have found useful.

1. *Place common operations and fields in the superclass.*

    This is why we put the name field into the `Person` class, rather than replicating it in `Employee` and `Student`.

2. *Don't use protected fields.*

    Some programmers think it is a good idea to define most instance fields as `protected`, "just in case," so that subclasses can access these fields if they need to. However, the `protected` mechanism doesn't give much protection, for two reasons. First, the set of subclasses is unbounded—anyone can form a subclass of your classes and then write code that directly accesses `protected` instance fields, thereby breaking encapsulation. And in the Java programming language, all classes in the same package have access to `protected` fields, whether or not they are subclasses.

However, `protected` methods can be useful to indicate methods that are not ready for general use and should be redefined in subclasses. The `clone` method is a good example.

3. *Use inheritance to model the "is–a" relationship.*

Inheritance is a handy code-saver, and sometimes people overuse it. For example, suppose we need a `Contractor` class. Contractors have names and hire dates, but they do not have salaries. Instead, they are paid by the hour, and they do not stay around long enough to get a raise. There is the temptation to derive `Contractor` from `Employee` and add an `hourlyWage` field.

```
class Contractor extends Employee
{  . . .
   private double hourlyWage;
}
```

This is *not* a good idea, however, because now each contractor object has both a salary and hourly wage field. It will cause you no end of grief when you implement methods for printing paychecks or tax forms. You will end up writing more code than you would have by not inheriting in the first place.

The contractor/employee relationship fails the "is–a" test. A contractor is not a special case of an employee.

4. *Don't use inheritance unless all inherited methods make sense.*

Suppose we want to write a `Holiday` class. Surely every holiday is a day, and days can be expressed as instances of the `GregorianCalendar` class, so we can use inheritance.

```
class Holiday extends GregorianCalendar { . . . }
```

Unfortunately, the set of holidays is not *closed* under the inherited operations. One of the public methods of `GregorianCalendar` is add. And add can turn holidays into nonholidays:

```
Holiday christmas;
christmas.add(GregorianCalendar.DAY, 12);
```

Therefore, inheritance is not appropriate in this example.

5. *Use polymorphism, not type information.*

Whenever you find code of the form

```
if (x is of type 1)
   action1(x);
```

```
else if (x is of type 2)
   action2(x);
```

think polymorphism.

Do `action1` and `action2` represent a common concept? If so, make the concept a method of a common superclass or interface of both types. Then, you can simply call

```
x.action();
```

and have the dynamic dispatch mechanism inherent in polymorphism launch the correct action.

Code using polymorphic methods or interface implementations is much easier to maintain and extend than code that uses multiple type tests.

6.   *Don't overuse reflection.*

The reflection mechanism lets you write programs with amazing generality, by detecting fields and methods at run time. This capability can be extremely useful for systems programming, but it is usually not appropriate in applications. Reflection is fragile—the compiler cannot help you find programming errors. Any errors are found at run time and result in exceptions.

Chapter 6

Interfaces and Inner Classes

▼ INTERFACES
▼ OBJECT CLONING
▼ INNER CLASSES
▼ PROXIES

You have now seen all the basic tools for object-oriented programming in Java. This chapter shows you two advanced techniques that are very commonly used. Despite their less obvious nature, you will need to master them to complete your Java tool chest.

The first, called an *interface*, is a way of describing *what* classes should do, without specifying *how* they should do it. A class can *implement* one or more interfaces. You can then use objects of these implementing classes anytime that conformance to the interface is required. After we cover interfaces, we take up cloning an object (or deep copying as it is sometimes called). A clone of an object is a new object that has the same state as the original but a different identity. In particular, you can modify the clone without affecting the original. Finally, we move on to the mechanism of *inner classes*. Inner classes are technically somewhat complex—they are defined inside other classes, and their methods can access the fields of the surrounding class. Inner classes are useful when you design collections of cooperating classes.

In particular, inner classes are important to write concise, professional-looking code to handle graphical user interface events.

This chapter concludes with a discussion of *proxies*, objects that implement arbitrary interfaces. A proxy is a very specialized construct that is useful for building system-level tools. You can safely skip that section on first reading.

Interfaces

In the Java programming language, an interface is not a class but a set of *requirements* for classes that want to conform to the interface.

Typically, the supplier of some service states: "If your class conforms to a particular interface, then I'll perform the service." Let's look at a concrete example. The `sort` method of the `Arrays` class promises to sort an array of objects, but under one condition: The objects must belong to classes that implement the `Comparable` interface.

Here is what the `Comparable` interface looks like:

```
public interface Comparable
{
    int compareTo(Object other);
}
```

This means that any class that implements the `Comparable` interface is required to have a `compareTo` method, and the method must take an `Object` parameter and return an integer.

All methods of an interface are automatically `public`. For that reason, it is not necessary to supply the keyword `public` when declaring a method in an interface.

Of course, there is an additional requirement that the interface cannot spell out: when calling `x.compareTo(y)`, the `compareTo` method must actually be able to compare two objects and return an indication whether x or y is larger. The method is supposed to return a negative number if x is smaller than y, zero if they are equal, and a positive number otherwise.

This particular interface has a single method. Some interfaces have more than one method. As you will see later, interfaces can also define constants. What is more important, however, is what interfaces *cannot* supply. Interfaces never have instance fields, and the methods are never implemented in the interface. Supplying instance fields and method implementations is the job of the classes that implement the interface. You can think of an interface as being similar to an abstract class with no instance fields. However, there are some differences between these two concepts—we will look at them later in some detail.

Now suppose we want to use the `sort` method of the `Arrays` class to sort an array of `Employee` objects. Then the `Employee` class must *implement* the `Comparable` interface.

To make a class implement an interface, you have to carry out two steps:

1. You declare that your class intends to implement the given interface.
2. You supply definitions for all methods in the interface.

To declare that a class implements an interface, use the `implements` keyword:

```
class Employee implements Comparable
```

Of course, now the `Employee` class needs to supply the `compareTo` method. Let's suppose that we want to compare employees by their salary. Here is a compareTo method that returns −1 if the first employee's salary is less than 0, 0 if they are equal, and 1 otherwise.

```
public int compareTo(Object otherObject)
{
    Employee other = (Employee)otherObject;
    if (salary < other.salary) return -1;
    if (salary > other.salary) return 1;
    return 0;
}
```

CAUTION: In the interface declaration, the `compareTo` method was not declared `public` because all methods in an *interface* are automatically public. However, when implementing the interface, you must declare the method as `public`. Otherwise, the compiler assumes that the method has package visibility—the default for a *class*. Then the compiler complains that you try to supply a weaker access privilege.

TIP: The `compareTo` method of the `Comparable` interface returns an integer. If the objects are not equal, it does not matter what negative or positive value you return. This flexibility can be useful when comparing integer fields. For example, suppose each employee has a unique integer `id`, and you want to sort by employee ID number. Then you can simply return `id - other.id`. That value will be some negative value if the first ID number is less than the other, 0 if they are the same ID, and some positive value otherwise. However, there is one caveat: The range of the integers must be small enough that the subtraction does not overflow. If you know that the IDs are between 0 and `(Integer.MAX_VALUE - 1) / 2`, you are safe.

Of course, the subtraction trick doesn't work for floating-point numbers. The difference `salary - other.salary` can round to 0 if the salaries are close together but not identical.

Now you saw what a class must do to avail itself of the sorting service—it must implement a `compareTo` method. That's eminently reasonable. There needs to be some way for the `sort` method to compare objects. But why can't the `Employee` class simply provide a `compareTo` method without implementing the `Comparable` interface?

The reason for interfaces is that the Java language is *strongly typed*. When making a method call, the compiler needs to be able to check that the method actually exists. Somewhere in the `sort` method, there will be statements like this:

```
if (a[i].compareTo(a[j]) > 0)
{
    // rearrange a[i] and a[j]
    . . .
}
```

The compiler must know that `a[i]` actually has a `compareTo` method. If `a` is an array of `Comparable` objects, then the existence of the method is assured, because every class that implements the `Comparable` interface must supply the method.

> NOTE: You would expect that the `sort` method in the `Arrays` class is defined to accept a `Comparable[]` array, so that the compiler can complain if anyone ever calls `sort` with an array whose element type doesn't implement the `Comparable` interface. Sadly, that is not the case. Instead, the `sort` method accepts an `Object[]` array and uses a clumsy cast:
>
> ```
> // from the standard library--not recommended
> if (((Comparable)a[i]).compareTo((Comparable)a[j]) > 0)
> {
>     // rearrange a[i] and a[j]
>     . . .
> }
> ```
>
> If `a[i]` does not belong to a class that implements the `Comparable` interface, then the virtual machine throws an exception. (Note that the second cast to `Comparable` is not necessary because the explicit parameter of the `compareTo` method has type `Object`, not `Comparable`.)

See Example 6–1 for the full code for sorting of an employee array.

Example 6–1: EmployeeSortTest.java

```
1. import java.util.*;
2.
3. public class EmployeeSortTest
4. {  public static void main(String[] args)
5.    {  Employee[] staff = new Employee[3];
6.
7.       staff[0] = new Employee("Harry Hacker", 35000);
8.       staff[1] = new Employee("Carl Cracker", 75000);
9.       staff[2] = new Employee("Tony Tester", 38000);
10.
11.      Arrays.sort(staff);
12.
```

```
13.       // print out information about all Employee objects
14.       for (int i = 0; i < staff.length; i++)
15.       {  Employee e = staff[i];
16.          System.out.println("name=" + e.getName()
17.             + ",salary=" + e.getSalary());
18.       }
19.    }
20. }
21.
22. class Employee implements Comparable
23. {  public Employee(String n, double s)
24.    {  name = n;
25.       salary = s;
26.    }
27.
28.    public String getName()
29.    {  return name;
30.    }
31.
32.    public double getSalary()
33.    {  return salary;
34.    }
35.
36.    public void raiseSalary(double byPercent)
37.    {  double raise = salary * byPercent / 100;
38.       salary += raise;
39.    }
40.
41.    /**
42.       Compares employees by salary
43.       @param otherObject another Employee object
44.       @return a negative value if this employee has a lower
45.       salary than otherObject, 0 if the salaries are the same,
46.       a positive value otherwise
47.    */
48.    public int compareTo(Object otherObject)
49.    {  Employee other = (Employee)otherObject;
50.       if (salary < other.salary) return -1;
51.       if (salary > other.salary) return 1;
52.       return 0;
53.    }
54.
55.    private String name;
56.    private double salary;
57. }
```

java.lang.Comparable

- `int compareTo(Object otherObject)`

  compares this object with `otherObject` and returns a negative integer if this object is less than `otherObject`, zero if they are equal, and a positive integer otherwise.

NOTE: According to the language standard: "The implementor must ensure sgn(`x.compareTo(y)`) = -sgn(`y.compareTo(x)`) for all `x` and `y`. (This implies that `x.compareTo(y)` must throw an exception if `y.compareTo(x)` throws an exception.)" Here, "sgn" is the *sign* of a number: sgn(n) is -1 if n is negative, 0 if n equals 0, and 1 if n is positive. In plain English, if you flip the parameters of `compareTo`, the sign (but not necessarily the actual value) of the result must also flip. That's not a problem, but the implication about exceptions is tricky. Suppose `Manager` has its own comparison method that compares two managers. It might start like this:

```
public int compareTo(Object otherObject)
{
    Manager other = (Manager)otherObject;
    . . .
}
```

That violates the "antisymmetry" rule. If `x` is an `Employee` and `y` is a `Manager`, then the call `x.compareTo(y)` doesn't throw an exception—it simply compares `x` and `y` as employees. But the reverse, `y.compareTo(x)` throws a `ClassCastException`.

The same issue comes up when programming an `equals` method. However, in that case, you simply test if the two classes are identical, and if they aren't, you know that you should return `false`. However, if `x` and `y` aren't of the same class, it is not clear whether `x.compareTo(y)` should return a negative or a positive value. Maybe managers think that they should compare larger than any employee, no matter what the salary. But then they need to explicitly implement that check.

If you don't trust the implementors of your subclasses to grasp this subtlety, you can declare `compareTo` as a `final` method. Then the problem never arises because subclasses can't supply their own version. Conversely, if you implement a `compareTo` method of a subclass, you need to provide a thorough test. Here is an example:

```
if (otherObject instanceof Manager)
{
    Manager other = (Manager)otherObject;
    . . .
}
else if (otherObject instanceof Employee)
{
    return 1; // managers are always better :-(
}
else
    return -((Comparable)otherObject).compareTo(this);
```

`java.util.Arrays`

- `static void sort(Object[] a)`

  sorts the elements in the array `a`, using a tuned mergesort algorithm. All elements in the array must belong to classes that implement the `Comparable` interface, and they must all be comparable to each other.

Properties of Interfaces

Interfaces are not classes. In particular, you can never use the `new` operator to instantiate an interface:

```
x = new Comparable(. . .); // ERROR
```

However, even though you can't construct interface objects, you can still declare interface variables.

```
Comparable x; // OK
```

An interface variable must refer to an object of a class that implements the interface:

```
x = new Employee(. . .);
   // OK provided Employee implements Comparable
```

Next, just as you use `instanceof` to check if an object is of a specific class, you can use `instanceof` to check if an object implements an interface:

```
if (anObject instanceof Comparable) { . . . }
```

Just as you can build hierarchies of classes, you can extend interfaces. This allows for multiple chains of interfaces that go from a greater degree of generality to a greater degree of specialization. For example, suppose you had an interface called `Moveable`.

```
public interface Moveable
{
   void move(double x, double y);
}
```

Then, you could imagine an interface called `Powered` that extends it:

```
public interface Powered extends Moveable
{
   double milesPerGallon();
}
```

Although you cannot put instance fields or static methods in an interface, you can supply constants in them. For example:

```
public interface Powered extends Moveable
{
   double milesPerGallon();
   double SPEED_LIMIT = 95; // a public static final constant
}
```

Just as methods in an interface are automatically `public`, fields are always
`public static final`.

> NOTE: It is legal to tag interface methods as `public`, and fields as `public static`
> `final`. Some programmers do that, either out of habit or for greater clarity. However,
> the Java Language Specification recommends not to supply the redundant keywords,
> and we follow that recommendation.

Some interfaces define just constants and no methods. For example, the standard library contains an interface `SwingConstants` that defines constants
`NORTH`, `SOUTH`, `HORIZONTAL`, and so on. Any class that chooses to implement
the `SwingConstants` interface automatically inherits these constants. Its
methods can simply refer to `NORTH` rather than the more cumbersome
`SwingConstants.NORTH`.

While each class can only have one superclass, classes can implement *multiple* interfaces. This gives you the maximum amount of flexibility in defining a class's behavior. For example, the Java programming language has an important interface built
into it, called `Cloneable`. (We will discuss this interface in detail in the next section.) If your class implements `Cloneable`, the `clone` method in the `Object` class
will make an exact copy of your class's objects. Suppose, therefore, you want clone-
ability and comparability. Then you simply implement both interfaces.

```
class Employee implements Cloneable, Comparable
```

Use commas to separate the interfaces that describe the characteristics that you
want to supply.

Interfaces and Abstract Classes

If you read the section about abstract classes in Chapter 5, you may wonder why
the designers of the Java programming language bothered with introducing the
concept of interfaces. Why can't `Comparable` simply be an abstract class:

```
abstract class Comparable // why not?
{
   public abstract int compareTo(Object other);
}
```

Then the `Employee` class would simply extend this abstract class and supply the
`compareTo` method:

```
class Employee extends Comparable // why not?
{
   public int compareTo(Object other) { . . . }
}
```

There is, unfortunately, a major problem with using an abstract base class to
express a generic property. A class can only extend a single class. Suppose that

the `Employee` class already extends a different class, say `Person`. Then it can't extend a second class.

```
class Employee extends Person, Comparable // ERROR
```

But each class can implement as many interfaces as it likes:

```
class Employee extends Person implements Comparable // OK
```

Other programming languages, in particular C++, allow a class to have more than one superclass. This feature is called *multiple inheritance*. The designers of Java chose not to support multiple inheritance because it makes the language either very complex (as in C++) or less efficient (as in Eiffel).

Instead, interfaces give most of the benefits of multiple inheritance while avoiding the complexities and inefficiencies.

C++ NOTE: C++ has multiple inheritance and all the complications that come with it, such as virtual base classes, dominance rules, and transverse pointer casts. Few C++ programmers use multiple inheritance, and some say it should never be used. Other programmers recommend using multiple inheritance only for "mix-in" style inheritance. In the mix-in style, a primary base class describes the parent object, and additional base classes (the so-called mix-ins) may supply auxiliary characteristics. That style is similar to a Java class with a single base class and additional interfaces. However, in C++, mix-ins can add default behavior, whereas Java interfaces cannot.

NOTE: Microsoft has long been a proponent of using interfaces instead of using multiple inheritance. In fact, the Java notion of an interface is essentially equivalent to how Microsoft's COM technology uses interfaces. As a result of this unlikely convergence of minds, it is easy to supply tools based on the Java programming language to build COM objects (such as ActiveX controls). This is done (pretty much transparently to the coder) in, for example, Microsoft's J++ product and is also the basis for Sun's JavaBeans-to-ActiveX bridge.

Interfaces and Callbacks

A common pattern in programming is the *callback* pattern. In this pattern, you want to specify the action that should occur whenever a particular event happens. For example, you may want a particular action to occur when a button is clicked or a menu item is selected. However, since you have not yet seen how to implement user interfaces, we will consider a similar but simpler situation.

The `javax.swing` class contains a `Timer` class that is useful if you want to be notified whenever a time interval has elapsed. For example, if a part of your program contains a clock, then you can ask to be notified every second so that you can update the clock face.

When you construct a timer, you set the time interval, and you tell it what it should do whenever the time interval has elapsed.

How do you tell the timer what it should do? In many programming languages, you supply the name of a function that the timer should call periodically. However, the classes in the Java standard library take an object-oriented approach. You pass an object of some class. The timer then calls one of the methods on that object. Passing an object is more flexible than passing a function because the object can carry additional information.

Of course, the timer needs to know what method to call. The timer requires that you specify an object of a class that implements the `ActionListener` interface of the `java.awt.event` package. Here is that interface:

```
public interface ActionListener
{
    void actionPerformed(ActionEvent event);
}
```

The timer calls the `actionPerformed` method when the time interval has expired.

> C++ NOTE: As you saw in Chapter 5, Java does have the equivalent of function point-
> ers, namely, `Method` objects. However, they are difficult to use, slower, and cannot be
> checked for type safety at compile time. Whenever you would use a function pointer in
> C++, you should consider using an interface in Java.

Suppose you want to print a message "At the tone, the time is . . .," followed by a beep, once every ten seconds. You need to define a class that implements the `ActionListener` interface. Then place whatever statements you want to have executed inside the `actionPerformed` method.

```
class TimePrinter implements ActionListener
{
    public void actionPerformed(ActionEvent event)
    {
        Date now = new Date();
        System.out.println("At the tone, the time is " + now);
        Toolkit.getDefaultToolkit().beep();
    }
}
```

Note the `ActionEvent` parameter of the `actionPerformed` method. This parameter gives information about the event, such as the source object that generated it—see Chapter 8 for more information. However, detail information about the event is not important in this program, and you can safely ignore the parameter.

Next, you construct an object of this class and pass it to the `Timer` constructor.

```
ActionListener listener = new TimePrinter();
Timer t = new Timer(10000, listener);
```

The first parameter of the `Timer` constructor is the time interval that must elapse between notifications, measured in milliseconds. We want to be notified every ten seconds. The second parameter is the listener object.

Finally, you start the timer.

```
t.start();
```

Every ten seconds, a message like

```
At the tone, the time is Thu Apr 13 23:29:08 PDT 2000
```

is displayed, followed by a beep.

Example 6–2 puts the timer and its action listener to work. After the timer is started, the program puts up a message dialog and waits for the user to click the Ok button to stop. While the program waits for the user, the current time is displayed in ten second intervals.

Be patient when running the program. The "Quit program?" dialog box appears right away, but the first timer message is displayed after ten seconds.

Note that the program imports the `javax.swing.Timer` class by name, in addition to importing `javax.swing.*` and `java.util.*`. This breaks the ambiguity between `javax.swing.Timer` and `java.util.Timer`, an unrelated class for scheduling background tasks.

Example 6–2: TimerTest.java

```
1. import java.awt.*;
2. import java.awt.event.*;
3. import java.util.*;
4. import javax.swing.*;
5. import javax.swing.Timer;
6. // to resolve conflict with java.util.Timer
7.
8. public class TimerTest
9. {
10.    public static void main(String[] args)
11.    {
12.       ActionListener listener = new TimePrinter();
13.
14.       // construct a timer that calls the listener
15.       // once every 10 seconds
16.       Timer t = new Timer(10000, listener);
17.       t.start();
18.
19.       JOptionPane.showMessageDialog(null, "Quit program?");
20.       System.exit(0);
21.    }
22. }
```

```
23.
24. class TimePrinter implements ActionListener
25. {
26.    public void actionPerformed(ActionEvent event)
27.    {
28.       Date now = new Date();
29.       System.out.println("At the tone, the time is " + now);
30.       Toolkit.getDefaultToolkit().beep();
31.    }
32. }
```

javax.swing.JOptionPane

• static void showMessageDialog(Component parent, Object message)
displays a dialog box with a message prompt and an Ok button. The dialog is centered over the `parent` component. If `parent` is `null`, the dialog is centered on the screen.

javax.swing.Timer

• Timer(int interval, ActionListener listener)
constructs a timer that notifies `listener` whenever `interval` milliseconds have elapsed.

• void start()
starts the timer. Once started, the timer calls `actionPerformed` on its listeners.

• void stop()
stops the timer. Once stopped, the timer no longer calls `actionPerformed` on its listeners.

java.awt.Toolkit

• static Toolkit getDefaultToolkit()
gets the default toolkit. A toolkit contains information about the graphical user interface environment.

• void beep()
Emits a beep sound.

Object Cloning

When you make a copy of a variable, the original and the copy are references to the same object. (See Figure 6–1.) This means a change to either variable also affects the other.

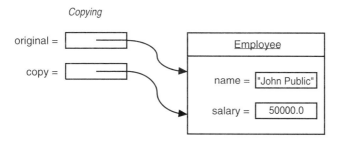

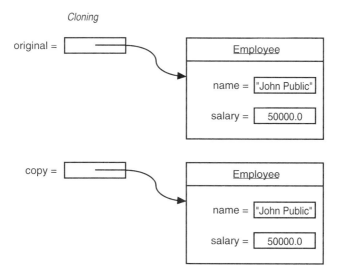

Figure 6–1: Copying and cloning

```
Employee original = new Employee("John Public", 50000);
Employee copy = original;
copy.raiseSalary(10); // oops--also changed original
```

If you would like copy to be a new object that begins its life being identical to original but whose state can diverge over time, then you use the clone() method.

```
Employee copy = (Employee)original.clone();
    // must cast—clone returns an Object
copy.raiseSalary(10); // OK--original unchanged
```

But it isn't quite so simple. The clone method is a protected method of Object, which means that your code cannot simply call it. Only the Employee class can clone Employee objects. There is a reason for this restriction. Think about the way in which the Object class can implement clone. It knows nothing about the object at all, so it can make only a field-by-field copy. If all data fields in the object are numbers or other basic types, copying the fields is just fine. But if the object contains references to subobjects, then copying the field gives you another reference to the subobject, so the original and the cloned objects still share some information.

To visualize that phenomenon, let's consider an `Employee` class that also has a `payDay` field. Figure 6–2 shows what happens when you use the `clone` method of the `Object` class to clone such an `Employee` object. As you can see, the default cloning operation is "shallow"—it doesn't clone objects that are referenced inside other objects.

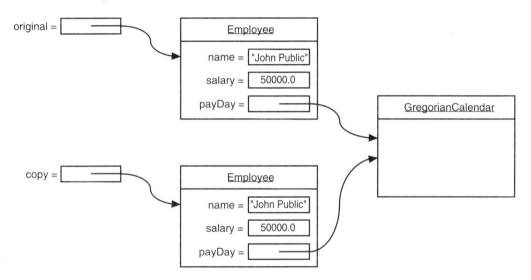

Figure 6–2: A shallow copy

Does it matter if the copy is shallow? It depends. If the subobject that is shared between the original and the shallow clone is *immutable*, then the sharing is safe. This happens in two situations. The subobject may belong to an immutable class, such as `String` and `Date`. Alternatively, the subobject may simply remain constant throughout the lifetime of the object, with no mutators touching it and no methods yielding a reference to it.

Quite frequently, however, subobjects are mutable, and you must redefine the `clone` method to make a *deep copy* that clones the subobjects as well. In our example, the `payDay` field is a `GregorianCalendar`, which is mutable.

For every class, you need to decide whether or not

1. The default `clone` method is good enough
2. The default `clone` method can be patched up by calling `clone` on the mutable subobjects

3.   `clone` should not be attempted

The third option is actually the default. To choose either the first or the second option, a class must

1.   Implement the `Cloneable` interface, and

2.   Redefine the `clone` method with the `public` access modifier.

> NOTE: The `clone` method is declared `protected` in the `Object` class so that your code can't simply call `anObject.clone()`. But aren't protected methods accessible from any subclass, and isn't every class a subclass of `Object`? Fortunately, the rules for protected access are more subtle (see Chapter 5). A subclass can call a protected `clone` method only to clone *its own* objects. You must redefine `clone` to be public to allow objects to be cloned by any method.

> NOTE: Users of your `clone` method still have to cast the result. The `clone` method always has return type `Object`.

In this case, the appearance of the `Cloneable` interface has nothing to do with the normal use of interfaces. In particular, it does *not* specify the `clone` method— that method is inherited from the `Object` class. The interface merely serves as a tag, indicating that the class designer understands the cloning process. Objects are so paranoid about cloning that they generate a checked exception if an object requests cloning but does not implement that interface.

> NOTE: The `Cloneable` interface is one of a handful of *tagging interfaces* that Java provides. Recall that the usual purpose of an interface such as `Comparable` is to ensure that a class implements a particular method or set of methods. A tagging interface has no methods; its only purpose is to allow the use of `instanceof` in a type inquiry:
>
>   if (obj instanceof Cloneable) . . .

Even if the default (shallow copy) implementation of `clone` is adequate, you still need to implement the `Cloneable` interface, redefine `clone` to be public, call `super.clone()` and catch the `CloneNotSupportedException`. Here is an example:

```
class Person implements Cloneable
{
   public Object clone() // raise visibility level to public
   {
      try
      {
         return super.clone();
      }
```

```
         catch (CloneNotSupportedException e) { return null; }
         // this won't happen, since we are Cloneable
      }
      . . .
   }
```

The `clone` method of the `Object` class threatens to throw a `CloneNotSupportedException`—it does that whenever `clone` is invoked on an object whose class does not implement the `Cloneable` interface. Of course, the `Person` class is cloneable, so the exception won't be thrown. However, the compiler does not know that. Therefore, you still need to catch the exception and return a dummy value.

Here is an example of a `clone` method that creates a deep copy:

```
   class Employee implements Cloneable
   {
      . . .
      public Object clone()
      {
         try
         {
            // call Object.clone()
            Employee cloned = (Employee)super.clone();

            // clone mutable fields
            cloned.payDay = (GregorianCalendar)payDay.clone()

            return cloned;
         }
         catch (CloneNotSupportedException e) { return null; }
      }
   }
```

As you can see, cloning is a subtle business, and it makes sense that it is defined as `protected` in the `Object` class. (See Chapter 12 for an elegant method for cloning objects, using the object serialization feature of Java.)

CAUTION: When you define a `public clone` method, you have lost a safety mechanism. Your `clone` method is inherited by the subclasses, whether or not it makes sense for them. For example, once you have defined the `clone` method for the `Employee` class, anyone can also clone `Manager` objects. Can the `Employee` clone method do the job? It depends on the fields of the `Manager` class. In our case, there is no problem because the `bonus` field has primitive type. But in general, you need to make sure to check the `clone` method of any class that you extend.

The program in Example 6–3 clones an `Employee` object, then invokes two mutators. The `raiseSalary` method changes the value of the `salary` field, while the `addPayDay` method changes the state of the `payDay` field. Neither mutation affects the original object because `clone` has been defined to make a deep copy.

Example 6–3: CloneTest.java

```
1. import java.util.*;
2.
3. public class CloneTest
4. {
5.    public static void main(String[] args)
6.    {
7.       Employee original = new Employee("John Q. Public", 50000);
8.       original.setPayDay(2000, 1, 1);
9.       Employee copy = (Employee)original.clone();
10.      copy.raiseSalary(10);
11.      copy.addPayDay(14);
12.      System.out.println("original=" + original);
13.      System.out.println("copy=" + copy);
14.   }
15. }
16.
17. /**
18.    An employee class with a mutable payDay field
19. */
20. class Employee implements Cloneable
21. {
22.    public Employee(String n, double s)
23.    {
24.       name = n;
25.       salary = s;
26.    }
27.
28.    public Object clone()
29.    {
30.       try
31.       {
32.          // call Object.clone()
33.          Employee cloned = (Employee)super.clone();
34.
35.          // clone mutable fields
36.          cloned.payDay = (GregorianCalendar)payDay.clone();
37.
38.          return cloned;
39.       }
40.       catch (CloneNotSupportedException e) { return null; }
41.    }
42.
43.    /**
44.       Set the pay day to a given date
45.       @param year the year of the pay day
46.       @param month the month of the pay day
47.       @param day the day of the pay day
48.    */
```

```
49.    public void setPayDay(int year, int month, int day)
50.    {
51.       payDay = new GregorianCalendar(year, month - 1, day);
52.    }
53.
54.
55.    /**
56.       Add a number of days to the pay day (e.g. add 14 days)
57.       @param days the number of days to add
58.    */
59.    public void addPayDay(int days)
60.    {
61.       payDay.add(Calendar.DAY_OF_MONTH, days);
62.    }
63.
64.    public Date getPayDay()
65.    {
66.       return payDay.getTime();
67.    }
68.
69.    public void raiseSalary(double byPercent)
70.    {
71.       double raise = salary * byPercent / 100;
72.       salary += raise;
73.    }
74.
75.    public String toString()
76.    {
77.       return "Employee[name=" + name
78.          + ",salary=" + salary
79.          + ",payDay=" + getPayDay()
80.          + "]";
81.    }
82.
83.    private String name;
84.    private double salary;
85.    private GregorianCalendar payDay;
86. }
```

Inner Classes

An *inner class* is a class that is defined inside another class. Why would you want to do that? There are four reasons:

- An object of an inner class can access the implementation of the object that created it—including data that would otherwise be private.
- Inner classes can be hidden from other classes in the same package.
- *Anonymous* inner classes are handy when you want to define callbacks on the fly.

• Inner classes are very convenient when you are writing event-driven programs.

You will soon see examples that demonstrate the first three benefits. (For more information on the event model, please turn to Chapter 8.)

C++ NOTE: C++ has *nested classes*. A nested class is contained inside the scope of the enclosing class. Here is a typical example: a linked list class defines a class to hold the links, and a class to define an iterator position.

```
class LinkedList
{
public:
   class Iterator // a nested class
   {
   public:
      void insert(int x);
      int erase();
      . . .
   };
   . . .
private:
   class Link // a nested class
   {
   public:
      Link* next;
      int data;
   };
   . . .
};
```

The nesting is a relationship between *classes*, not *objects*. A `LinkedList` object does *not* have subobjects of type `Iterator` or `Link`.

There are two benefits: *name control* and *access control*. Because the name `Iterator` is nested inside the `LinkedList` class, it is externally known as `LinkedList::Iterator` and cannot conflict with another class called `Iterator`. In Java, this benefit is not as important since Java *packages* give the same kind of name control. Note that the `Link` class is in the *private* part of the `LinkedList` class. It is completely hidden from all other code. For that reason, it is safe to make its data fields public. They can be accessed by the methods of the `LinkedList` class (which has a legitimate need to access them), and they are not visible elsewhere. In Java, this kind of control was not possible until inner classes were introduced.

However, the Java inner classes have an additional feature that makes them richer and more useful than nested classes in C++. An object that comes from an inner class has an implicit reference to the outer class object that instantiated it. Through this pointer, it gains access to the total state of the outer object. You will see the details of the Java mechanism later in this chapter.

Only `static` inner classes do not have this added pointer. They are the exact Java analog to nested classes in C++.

Using an Inner Class to Access Object State

The syntax for inner classes is somewhat complex. For that reason, we will use a simple but somewhat artificial example to demonstrate the use of inner classes. We will write a program in which a timer controls a bank account. The timer's action listener object adds interest to the account once per second. However, we don't want to use public methods (such as `deposit` or `withdraw`) to manipulate the bank balance because anyone could call those public methods to modify the balance for other purposes. Instead, we will use an *inner class* whose methods can manipulate the bank balance directly.

Here is the outline of the `BankAccount` class:

```
class BankAccount
{
   public BankAccount(double initialBalance) { . . . }
   public void start(double rate) { . . . }

   private double balance;

   private class InterestAdder implements ActionListener
      // an inner class
   {
      . . .
   }
}
```

Note the `InterestAdder` class that is located inside the `BankAccount` class. This does *not* mean that every `BankAccount` has an `InterestAdder` instance field. Of course, we will construct objects of the inner class, but those objects aren't instance fields of the outer class. Instead, they will be local to the methods of the outer class.

The `InterestAdder` class is a *private inner class* inside `BankAccount`. This is a safety mechanism—since only `BankAccount` methods can generate `Interest-Adder` objects, we don't have to worry about breaking encapsulation. Only inner classes can be private. Regular classes always have either package or public visibility.

The `InterestAdder` class has a constructor which sets the interest rate that should be applied at each step. Since this inner class implements the `Action-Listener` interface, it also has an `actionPerformed` method. That method actually increments the account balance. Here is the inner class in more detail:

```
class BankAccount
{
   public BankAccount(double initialBalance)
   {
      balance = initialBalance;
```

```
   }
   . . .
   private double balance;

   private class InterestAdder implements ActionListener
   {
      public InterestAdder(double aRate)
      {
         rate = aRate;
      }

      public void actionPerformed(ActionEvent event) { . . . }

      private double rate;
   }
}
```

The `start` method of the `BankAccount` class constructs an `InterestAdder` object for the given interest rate, makes it the action listener for a timer, and starts the timer.

```
public void start(double rate)
{
   ActionListener adder = new InterestAdder(rate);
   Timer t = new Timer(1000, adder);
   t.start();
}
```

As a result, the `actionPerformed` method of the `InterestAdder` class will be called once per second. Now let's look inside this method more closely:

```
public void actionPerformed(ActionEvent event)
{
   double interest = balance * rate / 100;
   balance += interest;

   NumberFormat formatter
      = NumberFormat.getCurrencyInstance();
   System.out.println("balance="
      + formatter.format(balance));
}
```

The name `rate` refers to the instance field of the `InterestAdder` class, which is not surprising. However, there is no `balance` field in the `InterestAdder` class. Instead, `balance` refers to the field of the `BankAccount` object that created this `InstanceAdder`. This is quite innovative. Traditionally, a method could refer to the data fields of the object invoking the method. An inner class method gets to access both its own data fields *and* those of the outer object creating it.

For this to work, of course, an object of an inner class always gets an implicit reference to the object that created it. (See Figure 6–3.)

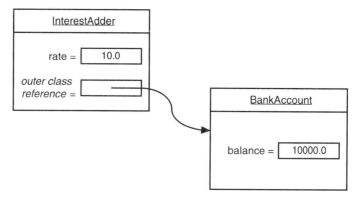

Figure 6–3: An inner class object has a reference to an outer class object

This reference is invisible in the definition of the inner class. However, to illuminate the concept, let us call the reference to the outer object *outer*. Then, the `actionPerformed` method is equivalent to the following:

```
public void actionPerformed(ActionEvent event)
{
   double interest = outer.balance * this.rate / 100;
      // "outer" isn't the actual name
   outer.balance += interest;

   NumberFormat formatter
      = NumberFormat.getCurrencyInstance();
   System.out.println("balance="
      + formatter.format(outer.balance));
}
```

The outer class reference is set in the constructor. That is, the compiler adds a parameter to the constructor, generating code like this:

```
public InterestAdder(BankAccount account, double aRate)
{
   outer = account;
      // automatically generated code
   rate = aRate;
}
```

Again, please note, *outer* is not a Java keyword. We just use it to illustrate the mechanism involved in an inner class.

When an `InterestAdder` object is constructed in the `start` method, the compiler passes the `this` reference to the current bank account into the constructor:

```
ActionListener adder = new InterestAdder(this, rate);
   // automatically generated code
```

Example 6–4 shows the complete program that tests the inner class. Have another look at the access control. The Timer object requires an object of some class that implements the ActionListener interface. Had that class been a regular class, then it would have needed to access the bank balance through a public method. As a consequence, the BankAccount class would have to provide those methods to all classes, which it might have been reluctant to do. Using an inner class is an improvement. The InterestAdder inner class is able to access the bank balance, but no other class has the same privilege.

Example 6–4: InnerClassTest.java

```
1. import java.awt.event.*;
2. import java.text.*;
3. import javax.swing.*;
4.
5. public class InnerClassTest
6. {
7.    public static void main(String[] args)
8.    {
9.       // construct a bank account with initial balance of $10,000
10.      BankAccount account = new BankAccount(10000);
11.      // start accumulating interest at 10%
12.      account.start(10);
13.
14.      // keep program running until user selects "Ok"
15.      JOptionPane.showMessageDialog(null, "Quit program?");
16.      System.exit(0);
17.   }
18. }
19.
20. class BankAccount
21. {
22.    /**
23.       Constructs a bank account with an initial balance
24.       @param initialBalance the initial balance
25.    */
26.    public BankAccount(double initialBalance)
27.    {
28.       balance = initialBalance;
29.    }
30.
31.    /**
32.       Starts a simulation in which interest is added once per
33.       second
34.       @param rate the interest rate in percent
35.    */
36.    public void start(double rate)
37.    {
```

```
38.        ActionListener adder = new InterestAdder(rate);
39.        Timer t = new Timer(1000, adder);
40.        t.start();
41.    }
42.
43.    private double balance;
44.
45.    /**
46.        This class adds the interest to the bank account.
47.        The actionPerformed method is called by the timer.
48.    */
49.    private class InterestAdder implements ActionListener
50.    {
51.        public InterestAdder(double aRate)
52.        {
53.            rate = aRate;
54.        }
55.
56.        public void actionPerformed(ActionEvent event)
57.        {
58.            // update interest
59.            double interest = balance * rate / 100;
60.            balance += interest;
61.
62.            // print out current balance
63.            NumberFormat formatter
64.                = NumberFormat.getCurrencyInstance();
65.            System.out.println("balance="
66.                + formatter.format(balance));
67.        }
68.
69.        private double rate;
70.    }
71. }
```

Special Syntax Rules for Inner Classes

In the preceding section, we explained the outer class reference of an inner class by calling it *outer*. Actually, the proper syntax for the outer reference is a bit more complex. The expression

```
OuterClass.this
```

denotes the outer class reference. For example, you can write the actionPerformed method of the InterestAdder inner class as

```
public void actionPerformed(ActionEvent event)
{
    double interest = BankAccount.this.balance * this.rate / 100;
    BankAccount.this.balance += interest;
```

```
    . . .
  }
```

Conversely, you can write the inner object constructor more explicitly, using the syntax:

```
outerObject.new InnerClass(construction parameters)
```

For example,

```
ActionListener adder = this.new InterestAdder(rate);
```

Here, the outer class reference of the newly constructed `InterestAdder` object is set to the `this` reference of the method that creates the inner class object. This is the most common case. As always, the `this.` qualifier is redundant. However, it is also possible to set the outer class reference to another object by explicitly naming it. For example, if `InterestAdder` was a public inner class, you could construct an `InterestAdder` for any bank account:

```
BankAccount mySavings = new BankAccount(10000);
BankAccount.InterestAdder adder
   = mySavings.new InterestAdder(10);
```

Note that you refer to an inner class as

```
OuterClass.InnerClass
```

when it occurs outside the scope of the outer class. For example, if `InterestAdder` had been a public class, you could have referred to it as `BankAccount.InterestAdder` elsewhere in your program.

Are Inner Classes Useful? Are They Actually Necessary? Are They Secure?

Inner classes are a major addition to the language. Java started out with the goal of being simpler than C++. But inner classes are anything but simple. The syntax is complex. (It will get more complex as we study anonymous inner classes later in this chapter.) It is not obvious how inner classes interact with other features of the language, such as access control and security.

Has Java started down the road to ruin that has afflicted so many other languages, by adding a feature that was elegant and interesting rather than needed?

While we won't try to answer this question completely, it is worth noting that inner classes are a phenomenon of the *compiler,* not the virtual machine. Inner classes are translated into regular class files with $ (dollar signs) delimiting outer and inner class names, and the virtual machine does not have any special knowledge about them.

For example, the `InterestAdder` class inside the `BankAccount` class is translated to a class file `BankAccount$InterestAdder.class`. To see this at work, try out the following experiment: run the `ReflectionTest` program of Chapter 5, and give it the class `BankAccount$InterestAdder` to reflect upon. You will get the following printout:

```
class BankAccount$InterestAdder
{
   public BankAccount$InterestAdder(BankAccount, double);

   public void actionPerformed(java.awt.event.ActionEvent);

   private double rate;
   private final BankAccount this$0;
}
```

> **NOTE:** If you use Unix, remember to escape the `$` character if you supply the class name on the command line. That is, run the `ReflectionTest` program as
>
> ```
> java ReflectionTest 'BankAccount$InterestAdder'
> ```

You can plainly see that the compiler has generated an additional instance field, `this$0`, for the reference to the outer class. (The name `this$0` is synthesized by the compiler—you cannot refer to it in your code.) You can also see the added parameter for the constructor.

If the compiler can do this transformation, couldn't you simply program the same mechanism by hand? Let's try it. We would make `InterestAdder` a regular class, outside the `BankAccount` class. When constructing an `InterestAdder` object, we pass it the `this` reference of the object that is creating it.

```
class BankAccount
{  . . .

   public void start(double rate)
   {
      ActionListener adder = new InterestAdder(this, rate);
      Timer t = new Timer(1000, adder);
      t.start();
   }
}

class InterestAdder implements ActionListener
{
   public InterestAdder(BankAccount account, double aRate)
   {
      outer = account;
      rate = aRate;
   }
   . . .
   private BankAccount outer;
   private double rate;
}
```

Now let us look at the `actionPerformed` method. It needs to access `outer.balance`.

```
public void actionPerformed(ActionEvent event)
{
   double interest = outer.balance * rate / 100; // ERROR
   outer.balance += interest; // ERROR
   . . .
}
```

Here we run into a problem. The inner class can access the private data of the outer class, but our external `InterestAdder` class cannot.

Thus, inner classes are genuinely more powerful than regular classes, since they have more access privileges.

You may well wonder how inner classes manage to acquire those added access privileges, since inner classes are translated to regular classes with funny names— the virtual machine knows nothing at all about them. To solve this mystery, let's again use the `ReflectionTest` program to spy on the `BankAccount` class:

```
class BankAccount
{
   public BankAccount(double);

   static double access$000(BankAccount);
   public void start(double);
   static double access$018(BankAccount, double);

   private double balance;
}
```

Notice the static `access$000` and `access$018` methods that the compiler added to the outer class. The inner class methods call those methods. For example, the statement

```
balance += interest
```

in the `actionPerformed` method of the `InterestAdder` class effectively makes the following call:

```
access$018(outer, access$000(outer) + interest);
```

Is this a security risk? You bet it is. It is an easy matter for someone else to invoke the `access$000` method to read the private `balance` field or, even worse, to call the `access$018` method to set it. The Java language standard reserves $ characters in variable and method names for system usage. However, for those hackers who are familiar with the structure of class files, it is an easy (if tedious) matter to produce a class file with virtual machine instructions to call that method. Of course, such a class file would need to be generated manually (for example, with a hex editor). Because the secret access methods have package visibility, the attack code would need to be placed inside the same package as the class under attack.

To summarize, if an inner class accesses a private data field, then it is possible to access that data field through other classes that are added to the package of the outer class, but to do so requires skill and determination. A programmer cannot accidentally obtain access but must intentionally build or modify a class file for that purpose.

Local Inner Classes

If you look carefully at the code of the `BankAccount` example, you will find that you need the name of the type `InterestAdder` only once: when you create an object of that type in the `start` method.

When you have a situation like this, you can define the class *locally in a single method*.

```java
public void start(double rate)
{
   class InterestAdder implements ActionListener
   {
      public InterestAdder(double aRate)
      {
         rate = aRate;
      }

      public void actionPerformed(ActionEvent event)
      {
         double interest = balance * rate / 100;
         balance += interest;

            = NumberFormat.getCurrencyInstance();
         System.out.println("balance="
            + formatter.format(balance));
      }

      private double rate;
   }

   ActionListener adder = new InterestAdder(rate);
   Timer t = new Timer(1000, adder);
   t.start();
}
```

Local classes are never declared with an access specifier (that is, `public` or `private`). Their scope is always restricted to the block in which they are declared.

Local classes have a great advantage—they are completely hidden from the outside world—not even other code in the `BankAccount` class can access them. No method except `start` has any knowledge of the `InterestAdder` class.

Local classes have another advantage over other inner classes. Not only can they access the fields of their outer classes, they can even access local variables! However, those local variables must be declared `final`. Here is a typical example.

```
public void start(final double rate)
{
   class InterestAdder implements ActionListener
   {
     public void actionPerformed(ActionEvent event)
     {
        double interest = balance * rate / 100;
        balance += interest;

        NumberFormat formatter
           = NumberFormat.getCurrencyInstance();
        System.out.println("balance="
           + formatter.format(balance));
     }
   }

   ActionListener adder = new InterestAdder();
   Timer t = new Timer(1000, adder);
   t.start();
}
```

Note that the `InterestAdder` class no longer needs to store a `rate` instance variable. It simply refers to the parameter variable of the method that contains the class definition.

Maybe this should not be so surprising. The line

```
double interest = balance * rate / 100;
```

is, after all, ultimately inside the `start` method, so why shouldn't it have access to the value of the `rate` variable?

To see why there is a subtle issue here, let's consider the flow of control more closely.

1. The `start` method is called.

2. The object variable `adder` is initialized via a call to the constructor of the inner class `InterestAdder`.

3. The `adder` reference is passed to the `Timer` constructor, the timer is started, and the `start` method exits. At this point, the `rate` parameter variable of the `start` method no longer exists.

4. A second later, the `actionPerformed` method calls `double interest = balance * rate / 100;`.

For the code in the `actionPerformed` method to work, the `InterestAdder` class must have made a copy of the `rate` field before it went away as a local variable of the `start` method. That is indeed exactly what happens. In our example, the compiler synthesizes the name `BankAccount$1$InterestAdder` for the local inner class. If you use the `ReflectionTest` program again to spy on the `BankAccount$1$InterestAdder` class, you get the following output:

```
class BankAccount$1$InterestAdder
{
    BankAccount$1$InterestAdder(BankAccount, double);

    public void actionPerformed(java.awt.event.ActionEvent);

    private final double val$rate;
    private final BankAccount this$0;
}
```

Note the extra `double` parameter to the constructor and the `val$rate` instance variable. When an object is created, the value `rate` is passed into the constructor and stored in the `val$rate` field. This sounds like an extraordinary amount of trouble for the implementors of the compiler. The compiler must detect access of local variables, make matching data fields for each one of them, and copy the local variables into the constructor so that the data fields can be initialized as copies of them.

From the programmer's point of view, however, local variable access is quite pleasant. It makes your inner classes simpler by reducing the instance fields that you need to program explicitly.

As we already mentioned, the methods of a local class can refer only to local variables that are declared `final`. For that reason, the `rate` parameter was declared `final` in our example. A local variable that is declared `final` cannot be modified. Thus, it is guaranteed that the local variable and the copy that is made inside the local class always have the same value.

NOTE: You have seen `final` variables used for constants, such as

```
public static final double SPEED_LIMIT = 55;
```

The `final` keyword can be applied to local variables, instance variables, and static variables. In all cases it means the same thing: You can assign to this variable *once* after it has been created. Afterwards, you cannot change the value—it is final.

However, you don't have to initialize a `final` variable when you define it. For example, the `final` parameter variable `rate` is initialized once after its creation, when the `start` method is called. (If the method is called multiple times, each call has its own newly created `rate` parameter.) The `val$rate` instance variable that you can see in the `BankAccount$1$InterestAdder` inner class is set once, in the inner class constructor. A final variable that isn't initialized when it is defined is often called a *blank final* variable.

Anonymous inner classes

When using local inner classes, you can often go a step further. If you want to make only a single object of this class, you don't even need to give the class a name. Such a class is called *anonymous inner class*.

```
public void start(final double rate)
{
 ActionListener adder = new
   ActionListener()
   {
      public void actionPerformed(ActionEvent event)
      {
         double interest = balance * rate / 100;
         balance += interest;

         NumberFormat formatter
            = NumberFormat.getCurrencyInstance();
         System.out.println("balance="
            + formatter.format(balance));
      }
   };
 Timer t = new Timer(1000, adder);
 t.start();
 }
```

This is a very cryptic syntax indeed. What it means is:

Create a new object of a class that implements the ActionListener interface, where the required method actionPerformed is the one defined inside the braces { }.

Any parameters used to construct the object are given inside the parentheses ( ) following the supertype name. In general, the syntax is

```
new SuperType(construction parameters)
{
    inner class methods and data
}
```

Here, *SuperType* can be an interface, such as ActionListener; then, the inner class *implements* that interface. Or, *SuperType* can be a class; then, the inner class *extends* that class.

An anonymous inner class cannot have constructors because the name of a constructor must be the same as the name of a class, and the class has no name. Instead, the construction parameters are given to the *superclass* constructor. In particular, whenever an inner class implements an interface, it cannot have any construction parameters. Nevertheless, you must supply a set of parentheses as in:

```
new InterfaceType() { methods and data }
```

You have to look very carefully to see the difference between the construction of a new object of a class and the construction of an object of an anonymous inner class extending that class. If the closing parenthesis of the construction parameter list is followed by an opening brace, then an anonymous inner class is being defined.

```
Person queen = new Person("Mary");
   // a Person object
Person count = new Person("Dracula") { ... };
   // an object of an inner class extending Person
```

Are anonymous inner classes a great idea or are they a great way of writing obfuscated code? Probably a bit of both. When the code for an inner class is short, just a few lines of simple code, then they can save typing time, but it is exactly timesaving features like this that lead you down the slippery slope to "Obfuscated Java Code Contests."

It is a shame that the designers of Java did not try to improve the syntax of anonymous inner classes, since, generally, Java syntax is a great improvement over C++. The designers of the inner class feature could have helped the human reader with a syntax such as:

```
Person count = new class extends Person("Dracula") { ... };
   // not the actual Java syntax
```

But they didn't. Because many programmers find code with too many anonymous inner classes hard to read, we recommend restraint when using them.

Example 6–5 contains the complete source code for the bank account program with an anonymous inner class. If you compare this program with Example 6–4, you will find that in this case the solution with the anonymous inner class is quite a bit shorter, and, hopefully, with a bit of practice, as easy to comprehend.

Example 6–5: AnonymousInnerClassTest.java

```
1. import java.awt.event.*;
2. import java.text.*;
3. import javax.swing.*;
4.
5. public class AnonymousInnerClassTest
6. {
7.    public static void main(String[] args)
8.    {
9.       // construct a bank account with initial balance of $10,000
10.      BankAccount account = new BankAccount(10000);
11.      // start accumulating interest at 10%
12.      account.start(10);
13.
14.      // keep program running until user selects "Ok"
15.      JOptionPane.showMessageDialog(null, "Quit program?");
16.      System.exit(0);
```

```
17.     }
18. }
19.
20. class BankAccount
21. {
22.     /**
23.         Constructs a bank account with an initial balance
24.         @param initialBalance the initial balance
25.     */
26.     public BankAccount(double initialBalance)
27.     {
28.         balance = initialBalance;
29.     }
30.
31.     /**
32.         Starts a simulation in which interest is added once per
33.         second
34.         @param rate the interest rate in percent
35.     */
36.     public void start(final double rate)
37.     {
38.         ActionListener adder = new
39.             ActionListener()
40.             {
41.                 public void actionPerformed(ActionEvent event)
42.                 {
43.                     // update interest
44.                     double interest = balance * rate / 100;
45.                     balance += interest;
46.
47.                     // print out current balance
48.                     NumberFormat formatter
49.                         = NumberFormat.getCurrencyInstance();
50.                     System.out.println("balance="
51.                         + formatter.format(balance));
52.                 }
53.             };
54.
55.         Timer t = new Timer(1000, adder);
56.         t.start();
57.     }
58.
59.     private double balance;
60. }
```

Static Inner Classes

Occasionally, you want to use an inner class simply to hide one class inside another, but you don't need the inner class to have a reference to the outer class object. You can suppress the generation of that reference by declaring the inner class `static`.

Here is a typical example of where you would want to do this. Consider the task of computing the minimum and maximum value in an array. Of course, you write one function to compute the minimum and another function to compute the maximum. When you call both functions, then the array is traversed twice. It would be more efficient to traverse the array only once, computing both the minimum and the maximum simultaneously.

```
double min = d[0];
double max = d[0];
for (int i = 1; i < d.length; i++)
{  if (min > d[i]) min = d[i];
   if (max < d[i]) max = d[i];
}
```

However, the function must return two numbers. We can achieve that by defining a class `Pair` that holds two values:

```
class Pair
{  public Pair(double f, double s)
   {  first = f;
      second = s;
   }
   public double getFirst()
   {  return first;
   }
   public double getSecond()
   {  return second;
   }

   private double first;
   private double second;
}
```

The `minmax` function can then return an object of type `Pair`.

```
class ArrayAlg
{  public static Pair minmax(double[] d)
   {  . . .
      return new Pair(min, max);
   }
}
```

The caller of the function then uses the `getFirst` and `getSecond` methods to retrieve the answers:

```
Pair p = ArrayAlg.minmax(d);
System.out.println("min = " + p.getFirst());
System.out.println("max = " + p.getSecond());
```

Of course, the name `Pair` is an exceedingly common name, and in a large project, it is quite possible that some other programmer had the same bright idea, except that the other programmer made a `Pair` class that contains a pair of strings. We can solve this potential name clash by making `Pair` a public inner class inside `ArrayAlg`. Then the class will be known to the public as `ArrayAlg.Pair`:

```
ArrayAlg.Pair p = ArrayAlg.minmax(d);
```

However, unlike the inner classes that we used in previous examples, we do not want to have a reference to any other object inside a `Pair` object. That reference can be suppressed by declaring the inner class `static`:

```
class ArrayAlg
{   public static class Pair
    {   . . .
    }
    . . .
}
```

Of course, only inner classes can be declared static. A static inner class is exactly like any other inner class, except that an object of a static inner class does not have a reference to the outer class object that generated it. In our example, we must use a static inner class because the inner class object is constructed inside a static method:

```
public static Pair minmax(double[] d)
{   . . .
    return new Pair(min, max);
}
```

Had the `Pair` class not been declared as `static`, the compiler would have complained that there was no implicit object of type `ArrayAlg` available to initialize the inner class object.

NOTE: You use a static inner class whenever the inner class does not need to access an outer class object. Some programmers use the term *nested class* to describe static inner classes.

Example 6–6 contains the complete source code of the `ArrayAlg` class and the nested `Pair` class.

Example 6–6: StaticInnerClassTest.java

```
1. public class StaticInnerClassTest
2. {
3.     public static void main(String[] args)
4.     {
5.         double[] d = new double[20];
6.         for (int i = 0; i < d.length; i++)
7.             d[i] = 100 * Math.random();
```

```
8.         ArrayAlg.Pair p = ArrayAlg.minmax(d);
9.         System.out.println("min = " + p.getFirst());
10.        System.out.println("max = " + p.getSecond());
11.     }
12. }
13.
14. class ArrayAlg
15. {
16.     /**
17.        A pair of floating point numbers
18.     */
19.     public static class Pair
20.     {
21.        /**
22.           Constructs a pair from two floating point numbers
23.           @param f the first number
24.           @param s the second number
25.        */
26.        public Pair(double f, double s)
27.        {
28.           first = f;
29.           second = s;
30.        }
31.
32.        /**
33.           Returns the first number of the pair
34.           @return the first number
35.        */
36.        public double getFirst()
37.        {
38.           return first;
39.        }
40.
41.        /**
42.           Returns the second number of the pair
43.           @return the second number
44.        */
45.        public double getSecond()
46.        {
47.           return second;
48.        }
49.
50.        private double first;
51.        private double second;
52.     }
53.
54.     /**
55.        Computes both the minimum and the maximum of an array
56.        @param a an array of floating point numbers
```

```
57.        @return a pair whose first element is the minimum and whose
58.        second element is the maximum
59.     */
60.     public static Pair minmax(double[] d)
61.     {
62.        if (d.length == 0) return new Pair(0, 0);
63.        double min = d[0];
64.        double max = d[0];
65.        for (int i = 1; i < d.length; i++)
66.        {
67.           if (min > d[i]) min = d[i];
68.           if (max < d[i]) max = d[i];
69.        }
70.        return new Pair(min, max);
71.     }
72. }
```

Proxies

In the final section of this chapter, we will discuss *proxies*, a new feature that became available with version 1.3 of the Java SDK. You use a proxy to create new classes at runtime that implement a given set of interfaces. Proxies are only necessary when you don't yet know at compile time which interfaces you need to implement. This is not a common situation for application programmers. However, for certain system programming applications the flexibility that proxies offer can be very important. By using proxies, you can often avoid the mechanical generation and compilation of "stub" code.

NOTE: In versions 1.2 and below of the Java SDK, you encounter stub code in a number of situations. When you use *remote method invocation* (RMI), a special utility called `rmic` produces stub classes that you need to add to your program. (See Chapter 4 of Volume 2 for more information on RMI.) And when you use the *bean box*, stub classes are produced and compiled on the fly when you connect beans to each other. (See Chapter 7 of Volume 2 for more information on Java beans.) It is expected that these mechanisms will be updated soon to take advantage of the proxy capability.

Suppose you have an array of `Class` objects representing interfaces (maybe only containing a single interface), whose exact nature you may not know at compile time. Now you want to construct an object of a class that implements these interfaces. This is a difficult problem. If a `Class` object represents an actual class, then you can simply use the `newInstance` method or use reflection to find a constructor of that class. But you can't instantiate an interface. And you can't define new classes in a running program.

To overcome this problem, some programs—such as the BeanBox in early versions of the Bean Development Kit—generate code, place it into a file, invoke the compiler and then load the resulting class file. Naturally, this is slow, and it also requires deployment of the compiler together with the program. The *proxy* mechanism is a better solution. The proxy class can create brand-new classes at runtime. Such a proxy class implements the interfaces that you specify. In particular, the proxy class has the following methods:

- All methods required by the specified interfaces;
- All methods defined in the `Object` class (`toString`, `equals`, and so on).

However, you cannot define new code for these methods at runtime. Instead, you must supply an *invocation handler*. An invocation handler is an object of any class that implements the `InvocationHandler` interface. That interface has a single method:

```
Object invoke(Object proxy, Method method, Object[] args)
```

Whenever a method is called on the proxy object, the `invoke` method of the invocation handler gets called, with the `Method` object and parameters of the original call. The invocation handler must then figure out how to handle the call.

To create a proxy object, you use the `newProxyInstance` method of the `Proxy` class. The method has three parameters:

1. A *class loader*. As part of the Java security model, it is possible to use different class loaders for system classes, classes that are downloaded from the Internet, and so on. We will discuss class loaders in Volume 2. For now, we will specify `null` to use the default class loader.
2. An array of `Class` objects, one for each interface to be implemented.
3. An invocation handler.

There are two remaining questions. How do we define the handler? And what can we do with the resulting proxy object? The answers depend, of course, on the problem that we want to solve with the proxy mechanism. Proxies can be used for many purposes, such as:

- Routing method calls to remote servers;
- Associating user interface events with actions in a running program;
- Tracing method calls for debugging purposes.

In our example program, we will use proxies and invocation handlers to trace method calls. We define a `TraceHandler` wrapper class that stores a wrapped object. Its `invoke` method simply prints out the name and parameters of the method to be called, and then calls the method with the wrapped object as the implicit parameter.

```
class TraceHandler implements InvocationHandler
{
```

```
    public TraceHandler(Object t)
    {
        target = t;
    }

    public Object invoke(Object proxy, Method m, Object[] args)
        throws Throwable
    {
        // print method name and parameters
        . . .
        // invoke actual method
        return m.invoke(target, args);
    }

    private Object target;
}
```

Here is how you construct a proxy object that causes the tracing behavior whenever one of its methods is called.

```
Object value = . . .;
// construct wrapper
InvocationHandler handler = new TraceHandler(value);
// construct proxy for all interfaces
Class[] interfaces = value.getClass().getInterfaces();
Object proxy = Proxy.newProxyInstance(null, interfaces, handler);
```

Now, whenever a method is called on `proxy`, the method name and parameters are printed out, and then the method is invoked on `value`.

In the program shown in Example 6–7, we use proxy objects to trace a binary search. We fill an array with proxies to the integers 1 . . . 1000. Then we invoke the `binarySearch` method of the `Arrays` class to search for a random integer in the array. Finally, we print out the matching element.

```
Object[] elements = new Object[1000];

// fill elements with proxies for the integers 1 ... 1000
for (int i = 0; i < elements.length; i++)
{
    Integer value = new Integer(i + 1);
    elements[i] = . . .; // proxy for value;
}

// construct a random integer
Random generator = new Random();
int r = generator.nextInt(elements.length);
Integer key = new Integer(r + 1);

// search for the key
int result = Arrays.binarySearch(elements, key);
```

```
// print match if found
if (result >= 0)
   System.out.println(elements[result]);
```

The `Integer` class implements the `Comparable` interface. The proxy objects belong to a class that is defined at runtime. (It has a name such as `$Proxy0`.) That class also implements the `Comparable` interface. However, its `compareTo` method calls the `invoke` method of the proxy object's handler.

The `binarySearch` method makes calls like this:

```
if (elements[i].compareTo(key) < 0) . . .
```

Because we filled the array with proxy objects, the `compareTo` calls call the `invoke` method of the `TraceHandler` class. That method prints out the method name and parameters and then invokes `compareTo` on the wrapped `Integer` object.

Finally, at the end of the sample program, we call:

```
System.out.println(elements[result]);
```

The `println` method calls `toString` on the proxy object, and that call is also redirected to the invocation handler.

Here is the complete trace of a program run:

```
500.compareTo(288)
250.compareTo(288)
375.compareTo(288)
312.compareTo(288)
281.compareTo(288)
296.compareTo(288)
288.compareTo(288)
288.toString()
```

You can see how the binary search algorithm homes in on the key, by cutting the search interval in half in every step.

Example 6–7: ProxyTest.java

```
1. import java.lang.reflect.*;
2. import java.util.*;
3.
4. public class ProxyTest
5. {
6.    public static void main(String[] args)
7.    {
8.       Object[] elements = new Object[1000];
9.
10.      // fill elements with proxies for the integers 1 ... 1000
11.      for (int i = 0; i < elements.length; i++)
12.      {
13.         Integer value = new Integer(i + 1);
```

```
14.            Class[] interfaces = value.getClass().getInterfaces();
15.            InvocationHandler handler = new TraceHandler(value);
16.            Object proxy = Proxy.newProxyInstance(null,
17.               interfaces, handler);
18.            elements[i] = proxy;
19.         }
20.
21.         // construct a random integer
22.         Random generator = new Random();
23.         int r = generator.nextInt(elements.length);
24.         Integer key = new Integer(r + 1);
25.
26.         // search for the key
27.         int result = Arrays.binarySearch(elements, key);
28.
29.         // print match if found
30.         if (result >= 0)
31.            System.out.println(elements[result]);
32.      }
33. }
34.
35. /**
36.    An invocation handler that prints out the method name
37.    and parameters, then invokes the original method
38. */
39. class TraceHandler implements InvocationHandler
40. {
41.    /**
42.       Constructs a TraceHandler
43.       @param t the implicit parameter of the method call
44.    */
45.    public TraceHandler(Object t)
46.    {
47.       target = t;
48.    }
49.
50.    public Object invoke(Object proxy, Method m, Object[] args)
51.       throws Throwable
52.    {
53.       // print implicit argument
54.       System.out.print(target);
55.       // print method name
56.       System.out.print("." + m.getName() + "(");
57.       // print explicit arguments
58.       if (args != null)
59.       {
60.          for (int i = 0; i < args.length; i++)
61.          {
62.             System.out.print(args[i]);
```

```
63.              if (i < args.length - 1)
64.                  System.out.print(", ");
65.          }
66.      }
67.      System.out.println(")");
68.
69.      // invoke actual method
70.      return m.invoke(target, args);
71.  }
72.
73.  private Object target;
74. }
```

Properties of Proxy Classes

Now that you have seen proxy classes in action, we want to go over some of their properties. Remember that proxy classes are created on the fly, in a running program. However, once they are created, they are regular classes, just like any other classes in the virtual machine.

All proxy classes extend the class `Proxy`. A proxy class has only one instance variable—the invocation handler which is defined in the `Proxy` superclass. Any additional data that is required to carry out the proxy objects' tasks must be stored in the invocation handler. For example, when we proxied `Comparable` objects in the program shown in Example 6–7, the `TraceHandler` wrapped the actual objects.

All proxy classes override the `toString`, `equals`, and `hashCode` methods of the `Object` class. Like all proxy methods, these methods simply call `invoke` on the invocation handler. The other methods of the `Object` class (such as `clone` and `getClass`) are not redefined.

The names of proxy classes are not defined. The `Proxy` class in the Java 2 SDK generates class names that begin with the string `$Proxy`.

There is only one proxy class for a particular class loader and ordered set of interfaces. That is, if you call the `newProxyInstance` method twice with the same class loader and interface array, then you get two objects of the same class. You can also obtain that class with the `getProxyClass` method:

```
Class proxyClass = Proxy.getProxyClass(null, interfaces);
```

A proxy class is always `public` and `final`. If all interfaces that the proxy class implements are `public`, then the proxy class does not belong to any particular package. Otherwise, all non-public interfaces must belong to the same package, and then the proxy class also belongs to that package.

You can test whether a particular `Class` object represents a proxy class, by calling the `isProxyClass` method of the `Proxy` class.

This ends our final chapter on the fundamentals of the Java programming language. Interfaces and inner classes are concepts that you will encounter frequently. However, as we already mentioned, proxies are an advanced technique that is of interest mainly to tool builders, not application programmers. You are now ready to go on to learn about graphics and user interfaces, starting with Chapter 7.

---

java.lang.reflect.InvocationHandler

- Object invoke(Object proxy, Method method, Object[] args)
  Define this method to contain the action that you want carried out whenever a method was invoked on the proxy object.

---

java.lang.reflect.Proxy

- static Class getProxyClass(ClassLoader loader, Class[] interfaces)
  Returns the proxy class that implements the given interfaces.

- static Object newProxyInstance(ClassLoader loader, Class[] interfaces, InvocationHandler handler)
  Constructs a new instance of the proxy class that implements the given interfaces. All methods call the invoke method of the given handler object.

- static boolean isProxyClass(Class c)
  Returns true if c is a proxy class.

Chapter 7

Graphics
Programming

- ▼ INTRODUCTION TO SWING
- ▼ CREATING A FRAME
- ▼ FRAME POSITIONING
- ▼ DISPLAYING INFORMATION IN A PANEL
- ▼ 2D SHAPES
- ▼ COLORS
- ▼ TEXT AND FONTS
- ▼ IMAGES

To this point, you have seen only how to write programs that take input from the keyboard, fuss with it, and then display the results on a console screen. This is not what most users want now. Modern programs don't work this way and neither do Web pages. This chapter starts you on the road to writing Java programs that use a graphical user interface (GUI). In particular, you will learn how to write programs that size and locate windows on the screen, display text with multiple fonts in a window, display images, and so on. This gives you a useful, valuable repertoire of skills that we will put to good use in the following chapters to write interesting programs.

The next two chapters show you how to process events such as keystrokes and mouse clicks, and how to add interface elements, such as menus and buttons, to your applications. When you finish these three chapters, you will know the essentials for writing *stand-alone* graphical applications. Chapter 10 shows how to program applets that use these features and are embedded in Web pages. For more sophisticated graphics programming techniques, we refer you to Volume 2.

Introduction to Swing

When Java 1.0 was introduced, it contained a class library, which Sun called the Abstract Window Toolkit (AWT), for basic GUI programming. The way the basic AWT library deals with user interface elements is to delegate their creation and behavior to the native GUI toolkit on each target platform (Windows, Solaris, Macintosh, and so on). For example, if you used the original AWT to put a text box on a Java window, an underlying "peer" text box actually handled the text input. When writing these kinds of AWT programs, the idea was that you simply specify the location and behavior of your user interface elements, and Java would create the peers. The resulting program could then, in theory, run on any of these platforms, with the "look and feel" of the target platform—hence Sun's trademarked slogan "Write Once, Run Anywhere."

The peer-based approach worked well for simple applications, but it soon became apparent that it was fiendishly difficult to write a high-quality portable graphics library that depended on native user interface elements. User interface elements such as menus, scrollbars, and text fields can have subtle differences in behavior on different platforms. It was hard, therefore, to give users a consistent and predictable experience with this approach. Moreover, some graphical environments (such as X11/Motif) do not have as rich a collection of user interface components as does Windows or the Macintosh. This in turn further limits a portable library based on peers to a "lowest common denominator" approach. As a result, GUI applications built with the AWT simply did not look as nice as native Windows or Macintosh applications, nor did they have the kind of functionality that users of those platforms had come to expect. More depressingly, there were *different* bugs in the AWT user interface library on the different platforms. Developers complained that they needed to test their applications on each platform, a practice derisively called "write once, debug everywhere."

In 1996, Netscape created a GUI library they called the *IFC* (Internet Foundation Classes) that used an entirely different approach. User interface elements, such as buttons, menus, and so on, were *painted* onto blank windows. The only peer functionality needed was a way to put up windows and to paint on the window. Thus, Netscape's IFC widgets looked and behaved the same no matter which platform the program ran on. Sun worked with Netscape to perfect this approach, creating a user interface library with the code name "Swing" (sometimes called the "Swing set").

Since, as Duke Ellington said, "It Don't Mean a Thing If It Ain't Got That Swing," Swing is now the official name for the non-peer-based GUI toolkit that is part of the Java Foundation Classes (JFC). The full JFC is vast and contains far more than the Swing GUI toolkit. JFC features not only include the Swing components but also an accessibility API, a 2D API, and a drag-and-drop API.

NOTE: Swing is not a complete replacement for the AWT. Swing simply gives you more capable user interface components. The basic architecture of the AWT, in particular, event handling, remains the same as it was in Java 1.1. (AWT event handling underwent a significant change between Java 1.0 and Java 1.1.) Swing uses the 1.1 event handling model, and a version of Swing can even be downloaded from Sun's web site for use in Java 1.1 programs. And, although the AWT peer-based user interface components are still available, you will rarely, if ever, want to use them. From now on, we'll say "Swing" when we mean the "painted" non-peer user interface classes, and we'll say "AWT" when we mean the underlying mechanisms of the windowing toolkit, such as event handling.

Of course, Swing-based user interface elements will be somewhat slower to appear on the user's screen than the peer-based components used by the AWT. Our experience is that on any reasonably modern machine, the speed difference shouldn't be a problem. On the other hand, the reasons to choose Swing are overwhelming:

- Swing has a much richer and more convenient set of user interface elements.

- Swing depends far less on the underlying platform; it is therefore less prone to platform-specific bugs.

- Swing will give a consistent user experience across platforms.

All this means Swing has the potential of finally fulfilling the promise of Sun's "Write Once, Run Anywhere" slogan.

Still, the third plus is also a potential drawback: if the user interface elements look the same on all platforms, then they will look *different* from the native controls on at least some platforms, and thus users will be less familiar with them.

Swing solves this problem in a very elegant way. Programmers writing Swing programs can give the program a specific "look and feel." For example, Figure 7–1 and 7–2 show the same program running with the Windows[1] and the Motif look and feel.

---

1. For what are apparently copyright reasons, the Windows and Macintosh look and feel are available only with the Java runtime environments for those platforms.

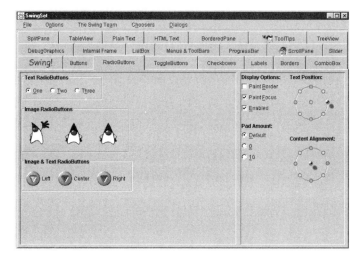

Figure 7–1: The Windows look and feel of Swing

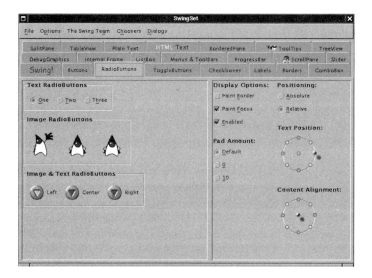

Figure 7–2: The Motif look and feel of Swing

NOTE: While we won't have space in this book to tell you how to do it, it is possible for Java programmers to extend an existing look and feel or even design a totally new look and feel. This is a tedious process that involves specifying how various Swing components need to be painted, but some developers have done just that, especially when porting Java to nontraditional platforms such as kiosk terminals or handheld terminals. See the "Swing Connection" at http://java.sun.com/products/jfc/tsc/ for more on this process.

Furthermore, Sun developed a platform-independent look and feel that they call "Metal," which we think looks very nice (see Figure 7–3). In this book, we will use Swing, with the Metal look and feel, for all our graphical programs.

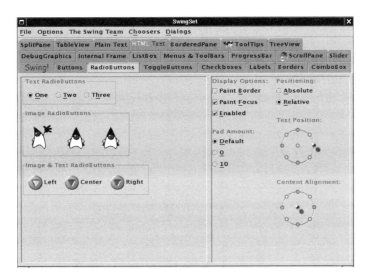

Figure 7–3: The Metal look and feel of Swing

In sum, Swing is more robust, has more features, is more portable, and is easier to use than the peer-based AWT user interface components. We feel strongly that Swing is the future of user interface programming in Java, and we think that you will want to use it for all your new Java programming projects.

Finally, we do have to warn you that if you have programmed Microsoft Windows applications using VB, Delphi, or Visual C++, you know about the ease of use that comes with the graphical layout tools and resource editors these products provide. These tools let you design the visual appearance of your application, and then they generate much (often all) of the GUI code for you. Although some GUI builders are now available for Java programming, these products are not as mature as the corresponding tools for Windows. In any case, to fully understand graphical user interface programming (or even, we feel, to use these tools effectively), you need to know how to build a user interface manually. Naturally, this often requires writing *a lot of code.*

Creating a Frame

A top-level window (that is, a window that is not contained inside another window) is called a *frame* in Java. The AWT library has a peer-based class, called Frame, for this top level. The Swing version of this class is called JFrame; JFrame extends the Frame class and is one of the few Swing components that is not painted on a canvas. Thus, the decorations (buttons, title bar, icons, and so on) are drawn by the user's windowing system, not by Swing.

 TIP: For users coming from an earlier version of Java, most of the AWT components have Swing equivalents whose class names simply add a "J"; hence, `JButton`, `JPanel`, etc.

Frames are examples of *containers*. This means that a frame can contain other user interface components such as buttons and text fields. In this section, we want to go over the most common methods for working with a Swing `JFrame`.

Example 7–1 lists a simple program that displays an empty frame on the screen, as illustrated in Figure 7–4.

Figure 7–4: The simplest visible frame

Example 7–1: SimpleFrameTest.java

```
1. import javax.swing.*;
2.
3. public class SimpleFrameTest
4. {
5.    public static void main(String[] args)
6.    {
7.       SimpleFrame frame = new SimpleFrame();
8.       frame.setDefaultCloseOperation(JFrame.EXIT_ON_CLOSE);
9.       frame.show();
10.   }
11. }
12.
13. class SimpleFrame extends JFrame
14. {
15.    public SimpleFrame()
16.    {
```

```
17.        setSize(WIDTH, HEIGHT);
18.    }
19.
20.    public static final int WIDTH = 300;
21.    public static final int HEIGHT = 200;
22. }
```

Let's work through this program, line by line.

The Swing classes are placed in the `javax.swing` package. The package name `javax` indicates a Java extension package, not a core package. The Swing classes are indeed an extension to Java 1.1. Because the Swing classes were not made a part of the core hierarchy, it is possible to load the Swing classes into a Java 1.1-compatible browser. (The security manager of the browser does not allow adding any packages that start with "`java.`".) On the Java 2 platform, the Swing package is no longer an extension, but is instead part of the core hierarchy. Any Java implementation that is compatible with Java 2 must supply the Swing classes. Nevertheless, the `javax` name remains, for compatibility with Java 1.1 code. (Actually, the Swing package started out as `com.sun.java.swing`, then briefly got moved to `java.awt.swing` during early Java 2 beta versions, then went back to `com.sun.java.swing` in late Java 2 beta versions, and after howls of protest by Java programmers, found its final resting place in `javax.swing`.)

By default, a frame has a rather useless size of 0 × 0 pixels. We define a subclass `SimpleFrame` whose constructor sets the size to 300 × 200 pixels. In the `main` method of the `SimpleFrameTest` class, we start out by constructing a `SimpleFrame` object.

Next, we define what should happen when the user closes this frame. For this particular program, we want the program to exit. To select this behavior, use the statement

```
frame.setDefaultCloseOperation(JFrame.EXIT_ON_CLOSE);
```

In other programs with multiple frames, you would not want the program to exit just because the user closes one of the frames. By default, a frame is hidden when the user closes it, but the program does not terminate.

NOTE: The `EXIT_ON_CLOSE` parameter for the `setDefaultCloseOperation` method was introduced with version 1.3 of the Java 2 SDK. If you are using an earlier version, you need to remove this line from the source code. (You will have to do that with the majority of programs in this book.)

Of course, after removing the call to `setDefaultCloseOperation`, the program won't exit when you close the window. To exit the program, you need to *kill* it. Under X

Windows, there is usually a menu option to "kill," "annihilate," or "destroy" the program. The details depend on the window manager. In Windows, you can summon the task list (with the CTRL+ALT+DEL "three-finger salute") and end the task.

Of course, these are drastic remedies. Alternatively, you can replace the call to the setDefaultCloseOperation method with the following code:

```
frame.addWindowListener(new
    WindowAdapter()
    {
        public void windowClosing(WindowEvent e)
        {
            System.exit(0);
        }
    });
```

You will see in Chapter 8 why this code fragment exits the application when the frame is closed.

TIP: The preceding note told you the "official" way of making a frame close on exit in a pre-1.3 version of the Java 2 SDK. However, in some of those versions, the call

```
frame.setDefaultCloseOperation(3);
```

magically works as well. Apparently, the functionality for the "exit on close" behavior had been added to the SDK before the EXIT_ON_CLOSE constant was added to the JFrame class.

Simply constructing a frame does not automatically display it. Frames start their life invisible. That gives the programmer the chance to add components into the frame before showing it for the first time. To show the frame, the main method calls the show method of the frame.

Afterwards, the main method exits. Note that exiting main does not terminate the program, just the main thread. Showing the frame activates a user interface thread that keeps the program alive.

NOTE: The JFrame class inherits the show method from the superclass Window. The Window class has a superclass Component that also has a show method. The Component.show method is deprecated, and you are supposed to call setVisible(true) instead if you want to show a component. However, the Window.show method is *not* deprecated. For windows and frames it makes sense to call show, not setVisible, because show makes the window visible *and* brings it to the front.

The running program is shown in Figure 7–4—it is a truly boring top-level window. As you can see in the figure, the title bar and surrounding decorations, such as resize corners, are drawn by the operating system and not the Swing library. If you run the same program in X Windows, the frame decorations are different. The Swing library draws everything inside the frame. In this program, it just fills the frame with a default background color.

NOTE: In the above example we wrote two classes, one to define a frame class and one that contains a `main` method that creates and shows a frame object. Frequently, you will see programs in which the `main` method is opportunistically tossed into a convenient class, like this:

```
class SimpleFrame extends JFrame
{
    public static void main(String[] args)
    {
        SimpleFrame frame = new SimpleFrame();
        frame.setDefaultCloseOperation(JFrame.EXIT_ON_CLOSE);
        frame.show();
    }

    public SimpleFrame()
    {
        setSize(WIDTH, HEIGHT);
    }

    public static final int WIDTH = 300;
    public static final int HEIGHT = 200;
}
```

Using the `main` method of the frame class for the code that launches the program is simpler in one sense. You do not have to introduce another auxiliary class. However, quite a few programmers find this code style a bit confusing. Therefore, we prefer to separate out the class that launches the program from the classes that define the user interface.

Frame Positioning

The JFrame class itself has only a few methods for changing how frames look. Of course, through the magic of inheritance, most of the methods for working with the size and position of a frame come from the various superclasses of JFrame. Probably the most important methods, inherited from the base class Frame, are the following ones:

- The dispose method that closes the window down and reclaims any system resources used in creating it;

- The `setIconImage` method, which takes an `Image` object to use as the icon when the window is minimized (often called *iconized* in Java terminology);

- The `setTitle` method for changing the text in the title bar;

- The `setResizable` method, which takes a `boolean` to determine if a frame will be resizeable by the user.

Figure 7–5 illustrates the inheritance chain for the `JFrame` class.

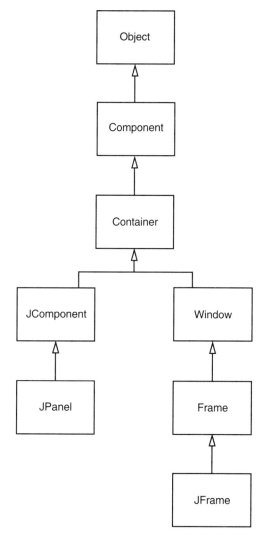

Figure 7–5: Inheritance hierarchy for the `JFrame` and `JPanel` classes

As the API notes indicate, the `Component` class (which is the ancestor of all GUI objects) and the `Window` class (which is the `Frame`'s class parent) are where you need to look to find the methods to resize and reshape frames. For example, the `show` method that you use to display the frame lives in the `Window` class. As another example, the `setLocation` method in the `Component` class is one way to reposition a component. If you make the call

```
setLocation(x, y)
```

the top-left corner is located x pixels across and y pixels down, where (0, 0) is the top-left corner of the screen. Similarly, the `setBounds` method in `Component` lets you resize and relocate a component (in particular, a `JFrame`) in one step, as

```
setBounds(x, y, width, height)
```

NOTE: For a frame, the coordinates of the `setLocation` and `setBounds` are taken relative to the whole screen. As you will see in Chapter 9, for other components inside a container, the measurements are taken relative to the container.

Remember: if you don't explicitly size a frame, all frames will default to being 0 by 0 pixels. To keep our example programs simple, we resize the frames to a size that we hope works acceptably on most displays. However, in a professional application, you should check the resolution of the user's screen and write code that resizes the frames accordingly: a window that looks nice on a laptop screen will look like a postage stamp on a high-resolution screen. As you will soon see, you can obtain the screen dimensions in pixels on the user's system. You can then use this information to compute the optimal window size for your program.

TIP: The API notes for this section give what we think are the most important methods for giving frames the proper look and feel. Some of these methods are defined in the `JFrame` class. Others come from the various parent classes of `JFrame`. At some point, you may need to search the API docs to see if there are methods for some special purpose. Unfortunately, that is a bit tedious to do with the SDK documentation. For subclasses, the API docs only explain *overridden* methods. For example, `show` is applicable to objects of type `JFrame`, but because it is simply inherited from the `Window` class, the `JFrame` documentation doesn't explain it. If you feel that there should be a method to do something and it isn't explained in the documentation for the class you are working with, try looking at the API docs for the methods of the *superclasses* of that class. The top of each API page has hyperlinks to the superclasses, and there is a list of inherited methods below the method summary for the new and overridden methods.

To give you an idea of what you can do with a window, we end this section by showing you a sample program that positions one of our closable frames so that:

• Its area is one-fourth that of the whole screen;

• It is centered in the middle of the screen.

For example, if the screen was 800×600 pixels, we need a frame that is 400×300 pixels and we need to move it so the top left-hand corner is at (200,150).

To do this, we need a method to find out the screen resolution. This method obviously requires interacting with the underlying operating system since this is the only place where this information is likely to be stored. In Java, you usually get at system-dependent information via what is called a *toolkit*. The Toolkit class has a method called getScreenSize that returns the screen size as a Dimension object. A Dimension object d simultaneously stores a width and a height, in public (!) instance variables width and height.

Here's a fragment you use to get the screen size:

```
Toolkit kit = Toolkit.getDefaultToolkit();
Dimension screenSize = kit.getScreenSize();
int screenWidth = screenSize.width;
int screenHeight = screenSize.height;
```

We also supply an icon. Because the representation of images is also system dependent, we again need to use the toolkit to load an image. Then, we set the image as the icon for the frame.

```
Image img = kit.getImage("icon.gif");
setIconImage(img);
```

Depending on your operating system, you can see the icon in various places. For example, in Windows, the icon is displayed in the top-left corner of the window, and you can see it in the list of active tasks when you press ALT+TAB.

Example 7–2 is the complete program. When you run the program, pay attention to the "Core Java" icon.

Example 7–2: CenteredFrameTest.java

```
1. import java.awt.*;
2. import java.awt.event.*;
3. import javax.swing.*;
4.
5. public class CenteredFrameTest
6. {
7.    public static void main(String[] args)
8.    {
9.       CenteredFrame frame = new CenteredFrame();
```

```
10.         frame.setDefaultCloseOperation(JFrame.EXIT_ON_CLOSE);
11.         frame.show();
12.     }
13. }
14.
15. class CenteredFrame extends JFrame
16. {
17.     public CenteredFrame()
18.     {
19.         // get screen dimensions
20.
21.         Toolkit kit = Toolkit.getDefaultToolkit();
22.         Dimension screenSize = kit.getScreenSize();
23.         int screenHeight = screenSize.height;
24.         int screenWidth = screenSize.width;
25.
26.         // center frame in screen
27.
28.         setSize(screenWidth / 2, screenHeight / 2);
29.         setLocation(screenWidth / 4, screenHeight / 4);
30.
31.         // set frame icon and title
32.
33.         Image img = kit.getImage("icon.gif");
34.         setIconImage(img);
35.         setTitle("CenteredFrame");
36.     }
37. }
```

java.awt.Component

- `boolean isVisible()`
  checks if this component is set to be visible. Components are initially visible, with the exception of top-level components such as `JFrame`.

- `void setVisible(boolean b)`
  shows or hides the component depending on whether b is `true` or `false`.

- `boolean isShowing()`
  checks if this component is showing on the screen. For this, it must be visible and be inside a container that is showing.

- `boolean isEnabled()`
  checks if this component is enabled. An enabled component can receive keyboard input. Components are initially enabled.

- `void setEnabled(boolean b)`
  enables or disables a component.

- `Point getLocation()`
  returns the location of the top-left corner of this component, relative to the top-left corner of the surrounding container. (A `Point` object p encapsulates an *x*- and a *y*-coordinate which are accessible by p.x and p.y.)

- `Point getLocationOnScreen()`
  returns the location of the top-left corner of this component, using the screen's coordinates.

- `void setBounds(int x, int y, int width, int height)`
  moves and resizes this component. The location of the top-left corner is given by x and y, and the new size is given by the width and height parameters.

- `void setLocation(int x, int y)`
- `void setLocation(Point p)`
  moves the component to a new location. The *x*- and *y*-coordinates (or p.x and p.y) use the coordinates of the container if the component is not a top-level component, or the coordinates of the screen if the component is top level (for example, a JFrame).

- `Dimension getSize()`
  gets the current size of this component.

- `void setSize(int width, int height)`
- `void setSize(Dimension d)`
  resizes the component to the specified width and height.

java.awt.Window

- `void toFront()`
  shows this window on top of any other windows.

- `void toBack()`
  moves this window to the back of the stack of windows on the desktop and rearranges all other visible windows accordingly.

java.awt.Frame

- `void setResizable(boolean b)`
  determines whether the user can resize the frame.

- `void setTitle(String s)`
  sets the text in the title bar for the frame to the string s.

- `void setIconImage(Image image)`

Parameters:	image	The image you want to appear as the icon for the frame

```
java.awt.Toolkit
```

- `Dimension getScreenSize()`
  gets the size of the user's screen.

- `Image getImage(String filename)`
  loads an image from the file with name `filename`.

Displaying Information in a Panel

In this section, we'll show you how to display information inside a frame. For example, rather than displaying "Not a Hello, World program" in text mode in a console window as we did in Chapter 3, we will display the message in a frame, as shown in Figure 7–6.

Figure 7–6: A simple graphical program

It would be possible to draw the message string directly onto a frame, but that is not considered good programming practice. In Java, frames are really designed to be containers for *components* such as a menu bar and other user interface elements. You normally draw on another component, called a *panel*, which you add to the frame.

The structure of a `JFrame` is surprisingly complex. Look at Figure 7–7 which shows the makeup of a `JFrame`. As you can see, four panes are layered in a `JFrame`. The root pane, layered pane, and glass pane are of no interest to us; they are required to organize the menu bar and content pane and to implement the look and feel. The part that most concerns Swing programmers is the *content pane*. When designing a frame, you add components into the content pane, using code such as the following:

```
Container contentPane = getContentPane();
Component c = . . .;
contentPane.add(c);
```

NOTE: If you are familiar with AWT programming, you know that you used to call the `add` method to add components directly into an AWT `Frame`. In Swing, that is not possible. You must add all components into the content pane.

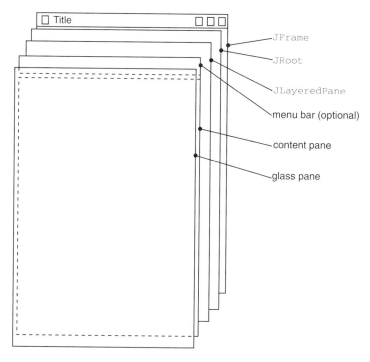

Figure 7–7: The internal structure of a `JFrame`

In our case, we want to add a single *panel* to the content pane onto which we will draw our message. Panels are implemented by the `JPanel` class. They are user interface elements with two useful properties:

*   They have a surface onto which you can draw;

*   They themselves are containers.

Thus, they can hold other user interface components such as buttons, sliders, and so on.

However, there is no sense in adding a plain `JPanel` to the content pane—it doesn't do anything interesting. To make it more interesting, you use inheritance to create a new class and then override or add methods to get the extra functionality you want.

In particular, to draw on a panel, you will need to:

* Define a class that extends `JPanel`;

* Override the `paintComponent` method in that class.

The `paintComponent` method is actually in `JComponent`—the parent class for all nonwindow Swing components. It takes one parameter of type `Graphics`. A `Graphics` object remembers a collection of settings for drawing images and text, such as the font you set or the current color. All drawing in Java must go through a `Graphics` object. It has methods that draw patterns, images, and text.

NOTE: The Graphics parameter is similar to a device context in Windows or a graphics context in X11 programming.

Here's how to make a panel onto which you can draw:

```
class MyPanel extends JPanel
{
   public void paintComponent(Graphics g)
   {
      . . . // code for drawing will go here
   }
}
```

Each time a window needs to be redrawn, no matter what the reason, the event handler notifies the component. This causes the `paintComponent` methods of all components to be executed.

Never call the `paintComponent` method yourself. It is called automatically whenever a part of your application needs to be redrawn, and you should not interfere with this automatic process.

What sorts of actions trigger this automatic response? For example, painting occurs because the user increased the size of the window or minimized and then restored the window. If the user popped up another window and it covered an existing window and then made the overlaid window disappear, the application window that was covered is now corrupted and will need to be repainted. (The graphics system does not save the pixels underneath.) And, of course, when the window is displayed for the first time, it needs to process the code that specifies how and where it should draw the initial elements.

TIP: If you need to force repainting of the screen, call the `repaint` method instead of `paintComponent`. The `repaint` method will cause `paintComponent` to be called for all components, with properly configured `Graphics` arguments.

As you saw in the code fragment above, the `paintComponent` method takes a single parameter of type `Graphics`. Measurement on a `Graphics` object for screen display is done in pixels. The (0, 0) coordinate denotes the top-left corner of the component on whose surface you are drawing.

Displaying text (usually called *rendering text*) is considered a special kind of drawing. The `Graphics` class has a `drawString` method that has the following syntax:

```
g.drawString(text, x, y)
```

In our case, we want to draw the string `"Not a Hello, World Program"` in our original window, roughly one-quarter of the way across and halfway down. Although we don't yet know how to measure the size of the string, we'll start the string at coordinates (75, 100). This means the first character in the string will start at a position 75 pixels to the right and 100 pixels down. (Actually, it is the baseline for the text that is 100 pixels down—see below for more on how text is measured.) Thus, our `paintComponent` method looks like this:

```
class NotHelloWorldPanel extends JPanel
{
   public void paintComponent(Graphics g)
   {
      . . . // see below

      g.drawString("Not a Hello, World program",
         MESSAGE_X, MESSAGE_Y);
   }

   public static final int MESSAGE_X = 75;
   public static final int MESSAGE_Y = 100;
}
```

However, this `paintComponent` method is not complete. The `NotHello-WorldPanel` class extends the `JPanel` class, which has its own idea how to paint the panel, namely, to fill it with the background color. To make sure that the superclass does its part of the job, we must call `super.paintComponent` before doing any painting on our own.

```
class NotHelloWorldPanel extends JPanel
{
   public void paintComponent(Graphics g)
   {
      super.paintComponent(g);
```

```
          . . . // code for drawing will go here
     }
}
```

NOTE: If you have programmed for the old AWT, you will have noticed quite a few differences. In the old AWT, you drew onto a `Canvas`, a subclass of `Component` just for drawing. In Swing, there is no special canvas class. You can draw onto any Swing component, but if you want to separate a drawing area from the remainder of your user interface, you should just render the drawing on the surface of a `JPanel` subclass.

More importantly, you no longer use the `paint` method for drawing. In fact, if you override `paint`, then your program will not work correctly. You then interfere with the `JComponent.paint` method which carries out a number of complex actions, such as setting up the graphics context and image buffering. In Swing, you should always use the `paintComponent` method.

In the old AWT, you may have defined the `update` method to call `paint` without erasing the window to avoid screen flicker. This is no longer necessary in Swing. The Swing components use buffering for flicker-free painting.

Example 7–3 shows the complete code.

Example 7–3: NotHelloWorld.java

```
1. import javax.swing.*;
2. import java.awt.*;
3.
4. public class NotHelloWorld
5. {
6.    public static void main(String[] args)
7.    {
8.       NotHelloWorldFrame frame = new NotHelloWorldFrame();
9.       frame.setDefaultCloseOperation(JFrame.EXIT_ON_CLOSE);
10.       frame.show();
11.    }
12. }
13.
14. /**
15.    A frame that contains a message panel
16. */
17. class NotHelloWorldFrame extends JFrame
18. {
19.    public NotHelloWorldFrame()
20.    {
21.       setTitle("NotHelloWorld");
```

```java
22.        setSize(WIDTH, HEIGHT);
23.
24.        // add panel to frame
25.
26.        NotHelloWorldPanel panel = new NotHelloWorldPanel();
27.        Container contentPane = getContentPane();
28.        contentPane.add(panel);
29.     }
30.
31.     public static final int WIDTH = 300;
32.     public static final int HEIGHT = 200;
33. }
34.
35. /**
36.    A panel that displays a message.
37. */
38. class NotHelloWorldPanel extends JPanel
39. {
40.     public void paintComponent(Graphics g)
41.     {
42.        super.paintComponent(g);
43.
44.        g.drawString("Not a Hello, World program",
45.           MESSAGE_X, MESSAGE_Y);
46.     }
47.
48.     public static final int MESSAGE_X = 75;
49.     public static final int MESSAGE_Y = 100;
50. }
```

javax.swing.JFrame

- `Container getContentPane()`
  returns the content pane object for this `JFrame`.

java.awt.Component

- `void repaint()`
  causes a repaint of the component "as soon as possible."

- `public void repaint(int x, int y, int width, int height)`
  causes a repaint of a part of the component "as soon as possible."

javax.swing.JComponent

- `void paintComponent(Graphics g)`
  Override this method to describe how your component needs to be painted.

2D Shapes

Since JDK version 1.0, the `Graphics` class had methods to draw lines, rectangles, ellipses, and so on. But those drawing operations are very limited. For example, you cannot vary the line thickness and you cannot rotate the shapes.

Beginning with SDK version 2.0, J2SE includes the *Java 2D* library which implements a very powerful set of graphical operations. In this chapter, we will only look at the basics of the Java 2D library—see the Advanced AWT chapter in Volume 2 for more information on the advanced features.

To draw shapes in the Java 2D library, you need to obtain an object of the `Graphics2D` class. This class is a subclass of the `Graphics` class. If you use a version of the SDK that is Java 2D enabled, methods such as `paintComponent` automatically receive an object of the `Graphics2D` class. Simply use a cast, as follows:

```
public void paintComponent(Graphics g)
{
    Graphics2D g2 = (Graphics2D)g;
    . . .
}
```

The Java 2D library organizes geometric shapes in an object-oriented fashion. In particular, there are classes to represent lines, rectangles and ellipses:

```
Line2D
Rectangle2D
Ellipse2D
```

These classes all implement the `Shape` interface.

NOTE: The Java 2D library supports more complex shapes—in particular, arcs, quadratic and cubic curves, and general paths. See Volume 2 for more information.

To draw a shape, you first create an object of a class that implements the `Shape` interface and then call the `draw` method of the `Graphics2D` class. For example,

```
Rectangle2D rect = . . .;
g2.draw(rect);
```

NOTE: Before the Java 2D library appeared, programmers used methods of the `Graphics` class such as `drawRectangle` to draw shapes. Superficially, the old-style method calls look a bit simpler. However, by using the Java 2D library, you keep your options open—you can later enhance your drawings with some of the many tools that the Java 2D library supplies.

There is a complexity when using the Java 2D shape classes. Unlike the 1.0 draw methods, which used integer pixel coordinates, the Java 2D shapes use floating-point coordinates. In many cases, that is a great convenience because it allows you to specify your shapes in coordinates that are meaningful to you (such as millimeters or inches) and then translate to pixels. The Java 2D library uses single-precision `float` quantities for many of its internal floating-point calculations. Single precision is sufficient—after all, the ultimate purpose of the geometric computations is to set pixels on the screen or printer. As long as any roundoff errors stay within one pixel, the visual outcome is not affected. Furthermore, `float` computations are faster on some platforms, and `float` values require half the storage of `double` values.

However, manipulating `float` values is sometimes inconvenient for the programmer because the Java programming language is adamant about requiring casts when converting `double` values into `float` values. For example, consider the following statement:

```
float f = 1.2; // Error
```

This statement does not compile because the constant `1.2` has type `double`, and the compiler is nervous about loss of precision. The remedy is to add an `F` suffix to the floating-point constant:

```
float f = 1.2F; // Ok
```

Now consider this statement:

```
Rectangle2D r = . . .
float f = r.getWidth(); // Error
```

This statement does not compile either, for the same reason. The `getWidth` method returns a `double`. This time, the remedy is to provide a cast:

```
float f = (float)r.getWidth(); // Ok
```

Because the suffixes and casts are a bit of a pain, the designers of the 2D library decided to supply *two versions* of each shape class: one with `float` coordinates for frugal programmers, and one with `double` coordinates for the lazy ones. (In this book, we'll fall into the second camp and use `double` coordinates whenever we can.)

The library designers chose a curious, and initially confusing, method for packaging these choices. Consider the `Rectangle2D` class. This is an abstract class with two concrete subclasses, which are also static inner classes:

```
Rectangle2D.Float
Rectangle2D.Double
```

Figure 7–8 shows the inheritance diagram.

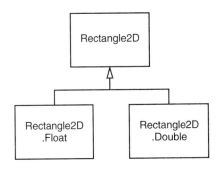

Figure 7–8: 2D rectangle classes

It is best to try to ignore the fact that the two concrete classes are static inner classes—that is just a gimmick to avoid names such as FloatRectangle2D and DoubleRectangle2D. (For more information on static inner classes, see Chapter 6.)

When you construct a Rectangle2D.Float object, you supply the coordinates as float numbers. For a Rectangle2D.Double object, you supply them as double numbers.

```
Rectangle2D.Float floatRect = new Rectangle2D.Float(10.0F,
    25.0F, 22.5F, 20.0F);
Rectangle2D.Double doubleRect = new Rectangle2D.Double(10.0,
    25.0, 22.5, 20.0);
```

Actually, since both Rectangle2D.Float and Rectangle2D.Double extend the common Rectangle2D class, and the methods in the subclasses simply override methods in the Rectangle2D superclass, there is no benefit in remembering the exact shape type. You can simply use Rectangle2D variables to hold the rectangle references.

```
Rectangle2D floatRect = new Rectangle2D.Float(10.0F,
    25.0F, 22.5F, 20.0F);
Rectangle2D doubleRect = new Rectangle2D.Double(10.0,
    25.0, 22.5, 20.0);
```

That is, you only need to use the pesky inner classes when you construct the shape objects.

The construction parameters denote the top-left corner, width, and height of the rectangle.

NOTE: Actually, the Rectangle2D.Float class has one additional method that is not inherited from Rectangle2D, namely, setRect(float x, float y, float h, float w). You lose that method if you store the Rectangle2D.Float reference in a Rectangle2D variable. But it is not a big loss—the Rectangle2D class has a setRect method with double parameters.

The `Rectangle2D` methods use `double` parameters and return values. For example, the `getWidth` method returns a `double` value, even if the width is stored as a `float` in a `Rectangle2D.Float` object.

> TIP: Simply use the `Double` shape classes to avoid dealing with `float` values altogether. However, if you are constructing thousands of shape objects, then you can consider using the `Float` classes to conserve memory.

What we just discussed for the `Rectangle2D` classes holds for the other shape classes as well. Furthermore, there is a `Point2D` class with subclasses `Point2D.Float` and `Point2D.Double`. Here is how to make a point object.

```
Point2D p = new Point2D.Double(10, 20);
```

> TIP: The `Point2D` class is very useful—it is more object oriented to work with `Point2D` objects than with separate *x*- and *y*- values. Many constructors and methods accept `Point2D` parameters. We suggest that you use `Point2D` objects when you can—they usually make geometric computations easier to understand.

The classes `Rectangle2D` and `Ellipse2D` both inherit from a common superclass `RectangularShape`. Admittedly, ellipses are not rectangular, but they have a *bounding rectangle* (see Figure 7–9).

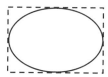

Figure 7–9: The bounding rectangle of an ellipse

The `RectangularShape` class defines over 20 methods that are common to these shapes, among them such useful methods as `getWidth`, `getHeight`, `getCenterX`, and `getCenterY` (but sadly, at the time of this writing, not a `getCenter` method that returns the center as a `Point2D` object).

Finally, there are a couple of legacy classes from JDK 1.0 that have been fit into the shape class hierarchy. The `Rectangle` and `Point` classes, which store a rectangle and a point with integer coordinates, extend the `Rectangle2D` and `Point2D` classes.

Figure 7–10 shows the relationships between the shape classes. However, the `Double` and `Float` subclasses are omitted. Legacy classes are marked with a gray fill.

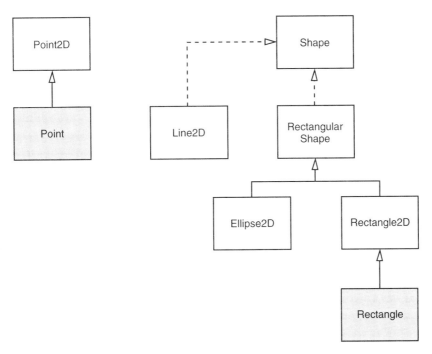

Figure 7–10: Relationships between the shape classes

`Rectangle2D` and `Ellipse2D` objects are simple to construct. You need to specify

*   The *x*- and *y*-coordinates of the top-left corner;

*   The width and height.

For ellipses, these refer to the bounding rectangle.

For example,

```
Ellipse2D e = new Ellipse2D.Double(150, 200, 100, 50);
```

constructs an ellipse that is bounded by a rectangle with the top-left corner at (150, 200), width 100, and height 50.

However, sometimes you don't have the top-left corner readily available. It is quite common to have two diagonal corner points of a rectangle, but perhaps they aren't the top-left and bottom-right corners. You can't simply construct a rectangle as

```
Rectangle2D rect = new Rectangle2D.Double(px, py,
    qx - px, qy - py); // Error
```

If `p` isn't the top-left corner, one or both of the coordinate differences will be negative and the rectangle will come out empty. In that case, first create a blank rectangle and use the `setFrameFromDiagonal` method.

```
Rectangle2D rect = new Rectangle2D.Double();
rect.setFrameFromDiagonal(px, py, qx, qy);
```

Or, even better, if you know the corner points as `Point2D` objects p and q,

```
rect.setFrameFromDiagonal(p, q);
```

When constructing an ellipse, you usually know the center, width, and height, and not the corner points of the bounding rectangle (which don't even lie on the ellipse). There is a `setFrameFromCenter` method that uses the center point, but it still requires one of the four corner points. Thus, you will usually end up constructing an ellipse as follows:

```
Ellipse2D ellipse = new Ellipse2D.Double(centerX - width / 2,
    centerY - height / 2, width, height);
```

To construct a line, you supply the start and end points, either as `Point2D` objects or as pairs of numbers:

```
Line2D line = new Line2D.Double(start, end);
```

or

```
Line2D line = new Line2D.Double(startX, startY, endX, endY);
```

The program in Example 7–4 draws

- A rectangle;

- The ellipse that is enclosed in the rectangle;

- A diagonal of the rectangle;

- A circle that has the same center as the rectangle.

Figure 7–11 shows the result.

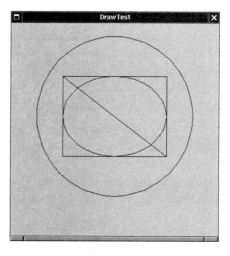

Figure 7–11: Rectangles and ellipses

Example 7–4: DrawTest.java

```
1. import java.awt.*;
2. import java.awt.geom.*;
3. import javax.swing.*;
4.
5. public class DrawTest
6. {
7.    public static void main(String[] args)
8.    {
9.       DrawFrame frame = new DrawFrame();
10.       frame.setDefaultCloseOperation(JFrame.EXIT_ON_CLOSE);
11.       frame.show();
12.    }
13. }
14.
15. /**
16.    A frame that contains a panel with drawings
17. */
18. class DrawFrame extends JFrame
19. {
20.    public DrawFrame()
21.    {
22.       setTitle("DrawTest");
23.       setSize(WIDTH, HEIGHT);
24.
25.       // add panel to frame
26.
27.       DrawPanel panel = new DrawPanel();
28.       Container contentPane = getContentPane();
29.       contentPane.add(panel);
30.    }
31.
32.    public static final int WIDTH = 400;
33.    public static final int HEIGHT = 400;
34. }
35.
36. /**
37.    A panel that displays rectangles and ellipses.
38. */
39. class DrawPanel extends JPanel
40. {
41.    public void paintComponent(Graphics g)
42.    {
43.       super.paintComponent(g);
44.       Graphics2D g2 = (Graphics2D)g;
45.
46.       // draw a rectangle
47.
48.       double leftX = 100;
```

```
49.     double topY = 100;
50.     double width = 200;
51.     double height = 150;
52.
53.     Rectangle2D rect = new Rectangle2D.Double(leftX, topY,
54.         width, height);
55.     g2.draw(rect);
56.
57.     // draw the enclosed ellipse
58.
59.     Ellipse2D ellipse = new Ellipse2D.Double();
60.     ellipse.setFrame(rect);
61.     g2.draw(ellipse);
62.
63.     // draw a diagonal line
64.
65.     g2.draw(new Line2D.Double(leftX, topY,
66.         leftX + width, topY + height));
67.
68.     // draw a circle with the same center
69.
70.     double centerX = rect.getCenterX();
71.     double centerY = rect.getCenterY();
72.     double radius = 150;
73.
74.     Ellipse2D circle = new Ellipse2D.Double();
75.     circle.setFrameFromCenter(centerX, centerY,
76.         centerX + radius, centerY + radius);
77.     g2.draw(circle);
78.   }
79. }
```

java.awt.geom.RectangularShape

- double getCenterX()
- double getCenterY()
- double getMinX()
- double getMinY()
- double getMaxX()
- double getMaxY()

   return the center, minimum, or maximum *x*- or *y*-value of the enclosing rectangle.

- double getWidth()
- double getHeight()

   return the width or height of the enclosing rectangle.

- double getX()
- double getY()

   return the *x*- or *y*-coordinate of the top-left corner of the enclosing rectangle.

`java.awt.geom.Rectangle2D.Double`

- `Rectangle2D.Double(double x, double y, double w, double h)`
  constructs a rectangle with the given top-left corner, width, and height.

`java.awt.geom.Rectangle2D.Float`

- `Rectangle2D.Float(float x, float y, float w, float h)`
  constructs a rectangle with the given top-left corner, width, and height.

`java.awt.geom.Ellipse2D.Double`

- `Ellipse2D.Double(double x, double y, double w, double h)`
  constructs an ellipse whose bounding rectangle has the given top-left corner, width, and height.

`java.awt.geom.Point2D.Double`

- `Point2D.Double(double x, double y)`
  constructs a point with the given coordinates.

`java.awt.geom.Line2D.Double`

- `Line2D.Double(Point2D start, Point2D end)`
- `Line2D.Double(double startX, double startY, double endX, double endY)`
  construct a line with the given start and end points.

Colors

The `setPaint` method of the `Graphics2D` class lets you select a color that is used for all subsequent drawing operations on the graphics context or component. To draw in multiple colors, you select a color, draw, then select another color, and draw again.

You define colors with the `Color` class. The `java.awt.Color` class offers predefined constants for the 13 standard colors listed in Table 7–1.

For example,

```
g2.setPaint(Color.red);
g2.drawString("Warning!", 100, 100);
```

You can specify a custom color by creating a `Color` object by its red, green, and blue components. Using a scale of 0–255 (that is, one byte) for the redness, blueness, and greenness, call the `Color` constructor like this:

```
Color(int redness, int  greenness, int blueness)
```

Here is an example of setting a custom color:

```
g.setPaint(new Color(0, 128, 128)); // a dull blue-green
g.drawString("Welcome!", 75, 125);
```

NOTE: In addition to solid colors, you can select more complex "paint" settings, such as varying hues or images. See the Advanced AWT chapter in Volume 2 for more details. If you use a `Graphics` object instead of a `Graphics2D` object, you need to use the `setColor` method to set colors.

Table 7–1: Standard colors

black	green	red
blue	lightGray	white
cyan	magenta	yellow
darkGray	orange	
gray	pink	

To set the *background color*, you use the `setBackground` method of the `Component` class, an ancestor of `JPanel`. In fact, you should set the background before displaying the frame for the first time.

```
MyPanel p = new MyPanel();
p.setBackground(Color.white);
contentPane.add(p);
```

There is also a `setForeground` method. It specifies the default color that is used for drawing on the component.

TIP: The `brighter()` and `darker()` methods of the `Color` class produce, as their names suggest, either brighter or darker versions of the current color. Using the `brighter` method is also a good way to highlight an item. Actually, `brighter()` is just a little bit brighter. To make a color really stand out, apply it three times: `c.brighter().brighter().brighter()`.

Java gives you predefined names for many more colors in its `SystemColor` class. The constants in this class encapsulate the colors used for various elements of the user's system. For example,

```
frame.setBackground(SystemColor.window)
```

sets the background color of the frame to the default used by all windows on the user's desktop. (The background is filled in whenever the window is repainted.) Using the colors in the `SystemColor` class is particularly useful when you want to draw user interface elements so that the colors match those already found on the user's desktop. Table 7–2 lists the system color names and their meanings.

Table 7–2: System colors

`desktop`	Background color of desktop
`activeCaption`	Background color for captions
`activeCaptionText`	Text color for captions
`activeCaptionBorder`	Border color for caption text
`inactiveCaption`	Background color for inactive captions
`inactiveCaptionText`	Text color for inactive captions
`inactiveCaptionBorder`	Border color for inactive captions
`window`	Background for windows
`windowBorder`	Color of window border frame
`windowText`	Text color inside windows
`menu`	Background for menus
`menuText`	Text color for menus
`text`	Background color for text
`textText`	Text color for text
`textInactiveText`	Text color for inactive controls
`textHighlight`	Background color for highlighted text
`textHighlightText`	Text color for highlighted text
`control`	Background color for controls
`controlText`	Text color for controls
`controlLtHighlight`	Light highlight color for controls
`controlHighlight`	Highlight color for controls
`controlShadow`	Shadow color for controls
`controlDkShadow`	Dark shadow color for controls
`scrollbar`	Background color for scrollbars
`info`	Background color for spot-help text
`infoText`	Text color for spot-help text

java.awt.Color

- Color(int r, int g, int b)

  creates a color object.

Parameters:	r	The red value (0–255)
	g	The green value (0–255)
	b	The blue value (0–255)

java.awt.Graphics

- void setColor(Color c)

  changes the current color. All subsequent graphics operations will use the new color.

Parameters:	c	The new color

java.awt.Graphics2D

- void setPaint(Paint p)

  Sets the paint attribute of this graphics context. The Color class implements the Paint interface. Therefore, you can use this method to set the paint attribute to a solid color.

java.awt.Component

- void setBackground(Color c)

  sets the background color.

Parameters:	c	The new background color

- void setForeground(Color c)

  sets the foreground color.

Parameters:	c	The new foreground color

Filling Shapes

You can fill the interiors of closed shapes (such as rectangles or ellipses) with a color (or, more generally, the current paint setting). Simply call fill instead of draw:

```
Rectangle2D rect = . . .;
g2.setPaint(Color.red);
g2.fill(rect); // fills rect with red color
```

The program in Example 7–5 fills a rectangle in red, then an ellipse with the same boundary in a dull green (see Figure 7–12).

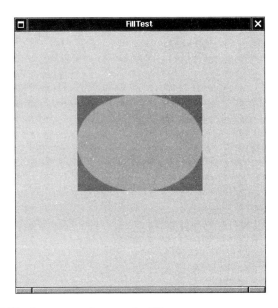

Figure 7–12: Filled rectangles and ellipses

Example 7–5: FillTest.java

```
1. import java.awt.*;
2. import java.awt.geom.*;
3. import javax.swing.*;
4.
5. public class FillTest
6. {
7.    public static void main(String[] args)
8.    {
9.       FillFrame frame = new FillFrame();
10.      frame.setDefaultCloseOperation(JFrame.EXIT_ON_CLOSE);
11.      frame.show();
12.   }
13. }
14.
15. /**
16.    A frame that contains a panel with drawings
17. */
18. class FillFrame extends JFrame
19. {
20.    public FillFrame()
21.    {
22.       setTitle("FillTest");
23.       setSize(WIDTH, HEIGHT);
24.
```

```
25.          // add panel to frame
26.
27.          FillPanel panel = new FillPanel();
28.          Container contentPane = getContentPane();
29.          contentPane.add(panel);
30.      }
31.
32.      public static final int WIDTH = 400;
33.      public static final int HEIGHT = 400;
34. }
35.
36. /**
37.     A panel that displays filled rectangles and ellipses
38. */
39. class FillPanel extends JPanel
40. {
41.     public void paintComponent(Graphics g)
42.     {
43.         super.paintComponent(g);
44.         Graphics2D g2 = (Graphics2D)g;
45.
46.         // draw a rectangle
47.
48.         double leftX = 100;
49.         double topY = 100;
50.         double width = 200;
51.         double height = 150;
52.
53.         Rectangle2D rect = new Rectangle2D.Double(leftX, topY,
54.             width, height);
55.         g2.setPaint(Color.red);
56.         g2.fill(rect);
57.
58.         // draw the enclosed ellipse
59.
60.         Ellipse2D ellipse = new Ellipse2D.Double();
61.         ellipse.setFrame(rect);
62.         g2.setPaint(new Color(0,  128, 128)); // a dull blue-green
63.         g2.fill(ellipse);
64.     }
65. }
```

Text and Fonts

The "Not a Hello, World" program at the beginning of this chapter displayed a string in the default font. Often, you want to show text in a different font. You specify a font by its *font face name* (or font name for short). A font face name is composed of a *font family name*, such as "Helvetica," and an optional suffix such as "Bold." For example, the font faces "Helvetica" and "Helvetica Bold" are both considered to be part of the family named "Helvetica."

To find out which fonts are available on a particular computer, call the getAvailableFontFamilyNames method of the GraphicsEnvironment class. The method returns an array of strings that contains the names of all available fonts. To obtain an instance of the GraphicsEnvironment class that describes the graphics environment of the user's system, use the static getLocalGraphicsEnvironment method. Thus, the following program gives you a printout of the names of all fonts on your system:

```
import java.awt.*;

public class ListFonts
{
    public static void main(String[] args)
    {
        String[] fontNames = GraphicsEnvironment
            .getLocalGraphicsEnvironment()
            .getAvailableFontFamilyNames();
        for (int i = 0; i < fontNames.length; i++)
            System.out.println(fontNames[i]);
    }
}
```

On one system, the list starts out like this:

```
Abadi MT Condensed Light
Arial
Arial Black
Arial Narrow
Arioso
Baskerville
Binner Gothic
. . .
```

and goes on for another 70 fonts or so.

NOTE: The SDK documentation claims that suffixes such as "heavy," "medium," "oblique," or "gothic" are variations within inside a single family. In our experience, that is not the case. The "Bold," "Italic," and "Bold Italic" suffixes are recognized as family variations, but other suffixes aren't.

Unfortunately, there is no absolute way of knowing whether a user has a font with a particular "look" installed. Font names can be trademarked, and font designs can be copyrighted in some jurisdictions. Thus, the distribution of fonts often involves royalty payments to a font foundry. Of course, just as there are inexpensive imitations of famous perfumes, there are lookalikes for name-brand fonts. For example, the Helvetica and Times Roman imitations that are shipped with Windows are called Arial and Times New Roman.

To establish a common baseline, the AWT defines five *logical* font names:

```
SansSerif
Serif
Monospaced
Dialog
DialogInput
```

These font names are always mapped to fonts that actually exist on the client machine. For example, on a Windows system, SansSerif is mapped to Arial.

To draw characters in a font, you must first create an object of the class `Font`. You specify the font name, the font style, and the point size. Here is an example of how you construct a `Font` object:

```
Font helvb14 = new Font("Helvetica", Font.BOLD, 14);
```

The third argument is the point size.

You can use a logical font name in the place of a font face name in the `Font` constructor. You specify the style (plain, **bold**, *italic*, or ***bold italic***) by setting the second `Font` constructor argument to one of the following values:

```
Font.PLAIN
Font.BOLD
Font.ITALIC
Font.BOLD + Font.ITALIC
```

Here is an example:

```
Font sansbold14 = new Font("SansSerif", Font.BOLD, 14)
```

NOTE: Prior versions of Java used the names Helvetica, TimesRoman, Courier, and ZapfDingbats as logical font names. For backward compatibility, these font names are still treated as logical font names even though Helvetica is really a font face name and TimesRoman and ZapfDingbats are not font names at all—the actual font face names are "Times Roman" and "Zapf Dingbats."

TIP: Starting with J2SE version 1.3, you can read TrueType fonts. You need an input stream for the font—typically from a disk file or URL. (See Chapter 12 for more information on streams.) Then call the static `Font.createFont` method:

```
URL url = new URL(http://www.fonts.com/Wingbats.ttf");
InputStream in = url.openStream();
Font f = Font.createFont(Font.TRUETYPE_FONT, in);
```

The font is plain with a font size of 1 point. Use the `deriveFont` method to get a font of the desired size:

```
Font df = f.deriveFont(14);
```

The Java fonts contain the usual ASCII characters as well as symbols. For example, if you print the character `'\u2297'` in the Dialog font, then you get a ⊗ character. Only those symbols that are defined in the Unicode character set are available. (See the sidebar at the end of this section for more information about available symbols and adding more fonts.)

Here's the code that displays the string "Hello, World!" in the standard sans serif font on your system, using 14-point bold type:

```
Font sansbold14 = new Font("SansSerif", Font.BOLD, 14);
g2.setFont(sansbold14);
String message = "Hello, World!";
g2.drawString(message, 75, 100);
```

Next, let's *center* the string in its panel rather than drawing it at an arbitrary position. We need to know the width and height of the string in pixels. These dimensions depend on three factors:

- The font used (in our case, sans serif, bold, 14-point);

- The string (in our case, "Hello, World!");

- The device on which the font is drawn (in our case, the user's screen).

To obtain an object that represents the font characteristics of the screen device, you call the `getFontRenderContext` method of the `Graphics2D` class. It returns an object of the `FontRenderContext` class. You simply pass that object to the `getStringBounds` method of the `Font` class:

```
FontRenderContext context = g2.getFontRenderContext();
Rectangle2D bounds = f.getStringBounds(message, context);
```

The `getStringBounds` method returns a rectangle that encloses the string.

To interpret the dimensions of that rectangle, it is helpful to consider some basic typesetting terms (see Figure 7–13). The *baseline* is the imaginary line where, for example, the bottom of a character like "e" rests. The *ascent* is the distance from the baseline to the top of an *ascender*, which is the upper part of a letter like "b" or "k," or an uppercase character. The *descent* is the distance from the baseline to a *descender,* which is the lower portion of a letter like "p" or "g."

Figure 7–13: Typesetting terms illustrated

Leading is the space between the descent of one line and the ascent of the next line. (The term has its origin from the strips of lead that typesetters used to separate lines.) The *height* of a font is the distance between successive baselines, which is the same as descent + leading + ascent.

The width of the rectangle that the getStringBounds method returns is the horizontal extent of the string. The height of the rectangle is the sum of ascent and descent. The rectangle has its origin at the baseline of the string. The top *y*-coordinate of the rectangle is negative. Thus, you can obtain string width, height, ascent, and descent as follows:

```
double stringWidth = bounds.getWidth();
double stringHeight = bounds.getHeight();
double ascent = -bounds.getY();
double descent = bounds.getHeight() + bounds.getY();
```

If you need to know the leading or total height, you need to use the get-LineMetrics method of the Font class. That method returns an object of the LineMetrics class, which has methods to obtain the leading and font height:

```
LineMetrics metrics = f.getLineMetrics(message, context);
float fontHeight = metrics.getHeight();
float leading = metrics.getLeading();
```

The following code uses all this information to center a string in its surrounding panel:

```
FontRenderContext context = g2.getFontRenderContext();
Rectangle2D bounds = f.getStringBounds(message, context);

// (x,y) = top left corner of text
double x = (getWidth() - bounds.getWidth()) / 2;
double y = (getHeight() - bounds.getHeight()) / 2;

// add ascent to y to reach the baseline
```

```
double ascent = -bounds.getY();
double baseY = y + ascent;
g2.drawString(message, (int)x, (int)(baseY));
```

To understand the centering, consider that `getWidth()` returns the width of the panel. A portion of that width, namely `bounds.getWidth()`, is occupied by the message string. The remainder should be equally distributed on both sides. Therefore the blank space on each side is half of the difference. The same reasoning applies to the height.

Finally, the program draws the baseline and the bounding rectangle.

Figure 7–14 shows the screen display; Example 7–6 is the program listing.

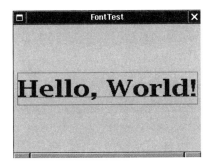

Figure 7–14: Drawing the baseline and string bounds

Example 7–6: FontTest.java

```
1. import java.awt.*;
2. import java.awt.font.*;
3. import java.awt.geom.*;
4. import javax.swing.*;
5.
6. public class FontTest
7. {
8.    public static void main(String[] args)
9.    {
10.       FontFrame frame = new FontFrame();
11.       frame.setDefaultCloseOperation(JFrame.EXIT_ON_CLOSE);
12.       frame.show();
13.    }
14. }
15.
16. /**
17.    A frame with a text message panel
18. */
19. class FontFrame extends JFrame
20. {
21.    public FontFrame()
```

```
22.     {
23.        setTitle("FontTest");
24.        setSize(WIDTH, HEIGHT);
25.
26.        // add panel to frame
27.
28.        FontPanel panel = new FontPanel();
29.        Container contentPane = getContentPane();
30.        contentPane.add(panel);
31.     }
32.
33.     public static final int WIDTH = 300;
34.     public static final int HEIGHT = 200;
35. }
36.
37. /**
38.    A panel that shows a centered message in a box.
39. */
40. class FontPanel extends JPanel
41. {
42.     public void paintComponent(Graphics g)
43.     {
44.        super.paintComponent(g);
45.        Graphics2D g2 = (Graphics2D)g;
46.
47.        String message = "Hello, World!";
48.
49.        Font f = new Font("Serif", Font.BOLD, 36);
50.        g2.setFont(f);
51.
52.        // measure the size of the message
53.
54.        FontRenderContext context = g2.getFontRenderContext();
55.        Rectangle2D bounds = f.getStringBounds(message, context);
56.
57.        // set (x,y) = top left corner of text
58.
59.        double x = (getWidth() - bounds.getWidth()) / 2;
60.        double y = (getHeight() - bounds.getHeight()) / 2;
61.
62.        // add ascent to y to reach the baseline
63.
64.        double ascent = -bounds.getY();
65.        double baseY = y + ascent;
66.
67.        // draw the message
68.
69.        g2.drawString(message, (int)x, (int)(baseY));
70.
71.        g2.setPaint(Color.gray);
72.
```

```
73.        // draw the baseline
74.
75.        g2.draw(new Line2D.Double(x, baseY,
76.            x + bounds.getWidth(), baseY));
77.
78.        // draw the enclosing rectangle
79.
80.        Rectangle2D rect = new Rectangle2D.Double(x, y,
81.            bounds.getWidth(),
82.            bounds.getHeight());
83.        g2.draw(rect);
84.    }
85. }
```

`java.awt.Font`

- `Font(String name, int style, int size)`
  creates a new font object.

Parameters:	name	The font name. This is either a font face name (such as "Helvetica Bold") or a logical font name (such as "Serif", "SansSerif")
	style	The style (`Font.PLAIN`, `Font.BOLD`, `Font.ITALIC` or `Font.BOLD + Font.ITALIC`)
	size	The point size (for example, 12)

- `String getFontName()`
  gets the font face name (such as "Helvetica Bold").

- `String getFamily()`
  gets the font family name (such as "Helvetica").

- `String getName()`
  gets the logical name (such as "SansSerif") if the font was created with a logical font name; otherwise gets the font face name.

- `Rectangle2D getStringBounds(String s, FontRenderContext context)`
  returns a rectangle that encloses the string. The origin of the rectangle falls on the baseline. The top *y*-coordinate of the rectangle equals the negative of the ascent. The height of the rectangle equals the sum of ascent and descent. The width equals the string width.

- `LineMetrics getLineMetrics(String s, FontRenderContext context)`
  returns a line metrics object to determine the extent of the string.

- `Font deriveFont(int style)`
- `Font deriveFont(float size)`
- `Font deriveFont(int style, float size)`
  return a new font that equals this font, except that it has the given size and style.

---

java.awt.font.LineMetrics

- float getAscent()
  gets the font ascent—the distance from the baseline to the tops of uppercase characters.

- float getDescent()
  gets the font descent—the distance from the baseline to the bottoms of descenders.

- float getLeading()
  gets the font leading—the space between the bottom of one line of text and the top of the next line.

- float getHeight()
  gets the total height of the font—the distance between the two baselines of text (descent + leading + ascent).

---

java.awt.Graphics

- void setFont(Font font)
  selects a font for the graphics context. That font will be used for subsequent text-drawing operations.

  Parameters: font   A font

- void drawString(String str, int x, int y)
  draws a string in the current font and color.

  Parameters: str   The string to be drawn

                        x   The x-coordinate of the start of the string

                        y   The y-coordinate of the baseline of the string

---

java.awt.Graphics2D

- FontRenderContext getFontRenderContext()
  gets a font render context that specifies font characteristics in this graphics context.

- void drawString(String str, float x, float y)
  draws a string in the current font and color.

  Parameters: str   The string to be drawn

                        x   The x-coordinate of the start of the string

                        y   The y-coordinate of the baseline of the string

Fonts and the `font.properties` File

Sun's Java runtime looks at the `font.properties` file in the `jre/lib` directory to find out which logical fonts are available and which symbol sets are contained in a specific font. To be able to use more logical fonts in Java than the default ones, you need to modify this file. Let us look at a typical entry in this file:

```
serif.0=Times New Roman,ANSI_CHARSET
serif.1=WingDings,SYMBOL_CHARSET,NEED_CONVERTED
serif.2=Symbol,SYMBOL_CHARSET,NEED_CONVERTED
exclusion.serif.0=0100-ffff
fontcharset.serif.1=sun.awt.windows.CharToByteWingDingsfont-
charset.serif.2=sun.awt.CharToByteSymbolfontchar-
set.serif.2=sun.awt.CharToByteSymbol
```

This means: To render a character in the serif font, first check that it is in the "0" range, that is, it is not in the excluded area `0100-ffff`. If it is not excluded, use the Times New Roman font to render it. Next, check that the class `sun.awt.windows.Char-ToByteWingDings` will accept the character. This (undocumented) class extends the (equally undocumented) class `sun.io.CharToByteConverter`. There are two key methods in these classes that you work with. The method call:

```
boolean canConvert(char)
```

tests whether Java can convert a character. To actually perform the conversion, you need to supply two arrays: one for source characters, and one for the target bytes. Then you call:

```
int convert(char[] input, int inStart, int inPastEnd,
    byte[] output, int outStart, int outPastEnd)
```

This method converts the `inPastEnd - inStart` characters in the array `input`, starting from `inStart`, and places them into the byte array `output`, starting at `out-Start`. It also fills out at most `outPastEnd - outStart` bytes. (You may wonder why the `convert` method uses arrays instead of simply converting one character into a byte. The reason is that in some encoding schemes, such as the Japanese JIS code, some characters are encoded as single bytes, others as multiple bytes, with control codes switching between character sets.)

If the `canConvert` method returns `true`, then Java will render the character in the `WingDings` font. Otherwise, Java tries the `Symbol` font. If this fails as well, Java renders the character as a `?` (question mark).

Note that font descriptions are dependent on the operating system. The lines in these examples describe fonts for Windows. In other operating systems, the font descriptions will be different. For example, in Solaris, the description of the Times font looks like this:

```
serif.plain.0=
    -linotype-times-medium-r-normal—*-%d-*-*-p-*-iso8859-1
```

You can add your own fonts to the `font.properties` file. For example, if you run Java under Windows, add the following lines:

```
oldstyle.0=Bookman Old Style,ANSI_CHARSET
exclusion.oldstyle.0=0100-ffff
```

You can then make a font:

```
new Font("OldStyle", Font.PLAIN, 12)
```

You can even add your own font maps. Let us consider the most common case, that is, when characters in your font are described by single bytes. To add your own font map:

- Extend the (undocumented and poorly named) class
  `sun.io.CharToByte8859_1`. (ISO 8859-1 is the Latin-1 8-bit character set,
  one of ten 8-bit character sets in the ISO 8859 standard. This Java class can be
  used as the base class for any Unicode to 8-bit code conversion, not just Latin-1.)
- Override two methods: `canConvert`, which returns `true` for those Unicode
  characters that are part of your font, and `convert`, which converts a character
  array into the equivalent byte arrays.

Here is a practical example. Suppose that you have a Russian font in ISO 8859-5 format. Omitting a couple of technical exceptions, the mapping from Unicode to ISO 8859-5 is simple:

```
'\u0021'...'\u007E': ch -> ch
'\u0401'...'\u045F': ch -> ch - 0x0360
```

Here is a converter class that does the conversion.

```
public class CharToByteRussian extends sun.io.CharToByte8859_1
{
   public boolean canConvert(char ch)
   {
      return 0x0021 <= ch && ch <= 0x007E
         || 0x0401 <= ch && ch <= 0x45F;
   }

   public int convert(char[] input, int inStart, int inPastEnd,
         byte[] output, int outStart, int outPastEnd)
      throws ConversionBufferFullException
   {
      int outIndex = outStart;
      for (int i = inStart; i < inPastEnd; i++)
      {
         char ch = input[i];
         byte b = 0;
         if (0x0021 <= ch && ch <= 0x007E)
            b = (byte)ch;
         if (0x0401 <= ch && ch <= 0x45F)
            b = (byte)(ch - 0x0360);
         if (b != 0)
         {
            if (outIndex >= outPastEnd)
               throw new ConversionBufferFullException();
            output[outIndex] = b;
            outIndex++;
         }
      }
      return outIndex - outStart;
   }
}
```

To add the Russian font to the Java runtime, you need to place the class
`CharToByteRussian` somewhere on your class path. Then, add the following lines
to `font.properties`:

```
russian.0=Cyrillic,SYMBOL_CHARSET,NEED_CONVERTED
fontcharset.russian.0=CharToByteRussian
```

Images

You have already seen how to build up simple images by drawing lines and shapes. Complex images, such as photographs, are usually generated externally, for example, with a scanner or special image-manipulation software. (As you will see in Volume 2, it is also possible to produce an image, pixel by pixel, and store the result in an array. This procedure is common for fractal images, for example.)

Once images are stored in local files or someplace on the Net, you can read them into a Java application and display them on `Graphics` objects. To read a graphics file into an application, you use a `Toolkit` object. A `Toolkit` object can read in GIF and JPEG files.

TIP: Most image-manipulation programs can convert image formats (such as Windows bitmaps or icon files) to one of the formats that Java can use. This conversion will be necessary when you want, for example, to use standard Windows icons in the `setIconImage` method to set the icon for your frames.)

To get a `Toolkit` object, use the static `getDefaultToolkit` method of the `Toolkit` class. Here is the code to get a local image file from the current user's directory (supply a full pathname if the image file isn't in the current user's directory):

```
String name = "blue-ball.gif";
Image image = Toolkit.getDefaultToolkit().getImage(name);
```

To get an image file from the Net, you must supply the URL. For example,

```
URL u = new URL("http://www.someplace.com/anImage.gif");
Image image = Toolkit.getDefaultToolkit().getImage(u);
```

Now the variable `image` contains a reference to an object that encapsulates the GIF file image. You can display it with the `drawImage` method of the `Graphics` class.

```
public void paintComponent(Graphics g)
{
   . . .
   g.drawImage(image, x, y, null);
}
```

Example 7–7 takes this a little bit further and *tiles* the window with the graphics image. The result looks like the screen shown in Figure 7–15. We do the tiling in the `paintComponent` method. We first draw one copy of the image in the top-left corner and then use the `copyArea` call to copy it into the entire window:

```
for (int i = 0; i * imageWidth <= getWidth(); i++)
   for (int j = 0; j * imageHeight <= getHeight(); j++)
      if (i + j > 0)
         g.copyArea(0, 0, imageWidth, imageHeight,
            i * imageWidth, j * imageHeight);
```

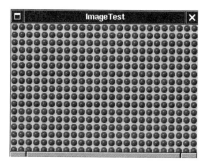

Figure 7–15: Window with tiled graphics image

However, there is a catch. The AWT was written with the assumption that an image may arrive slowly over a network connection. The *first* call to the `drawImage` method recognizes that the GIF file has not yet been loaded. Instead of loading the file and returning to the caller when the image is actually loaded, Java spawns a new thread of execution to load the image *and then returns to the caller without actually having completed that task*. (See the Multithreading chapter of Volume 2 for more on threads.)

This is—to say the least—surprising to anyone who expects that a method won't return until it has done its job. But here, the multithreaded aspect of Java works against your assumptions. What will happen is that the code in your program runs in parallel with the code to load the image. Eventually, the image will be loaded and available. Of course, in the meantime, our code has tiled the entire buffer with copies of a blank image.

There is a mechanism for tracking the image acquisition process. Using this mechanism, you can be notified when the image size is known, each time that a chunk of the image is ready, and finally, when the entire image is complete. When you use an Internet browser and look at a web page that contains an image, you can see how these notifications are translated into actions. An Internet browser lays out a web page as soon as it knows the sizes of the images in the page. Then it gradually fills in the images, as more detailed information becomes available. The fourth parameter of the `drawImage` call, which we set to `null`, can optionally point to an `ImageObserver` object that receives these notifications.

However, we are not interested in incremental rendering. We just want to find out when the GIF image is completely loaded and *then* tile the buffer. A special class, called `MediaTracker`, makes it easy to program this delay. A media tracker can track the acquisition of one or more images. (The name "media" suggests that the class should also be able to track audio files or other media. While such an extension may be available in the future, the current implementation tracks images only.)

You add an image to a tracker object with the following command:

```
MediaTracker tracker = new MediaTracker();
Image img = Toolkit.getDefaultToolkit().getImage(name);
int id = 1; // the ID used to track the image loading process
tracker.addImage(img, id);
```

You can add as many images as you like to a single media tracker. Each of the images should have a different ID number, but you can choose any numbering that is convenient. To wait for an image to be loaded completely, you use code like this:

```
try { tracker.waitForID(id); }
catch (InterruptedException e) {}
```

The try/catch statements are necessary for a technical reason; we will discuss the general topic of exception handling in Chapter 12 and the InterruptedException in the Multithreading chapter of Volume 2. In our sample program, we just insert this code into the constructor as shown here:

```
public ImagePanel()
{
    image = Toolkit.getDefaultToolkit().getImage
        ("blue-ball.gif");
    MediaTracker tracker = new MediaTracker(this);
    tracker.addImage(image, 0);
    try { tracker.waitForID(0); }
    catch (InterruptedException e) {}
}
```

This code has the effect of waiting until the image is loaded completely before more code will be processed.

If you want to acquire multiple images, then you can add them all to the media tracker object and wait until they are all loaded. You can achieve this with the following code:

```
try { tracker.waitForAll(); }
catch (InterruptedException e) {}
```

NOTE: When programming with the basic AWT, you need to work harder to produce flicker-free images: you need to use buffering. With Swing, buffering is automatically done for you by default. (You can turn it off but there is rarely a reason to do so.) If you need to acquire an image for an AWT component, first assemble your drawing in a background image, then draw the background image.

```
Image buffered_image = createImage(width, height);
Graphics bg = buffered_image.getGraphics();
// all drawing commands that use bg fill the buffered_image
// . . .
// finally, draw the buffer
g.drawImage(buffered_image, 0, 0, null);
bg.dispose();
buffered_image.flush();
```

Example 7–7 shows the full source code of the image display program. This concludes our introduction to Java graphics programming. For more advanced techniques, you will want to turn to the discussion about 2D graphics and image manipulation in Volume 2.

Example 7–7: ImageTest.java

```
1. import java.awt.*;
2. import java.awt.event.*;
3. import javax.swing.*;
4.
5. public class ImageTest
6. {
7.    public static void main(String[] args)
8.    {
9.       ImageFrame frame = new ImageFrame();
10.      frame.setDefaultCloseOperation(JFrame.EXIT_ON_CLOSE);
11.      frame.show();
12.   }
13. }
14.
15. /**
16.    A frame with an image panel
17. */
18. class ImageFrame extends JFrame
19. {
20.    public ImageFrame()
21.    {
22.       setTitle("ImageTest");
23.       setSize(WIDTH, HEIGHT);
24.
25.       // add panel to frame
26.
27.       ImagePanel panel = new ImagePanel();
28.       Container contentPane = getContentPane();
29.       contentPane.add(panel);
30.    }
31.
32.    public static final int WIDTH = 300;
33.    public static final int HEIGHT = 200;
34. }
35.
36. /**
37.    A panel that displays a tiled image
38. */
39. class ImagePanel extends JPanel
40. {
```

```
41.    public ImagePanel()
42.    {
43.       // acquire the image
44.
45.       image = Toolkit.getDefaultToolkit().getImage
46.          ("blue-ball.gif");
47.       MediaTracker tracker = new MediaTracker(this);
48.       tracker.addImage(image, 0);
49.       try { tracker.waitForID(0); }
50.       catch (InterruptedException exception) {}
51.    }
52.
53.    public void paintComponent(Graphics g)
54.    {
55.       super.paintComponent(g);
56.
57.       int imageWidth = image.getWidth(this);
58.       int imageHeight = image.getHeight(this);
59.
60.       // draw the image in the upper-left corner
61.
62.       g.drawImage(image, 0, 0, null);
63.
64.       // tile the image across the panel
65.
66.       for (int i = 0; i * imageWidth <= getWidth(); i++)
67.         for (int j = 0; j * imageHeight <= getHeight(); j++)
68.            if (i + j > 0)
69.                g.copyArea(0, 0, imageWidth, imageHeight,
70.                   i * imageWidth, j * imageHeight);
71.    }
72.
73.    private Image image;
74. }
```

`java.awt.Toolkit`

- `Toolkit getDefaultToolkit()`
  returns the default toolkit.

- `Image getImage(String filename)`
  returns an image that will read its pixel data from a file.

  Parameters: `filename`   The file containing the image (for example, a GIF
                                or JPEG file)

java.awt.Graphics

- boolean drawImage(Image img, int x, int y, ImageObserver observer)

  draws a scaled image. Note: This call may return before the image is drawn.

Parameters:	img	The image to be drawn
	x	The *x*-coordinate of the upper-left corner
	y	The *y*-coordinate of the upper-left corner
	observer	The object to notify of the progress of the rendering process (may be null)

- boolean drawImage(Image img, int x, int y, int width, int height, ImageObserver observer)

  draws a scaled image. The system scales the image to fit into a region with the given width and height. Note: This call may return before the image is drawn.

Parameters:	img	The image to be drawn
	x	The *x*-coordinate of the upper-left corner
	y	The *y*-coordinate of the upper-left corner
	width	The desired width of image
	height	The desired height of image
	observer	The object to notify of the progress of the rendering process (may be null)

- void copyArea(int x, int y, int width, int height, int dx, int dy)

  copies an area of the screen.

Parameters:	x	The *x*-coordinate of the upper-left corner of the source area
	y	The *y*-coordinate of the upper-left corner of the source area
	width	The width of the source area
	height	The height of the source area
	dx	The horizontal distance from the source area to the target area
	dy	The vertical distance from the source area to the target area

- void dispose()

  disposes of this graphics context and releases operating system resources. You should always dispose of the graphics contexts that you receive from calls to methods such as Image.getGraphics, but not the ones handed to you by paintComponent.

`java.awt.Component`

- `Image createImage(int width, int height)`
  creates an off-screen image buffer to be used for double buffering.

  Parameters: `width`   The width of the image

                       `height`   The height of the image

`java.awt.Image`

- `Graphics getGraphics()`
  gets a graphics context to draw into this image buffer.

- `void flush()`
  releases all resources held by this image object.

`java.awt.MediaTracker`

- `void addImage(Image image, int id)`
  adds an image to the list of images being tracked. When the image is added, the image loading process is started.

  Parameters: `image`   The image to be tracked

                       `id`   The identifier used to later refer to this image

- `void waitForID(int id)`
  waits until all images with the specified ID are loaded.

- `void waitForAll()`
  waits until all images that are being tracked are loaded.

Chapter **8**

Event Handling

Event handling is of fundamental importance to programs with a graphical user interface. To implement graphical user interfaces, you must master how Java handles events. This chapter explains how the Java AWT event model works. You will see how to capture events from the mouse and the keyboard. This chapter also shows you how to use the simplest GUI elements, such as buttons. In particular, this chapter discusses how to work with the basic events generated by these components. The next chapter shows you how to put together the most common of the components that Swing offers, along with a full coverage of the events they generate.

The current Java event model is different from the one used in Java 1.0. If you are already familiar with Java 1.0, you will need to learn a new way of coding: one that bears little, if any, relation to the way you used to do things. Note, however, that while Sun has said that code written following the older event model should still work in later versions of Java, moving to the new event model promises both performance improvements and a greater degree of flexibility. We only briefly discuss the older event model in this chapter. You can tell the compiler to flag all lines that use one of the older event handling methods by compiling your source code with the `-deprecation` switch. (There is some potential for incompatibility down the road. Sun has not said they will be supporting the older event model indefinitely. And, of course, if you use Swing components, then you must use the new event model.)

NOTE: If you need to write applets that can run under old browsers that are still using Java 1.0, such as Netscape Navigator 2 or 3 or Internet Explorer before version 4, then you must use the Java 1.0 event model.

Basics of Event Handling

Any operating environment that supports GUIs constantly monitors events such as keystrokes or mouse clicks. The operating environment reports these events to the programs that are running. Each program then decides what, if anything, to do in response to these events. In languages like Visual Basic, the correspondence between events and code is obvious. One writes code for each specific event of interest and places the code in what is usually called an *event procedure*. For example, a Visual Basic button named HelpButton would have a HelpButton_Click event procedure associated with it, and VB would activate the code in this procedure in response to that button being clicked. Each Visual Basic user interface component responds to a fixed set of events, and it is impossible to change the events to which a Visual Basic component responds.

On the other hand, if you use a language like raw C to do event-driven programming, you need to write the code that checks the event queue constantly for what the operating environment is reporting. (You usually do this by encasing your code in a giant loop with a massive switch statement!) This technique is obviously rather ugly, and, in any case, it is much more difficult to code. The advantage is that the events you can respond to are not as limited as in languages, like Visual Basic, that go to great lengths to hide the event queue from the programmer.

Java takes an approach somewhat between the Visual Basic approach and the raw C approach in terms of power and, therefore, in resulting complexity. Within the limits of the events that the AWT knows about, you completely control how events are transmitted from the *event sources* (such as buttons or scrollbars) to *event listeners*. You can designate *any* object to be an event listener—in practice, you pick an object that can conveniently carry out the desired response to the event. This *event delegation model* gives you much more flexibility than is possible with Visual Basic, where the listener is predetermined, but it requires more code and is more difficult to untangle (at least until you get used to it).

Event sources have methods that allow you to register event listeners with them. When an event happens to the source, the source sends a notification of that event to all the listener objects that were registered for that event.

As one would expect in an object-oriented language like Java, the information about the event is encapsulated in an *event* object. In Java, all event objects ultimately derive from the class `java.util.EventObject`. Of course, there are subclasses for each event type, such as `ActionEvent` and `WindowEvent`.

Different event sources can produce different kinds of events. For example, a button can send `ActionEvent` objects, whereas a window can send `WindowEvent` objects.

To sum up, here's an overview of how event handling in the AWT works.

- A listener object is an instance of a class that implements a special interface called (naturally enough) a *listener interface.*
- An event source is an object that can register listener objects and send them event objects.
- The event source sends out event objects to all registered listeners when that event occurs.
- The listener objects will then use the information in the event object to determine their reaction to the event.

You register the listener object with the source object by using lines of code that follow the model:

```
eventSourceObject.addEventListener(eventListenerObject);
```

For example,

```
ActionListener listener = . . .;
JButton button = new JButton("Ok");
button.addActionListener(listener);
```

Now the `listener` object is notified whenever an "action event" occurs in the button. For buttons, as you might expect, an action event is a button click.

Code like the above requires that the class to which the listener object belongs implements the appropriate interface (which in this case is the `ActionListener` interface). As with all interfaces in Java, implementing an interface means supplying methods with the right signatures. To implement the `ActionListener` interface, the listener class must have a method called `actionPerformed` that receives an `ActionEvent` object as a parameter.

```
class MyListener
   implements ActionListener
{
   . . .
   public void actionPerformed(ActionEvent event)
   {
      // reaction to button click goes here
      . . .
   }
}
```

Whenever the user clicks the button, the JButton object creates an ActionEvent object and calls listener.actionPerformed(event) passing that event object. It is possible for multiple objects to be added as listeners to an event source such as a button. In that case, the button calls the actionPerformed methods of all listeners whenever the user clicks the button.

Figure 8–1 shows the interaction between the event source, event listener, and event object.

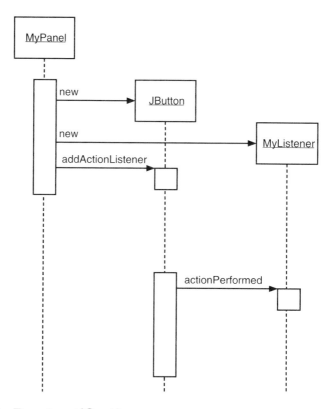

Figure 8–1: Event notification

> NOTE: In this chapter, we put particular emphasis on event handling for *user interface* events such as button clicks and mouse moves. However, the basic event handling architecture is not specific to user interfaces. For example, in the JavaBeans chapter of Volume 2 you will see how to a component can fire events when its properties change.

Example: Handling a button click

As a way of getting comfortable with the event delegation model, let's work through all details needed for the simple example of responding to a button click. For this example, we will want:

- A panel populated with three buttons;
- Three listener objects that are added as action listeners to the buttons.

With this scenario, each time a user clicks on any of the buttons on the panel, the associated listener object then receives an `ActionEvent` that indicates a button click. In our sample program, the listener object will then change the background color of the panel.

Before we can show you the program that listens to button clicks, we first need to explain how to create buttons and how to add them to a panel. (For more on GUI elements, please see Chapter 9.)

You create a button by specifying a label string, an icon, or both in the button constructor. Here are two examples:

```
JButton yellowButton = new JButton("Yellow");
JButton blueButton = new JButton(new ImageIcon("blue-ball.gif"));
```

Adding buttons to a panel occurs through a call to a method named (quite mnemonically) `add`. The `add` method takes as a parameter the specific component to be added to the container. For example,

```
class ButtonPanel extends JPanel
{
   public ButtonPanel()
   {
      JButton yellowButton = new JButton("Yellow");
      JButton blueButton = new JButton("Blue");
      JButton redButton = new JButton("Red");

      add(yellowButton);
      add(blueButton);
      add(redButton);
   }
}
```

Figure 8–2 shows the result.

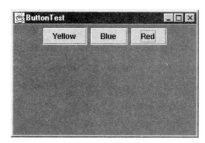

Figure 8–2: A panel filled with buttons

Now that you know how to add buttons to a panel, you'll need to add code that lets the panel listen to these buttons. This requires classes that implement the ActionListener interface, which, as we just mentioned, has one method: actionPerformed, whose signature looks like this:

```
public void actionPerformed(ActionEvent event)
```

NOTE: The ActionListener interface we used in the button example is not restricted to button clicks. It is used in many separate situations such as:

- When an item is selected from a list box with a double click;
- When a menu item is selected;
- When the ENTER key is clicked in a text field;
- When a certain amount of time has elapsed for a Timer component.

You will see more details in this chapter and the next.

The way to use the ActionListener interface is the same in all situations: the actionPerformed method (which is the only method in ActionListener) takes an object of type ActionEvent as a parameter. This event object gives you information about the event that happened.

When a button is clicked, then we want to set the background color of the panel to a particular color. We store the desired color in our listener class.

```
class ColorAction implements ActionListener
{
   public ColorAction(Color c)
   {
      backgroundColor = c;
   }
```

```
   public void actionPerformed(ActionEvent event)
   {
      // set panel background color
      . . .
   }

   private Color backgroundColor;
}
```

We then construct one object for each color and set the objects as the button listeners.

```
ColorAction yellowAction = new ColorAction(Color.yellow);
ColorAction blueAction = new ColorAction(Color.blue);
ColorAction redAction = new ColorAction(Color.red);

yellowButton.addActionListener(yellowAction);
blueButton.addActionListener(blueAction);
redButton.addActionListener(redAction);
```

For example, if a user clicks on the button marked "Yellow," then the `action-Performed` method of the `yellowAction` object is called. Its `background-Color` instance field is set to `Color.yellow`, and it can now proceed to set the panel's background color.

There is just one remaining issue. The `ColorAction` object doesn't have access to the `panel` variable. You can solve this problem in two ways. You can store the panel in the `ColorAction` object and set it in the `ColorAction` constructor. Or, more conveniently, you can make `ColorAction` into an inner class of the `ButtonPanel` class. Then its methods can access the outer panel automatically. (For more information on inner classes, see Chapter 6.)

We will follow the latter approach. Here is how you place the `ColorAction` class inside the `ButtonPanel` class.

```
class ButtonPanel extends JPanel
{
   . . .

   private class ColorAction implements ActionListener
   {
      . . .

      public void actionPerformed(ActionEvent event)
      {
         setBackground(backgroundColor);
         // i.e. outer.setBackground(...)
         repaint();
```

```
              // i.e. outer.repaint();
          }

          private Color backgroundColor;
      }
  }
```

Look closely at the `actionPerformed` method. The `ColorAction` class doesn't have `setBackground` or `repaint` methods. But the outer `ButtonPanel` class does. The methods are invoked on the `ButtonPanel` object that constructed the inner class objects. (Note again that *outer* is not a keyword in the Java programming language. We just use it as an intuitive symbol for the invisible outer class reference in the inner class object.)

This situation is very common. Event listener objects usually need to carry out some action that affects other objects. You can often strategically place the listener class inside the class whose state the listener should modify.

Example 8–1 contains the complete program. Whenever you click one of the buttons, the appropriate action listener changes the background color of the panel.

Example 8–1: ButtonTest.java

```
1. import java.awt.*;
2. import java.awt.event.*;
3. import javax.swing.*;
4.
5. public class ButtonTest
6. {
7.    public static void main(String[] args)
8.    {
9.       ButtonFrame frame = new ButtonFrame();
10.       frame.setDefaultCloseOperation(JFrame.EXIT_ON_CLOSE);
11.       frame.show();
12.    }
13. }
14.
15. /**
16.    A frame with a button panel
17. */
18. class ButtonFrame extends JFrame
19. {
20.    public ButtonFrame()
21.    {
22.       setTitle("ButtonTest");
23.       setSize(WIDTH, HEIGHT);
24.
25.       // add panel to frame
26.
```

```
27.        ButtonPanel panel = new ButtonPanel();
28.        Container contentPane = getContentPane();
29.        contentPane.add(panel);
30.     }
31.
32.     public static final int WIDTH = 300;
33.     public static final int HEIGHT = 200;
34. }
35.
36. /**
37.    A panel with three buttons.
38. */
39. class ButtonPanel extends JPanel
40. {
41.     public ButtonPanel()
42.     {
43.        // create buttons
44.
45.        JButton yellowButton = new JButton("Yellow");
46.        JButton blueButton = new JButton("Blue");
47.        JButton redButton = new JButton("Red");
48.
49.        // add buttons to panel
50.
51.        add(yellowButton);
52.        add(blueButton);
53.        add(redButton);
54.
55.        // create button actions
56.
57.        ColorAction yellowAction = new ColorAction(Color.yellow);
58.        ColorAction blueAction = new ColorAction(Color.blue);
59.        ColorAction redAction = new ColorAction(Color.red);
60.
61.        // associate actions with buttons
62.
63.        yellowButton.addActionListener(yellowAction);
64.        blueButton.addActionListener(blueAction);
65.        redButton.addActionListener(redAction);
66.     }
67.
68.     /**
69.        An action listener that sets the panel's background color.
70.     */
71.     private class ColorAction implements ActionListener
72.     {
73.        public ColorAction(Color c)
74.        {
75.           backgroundColor = c;
```

```
76.          }
77.
78.      public void actionPerformed(ActionEvent event)
79.      {
80.          setBackground(backgroundColor);
81.          repaint();
82.      }
83.
84.      private Color backgroundColor;
85.   }
86. }
```

NOTE: If you have programmed graphical user interfaces in Java 1.0, then you may well be horribly confused after reading this section. In Java 1.0, life was simple: you didn't need to worry about listeners. Instead, you added code in methods like `action` and `handleEvent` to the classes that contained the user interface elements. For example, testing a button click would look like this:

```
class ButtonPanel
{
    . . .
    public boolean action(Event event, Object arg)
    {
        if (arg.equals("Yellow")) setBackground(Color.yellow);
        else if (arg.equals("Blue")) setBackground(Color.blue);
        else if (arg.equals("Red")) setBackground(Color.red);
        repaint();
        return true;
    }
}
```

There are two important differences between the new event model and the older one:

1. In Java 1.0, a button click is always received by the object that contains the button (that is, the panel). Now, information about the button click is sent only to objects that were added as an `actionListener` for the button.

2. In Java 1.0, all events are caught in the `action` and `handleEvent` methods. Now, there are many separate methods (such as `actionPerformed` and `windowClosing`) that can react to events.

For simple programs, the old event model is easier to program (although whether it is conceptually as simple is another question). But for complex programs, the old event model has severe limitations. The new model, while initially more involved, is far more flexible and is potentially faster since events are sent only to the listeners that are actually interested in them.

`javax.swing.JButton`

- `JButton(String label)`
  constructs a button. The label string can be plain text, or, starting with
  J2SE 1.3, HTML; for example, `"<HTML><B>Ok</B></HTML>"`.

  Parameters: `label`   The text you want on the face of the button

- `JButton(Icon icon)`
  constructs a button.

  Parameters: `icon`   The icon you want on the face of the button

- `JButton(String label, Icon icon)`
  constructs a button.

  Parameters: `label`   The text you want on the face of the button

                `icon`   The icon you want on the face of the button

---

`java.awt.Container`

- `Component add(Component c)`
  adds a component to this container and adds `c`.

`javax.swing.ImageIcon`

- `ImageIcon(String filename)`
  constructs an icon whose image is stored in a file. The image is automatically
  loaded with a media tracker (see Chapter 7).

Selecting Event Listeners

You are completely free to designate *any* object of a class that implements the `Action-`
`Listener` interface as a button listener. In our example, we use objects of a new class
that was expressly created for carrying out the desired button actions. Many programmers choose a different strategy and add an `actionPerformed` method to an existing class. Of course, that class must implement the `ActionListener` interface. For
example, you can turn the `ButtonPanel` into an action listener:

```
class ButtonPanel extends JPanel
    implements ActionListener
{
    . . .
    public void actionPerformed(ActionEvent event)
    {
       // set background color
       . . .
    }
}
```

Then the panel sets *itself* as the listener to all three buttons:

```
yellowButton.addActionListener(this);
blueButton.addActionListener(this);
redButton.addActionListener(this);
```

Note that now the three buttons no longer have individual listeners. They share a single listener object, namely the button panel. Therefore, the `actionPerformed` method must figure out *which* button was clicked.

The `getSource` method of the `EventObject` class, the superclass of all other event classes, will tell you the *source* of every event. The event source is the object that generated the event and notified the listener:

```
Object source = event.getSource();
```

The `actionPerformed` method can then check which of the buttons was the source:

```
if (source == yellowButton) . . .
else if (source == blueButton) . . .
else if (source == redButton ) . . .
```

Of course, this approach requires that you keep references to the buttons as instance fields in the surrounding panel.

CAUTION: Some programmers use a different way to find out the event source in a listener object that is shared among multiple sources. The `ActionEvent` class has a `getActionCommand` method that returns the *command string* associated with this action. For buttons, it turns out that the command string defaults to being the button label. If you take this approach, an `actionPerformed` method contains code like this:

```
String command = event.getActionCommand();
if (command.equals("Yellow")) . . .;
else if (command.equals("Blue")) . . .;
else if (command.equals("Red")) . . .;
```

Of course, relying on the button strings is dangerous. It is an easy mistake to label a button `"Gray"` and then spell the string slightly differently in the test:

```
if (command.equals("Grey")) . . .
```

And button strings give you grief when the time comes to internationalize your application. To make the German version with button labels "Gelb," "Blau," and "Rot," you have to change *both* the button labels and the strings in the `action-Performed` method.

As you can see, turning the button panel into the action listener isn't really any simpler than defining an inner class. It also becomes *really* messy when the panel contains multiple user interface elements. Nevertheless, this programming strategy is quite widespread. We believe that many programmers (ourselves included) were initially uncomfortable with inner classes, mainly because of the mysterious syntax.

Some people dislike inner classes because they feel that a proliferation of classes and objects makes their programs slower. Let's have a look at that claim. First of all, you don't need a new class for every user interface component. In our example, all three buttons share the same listener class. Of course, each of them has a separate listener object. But these objects aren't large. They each contain a color value and a reference to the panel. And the traditional solution, with `if . . . else` statements, also references the same color objects that the action listeners store, just as local variables and not as instance variables.

We believe the time has come to get used to inner classes. We recommend that you use dedicated inner classes for event handlers rather than turning existing classes into listeners. We think that even anonymous inner classes have their place.

Here is a good example how anonymous inner classes can actually simplify your code. If you look at the code of Example 8–1, you will note that each button requires the same treatment:

1.   Construct the button with a label string.

2.   Add the button to the panel.

3.   Construct an action listener with the appropriate color.

4.   Add that action listener.

Let's implement a helper method to simplify these tasks:

```
void makeButton(String name, Color backgroundColor)
{
   JButton button = new JButton(name);
   add(button);
   ColorAction action = new ColorAction(backgroundColor);
   button.addActionListener(action);
}
```

Then the `ButtonPanel` constructor simply becomes

```
public ButtonPanel()
{
   makeButton("yellow", Color.yellow);
   makeButton("blue", Color.blue);
   makeButton("red", Color.red);
}
```

Now you can make a further simplification. Note that the `ColorAction` class is only needed *once*: in the `makeButton` method. Therefore, you can make it into an anonymous class:

```
void makeButton(String name, final Color backgroundColor)
{
   JButton button = new JButton(name);
   add(button);
   button.addActionListener(new
      ActionListener()
      {
         public void actionPerformed(ActionEvent event)
         {
            setBackground(backgroundColor);
            repaint();
         }
      });
}
```

The action listener code has become quite a bit simpler. The `actionPerformed` method simply refers to the parameter variable `backgroundColor`. (As with all local variables that are accessed in the inner class, the parameter needs to be declared as `final`.)

No explicit constructor is needed. As you saw in Chapter 6, the inner class mechanism automatically generates a constructor that stores all local `final` variables that are used in one of the methods of the inner class.

TIP: Anonymous inner classes can look confusing. But you can get used to deciphering them if you train your eyes to glaze over the routine code, like this:

```
button.addActionListener(new
   ActionListener()
   {
      public void actionPerformed(ActionEvent event)
      {
         setBackground(backgroundColor);
         repaint();
      }
   });
```

That is, the button action is to set the background color and repaint. As long as the event handler consists of just a few statements, we think this can be quite readable, particularly if you don't worry about the inner class mechanics.

java.util.EventObject

- `Object getSource()`

  returns a reference to the object where the event initially occurred.

```
java.awt.event.ActionEvent
```

- `String getActionCommand()`

  returns the command string associated with this action event. If the action event originated from a button, the command string equals the button label, unless it has been changed with the `setActionCommand` method.

Example: Changing the Look and Feel

By default, Swing programs use the Metal look and feel. There are two ways to change to a different look and feel. You can supply a file `swing.properties` in the `jdk/jre/lib` directories that sets the property `swing.defaultlaf` to the class name of the look and feel that you want. For example,

```
swing.defaultlaf=com.sun.java.swing.plaf.motif.MotifLookAndFeel
```

Note that the Metal look and feel is located in the `javax.swing` package. The other look and feel packages are located in the `com.sun.java` package and need not be present in every Java implementation. Currently, for copyright reasons, the Windows and Mac look and feel packages are only shipped with the Windows and Mac versions of the Java Runtime Environment.

TIP: Here is a useful tip for testing. Since lines starting with a # character are ignored in property files, you can supply several look and feel selections in the `swing.properties` file and move around the # to select one of them:

```
#swing.defaultlaf=javax.swing.plaf.metal.MetalLookAndFeel
swing.defaultlaf=com.sun.java.swing.plaf.motif.MotifLookAndFeel
#swing.defaultlaf=com.sun.java.swing.plaf.windows.WindowsLookAndFeel
```

You must restart your program to switch the look and feel in this way. A Swing program reads the `swing.properties` file only once, at startup.

To change the look and feel dynamically, call the static `UIManager.setLookAndFeel` method and give it the name of the look and feel that you want. Then call the static method `SwingUtilities.updateComponentTreeUI` to refresh the entire set of components. You need to supply one component to that method; it will find all others. The `UIManager.setLookAndFeel` method may throw a number of exceptions when it can't find the look and feel that you request, or when there is an error loading it. As always, we ask you to gloss over the exception handling code and wait until Chapter 11 for a full explanation.

Here is an example showing how you can switch to the Motif look and feel in your program:

```
String plaf = "com.sun.java.swing.plaf.motif.MotifLookAndFeel";
try
```

```
{
    UIManager.setLookAndFeel(plaf);
    SwingUtilities.updateComponentTreeUI(panel);
}
catch(Exception e) { e.printStackTrace(); }
```

Example 8–2 is a complete program that demonstrates how to switch the look and feel (see Figure 8–3). The program is very similar to Example 8–1. Following the advice of the preceding section, we use a helper method `makeButton` and an anonymous inner class to specify the button action, namely to switch the look and feel.

There is one fine point to this program. The `actionPerformed` method of the inner action listener class needs to pass the `this` reference of the outer `PlafPanel` class to the `updateCompnentTreeUI` method. Recall from Chapter 6 that the outer object's `this` pointer must be prefixed by the outer class name:

```
SwingUtilities.updateComponentTreeUI(PlafPanel.this);
```

Note that the "Windows" button will only work on Windows since Sun does not supply the Windows look and feel on other platforms.

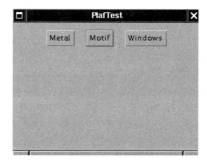

Figure 8–3: Switching the Look and Feel

Example 8–2: PlafTest.java

```
1. import java.awt.*;
2. import java.awt.event.*;
3. import javax.swing.*;
4.
5. public class PlafTest
6. {
7.     public static void main(String[] args)
8.     {
9.         PlafFrame frame = new PlafFrame();
10.        frame.setDefaultCloseOperation(JFrame.EXIT_ON_CLOSE);
11.        frame.show();
12.    }
```

```
13. }
14.
15. /**
16.    A frame with a button panel for changing look and feel
17. */
18. class PlafFrame extends JFrame
19. {
20.    public PlafFrame()
21.    {
22.       setTitle("PlafTest");
23.       setSize(WIDTH, HEIGHT);
24.
25.       // add panel to frame
26.
27.       PlafPanel panel = new PlafPanel();
28.       Container contentPane = getContentPane();
29.       contentPane.add(panel);
30.    }
31.
32.    public static final int WIDTH = 300;
33.    public static final int HEIGHT = 200;
34. }
35.
36. /**
37.    A panel with buttons to change the pluggable look and feel
38. */
39. class PlafPanel extends JPanel
40. {
41.    public PlafPanel()
42.    {
43.       makeButton("Metal",
44.          "javax.swing.plaf.metal.MetalLookAndFeel");
45.       makeButton("Motif",
46.          "com.sun.java.swing.plaf.motif.MotifLookAndFeel");
47.       makeButton("Windows",
48.          "com.sun.java.swing.plaf.windows.WindowsLookAndFeel");
49.    }
50.
51.    /**
52.       Makes a button to change the pluggable look and feel.
53.       @param name the button name
54.       @param plafName the name of the look and feel class
55.    */
56.    void makeButton(String name, final String plafName)
57.    {
58.       // add button to panel
59.
60.       JButton button = new JButton(name);
61.       add(button);
62.
```

```
63.        // set button action
64.
65.        button.addActionListener(new
66.           ActionListener()
67.           {
68.             public void actionPerformed(ActionEvent event)
69.             {
70.                // button action: switch to the new look and feel
71.                try
72.                {
73.                   UIManager.setLookAndFeel(plafName);
74.                   SwingUtilities.updateComponentTreeUI
75.                      (PlafPanel.this);
76.                }
77.                catch(Exception e) { e.printStackTrace(); }
78.             }
79.           });
80.    }
81. }
```

Example: Capturing Window Events

Not all events are as simple to handle as button clicks. Here is an example of a more complex case that we already briefly noted in chapter 7. Prior to the appearance of the EXIT_ON_CLOSE option in the Java SDK 1.3, programmers had to manually exit the program when the main frame was closed. In a non-toy program, you will want to do that as well, because you only want to close the program after you checked that the user won't lose work. For example, when the user closes the frame, you may want to put up a dialog to warn the user if unsaved work is about to be lost, and only exit the program when the user agrees.

When the program user tries to close a frame window, the JFrame object is the source of a WindowEvent. If you want to catch that event, you must have an appropriate listener object and add it to the list of window listeners.

```
WindowListener listener = . . .;
frame.addWindowListener(listener);
```

The window listener must be an object of a class that implements the WindowListener interface. There are actually seven methods in the WindowListener interface. The frame calls them as the responses to seven distinct events that could happen to a window. The names are self-explanatory, except that "iconified" is usually called "minimized" under Windows. Here is the complete WindowListener interface:

```
public interface WindowListener
{
   void windowOpened(WindowEvent e);
   void windowClosing(WindowEvent e);
   void windowClosed(WindowEvent e);
```

```
    void windowIconified(WindowEvent e);
    void windowDeiconified(WindowEvent e);
    void windowActivated(WindowEvent e);
    void windowDeactivated(WindowEvent e);
}
```

As is always the case in Java, any class that implements an interface must implement all its methods; in this case, this means implementing *seven* methods. Recall that we are only interested in one of these seven methods, namely the windowClosing method.

Of course, we can define a class that implements the interface, add a call to System.exit(0) in the windowClosing method, and write do-nothing functions for the other six methods:

```
class Terminator implements WindowListener
{
    public void windowClosing(WindowEvent e)
    {
        System.exit(0);
    }

    public void windowOpened(WindowEvent e) {}
    public void windowClosed(WindowEvent e) {}
    public void windowIconified(WindowEvent e) {}
    public void windowDeiconified(WindowEvent e) {}
    public void windowActivated(WindowEvent e) {}
    public void windowDeactivated(WindowEvent e) {}
}
```

Adapter Classes

Typing code for six methods that don't do anything is the kind of tedious busy-work that nobody likes. To simplify this task, each of the AWT listener interfaces that has more than one method comes with a companion *adapter* class that implements all the methods in the interface but does nothing with them. For example, the WindowAdapter class has seven do-nothing methods. This means the adapter class automatically satisfies the technical requirements that Java imposes for implementing the associated listener interface. You can extend the adapter class to specify the desired reactions to some, but not all, of the event types in the interface. (An interface such as ActionListener that has only a single method does not need an adapter class.)

Let us make use of the window adapter. We can extend the WindowAdapter class, inherit six of the do-nothing methods, and override the windowClosing method:

```
class Terminator extends WindowAdapter
{
    public void windowClosing(WindowEvent e)
    {
```

```
        System.exit(0);
    }
}
```

> NOTE: You may recall that some programmers like to turn components into event listeners. But that trick won't work here. You cannot make `MyFrame` into a subclass of `WindowAdapter` since `MyFrame` already extends `JFrame`. Therefore, you cannot simply set the window listener to `this`, and you must come up with a new class.

Now you can register an object of type `Terminator` as the event listener:

```
WindowListener listener = new Terminator();
frame.addWindowListener(listener);
```

Now, whenever the frame generates a window event, it passes it to the `listener` object by calling one of its seven methods (see Figure 8–4). Six of those methods do nothing; the `windowClosing` method calls `System.exit(0)`, terminating the application.

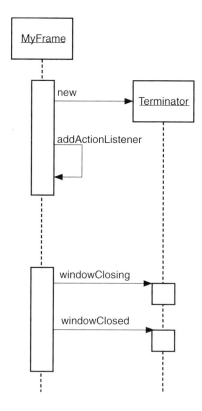

Figure 8–4: A window listener

Creating a listener class that extends the `WindowAdapter` is an improvement, but we can go even further. There is no need to give a name to the `listener` object. Simply write

```
frame.addWindowListener(new Terminator());
```

But why stop there? We can make the listener class into an anonymous inner class of the frame.

```
frame.addWindowListener(new
    WindowAdapter()
    {
        public void windowClosing(WindowEvent e)
        {
            System.exit(0);
        }
    } );
```

This code does the following:

- Defines a class without a name that extends the `WindowAdapter` class.

- Adds a `windowClosing` method to that anonymous class. (As before, this method exits the program.)

- Inherits the remaining six do-nothing methods from `WindowAdapter`.

- Creates an object of this class. That object does not have a name, either.

- Passes that object to the `addWindowListener` method.

As we already mentioned, the syntax for using anonymous inner classes for event listeners takes some getting used to. The payoff is that the resulting code is as short as possible.

NOTE: We want to stress that using an anonymous inner adapter class is purely technical. Instead of using an anonymous inner class, you can always define a regular class with a name and then create an object of that named class.

You will see this code in many example programs. Before the `EXIT_ON_CLOSE` option came along, all graphical applications needed to supply it.

The AWT Event Hierarchy

Having given you a taste of how event handling works, we want to turn to a more general discussion of event handling in Java. As we briefly mentioned earlier, event handling in Java is object oriented, with all events descending from the `EventObject` class in the `java.util` package. (The common super-class is not called `Event` since that is the name of the event class in the old event model. Although the old model is now deprecated, its classes are still a part of the current AWT.)

The `EventObject` class has a subclass `AWTEvent`, which is the parent of all AWT event classes. Figure 8–5 shows the inheritance diagram of the AWT events.

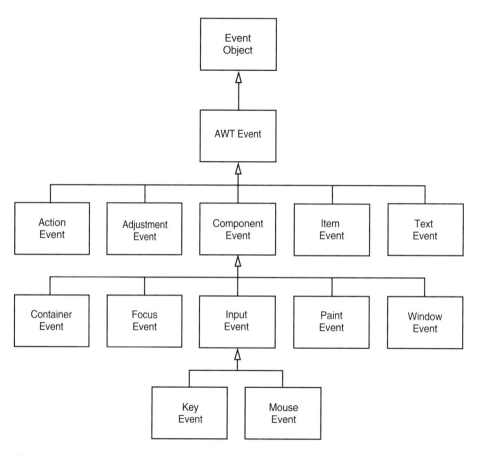

Figure 8–5: Inheritance diagram of the AWT event classes

Some of the Swing components generate event objects of yet more event types; these directly extend `EventObject`, not `AWTEvent`.

You can even add your own custom events by subclassing `EventObject` or one of the other event classes, as you will see at the end of this chapter.

The event objects encapsulate information about the event that the event source communicates to its listeners. When necessary, you can then analyze the event objects that were passed to the listener object, as we did in the button example with the `getSource` and `getActionCommand` methods.

Some of the AWT event classes are of no practical use for the Java programmer. For example, the AWT inserts `PaintEvent` objects into the event queue, but these objects are not delivered to listeners. Java programmers should override the `paintComponent` method to control repainting. Here is a list of those AWT event types that are actually passed to listeners.

```
ActionEvent          ItemEvent
AdjustmentEvent      KeyEvent
ComponentEvent       MouseEvent
ContainerEvent       TextEvent
FocusEvent           WindowEvent
```

You will see examples of all of these event types in this chapter and the next.

The `javax.swing.event` package contains additional events that are specific to Swing components. We will cover some of them in the next chapter.

There are eleven listener interfaces altogether in the `java.awt.event` package:

```
ActionListener       KeyListener
AdjustmentListener   MouseListener
ComponentListener    MouseMotionListener
ContainerListener    TextListener
FocusListener        WindowListener
ItemListener
```

You have already seen the `ActionListener` and `WindowListener` interface.

Although the `javax.swing.event` package contains many more listener interfaces that are specific to Swing user interface components, it still uses the basic AWT listener interfaces extensively for general event processing.

Seven of the AWT listener interfaces, namely, those that have more than one method, come with a companion *adapter* class that implements all the methods in the interface to do nothing. (The remaining four interfaces have only a single method each, so there is no benefit in having adapter classes for these interfaces.) For example, the `WindowAdapter` class has seven do-nothing methods.

Here is a list of the names of these adapter classes:

```
ComponentAdapter     MouseAdapter
ContainerAdapter     MouseMotionAdapter
FocusAdapter         WindowAdapter
KeyAdapter
```

Obviously, there are a lot of classes and interfaces to keep track of—it can all be a bit overwhelming. Fortunately, the principle is simple. A class that is interested in receiving events must implement a listener interface. It registers itself with the event source. It then gets the events that it asked for, and processes them through the methods of the listener interface.

C++ NOTE: People coming from a C/C++ background may be wondering: why the proliferation of objects, methods, and interfaces needed for event handling? You are used to doing GUI programming by writing callbacks with generic pointers or handles. This won't work in Java. The Java event model is strongly typed: the compiler watches out that events are sent only to objects that are capable of handling them.

Semantic and Low-Level Events in the AWT

The AWT makes a useful distinction between *low-level* and *semantic* events. A semantic event is one that expresses what the user is doing, such as "clicking that button"; hence, an `ActionEvent` is a semantic event. Low-level events are those events that make this possible. In the case of a button click, this is a mouse down, a series of mouse moves, and a mouse up (but only if the mouse up is inside the button area). Or it might be a keystroke, which happens if the user selects the button with the TAB key and then activates it with the space bar. Similarly, adjusting a scrollbar is a semantic event, but dragging the mouse is a low-level event.

There are four semantic event classes in the `java.awt.event` package:

- `ActionEvent` (for a button click, a menu selection, selecting a list item, or ENTER typed in a text field)

- `AdjustmentEvent` (the user adjusted a scroll bar)

- `ItemEvent` (the user made a selection from a set of checkbox or list items)

- `TextEvent` (the contents of a text field or text area were changed)

There are six low-level event classes:

- `ComponentEvent` (the component was resized, moved, shown, or hidden); also is the base class for all low-level events

- `KeyEvent` (a key was pressed or released)

- `MouseEvent` (the mouse button was pressed, released, moved, or dragged)

- `FocusEvent` (a component got focus, or lost focus)

- `WindowEvent` (the window was activated, deactivated, iconified, deiconified, or closed)

- `ContainerEvent` (a component has been added or removed)

Event Handling Summary

Table 8–1 shows all AWT listener interfaces, events, and event sources. Notice that this table gives a number of events that track the *focus* of components and the *activation* of windows—these concepts are explained in the sections that follow.

Table 8–1: Event handling summary

Interface	Methods	Parameter/Accessors	Events Generated By
ActionListener	actionPerformed	ActionEvent getActionCommand getModifiers	AbstractButton JComboBox JTextField Timer
AdjustmentListener	adjustmentValueChanged	AdjustmentEvent getAdjustable getAdjustmentType getValue	JScrollbar
ItemListener	itemStateChanged	ItemEvent getItem getItemSelectable getStateChange	AbstractButton JComboBox
TextListener	textValueChanged	TextEvent	
ComponentListener	componentMoved componentHidden componentResized componentShown	ComponentEvent getComponent	Component
ContainerListener	componentAdded componentRemoved	ContainerEvent getChild getContainer	Container
FocusListener	focusGained focusLost	FocusEvent isTemporary	Component
KeyListener	keyPressed keyReleased keyTyped	KeyEvent getKeyChar getKeyCode getKeyModifiersText getKeyText isActionKey	Component
MouseListener	mousePressed mouseReleased mouseEntered mouseExited mouseClicked	MouseEvent getClickCount getX getY getPoint translatePoint isPopupTrigger	Component
MouseMotionListener	mouseDragged mouseMoved	MouseEvent	Component
WindowListener	windowClosing windowOpened windowIconified windowDeiconified windowClosed windowActivated windowDeactivated	WindowEvent getWindow	Window

Let's go over the event delegation mechanism one more time to make sure that you understand the relationship between event classes, listener interfaces, and adapter classes.

Event *sources* are user interface components, windows, and menus. The operating system notifies an event source about interesting activities, such as mouse moves and keystrokes. The event source describes the nature of the event in an *event object*. It also keeps a set of *listeners*—objects that want to be called when the event happens (see Figure 8–6). The event source then calls the appropriate method of the *listener interface* to deliver information about the event to the various listeners. The source does this by passing the appropriate event object to the method in the listener class. The listener analyzes the event object to find out more about the event. For example, you can use the `getSource` method to find out the source, or the `getX` and `getY` methods of the `MouseEvent` class to find out the current location of the mouse.

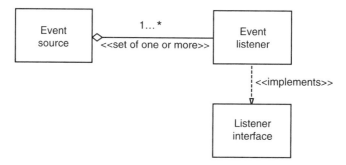

Figure 8–6: Relationship between event sources and listeners

With one exception, each AWT event type corresponds to a listener interface. The one exception is that both `MouseListener` and `MouseMotionListener` receive `MouseEvent` objects. This is done for efficiency—there are a lot of mouse events as the user moves the mouse around, and a listener that just cares about mouse *clicks* will not be bothered with unwanted mouse *moves*.

Furthermore, Java supplies a corresponding *adapter* class to all AWT listener interfaces with more than one method. The adapter class defines all the methods of the interface to do nothing. You use adapter classes as a time-saving tool: use them when you want to override just a few of the listener interface methods.

NOTE: In the AWT 1.0 event mechanism, events originated in a particular component and were then propagated to all containers of the compontent. Starting with the AWT 1.1, events are only sent to listeners who registered their interest in receiving them.

The high-level semantic events are quite natural for GUI programming—they correspond to user input. To better understand the low-level events in Table 8–1, we will need to briefly review some terminology.

- A *component* is a user interface element such as a button, text field, or scrollbar.
- A *container* is a screen area or component that can contain components, such as a window or a panel.

All low-level events inherit from `ComponentEvent`. This class has a method, called `getComponent`, which reports the component that originated the event; you can use `getComponent` instead of `getSource`. The `getComponent` method returns the same value as `getSource`, but already cast as a `Component`. For example, if a key event was fired because of an input into a text field, then `getComponent` returns a reference to that text field.

A `ContainerEvent` is generated whenever a component is added or removed. This is quite different from the other events that we saw. Button clicks and keystrokes come from the user in a random fashion, but adding or removing components is a consequence of your programming. Therefore, you don't need an event notification mechanism—you could have programmed the notification yourself. This event was provided to make user interface generators simpler to program. Unless you have a dynamically changing user interface, you will not need to worry about it.

`java.awt.event.ComponentEvent`

- `Component getComponent()`
  returns a reference to the component that is the source for the event. This is the same as `(Component)getSource()`.

Low-Level Event Types

In the sections that follow, we will discuss in more detail the focus and window events that we have already briefly mentioned. After that, we take up the events that are not linked to specific user interface components, in particular, events related to keystrokes and mouse activity. You can find a detailed discussion of semantic events generated by user interface components in the next chapter.

Focus Events

When you use a mouse, you can point to any object on the screen. But when you type, your keystrokes must go to a specific screen object. The *window manager* (such as Windows or X Windows) directs all keystrokes to the *active window*. Often, the active window is distinguished by a highlighted title bar. Only one window can be active at any one time.

Now suppose the active window is controlled by a Java program. The Java window receives the keystrokes, and it in turn directs them towards a particular *component*. That component is said to have *focus*. Just like the active window is usually distinguished in some way, most Swing components give a visual cue if they currently have focus. A text field has a blinking caret, a button has a rectangle around the label, and so on. When a text field has focus, you can enter text into the text field. When a button has focus, you can "click" it by pressing the space bar.

There is at most one component in a window that has focus. A component can *lose focus* if the user selects another component, which then *gains focus*. A component gains focus if the user clicks the mouse inside it. The user can also use the TAB key to give focus to each component in turn. This traverses all components that are able to receive input focus. By default, Swing components are traversed from left to right, then top to bottom, as they are shown in the ambient container. You can change the focus traversal order; see the next chapter for more on this subject.

Finally, you can use the `requestFocus` method to move the focus to any specific visible component at run time, or you can use the `transferFocus` method to move the focus to the next component in the traversal order. Most components can receive the focus; however, by default, some components, such as labels and panels, do not.

TIP: You can prevent a Swing component from receiving the focus by overriding the `isFocusTraversable` method to return `false`.

A focus listener must implement two methods, `focusGained` and `focusLost`. These methods are triggered when the event *source* gains or loses the focus. Each of these methods has a `FocusEvent` parameter. There are two useful methods for this class. The `getComponent` method reports the component that gained or lost the focus, and the `isTemporary` method returns `true` if the focus change was *temporary*. A temporary focus change occurs when a component loses control temporarily but will automatically get it back. This happens, for example, when the user selects a different active window. As soon as the user selects the current window again, the same component regains the focus.

One use for trapping focus events is error checking or data validation. Suppose you have a text field that contains a credit card number. When the user is done editing the field and moves to another field, you trap the lost focus event. If the credit card format was not formatted properly, you call `requestFocus()` to give the focus back to the credit card field.

```
public void focusLost(FocusEvent event)
{
   if (event.getComponent() == ccField && !event.isTemporary())
   {
      if (!checkFormat(ccField.getText()))
         ccField.requestFocus();
   }
}
```

`java.awt.Component`

• `void requestFocus()`

moves the focus to this component. The component must be visible for this to happen.

• `void transferFocus()`

transfers the focus to the next component in the traversal order.

• `boolean isFocusTraversable()`

tells whether a component can be reached by using TAB or SHIFT-TAB. Override this method to return `false` if you don't want the component to be reachable with TAB/SHIFT+TAB. (You can still set the focus explicitly by using `requestFocus`.)

Keyboard Events

When the user pushes a key, a `KEY_PRESSED` KeyEvent is generated. When the user releases the key, a `KEY_RELEASE` KeyEvent is triggered. You trap these events in the `keyPressed` and `keyReleased` methods of any class that implements the `KeyListener` interface. Use these methods to trap raw keystrokes. A third method, `keyTyped`, combines the two: it reports on the *characters* that were generated by the user's keystrokes.

The best way to see what happens is with an example. But before we can do that, we have to add a little more terminology. Java makes a distinction between characters and *virtual key codes*. Virtual key codes are indicated with a prefix of `VK_`, such as `VK_A` or `VK_SHIFT`. Virtual key codes correspond to keys on the keyboard. For example, `VK_A` denotes the key marked A. There is no separate lowercase virtual key code—the keyboard does not have separate lowercase keys.

NOTE: Virtual key codes are similar (and related to) the scan codes of a PC keyboard.

So, suppose that the user types an uppercase "A" in the usual way, by pressing the SHIFT key along with the A key. Java reports *five* events in response to this user action. Here are the actions and the associated events:

1. Pressed the SHIFT key (keyPressed called for VK_SHIFT)
2. Pressed the A key (keyPressed called for VK_A)
3. Typed "A" (keyTyped called for an "A")
4. Released the A key (keyReleased called for VK_A)
5. Released the SHIFT key (keyReleased called for VK_SHIFT)

On the other hand, if the user typed a lowercase "a" by simply pressing the A key, then there are only three events:

1. Pressed the A key (keyPressed called for VK_A)
2. Typed "a" (keyTyped called for an "a")
3. Released the A key (keyReleased called for VK_A)

Thus, the keyTyped procedure reports the *character* that was typed ("A" or "a"), whereas the keyPressed and keyReleased methods report on the actual *keys* that the user pressed.

To work with the keyPressed and keyReleased methods, you want to first check the *key code*.

```
public void keyPressed(KeyEvent event)
{
    int keyCode = event.getKeyCode();
    . . .
}
```

The key code will equal one of the following (reasonably mnemonic) constants. They are defined in the KeyEvent class.

```
VK_A . . . VK_Z
VK_0 . . . VK_9
VK_COMMA, VK_PERIOD, VK_SLASH, VK_SEMICOLON, VK_EQUALS
VK_OPEN_BRACKET, VK_BACK_SLASH, VK_CLOSE_BRACKET
VK_BACK_QUOTE, VK_QUOTE
VK_GREATER, VK_LESS, VK_UNDERSCORE, VK_MINUS
VK_AMPERSAND, VK_ASTERISK, VK_AT, VK_BRACELEFT, VK_BRACERIGHT
VK_LEFT_PARENTHESIS, VK_RIGHT_PARENTHESIS
VK_CIRCUMFLEX, VK_COLON, VK_NUMBER_SIGN, VK_QUOTEDBL
VK_EXCLAMATION_MARK, VK_INVERTED_EXCLAMATION_MARK
VK_DEAD_ABOVEDOT, VK_DEAD_ABOVERING, VK_DEAD_ACUTE
VK_DEAD_BREVE
VK_DEAD_CARON, VK_DEAD_CEDILLA, VK_DEAD_CIRCUMFLEX
VK_DEAD_DIAERESIS
VK_DEAD_DOUBLEACUTE, VK_DEAD_GRAVE, VK_DEAD_IOTA, VK_DEAD_MACRON
```

```
VK_DEAD_OGONEK, VK_DEAD_SEMIVOICED_SOUND, VK_DEAD_TILDE
  VK_DEAD_VOICED_SOUND
VK_DOLLAR, VK_EURO_SIGN
VK_SPACE, VK_ENTER, VK_BACK_SPACE, VK_TAB, VK_ESCAPE
VK_SHIFT, VK_CONTROL, VK_ALT, VK_ALT_GRAPH, VK_META
VK_NUM_LOCK, VK_SCROLL_LOCK, VK_CAPS_LOCK
VK_PAUSE, VK_PRINTSCREEN
VK_PAGE_UP, VK_PAGE_DOWN, VK_END, VK_HOME, VK_LEFT, VK_UP VK_RIGHT
  VK_DOWN
VK_F1 . . .VK_F24
VK_NUMPAD0 . . . VK_NUMPAD9
VK_KP_DOWN, VK_KP_LEFT, VK_KP_RIGHT, VK_KP_UP
VK_MULTIPLY, VK_ADD, VK_SEPARATER [sic], VK_SUBTRACT, VK_DECIMAL
  VK_DIVIDE
VK_DELETE, VK_INSERT
VK_HELP, VK_CANCEL, VK_CLEAR, VK_FINAL
VK_CONVERT, VK_NONCONVERT, VK_ACCEPT, VK_MODECHANGE
VK_AGAIN, VK_ALPHANUMERIC, VK_CODE_INPUT, VK_COMPOSE, VK_PROPS
VK_STOP
VK_ALL_CANDIDATES, VK_PREVIOUS_CANDIDATE
VK_COPY, VK_CUT, VK_PASTE, VK_UNDO
VK_FULL_WIDTH, VK_HALF_WIDTH
VK_HIRAGANA, VK_KATAKANA, VK_ROMAN_CHARACTERS
VK_KANA, VK_KANJI
VK_JAPANESE_HIRAGANA, VK_JAPANESE_KATAKANA, VK_JAPANESE_ROMAN
VK_UNDEFINED
```

To find the current state of the SHIFT, CONTROL, ALT, and META keys, you can, of course, track the VK_SHIFT, VK_CONTROL, VK_ALT, and VK_META key presses, but that is tedious. Instead, simply use the isShiftDown, isControlDown, isAltDown, and isMetaDown methods.

For example, the following code tests whether the user presses SHIFT + RIGHT ARROW:

```
public void keyPressed(KeyEvent event)
{
    int keyCode = event.getKeyCode();
    if (keyCode == keyEvent.VK_RIGHT && event.isShiftDown())
    {
        . . .
    }
}
```

In the keyTyped method, you call the getKeyChar method to obtain the actual character that was typed.

NOTE: Not all keystrokes result in a call to keyTyped. Only those keystrokes that generate a Unicode character can be captured in the keyTyped method. You need to use the keyPressed method to check for cursor keys and other command keys.

Example 8–3 shows how to handle keystrokes. The program (shown in Figure 8–7) is a simple implementation of the Etch-A-Sketch^{TM} toy.

You move a pen up, down, left, and right with the cursor keys. If you hold down the SHIFT key, the pen moves by a larger increment. Or, if you are experienced using the vi editor, you can bypass the cursor keys and use the lowercase h, j, k, and l keys to move the pen. The uppercase H, J, K, and L move the pen by a larger increment. We trap the cursor keys in the `keyPressed` method and the characters in the
`keyTyped` method.

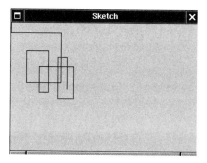

Figure 8–7: A sketch program

There is one technicality: Normally, a panel cannot get keyboard focus. That is, it will not receive any key events. To allow it to gain focus, we override the `isFocusTraversable` method of the `SketchPanel` class to return `true`.

Example 8–3: Sketch.java

```
1. import java.awt.*;
2. import java.awt.geom.*;
3. import java.util.*;
4. import java.awt.event.*;
5. import javax.swing.*;
6.
7. public class Sketch
8. {
9.    public static void main(String[] args)
10.    {
11.       SketchFrame frame = new SketchFrame();
12.       frame.setDefaultCloseOperation(JFrame.EXIT_ON_CLOSE);
13.       frame.show();
14.    }
15. }
16.
17. /**
```

```
18.    A frame with a panel for sketching a figure
19. */
20. class SketchFrame extends JFrame
21. {
22.    public SketchFrame()
23.    {
24.       setTitle("Sketch");
25.       setSize(WIDTH, HEIGHT);
26.
27.       // add panel to frame
28.
29.       SketchPanel panel = new SketchPanel();
30.       Container contentPane = getContentPane();
31.       contentPane.add(panel);
32.    }
33.
34.    public static final int WIDTH = 300;
35.    public static final int HEIGHT = 200;
36. }
37.
38. /**
39.    A panel for sketching with the keyboard.
40. */
41. class SketchPanel extends JPanel
42. {
43.    public SketchPanel()
44.    {
45.       last = new Point2D.Double(100, 100);
46.       lines = new ArrayList();
47.       KeyHandler listener = new KeyHandler();
48.       addKeyListener(listener);
49.    }
50.
51.    public boolean isFocusTraversable()
52.    {
53.       return true; // allow panel to get input focus
54.    }
55.
56.    /**
57.       Add a new line segment to the sketch.
58.       @param dx the movement in x direction
59.       @param dy the movement in y direction
60.    */
61.    public void add(int dx, int dy)
62.    {
63.       // compute new end point
64.       Point2D end = new Point2D.Double(last.getX() + dx,
65.          last.getY() + dy);
```

```
66.
67.        // add line segment
68.        Line2D line = new Line2D.Double(last, end);
69.        lines.add(line);
70.        repaint();
71.
72.        // remember new end point
73.        last = end;
74.     }
75.
76.     public void paintComponent(Graphics g)
77.     {
78.        super.paintComponent(g);
79.        Graphics2D g2 = (Graphics2D)g;
80.
81.        // draw all lines
82.        for (int i = 0; i < lines.size(); i++)
83.           g2.draw((Line2D)lines.get(i));
84.     }
85.
86.     private Point2D last;
87.     private ArrayList lines;
88.
89.     private static final int SMALL_INCREMENT = 1;
90.     private static final int LARGE_INCREMENT = 5;
91.
92.     private class KeyHandler implements KeyListener
93.     {
94.        public void keyPressed(KeyEvent event)
95.        {
96.           int keyCode = event.getKeyCode();
97.
98.           // set distance
99.           int d;
100.          if (event.isShiftDown())
101.             d = LARGE_INCREMENT;
102.          else
103.             d = SMALL_INCREMENT;
104.
105.          // add line segment
106.          if (keyCode == KeyEvent.VK_LEFT) add(-d, 0);
107.          else if (keyCode == KeyEvent.VK_RIGHT) add(d, 0);
108.          else if (keyCode == KeyEvent.VK_UP) add(0, -d);
109.          else if (keyCode == KeyEvent.VK_DOWN) add(0, d);
110.        }
111.
112.        public void keyReleased(KeyEvent event) {}
```

```
113.
114.      public void keyTyped(KeyEvent event)
115.      {
116.         char keyChar = event.getKeyChar();
117.
118.         // set distance
119.         int d;
120.         if (Character.isUpperCase(keyChar))
121.         {
122.            d = LARGE_INCREMENT;
123.            keyChar = Character.toLowerCase(keyChar);
124.         }
125.         else
126.            d = SMALL_INCREMENT;
127.
128.         // add line segment
129.         if (keyChar == 'h') add(-d, 0);
130.         else if (keyChar == 'l') add(d, 0);
131.         else if (keyChar == 'k') add(0, -d);
132.         else if (keyChar == 'j') add(0, d);
133.      }
134.   }
135. }
```

java.awt.event.KeyEvent

- `char getKeyChar()`

  returns the character that the user typed.

- `int getKeyCode()`

  returns the virtual key code of this key event.

- `boolean isActionKey()`

  returns `true` if the key in this event is an "action" key. The following keys are action keys: HOME, END, PAGE UP, PAGE DOWN, UP, DOWN, LEFT, RIGHT, F1 ... F24, PRINT SCREEN, SCROLL LOCK, CAPS LOCK, NUM LOCK, PAUSE, INSERT, DELETE, ENTER, BACKSPACE, DELETE, and TAB.

- `static String getKeyText(int keyCode)`

  returns a string describing the key code. For example, `getKeyText(KeyEvent.VK_END)` is the string `"End"`.

- `static String getKeyModifiersText(int modifiers)`

  returns a string describing the modifier keys, such as SHIFT or CTRL + SHIFT.

  Parameters: `modifiers` The modifier state, as reported by `getModifiers`

java.awt.event.InputEvent

• `int getModifiers()`

returns an integer whose bits describe the state of the modifiers SHIFT, CONTROL, ALT, and META. This method applies to both keyboard and mouse events. To see if a bit is set, test the return value against one of the bit masks SHIFT_MASK, CONTROL_MASK, ALT_MASK, META_MASK, or use one of the following methods.

- `boolean isAltDown()`
- `boolean isControlDown()`
- `boolean isMetaDown()`
- `boolean isShiftDown()`

The methods return `true` if the modifier key was held down when this event was generated.

Consuming Events

Occasionally, you will want to capture an event so that it is not passed on to a user interface component. Suppose you want to write a text input field that accepts only numbers. Start out with a regular text field. (Text fields are covered in detail in Chapter 9.) Simply listen to all key events and *consume* all events that don't correspond to digit keys.

```
textField.addKeyListener(new
   KeyAdapter()
   {
      public void keyTyped(KeyEvent event)
      {
         char ch = event.getKeyChar();
         if (ch < '0' || ch > '9') // not a digit
            event.consume();
      }
   });
```

The result is that as far as the text field is concerned, the "key typed" event never happened if the user typed a wrong key.

Only input events (that is, mouse and keyboard events) can be consumed.

 NOTE: Actually, you need to work harder to create a text field that is suitable for editing numbers. See Chapter 9 for details.

`java.awt.event.InputEvent`

- `void consume()`

    consumes a low-level event and thereby prevents it from being sent to a user interface component.

- `boolean isConsumed()`

    returns `true` if the event was consumed.

Mouse Events

You do not need to handle mouse events explicitly if you just want the user to be able to click on a button or menu. These mouse operations are handled internally by the various components in the user interface and then translated into the appropriate semantic event. However, if you want to enable the user to draw with the mouse, you will need to trap mouse move, click, and drag events.

In this section, we will show you a simple graphics editor application that allows the user to place, move, and erase squares on a canvas (see Figure 8–8).

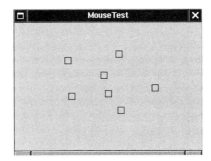

Figure 8–8: A mouse test program

When the user clicks a mouse button, three listener methods are called: `mouse-Pressed` when the mouse is first pressed, `mouseReleased` when the mouse is released, and, finally, `mouseClicked`. If you are only interested in complete clicks, you can ignore the first two methods. By using the `getX` and `getY` methods on the `MouseEvent` argument, you can obtain the *x*- and *y*-coordinates of the mouse pointer when the mouse was clicked. If you want to distinguish between single and double clicks, use the `getClickCount` method.

You can even get triple clicks, but your users will hate you if you force them to exercise their fingers too much. Unless they come from a Macintosh background, they will also hate you if you inflict keystroke + mouse click combinations, such as CONTROL + SHIFT + CLICK, on them. If you do want to check the state of the SHIFT, CONTROL, ALT, and META keys, you do it in the same way as you just saw for key events: use the `isShiftDown`, `isControlDown`, `isAltDown`, and `isMetaDown` methods.

For example, here is a handler for the CONTROL + SHIFT + triple click command.

```
public void mouseClicked(MouseEvent event)
{
   int x = event.getX();
   int y = event.getY();

   int clickCount = event.getClickCount();
   if (event.isShiftDown() && event.isControlDown()
      && clickCount >= 3)
   {
      Graphics g = getGraphics();
      g.drawString("Yikes", x, y);
      g.dispose();
   }
}
```

NOTE: In this example, we use the `Component.getGraphics` method to draw immediately when the mouse is clicked, rather than waiting for the next call to `paintComponent`. We must therefore call `g.dispose()` to recycle the resources that a `Graphics` object holds. You must always call `dispose` for the `Graphics` objects that you obtain yourself, but never for the ones that you receive as arguments of paint methods.

You can distinguish between the mouse buttons by testing the return value of `getModifiers` against the values BUTTON1_MASK, BUTTON2_MASK, and BUTTON3_MASK. Note that BUTTON3_MASK tests for the right (nonprimary) mouse button under Windows. For example, you can use code like this to detect if the right mouse button is down:

```
if ((event.getModifiers() & InputEvent.BUTTON3_MASK) != 0)
   // code for right click
```

In our sample program, we supply both a `mousePressed` and a `mouseClicked` method. When you click onto a pixel that is not inside any of the squares that have been drawn, a new square is added. We implemented this in the `mousePressed` method so that the user receives immediate feedback and does not have to wait until the mouse button is released. When a user double-clicks inside an existing square, it is erased. We implemented this in the `mouseClicked` method because we need the click count.

```
public void mousePressed(MouseEvent event)
{
   current = find(event.getPoint());
   if (current == null) // not inside a square
      add(event.getPoint());
}
```

```
public void mouseClicked(MouseEvent event)
{
   current = find(event.getPoint());
   if (current != null && event.getClickCount() >= 2)
      remove(current);
}
```

Table 8–2: Sample cursor shapes

Icon	Constant
	DEFAULT_CURSOR
	CROSSHAIR_CURSOR
	HAND_CURSOR
	MOVE_CURSOR
	TEXT_CURSOR
	WAIT_CURSOR
	N_RESIZE_CURSOR
	NE_RESIZE_CURSOR
	E_RESIZE_CURSOR
	SE_RESIZE_CURSOR
	S_RESIZE_CURSOR
	SW_RESIZE_CURSOR
	W_RESIZE_CURSOR
	NW_RESIZE_CURSOR

As the mouse moves over a window, the window receives a steady stream of mouse movement events. These are ignored by most applications. However, our test application traps the events to change the cursor to a different shape (a cross hair) when it is over a square. This is done with the `getPredefinedCursor` method of the `Cursor` class. Table 8–2 lists the constants to use with this method along with what the cursors look like under Windows. (Note that several of these cursors look the same, but you should check how they look on your platform.)

TIP: You can find cursor images in the `jre/lib/images/cursors/cursors.properties` directory. The file `cursors.properties` defines the cursor "hot spots." This is the point that the user associates with the pointing action of the cursor. For example, if the cursor has the shape of a pointing hand, the hot spot would be the tip of the index finger. If the cursor has the shape of a magnifying glass, the hot spot would be the center of the lens.

Here is the `mouseMoved` method of the `MouseMotionListener` in our example program:

```
public void mouseMoved(MouseEvent event)
{
   if (find(event.getPoint()) == null)
      setCursor(Cursor.getDefaultCursor());
   else
      setCursor(Cursor.getPredefinedCursor
         (Cursor.CROSSHAIR_CURSOR));
}
```

NOTE: You can also define your own cursor types through the use of the `createCustomCursor` method in the `Toolkit` class:

```
Toolkit tk = Toolkit.getDefaultToolkit();
Image img = tk.getImage("dynamite.gif");
Cursor dynamiteCursor = tk.createCustomCursor(img,
   new Point(10, 10), "dynamite stick");
```

The first parameter of the `createCustomCursor` points to the cursor image. The second parameter gives the offset of the "hot spot" of the cursor. The third parameter is a string that describes the cursor. This string can be used for accessibility support, for example, to read the cursor shape to a user who is visually impaired or who simply is not facing the screen.

If the user presses a mouse button while the mouse is in motion, `mouseDragged` calls are generated instead of `mouseClicked` calls. Our test application lets you drag the square under the cursor. We simply update the currently dragged rectangle to be centered under the mouse position. Then, we repaint the canvas to show the new mouse position.

```
public void mouseDragged(MouseEvent event)
{
   if (current >= 0)
   {
      int x = event.getX();
      int y = event.getY();

      current.setFrame(
         x - SIDELENGTH / 2,
         y - SIDELENGTH / 2,
         SIDELENGTH,
         SIDELENGTH);
      repaint();
   }
}
```

NOTE: The `mouseMoved` method is only called as long as the mouse stays inside the component. However, the `mouseDragged` method keeps getting called even when the mouse is being dragged outside the component.

There are two other mouse event methods: `mouseEntered` and `mouseExited`. These methods are called when the mouse enters or exits a component.

Finally, we need to explain how to listen to mouse events. Mouse clicks are reported through the `mouseClicked` procedure, which is part of the `MouseListener` interface. Because many applications are interested only in mouse clicks and not in mouse moves, and because mouse move events occur so frequently, the mouse move and drag events are defined in a separate interface called `MouseMotionListener`.

In our program we are interested in both types of mouse events. We define two inner classes: `MouseHandler` and `MouseMotionHandler`. The `Mouse-Handler` class extends the `MouseAdapter` class because it only defines two of the five `MouseListener` methods. The `MouseMotionHandler` implements the `MouseMotionListener`, and defines both methods of that interface. Example 8–4 is the program listing.

Example 8–4: MouseTest.java

```
1. import java.awt.*;
2. import java.awt.event.*;
3. import java.util.*;
```

```
 4. import java.awt.geom.*;
 5. import javax.swing.*;
 6.
 7. public class MouseTest
 8. {
 9.    public static void main(String[] args)
10.    {
11.       MouseFrame frame = new MouseFrame();
12.       frame.setDefaultCloseOperation(JFrame.EXIT_ON_CLOSE);
13.       frame.show();
14.    }
15. }
16.
17. /**
18.    A frame containing a panel for testing mouse operations
19. */
20. class MouseFrame extends JFrame
21. {
22.    public MouseFrame()
23.    {
24.       setTitle("MouseTest");
25.       setSize(300, 200);
26.
27.       // add panel to frame
28.
29.       MousePanel panel = new MousePanel();
30.       Container contentPane = getContentPane();
31.       contentPane.add(panel);
32.    }
33.
34.    public static final int WIDTH = 300;
35.    public static final int HEIGHT = 200;
36. }
37.
38. /**
39.    A panel with mouse operations for adding and removing squares.
40. */
41. class MousePanel extends JPanel
42. {
43.    public MousePanel()
44.    {
45.       squares = new ArrayList();
46.       current = null;
47.
48.       addMouseListener(new MouseHandler());
49.       addMouseMotionListener(new MouseMotionHandler());
50.    }
51.
52.    public void paintComponent(Graphics g)
```

```
53.     {
54.        super.paintComponent(g);
55.        Graphics2D g2 = (Graphics2D)g;
56.
57.        // draw all squares
58.        for (int i = 0; i < squares.size(); i++)
59.           g2.draw((Rectangle2D)squares.get(i));
60.     }
61.
62.     /**
63.        Finds the first square containing a point.
64.        @param p a point
65.        @return the index of the first square that contains p
66.     */
67.     public Rectangle2D find(Point2D p)
68.     {
69.        for (int i = 0; i < squares.size(); i++)
70.        {
71.           Rectangle2D r = (Rectangle2D)squares.get(i);
72.           if (r.contains(p)) return r;
73.        }
74.
75.        return null;
76.     }
77.
78.     /**
79.        Adds a square to the collection.
80.        @param p the center of the square
81.     */
82.     public void add(Point2D p)
83.     {
84.        double x = p.getX();
85.        double y = p.getY();
86.
87.        current = new Rectangle2D.Double(
88.           x - SIDELENGTH / 2,
89.           y - SIDELENGTH / 2,
90.           SIDELENGTH,
91.           SIDELENGTH);
92.        squares.add(current);
93.        repaint();
94.     }
95.
96.     /**
97.        Removes a square from the collection.
98.        @param s the square to remove
99.     */
100.    public void remove(Rectangle2D s)
101.    {
```

```
102.       if (s == null) return;
103.       if (s == current) current = null;
104.       squares.remove(s);
105.       repaint();
106.    }
107.
108.
109.    private static final int SIDELENGTH = 10;
110.    private ArrayList squares;
111.    private Rectangle2D current;
112.    // the square containing the mouse cursor
113.
114.    private class MouseHandler extends MouseAdapter
115.    {
116.       public void mousePressed(MouseEvent event)
117.       {
118.          // add a new square if the cursor isn't inside a square
119.          current = find(event.getPoint());
120.          if (current == null)
121.             add(event.getPoint());
122.       }
123.
124.       public void mouseClicked(MouseEvent event)
125.       {
126.          // remove the current square if double clicked
127.          current = find(event.getPoint());
128.          if (current != null && event.getClickCount() >= 2)
129.             remove(current);
130.       }
131.    }
132.
133.    private class MouseMotionHandler
134.       implements MouseMotionListener
135.    {
136.       public void mouseMoved(MouseEvent event)
137.       {
138.          // set the mouse cursor to cross hairs if it is inside
139.          // a rectangle
140.
141.          if (find(event.getPoint()) == null)
142.             setCursor(Cursor.getDefaultCursor());
143.          else
144.             setCursor(Cursor.getPredefinedCursor
145.                (Cursor.CROSSHAIR_CURSOR));
146.       }
147.
148.       public void mouseDragged(MouseEvent event)
149.       {
```

```
150.        if (current != null)
151.        {
152.            int x = event.getX();
153.            int y = event.getY();
154.
155.            // drag the current rectangle to center it at (x, y)
156.            current.setFrame(
157.                x - SIDELENGTH / 2,
158.                y - SIDELENGTH / 2,
159.                SIDELENGTH,
160.                SIDELENGTH);
161.            repaint();
162.        }
163.     }
164.   }
165. }
```

java.awt.event.MouseEvent

- `int getX()`
- `int getY()`
- `Point getPoint()`

  return the *x*- (horizontal) and *y*- (vertical) coordinate, or point where the event happened, using the coordinate system of the source.

- `void translatePoint(int x, int y)`

  translates the coordinates of the event by moving x units horizontally and y units vertically.

- `int getClickCount()`

  returns the number of consecutive mouse clicks associated with this event. (The time interval for what constitutes "consecutive" is system dependent.)

java.awt.Toolkit

- `public Cursor createCustomCursor(Image image, Point hotSpot, String name)`

  creates a new custom cursor object.

Parameters:	image	The image to display when the cursor is active
	hotSpot	The cursor's hot spot (such as the tip of an arrow or the center of cross hairs)
	name	A description of the cursor, to support special accessibility environments

java.awt.Component

- `public void setCursor(Cursor cursor)`
  sets the cursor image to one of the predefined cursors specified by the `cursor` parameter.

Actions

It is common to have multiple ways to activate the same command. The user can choose a certain function through a menu, a keystroke, or a button on a toolbar. This is easy to achieve in the AWT event model: link all events to the same listener. For example, suppose `blueAction` is an object of a class (such as `ColorAction`) implementing the `ActionListener` interface that changes the color to blue. You can attach the same object as a listener to several event sources:

- A toolbar button labeled "Blue"
- A menu item labeled "Blue"
- A keystroke CTRL+B

Then the color change command is handled in a uniform way, no matter whether it was caused by a button click, a menu selection, or a key press.

The Swing package provides a very useful mechanism to encapsulate commands and to attach them to multiple event sources: the `Action` interface. An *action* is an object that encapsulates the following:

- A description of the command (as a text string and an optional icon)
- Parameters that are necessary to carry out the command (such as the requested color in our example)

The `Action` interface has the following methods:

```
void actionPerformed(ActionEvent event)
void setEnabled(boolean b)
boolean isEnabled()
void putValue(String key, Object value)
Object getValue(String key)
void addPropertyChangeListener(PropertyChangeListener listener)
void removePropertyChangeListener(PropertyChangeListener listener)
```

The first method is the familiar method in the `ActionListener` interface: in fact, the `Action` interface extends the `ActionListener` interface. Therefore, you can use an `Action` object whenever an `ActionListener` object is expected.

The next two methods let you enable or disable the action and check whether the action is currently enabled. When an action is attached to a menu or toolbar and the action is disabled, then the option is grayed out.

The `putValue` and `getValue` methods let you store and retrieve arbitrary name/value pairs in the action object. There are a couple of important predefined strings, namely, `Action.NAME` and `Action.SMALL_ICON`, for storing action names and icons into an action object:

```
action.putValue(Action.NAME, "Blue");
action.putValue(Action.SMALL_ICON,
   new ImageIcon("blue-ball.gif"));
```

Table 8–3 shows all predefined action table names.

Table 8–3: Predefined action table names

Name	Value
NAME	The name of the action; displayed on buttons and menu items.
SMALL_ICON	A place to store a small icon; for display in a button, menu item or toolbar.
SHORT_DESCRIPTION	A short description of the icon; for display in a tooltip.
LONG_DESCRIPTION	A long description of the icon; for potential use in online help. No Swing component uses this value.
MNEMONIC_KEY	A mnemonic abbreviation; for display in menu items (see Chapter 9).
ACCELERATOR_KEY	A place to store an accelerator keystroke. No Swing component uses this value.
ACTION_COMMAND_KEY	Historically, used in the now obsolete `registerKeyboardAction` method.
DEFAULT	Potentially useful catchall property. No Swing component uses this value.

If the action object is added to a menu or toolbar, then the name and icon are automatically retrieved and displayed in the menu item or toolbar button. The `SHORT_DESCRIPTION` value turns into a tooltip.

The final two methods of the `Action` interface allow other objects, in particular menus or toolbars that trigger the action, to be notified when the properties of the action object change. For example, if a menu is added as a property change listener of an action object and the action object is subsequently disabled, then the menu is called and can gray out the action name. Property change listeners are a general construct that is a part of the "Java beans" component model. You can find out more about Java beans and their properties in Volume 2.

Note that `Action` is an *interface*, not a class. Any class implementing this interface must implement the seven methods that we just discussed. Fortunately, that is easy because a friendly soul has implemented all but the first method in a class `AbstractAction`. That class takes care of storing all name/value pairs and

managing the property change listeners. All you have to add is an `actionPer-`
`formed` method.

Let's build an action object that can execute color change commands. We store the
name of the command, an icon, and the desired color. We will store the color in
the table of name/value pairs that the `AbstractAction` class provides. Here is
the code for the `ColorAction` class. The constructor sets the name/value pairs,
and the `actionPerformed` method carries out the color change action.

```
public class ColorAction extends AbstractAction
{
   public ColorAction(String name, Icon icon, Color c)
   {
      putValue(Action.NAME, name);
      putValue(Action.SMALL_ICON, icon);
      putValue("color", c);
   }

   public void actionPerformed(ActionEvent event)
   {
      Color c = (Color)getValue("color");
      setBackground(c);
      repaint();
   }
}
```

Our test program creates three objects of this class, such as:

```
Action blueAction = new ColorAction("Blue",
   new ImageIcon("blue-ball.gif"), Color.blue);
```

Next, let's associate this action with a button. That is easy because there is a
`JButton` constructor that takes an `Action` object.

```
JButton blueButton = new JButton(blueAction);
```

That constructor reads the name and icon from the action, sets the short description as the tooltip, and sets the action as the listener. You can see the icons and a
tool tip in Figure 8–9.

As you will see in the next chapter, it is just as easy to add the same action to a menu.

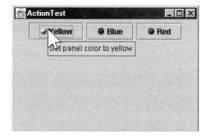

Figure 8–9: Buttons display the icons from the Action objects

Finally, we want to add the action objects to keystrokes. Now we run into a technical complexity. Keystrokes are delivered to the component that has focus. Our sample application is made up of several components, namely, three buttons inside a panel. Therefore, at any time, any one of the three buttons may have focus. *Each* of the buttons would need to handle key events and listen to the CTRL+Y, CTRL+B, and CTRL+R keys.

This is a common problem, and the Swing designers came up with a convenient solution for solving it.

> NOTE: In fact, in J2SE version 1.2, there were two different solutions for binding keys to actions: the `registerKeyboardAction` method of the `JComponent` class, and the `KeyMap` concept for `JTextComponent` commands. As of Java SDK version 1.3, these two mechanisms are unified. This section describes the unified approach.

To associate actions with keystrokes, you first need to generate objects of the `KeyStroke` class. This is a convenience class that encapsulates the description of a key. To generate a `KeyStroke` object, you don't call a constructor, but instead use the static `getKeyStroke` method of the `KeyStroke` class. You specify the virtual key code and the flags (such as SHIFT and CONTROL key combinations):

```
KeyStroke ctrlBKey = KeyStroke.getKeyStroke(KeyEvent.VK_B,
    Event.CTRL_MASK);
```

There is a convenient method that lets you describe the keystroke as a string:

```
KeyStroke ctrlBKey = KeyStroke.getKeyStroke("ctrl B");
```

Every `JComponent` has three *input maps* that map `KeyStroke` objects to actions. The three input maps correspond to three different conditions (see Table 8–4).

Table 8–4: Input map conditions

Flag	Invoke Action
`WHEN_FOCUSED`	When this component has keyboard focus
`WHEN_ANCESTOR_OF_FOCUSED_COMPONENT`	When this component contains the component that has keyboard focus
`WHEN_IN_FOCUSED_WINDOW`	When this component is contained in the same window as the component that has keyboard focus

Keystroke processing checks these maps in the following order:

1. Check the `WHEN_FOCUSED` map of the component with input focus. If the keystroke exists, execute the corresponding action. If the action is enabled, stop processing.

2. Starting from the component with input focus, check the WHEN_ANCESTOR_OF_FOCUSED_COMPONENT maps of its parent components. As soon as a map with the keystroke is found, execute the corresponding action. If the action is enabled, stop processing.

3. Look at all *visible* and *enabled* components in the window with input focus that have this keystroke registered in a WHEN_IN_FOCUSED_WINDOW map. Give these components (in the order of their keystroke registration) a chance to execute the corresponding action. As soon as the first enabled action is executed, stop processing. This part of the process is somewhat fragile if a keystroke appears in more than one WHEN_IN_FOCUSED_WINDOW map.

You obtain an input map from the component with the getInputMap method, for example:

```
InputMap imap = panel.getInputMap(JComponent.WHEN_FOCUSED);
```

The WHEN_FOCUSED condition means that this map is consulted when the current component has the keyboard focus. In our situation, that isn't the map we want. One of the buttons, not the panel, has the input focus. Either of the other two map choices works fine for inserting the color change key strokes. We use WHEN_ANCESTOR_OF_FOCUSED_COMPONENT in our example program.

The InputMap doesn't directly map KeyStroke objects to Action objects. Instead, it maps to arbitrary objects, and a second map, implemented by the ActionMap class, maps objects to actions. That makes it easier to share the same actions among keystrokes that come from different input maps.

Thus, each component has three input maps and one action map. To tie them together, you need to come up with names for the actions. Here is how you can tie a key to an action:

```
imap.put(KeyStroke.getKeyStroke("ctrl Y"), "panel.yellow");
ActionMap amap = panel.getActionMap();
amap.put("panel.yellow", yellowAction);
```

It is customary to use the string "none" for a do-nothing action. That makes it easy to deactivate a key:

```
imap.put(KeyStroke.getKeyStroke("ctrl C"), "none");
```

CAUTION: The SDK documentation suggests to use the action name as the action's key. We don't think that is a good idea. The action name is displayed on buttons and menu items; thus, it can change at the whim of the UI designer and it may be translated into multiple languages. Such unstable strings are poor choices for lookup keys. Instead, we recommend that you come up with action names that are independent of the displayed names.

To summarize, here is what you do to carry out the same action in response to a button, a menu item, or a keystroke:

1. Make a class that extends the `AbstractAction` class. You may be able to use the same class for multiple related actions.

2. Make an object of the action class.

3. Construct a button or menu item from the action object. The constructor will read the label text and icon from the action object.

4. For actions that can be triggered by keystrokes, you have to carry out additional steps. First locate the top-level component of the window, such as a panel that contains all other components.

5. Then get the `WHEN_ANCESTOR_OF_FOCUSED_COMPONENT` input map of the top-level component. Make a `KeyStroke` object for the desired keystroke. Make an action key object, such as a string that describes your action. Add the pair (keystroke, action key) into the input map.

6. Finally, get the action map of the top-level component. Add the pair (action key, action object) into the map.

Example 8–5 shows the complete code of the program that maps both buttons and keystrokes to action objects. Try it out—clicking either the buttons or pressing CTRL+Y, CTRL+B, or CTRL+R changes the panel color.

Example 8–5: ActionTest.java

```
1. import java.awt.*;
2. import java.awt.event.*;
3. import javax.swing.*;
4.
5. public class ActionTest
6. {
7.    public static void main(String[] args)
8.    {
9.       ActionFrame frame = new ActionFrame();
10.      frame.setDefaultCloseOperation(JFrame.EXIT_ON_CLOSE);
11.      frame.show();
12.   }
13. }
14.
15. /**
16.    A frame with a panel that demonstrates color change actions.
17. */
18. class ActionFrame extends JFrame
19. {
20.    public ActionFrame()
```

```
21.     {
22.         setTitle("ActionTest");
23.         setSize(WIDTH, HEIGHT);
24.
25.         // add panel to frame
26.
27.         ActionPanel panel = new ActionPanel();
28.         Container contentPane = getContentPane();
29.         contentPane.add(panel);
30.     }
31.
32.     public static final int WIDTH = 300;
33.     public static final int HEIGHT = 200;
34. }
35.
36. /**
37.     A panel with buttons and keyboard shortcuts to change
38.     the background color.
39. */
40. class ActionPanel extends JPanel
41. {
42.     public ActionPanel()
43.     {
44.         // define actions
45.
46.         Action yellowAction = new ColorAction("Yellow",
47.             new ImageIcon("yellow-ball.gif"),
48.             Color.yellow);
49.         Action blueAction = new ColorAction("Blue",
50.             new ImageIcon("blue-ball.gif"),
51.             Color.blue);
52.         Action redAction = new ColorAction("Red",
53.             new ImageIcon("red-ball.gif"),
54.             Color.red);
55.
56.         // add buttons for these actions
57.
58.         add(new JButton(yellowAction)); // since 1.3
59.         add(new JButton(blueAction));
60.         add(new JButton(redAction));
61.
62.         // associate the Y, B, and R keys with names
63.
64.         InputMap imap = getInputMap( // since 1.3
65.             JComponent.WHEN_ANCESTOR_OF_FOCUSED_COMPONENT);
66.
67.         imap.put(KeyStroke.getKeyStroke("ctrl Y"), "panel.yellow");
68.         imap.put(KeyStroke.getKeyStroke("ctrl B"), "panel.blue");
```

```
69.        imap.put(KeyStroke.getKeyStroke("ctrl R"), "panel.red");
70.
71.        // associate the names with actions
72.
73.        ActionMap amap = getActionMap();
74.        amap.put("panel.yellow", yellowAction);
75.        amap.put("panel.blue", blueAction);
76.        amap.put("panel.red", redAction);
77.     }
78.
79.     public class ColorAction extends AbstractAction
80.     {
81.        /**
82.           Constructs a color action.
83.           @param name the name to show on the button
84.           @param icon the icon to display on the button
85.           @param c the background color
86.        */
87.        public ColorAction(String name, Icon icon, Color c)
88.        {
89.           putValue(Action.NAME, name);
90.           putValue(Action.SMALL_ICON, icon);
91.           putValue(Action.SHORT_DESCRIPTION,
92.              "Set panel color to " + name.toLowerCase());
93.           putValue("color", c);
94.        }
95.
96.        public void actionPerformed(ActionEvent event)
97.        {
98.           Color c = (Color)getValue("color");
99.           setBackground(c);
100.          repaint();
101.       }
102.    }
103. }
```

javax.swing.Action

- `void setEnabled(boolean b)`
  enables or disables this action. User interface elements may query this status and disable themselves if the associated action is disabled.

- `boolean isEnabled()`
  returns `true` if this action is enabled.

- `void putValue(String key, Object value)`
  places a name/value pair inside the action object.

Parameters: `key`   The name of the feature to store with the action object. This can be any string, but four names have predefined meanings:

Name	Value
`Action.NAME`	The action name, to be displayed in UI components
`Action.SMALL_ICON`	The action icon, to be displayed in UI components
`Action.SHORT_DESCRIPTION`	A short description, for example, for a tool tip hint
`Action.LONG_DESCRIPTION`	A longer description for on-line help

             `value`   The object associated with the name.

- `Object getValue(String key)`
  returns the value of a stored name/value pair.

javax.swing.JMenu

- `JMenuItem add(Action a)`
  adds a menu item to the menu that invokes the action `a` when selected; returns the added menu item.

javax.swing.KeyStroke

- `static KeyStroke getKeyStroke(char keyChar)`
  creates a `KeyStroke` object that encapsulates a key stroke corresponding to a `KEY_TYPED` event.

- `static KeyStroke getKeyStroke(int keyCode, int modifiers)`
- `static KeyStroke getKeyStroke(int keyCode, int modifiers, boolean onRelease)`
  create a `KeyStroke` object that encapsulates a key stroke corresponding to a `KEY_PRESSED` or `KEY_RELEASED` event.

- `static KeyStroke getKeyStroke(String description)`
  constructs a keystroke from a humanly readable description. The description is a sequence of white-space-delimited tokens in the following format:

  1. Tokens that match `shift control ctrl meta alt button1 button2 button3` are translated to the appropriate mask bits.

  2. A token `typed` must be followed by a one-character string, for example, `"typed a"`.

Parameters:	keyCode	The virtual key code
	modifiers	Any combination of
		InputEvent.SHIFT_MASK,
		InputEvent.CONTROL_MASK,
		InputEvent.ALT_MASK,
		InputEvent.META_MASK
	onRelease	true if the keystroke is to be recognized when the key is released

3. A token `pressed` or `released` indicates a key press or release. (Key press is the default.)

4. Otherwise, the token, when prefixed with `VK_`, should correspond to a `KeyEvent` constant, for example, `"INSERT"` corresponds to `KeyEvent.VK_INSERT`.

For example, `"released ctrl Y"` corresponds to:
`getKeyStroke(KeyEvent.VK_Y, Event.CTRL_MASK, true)`

---

javax.swing.JComponent

*   `ActionMap getActionMap()`
    returns the action map that maps keystrokes to action keys

*   `InputMap getInputMap(int flag)`
    gets the input map that maps action keys to action objects.

    | *Parameters:* | flag | A condition on the keyboard focus to trigger the action, one of: |

Name	Value
WHEN_FOCUSED	In this component
WHEN_IN_FOCUSED_WINDOW	Anywhere in the window containing this component
WHEN_ANCESTOR_OF_FOCUSED_COMPONENT	Anywhere in a subcomponent contained in this component

Multicasting

In the preceding section, we had several event sources report to the same event listener. In this section, we will do the opposite. All AWT event sources support a *multicast* model for listeners. This means that the same event can be sent to more than one listener object. Multicasting is useful if an event is *potentially* of interest to many parties. Simply add multiple listeners to an event source to give all registered listeners a chance to react to the events.

CAUTION: According to the SDK documentation, "The API makes no guarantees about the order in which the events are delivered to a set of registered listeners for a given event on a given source." In particular, don't implement program logic that consumes a multicast event. Consumption yields unpredictable effects when the delivery order is random. (See the section entitled "Consuming Events" in this chapter for details on event consumption.)

Here we will show a simple application of multicasting. We will have a frame that can spawn multiple windows with the New button. And, it can close all windows with the Close all button—see Figure 8–10.

The listener to the New button of the `MulticastPanel` is the `newListener` object constructed in the `MulticastPanel` constructor—it makes a new frame whenever the button is clicked.

But the Close all button of the `MulticastPanel` has *multiple listeners.* Each time the `makeNewFrame` method executes, it adds another action listener to the Close all button. Each of those listeners is responsible for closing a single frame in its `actionPerformed` method. When the user clicks the Close all button, each of the listeners is activated, and each of them closes its frame.

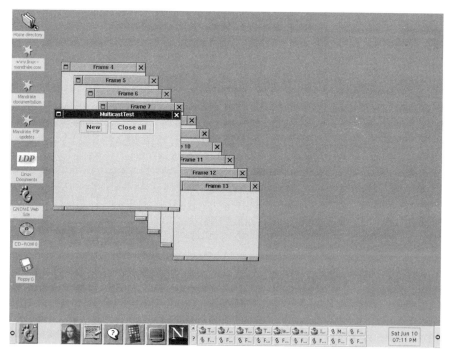

Figure 8–10: All frames listen to the Close all command

Example 8–6 shows the source code.

Example 8–6: MulticastTest.java

```
1. import java.awt.*;
2. import java.awt.event.*;
3. import javax.swing.*;
4.
5. public class MulticastTest
6. {
7.    public static void main(String[] args)
8.    {
9.       MulticastFrame frame = new MulticastFrame();
10.      frame.setDefaultCloseOperation(JFrame.EXIT_ON_CLOSE);
11.      frame.show();
12.   }
13. }
14.
15. /**
16.    A frame with buttons to make and close secondary frames
17. */
18. class MulticastFrame extends JFrame
19. {
20.    public MulticastFrame()
21.    {
22.       setTitle("MulticastTest");
23.       setSize(WIDTH, HEIGHT);
24.
25.       // add panel to frame
26.
27.       MulticastPanel panel = new MulticastPanel();
28.       Container contentPane = getContentPane();
29.       contentPane.add(panel);
30.    }
31.
32.    public static final int WIDTH = 300;
33.    public static final int HEIGHT = 200;
34. }
35.
36. /**
37.    A panel with buttons to create and close sample frames.
38. */
39. class MulticastPanel extends JPanel
40. {
41.    public MulticastPanel()
42.    {
43.       // add "New" button
```

```
44.
45.         JButton newButton = new JButton("New");
46.         add(newButton);
47.
48.         ActionListener newListener = new
49.             ActionListener()
50.             {
51.                 public void actionPerformed(ActionEvent event)
52.                 {
53.                     makeNewFrame();
54.                 }
55.             };
56.         newButton.addActionListener(newListener);
57.
58.         // add "Close all" button
59.
60.         closeAllButton = new JButton("Close all");
61.         add(closeAllButton);
62.     }
63.
64.     private void makeNewFrame()
65.     {
66.         // make new blank frame
67.         final BlankFrame frame = new BlankFrame();
68.         frame.show();
69.
70.         // create action listener that disposes of this frame
71.
72.         ActionListener closeAllListener = new
73.             ActionListener()
74.             {
75.                 public void actionPerformed(ActionEvent event)
76.                 {
77.                     frame.dispose();
78.                 }
79.             };
80.
81.         // add the listener to the "Close all" button of
82.         // the panel--note that this button has multiple
83.         // listeners added, one for each frame
84.         closeAllButton.addActionListener(closeAllListener);
85.     }
86.
87.     private JButton closeAllButton;
88. }
89.
90. class BlankFrame extends JFrame
91. {
```

```
92.    public BlankFrame()
93.    {
94.       counter++;
95.       setTitle("Frame " + counter);
96.       setSize(WIDTH, HEIGHT);
97.       setLocation(SPACING * counter, SPACING * counter);
98.    }
99.
100.   public static final int WIDTH = 300;
101.   public static final int HEIGHT = 200;
102.   public static final int SPACING = 30;
103.   private static int counter = 0;
104. }
```

The Event Queue

When the operating environment generates an event in response to a user action such as a mouse click, the part of the AWT that communicates with the operating environment receives a notification and turns it into an AWT event. The AWT then deposits the event into an *event queue*. The part of the AWT that dispatches events to listeners:

- Fetches events from the event queue;
- Locates the listener object for that event;
- Invokes the appropriate listener procedure for that event.

An event queue is important for performance reasons. Events that occur frequently (such as mouse moves) or that are slow to carry out (such as painting) can be *combined* in the queue. If the program has not managed to extract mouse move or paint events and a new event is inserted, then the AWT can combine it with the existing event to make a single, new event. For example, we can have the new mouse position update the old one, or a new paint event can contain a request to repaint the combined areas of the old paint events.

Occasionally, it is useful to manipulate the event queue directly. For example, you can remove events from the queue, thereby bypassing how events would normally be delivered. Or, you can add new events into the queue, allowing a richer event handling than is possible in the basic Java event model.

You obtain an object representing the event queue by using the method call

```
EventQueue queue
    = Toolkit.getDefaultToolkit().getSystemEventQueue();
```

You insert a new event into the event queue with the postEvent method:

```
queue.postEvent(new ActionEvent(this,
    ActionEvent.ACTION_PERFORMED, "Blue"));
```

You remove an event with the `getNextEvent` method. The `peekEvent` method returns the next event in the queue, but it does not remove it.

> NOTE: Inserting or removing events is an advanced technique. If performed improperly or maliciously, it can wreak havoc with an application. For that reason, applets—the Java applications that are downloaded from foreign computers and run inside your browser—are not allowed access to the system event queue.

`java.awt.EventQueue`

- `AWTEvent peekEvent()`

  returns a reference to the `AWTEvent` object that describes the next event.

- `AWTEvent getNextEvent()`

  returns a reference to the `AWTEvent` object that describes the next event and removes it from the queue.

- `void postEvent(AWTEvent anEvent)`

  places the event on the event queue.

  Parameters: `anEvent`   The event you want to post

Adding Custom Events

In the last section of this chapter, we will do some fairly sophisticated programming. We want to show you how to build a *custom event type* that you can insert into the AWT event queue and then have it dispatched to a listener, just like regular AWT events. For the example in this section, we will implement our own timer. The timer sends an event to its listener whenever a certain time interval has elapsed. For this event, we make a new event type that we call `TimerEvent`. The associated listener will have one method, called `timeElapsed`.

Using our timer is simple. Construct a timer object and specify the interval (in milliseconds) in the constructor. Then, add a listener. The listener will be notified whenever the time interval has elapsed. Here is how you can put the timer to work:

```
Timer t = new Timer(100);
   // deliver timer clicks every 100 milliseconds
TimerListener listener = . . .;
t.addTimerListener(listener);
   // notify the timeElapsed method of this class
```

You need to define a class that implements the `TimerListener` interface:

```
class TimerAction implements TimerListener
{
   public void timeElapsed(TimerEvent event)
```

```
    {
        // this code is executed every 100 milliseconds
    }
}
```

NOTE: As you know from Chapter 6, the Swing package has its own `Timer` class, which is slightly different from ours. The Swing timer does not introduce a new event type but instead sends action events to the listener. More importantly, the Swing timer does not smuggle its events inside the AWT queue but keeps its own separate queue for timer events. We are implementing our own class to show you how to add new event types to the AWT, not to build a better timer. If you need a timer in your own code, you should simply use the Swing timer, not ours.

Now, let us see how to implement a custom event. Whenever you define a custom event, you need three ingredients:

- an *event type*. We will define a `TimerEvent` class.
- an *event listener interface*. We will use:
  ```
  public interface TimerListener extends EventListener
  {
      void timeElapsed(TimerEvent event);
  }
  ```
- an *event source* (that is, our `Timer`). Listeners are attached to the event source.

The `TimerEvent` class is pretty simple:

- It extends the `AWTEvent` superclass since all events in the AWT event queue must have type `AWTEvent`.
- The constructor for the timer event receives the object that is the source of the event (that is, the timer object).

We also need to give an *event ID number* to the superclass. It does not matter what positive integer we choose, as long as we stay outside the range that the AWT uses for its own events.

How to find an unused ID? To quote the SDK documentation: "Programs should choose event ID values which are greater than the integer constant `java.awt.AWTEvent.RESERVED_ID_MAX`."

```
class TimerEvent extends AWTEvent
{
    public TimerEvent(Timer t) { super(t, TIMER_EVENT); }
    public static final int TIMER_EVENT =
        AWTEvent.RESERVED_ID_MAX  + 5555;
}
```

Finally, we need to implement the `Timer` class itself. The AWT event mechanism requires that event sources extend the class `Component`. Normally, components are user interface elements that are placed inside a window. We will simply take the attitude that a timer is an invisible component and have it extend the `JComponent` class.

To write the code that constructs the interval that the timer "ticks," we need to use threads. (Threads are discussed in the second volume of this book, so you will need to take the thread handling code on faith for now.) Whenever the specified time interval has elapsed, we make a new timer event and insert it into the event queue. Here's the code for this, with the pieces that are needed to post the event in bold:

```
class Timer extends JComponent implements Runnable
{
    public Timer(int i)
    {
        interval = i;
        Thread t = new Thread(this);
        t.start();
    }

    public void run()
    {
        while (true)
        {
            try { Thread.sleep(interval); }
            catch(InterruptedException e) {}

            EventQueue queue
                = Toolkit.getDefaultToolkit().getSystemEventQueue();
            TimerEvent event = new TimerEvent(this);
            queue.postEvent(event);
        }
    }
    . . .
    private int interval;
```

After this code is processed, our custom timer events are inserted into the queue. Event delivery is not automatic however, so our custom timer event will not be sent to anyone without additional code.

How do we make sure our custom event is sent to interested parties? The answer is that is the responsibility of the *event source* to:

• Manage the listeners for the events that it generates;
• Dispatch the events to the listeners that are registered for them.

Event management is a common task, and the Swing designers provide a convenience class `EventListenerList` to make it easy to implement the methods for adding and removing listeners and for firing events. The class takes care of the tricky details that can arise when multiple threads attempt to add, remove, or dispatch events at the same time.

Because some event sources accept listeners of multiple types, each listener in the event listener list is associated with a particular class. The `add` and `remove` methods are intended for the implementation of add*Xxx*`Listener` methods. For example,

```
public void addTimerListener(TimerListener listener)
{
    listenerList.add(TimerListener.class, listener);
}

public void removeTimerListener(TimerListener listener)
{
    listenerList.remove(TimerListener.class, listener);
}
```

NOTE: You may wonder why the `EventListenerList` doesn't simply check which interface the listener object implements. But it is possible for an object to implement multiple interfaces. For example, it is possible that `listener` happens to implement both the `TimerListener` and the `ActionListener` interface, but a programmer may choose only to add it as a `TimerListener` by calling the `addTimerListener`. The `EventListenerList` must respect that choice.

Whenever the AWT removes an event from the queue, it calls the `processEvent` method. For timers, we define that method to call the `timeElapsed` method on the single listener. We use the `getListeners` method of the `EventListener-List` class to obtain all timer listeners. Then we call the `timeElapsed` method for each of them:

```
public void processEvent(AWTEvent event)
{
    if (event instanceof TimerEvent)
    {
        EventListener[] listeners = listenerList.getListeners(
            TimerListener.class);
        for (int i = 0; i < listeners.length; i++)
            ((TimerListener)listeners[i]).timeElapsed(
                (TimerEvent)event);
    }
    else super.processEvent(event);
}
```

> NOTE: The `getListeners` method is a J2SE 1.3 feature. Use `getListenerList` if you use J2SE 1.2.

> CAUTION: Our timer extends the `JComponent` class. If you instead use the `Component` class as the superclass, you will run into a problem. The AWT code that removes events from the queue and dispatches them to the event source will deliver them only if it is convinced that the component supports the new event model. One way to convince it is to call the `enableEvents` method in the `Component` class. This method takes a parameter that gives a mask for the AWT events that you want to enable for this component. If you don't care about AWT events at all—as is the case for a source of custom events— you can pass pass a mask of 0. Therefore, if your event source extends the `Component` class, you should place a call `enableEvents(0)` into the constructor.

As you can see, it is possible to add custom events to the AWT mechanism using relatively little code.

Example 8–7 shows the complete source code of a sample program that uses the timer. For fun, we generate a new random circle and shift the screen display down a pixel with every timer tick. The effect is an animation that simulates rainfall. (See Figure 8–11.)

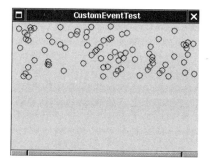

Figure 8–11: Using custom timer events to simulate rainfall

This ends our discussion of event handling. In the next chapter, you will learn more about user interface components. Of course, to program user interfaces, you will put your knowledge of event handling to work by capturing the events that the user interface components generate.

Example 8–7: CustomEventTest.java

```
1. import java.awt.*;
2. import java.awt.geom.*;
3. import java.util.*;
```

```
 4. import java.awt.event.*;
 5. import javax.swing.*;
 6. import javax.swing.event.*;
 7.
 8. public class CustomEventTest
 9. {
10.    public static void main(String[] args)
11.    {
12.       CustomEventFrame frame = new CustomEventFrame();
13.       frame.setDefaultCloseOperation(JFrame.EXIT_ON_CLOSE);
14.       frame.show();
15.    }
16. }
17.
18. /**
19.    A frame with a panel that displays falling raindrops
20. */
21. class CustomEventFrame extends JFrame
22. {
23.    public CustomEventFrame()
24.    {
25.       setTitle("CustomEventTest");
26.       setSize(WIDTH, HEIGHT);
27.
28.       // add frame to panel
29.
30.       CustomEventPanel panel = new CustomEventPanel();
31.       Container contentPane = getContentPane();
32.       contentPane.add(panel);
33.    }
34.
35.    public static final int WIDTH = 300;
36.    public static final int HEIGHT = 200;
37. }
38.
39. /**
40.    A panel that displays falling rain drops
41. */
42. class CustomEventPanel extends JPanel
43. {
44.    public CustomEventPanel()
45.    {
46.       y = 0;
47.       circles = new ArrayList();
48.
49.       Timer t = new Timer(100);
50.       TimerAction listener = new TimerAction();
```

```
51.        t.addTimerListener(listener);
52.    }
53.
54.    public void paintComponent(Graphics g)
55.    {
56.        super.paintComponent(g);
57.        Graphics2D g2 = (Graphics2D)g;
58.
59.        // translate the origin to create illusion of falling drops
60.        g2.translate(0, y);
61.
62.        // draw all circles
63.        for (int i = 0; i < circles.size(); i++)
64.            g2.draw((Ellipse2D)circles.get(i));
65.    }
66.
67.    private ArrayList circles;
68.    private int y;
69.
70.    private class TimerAction implements TimerListener
71.    {
72.        public void timeElapsed(TimerEvent event)
73.        {
74.            if (getWidth() == 0) return; // panel not yet shown
75.
76.            // add another circle
77.            int x = generator.nextInt(getWidth());
78.            Ellipse2D circle = new Ellipse2D.Double(x, -y,
79.                SIZE, SIZE);
80.            circles.add(circle);
81.
82.            // shift up the origin
83.            y++;
84.
85.            repaint();
86.        }
87.
88.        private Random generator = new Random();
89.        private static final int SIZE = 9;
90.    }
91. }
92.
93. /**
94.    A custom event class.
95. */
96. class TimerEvent extends AWTEvent
```

```
97.  {
98.     public TimerEvent(Timer t) { super(t, TIMER_EVENT); }
99.     public static final int TIMER_EVENT
100.        = AWTEvent.RESERVED_ID_MAX  + 5555;
101. }
102.
103. /**
104.    A custom event listener interface.
105. */
106. interface TimerListener extends EventListener
107. {
108.    public void timeElapsed(TimerEvent event);
109. }
110.
111. /**
112.    A custom timer class that is the source of timer events.
113. */
114. class Timer extends JComponent implements Runnable
115. {
116.    public Timer(int i)
117.    {
118.       listenerList = new EventListenerList();
119.       interval = i;
120.       Thread t = new Thread(this);
121.       t.start();
122.    }
123.
124.    /**
125.       Adds a timer listener
126.       @param listener the listener to add
127.    */
128.    public void addTimerListener(TimerListener listener)
129.    {
130.       listenerList.add(TimerListener.class, listener);
131.    }
132.
133.    /**
134.       Removes a timer listener
135.       @param listener the listener to remove
136.    */
137.    public void removeTimerListener(TimerListener listener)
138.    {
139.       listenerList.remove(TimerListener.class, listener);
140.    }
141.
142.
143.    /**
```

```
144.        Posts a new timer event every <code>interval</code>
145.        milliseconds.
146.     */
147.     public void run()
148.     {
149.        while (true)
150.        {
151.           try { Thread.sleep(interval); }
152.           catch(InterruptedException e) {}
153.
154.           TimerEvent event = new TimerEvent(this);
155.
156.           EventQueue queue
157.              = Toolkit.getDefaultToolkit().getSystemEventQueue();
158.           queue.postEvent(event);
159.        }
160.     }
161.
162.     public void processEvent(AWTEvent event)
163.     {
164.        if (event instanceof TimerEvent)
165.        {
166.           EventListener[] listeners = listenerList.getListeners(
167.              TimerListener.class);
168.           for (int i = 0; i < listeners.length; i++)
169.              ((TimerListener)listeners[i]).timeElapsed(
170.                 (TimerEvent)event);
171.        }
172.        else
173.           super.processEvent(event);
174.     }
175.
176.     private int interval;
177.     private EventListenerList listeners;
178. }
```

javax.swing.event.EventListenerList

- `void add(Class t, EventListener l)`
  adds an event listener and its class to the list. The class is stored so that event firing methods can selectively call events. Typical usage is in an add*Xxx*Listener method:

  ```
  public void addXxxListener(XxxListener l)
  {
  ```

```
        listenerList.add(XxxListener.class, l);
    }
```

Parameters:	t	The listener type
	l	The listener

- `void remove(Class t, EventListener l)`
  removes an event listener and its class from the list. Typical usage is in a
  remove*Xxx*Listener method:

```
    public void removeXxxListener(XxxListener l)
    {
        listenerList.remove(XxxListener.class, l);
    }
```

Parameters:	t	The listener type
	l	The listener

- `EventListener[] getListeners(Class t)`
  returns an array of all the listeners of the given type. The array is guaranteed
  to be non-`null`.

- `Object[] getListenerList()`
  returns an array whose elements with even-numbered index are listener
  classes, and whose elements with odd-numbered index are listener objects. The
  array is guaranteed to be non-`null`.

java.awt.Component

- `void enableEvents(long maskForEvents)`
  enables the component to insert events into the event queue even when there
  is no listener for a particular event type.

Parameters:	maskForEvents	A mask of event types to enable, made up of constants, such as `ACTION_EVENT_MASK`, that are defined in the `AWTEvent` class.

Chapter *9*

User Interface Components with Swing

The last chapter was primarily designed to show you how to use the event model in Java. In the process you did take the first steps toward learning how to build a graphical user interface. This chapter shows you the most important tools you'll need to build more full-featured graphical user interfaces.

We'll start out with a tour of the architectural underpinnings of Swing. Knowing what goes on "under the hood" is important in understanding how to use some of the more advanced components effectively. We'll then show you how to use the most common user interface components in Swing such as text fields, radio buttons, and menus. Next, you will learn how to use the nifty layout manager features of Java to arrange these components in a window, regardless of the look and feel of a particular user interface. Finally, you'll see how to implement dialog boxes in Swing.

This chapter covers basic Swing components such as text components, buttons, and sliders. These are the essential user interface components that you will need most frequently. We will cover advanced Swing components in Volume 2. For an even more comprehensive look into all details of the Swing framework, we recommend the book *Core Java Foundation Classes* by Kim Topley (Prentice-Hall 1998).

The Model-View-Controller Design Pattern

As promised, we start this chapter with a section describing the architecture of Swing components. Before we explain just what the title of this section means, let's step back for a minute and think about the pieces that make up a user interface component such as a button, a check box, a text field, or a sophisticated tree control. Every component has three characteristics:

- Its *contents*, such as the state of a button (pushed in or not), or the text in a text field;

- Its *visual appearance* (color, size, and so on);

- Its *behavior* (reaction to events).

Even a seemingly simple component such as a button exhibits some moderately complex interaction between these characteristics. Obviously, the visual appearance of a button depends on the look and feel. A Metal button looks different from a Windows button or a Motif button. In addition, the appearance depends on the button state: when a button is pushed in, it needs to be redrawn to look different. The state depends on the events that the button receives. When the user depresses the mouse inside the button, the button is pushed in.

Of course, when you use a button in your programs, you simply consider it as a *button*, and you don't think too much about the inner workings and characteristics. That, after all, is the job of the programmer who implemented the button. However, those programmers that implement buttons are motivated to think a little harder about them. After all, they have to implement buttons, and all other user interface components, so that they work well no matter what look and feel is installed.

To do this, the Swing designers turned to a well-known *design pattern*: the *model-view-controller* pattern. This pattern, like many other design patterns, goes back to one of the principles of object-oriented design that we mentioned way back in Chapter 5: don't make one object responsible for too much. Don't have a single button class do everything. Instead, have the look and feel of the component associated with one object and store the contents in *another* object. The model-view-controller (MVC) design pattern teaches how to accomplish this. Implement three separate classes:

- The *model*, which stores the contents;

- The *view*, which displays the contents;

- The *controller,* which handles user input.

The pattern specifies precisely how these three objects interact. The model stores the contents and has *no user interface.* For a button, the content is pretty trivial—it is just a small set of flags that tells whether the button is currently pushed in or out, whether it is active or inactive, and so on. For a text field, the content is a bit more interesting. It is a string object that holds the current text. This is *not the same* as the view of the content—if the content is larger than the text field, the user sees only a portion of the text displayed (see Figure 9–1).

model   "The quick brown fox jumped over the lazy dog"

view   brown |fox jump

Figure 9–1: Model and view of a text field

The model must implement methods to change the contents and to discover what the contents are. For example, a text model has methods to add or remove characters in the current text and to return the current text as a string. Again, keep in mind that the model is completely nonvisual. It is the job of a view to draw the data that is stored in the model.

NOTE: The term "model" is perhaps unfortunate because we often think of a model as a representation of an abstract concept. Car and airplane designers build models to simulate real cars and planes. But that analogy really leads you astray when thinking about the model-view-controller pattern. In the design pattern, the model stores the complete contents, and the view gives a (complete or incomplete) visual representation of the contents. A better analogy might be the model that poses for an artist. It is up to the artist to look at the model and create a view. Depending on the artist, that view might be a formal portrait, an impressionist painting, or a cubist drawing that shows the limbs in strange contortions.

One of the advantages of the model-view-controller pattern is that a model can have multiple views, each showing a different part or aspect of the full contents. For example, an HTML editor can offer two *simultaneous* views of the same contents: a WYSIWYG view and a "raw tag" view (see Figure 9–2). When the model is updated through the controller of one of the views, it tells both attached views about the change. When the views are notified, they refresh themselves automatically. Of course, for a simple user interface component such as a button, you won't have multiple views of the same model.

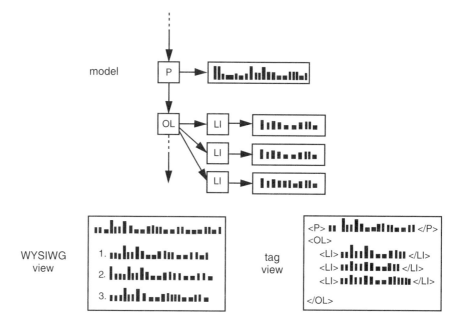

Figure 9–2: Two separate views of the same model

The controller handles the user input events such as mouse clicks and keystrokes. It then decides whether to translate these events into changes in the model or the view. For example, if the user presses a character key in a text box, the controller calls the "insert character" command of the model. The model then tells the view to update itself. The view never knows why the text changed. But if the user presses a key, then the controller may tell the view to scroll. Scrolling the view has no effect on the underlying text, so the model never knows that this event happened.

Design Patterns

When solving a problem, you don't usually figure out a solution from first principles. Instead, you are likely to be guided by past experience, or you may ask other experts for advice on what has worked for them. Design patterns are a method for presenting this expertise in a structured way.

In recent years, software engineers have begun to assemble catalogs of such patterns. The pioneers in this area were inspired by the architectural design patterns of the architect Christopher Alexander. In his book *The Timeless Way of Building* (Oxford University Press 1979), Alexander gives a catalog of patterns for designing public and private living spaces. Here is a typical example:

Window Place

Everybody loves window seats, bay windows, and big windows with low sills and comfortable chairs drawn up to them . . . A room which does not have a place like this seldom allows you to feel comfortable or perfectly at ease . . .

If the room contains no window which is a "place," a person in the room will be torn between two forces:

1. He wants to sit down and be comfortable.
2. He is drawn toward the light.

Obviously, if the comfortable places—those places in the room where you most want to sit—are away from the windows, there is no way of overcoming this conflict . . .

Therefore: In every room where you spend any length of time during the day, make at least one window into a "window place."

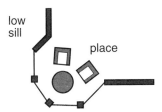

Figure 9–3: A window place

Each pattern in Alexander's catalog, as well as those in the catalogs of software patterns, follows a particular format. The pattern first describes a context, a situation that gives rise to a design problem. Then, the problem is explained, usually as a set of conflicting forces. Finally, the solution shows a configuration that balances these forces.

In the "window place" pattern, the context is a room in which you spend any length of time during the day. The conflicting forces are that you want to sit down and be comfortable and that you are drawn to the light. The solution is to make a "window place."

In the model-view-controller pattern, the context is a user interface system that presents information and receives user input. There are several forces. There may be multiple visual representations of the same data that need to be updated together. The visual representation may change, for example, to accommodate various look-and-feel standards. The interaction mechanisms may change, for example, to support voice commands. The solution is to distribute responsibilities into three separate interacting components: the model, view, and controller.

Of course, the model-view-controller pattern is more complex than the "window place" pattern, and it needs to teach in some detail how to make this distribution of responsibilities work.

You will find a formal description of the model-view-controller pattern, as well as numerous other useful software patterns, in the seminal book of the pattern movement, *Design Patterns—Elements of Reusable Object-Oriented Software*, by Erich Gamma et al., Addison-Wesley 1995. We also highly recommend the excellent book *A System of Patterns* by Frank Buschmann et al., John Wiley & Sons 1996, which we find less seminal and more approachable.

The model-view-controller pattern is not the only pattern used in the design of Java. For example, the AWT event handling mechanism follows the "observer" pattern.

> One important aspect of design patterns is that they become part of the culture. Programmers all over the world know what you mean when you talk about the model-view-controller pattern or the "observer" pattern. Thus, patterns become an efficient way of talking about design problems.

Figure 9–4 shows the interactions between model, view, and controller objects.

As a programmer using Swing components, you generally don't need to think about the model-view-controller architecture. Each user interface has a wrapper class (such as `JButton` or `JTextField`) that stores the model and the view. When you want to inquire about the contents (for example, the text in a text field), the wrapper class asks the model and returns the answer to you. When you want to change the view (for example, move the caret position in a text field), the wrapper class forwards that request to the view. However, there are occasions where the wrapper class doesn't work hard enough on forwarding commands. Then, you have to ask it to retrieve the model and work directly with the model. (You don't have to work directly with the view—that is the job of the look-and-feel code.)

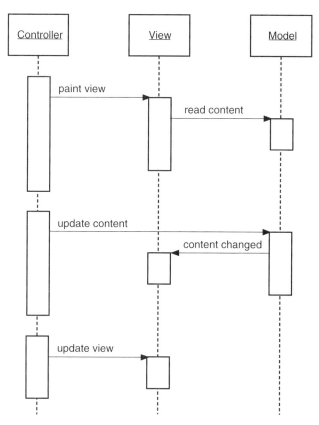

Figure 9–4: Interactions between model, view, and controller objects

Besides being "the right thing to do," the model-view-controller pattern was attractive for the Swing designers because it allowed them to implement pluggable look and feel. The model of a button or text field is independent of the look-and-feel. But of course the visual representation is completely dependent on the user interface design of a particular look and feel. The controller can vary as well. For example, in a voice-controlled device, the controller must cope with an entirely different set of events than in a standard computer with a keyboard and a mouse. By separating out the underlying model from the user interface, the Swing designers are able to reuse the code for the models and even to switch user interfaces in a running program.

Of course, patterns are only intended as guidance, not as religion. Not every pattern is applicable in all situations. For example, you may find it difficult to follow the "window places" pattern (see the sidebar on design patterns) to rearrange your cubicle. Similarly, the Swing designers found that the harsh reality of pluggable look-and-feel implementation does not always allow for a neat realization of the model-view-controller pattern. Models are easy to separate, and each user interface component has a model class. But, the responsibilities of the view and controller are not always clearly separated and are distributed over a number of different classes. Of course, as a user of these classes, you won't be concerned about this. In fact, as we pointed out before, you often won't have to worry about the models either—you can just use the component wrapper classes.

A Model-View-Controller Analysis of Swing Buttons

You already learned how to use buttons in the previous chapter, without having to worry about the controller, model, or view for them. Still, buttons are about the simplest user interface elements, so they are a good place to become comfortable with the model-view-controller pattern. You will encounter similar kinds of classes and interfaces for the more sophisticated Swing components.

For most components, the model class implements an interface whose name ends in `Model`. Thus, there is an interface called `ButtonModel`. Classes implementing that interface can define the state of the various kinds of buttons. Actually, buttons aren't all that complicated, and the Swing library contains a single class, called `DefaultButtonModel`, that implements this interface.

You can get a sense of what sort of data is maintained by a button model by looking at the methods of the `ButtonModel` interface. Table 9–1 shows the accessor methods.

Table 9–1: The accessor methods of the `ButtonModel` interface

`getActionCommand()`	The action command string associated with this button
`getMnemonic()`	The keyboard mnemonic for this button
`isArmed()`	`true` if the button was pressed and the mouse is still over the button
`isEnabled()`	`true` if the button is selectable
`isPressed()`	`true` if the button was pressed but the mouse button hasn't yet been released
`isRollover()`	`true` if the mouse is over the button
`isSelected()`	`true` if the button has been toggled on (used for check boxes and radio buttons)

Each `JButton` object stores a button model object, which you can retrieve.

```
JButton button = new JButton("Blue");
ButtonModel model = button.getModel();
```

In practice, you won't care—the minutiae of the button state are only of interest to the view that draws it. And the important information—such as whether a button is enabled—is available from the `JButton` class. (The `JButton` then asks its model, of course, to retrieve that information.)

Have another look at the `ButtonModel` interface to see what *isn't* there. The model does *not* store the button label or icon. There is no way to find out what's on the face of a button just by looking at its model. (Actually, as you will see in the section on radio button groups, that purity of design is the source of some grief for the programmer.)

It is also worth noting that the *same* model (namely, `DefaultButtonModel`) is used for push buttons, radio buttons, check boxes, and even menu items. Of course, each of these button types has different views and controllers. When using the Metal look and feel, the `JButton` uses a class called `BasicButtonUI` for the view and a class called `ButtonUIListener` as controller. In general, each Swing component has an associated view object that ends in `UI`. But not all Swing components have dedicated controller objects.

So, having given you this short introduction to what is going on under the hood in a `JButton`, you may be wondering: just what is a `JButtton` really?

It is simply a wrapper class inheriting from `JComponent` that holds the `DefaultButtonModel` object, some view data (such as the button label and icons), and a `DefaultButtonUI` object that is responsible for the button view.

An Introduction to Layout Management

Before we go on to discussing individual Swing components, such as text fields and radio buttons, we need to briefly cover how to arrange these components inside a frame. Since the Java SDK has no form designer like those in Visual Basic or Delphi, you need to write code to position (lay out) the user interface components where you want them to be.

Of course, if you have a Java-enabled development environment, it will probably have a layout tool that automates some or all of these tasks. Nevertheless, it is important to know exactly what goes on "under the hood" since even the best of these tools will usually require hand-tweaking to get a professional look and feel.

Let's start by reviewing the program from the last chapter that used buttons to change the background color of a frame (see Figure 9–5).

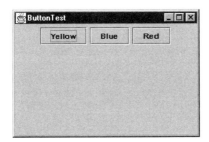

Figure 9–5: A panel with three buttons

Let us quickly recall how we built this program:

1. We defined the look of each button by setting the label string in the constructor, for example:

    ```
    JButton yellowButton = new JButton("Yellow")
    ```

2. We then added the individual buttons to a panel, for example, with:

    ```
    add(yellowButton);
    ```

3. Then, we added the needed event handlers, for example:

    ```
    yellowButton.addActionListener(listener);
    ```

What happens if we add more buttons? Figure 9–6 shows what happens when you add six buttons to the panel. As you can see, they are centered in a row, and when there isn't any more room, a new row is started.

Figure 9–6: A panel with six buttons managed by a flow layout

Moreover, the buttons stay centered in the panel, even when the user resizes the frame (see Figure 9–7).

Java has a very elegant concept to enable this dynamic layout: all components in a container are managed by a *layout manager*. In our example, the buttons are managed by the *flow layout manager*, the default layout manager for a panel.

The flow layout manager lines the components horizontally until there is no more room and then starts a new row of components.

When the user resizes the container, the layout manager automatically reflows the components to fill the available space.

You can choose how you want to arrange the components in each row. The default is to center them in the container. The other choices are to align them to the left or to the right of the container. To use one of these alignments, specify `LEFT` or `RIGHT` in the constructor of the `FlowLayout` object.

```
setLayout(new FlowLayout(FlowLayout.LEFT));
```

Figure 9–7: Changing the panel size rearranges the buttons automatically

 NOTE: Normally, you just let the flow layout manager control the vertical and horizontal gaps between the components. You can, however, force a specific horizontal or vertical gap by using another version of the flow layout constructor. (See the API notes.)

java.awt.Container

- `setLayout(LayoutManager m)`
  sets the layout manager for this container.

java.awt.FlowLayout

- `FlowLayout(int align)`
  constructs a new `FlowLayout` with the specified alignment.

  Parameters: `align`   One of `LEFT`, `CENTER`, or `RIGHT`

- `FlowLayout(int align, int hgap, int vgap)`
  constructs a new `FlowLayout` with the specified alignment and the specified horizontal and vertical gaps between components.

  Parameters: `align`   One of `LEFT`, `CENTER`, or `RIGHT`

  `hgap`   The horizontal gap to use in pixels (negative values force an overlap)

  `vgap`   The vertical gap to use in pixels (negative values force an overlap)

Border Layout

Java comes with several layout managers, and you can also make your own layout managers: we will cover all of them later on in this chapter. However, to enable us to give you more interesting examples right away, we need to briefly describe another layout manager called the *border layout manager*. This is the default layout manager of the content pane of every `JFrame`. Unlike the flow layout manager, which completely controls the position of each component, the border layout manager lets you choose where you want to place each component. You can choose to place the component in the center, north, south, east, or west of the content pane (see Figure 9–8).

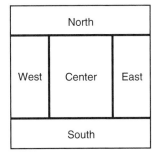

Figure 9–8: Border layout

For example:

```
class MyPanel extends JPanel
{
   setLayout(new BorderLayout());
   . . .
   add(yellowButton, BorderLayout.SOUTH);
}
```

The edge components are laid out first, and the remaining available space is occupied by the center. When the container is resized, the thickness of the edge components is unchanged, but the center component changes its size. You add components by specifying a constant CENTER, NORTH, SOUTH, EAST, or WEST of the BorderLayout class. Not all of the positions need to be occupied. If you don't supply any value, CENTER is assumed.

NOTE: The BorderLayout constants are defined as strings. For example, Border-Layout.SOUTH is defined as the string "South". Many programmers prefer to use the strings directly because they are shorter, for example, contentPane.add(component, "South"). However, if you accidentally misspell a string, the compiler won't catch that error.

Unlike the flow layout, the border layout grows all components to fill the available space. (The flow layout leaves each component at its preferred size.)

As with flow layouts, if you want to specify a gap between the regions, you can do so in the constructor of the BorderLayout.

As previously noted, the content pane of a JFrame uses a border layout. Up to now, we never took advantage of this—we simply added panels into the default (center) area. But you can add components into the other areas as well:

```
Container contentPane = getContentPane();
contentPane.add(yellowButton, BorderLayout.SOUTH);
```

However, there is a problem with this code fragment that we take up in the next section.

java.awt.Container

* void add(Component c, Object constraints)
  adds a component to this container.

Parameters:	c	The component to add
	constraints	An identifier understood by the layout manager

`java.awt.BorderLayout`

- `BorderLayout(int hgap, int vgap)`
  constructs a new `BorderLayout` with the specified horizontal and vertical gaps between components.

  Parameters: hgap   The horizontal gap to use in pixels (negative values force an overlap)

                   vgap   The vertical gap to use in pixels (negative values force an overlap)

Panels

A `BorderLayout` is not very useful by itself. Figure 9–9 shows what happens when you use the code fragment above. The button has grown to fill the entire southern region of the frame. And, if you were to add another button to the southern region, it would just displace the first button.

One common method to overcome this problem is to use additional *panels.* Panels act as (smaller) containers for interface elements and can themselves be arranged inside a larger panel under the control of a layout manager. For example, you can have one panel in the southern area for the buttons and another in the center for text. By nesting panels and using a mixture of border layouts and flow layouts, you can achieve fairly precise positioning of components. This approach to layout is certainly enough for prototyping, and it is the approach that we will use for the example programs in the first part of this chapter. See the section on the `GridBagLayout` later in this chapter for the most precise way to position components.

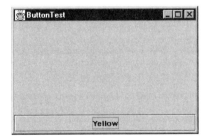

Figure 9–9: A single button managed by a border layout

For example, look at Figure 9–10. The three buttons at the bottom of the screen are all contained in a panel. The panel is put into the southern end of the content pane.

So, suppose you want to add a panel with three buttons as in Figure 9–10. As you might expect, you first create a new instance of a `JPanel` object before you add the individual buttons to it. The default layout manager for a panel is a `FlowLayout`, which is a good choice for this situation. Finally, you add the individual buttons, using the `add` method you have seen before. Since you are adding buttons to a panel and haven't changed the default layout manager, the position of the buttons is under the control of the `FlowLayout` manager. This means the buttons stay centered within the panel and they do not expand to fill the entire panel area. Here's a code fragment that adds a panel containing three buttons in the south end of a container.

Figure 9–10: A panel placed at the south end of the frame

```
Container contentPane = getContentPane();
JPanel panel = new JPanel();
panel.add(yellowButton);
panel.add(blueButton);
panel.add(redButton);
contentPane.add(panel, BorderLayout.SOUTH);
```

NOTE: The panel boundaries are not visible to the user. Panels are just an organizing mechanism for the user interface designer.

As you just saw, the `JPanel` class uses a `FlowLayout` as the default layout manager. For a `JPanel`, you can supply a different layout manager object in the constructor. However, most other containers do not have such a constructor. But all containers have a `setLayout` method to set the layout manager to something other than the default for the container.

javax.swing.JPanel

• `JPanel(LayoutManager m)`
  sets the layout manager for the panel.

Text Input

We are finally ready to start introducing the Swing user interface components. We'll start with components that let a user input and edit text. In Java, two components are used to get text input: *text fields* and *text areas*. The difference between them is that a text field can accept only one line of text and a text area can accept multiple lines of text. The classes are called `JTextField` for single-line input and `JTextArea` for multiple lines of text.

Both of these classes inherit from a class called `JTextComponent`. You will not be able to construct a `JTextComponent` yourself since it is an abstract class. On the other hand, as is so often the case in Java, when you go searching through the API documentation, you may find that the methods you are looking for are actually in the parent class `JTextComponent` rather than in the derived class. For example, the methods that get or set the text in a text field or text area are actually methods in `JTextComponent`.

`javax.swing.text.JTextComponent`

- `void setText(String t)`
  changes the text of a text component.

  Parameters: t   The new text

- `String getText()`
  returns the text contained in this text component.

- `void setEditable(boolean b)`
  determines whether the user can edit the contents of the `JTextComponent`.

Text Fields

The usual way to add a text field to a window is to add it to a panel or other container—just as you would a button:

```
JPanel panel = new JPanel();
JTextField textField = new JTextField("Default input", 20);
panel.add(textField);
```

This code adds a text field and initializes the text field by placing the string `"Default input"` inside it. The second parameter of this constructor sets the width. In this case, the width is 20 "columns." Unfortunately, a column is a rather imprecise measurement. One column is the expected width of one character in the font you are using for the text. The idea is that if you expect the inputs to be *n* characters or less, you are supposed to specify *n* as the column width. In practice, this measurement doesn't work out too well, and you should add 1 or 2 to the maximum input length to be on the safe side. Also, keep in mind that the number of columns is only a hint to the AWT that gives the *preferred* size. If the layout manager needs to grow or shrink the text field, it can adjust its size. The column width that you set in the `JTextField` constructor is not an upper limit on the number of characters the user can enter. The user can still type in longer strings, but the input scrolls when the text exceeds the length of the field. Users tend to find scrolling text fields irritating, so you should size the fields generously. If you need to reset the number of columns at run time, you can do that with the `setColumns` method.

> TIP: After changing the size of a text box with the `setColumns` method, you need to call the `validate` method of the surrounding container.
>
> ```
> textField.setColumns(10);
> panel.validate();
> ```
>
> The `validate` method recomputes the size and layout of all components in a container. After you use the `validate` method, the layout manager repaints the container, and the changed size of the text field will be visible.

In general, you want to let the user add text (or edit the existing text) in a text field. Quite often these text fields start out blank. To make a blank text field, just leave out the string as a parameter for the `JTextField` constructor:

```
JTextField textField = new JTextField(20);
```

You can change the contents of the text field at any time by using the `setText` method from the `TextComponent` parent class mentioned in the previous section. For example:

```
textField.setText("Hello!");
```

And, as was also mentioned in the previous section, you can find out what the user typed by calling the `getText` method. This method returns the exact text that the user typed. To trim any extraneous leading and trailing spaces from the data in a text field, apply the `trim` method to the return value of `getText`:

```
String text = textField.getText().trim();
```

To change the font in which the user text appears, use the `setFont` method.

Let us put a few text fields to work. Figure 9–11 shows the running application. The program shows a clock, and there are two text fields for entering the hours and minutes. Whenever the contents of the text fields change, the clock is updated.

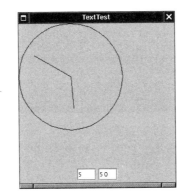

Figure 9–11: Text field example

To track every change in the text field requires a bit of an effort. First of all, note that it is not a good idea to monitor keystrokes. Some keystrokes (such as the arrow keys) don't change the text. And, depending on the look and feel, there may be mouse actions that result in text changes. As you saw in the beginning of this chapter, the Swing text field is implemented in a rather general way: the string that you see in the text field is just a visible manifestation (the *view*) of an underlying data structure (the *model*). Of course, for a humble text field, there is no great difference between the two. The view is a displayed string, and the model is a string object. But the same architecture is used in more advanced editing components to present formatted text, with fonts, paragraphs, and other attributes that are internally represented by a more complex data structure. The model for all text components is described by the `Document` interface, which covers both plain text and formatted text (such as HTML). The point is that you can ask the *document* (and not the text component) to notify you whenever the data has changed, by installing a *document listener*:

```
textField.getDocument().addDocumentListener(listener);
```

When the text has changed, one of the following three methods is called:

```
void insertUpdate(DocumentEvent e)
void removeUpdate(DocumentEvent e)
void changedUpdate(DocumentEvent e)
```

The first two methods are called when characters have been inserted or removed. The third method is not called at all for text fields. For more complex document types, it would be called when some other change, such as a change in formatting, has occurred. Unfortunately, there is no single callback to tell you that the text has changed—usually you don't care so much how it has changed. And there is no adapter class either. Thus, your document listener must implement all three methods. Here is what we do in our sample program:

```
private class ClockFieldListener implements DocumentListener
{
    public void insertUpdate(DocumentEvent e) { setClock(); }
    public void removeUpdate(DocumentEvent e) { setClock(); }
    public void changedUpdate(DocumentEvent e) {}
}
```

The `setClock` method uses the `getText` method to obtain the current user input strings from the text fields. Unfortunately, that is what we get: strings. We need to convert the strings to integers, using the familiar, if cumbersome, incantation:

```
int hours = Integer.parseInt(hourField.getText().trim());
int minutes = Integer.parseInt(minuteField.getText().trim());
```

But this code won't work right when the user types a noninteger string, such as `"two"`, into the text field or even leaves the field blank. For now, we catch the `NumberFormatException` that the `parseInt` method throws, and we simply don't update the clock when the text field entry is not a number. In the next section, you will see how you can prevent the user from entering invalid input in the first place.

NOTE: Instead of listening to document events, you can also add an action event listener to a text field. The action listener is notified whenever the user presses the ENTER key. We don't recommend this approach since users don't always remember to press ENTER when they are done entering data. If you use an action listener, you should also install a focus listener so that you can track when the user leaves the text field.

Example 9–1: TextTest.java

```
1. import java.awt.*;
2. import java.awt.event.*;
3. import java.awt.geom.*;
4. import javax.swing.*;
5. import javax.swing.event.*;
6.
7. public class TextTest
8. {
9.     public static void main(String[] args)
10.    {
11.        TextTestFrame frame = new TextTestFrame();
12.        frame.setDefaultCloseOperation(JFrame.EXIT_ON_CLOSE);
13.        frame.show();
14.    }
15. }
16.
```

```
17. /**
18.    A frame with two text fields to set a clock.
19. */
20. class TextTestFrame extends JFrame
21. {
22.    public TextTestFrame()
23.    {
24.       setTitle("TextTest");
25.       setSize(WIDTH, HEIGHT);
26.
27.       Container contentPane = getContentPane();
28.
29.       DocumentListener listener = new ClockFieldListener();
30.
31.       // add a panel with text fields
32.
33.       JPanel panel = new JPanel();
34.
35.       hourField = new JTextField("12", 3);
36.       panel.add(hourField);
37.       hourField.getDocument().addDocumentListener(listener);
38.
39.       minuteField = new JTextField("00", 3);
40.       panel.add(minuteField);
41.       minuteField.getDocument().addDocumentListener(listener);
42.
43.       contentPane.add(panel, BorderLayout.SOUTH);
44.
45.       // add the clock
46.
47.       clock = new ClockPanel();
48.       contentPane.add(clock, BorderLayout.CENTER);
49.    }
50.
51.    /**
52.       Set the clock to the values stored in the text fields.
53.    */
54.    public void setClock()
55.    {
56.       try
57.       {
58.          int hours
59.             = Integer.parseInt(hourField.getText().trim());
60.          int minutes
61.             = Integer.parseInt(minuteField.getText().trim());
62.          clock.setTime(hours, minutes);
63.       }
64.       catch (NumberFormatException e) {}
65.       // don't set the clock if the input can't be parsed
66.    }
67.
```

```
68.     public static final int WIDTH = 300;
69.     public static final int HEIGHT = 300;
70.
71.     private JTextField hourField;
72.     private JTextField minuteField;
73.     private ClockPanel clock;
74.
75.     private class ClockFieldListener implements DocumentListener
76.     {
77.        public void insertUpdate(DocumentEvent e) { setClock(); }
78.        public void removeUpdate(DocumentEvent e) { setClock(); }
79.        public void changedUpdate(DocumentEvent e) {}
80.     }
81. }
82.
83. /**
84.    A panel that draws a clock.
85. */
86. class ClockPanel extends JPanel
87. {
88.    public void paintComponent(Graphics g)
89.    {
90.       // draw the circular boundary
91.
92.       super.paintComponent(g);
93.       Graphics2D g2 = (Graphics2D)g;
94.       Ellipse2D circle
95.          = new Ellipse2D.Double(0, 0, 2 * RADIUS, 2 * RADIUS);
96.       g2.draw(circle);
97.
98.       // draw the hour hand
99.
100.      double hourAngle
101.         = Math.toRadians(90 - 360 * minutes / (12 * 60));
102.      drawHand(g2, hourAngle, HOUR_HAND_LENGTH);
103.
104.      // draw the minute hand
105.
106.      double minuteAngle
107.         = Math.toRadians(90 - 360 * minutes / 60);
108.      drawHand(g2, minuteAngle, MINUTE_HAND_LENGTH);
109.   }
110.
111.   public void drawHand(Graphics2D g2,
112.      double angle, double handLength)
113.   {
114.      Point2D end = new Point2D.Double(
115.         RADIUS + handLength * Math.cos(angle),
116.         RADIUS - handLength * Math.sin(angle));
117.      Point2D center = new Point2D.Double(RADIUS, RADIUS);
118.      g2.draw(new Line2D.Double(center, end));
```

```
119.      }
120.
121.      /**
122.         Set the time to be displayed on the clock
123.         @param h hours
124.         @param m minutes
125.      */
126.      public void setTime(int h, int m)
127.      {
128.         minutes = h * 60 + m;
129.         repaint();
130.      }
131.
132.      private double minutes = 0;
133.      private double RADIUS = 100;
134.      private double MINUTE_HAND_LENGTH = 0.8 * RADIUS;
135.      private double HOUR_HAND_LENGTH = 0.6 * RADIUS;
136. }
```

`java.awt.Component`

* `void validate()`

  recomputes the size of a component or the size and layout of the components in a container.

`javax.swing.JTextField`

* `JTextField(int cols)`

  constructs an empty `JTextField` with a specified number of columns.

  Parameters: `cols`   The number of columns in the field

* `JTextField(String text, int cols)`

  constructs a new `JTextField` with an initial string and the specified number of columns.

  Parameters: `text`   The text to display

                       `cols`   The number of columns

* `void setColumns(int cols)`

  tells the text field the number of columns it should use.

  Parameters: `cols`   The number of columns

`javax.swing.text.Document`

* `int getLength()`

  returns the number of characters currently in the document.

- String getText(int offset, int length)

  returns the text contained within the given portion of the document.

  Parameters: offset   The start of the text

                    length   The length of the desired string

- void addDocumentListener(DocumentListener listener)

  registers the listener to be notified when the document changes.

javax.swing.event.DocumentEvent

- Document getDocument()

  gets the document that is the source of the event.

javax.swing.event.DocumentListener

- void changedUpdate(DocumentEvent e)

  is called whenever an attribute or set of attributes changes.

- void insertUpdate(DocumentEvent e)

  is called whenever there was an insert into the document.

- void removeUpdate(DocumentEvent e)

  is called whenever a portion of the document has been removed.

Input Validation

The problems mentioned in the last section are commonplace—if you have a place to enter information, you will need to check that the input makes sense before you work with it. In our example, we need to make sure that the user types in a number. That is, the user is allowed to enter only digits 0 through 9 and a hyphen (–). The hyphen, if present at all, must be the *first* symbol of the input string. In this section, we will develop a class, IntTextField, that extends the JTextField class and enforces these rules. The technique discussed in this section is somewhat advanced—feel free to skip this section if you have no interest in input validation. If you use a professional development environment, you will likely find a validating text component on the toolbar of your layout editor. But if you want to find out how to implement such a component from scratch, read on.

On the surface, input validation sounds simple. We can install a key listener to the text field, and then *consume* all key events that aren't digits or a hyphen. (See Chapter 8 for consuming events.) Unfortunately, this simple approach, although commonly recommended as a method for input validation, does not work well in practice. First, not every combination of the valid input characters is a valid number. For example, --3 and 3-3 aren't valid, even though they are made up from valid input characters. But, more importantly, there are other ways of changing the text that don't involve typing character keys.

Depending on the look and feel, certain key combinations can be used to cut, copy, and paste text. For example, in the Metal look and feel, the CTRL+V key combination pastes the contents of the paste buffer into the text field. That is, we also need to monitor that the user doesn't paste in an invalid character. Clearly, trying to filter keystrokes to ensure that the content of the text field is always valid begins to look like a real chore.

Fortunately, there is another way that takes advantage of the model-view-controller architecture of the Swing text components. Recall that in the model- view-controller architecture, the controller collects the input events and translates them into commands. For example, whenever the controller processes a command that causes text to be inserted into the document, it calls the `insertString` method of the `Document` class, telling it to insert a string at the position of the caret. (The caret is the vertical bar that indicates the current editing position.) The string to be inserted can be either a single character or the contents of the paste buffer.

This is the key to solving our validation problem. The `TextField` stores its text in a `PlainDocument`, a class that implements the `Document` interface and stores a single string. We will supply a different document type that we call `IntTextDocument`. Our new class extends the `PlainDocument` class and overrides the `insertString` method. The `insertString` method of the subclass will refuse to insert any string that would produce an illegal result.

There is a subtle point that you often run into when performing data validation. It not not always obvious which insertions are legal. Sometimes, the only way to get to a valid string is to start with an invalid one. Consider the steps necessary to type the number -3. First, the user starts out with an empty field, which of course is not a valid number. Then, the user types a minus sign, resulting in a string "-", again, not a valid number. Finally, when the user adds a digit, the string becomes valid. The `canBecomeValid` method of our `IntTextDocument` class tests whether a string can become a valid string. The empty string, the string "-", and all strings representing numbers pass this test.

In the `insertString` method of the `IntTextDocument` class, we first compute the string that would result from inserting the new string at the caret position. Then, we test whether that string can become valid. If the test passes, we call `super.insertString` and permit the `PlainDocument.insertString` method to insert the string to the document text. Otherwise, we do not insert the string. Here is the source code for the `insertString` method of the `IntTextDocument` subclass.

```
class IntTextDocument extends PlainDocument
{
    public void insertString(int offs, String str,
        AttributeSet a)
        throws BadLocationException
```

```
    {
        if (str == null) return;

        String oldString = getText(0, getLength());
        String newString = oldString.substring(0, offs)
            + str + oldString.substring(offs);

        if (canBecomeValid(newString))
            super.insertString(offs, str, a);
    }
    . . .
}
```

Next, we define an `IntTextField` class that extends the `JTextField` class. Its
`createDefaultModel` method creates an `IntTextDocument` instead of a
`PlainDocument`.

```
class IntTextField extends JTextField
{   public IntTextField(int defval, int size)
    {
        super("" + defval, size);
    }

    protected Document createDefaultModel()
    {
        return new IntTextDocument();
    }
    . . .
}
```

Our `IntTextField` class supplies convenience methods, `isValid` and
`getValue`. The `getValue` method returns the contents of the field, already
converted into an integer. Before calling `getValue`, you should call
`isValid` to check that the value is correct.

Starting with J2SE version 1.3, there is a second mechanism that you can use to force
users to enter valid information into text fields. If you set an *input verifier*, then the user
can't leave the component until the `verify` method of the verifier returns `true`. That
is, if the user tries to leave the component that contains invalid information—by hitting
the TAB key or clicking the mouse on a different component—then the original component immediately regains the focus.

CAUTION: We found that the verifier mechanism isn't as reliable as it should be. For
example, in the example program of this section, if you enter an invalid number into one
of the text fields and then click the Set button, the button first gains focus, gets clicked,
and notifies its action listener, before the text field regains focus. Thus, the action listener
cannot rely on the fact that a text field with an attached verifier always has valid contents.

A verifier must extend the abstract `InputVerifier` class and define a `verify` method. For example, this verifier checks if a component contains a valid integer. If the text content of the component does not pass the validity test, then the `verify` method returns `false`.

```
class IntTextFieldVerifier extends InputVerifier
{
   public boolean verify(JComponent component)
   {
      String text = ((JTextComponent)component).getText();
      return IntTextDocument.isValid(text);
   }
}
```

You use the `setInputVerifier` method to attach a verifier to a component:

```
InputVerifier verifier = new IntTextFieldVerifier();
textField.setInputVerifier(verifier);
```

Now the text field won't lose focus until the verifier is satisfied with its contents.

Example 9–2 shows how to put the `IntTextField` class to use. Try typing letters into one of the text fields. Those inputs are immediately undone, and you never see the letters. Try leaving a text field that is blank or contains a single "-". The text field immediately regains focus.

NOTE: If the character the user enters is not one of the allowable ones, some user interface designs insist that the computer beep at the user in response to an illegal keypress. This is certainly not something that we would recommend, but you can do this in Java with the `beep` method of the `Toolkit` class:

```
      Toolkit.getDefaultToolkit().beep();
```

Example 9–2: ValidationTest.java

```
1. import java.awt.*;
2. import java.awt.event.*;
3. import java.awt.geom.*;
4. import javax.swing.*;
5. import javax.swing.event.*;
6. import javax.swing.text.*;
7. import javax.swing.undo.*;
8.
9. public class ValidationTest
10. {
11.    public static void main(String[] args)
12.    {
13.       ValidationTestFrame frame = new ValidationTestFrame();
14.       frame.setDefaultCloseOperation(JFrame.EXIT_ON_CLOSE);
15.       frame.show();
```

```
16.      }
17. }
18.
19. /**
20.    A frame with a clock and text fields to set the time.
21. */
22. class ValidationTestFrame extends JFrame
23. {
24.    public ValidationTestFrame()
25.    {
26.       setTitle("ValidationTest");
27.       setSize(WIDTH, HEIGHT);
28.
29.       Container contentPane = getContentPane();
30.
31.       JPanel panel = new JPanel();
32.
33.       // add text fields
34.
35.       hourField = new IntTextField(12, 3);
36.       panel.add(hourField);
37.
38.       minuteField = new IntTextField(0, 3);
39.       panel.add(minuteField);
40.
41.       // add Set button
42.
43.       JButton setButton = new JButton("Set");
44.       panel.add(setButton);
45.       setButton.addActionListener(new
46.          ActionListener()
47.          {
48.             public void actionPerformed(ActionEvent event)
49.             {
50.                if (hourField.isValid() && minuteField.isValid())
51.                   clock.setTime(
52.                      hourField.getValue(),
53.                      minuteField.getValue());
54.             }
55.          });
56.
57.       contentPane.add(panel, BorderLayout.SOUTH);
58.
59.       // add clock
60.
61.       clock = new ClockPanel();
62.       contentPane.add(clock, BorderLayout.CENTER);
63.    }
64.
65.    public static final int WIDTH = 300;
66.    public static final int HEIGHT = 300;
```

```
67.
68.   private IntTextField hourField;
69.   private IntTextField minuteField;
70.   private ClockPanel clock;
71. }
72.
73. /**
74.    A document that can only hold valid integers or their
75.    substrings
76. */
77. class IntTextDocument extends PlainDocument
78. {
79.    public void insertString(int offs, String str,
80.       AttributeSet a)
81.       throws BadLocationException
82.    {
83.       if (str == null) return;
84.
85.       String oldString = getText(0, getLength());
86.       String newString = oldString.substring(0, offs)
87.          + str + oldString.substring(offs);
88.
89.       if (canBecomeValid(newString))
90.          super.insertString(offs, str, a);
91.    }
92.
93.    /**
94.       A helper function that tests whether a string is a valid
95.       integer
96.       @param s a string
97.       @return true if s is a valid integer
98.    */
99.    public static boolean isValid(String s)
100.   {
101.      try
102.      {
103.         Integer.parseInt(s);
104.         return true;
105.      }
106.      catch(NumberFormatException e)
107.      {
108.         return false;
109.      }
110.   }
111.
112.   /**
113.      A helper function that tests whether a string is a
114.      substring of a valid integer
115.      @param s a string
116.      @return true if s can be extended to a valid integer
117.   */
```

```
118.    public static boolean canBecomeValid(String s)
119.    {
120.        return s.equals("") || s.equals("-") || isValid(s);
121.    }
122. }
123.
124. /**
125.    A text field for editing integer values
126. */
127. class IntTextField extends JTextField
128. {
129.    /**
130.        Constructs an IntTextField.
131.        @param defval the default value
132.        @param size the field size
133.    */
134.    public IntTextField(int defval, int size)
135.    {
136.        super("" + defval, size);
137.        setInputVerifier(new IntTextFieldVerifier());
138.        //      Document doc = getDocument();
139.        //      doc.addUndoableEditListener(new UndoListener());
140.    }
141.
142.    protected Document createDefaultModel()
143.    {
144.        return new IntTextDocument();
145.    }
146.
147.    /**
148.        Checks if the contents of this field is a valid integer.
149.        @return true of the field contents is valid
150.    */
151.    public boolean isValid()
152.    {
153.        return IntTextDocument.isValid(getText());
154.    }
155.
156.    /**
157.        Gets the numeric value of the field contents.
158.        @param the number that the user typed into the field, or
159.        0 if the field contents is not valid.
160.    */
161.    public int getValue()
162.    {
163.        try
164.        {
165.            return Integer.parseInt(getText());
166.        }
167.        catch(NumberFormatException e)
168.        {
169.            return 0;
```

```
170.          }
171.      }
172. }
173.
174. /**
175.    A verifier that checks if the contents of a text component
176.    is a valid integer.
177. */
178. class IntTextFieldVerifier extends InputVerifier
179. {
180.    public boolean verify(JComponent component)
181.    {
182.       String text = ((JTextComponent)component).getText();
183.       return IntTextDocument.isValid(text);
184.    }
185. }
186.
187. /**
188.    A panel that draws a clock. (Unchanged from TextTest.)
189. */
190. class ClockPanel extends JPanel
191. {
192.    public void paintComponent(Graphics g)
193.    {
194.       // draw the circular boundary
195.
196.       super.paintComponent(g);
197.       Graphics2D g2 = (Graphics2D)g;
198.       Ellipse2D circle
199.          = new Ellipse2D.Double(0, 0, 2 * RADIUS, 2 * RADIUS);
200.       g2.draw(circle);
201.
202.       // draw the hour hand
203.
204.       double hourAngle
205.          = Math.toRadians(90 - 360 * minutes / (12 * 60));
206.       drawHand(g2, hourAngle, HOUR_HAND_LENGTH);
207.
208.       // draw the minute hand
209.
210.       double minuteAngle
211.          = Math.toRadians(90 - 360 * minutes / 60);
212.       drawHand(g2, minuteAngle, MINUTE_HAND_LENGTH);
213.    }
214.
215.    public void drawHand(Graphics2D g2,
216.       double angle, double handLength)
217.    {
218.       Point2D end = new Point2D.Double(
219.          RADIUS + handLength * Math.cos(angle),
220.          RADIUS - handLength * Math.sin(angle));
```

```
221.        Point2D center = new Point2D.Double(RADIUS, RADIUS);
222.        g2.draw(new Line2D.Double(center, end));
223.     }
224.
225.     /**
226.        Set the time to be displayed on the clock
227.        @param h hours
228.        @param m minutes
229.     */
230.     public void setTime(int h, int m)
231.     {
232.        minutes = h * 60 + m;
233.        repaint();
234.     }
235.
236.     private double minutes = 0;
237.     private double RADIUS = 100;
238.     private double MINUTE_HAND_LENGTH = 0.8 * RADIUS;
239.     private double HOUR_HAND_LENGTH = 0.6 * RADIUS;
240. }
```

javax.swing.JComponent

- void setInputVerifier(InputVerifier verifier)
- Verifier getInputVerifier()

  set or get the input verifier that is called when the component loses focus.

- void setVerifyInputWhenFocusTarget(boolean flag)
- boolean getVerifyInputWhenFocusTarget()

  set or get the flag that determines whether the input verifier for the current focus owner will be called before this component requests focus. The default is true. You should set this property to false on components such as a Cancel button or a scroll bar, which should gain focus even if the the current component does not pass verification.

javax.swing.InputVerifier

- abstract boolean verify(JComponent component)

  Override this method to verify the contents of the given component.

javax.swing.text.Document

- void addUndoableEditListener(UndoableEditListener listener)

  adds a listener that is notified whenever an undoable edit operation modifies the document.

javax.swing.undo.UndoableEditListener

- void undoableEditHappened(UndoableEditEvent event)
  This method is called whenever an undoable edit operation has modified the event source document.

javax.swing.undo.UndoableEditEvent

- UndoableEdit getEdit()
  returns the edit operation that caused this event.

javax.swing.undo.UndoableEdit

- void undo()
  undoes this edit operation.

Password Fields

Password fields are a special kind of text field. To avoid nosy bystanders being able to glance at a password, the characters that the user entered are not actually displayed. Instead, each typed character is represented by an *echo character*, typically an asterisk (*). The Swing set supplies a JPasswordField class that implements such a text field.

The password field is another example of the power of the model-view-controller architecture pattern. The password field uses the same model to store the data as a regular text field, but its view has been changed to display all characters as echo characters.

javax.swing.JPasswordField

- JPasswordField(String text, int columns)
  constructs a new password field.

Parameters:	text	The text to be displayed, null if none
	columns	The number of columns

- void setEchoChar(char echo)
  sets the echo character for this password field. This is advisory; a particular look and feel may insist on its own choice of echo character. A value of 0 resets the echo character to the default.

Parameters:	echo	The echo character to display instead of the text characters

- `char[] getPassword()`

    returns the text contained in this password field. For stronger security, you should overwrite the contents of the returned array after use. (The password is not returned as a `String` because a string would stay in the virtual machine until it is garbage-collected.)

Text Areas

Sometimes, you need to collect user input that is more than one line long. As mentioned earlier, you use the `JTextArea` component for this collection. When you place a text area component in your program, a user can enter any number of lines of text, using the ENTER key to separate them. Each line ends with a '`\n`' as far as Java is concerned. If you need to break up what the user enters into separate lines, you can use the `StringTokenizer` class (see Chapter 12). Figure 9–12 shows a text area at work.

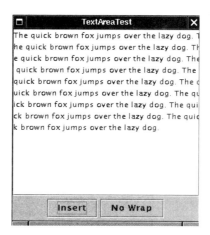

Figure 9–12: A text area

In the constructor for the `JTextArea` component, you specify the number of rows and columns for the text area. For example:

```
textArea = new JTextArea(8, 40); // 8 lines of 40 columns each
contentPane.add(textArea);
```

where the columns parameter works as before—and you still need to add a few more columns for safety's sake. Also, as before, the user is not restricted to the number of rows and columns; the text simply scrolls when the user inputs too much. You can also use the `setColumns` method to change the number of columns, and the `setRows` method to change the number of rows. These numbers only indicate the preferred size—the layout manager can still grow or shrink the text area.

If there is more text than the text area can display, then the remaining text is simply clipped. You can avoid clipping long lines by turning on line-wrapping:

```
textArea.setLineWrap(true); // long lines are wrapped
```

This wrapping is a visual effect only; the text in the document is not changed—no '\n' characters are inserted into the text.

In Swing, a text area does not have scroll bars. If you want scroll bars, you have to insert the text area inside a *scroll pane*. Then, insert the scroll pane inside the content pane.

```
textArea = new JTextArea(8, 40);
JScrollPane scrollPane = new JScrollPane(textArea);
contentPane.add(scrollPane, BorderLayout.CENTER);
```

The scroll pane now manages the view of the text area. Scroll bars automatically appear if there is more text than the text area can display, and they vanish again if text is deleted and the remaining text fits inside the area. The scrolling is handled internally in the scroll pane—your program does not need to process scroll events.

TIP: This is a general mechanism that you will encounter many times when working with Swing—to add scroll bars to a component, put them inside a scroll pane.

Example 9–3 is the complete code for the text area demo. This program simply lets you edit text in a text area. Click on "Insert" to insert a sentence at the end of the text. Click the second button to turn line-wrapping on and off. (Its name toggles between "Wrap" and "No wrap.") Of course, you can simply use the keyboard to edit the text in the text area. Note how you can highlight a section of text, and how you can cut, copy, and paste with the CTRL+X, CTRL+C, and CTRL+V keys. (Keyboard shortcuts are specific to the look and feel. These particular key combinations work for the Metal, Windows, and Mac look and feel.)

NOTE: The JTextArea component displays plain text only, without special fonts or formatting. To display formatted text (such as HTML or RTF), you can use the JEditorPane and JTextPane classes. These classes are discussed in Volume 2.

Example 9–3: TextAreaTest.java

```
1. import java.awt.*;
2. import java.awt.event.*;
3. import javax.swing.*;
4.
5. public class TextAreaTest
6. {
7.    public static void main(String[] args)
```

```
8.      {
9.         TextAreaFrame frame = new TextAreaFrame();
10.        frame.setDefaultCloseOperation(JFrame.EXIT_ON_CLOSE);
11.        frame.show();
12.     }
13. }
14.
15. /**
16.    A frame with a text area and buttons for text editing
17. */
18. class TextAreaFrame extends JFrame
19. {
20.    public TextAreaFrame()
21.    {
22.       setTitle("TextAreaTest");
23.       setSize(WIDTH, HEIGHT);
24.
25.       Container contentPane = getContentPane();
26.
27.       buttonPanel = new JPanel();
28.
29.       // add button to append text into the text area
30.
31.       JButton insertButton = new JButton("Insert");
32.       buttonPanel.add(insertButton);
33.       insertButton.addActionListener(new
34.          ActionListener()
35.          {
36.             public void actionPerformed(ActionEvent event)
37.             {
38.                textArea.append("The quick brown fox "
39.                   + "jumps over the lazy dog. ");
40.             }
41.          });
42.
43.       // add button to turn line wrapping on and off
44.
45.       wrapButton = new JButton("Wrap");
46.       buttonPanel.add(wrapButton);
47.       wrapButton.addActionListener(new
48.          ActionListener()
49.          {
50.             public void actionPerformed(ActionEvent evt)
51.             {
52.                boolean wrap = !textArea.getLineWrap();
53.                textArea.setLineWrap(wrap);
54.                scrollPane.validate();
55.                wrapButton.setText(wrap ? "No Wrap" : "Wrap");
56.             }
57.          });
```

```
58.
59.         contentPane.add(buttonPanel, BorderLayout.SOUTH);
60.
61.         // add a text area with scroll bars
62.
63.         textArea = new JTextArea(8, 40);
64.         scrollPane = new JScrollPane(textArea);
65.
66.         contentPane.add(scrollPane, BorderLayout.CENTER);
67.      }
68.
69.      public static final int WIDTH = 300;
70.      public static final int HEIGHT = 300;
71.
72.      private JTextArea textArea;
73.      private JScrollPane scrollPane;
74.      private JPanel buttonPanel;
75.      private JButton wrapButton;
76. }
```

`javax.swing.JTextArea`

- `JTextArea(int rows, int cols)`
  constructs a new text area.

  Parameters: `rows`   The number of rows

  　　　　　　　　`cols`   The number of columns

- `JTextArea(String text, int rows, int cols)`
  constructs a new text area with an initial text.

  Parameters: `text`   The initial text

  　　　　　　　　`rows`   The number of rows

  　　　　　　　　`cols`   The number of columns

- `void setColumns(int cols)`
  tells the text area the preferred number of columns it should use.

  Parameters: `cols`   The number of columns

- `void setRows(int rows)`
  tells the text area the preferred number of rows it should use.

  Parameters: `rows`   The number of rows

- `void append(String newText)`
  appends the given text to the end of the text already in the text area.

  Parameters: `newText`   The text to append

- void setLineWrap(boolean wrap)
  turns line-wrapping on or off.

  Parameters: wrap   true if lines should be wrapped

- void setWrapStyleWord(boolean word)
  If word is true, then long lines are wrapped at word boundaries. If it is false, then long lines are broken without taking word boundaries into account.

- void setTabSize(int c)
  sets tab stops every c columns. Note that the tabs aren't converted to spaces, but they cause alignment with the next tab stop.

  Parameters: c   The number of columns for a tab stop

javax.swing.JScrollPane

- JScrollPane(Component c)
  creates a scroll pane that displays the contents of the specified component. Scroll bars are supplied when the component is larger than the view.

  Parameters: c   The component to scroll

Labels and Labeling Components

Labels are components that hold text. They have no decorations (for example, no boundaries). They also do not react to user input. You can use a label to identify components. For example, unlike buttons, text components have no label to identify them. To label a component that does not itself come with an identifier:

1. Construct a JLabel component with the correct text.

2. Place it close enough to the component you want to identify so that the user can see that the label identifies the correct component.

The constructor for a JLabel lets you specify the initial text or icon, and optionally, the alignment of the contents. You use constants from the Swing-Constants interface to specify alignment. That interface defines a number of useful constants such as LEFT, RIGHT, CENTER, NORTH, EAST, and so on. The JLabel class is one of several Swing classes that implements this interface. Therefore, you can specify a left-aligned label either as:

```
JLabel label = new JLabel("Text", SwingConstants.LEFT);
```
or
```
JLabel label = new JLabel("Text", JLabel.LEFT);
```
The setText and setIcon methods let you set the text and icon of the label at run time.

TIP: Beginning with J2SE 1.3, you can use both plain and HTML text in buttons, labels, and menu items. We don't recommend HTML in buttons—it interferes with the look and feel. But HTML in labels can be very effective. Simply surround the label string with `<HTML>. . .</HTML>`, like this:

```
label = new JLabel("<HTML><B>Required</B> entry:</HTML>");
```

Fair warning—the first component with an HTML label takes some time to be displayed because the rather complex HTML rendering code must be loaded.

Labels can be positioned inside a container like any other component. This means you can use the techniques you have seen before to place labels where you need them. For example, if you look at Figure 9–13, you can see how one of the text fields is preceded by a label with the text "with."

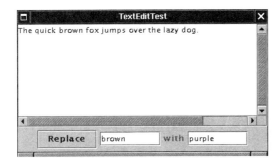

Figure 9–13: Testing text editing

`javax.swing.JLabel`

- `JLabel(String text)`
  constructs a label with left-aligned text.

  Parameters: `text`   The text in the label

- `JLabel(Icon icon)`
  constructs a label with a left-aligned icon.

  Parameters: `icon`   The icon in the label

- `JLabel(String text, int align)`

  Parameters: `text`   The text in the label

  `align`   One of `SwingConstants.LEFT`,
  `SwingConstants.CENTER`, or
  `SwingConstants.RIGHT`

- `JLabel(String text, Icon icon, int align)`
  constructs a label with both text and an icon. The icon is to the left of the text.

Parameters:	text	The text in the label
	icon	The icon in the label
	align	One of `SwingConstants.LEFT`, `SwingConstants.CENTER`, or `SwingConstants.RIGHT`

- `void setText(String text)`

Parameters:	text	The text in the label

- `void setIcon(Icon icon)`

Parameters:	icon	The icon in the label

Selecting Text

The text field and text area classes inherit methods from the `JTextComponent` superclass to select (highlight) the text contained in the component. They can also check for text that is currently selected.

First, there is the `selectAll` method, which highlights all the text in the field. You would use this method when presenting users with an input that they either will want to use exactly as provided or that they won't want to use at all. In the latter case, they can just type their own input, and the first keystroke replaces the selection.

The `select` method selects a part of the text. The arguments of `select` are the same as for `substring`: the first index is the start of the substring; the last is one more than the end. For example, `t.select(10, 15)` selects the tenth to fourteenth characters in the text control. End-of-line markers count as one character.

The `getSelectionStart` and `getSelectionEnd` methods return the start and end of the current selection, and `getSelectedText` returns the highlighted text. How users highlight text is system dependent. In the Metal look and feel, you can use the mouse or the standard SHIFT + arrow keys.

javax.swing.text.JTextComponent

- `void selectAll()`
  selects all text in the component.
- `void select(int selStart,int selEnd)`
  selects a range of text in the component.

Parameters:	selStart	The first position to select
	selEnd	One past the last position to select

- `int getSelectionStart()`
  returns the first position of the selected text.
- `int getSelectionEnd()`
  returns one past the last position of the selected text.
- `String getSelectedText()`
  returns the selected text.

Editing Text

The `JTextArea` class contains a number of methods to modify the contents of a text area. You can append text at the end, insert text in the middle, and replace text. To delete text, simply replace the text to be deleted with an empty string. Example 9–4 shows how to implement a simple find-and-replace feature. In the program illustrated in Figure 9–13, each time you click on the Replace button, the first match of the text in the first field is replaced by the text in the second field. This is not a very realistic application, but you could use this feature to correct spelling or typing errors in URLs.

Example 9–4: TextEditTest.java

```
1. import java.awt.*;
2. import java.awt.event.*;
3. import javax.swing.*;
4.
5. public class TextEditTest
6. {
7.    public static void main(String[] args)
8.    {
9.       TextEditFrame frame = new TextEditFrame();
10.      frame.setDefaultCloseOperation(JFrame.EXIT_ON_CLOSE);
11.      frame.show();
12.   }
13. }
14.
15. /**
16.    A frame with a text area and components for search/replace.
17. */
18. class TextEditFrame extends JFrame
19. {
20.    public TextEditFrame()
21.    {
22.       setTitle("TextEditTest");
23.       setSize(WIDTH, HEIGHT);
24.
25.       Container contentPane = getContentPane();
26.
27.       JPanel panel = new JPanel();
28.
29.       // add button, text fields and labels
30.
31.       JButton replaceButton = new JButton("Replace");
32.       panel.add(replaceButton);
```

```
33.        replaceButton.addActionListener(new ReplaceAction());
34.
35.        from = new JTextField("brown", 8);
36.        panel.add(from);
37.
38.        panel.add(new JLabel("with"));
39.
40.        to = new JTextField("purple", 8);
41.        panel.add(to);
42.        contentPane.add(panel, BorderLayout.SOUTH);
43.
44.        // add text area with scroll bars
45.
46.        textArea = new JTextArea(8, 40);
47.        textArea.setText
48.           ("The quick brown fox jumps over the lazy dog.");
49.        JScrollPane scrollPane = new JScrollPane(textArea);
50.        contentPane.add(scrollPane, BorderLayout.CENTER);
51.     }
52.
53.     public static final int WIDTH = 400;
54.     public static final int HEIGHT = 200;
55.
56.     private JTextArea textArea;
57.     private JTextField from;
58.     private JTextField to;
59.
60.     /**
61.        The action listener for the replace button.
62.     */
63.     private class ReplaceAction implements ActionListener
64.     {
65.        public void actionPerformed(ActionEvent event)
66.        {
67.           String f = from.getText();
68.           int n = textArea.getText().indexOf(f);
69.           if (n >= 0 && f.length() > 0)
70.              textArea.replaceRange(to.getText(), n,
71.                 n + f.length());
72.        }
73.     }
74. }
```

javax.swing.JTextArea

- void insert(String str, int pos)

  inserts a string into the text area.

Parameters:	str	The text to insert
	pos	The position at which to insert (0 = first position; newlines count as one character)

- `void replaceRange(String str, int start, int end)`
  replaces a range of text with another string.

  Parameters: `str`   The new text

                         `start`   The start position of the text to be replaced

                         `end`   One past the end position of the text to be replaced

Making Choices

You now know how to collect text input from users, but there are many occasions where you would rather give users a finite set of choices than have them enter the data in a text component. Using a set of buttons or a list of items tells your users what choices they have. (It also saves you the trouble of error checking.) In this section, you will learn how to program check boxes, radio buttons, lists of choices, and sliders.

Check Boxes

If you want to collect just a "yes" or "no" input, use a check box component. Check boxes automatically come with labels that identify them. The user usually checks the box by clicking inside it, and turns off the check mark by clicking inside the box again. To toggle the check mark, the user can also press the space bar when the focus is in the check box.

Figure 9–14 shows a simple program with two check boxes, one to turn on or off the italic attribute of a font, and the other for boldface. Note that the first check box has focus, as indicated by the rectangle around the label. Each time the user clicks one of the check boxes, we refresh the screen, using the new font attributes.

Check boxes need a label next to them to identify their purpose. You give the label text in the constructor.

```
bold = new JCheckBox("Bold");
```

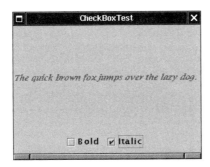

Figure 9–14: Check boxes

You use the `setSelected` method to turn a check box on or off. For example,

```
bold.setSelected(true);
```

The `isSelected` method then retrieves the current state of each check box. It is `false` if unchecked; `true` if checked.

When the user clicks on a check box, this triggers an action event. As always, you attach an action listener. In our program, the two buttons share the same action listener.

```
ActionListener listener = . . .
bold.addActionListener(listener);
italic.addActionListener(listener);
```

Its `actionPerformed` method queries the state of the `bold` and `italic` check boxes and sets the font of the panel to plain, bold, italic, or both.

```
public void actionPerformed(ActionEvent event)
{
    int mode = 0;
    if (bold.isSelected()) mode += Font.BOLD;
    if (italic.isSelected()) mode += Font.ITALIC;
    label.setFont(new Font("Serif", mode, FONTSIZE));
}
```

Example 9–5 is the complete program listing for the check box example.

 NOTE: In AWT, the equivalent component to a `JCheckBox` is called a `Checkbox` (with a lowercase "b"). It generates item events, not action events.

Example 9–5: CheckBoxTest.java

```
1. import java.awt.*;
2. import java.awt.event.*;
3. import javax.swing.*;
4.
5. public class CheckBoxTest
6. {
7.    public static void main(String[] args)
8.    {
9.       CheckBoxFrame frame = new CheckBoxFrame();
10.      frame.setDefaultCloseOperation(JFrame.EXIT_ON_CLOSE);
11.      frame.show();
12.   }
13. }
14.
15. /**
16.    A frame with a sample text label and check boxes for
17.    selecting font attributes.
18. */
19. class CheckBoxFrame extends JFrame
20. {
21.    public CheckBoxFrame()
```

```
22.    {
23.       setTitle("CheckBoxTest");
24.       setSize(WIDTH, HEIGHT);
25.
26.       Container contentPane = getContentPane();
27.
28.       // add the sample text label
29.
30.       label = new JLabel(
31.          "The quick brown fox jumps over the lazy dog.");
32.       label.setFont(new Font("Serif", Font.PLAIN, FONTSIZE));
33.       contentPane.add(label, BorderLayout.CENTER);
34.
35.       // this listener sets the font attribute of
36.       // the label to the check box state
37.
38.       ActionListener listener = new
39.          ActionListener()
40.          {
41.             public void actionPerformed(ActionEvent event)
42.             {
43.                int mode = 0;
44.                if (bold.isSelected()) mode += Font.BOLD;
45.                if (italic.isSelected()) mode += Font.ITALIC;
46.                label.setFont(new Font("Serif", mode, FONTSIZE));
47.             }
48.          };
49.
50.       // add the check boxes
51.
52.       JPanel buttonPanel = new JPanel();
53.
54.       bold = new JCheckBox("Bold");
55.       bold.addActionListener(listener);
56.       buttonPanel.add(bold);
57.
58.       italic = new JCheckBox("Italic");
59.       italic.addActionListener(listener);
60.       buttonPanel.add(italic);
61.
62.       contentPane.add(buttonPanel, BorderLayout.SOUTH);
63.    }
64.
65.    public static final int WIDTH = 300;
66.    public static final int HEIGHT = 200;
67.
68.    private JLabel label;
69.    private JCheckBox bold;
70.    private JCheckBox italic;
71.
72.    private static final int FONTSIZE = 12;
73. }
```

javax.swing.JCheckBox

- JCheckBox(String label)

  Parameters: label   The label on the check box

- JCheckBox(String label, boolean state)

  Parameters: label   The label on the check box

                  state   The initial state of the check box

- JCheckBox(String label, Icon icon)

  constructs a check box that is initially unselected.

  Parameters: label   The label on the check box

                  icon   The icon on the check box

- boolean isSelected ()

  returns the state of the check box.

- void setSelected(boolean state)

  sets the check box to a new state.

Radio Buttons

In the previous example, the user could check either, both, or none of the two check boxes. In many cases, we want to require the user to check only one of several boxes. When another box is checked, the previous box is automatically unchecked. Such a group of boxes is often called a *radio button group* because the buttons work like the station selector buttons on a radio. When you push in one button, the previously depressed button pops out. Figure 9–15 shows a typical example. We allow the user to select a font size among the choices—Small, Medium, Large, and Extra large—but, of course, we will allow the user to select only one size at a time.

Implementing radio button groups is easy in Swing. You construct one object of type ButtonGroup for every group of buttons. Then, you add objects of type JRadioButton to the button group. The button group object is responsible for turning off the previously set button when a new button is clicked.

```
ButtonGroup group = new ButtonGroup();

JRadioButton smallButton
   = new JRadioButton("Small", false);
group.add(smallButton);

JRadioButton mediumButton
   = new JRadioButton("Medium", true);
group.add(mediumButton);
. . .
```

Figure 9–15: A radio button group

The second argument of the constructor is `true` for the button that should be checked initially, and `false` for all others. Note that the button group controls only the *behavior* of the buttons; if you want to group the buttons together for layout purposes, you also need to add them to a container such as a `JPanel`.

If you look again at Figures 9–14 and 9–15, you will note that the appearance of the radio buttons is different from check boxes. Check boxes are square and contain a check mark when selected. Radio buttons are round and contain a dot when selected.

The event notification mechanism for radio buttons is the same as for any other buttons. When the user checks a radio button, the radio button generates an action event. In our example program, we define an action listener that sets the font size to a particular value:

```
ActionListener listener = new
   ActionListener()
   {
      public void actionPerformed(ActionEvent evt)
      {
         // size refers to the final parameter of the
         // addRadioButton method
         label.setFont(new Font("Serif", Font.PLAIN,
            size));
      }
   };
```

Compare this listener set-up with that of the check box example. Each radio button gets a different listener object. Each listener object knows exactly what it needs to do—set the font size to a particular value. In the case of the check boxes, we used a different approach. Both check boxes have the same action listener. It called a method that looked at the current state of both check boxes.

Could we follow the same approach here? We could have a single listener that computes the size as follows:

```
if (smallButton.isSelected()) size = 8;
else is (mediumButton.isSelected()) size = 12;
. . .
```

However, we prefer to use separate action listener objects because they tie the size values more closely to the buttons.

> NOTE: If you have a group of radio buttons, you know that only one of them is selected. It would be nice to be able to quickly find out which one, without having to query all the buttons in the group. Since the `ButtonGroup` object controls all buttons, it would be convenient if this object could give us a reference to the selected button. Indeed, the `ButtonGroup` class has a `getSelection` method, but that method doesn't return the radio button that is selected. Instead, it returns a `ButtonModel` reference to the model attached to the button. Unfortunately, none of the `Button-Model` methods are very helpful. The `ButtonModel` interface inherits a method `getSelectedObjects` from the `ItemSelectable` interface that, rather uselessly, returns `null`. The `getActionCommand` method looks promising because the "action command" of a radio button is its text label. But the action command of its model is `null`. Only if you explicitly set the action commands of all radio buttons with the `setActionCommand` method do the models' action command values also get set. Then you can retrieve the action command of the currently selected button with `buttonGroup.getSelection().getActionCommand()`.

Example 9–6 is the complete program for font size selection that puts a set of radio buttons to work.

Example 9–6: RadioButtonTest.java

```
1. import java.awt.*;
2. import java.awt.event.*;
3. import javax.swing.*;
4.
5. public class RadioButtonTest
6. {
7.    public static void main(String[] args)
8.    {
9.       RadioButtonFrame frame = new RadioButtonFrame();
10.      frame.setDefaultCloseOperation(JFrame.EXIT_ON_CLOSE);
11.      frame.show();
12.   }
13. }
14.
15. /**
16.    A frame with a sample text label and radio buttons for
17.    selecting font sizes.
18. */
19. class RadioButtonFrame extends JFrame
```

```
20. {
21.    public RadioButtonFrame()
22.    {
23.       setTitle("RadioButtonTest");
24.       setSize(WIDTH, HEIGHT);
25.
26.       Container contentPane = getContentPane();
27.
28.       // add the sample text label
29.
30.       label = new JLabel(
31.          "The quick brown fox jumps over the lazy dog.");
32.       label.setFont(new Font("Serif", Font.PLAIN,
33.          DEFAULT_SIZE));
34.       contentPane.add(label, BorderLayout.CENTER);
35.
36.       // add the radio buttons
37.
38.       buttonPanel = new JPanel();
39.       group = new ButtonGroup();
40.
41.       addRadioButton("Small", 8);
42.       addRadioButton("Medium", 12);
43.       addRadioButton("Large", 18);
44.       addRadioButton("Extra large", 36);
45.
46.       contentPane.add(buttonPanel, BorderLayout.SOUTH);
47.    }
48.
49.    /**
50.       Adds a radio button that sets the font size of the
51.       sample text.
52.       @param name the string to appear on the button
53.       @param size the font size that this button sets
54.    */
55.    public void addRadioButton(String name, final int size)
56.    {
57.       boolean selected = size == DEFAULT_SIZE;
58.       JRadioButton button = new JRadioButton(name, selected);
59.       group.add(button);
60.       buttonPanel.add(button);
61.
62.       // this listener sets the label font size
63.
64.       ActionListener listener = new
65.          ActionListener()
66.          {
67.             public void actionPerformed(ActionEvent evt)
68.             {
69.                // size refers to the final parameter of the
70.                // addRadioButton method
```

```
71.                    label.setFont(new Font("Serif", Font.PLAIN,
72.                        size));
73.                }
74.            };
75.
76.        button.addActionListener(listener);
77.    }
78.
79.    public static final int WIDTH = 400;
80.    public static final int HEIGHT = 200;
81.
82.    private JPanel buttonPanel;
83.    private ButtonGroup group;
84.    private JLabel label;
85.
86.    private static final int DEFAULT_SIZE = 12;
87. }
```

javax.swing.JRadioButton

• JRadioButton(String label, boolean state)

Parameters: label   The label on the check box

state   The initial state of the check box

• JRadioButton(String label, Icon icon)
constructs a radio button that is initially unselected.

Parameters: label   The label on the radio button

icon   The icon on the radio button

javax.swing.ButtonGroup

• void add(AbstractButton b)
adds the button to the group.

• ButtonModel getSelection()
returns the button model of the selected button.

javax.swing.ButtonModel

• String getActionCommand()
returns the action command for this button model.

javax.swing.AbstractButton

• void setActionCommand(String s)
sets the action command for this button and its model.

Borders

If you have multiple groups of radio buttons in a window, you will want to visually indicate which buttons are grouped together. The Swing set provides a set of useful *borders* for this purpose. You can apply a border to any component that extends `JComponent`. The most common usage is to place a border around a panel and fill that panel with other user interface elements such as radio buttons.

There are quite a few borders to choose from, but you follow the same steps for all of them.

1. Call a static method of the `BorderFactory` to create a border. You can choose among the following styles (see Figure 9–16):

    *   Lowered bevel

    *   Raised bevel

    *   Etched

    *   Line

    *   Matte

    *   Empty (just to create some blank space around the component)

2. If you like, add a title to your border by passing your border to `BorderFactory.createTitledBorder`.

3. If you really want to go all out, combine several borders with a call to `BorderFactory.createCompoundBorder`.

4. Add the resulting border to your component by calling the `setBorder` method of the `JComponent` class.

For example, here is how you add an etched border with a title to a panel:

```
Border etched = BorderFactory.createEtchedBorder()
Border titled = BorderFactory.createTitledBorder(etched,
   "A Title");
panel.setBorder(titled);
```

Run the program in Example 9–7 to get an idea what the various borders look like.

The various borders have different options for setting border widths and colors. See the API notes for details. True border enthusiasts will appreciate that there is also a `SoftBevelBorder` class for beveled borders with softened corners, and that a `LineBorder` can have rounded corners as well. These borders can be constructed only by using one of the class constructors—there is no `BorderFactory` method for them.

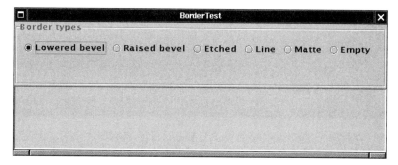

Figure 9–16: Testing border types

Example 9–7: BorderTest.java

```
1. import java.awt.*;
2. import java.awt.event.*;
3. import javax.swing.*;
4. import javax.swing.border.*;
5.
6. public class BorderTest
7. {
8.    public static void main(String[] args)
9.    {
10.       BorderFrame frame = new BorderFrame();
11.       frame.setDefaultCloseOperation(JFrame.EXIT_ON_CLOSE);
12.       frame.show();
13.    }
14. }
15.
16. /**
17.    A frame with radio buttons to pick a border style.
18. */
19. class BorderFrame extends JFrame
20. {
21.    public BorderFrame()
22.    {
23.       setTitle("BorderTest");
24.       setSize(WIDTH, HEIGHT);
25.
26.       demoPanel = new JPanel();
27.       buttonPanel = new JPanel();
28.       group = new ButtonGroup();
29.
30.       addRadioButton("Lowered bevel",
31.          BorderFactory.createLoweredBevelBorder());
32.       addRadioButton("Raised bevel",
```

```
33.              BorderFactory.createRaisedBevelBorder());
34.         addRadioButton("Etched",
35.              BorderFactory.createEtchedBorder());
36.         addRadioButton("Line",
37.              BorderFactory.createLineBorder(Color.blue));
38.         addRadioButton("Matte",
39.              BorderFactory.createMatteBorder(
40.                  10, 10, 10, 10, Color.blue));
41.         addRadioButton("Empty",
42.              BorderFactory.createEmptyBorder());
43.
44.         Border etched = BorderFactory.createEtchedBorder();
45.         Border titled = BorderFactory.createTitledBorder
46.              (etched, "Border types");
47.         buttonPanel.setBorder(titled);
48.
49.         Container contentPane = getContentPane();
50.
51.         contentPane.setLayout(new GridLayout(2, 1));
52.         contentPane.add(buttonPanel);
53.         contentPane.add(demoPanel);
54.     }
55.
56.     public void addRadioButton(String buttonName, final Border b)
57.     {
58.         JRadioButton button = new JRadioButton(buttonName);
59.         button.addActionListener(new
60.              ActionListener()
61.              {
62.                  public void actionPerformed(ActionEvent event)
63.                  {
64.                      demoPanel.setBorder(b);
65.                      validate();
66.                  }
67.              });
68.         group.add(button);
69.         buttonPanel.add(button);
70.     }
71.
72.     public static final int WIDTH = 600;
73.     public static final int HEIGHT = 200;
74.
75.     private JPanel demoPanel;
76.     private JPanel buttonPanel;
77.     private ButtonGroup group;
78. }
```

javax.swing.BorderFactory

- `static Border createLineBorder(Color color)`
- `static Border createLineBorder(Color color, int thickness)`

create a simple line border.

- `static MatteBorder createMatteBorder(int top, int left, int bottom, int right, Color color)`
- `static MatteBorder createMatteBorder(int top, int left, int bottom, int right, Icon tileIcon)`

create a thick border that is filled with a color or a repeating icon.

- `static Border createEmptyBorder()`
- `static Border createEmptyBorder(int top, int left, int bottom, int right)`

create an empty border.

- `static Border createEtchedBorder()`
- `static Border createEtchedBorder(Color highlight, Color shadow)`
- `static Border createEtchedBorder(int type)`
- `static Border createEtchedBorder(int type, Color highlight, Color shadow)`

create a line border with a 3D effect.

Parameters:	highlight, shadow	Colors for 3D effect
	type	One of `EtchedBorder.RAISED`, `EtchedBorder.LOWERED`

- `static Border createBevelBorder(int type)`
- `static Border createBevelBorder(int type, Color highlight, Color shadow)`
- `static Border createLoweredBevelBorder()`
- `static Border createRaisedBevelBorder()`

create a border that gives the effect of a lowered or raised surface.

Parameters:	type	One of `BevelBorder.LOWERED`, `BevelBorder.RAISED`
	highlight, shadow	Colors for 3D effect

- `static TitledBorder createTitledBorder(String title)`
- `static TitledBorder createTitledBorder(Border border)`
- `static TitledBorder createTitledBorder(Border border, String title)`

- `static TitledBorder createTitledBorder(Border border, String title, int justification, int position)`
- `static TitledBorder createTitledBorder(Border border, String title, int justification, int position, Font font)`
- `static TitledBorder createTitledBorder(Border border, String title, int justification, int position, Font font, Color color)`

Parameters:	`title`	The title string
	`border`	The border to decorate with the title
	`justification`	One of `TitledBorder.LEFT`, `TitledBorder.CENTER`, `TitledBorder.RIGHT`
	`position`	One of the `TitledBorder` constants `ABOVE_TOP`, `TOP`, `BELOW_TOP`, `ABOVE_BOTTOM`, `BOTTOM`, `BELOW_BOTTOM`
	`font`	The font for the title
	`color`	The color of the title

- `static CompoundBorder createCompoundBorder(Border outsideBorder, Border insideBorder)`
  combines two borders to a new border.

`javax.swing.border.SoftBevelBorder`

- `SoftBevelBorder(int type)`
- `SoftBevelBorder(int type, Color highlight, Color shadow)`
  create a bevel border with softened corners.

Parameters:	`type`	One of `BevelBorder.LOWERED`, `BevelBorder.RAISED`
	`color, shadow`	Colors for 3D effect

`javax.swing.border.LineBorder`

- `public LineBorder(Color color, int thickness, boolean roundedCorners)`
  creates a line border with the given color and thickness. If `roundedCorners` is true, the border has rounded corners.

`javax.swing.JComponent`

- `void setBorder(Border border)`
  sets the border of this component.

Combo Boxes

If you have more than a handful of alternatives, radio buttons are not a good choice because they take up too much screen space. Instead, you can use a combo box. When the user clicks on the component, a list of choices drops down, and the user can then select one of them (see Figure 9–17).

Figure 9–17: A combo box

If the drop-down list box is set to be *editable*, then you can edit the current selection as if it was a text field. For that reason, this component is called a *combo box*—it combines the flexibility of an edit box with a set of predefined choices. The JComboBox class provides a combo box component.

You call the setEditable method to make the combo box editable. Note that editing affects only the current item. It does not change the contents of the list.

You can obtain the current selection or edited text by calling the getSelectedItem method.

In the example program, the user can choose a font style from a list of styles (Serif, SansSerif, Monospaced, etc.). The user can also type in another font.

You add the choice items with the addItem method. In our program, addItem is called only in the constructor, but you can call it any time.

```
faceCombo = new JComboBox();
faceCombo.setEditable(true);
faceCombo.addItem("Serif");
faceCombo.addItem("SansSerif");
. . .
```

This method adds the string at the end of the list. You can add new items any-where in the list with the `insertItemAt` method:

```
faceCombo.insertItemAt("Monospaced", 0); // add at the beginning
```

You can add items of any type—the combo box invokes each item's `toString` method to display it.

If you need to remove items at run time, you use the `removeItem` or `removeItemAt` method, depending on whether you supply the item to be removed or its position.

```
faceCombo.removeItem("Monospaced");
faceCombo.removeItemAt(0); // remove first item
```

There is also a `removeAllItems` method to remove all items at once.

When the user selects an item from a combo box, the combo box generates an action event. To find out which item was selected, call `getSource` on the event parameter to get a reference to the combo box that sent the event. Then call the `getSelectedItem` method to retrieve the currently selected item. You need to cast the returned value to the appropriate type, usually `String`.

```
public void actionPerformed(ActionEvent event)
{
    label.setFont(new Font(
        (String)faceCombo.getSelectedItem(),
        Font.PLAIN,
        DEFAULT_SIZE));
}
```

Example 9–8 shows the complete program.

Example 9–8: ComboBoxTest.java

```
1. import java.awt.*;
2. import java.awt.event.*;
3. import javax.swing.*;
4.
5. public class ComboBoxTest
6. {
7.    public static void main(String[] args)
8.    {
9.       ComboBoxFrame frame = new ComboBoxFrame();
10.      frame.setDefaultCloseOperation(JFrame.EXIT_ON_CLOSE);
11.      frame.show();
12.   }
13. }
14.
15. /**
16.    A frame with a sample text label and a combo box for
17.    selecting font faces.
```

```
18. */
19. class ComboBoxFrame extends JFrame
20. {
21.    public ComboBoxFrame()
22.    {
23.       setTitle("ComboBoxTest");
24.       setSize(WIDTH, HEIGHT);
25.
26.       Container contentPane = getContentPane();
27.
28.       // add the sample text label
29.
30.       label = new JLabel(
31.          "The quick brown fox jumps over the lazy dog.");
32.       label.setFont(new Font("Serif", Font.PLAIN,
33.          DEFAULT_SIZE));
34.       contentPane.add(label, BorderLayout.CENTER);
35.
36.       // make a combo box and add face names
37.
38.       faceCombo = new JComboBox();
39.       faceCombo.setEditable(true);
40.       faceCombo.addItem("Serif");
41.       faceCombo.addItem("SansSerif");
42.       faceCombo.addItem("Monospaced");
43.       faceCombo.addItem("Dialog");
44.       faceCombo.addItem("DialogInput");
45.
46.       // the combo box listener changes the label font to the
47.       // selected face name
48.
49.       faceCombo.addActionListener(new
50.          ActionListener()
51.          {
52.             public void actionPerformed(ActionEvent event)
53.             {
54.                label.setFont(new Font(
55.                   (String)faceCombo.getSelectedItem(),
56.                   Font.PLAIN,
57.                   DEFAULT_SIZE));
58.             }
59.          });
60.
61.       // add combo box to a panel at the frame's southern border
62.
63.       JPanel comboPanel = new JPanel();
64.       comboPanel.add(faceCombo);
65.       contentPane.add(comboPanel, BorderLayout.SOUTH);
66.    }
67.
```

```
68.    public static final int WIDTH = 300;
69.    public static final int HEIGHT = 200;
70.
71.    private JComboBox faceCombo;
72.    private JLabel label;
73.    private static final int DEFAULT_SIZE = 12;
74. }
```

javax.swing.JComboBox

- void setEditable(boolean b)

  Parameters: b   true if the combo box field can be edited
  by the user, false otherwise

- void addItem(Object item)

  adds an item to the item list.

- void insertItemAt(Object item, int index)

  inserts an item into the item list at a given index.

- void removeItem(Object item)

  removes an item from the item list.

- void removeItemAt(int index)

  removes the item at an index.

- void removeAllItems()

  removes all items from the item list.

- Object getSelectedItem()

  returns the currently selected item.

Sliders

Combo boxes let users choose from a discrete set of values. Sliders offer a choice from a continuum of values, for example, any number between 1 and 100.

The most common way of constructing a slider is as follows:

```
JSlider slider = new JSlider(min, max, initialValue);
```

If you omit the minimum, maximum, and initial values, they are initialized with 0, 100, and 50, respectively.

Or, if you want the slider to be vertical, then use the following constructor call:

```
JSlider slider = new JSlider(SwingConstants.VERTICAL,
    min, max, initialValue);
```

These constructors create a plain slider, such as the top slider in Figure 9–18. You will see presently how to add decorations to a slider.

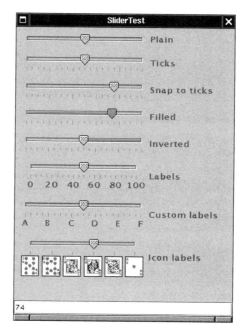

Figure 9–18: Sliders

As the user slides the slider bar, the *value* of the slider moves between the minimum and the maximum values. When the value changes, a `ChangeEvent` is sent to all change listeners. To be notified of the change, you need to call the `addChangeListener` method and install an object that implements the `ChangeListener` interface. That interface has a single method, `state-Changed`. In that method, you should retrieve the slider value:

```
public void stateChanged(ChangeEvent event)
{
    JSlider slider = (JSlider)event.getSource();
    int value = slider.getValue();
    . . .
}
```

You can embellish the slider by showing *ticks*. For example, in the sample program, the second slider uses the following settings:

```
slider.setMajorTickSpacing(20);
slider.setMinorTickSpacing(5);
```

The slider is decorated with large tick marks every 20 units and small tick marks every 5 units. The units refer to slider values, not pixels.

These instructions only set the units for the tick marks. To actually have the tick marks appear, you also need to call

```
slider.setPaintTicks(true);
```

The major and minor tick marks are independent. For example, you can set major tick marks every 20 units and minor tick marks every 7 units, but you'll get a very messy scale.

You can force the slider to *snap to ticks*. Whenever the user has finished dragging a slider in snap mode, it is immediately moved to the closest tick. You activate this mode with the call

```
slider.setSnapToTicks(true);
```

NOTE: In version 1.2 and 1.3, the "snap to ticks" behavior doesn't work as well as you might imagine. Until the slider has actually snapped, the change listener still reports slider values that don't correspond to ticks. And if you click next to the slider—an action that normally advances the slider a bit in the direction of the click—a slider with "snap to ticks" does not move to the next tick.

You can ask for *tick mark labels* for the major tick marks, by calling

```
slider.setPaintLabels(true);
```

For example, with a slider ranging from 0 to 100 and major tick spacing of 20, the ticks are labeled 0, 20, 40, 60, 80, and 100.

You can also supply other tick marks, such as strings or icons (see Figure 9–18). The process is a bit convoluted. You need to fill a hash table with keys `new Integer(tickValue)` and values of type `Component`. Then you call the `setLabelTable` method. The components are placed under the tick marks. Usually, you use `JLabel` objects. Here is how you can label ticks as A, B, C, D, E, and F.

```
Hashtable labelTable = new Hashtable();
labelTable.put(new Integer(0), new JLabel("A"));
labelTable.put(new Integer(20), new JLabel("B"));
. . .
labelTable.put(new Integer(100), new JLabel("F"));
slider.setLabelTable(labelTable);
```

See Chapter 2 of Volume 2 for more information about hash tables.

Example 9–9 also shows a slider with icons as tick labels.

TIP: If your tick marks or labels don't show, double-check that you called `setPaintTicks(true)` and `setPaintLabels(true)`.

Finally, if you use the Metal look and feel, you can add a visual enhancement to your sliders and have the portion from the minimum value to the current value

"filled in." The fourth and fifth sliders in Figure 9–18 are filled. You fill a slider by
setting a client property as follows:

```
slider.putClientProperty("JSlider.isFilled", Boolean.TRUE);
```

The fifth slider has its direction reversed by calling

```
slider.setInverted(true);
```

The example program shows all these visual effects with a collection of sliders.
Each slider has a change event listener installed that places the current slider
value into the text field at the bottom of the frame.

Example 9–9: SliderTest.java

```
1. import java.awt.*;
2. import java.awt.event.*;
3. import java.util.*;
4. import javax.swing.*;
5. import javax.swing.event.*;
6.
7. public class SliderTest
8. {
9.    public static void main(String[] args)
10.    {
11.       SliderTestFrame frame = new SliderTestFrame();
12.       frame.setDefaultCloseOperation(JFrame.EXIT_ON_CLOSE);
13.       frame.show();
14.    }
15. }
16.
17. /**
18.    A frame with many sliders and a text field to show slider
19.    values.
20. */
21. class SliderTestFrame extends JFrame
22. {
23.    public SliderTestFrame()
24.    {
25.       setTitle("SliderTest");
26.       setSize(WIDTH, HEIGHT);
27.
28.       sliderPanel = new JPanel();
29.       sliderPanel.setLayout(new FlowLayout(FlowLayout.LEFT));
30.
31.       // common listener for all sliders
32.       listener = new
33.          ChangeListener()
34.          {
35.             public void stateChanged(ChangeEvent event)
36.             {
37.                // update text field when the slider value changes
```

```
38.                   JSlider source = (JSlider)event.getSource();
39.                   textField.setText("" + source.getValue());
40.               }
41.           };
42.
43.       // add a plain slider
44.
45.       JSlider slider = new JSlider();
46.       addSlider(slider, "Plain");
47.
48.       // add a slider with major and minor ticks
49.
50.       slider = new JSlider();
51.       slider.setPaintTicks(true);
52.       slider.setMajorTickSpacing(20);
53.       slider.setMinorTickSpacing(5);
54.       addSlider(slider, "Ticks");
55.
56.       // add a slider that snaps to ticks
57.
58.       slider = new JSlider();
59.       slider.setPaintTicks(true);
60.       slider.setSnapToTicks(true);
61.       slider.setMajorTickSpacing(20);
62.       slider.setMinorTickSpacing(5);
63.       addSlider(slider, "Snap to ticks");
64.
65.       // add a filled slider
66.
67.       slider = new JSlider();
68.       slider.setPaintTicks(true);
69.       slider.setMajorTickSpacing(20);
70.       slider.setMinorTickSpacing(5);
71.       slider.putClientProperty("JSlider.isFilled",
72.           Boolean.TRUE);
73.       addSlider(slider, "Filled");
74.
75.       // add a filled and inverted slider
76.
77.       slider = new JSlider();
78.       slider.setPaintTicks(true);
79.       slider.setMajorTickSpacing(20);
80.       slider.setMinorTickSpacing(5);
81.       slider.putClientProperty("JSlider.isFilled",
82.           Boolean.TRUE);
83.       slider.setInverted(true);
84.       addSlider(slider, "Inverted");
85.
86.       // add a slider with numeric labels
87.
88.       slider = new JSlider();
```

```
89.       slider.setPaintTicks(true);
90.       slider.setPaintLabels(true);
91.       slider.setMajorTickSpacing(20);
92.       slider.setMinorTickSpacing(5);
93.       addSlider(slider, "Labels");
94.
95.       // add a slider with alphabetic labels
96.
97.       slider = new JSlider();
98.       slider.setPaintLabels(true);
99.       slider.setPaintTicks(true);
100.      slider.setMajorTickSpacing(20);
101.      slider.setMinorTickSpacing(5);
102.
103.      Hashtable labelTable = new Hashtable();
104.      labelTable.put(new Integer(0), new JLabel("A"));
105.      labelTable.put(new Integer(20), new JLabel("B"));
106.      labelTable.put(new Integer(40), new JLabel("C"));
107.      labelTable.put(new Integer(60), new JLabel("D"));
108.      labelTable.put(new Integer(80), new JLabel("E"));
109.      labelTable.put(new Integer(100), new JLabel("F"));
110.
111.      slider.setLabelTable(labelTable);
112.      addSlider(slider, "Custom labels");
113.
114.      // add a slider with icon labels
115.
116.      slider = new JSlider();
117.      slider.setPaintTicks(true);
118.      slider.setPaintLabels(true);
119.      slider.setSnapToTicks(true);
120.      slider.setMajorTickSpacing(20);
121.      slider.setMinorTickSpacing(20);
122.
123.      labelTable = new Hashtable();
124.
125.      // add card images
126.
127.      labelTable.put(new Integer(0),
128.         new JLabel(new ImageIcon("nine.gif")));
129.      labelTable.put(new Integer(20),
130.         new JLabel(new ImageIcon("ten.gif")));
131.      labelTable.put(new Integer(40),
132.         new JLabel(new ImageIcon("jack.gif")));
133.      labelTable.put(new Integer(60),
134.         new JLabel(new ImageIcon("queen.gif")));
135.      labelTable.put(new Integer(80),
136.         new JLabel(new ImageIcon("king.gif")));
137.      labelTable.put(new Integer(100),
138.         new JLabel(new ImageIcon("ace.gif")));
139.
```

```
140.        slider.setLabelTable(labelTable);
141.        addSlider(slider, "Icon labels");
142.
143.        // add the text field that displays the slider value
144.
145.        textField = new JTextField();
146.        Container contentPane = getContentPane();
147.        contentPane.add(sliderPanel, BorderLayout.CENTER);
148.        contentPane.add(textField, BorderLayout.SOUTH);
149.     }
150.
151.     /**
152.        Adds a slider to the slider panel and hooks up the listener
153.        @param s the slider
154.        @param description the slider description
155.     */
156.     public void addSlider(JSlider s, String description)
157.     {
158.        s.addChangeListener(listener);
159.        JPanel panel = new JPanel();
160.        panel.add(s);
161.        panel.add(new JLabel(description));
162.        sliderPanel.add(panel);
163.     }
164.
165.     public static final int WIDTH = 350;
166.     public static final int HEIGHT = 450;
167.
168.     private JPanel sliderPanel;
169.     private JTextField textField;
170.     private ChangeListener listener;
171. }
```

javax.swing.JSlider

- JSlider()
- JSlider(int direction)
- JSlider(int min, int max)
- JSlider(int min, int max, int initialValue)
- JSlider(int direction, int min, int max, int initialValue)

  construct a horizontal slider with the given direction, minimum, maximum, and initial values.

Parameters:	direction	One of SwingConstants.HORIZONTAL or SwingConstants.VERTICAL. The default is horizontal.
	min, max	The minimum and maximum for the slider values. Defaults are 0 and 100.

`initialValue`   The initial value for the slider. The
                              default is 50.

- `void setPaintTicks(boolean b)`
  If b is true, then ticks are displayed.

- `void setMajorTickSpacing(int units)`
- `void setMinorTickSpacing(int units)`
  set major or minor ticks at multiples of the given slider units.

- `void setPaintLabels(boolean b)`
  If b is true, then tick labels are displayed.

- `slider.setLabelTable(Dictionary table)`
  sets the components to use for the tick labels. Each key/value pair in the table has the form `new Integer(value)/component`.

- `void setSnapToTicks(boolean b)`
  If b is true, then the slider snaps to the closest tick after each adjustment.

Menus

We started this chapter by introducing the most common components that you might want to place into a window, such as various kinds of buttons, text fields, and combo boxes. Swing also supports another type of user interface elements, the pull-down menus that are familiar from GUI applications.

A *menu bar* on top of the window contains the names of the pull-down menus. Clicking on a name opens the menu containing *menu items* and *submenus*. When the user clicks on a menu item, all menus are closed and a message is sent to the program. Figure 9–19 shows a typical menu with a submenu.

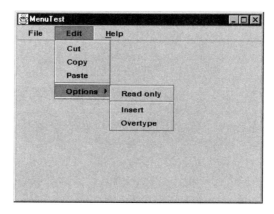

Figure 9–19: A menu with a submenu

Building Menus

Building menus is straightforward. You create a menu bar:

```
JMenuBar menuBar = new JMenuBar();
```

A menu bar is just a component that you can add anywhere you like. Normally, you want it to appear at the top of a frame. You can add it there with the `setJMenuBar` method:

```
frame.setJMenuBar(menuBar);
```

For each menu, you create a menu object:

```
JMenu editMenu = new JMenu("Edit");
```

You add the top-level menus to the menu bar:

```
menuBar.addMenu(editMenu);
```

You add menu items, separators, and submenus to the menu object:

```
JMenuItem pasteItem = new JMenuItem("Paste");
editMenu.add(pasteItem);
editMenu.addSeparator();
JMenu optionsMenu = . . .; // a submenu
editMenu.add(optionsMenu);
```

When the user selects a menu, an action event is triggered. You need to install an action listener for each menu item.

```
ActionListener listener = . . .;
pasteItem.addActionListener(listener);
```

There is a convenient method `JMenu.add(String s)` that adds a menu item to the end of a menu, for example:

```
editMenu.add("Paste");
```

The `add` method returns the created menu item, so that you can capture it and then add the listener, as follows:

```
JMenuItem pasteItem = editMenu.add("Paste");
pasteItem.addActionListener(listener);
```

It often happens that menu items trigger commands that can also be activated through other user interface elements such as toolbar buttons. In Chapter 8, you saw how to specify commands through `Action` objects. You define a class that implements the `Action` interface, usually by extending the `AbstractAction` convenience class. You specify the menu item label in the constructor of the `AbstractAction` object, and you override the `actionPerformed` method to hold the menu action handler. For example,

```
Action exitAction = new
   AbstractAction("Exit") // menu item text goes here
   {
```

```
public void actionPerformed(ActionEvent event)
{
    // action code goes here
    System.exit(0);
}
};
```

You can then add the action to the menu:

```
JMenuItem exitItem = fileMenu.add(exitAction);
```

This command adds a menu item to the menu, using the action name. The action object becomes its listener. This is just a convenient shortcut for

```
JMenuItem exitItem = new JMenuItem(exitAction);
fileMenu.add(exitItem);
```

NOTE: In Windows programs, menus are generally defined in an external resource file and tied to the application with resource identifiers. It is possible to build menus programmatically, but it is not commonly done. In Java, menus are still usually built inside the program because the mechanism for dealing with external resources is far more limited than it is in Windows.

javax.swing.JMenu

- JMenu(String label)

  Parameters: label   The label for the menu in the menu bar or parent menu

- JMenuItem add(JMenuItem item)

  adds a menu item (or a menu).

  Parameters: item   The item or menu to add

- JMenuItem add(String label)

  adds a menu item to this menu.

  Parameters: label   The label for the menu items

- JMenuItem add(Action a)

  adds a menu item and associates an action with it.

  Parameters: a   An action encapsulating a name, optional icon, and listener (see Chapter 8)

- void addSeparator()

  adds a separator line to the menu.

- JMenuItem insert(JMenuItem menu, int index)

  adds a new menu item (or submenu) to the menu at a specific index.

Parameters: `menu`   The menu to be added

                `index`   Where to add the item

- `JMenuItem insert(Action a, int index)`
  adds a new menu item at a specific index and associates an action with it.

  Parameters: `a`   An action encapsulating a name, optional icon, and listener

                  `index`   Where to add the item

- `void insertSeparator(int index)`
  adds a separator to the menu.

  Parameters: `index`   Where to add the separator

- `void remove(int index)`
  removes a specific item from the menu.

  Parameters: `index`   The position of the item to remove

- `void remove(JMenuItem item)`
  removes a specific item from the menu.

  Parameters: `item`   The item to remove

`javax.swing.JMenuItem`

- `JMenuItem(String label)`

  Parameters: `label`   The label for this menu item

- `JMenuItem(Action a)`

  Parameters: `a`   An action encapsulating a name, optional icon, and listener

---

`javax.swing.AbstractButton`

- `void setAction(Action a)`

  Parameters: `a`   An action encapsulating a name, optional icon, and listener

---

`javax.swing.JFrame`

- `void setJMenuBar(JMenuBar menubar)`
  sets the menu bar for this frame.

Icons in Menu Items

Menu items are very similar to buttons. In fact, the `JMenuItem` class extends the `AbstractButton` class. Just like buttons, menus can have just a text label, just an icon, or both. You can specify the icon with the `JMenuItem(String, Icon)` or `JMenuItem(Icon)` constructor, or you can set it with the `setIcon` method that the `JMenuItem` class inherits from the `AbstractButton` class. Here is an example:

```
JMenuItem cutItem = new JMenuItem("Cut", new ImageIcon("cut.gif"));
```

Figure 9–20 shows a menu with icons next to several menu items. As you can see, by default, the menu items are placed to the right of the menu text. If you prefer the icon to be placed on the right, call the `setHorizontalTextPosition` method that the `JMenuItem` class inherits from the `AbstractButton` class. For example, the call

```
cutItem.setHorizontalTextPosition(SwingConstants.RIGHT);
```

moves the menu item text to the right of the icon.

You can also add an icon to an action:

```
cutAction.putValue(Action.SMALL_ICON, new ImageIcon("cut.gif"));
```

Whenever you construct a menu item out of an action, the `Action.NAME` value becomes the text of the menu item, and the `Action.SMALL_ICON` value becomes the icon.

Alternatively, you can set the icon in the `AbstractAction` constructor:

```
cutAction = new
   AbstractAction("Cut", new ImageIcon("cut.gif"))
   {
      public void actionPerformed(ActionEvent event)
      {
         // action code goes here
      }
   };
```

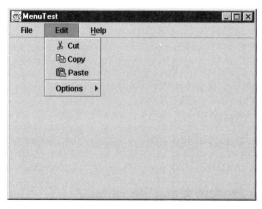

Figure 9–20: Icons in menu items

---

javax.swing.JMenuItem

- JMenuItem(String label, Icon icon)

    Parameters: label   The label for the menu item

                         icon   The icon for the menu item

---

javax.swing.AbstractButton

- void setHorizontalTextPosition(int pos)

    sets the horizontal position of the text relative to the icon.

    Parameters: pos   SwingConstants.RIGHT (text is to the right of icon) or SwingConstants.LEFT

---

javax.swing.AbstractAction

- AbstractAction(String name, Icon smallIcon)

    Parameters: name   the label for the action

                         smallIcon   the small icon for the action

Check Box and Radio Button Menu Items

Check box and *radio button* menu items display a check box or radio button next to the name (see Figure 9–21). When the user selects the menu item, the item automatically toggles between checked and unchecked.

Apart from the button decoration, you treat these menu items just as you would any others. For example, here is how you create a check box menu item.

```
JCheckBoxMenuItem readonlyItem
    = new JCheckBoxMenuItem("Read-only");
optionsMenu.add(readonlyItem);
```

The radio button menu items work just like regular radio buttons. You must add them to a button group. When one of the buttons in a group is selected, all others are automatically deselected.

```
ButtonGroup group = new ButtonGroup();
JRadioButtonMenuItem insertItem
    = new JRadioButtonMenuItem("Insert");
insertItem.setSelected(true);
JRadioButtonMenuItem overtypeItem
    = new JRadioButtonMenuItem("Overtype");
group.add(insertItem);
group.add(overtypeItem);
optionsMenu.add(insertItem);
optionsMenu.add(overtypeItem);
```

With these menu items, you don't necessarily want to be notified at the exact moment the user selects the item. Instead, you can simply use the `isSelected` method to test the current state of the menu item. (Of course, that means that you should keep a reference to the menu item stored in an instance variable.) Use the `setSelected` method to set the state.

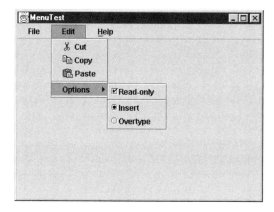

Figure 9–21: A checked menu item and menu items with radio buttons

javax.swing.JCheckBoxMenuItem

- `JCheckBoxMenuItem(String label)`
  constructs the check box menu item with the given label.
- `JCheckBoxMenuItem(String label, boolean state)`
  constructs the check box menu item with the given label and the given initial state (`true` is checked).

javax.swing.JRadioButtonMenuItem

- `JRadioButtonMenuItem(String label)`
  constructs the radio button menu item with the given label.
- `JRadioButtonMenuItem(String label, boolean state)`
  constructs the radio button menu item with the given label and the given initial state (`true` is checked).

javax.swing.AbstractButton

- `boolean isSelected()`
  returns the check state of this item (`true` is checked).
- `void setSelected(boolean state)`
  sets the check state of this item.

Pop-up Menus

A *pop-up menu* is a menu that is not attached to a menu bar but that floats some-where (see Figure 9–22).

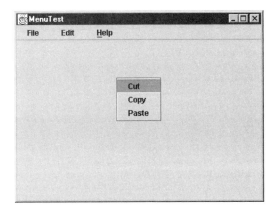

Figure 9–22: A pop-up menu

You create a pop-up menu similarly to the way you create a regular menu, but a pop-up menu has no title.

```
JPopupMenu popup = new JPopupMenu();
```

You then add menu items in the usual way:

```
JMenuItem item = new JMenuItem("Cut");
item.addActionListener(listener);
popup.add(item);
```

Unlike the regular menu bar that is always shown at the top of the frame, you must explicitly display a pop-up menu by using the show method. You specify the parent component and the location of the pop-up, using the coordinate system of the parent. For example:

```
popup.show(panel, x, y);
```

Usually you write code to pop up a menu when the user clicks a particular mouse button, the so-called *pop-up trigger*. In Windows, the pop-up trigger is the nonpri-mary (usually, the right) mouse button. To pop up a menu when the user clicks the pop-up trigger:

1.   Install a mouse listener.

2.   Add code like the following to the mouse listener:

```
public void mouseReleased(MouseEvent event)
{
    if (event.isPopupTrigger())
```

```
        popup.show(event.getComponent(),
            event.getX(), event.getY());
    }
```

This code will show the pop-up menu at the mouse location where the user clicked the pop-up trigger.

 CAUTION: With our version of the SDK, the `isPopupTrigger` method works correctly only in the `mouseReleased` method, not in the `mousePressed` or `mouse-Clicked` method.

 javax.swing.JPopupMenu

- `void show(Component c, int x, int y)`
  shows the pop-up menu.

  | *Parameters:* | c | The component over which the pop-up menu is to appear |
  | | x, y | The coordinates (in the coordinate space of c) of the top-left corner of the pop-up menu |

- `boolean isPopupTrigger(MouseEvent event)`
  returns `true` if the mouse event is the pop-up menu trigger.

 java.awt.event.MouseEvent

- `boolean isPopupTrigger()`
  returns `true` if this mouse event is the pop-up menu trigger.

Keyboard Mnemonics and Accelerators

It is a real convenience for the experienced user to select menu items by *keyboard mnemonics*. In Java, you can specify keyboard mnemonics for menu items by specifying a mnemonic letter in the menu item constructor:

```
JMenuItem cutItem = new JMenuItem("Cut", 'T');
```

The keyboard mnemonic is displayed automatically in the menu, by underlining the mnemonic letter (see Figure 9–23). For example, in the item defined in the last example, the label will be displayed as "Cu<u>t</u>" with an underlined letter "t". When the menu is displayed, the user just needs to press the "T" key, and the menu item is selected. (If the mnemonic letter is not part of the menu string, then typing it still selects the item, but the mnemonic is not displayed in the menu. Naturally, such invisible mnemonics are of dubious utility.)

If you have an `Action` object, you can add the mnemonic as the value of the
`Action.MNEMONIC_KEY` key, as follows:

```
cutAction.putValue(Action.MNEMONIC_KEY, new Integer('T'));
```

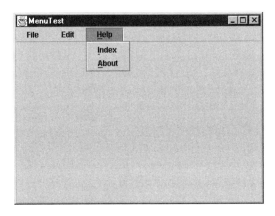

Figure 9–23: Keyboard mnemonics

You can only supply a mnemonic letter in the constructor of a menu item, not in
the constructor for a menu. Instead, to attach a mnemonic to a menu, you need to
call the `setMnemonic` method:

```
JMenu helpMenu = new JMenu("Help");
helpMenu.setMnemonic('H');
```

To select a top-level menu from the menu bar, you press the ALT key together with
the mnemonic letter. For example, you press ALT+H to select the Help menu from
the menu bar.

Keyboard mnemonics let you select a submenu or menu item from the currently
open menu. In contrast, *accelerators* are keyboard shortcuts that let you select
menu items without ever opening a menu. For example, many programs attach
the accelerators CTRL+O and CTRL+S to the Open and Save items in the File menu.
You use the `setAccelerator` method to attach an accelerator key to a menu
item. The `setAccelerator` method takes an object of type `Keystroke`. For
example, the following call attaches the accelerator CTRL+O to the `openItem`
menu item.

```
openItem.setAccelerator(KeyStroke.getKeyStroke(KeyEvent.VK_O,
    InputEvent.CTRL_MASK));
```

When the user presses the accelerator key combination, this automatically selects
the menu option and fires an action event, as if the user had selected the menu
option manually.

You can attach accelerators only to menu items, not to menus. Accelerator keys don't actually open the menu. Instead, they directly fire the action event that is associated with a menu.

Conceptually, adding an accelerator to a menu item is similar to the technique of adding an accelerator to a Swing component. (We discussed that technique in Chapter 8.) However, when the accelerator is added to a menu item, the key combination is automatically displayed in the menu (see Figure 9–24).

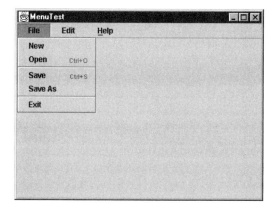

Figure 9–24: Accelerators

 CAUTION: `Action` objects can have a keystroke value associated with the `Action.ACCELERATOR_KEY` key. However, the `JMenuItem(Action)` constructor ignores that keystroke.

 NOTE: Under Windows, ALT+F4 closes a window. But this is not an accelerator that was programmed in Java. It is a shortcut defined by the operating system. This key combination will always trigger the `WindowClosing` event for the active window regardless of whether there is a Close item on the menu.

 `javax.swing.JMenuItem`

• `JMenuItem(String label, int mnemonic)`.

| *Parameters:* | `label` | The label for this menu item |
| | `mnemonic` | The mnemonic character for the item; this character will be underlined in the label |

- `void setAccelerator(KeyStroke k)`

  sets the keystroke `k` as accelerator for this menu item. The accelerator key is displayed next to the label.

`javax.swing.AbstractButton`

- `void setMnemonic(char mnemonic)`

  sets the mnemonic character for the button. This character will be underlined in the label.

  Parameters: `mnemonic`   The mnemonic character for the button

Enabling and Disabling Menu Items

Occasionally, a particular menu item should be selected only in certain contexts. For example, when a document is opened for reading only, then the Save menu item is not meaningful. Of course, we could remove the item from the menu with the `JMenu.remove` method, but users would react with some surprise to menus whose contents keeps changing. Instead, it is better to deactivate the menu items that lead to temporarily inappropriate commands. A deactivated menu item is shown in gray, and it cannot be selected (see Figure 9–25).

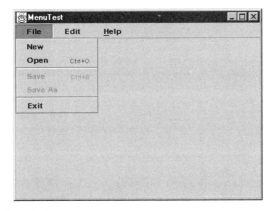

Figure 9–25: Disabled menu items

To enable or disable a menu item, use the `setEnabled` method:

```
saveItem.setEnabled(false);
```

There are two strategies for enabling and disabling menu items. Each time circumstances change, you can call `setEnabled` on the relevant menu items. For example, as soon as a document has been set to read-only mode, you can locate the Save and Save As menu items and disable them. However, if you use that strategy, you may find that your code gets cluttered up with menu management in many places. A smarter strategy is not to worry about the menu item states in the remainder of the program and to set them *just before displaying the menu.* To do this, you must register a listener for the "menu selected" event. The `javax.swing.event` package defines a `MenuListener` interface with three methods:

```
void menuSelected(MenuEvent evt)
void menuDeselected(MenuEvent evt)
void menuCanceled(MenuEvent evt)
```

The `menuSelected` method is called *before* the menu is displayed. It is therefore the perfect place to disable or enable menu items. The following code shows how to disable the Save and Save As menu items whenever the Read Only check box menu item is selected:

```
public void menuSelected(MenuEvent evt)
{
    saveItem.setEnabled(!readonlyItem.isSelected());
    saveAsItem.setEnabled(!readonlyItem.isSelected());
}
```

The `menuDeselected` method is called after the menu is again removed from the display. The `menuCanceled` method is called if the menu selection process is canceled, for example, by clicking with the mouse somewhere outside the menu. We are not interested in either of these two events, but there is no `MenuAdapter` class that allows us to override a single method, so we must define the latter two to do nothing.

`javax.swing.JMenuItem`

- `void setEnabled(boolean b)`
  enables or disables the menu item.

`javax.swing.event.MenuListener`

- `void menuSelected(MenuEvent e)`
  is called when the menu has been selected, before it is opened.
- `void menuDeselected(MenuEvent e)`
  is called when the menu has been deselected, after it has been closed.
- `void menuCanceled(MenuEvent e)`
  is called when the menu has been canceled, for example, by clicking outside the menu.

Example 9–10 is a sample program that generates a set of menus. It shows all the features that we saw in this section: nested menus, disabled menu items, check box and radio button menu items, a pop-up menu, and keyboard mnemonics and accelerators.

Example 9–10: MenuTest.java

```
1. import java.awt.*;
2. import java.awt.event.*;
```

```
3. import javax.swing.*;
4. import javax.swing.event.*;
5.
6. public class MenuTest
7. {
8.    public static void main(String[] args)
9.    {
10.       MenuFrame frame = new MenuFrame();
11.       frame.setDefaultCloseOperation(JFrame.EXIT_ON_CLOSE);
12.       frame.show();
13.    }
14. }
15.
16. /**
17.    A frame with a sample menu bar.
18. */
19. class MenuFrame extends JFrame
20. {
21.    public MenuFrame()
22.    {
23.       setTitle("MenuTest");
24.       setSize(WIDTH, HEIGHT);
25.
26.       JMenu fileMenu = new JMenu("File");
27.       JMenuItem newItem = fileMenu.add(new TestAction("New"));
28.
29.       // demonstrate accelerators
30.
31.       JMenuItem openItem = fileMenu.add(new TestAction("Open"));
32.       openItem.setAccelerator(KeyStroke.getKeyStroke(
33.          KeyEvent.VK_O, InputEvent.CTRL_MASK));
34.
35.       fileMenu.addSeparator();
36.
37.       saveItem = fileMenu.add(new TestAction("Save"));
38.       saveItem.setAccelerator(KeyStroke.getKeyStroke(
39.          KeyEvent.VK_S, InputEvent.CTRL_MASK));
40.
41.       saveAsItem = fileMenu.add(new TestAction("Save As"));
42.       fileMenu.addSeparator();
43.
44.       fileMenu.add(new
45.          AbstractAction("Exit")
46.          {
47.             public void actionPerformed(ActionEvent event)
48.             {
49.                System.exit(0);
50.             }
51.          });
52.
53.       // demonstrate enabled/disabled items
```

```
54.
55.        fileMenu.addMenuListener(new FileMenuListener());
56.
57.        // demonstrate check box and radio button menus
58.
59.        readonlyItem = new JCheckBoxMenuItem("Read-only");
60.
61.        ButtonGroup group = new ButtonGroup();
62.
63.        JRadioButtonMenuItem insertItem
64.           = new JRadioButtonMenuItem("Insert");
65.        insertItem.setSelected(true);
66.        JRadioButtonMenuItem overtypeItem
67.           = new JRadioButtonMenuItem("Overtype");
68.
69.        group.add(insertItem);
70.        group.add(overtypeItem);
71.
72.        // demonstrate icons
73.
74.        Action cutAction = new TestAction("Cut");
75.        cutAction.putValue(Action.SMALL_ICON,
76.           new ImageIcon("cut.gif"));
77.        Action copyAction = new TestAction("Copy");
78.        copyAction.putValue(Action.SMALL_ICON,
79.           new ImageIcon("copy.gif"));
80.        Action pasteAction = new TestAction("Paste");
81.        pasteAction.putValue(Action.SMALL_ICON,
82.           new ImageIcon("paste.gif"));
83.
84.        JMenu editMenu = new JMenu("Edit");
85.        editMenu.add(cutAction);
86.        editMenu.add(copyAction);
87.        editMenu.add(pasteAction);
88.
89.        // demonstrate nested menus
90.
91.        JMenu optionMenu = new JMenu("Options");
92.
93.        optionMenu.add(readonlyItem);
94.        optionMenu.addSeparator();
95.        optionMenu.add(insertItem);
96.        optionMenu.add(overtypeItem);
97.
98.        editMenu.addSeparator();
99.        editMenu.add(optionMenu);
100.
101.        // demonstrate mnemonics
102.
103.        JMenu helpMenu = new JMenu("Help");
104.        helpMenu.setMnemonic('H');
```

```
105.
106.        JMenuItem indexItem = new JMenuItem("Index");
107.        indexItem.setMnemonic('I');
108.        helpMenu.add(indexItem);
109.
110.        // you can also add the mnemonic key to an action
111.        Action aboutAction = new TestAction("About");
112.        aboutAction.putValue(Action.MNEMONIC_KEY,
113.           new Integer('A'));
114.        helpMenu.add(aboutAction);
115.
116.        // add all top-level menus to menu bar
117.
118.        JMenuBar menuBar = new JMenuBar();
119.        setJMenuBar(menuBar);
120.
121.        menuBar.add(fileMenu);
122.        menuBar.add(editMenu);
123.        menuBar.add(helpMenu);
124.
125.        // demonstrate pop-ups
126.
127.        popup = new JPopupMenu();
128.        popup.add(cutAction);
129.        popup.add(copyAction);
130.        popup.add(pasteAction);
131.
132.        getContentPane().addMouseListener(new
133.           MouseAdapter()
134.           {
135.              public void mouseReleased(MouseEvent event)
136.              {
137.                 if (event.isPopupTrigger())
138.                    popup.show(event.getComponent(),
139.                       event.getX(), event.getY());
140.              }
141.           });
142.    }
143.
144.    public static final int WIDTH = 300;
145.    public static final int HEIGHT = 200;
146.
147.    private JMenuItem saveItem;
148.    private JMenuItem saveAsItem;
149.    private JCheckBoxMenuItem readonlyItem;
150.    private JPopupMenu popup;
151.
152.    /**
153.       updates the state of the file menu. The Save
154.       menu option is disabled if the document is read only
155.    */
```

```
156.    private class FileMenuListener implements MenuListener
157.    {
158.       public void menuSelected(MenuEvent evt)
159.       {
160.          saveItem.setEnabled(!readonlyItem.isSelected());
161.          saveAsItem.setEnabled(!readonlyItem.isSelected());
162.       }
163.
164.       public void menuDeselected(MenuEvent evt) {}
165.
166.       public void menuCanceled(MenuEvent evt) {}
167.    }
168. }
169.
170. /**
171.    A sample action that prints the action name to System.out
172. */
173. class TestAction extends AbstractAction
174. {
175.    public TestAction(String name) { super(name); }
176.
177.    public void actionPerformed(ActionEvent event)
178.    {
179.       System.out.println(getValue(Action.NAME)
180.          + " selected.");
181.    }
182. }
```

Tool Bars

A tool bar is a button bar that gives quick access to the most commonly used commands in a program (see Figure 9–26).

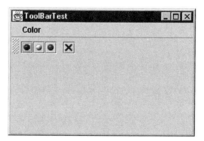

Figure 9–26: A tool bar

What makes tool bars special is that you can move them elsewhere. You can drag the tool bar to one of the four borders of the frame (see Figure 9–27). When you release the mouse button, the tool bar is dropped into the new location (see Figure 9–28).

NOTE: Tool bar dragging works if the tool bar is inside a container with a border layout, or any other layout manager that supports the `North`, `East`, `South`, and `West` constraints.

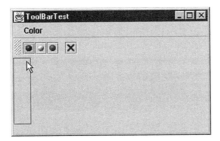

Figure 9–27: Dragging the tool bar

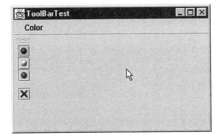

Figure 9–28: Dragging the tool bar to another border

The tool bar can even be completely detached from the frame. A detached tool bar is contained in its own frame (see Figure 9–29). When you close the frame containing a detached tool bar, the tool bar jumps back into the original frame.

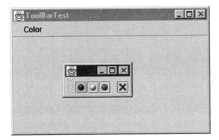

Figure 9–29: Detaching the tool bar

Tool bars are straightforward to program. You add components into the tool bar:

```
JToolBar bar = new JToolBar();
bar.add(blueButton);
```

The `JToolBar` class also has a method to add an `Action` object. Simply populate the tool bar with `Action` objects, like this:

```
bar.add(blueAction);
```

The small icon of the action is displayed in the tool bar.

> CAUTION: In J2SE version 1.2, the name of the action shows up on the tool bar, which makes the button far too large. Therefore, you cannot share an `Action` object between a menu and a toolbar in J2SE version 1.2. This problem has been fixed in version 1.3.

You can separate groups of buttons with a separator:

```
bar.addSeparator();
```

For example, the tool bar in Figure 9–26 has a separator between the third and fourth button.

Then, you add the tool bar to the container.

```
contentPane.add(bar, BorderLayout.NORTH);
```

You can also specify a title for the toolbar that appears when the toolbar is undocked:

```
bar = new JToolBar(titleString);
```

By default, toolbars are initially horizontal. To have a toolbar start out as vertical, use

```
bar = new JToolBar(SwingConstants.VERTICAL)
```

or

```
bar = new JToolBar(titleString, SwingConstants.VERTICAL)
```

Buttons are the most common components inside toolbars. But there is no restriction on the components that you can add to a tool bar. For example, you can add a combo box to a tool bar.

Tool Tips

A disadvantage of tool bars is that users are often mystified by the meanings of the tiny icons in tool bars. To solve this problem, *tool tips* were invented. A tool tip is activated when the cursor rests for a moment over a button. The tool tip text is displayed inside a colored rectangle. When the user moves the mouse away, the tool tip is removed.

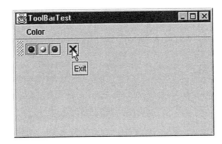

Figure 9–30: A tool tip

In Swing, you can add tool tips to any `JComponent` simply by calling the `setToolTipText` method:

```
exitButton.setToolTipText("Exit");
```

Alternatively, if you use `Action` objects, you associate the tool tip with the `SHORT_DESCRIPTION` key:

```
exitAction.putValue(Action.SHORT_DESCRIPTION, "Exit");
```

Example 9–11 is a program that shows how the same `Action` objects can be added to a menu and a tool bar. Note that the action names show up as the menu item names in the menu, and as the tool tips in the tool bar.

Example 9–11: ToolBarTest.java

```
 1. import java.awt.*;
 2. import java.awt.event.*;
 3. import java.beans.*;
 4. import javax.swing.*;
 5.
 6. public class ToolBarTest
 7. {
 8.    public static void main(String[] args)
 9.    {
10.       ToolBarFrame frame = new ToolBarFrame();
11.       frame.setDefaultCloseOperation(JFrame.EXIT_ON_CLOSE);
12.       frame.show();
13.    }
14. }
15.
16. /**
17.    A frame with a toolbar and menu for color changes.
18. */
19. class ToolBarFrame extends JFrame
20. {
21.    public ToolBarFrame()
```

```
22.    {
23.       setTitle("ToolBarTest");
24.       setSize(WIDTH, HEIGHT);
25.
26.       // add a panel for color change
27.
28.       Container contentPane = getContentPane();
29.       panel = new JPanel();
30.       contentPane.add(panel, BorderLayout.CENTER);
31.
32.       // set up actions
33.
34.       Action blueAction = new ColorAction("Blue",
35.          new ImageIcon("blue-ball.gif"), Color.blue);
36.       Action yellowAction = new ColorAction("Yellow",
37.          new ImageIcon("yellow-ball.gif"), Color.yellow);
38.       Action redAction = new ColorAction("Red",
39.          new ImageIcon("red-ball.gif"), Color.red);
40.
41.       Action exitAction = new
42.          AbstractAction("Exit", new ImageIcon("exit.gif"))
43.          {
44.             public void actionPerformed(ActionEvent event)
45.             {
46.                System.exit(0);
47.             }
48.          };
49.       exitAction.putValue(Action.SHORT_DESCRIPTION, "Exit");
50.
51.       // populate tool bar
52.
53.       JToolBar bar = new JToolBar();
54.       bar.add(blueAction);
55.       bar.add(yellowAction);
56.       bar.add(redAction);
57.       bar.addSeparator();
58.       bar.add(exitAction);
59.       contentPane.add(bar, BorderLayout.NORTH);
60.
61.       // populate menu
62.
63.       JMenu menu = new JMenu("Color");
64.       menu.add(yellowAction);
65.       menu.add(blueAction);
66.       menu.add(redAction);
67.       menu.add(exitAction);
68.       JMenuBar menuBar = new JMenuBar();
69.       menuBar.add(menu);
70.       setJMenuBar(menuBar);
```

```
71.      }
72.
73.      public static final int WIDTH = 300;
74.      public static final int HEIGHT = 200;
75.
76.      private JPanel panel;
77.
78.      /**
79.         The color action sets the background of the frame to a
80.         given color.
81.      */
82.      class ColorAction extends AbstractAction
83.      {
84.         public ColorAction(String name, Icon icon, Color c)
85.         {
86.            putValue(Action.NAME, name);
87.            putValue(Action.SMALL_ICON, icon);
88.            putValue(Action.SHORT_DESCRIPTION,
89.               name + " background");
90.            putValue("Color", c);
91.         }
92.
93.         public void actionPerformed(ActionEvent evt)
94.         {
95.            Color c = (Color)getValue("Color");
96.            panel.setBackground(c);
97.            panel.repaint();
98.         }
99.      }
100. }
```

---

javax.swing.JToolBar

- `JToolBar()`
- `JToolBar(String titleString)`
- `JToolBar(int orientation)`
- `JToolBar(String titleString, int orientation)`

  construct a tool bar with the given title string and orientation. `orientation` is one of `SwingConstants.HORIZONTAL` (the default) and `SwingConstants.VERTICAL`.

- `JButton add(Action a)`

  constructs a new button inside the tool bar with name, icon, and action callback from the given action, and adds the button to the end of the tool bar.

- `void addSeparator()`

  adds a separator to the end of the tool bar.

javax.swing.JComponent

- void setToolTipText(String text)

  sets the text that should be displayed as a tool tip when the mouse hovers over the component.

Sophisticated Layout Management

We have managed to lay out the user interface components of our sample applications so far by using only the border layout and flow layout. For more complex tasks, this is not going to be enough. In this section, we will give you a detailed discussion of all the layout managers that the standard Java library provides to organize components.

Windows programmers may well wonder why Java makes so much fuss about layout managers. After all, in Windows, layout management is not a big deal: First, you use a dialog editor to drag and drop your components onto the surface of the dialog, and then you use editor tools to line up components, to space them equally, to center them, and so on. If you are working on a big project, you probably don't have to worry about component layout at all—a skilled user interface designer does all this for you.

The problem with this approach is that the resulting layout must be manually updated if the size of the components changes. Why would the component size change? There are two common cases. First, a user may choose a larger font for button labels and other dialog text. If you try this out for yourself in Windows, you will find that many applications deal with this exceedingly poorly. The buttons do not grow, and the larger font is simply crammed into the same space as before. The same problem can occur when translating the strings in an application to a foreign language. For example, the German word for "Cancel" is "Abbrechen." If a button has been designed with just enough room for the string "Cancel," then the German version will look broken, with a clipped command string.

Why don't Windows buttons simply grow to accommodate the labels? Because the designer of the user interface gave no instructions in which direction they should grow. After the dragging and dropping and arranging, the dialog editor merely remembers the pixel position and size of each component. It does not remember *why* the components were arranged in this fashion.

The Java layout managers are a much better approach to component layout. With a layout manager, the layout comes with instructions about the relationships between the components. This was particularly important in the original AWT, which used native user interface elements. The size of a button or list box in Motif, Windows, and the Macintosh could vary widely, and an application or applet would not know *a priori* on which platform it would display its user interface. To some extent, that degree of variability has gone away with Swing. If your application forces a particular look and feel, such as the Metal look and feel, then it looks identical on all platforms. However, if you let users of your application choose their favorite look and feel, then you again need to rely on the flexibility of layout managers to arrange the components.

Of course, to achieve complex layouts, you will need to have more control over the layout than the border layout and flow layout give you. In this section, we will discuss the layout managers that the standard Java library has to offer. Using a sophisticated layout manager combined with the appropriate use of multiple panels will give you complete control over how your application will look.

TIP: If none of the layout schemes fit your needs, break the surface of your window into separate panels and lay out each panel separately. Then, use another layout manager to organize the panels.

First, let's review a few basic principles. As you know, in the AWT, *components* are laid out inside *containers*. Buttons, text fields, and other user interface elements are components and can be placed inside containers. Therefore, these classes extend the class `Component`. Containers such as panels can themselves be put inside other containers. Therefore, the class `Container` derives from `Component`. Figure 9–31 shows the inheritance hierarchy for `Component`.

NOTE: Note that some objects belong to classes extending `Component` even though they are not user interface components and cannot be inserted into containers. Top-level windows such as `JFrame` and `JApplet` cannot be contained inside another window or panel.

As you have seen, to organize the components in a container, you first specify a layout manager. For example, the statement

```
panel.setLayout(new GridLayout(4, 4));
```

will use the `GridLayout` class to lay out the panels. After you set the layout manager, you add components to the container. The `add` method of the container passes the component and any placement directions to the layout manager.

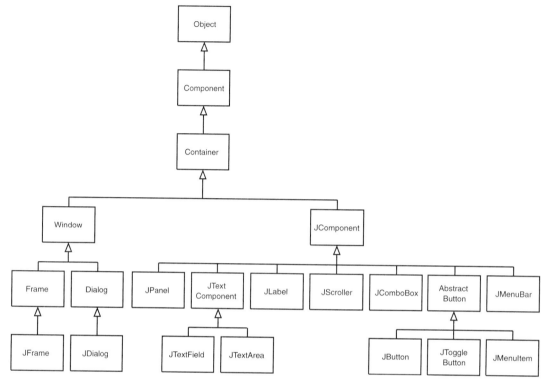

Figure 9–31: Inheritance hierarchy for the `Component` **class**

With the border layout manager, you give a string to indicate component placement:

```
panel.add(new JTextField(), BorderLayout.SOUTH);
```

With the grid layout that you will see shortly, you need to add components sequentially:

```
panel.add(new JCheckBox("italic"));
panel.add(new JCheckBox("bold"));
```

The grid layout is useful to arrange components in a grid, somewhat like the rows and columns of a spreadsheet. However, all rows and columns of the grid have *identical* size, which is not all that useful in practice.

To overcome the limitations of the grid layout, the AWT supplies the *grid bag layout*. It, too, lays out components in rows and columns, but the row and column sizes are flexible, and components can span multiple rows and columns. This layout manager is very flexible, but it is also very complex. The mere mention of the words "grid bag layout" has been known to strike fear in the hearts of Java programmers. Actually, in most common situations, the grid bag layout is not that hard to use, and we tell you a strategy that should make grid bag layouts relatively painless.

In an (unsuccessful) attempt to design a layout manager that would free programmers from the tyranny of the grid bag layout, the Swing designers came up with the *box layout*. The box layout simply arranges a sequence of components horizontally or vertically. When arranging components horizontally, it is similar to the flow layout; however, components do not "wrap" to a new row when one row is full. By placing a number of horizontal box layouts inside a vertical box layout (or the other way around), you can give some order to a set of components in a two-dimensional area. However, since each box is laid out independently, you cannot use box layouts to arrange neighboring components both horizontally and vertically.

The Swing set also contains an *overlay layout* that lets you place components on top of each other. This layout manager is not generally useful, and we won't discuss it.

Finally, there is a *card layout* that was used in the original AWT to produce tabbed dialogs. Since Swing has a much better tabbed dialog container (called `JTabbedPane`—see Volume 2), we do not cover the card layout here.

We end the discussion of layout managers by showing you how you can bypass layout management altogether and place components manually, and by showing you how you can write your own layout manager.

Grid Layout

The grid layout arranges all components in rows and columns like a spreadsheet. However, for a grid layout, cells are always the same size. The calculator program in Figure 9–32 uses a grid layout to arrange the calculator buttons. When you resize the window, the buttons grow and shrink, but all buttons have identical sizes.

Figure 9–32: A calculator

In the constructor of the grid layout object, you specify how many rows and columns you need.

```
panel.setLayout(new GridLayout(5, 4));
```

As with the border layout and flow layout managers, you can also specify the vertical and horizontal gaps you want.

```
panel.setLayout(new GridLayout(5, 4, 3, 3));
```

The last two parameters of this constructor specify the size of the horizontal and vertical gaps (in pixels) between the components.

You add the components, starting with the first entry in the first row, then the second entry in the first row, and so on.

```
panel.add(new JButton("1"));
panel.add(new JButton("2"));
```

Example 9–12 is the source listing for the calculator program. This is a regular calculator, not the "reverse Polish" variety that is so oddly popular in Java tutorials.

Example 9–12: Calculator.java

```
1. import java.awt.*;
2. import java.awt.event.*;
3. import javax.swing.*;
4.
5. public class Calculator
6. {
7.    public static void main(String[] args)
8.    {
9.       CalculatorFrame frame = new CalculatorFrame();
10.       frame.setDefaultCloseOperation(JFrame.EXIT_ON_CLOSE);
11.       frame.show();
12.    }
13. }
14.
15. /**
16.    A frame with a calculator panel.
17. */
18. class CalculatorFrame extends JFrame
19. {
20.    public CalculatorFrame()
21.    {
22.       setTitle("Calculator");
23.       setSize(WIDTH, HEIGHT);
24.
25.       Container contentPane = getContentPane();
26.       CalculatorPanel panel = new CalculatorPanel();
```

```
27.        contentPane.add(panel);
28.    }
29.
30.    public static final int WIDTH = 200;
31.    public static final int HEIGHT = 200;
32. }
33.
34.
35. /**
36.    A panel with calculator buttons and a result display.
37. */
38. class CalculatorPanel extends JPanel
39. {
40.    public CalculatorPanel()
41.    {
42.        setLayout(new BorderLayout());
43.
44.        result = 0;
45.        lastCommand = "=";
46.        start = true;
47.
48.        // add the display
49.
50.        display = new JTextField("0");
51.        display.setEditable(false);
52.        add(display, BorderLayout.NORTH);
53.
54.        ActionListener insert = new InsertAction();
55.        ActionListener command = new CommandAction();
56.
57.        // add the buttons in a 4 x 4 grid
58.
59.        panel = new JPanel();
60.        panel.setLayout(new GridLayout(4, 4));
61.
62.        addButton("7", insert);
63.        addButton("8", insert);
64.        addButton("9", insert);
65.        addButton("/", command);
66.
67.        addButton("4", insert);
68.        addButton("5", insert);
69.        addButton("6", insert);
70.        addButton("*", command);
71.
72.        addButton("1", insert);
73.        addButton("2", insert);
74.        addButton("3", insert);
```

```
75.        addButton("-", command);
76.
77.        addButton("0", insert);
78.        addButton(".", insert);
79.        addButton("=", command);
80.        addButton("+", command);
81.
82.        add(panel, BorderLayout.CENTER);
83.    }
84.
85.    /**
86.       Adds a button to the center panel.
87.       @param label the button label
88.       @param listener the button listener
89.    */
90.    private void addButton(String label, ActionListener listener)
91.    {
92.        JButton button = new JButton(label);
93.        button.addActionListener(listener);
94.        panel.add(button);
95.    }
96.
97.    /**
98.       This action inserts the button action string to the
99.       end of the display text.
100.   */
101.   private class InsertAction implements ActionListener
102.   {
103.       public void actionPerformed(ActionEvent event)
104.       {
105.           String input = event.getActionCommand();
106.           if (start)
107.           {
108.              display.setText("");
109.              start = false;
110.           }
111.           display.setText(display.getText() + input);
112.       }
113.   }
114.
115.   /**
116.      This action executes the command that the button
117.      action string denotes.
118.   */
119.   private class CommandAction implements ActionListener
120.   {
121.       public void actionPerformed(ActionEvent evt)
122.       {
```

```
123.        String command = evt.getActionCommand();
124.
125.        if (start)
126.        {
127.           if (command.equals("-"))
128.           {
129.              display.setText(command);
130.              start = false;
131.           }
132.           else
133.              lastCommand = command;
134.        }
135.        else
136.        {
137.           calculate(Double.parseDouble(display.getText()));
138.           lastCommand = command;
139.           start = true;
140.        }
141.     }
142.  }
143.
144.  /**
145.     Carries out the pending calculation.
146.     @param x the value to be accumulated with the prior result.
147.  */
148.  public void calculate(double x)
149.  {
150.     if (lastCommand.equals("+")) result += x;
151.     else if (lastCommand.equals("-")) result -= x;
152.     else if (lastCommand.equals("*")) result *= x;
153.     else if (lastCommand.equals("/")) result /= x;
154.     else if (lastCommand.equals("=")) result = x;
155.     display.setText("" + result);
156.  }
157.
158.  private JTextField display;
159.  private JPanel panel;
160.  private double result;
161.  private String lastCommand;
162.  private boolean start;
163. }
```

Of course, few applications have as rigid a layout as the face of a calculator. In practice, small grids (usually with just one row or one column) can be useful to organize partial areas of a window. For example, if you want to have a row of buttons with identical size, then you can put the buttons inside a panel that is governed by a grid layout with a single row. (You will need to set the gap size so that the buttons have some space between them.) But you will often find it inconvenient that each component in the grid is stretched to fill the entire cell and that all components are forced to have identical size. You can avoid these problems with the box layout that we describe next.

java.awt.GridLayout

• GridLayout(int rows, int cols)
  constructs a new GridLayout.

Parameters:	rows	The number of rows in the grid
	columns	The number of columns in the grid

• GridLayout(int rows, int columns, int hgap, int vgap)
  constructs a new GridLayout with horizontal and vertical gaps between components.

Parameters:	rows	The number of rows in the grid
	columns	The number of columns in the grid
	hgap	The horizontal gap to use in pixels (negative values force an overlap)
	vgap	The vertical gap to use in pixels (negative values force an overlap)

Box Layout

The box layout lets you lay out a single row or column of components with more flexibility than the grid layout. There is even a container—the Box class—whose default layout manager is the BoxLayout (unlike the JPanel class whose default layout manager is the FlowLayout). Of course, you can also set the layout manager of a JPanel to the box layout, but it is simpler to just start with a Box container. The Box class also contains a number of static methods that are useful for managing box layouts.

To create a new container with a box layout, you can simply call

```
Box b = Box.createHorizontalBox();
```

or

```
Box b = Box.createVerticalBox();
```

Then, you add components in the usual way:

```
b.add(okButton);
b.add(cancelButton);
```

In a horizontal box, the components are arranged left to right. In a vertical box, the components are arranged top to bottom. Let us look at the horizontal layout more closely.

Each component has three sizes:

*   The *preferred size* – the width and height at which the component would like to be displayed;
*   The *maximum size* – the largest width and height at which the component is willing to be displayed;
*   The *minimum size* – the smallest width and height at which the component is willing to be displayed.

Here are details about the box layout manager does:

1. It computes the maximum (!) height of the tallest component.

2. It tries to grow all components vertically to that height.

3. If a component does not actually grow to that height when requested, then its *y*-alignment is queried by calling its `getAlignmentY` method. That method returns a floating-point number between 0 (align on top) and 1 (align on bottom). The default in the `Component` class is 0.5 (center). The value is used to align the component vertically.

4. The preferred width of each component is obtained. All preferred widths are added up.

5. If the total preferred width is less than the box width, then the components are expanded, by letting them grow to their maximum width. Components are then placed, from left to right, with no additional space between them. If the total preferred width is greater than the box width, the components are shrunk, potentially down to their minimum width but no further. If the components don't all fit at their minimum width, some of them will not be shown.

For vertical layouts, the process is analogous.

TIP: It is unfortunate that `BoxLayout` tries to grow components beyond the preferred size. In particular, text fields have maximum width and height set to `Integer.MAX_VALUE`; that is, they are willing to grow as much as necessary. If you put a text field into a box layout, it will grow to monstrous proportions. Remedy: set the maximum size to the preferred size:

```
textField.setMaximumSize(textField.getPreferredSize());
```

Fillers

By default, there is no space between the components in a box layout. (Unlike the flow layout, the box layout does not have a notion of gaps between components.) To space the components out, you add invisible *fillers*. There are three kinds of fillers:

*   Struts;
*   Rigid areas;
*   Glue.

A strut simply adds some space between components. For example, here is how you can add ten pixels of space between two components in a horizontal box:

```
b.add(label);
b.add(Box.createHorizontalStrut(10));
b.add(textField);
```

You add a horizontal strut into a horizontal box, or a vertical strut into a vertical box, to add space between components. You can also add a vertical strut into a horizontal box, but that does not affect the horizontal layout. Instead, it sets the minimum height of the box.

The rigid area filler is similar to a pair of struts. It separates adjacent components but also adds a height or width minimum in the other direction. For example,

```
b.add(Box.createRigidArea(new Dimension(5, 20));
```

adds an invisible area with minimum, preferred, and maximum width of 5 pixels and height of 20 pixels, and centered alignment. If added into a horizontal box, it acts like a strut of width 5 and also forces the minimum height of the box to be 20 pixels.

By adding struts, you separate adjacent components by a fixed amount. Adding glue separates components *as much as possible*. The (invisible) glue expands to consume all available empty space, pushing the components away from each other. (We don't know why the designers of the box layout came up with the name "glue"—"spring" would have been a more appropriate name.)

For example, here is how you space apart two buttons in a box as much as possible:

```
b.add(button1);
b.add(Box.createGlue());
b.add(button2);
```

If the box contains no other components, then `button1` is moved all the way to the left and `button2` is moved all the way to the right.

The program in Example 9–13 arranges a set of labels, text fields, and buttons, using a set of horizontal and vertical box layouts. Each row is placed in a horizontal box. Struts separate the labels from the text fields. Glue pushes the two buttons away from each other. The three horizontal boxes are placed in a vertical box, with glue pushing the button box to the bottom (see Figure 9–33).

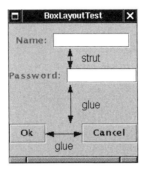

Figure 9–33: Box layouts

Example 9–13: BoxLayoutTest.java

```
1. import java.awt.*;
2. import java.awt.event.*;
3. import javax.swing.*;
4.
5. public class BoxLayoutTest
6. {
7.    public static void main(String[] args)
8.    {
9.       BoxLayoutFrame frame = new BoxLayoutFrame();
10.      frame.setDefaultCloseOperation(JFrame.EXIT_ON_CLOSE);
11.      frame.show();
12.   }
13. }
14.
15. /**
16.    A frame that uses box layouts to organize various components.
17. */
18. class BoxLayoutFrame extends JFrame
19. {
20.    public BoxLayoutFrame()
21.    {
22.       setTitle("BoxLayoutTest");
23.       setSize(WIDTH, HEIGHT);
24.
25.       // construct the top horizontal box
26.
27.       JLabel label1 = new JLabel("Name:");
28.       JTextField textField1 = new JTextField(10);
29.       textField1.setMaximumSize(textField1.getPreferredSize());
30.
31.       Box hbox1 = Box.createHorizontalBox();
32.       hbox1.add(label1);
```

```
33.        // separate with a 10-pixel strut
34.        hbox1.add(Box.createHorizontalStrut(10));
35.        hbox1.add(textField1);
36.
37.        // construct the middle horizontal box
38.
39.        JLabel label2 = new JLabel("Password:");
40.        JTextField textField2 = new JTextField(10);
41.        textField2.setMaximumSize(textField2.getPreferredSize());
42.
43.
44.        Box hbox2 = Box.createHorizontalBox();
45.        hbox2.add(label2);
46.        // separate with a 10-pixel strut
47.        hbox2.add(Box.createHorizontalStrut(10));
48.        hbox2.add(textField2);
49.
50.        // construct the bottom horizontal box
51.
52.        JButton button1 = new JButton("Ok");
53.        JButton button2 = new JButton("Cancel");
54.
55.        Box hbox3 = Box.createHorizontalBox();
56.        hbox3.add(button1);
57.        // use "glue" to push the two buttons apart
58.        hbox3.add(Box.createGlue());
59.        hbox3.add(button2);
60.
61.        // add the three horizontal boxes inside a vertical box
62.
63.        Box vbox = Box.createVerticalBox();
64.        vbox.add(hbox1);
65.        vbox.add(hbox2);
66.        vbox.add(Box.createGlue());
67.        vbox.add(hbox3);
68.
69.        Container contentPane = getContentPane();
70.        contentPane.add(vbox, BorderLayout.CENTER);
71.    }
72.
73.    public static final int WIDTH = 200;
74.    public static final int HEIGHT = 200;
75. }
```

 javax.swing.Box

- `static Box createHorizontalBox()`
- `static Box createVerticalBox()`

  create a container that arranges its contents horizontally or vertically.

- `static Component createHorizontalGlue()`
- `static Component createVerticalGlue()`

- `static Component createGlue()`

  create an invisible component that can expand infinitely horizontally, vertically, or in both directions.

- `static Component createHorizontalStrut(int width)`
- `static Component createVerticalStrut(int height)`
- `static Component createRigidArea(Dimension d)`

  create an invisible component with fixed width, fixed height, or fixed width and height.

`java.awt.Component`

- `float getAlignmentX()`
- `float getAlignmentY()`

  return the alignment along the *x*- or *y*-axis, a value between 0 and 1. The value 0 denotes alignment on top or left, 0.5 is centered, 1 is aligned on bottom or right.

Grid Bag Layout

The grid bag layout is the mother of all layout managers. You can think of a grid bag layout as a grid layout without the limitations. In a grid bag layout, the rows and columns can have variable sizes. You can join adjacent cells to make room for larger components. (Many word processors, as well as HTML, have the same capability when editing tables: you start out with a grid and then merge adjacent cells if need be.) The components need not fill the entire cell area, and you can specify their alignment within cells.

Fair warning: using grid bag layouts can be incredibly complex. The payoff is that they have the most flexibility and will work in the widest variety of situations. Keep in mind that the purpose of layout managers is to keep the arrangement of the components reasonable under different font sizes and operating systems, so it is not surprising that you need to work somewhat harder than when you design a layout just for one environment.

NOTE: According to the SDK documentation of the `BoxLayout` class: "Nesting multiple panels with different combinations of horizontal and vertical [*sic*] gives an effect similar to GridBagLayout, without the complexity." However, as you can see from Figure 9–33, the effect that you can achieve from multiple box layouts is plainly not useful in practice. No amount of fussing with boxes, struts, and glue will ensure that the components line up. When you need to arrange components so that they line up horizontally and vertically, you need to use the `GridBagLayout` class.

Consider the font selection dialog of Figure 9–34. It consists of the following components:

- Two combo boxes to specify the font face and size;
- Labels for these two combo boxes;
- Two check boxes to select bold and italic;
- A text area for the sample string.

Figure 9–34: Font dialog box

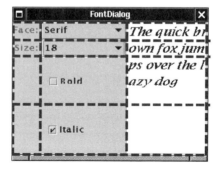

Figure 9–35: Dialog box grid used in design

Now, chop up the dialog box into a grid of cells, as shown in Figure 9–35. (The rows and columns do not need to have equal size.) As you can see, each check box spans two columns, and the text area spans four rows.

To describe the layout to the grid bag manager, you must go through the following convoluted procedure.

1. Create an object of type `GridBagLayout`. You don't tell it how many rows and columns the underlying grid has. Instead, the layout manager will try to guess it from the information you give it later.

2. Set this `GridBagLayout` object to be the layout manager for the component.

3. Create an object of type `GridBagConstraints`. The `GridBagConstraints` object will specify how the components are laid out within the grid bag.

4. For *each component*, fill in the `GridBagConstraints` object. Then (finally), add the component with the constraints by using the call:

```
add(component, constraints);
```

Here's an example of the code needed. (We will go over the various constraints in more detail in the sections that follow—so don't worry if you don't know what some of the constraints do.)

```
GridBagLayout layout = new GridBagLayout();
panel.setLayout(layout);
GridBagConstraints constraints = new GridBagConstraints();
constraints.weightx = 100;
constraints.weighty = 100;
constraints.gridx = 0;
constraints.gridy = 2;
constraints.gridwidth = 2;
constraints.gridheight = 1;
contentPane.add(style, bold);
```

It is obviously best to write a small helper function for this kind of repetitive code—see the listing in Example 9–13 for an example of one.

The trick is knowing how to set the state of the `GridBagConstraints` object. We will go over the most important constraints for using this object in the sections that follow.

The `gridx`, `gridy`, `gridwidth`, *and* `gridheight` *Parameters*

These constraints define where the component is located in the grid. The `gridx` and `gridy` values specify the column and row positions of the upper-left corner of the component to be added. The `gridwidth` and `gridheight` values determine how many columns and rows the component occupies.

The grid coordinates start with 0. In particular, `gridx = 0` and `gridy = 0` denotes the top left corner.

For example, the text area in our example has `gridx = 2`, `gridy = 0` because it starts in column 2 (that is, the third column) of row 0. It has `gridwidth = 1` and `gridheight = 4` because it spans one column and four rows.

Weight Fields

You always need to set the *weight* fields (`weightx` and `weighty`) for each area in a grid bag layout. If you set the weight to 0, then the area never grows or shrinks beyond its initial size in that direction. In the grid bag layout for Figure 9–34, we set the `weightx` field of the labels to be 0. This allows the labels to remain a constant width when you resize the window. On the other hand, if you set the weights for all areas to 0, the container will huddle in the center of its allotted area rather than stretching to fill it.

Conceptually, the problem with the weight parameters is that weights are properties of rows and columns, not individual cells. But you need to specify them in terms of cells, because the grid bag layout does not expose the rows and columns. The row and column weights are computed as the maxima of the cell weights in each row or column. Thus, if you want a row or column to stay at a fixed size, you need to set the weights of all components in it to zero.

Note that the weights don't actually give the relative sizes of the columns. They tell what proportion of the "slack" space should be allocated to each area if the container exceeds its preferred size. This isn't particularly intuitive. We recommend that you set all weights at 100. Then, run the program and see how the layout looks. Resize the dialog to see how the rows and columns adjust. If you find that a particular row or column should not grow, set the weights of all components in it to zero. You can tinker with other weight values, but it is usually not worth the effort.

The `fill` and `anchor` Parameters

If you don't want a component to stretch out and fill the entire area, you need to set the `fill` constraint. You have four possibilities for this parameter: the valid values are used in the forms `GridBagConstraints.NONE`, `GridBagConstraints.HORIZONTAL`, `GridBagConstraints.VERTICAL`, and `GridBagConstraints.BOTH`.

If the component does not fill the entire area, you can specify where in the area you want it by setting the `anchor` field. The valid values are `GridBagConstraints.CENTER` (the default), `GridBagConstraints.NORTH`, `GridBagConstraints.NORTHEAST`, `GridBagConstraints.EAST`, and so on.

Padding

You can surround a component with additional blank space by setting the `insets` field of the `GridBagLayout`. Set the `left`, `top`, `right` and `bottom` values of the `Insets` object to the amount of space that you want to have around the component. This is called the *external padding*.

The `ipadx` and `ipady` values set the *internal padding*. These values are added to the minimum width and height of the component. This ensures that the component does not shrink down to its minimum size.

An Alternative Method to Specify the `gridx`, `gridy`, `gridwidth`, *and* `gridheight` *Parameters*

The AWT documentation recommends that instead of setting the `gridx` and `gridy` values to absolute positions, you set them to the constant `GridBagConstraints.RELATIVE`. Then, add the components to the grid bag layout in a standardized order, going from left to right in the first row, then moving along the next row, and so on.

You still specify the number of rows and columns spanned, by giving the appropriate `gridheight` and `gridwidth` fields. Except, if the component extends to the *last* row or column, you aren't supposed to specify the actual number, but the constant `GridBagConstraints.REMAINDER`. This tells the layout manager that the component is the last one in its row.

This scheme does seem to work. But it sounds really goofy to hide the actual placement information from the layout manager and hope that it will rediscover it.

All this sounds like a lot of trouble and complexity. But in practice, the strategy in the following recipe makes grid bag layouts relatively trouble-free.

Recipe for Making a Grid Bag Layout

Step 1. Sketch out the component layout on a piece of paper.

Step 2. Find a grid such that the small components are each contained in a cell and the larger components span multiple cells.

Step 3. Label the rows and columns of your grid with 0, 1, 2, 3, . . . You can now read off the `gridx`, `gridy`, `gridwidth`, and `gridheight` values.

Step 4. For each component, ask yourself whether it needs to fill its cell horizontally or vertically. If not, how do you want it aligned? This tells you the `fill` and `anchor` parameters.

Step 5. Set all weights to 100. However, if you want a particular row or column to always stay at its default size, set the `weightx` or `weighty` to 0 in all components that belong to that row or column.

Step 6. Write the code. Carefully double-check your settings for the `GridBagConstraints`. One wrong constraint can ruin your whole layout.

Step 7. Compile, run, and enjoy.

Example 9–14 is the complete code to implement the font dialog example.

Example 9–14: FontDialog.java

```
1. import java.awt.*;
2. import java.awt.event.*;
3. import javax.swing.*;
```

```
4. import javax.swing.event.*;
5.
6. public class FontDialog
7. {
8.    public static void main(String[] args)
9.    {
10.       FontDialogFrame frame = new FontDialogFrame();
11.       frame.setDefaultCloseOperation(JFrame.EXIT_ON_CLOSE);
12.       frame.show();
13.    }
14. }
15.
16. /**
17.    A frame that uses a grid bag layout to arrange font
18.    selection components.
19. */
20. class FontDialogFrame extends JFrame
21. {
22.    public FontDialogFrame()
23.    {
24.       setTitle("FontDialog");
25.       setSize(WIDTH, HEIGHT);
26.
27.       Container contentPane = getContentPane();
28.       GridBagLayout layout = new GridBagLayout();
29.       contentPane.setLayout(layout);
30.
31.       ActionListener listener = new FontAction();
32.
33.       // construct components
34.
35.       JLabel faceLabel = new JLabel("Face: ");
36.
37.       face = new JComboBox(new String[]
38.          {
39.             "Serif", "SansSerif", "Monospaced",
40.             "Dialog", "DialogInput"
41.          });
42.
43.       face.addActionListener(listener);
44.
45.       JLabel sizeLabel = new JLabel("Size: ");
46.
47.       size = new JComboBox(new String[]
48.          {
49.             "8", "10", "12", "15", "18", "24", "36", "48"
50.          });
```

```
51.
52.       size.addActionListener(listener);
53.
54.       bold = new JCheckBox("Bold");
55.       bold.addActionListener(listener);
56.
57.       italic = new JCheckBox("Italic");
58.       italic.addActionListener(listener);
59.
60.       sample = new JTextArea();
61.       sample.setText(
62.          "The quick brown fox jumps over the lazy dog");
63.       sample.setEditable(false);
64.       sample.setLineWrap(true);
65.       sample.setBorder(BorderFactory.createEtchedBorder());
66.
67.       // add components to grid
68.
69.       GridBagConstraints constraints = new GridBagConstraints();
70.
71.       constraints.fill = GridBagConstraints.NONE;
72.       constraints.anchor = GridBagConstraints.EAST;
73.       constraints.weightx = 0;
74.       constraints.weighty = 0;
75.
76.       add(faceLabel, constraints, 0, 0, 1, 1);
77.       add(sizeLabel, constraints, 0, 1, 1, 1);
78.
79.       constraints.fill = GridBagConstraints.HORIZONTAL;
80.       constraints.weightx = 100;
81.
82.       add(face, constraints, 1, 0, 1, 1);
83.       add(size, constraints, 1, 1, 1, 1);
84.
85.       constraints.weighty = 100;
86.       constraints.fill = GridBagConstraints.NONE;
87.       constraints.anchor = GridBagConstraints.CENTER;
88.
89.       add(bold, constraints, 0, 2, 2, 1);
90.       add(italic, constraints, 0, 3, 2, 1);
91.
92.       constraints.fill = GridBagConstraints.BOTH;
93.       add(sample, constraints, 2, 0, 1, 4);
94.    }
95.
96.    /**
97.       A convenience method to add a component to given grid bag
```

```
 98.        layout locations.
 99.        @param c the component to add
100.        @param constraints the grid bag constraints to use
101.        @param x the x grid position
102.        @param y the y grid position
103.        @param w the grid width
104.        @param h the grid height
105.     */
106.     public void add(Component c, GridBagConstraints constraints,
107.        int x, int y, int w, int h)
108.     {
109.        constraints.gridx = x;
110.        constraints.gridy = y;
111.        constraints.gridwidth = w;
112.        constraints.gridheight = h;
113.        getContentPane().add(c, constraints);
114.     }
115.
116.     public static final int WIDTH = 300;
117.     public static final int HEIGHT = 200;
118.
119.     private JComboBox face;
120.     private JComboBox size;
121.     private JCheckBox bold;
122.     private JCheckBox italic;
123.     private JTextArea sample;
124.
125.     /**
126.        An action listener that changes the font of the
127.        sample text.
128.     */
129.     private class FontAction implements ActionListener
130.     {
131.        public void actionPerformed(ActionEvent event)
132.        {
133.           String fontFace = (String)face.getSelectedItem();
134.           int fontStyle = (bold.isSelected() ? Font.BOLD : 0)
135.              + (italic.isSelected() ? Font.ITALIC : 0);
136.           int fontSize = Integer.parseInt(
137.              (String)size.getSelectedItem());
138.           Font font = new Font(fontFace, fontStyle, fontSize);
139.           sample.setFont(font);
140.           sample.repaint();
141.        }
142.     }
143. }
```

java.awt.GridBagConstraints

- `int gridx, gridy`
  indicates the starting column and row of the cell.

- `int gridwidth, gridheight`
  indicates the column and row extent of the cell.

- `double weightx, weighty`
  indicates the capacity of the cell to grow.

- `int anchor`
  indicates the alignment of the component inside the cell, one of CENTER, NORTH, NORTHEAST, EAST, SOUTHEAST, SOUTH, SOUTHWEST, WEST, or NORTHWEST.

- `int fill`
  indicates the fill behavior of the component inside the cell, one of NONE, BOTH, HORIZONTAL, or VERTICAL.

- `int ipadx, ipady`
  indicates the "internal" padding around the component.

- `Insets insets`
  indicates the "external" padding along the cell boundaries.

- `GridBagConstraints(int gridx, int gridy, int gridwidth, int gridheight, double weightx, double weighty, int anchor, int fill, Insets insets, int ipadx, int ipady)`
  constructs a GridBagConstraints with all its fields specified in the arguments. Sun recommends that this constructor be used only by automatic code generators since it makes your source code very hard to read.

Using No Layout Manager

There will be times when you don't want to bother with layout managers but just want to drop a component at a fixed location (sometimes called *absolute positioning*). This is not a great idea for platform-independent applications, but there is nothing wrong with using it for a quick prototype.

Here is what you do to place a component at a fixed location:

1. Set the layout manager to `null`.
2. Add the component you want to the container.
3. Then specify the position and size that you want.
   ```
   contentPane.setLayout(null);
   JButton ok = new JButton("Ok");
   contentPane.add(ok);
   ok.setBounds(10, 10, 30, 15);
   ```

java.awt.Component

- void setBounds(int x, int y, int width, int height)

moves and resizes a component.

Parameters:	x, y	The new top-left corner of the component
	width, height	The new size of the component

Custom Layout Managers

In principle, it is possible to design your own LayoutManager class that manages components in a special way. For example, you could arrange all components in a container to form a circle. This will almost always be a major effort and a real time sink, but as Figure 9–36 shows, the results can be quite dramatic.

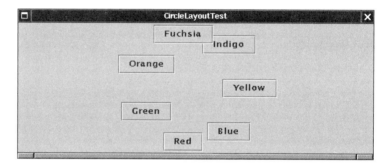

Figure 9–36: Circle layout

If you do feel you can't live without your own layout manager, here is what you do. Your own layout manager must implement the LayoutManager interface. You need to override the following five methods.

```
void addLayoutComponent(String s, Component c);
void removeLayoutComponent(Component c);
Dimension preferredLayoutSize(Container parent);
Dimension minimumLayoutSize(Container parent);
void layoutContainer(Container parent);
```

The first two functions are called when a component is added or removed. If you don't keep any additional information about the components, you can make them do nothing. The next two functions compute the space required for the minimum and the preferred layout of the components. These are usually the same quantity. The fifth function does the actual work and invokes setBounds on all components.

> **NOTE:** The AWT has a second interface called `LayoutManager2` with 10 methods to implement rather than 5. The main point of the `LayoutManager2` interface is to allow the user to use the `add` method with constraints. For example, the `BorderLayout` and `GridBagLayout` implement the `LayoutManager2` interface.

Example 9–15 is a simple implementation of the `CircleLayout` manager, which, amazingly and uselessly enough, lays out the components along a circle inside the parent.

Example 9–15: CircleLayoutTest.java

```
1. import java.awt.*;
2. import java.awt.event.*;
3. import javax.swing.*;
4.
5. public class CircleLayoutTest
6. {
7.    public static void main(String[] args)
8.    {
9.       CircleLayoutFrame frame = new CircleLayoutFrame();
10.      frame.setDefaultCloseOperation(JFrame.EXIT_ON_CLOSE);
11.      frame.pack();
12.      frame.show();
13.   }
14. }
15.
16. /**
17.    A frame that shows buttons arranged along a circle.
18. */
19. class CircleLayoutFrame extends JFrame
20. {
21.    public CircleLayoutFrame()
22.    {
23.       setTitle("CircleLayoutTest");
24.
25.       Container contentPane = getContentPane();
26.       contentPane.setLayout(new CircleLayout());
27.       contentPane.add(new JButton("Yellow"));
28.       contentPane.add(new JButton("Blue"));
29.       contentPane.add(new JButton("Red"));
30.       contentPane.add(new JButton("Green"));
31.       contentPane.add(new JButton("Orange"));
32.       contentPane.add(new JButton("Fuchsia"));
33.       contentPane.add(new JButton("Indigo"));
34.    }
35. }
36.
```

```
37.  /**
38.     A layout manager that lays out components along a circle.
39.  */
40.  class CircleLayout implements LayoutManager
41.  {
42.     public void addLayoutComponent(String name,
43.        Component comp)
44.     {}
45.
46.     public void removeLayoutComponent(Component comp)
47.     {}
48.
49.     public void setSizes(Container parent)
50.     {
51.        if (sizesSet) return;
52.        int n = parent.getComponentCount();
53.
54.        preferredWidth = 0;
55.        preferredHeight = 0;
56.        minWidth = 0;
57.        minHeight = 0;
58.        maxComponentWidth = 0;
59.        maxComponentHeight = 0;
60.
61.        // compute the maximum component widths and heights
62.        // and set the preferred size to the sum of
63.        // the component sizes.
64.        for (int i = 0; i < n; i++)
65.        {
66.           Component c = parent.getComponent(i);
67.           if (c.isVisible())
68.           {
69.              Dimension d = c.getPreferredSize();
70.              maxComponentWidth = Math.max(maxComponentWidth,
71.                 d.width);
72.              maxComponentHeight = Math.max(maxComponentHeight,
73.                 d.height);
74.              preferredWidth += d.width;
75.              preferredHeight += d.height;
76.           }
77.        }
78.        minWidth = preferredWidth / 2;
79.        minHeight = preferredHeight / 2;
80.        sizesSet = true;
81.     }
82.
83.     public Dimension preferredLayoutSize(Container parent)
84.     {
```

```
85.        setSizes(parent);
86.        Insets insets = parent.getInsets();
87.        int width = preferredWidth + insets.left
88.            + insets.right;
89.        int height = preferredHeight + insets.top
90.            + insets.bottom;
91.        return new Dimension(width, height);
92.     }
93.
94.     public Dimension minimumLayoutSize(Container parent)
95.     {
96.        setSizes(parent);
97.        Insets insets = parent.getInsets();
98.        int width = minWidth + insets.left + insets.right;
99.        int height = minHeight + insets.top + insets.bottom;
100.       return new Dimension(width, height);
101.    }
102.
103.    public void layoutContainer(Container parent)
104.    {
105.       setSizes(parent);
106.
107.       // compute center of the circle
108.
109.       Insets insets = parent.getInsets();
110.       int containerWidth = parent.getSize().width
111.           - insets.left - insets.right;
112.       int containerHeight = parent.getSize().height
113.           - insets.top - insets.bottom;
114.
115.       int xcenter = insets.left + containerWidth / 2;
116.       int ycenter = insets.top + containerHeight / 2;
117.
118.       // compute radius of the circle
119.
120.       int xradius = (containerWidth - maxComponentWidth) / 2;
121.       int yradius = (containerHeight - maxComponentHeight) / 2;
122.       int radius = Math.min(xradius, yradius);
123.
124.       // lay out components along the circle
125.
126.       int n = parent.getComponentCount();
127.       for (int i = 0; i < n; i++)
128.       {
129.          Component c = parent.getComponent(i);
130.          if (c.isVisible())
131.          {
132.             double angle = 2 * Math.PI * i / n;
```

```
133.
134.                  // center point of component
135.                  int x = xcenter + (int)(Math.cos(angle) * radius);
136.                  int y = ycenter + (int)(Math.sin(angle) * radius);
137.
138.                  // move component so that its center is (x, y)
139.                  // and its size is its preferred size
140.                  Dimension d = c.getPreferredSize();
141.                  c.setBounds(x - d.width / 2, y - d.height / 2,
142.                      d.width, d.height);
143.              }
144.          }
145.      }
146.
147.      private int minWidth = 0;
148.      private int minHeight = 0;
149.      private int preferredWidth = 0;
150.      private int preferredHeight = 0;
151.      private boolean sizesSet = false;
152.      private int maxComponentWidth = 0;
153.      private int maxComponentHeight = 0;
154. }
```

java.awt.LayoutManager

- void addLayoutComponent(String name, Component comp)
  adds a component to the layout.

  Parameters: name   An identifier for the component placement

                      comp   The component to be added

- void removeLayoutComponent(Component comp)
  removes a component from the layout.

  Parameters: comp   The component to be removed

- Dimension preferredLayoutSize(Container parent)
  returns the preferred size dimensions for the container under this layout.

  Parameters: parent   The container whose components are being laid out

- Dimension minimumLayoutSize(Container parent)
  returns the minimum size dimensions for the container under this layout.

  Parameters: parent   The container whose components are being laid out

- void layoutContainer(Container parent)
  lays out the components in a container.

  Parameters: parent   The container whose components are being laid out

Traversal Order

When you add many components into a window, you need to give some thought to the *traversal order*. When a window is first displayed, the first component in the traversal order has the keyboard focus. Each time the user presses the TAB key, the next component gains focus. (Recall that a component that has the keyboard focus can be manipulated with the keyboard. For example, a button can be "clicked" with the space bar when it has focus.) You may not personally care about using the TAB key to navigate through a set of controls, but there are plenty of users who do. Among them are the mouse haters and those who cannot use a mouse, perhaps because of a handicap or because they are navigating the user interface by voice. For that reason, you need to know how the Swing set handles traversal order.

The Swing set attempts to traverse your components in a reasonable way, first left-to-right and then top-to-bottom. For example, in the font dialog example, the components are traversed in the following order:

1. Face combo box
2. Sample text area
3. Size combo box
4. Bold check box
5. Italic combo box

Figure 9–37: Geometric traversal order

NOTE: In the old AWT, the traversal order was determined by the order in which you inserted components into a container. In Swing, the insertion order does not matter—only the layout of the components is considered.

The situation is more complex if your container contains other containers. When the focus is given to another container, it automatically ends up within the top-left component in that container and then it traverses all other components in that container. Finally, the focus is given to the component following the container.

You can use this to your advantage by grouping related elements in another container such as a panel.

Note that some components do not get focus, such as the labels in the `FontDialog` example.

Actually, the default focus order is not always appropriate. For example, run the `FontDialog` program. You'll notice that the program starts out with focus in the face combo box in the top left corner. (You may need to look carefully to see the thin rectangle indicating the focus.) When you press the TAB key, focus moves to the text area (without any visible indication). Unfortunately, pressing the TAB key again has no effect. Rather than moving the focus, the text area consumes the key, only to reject it because it is not editable. If the text area had been editable, the TAB key would simply have been inserted into the text.

If you are not happy with the default traversal order, you have a number of remedies.

You can transfer the focus explicitly to a particular component, with the `requestFocus` method:

```
size.requestFocus();
```

This works only in reaction to a particular event. It has no permanent effect on the traversal order.

You can change the traversal order with the `setNextFocusableComponent` method of the `JComponent` class. For example, suppose you want to skip from the face combo box directly to the size combo box. Use the command

```
face.setNextFocusableComponent(size);
```

The geometric order is preserved except for the transition that you set with the `setNextFocusableComponent` method.

You can also block a component from receiving the focus by having its `isFocusTraversable` method return `false`. In particular, the `isFocusTraversable` method of the `JComponent` class returns `false` if the text component is not enabled. To solve the focus problem of the `FontDialog` application, you can call

```
sample.setEnabled(false);
```

However, then the text in the text area is displayed in gray. You can do better by overriding the `isFocusTraversable` to do what it really should do anyway, namely return `true` only if the component is editable:

```
sample = new
   JTextArea()
   {
      public boolean isFocusTraversable()
      {
         return isEditable();
      }
   };
```

`java.awt.Component`

- `void requestFocus()`
  requests that this component have the input focus.

- `boolean isFocusTraversable()`
  returns `true` if this component can receive input focus.

`javax.swing.JComponent`

- `void setNextFocusableComponent(Component c)`
  makes `c` the next component to get the focus after this one in the traversal order, overriding the default traversal order.

Dialog Boxes

So far, all of our user interface components have appeared inside a frame window that was created in the application. This is the most common situation if you write *applets* that run inside a web browser. But if you write applications, you usually want separate dialog boxes to pop up to give information to or get information from the user.

Just as with most windowing systems, AWT distinguishes between *modal* and *modeless* dialog boxes. A modal dialog box won't let the user interact with the remaining windows of the application until he or she deals with it. You use a modal dialog box when you need information from the user before you can proceed with execution. For example, when the user wants to read a file, a modal file dialog box is the one to pop up. The user must specify a file name before the program can begin the read operation. Only when the user closes the (modal) dialog box can the application proceed.

A modeless dialog box lets the user enter information in both the dialog box and the remainder of the application. One example of a modeless dialog is a toolbar. The toolbar can stay in place as long as needed, and the user can interact with both the application window and the toolbar as needed.

We start this section with the simplest dialogs—modal dialogs with just a single message. Swing has a convenient `JOptionPane` class that lets you put up a simple dialog without writing any special dialog box code. Next, you will see how to write more complex dialogs by implementing your own dialog windows. Finally, you will see how to transfer data from your application into a dialog and back.

We conclude this section by looking at two standard dialogs: file dialogs and color dialogs. File dialogs are complex, and you definitely want to be familiar with the Swing `JFileChooser` for this purpose—it would be a real challenge

to write your own. The `JColorChooser` dialog is useful when you want users
to pick colors.

Option Dialogs

The Swing set has a set of ready-made simple dialogs that suffice when you need
to ask the user for a single piece of information. The `JOptionPane` has four static
methods to show these simple dialogs:

`showMessageDialog`	Show a message and wait for the user to click OK.
`showConfirmDialog`	Show a message and get a confirmation (like OK/Cancel).
`showOptionDialog`	Show a message and get a user option from a set of options.
`showInputDialog`	Show a message and get one line of user input.

Figure 9–38 shows a typical dialog. As you can see, the dialog has the
following components:

- An icon;

- A message;

- One or more option buttons.

The input dialog has an additional component for user input. This can be a
text field into which the user can type an arbitrary string, or a combo box from
which the user can select one item.

The exact layout of these dialogs, and the choice of icons for standard message
types, depend on the pluggable look and feel.

Figure 9–38: An option dialog

The icon on the left side depends on the *message type*. There are five
message types:

```
ERROR_MESSAGE
INFORMATION_MESSAGE
WARNING_MESSAGE
QUESTION_MESSAGE
PLAIN_MESSAGE
```

The `PLAIN_MESSAGE` type has no icon. For each of the dialog types, there is also a method that lets you supply your own icon instead.

For each dialog type, you can specify a message. This message can be a string, an icon, a user interface component, or any other object. Here is how the message object is displayed:

`String:`	Draw the string
`Icon:`	Show the icon
`Component:`	Show the component
`Object[]:`	Show all objects in the array, stacked on top of each other
any other object:	Apply `toString` and show the resulting string

You can see these options by running the program in Example 9–16.

Of course, supplying a message string is by far the most common case. Supplying a `Component` gives you ultimate flexibility since you can make the `paintComponent` method draw anything you want. Supplying an array of objects isn't all that useful since there isn't enough room in the dialog to show more than a couple of them—the dialog does not grow to accommodate all message objects.

The buttons on the bottom depend on the dialog type and the *option type*. When calling `showMessageDialog` and `showInputDialog`, you get only a standard set of buttons (OK and OK/Cancel, respectively). When calling `showConfirmDialog`, you can choose among four option types:

```
DEFAULT_OPTION
YES_NO_OPTION
YES_NO_CANCEL_OPTION
OK_CANCEL_OPTION
```

With the `showOptionDialog` you can specify an arbitrary set of options. You supply an array of objects for the options. Each array element is rendered as follows:

`String:`	Make a button with the string as label
`Icon:`	Make a button with the icon as label
`Component:`	Show the component
any other object:	Apply `toString` and make a button with the resulting string as label

The return values of these functions are as follows:

`showMessageDialog`	None
`showConfirmDialog`	An integer representing the chosen option

| `showOptionDialog` | An integer representing the chosen option |
| `showInputDialog` | The string that the user supplied or selected |

The `showConfirmDialog` and `showOptionDialog` return integers to indicate which button the user chose. For the option dialog, this is simply the index of the chosen option, or the value `CLOSED_OPTION` if the user closed the dialog instead of choosing an option. For the confirmation dialog, the return value can be one of the following:

```
OK_OPTION
CANCEL_OPTION
YES_OPTION
NO_OPTION
CLOSED_OPTION
```

This all sounds like a bewildering set of choices, but in practice it is simple:

1.   Choose the dialog type (message, confirmation, option or input).

2.   Choose the icon (error, information, warning, question, none, or custom).

3.   Choose the message (string, icon, custom component, or a stack of them).

4.   For a confirmation dialog, choose the option type (default, Yes/No, Yes/No/Cancel, or OK/Cancel).

5.   For an option dialog, choose the options (strings, icons, or custom components) and the default option.

6.   For an input dialog, choose between a text field and a combo box.

7.   Locate the appropriate method to call in the `JOptionPane` API.

For example, suppose you want to show the dialog in Figure 9–38. The dialog shows a message and asks the user to confirm or cancel. Thus, it is a confirmation dialog. The icon is a warning icon. The message is a string. The option type is `OK_CANCEL_OPTION`. Here is the call you need to make:

```
int selection = JOptionPane.showConfirmDialog(parent,
    "Message", "Title",
    JOptionPane.OK_CANCEL_OPTION,
    JOptionPane.WARNING_MESSAGE);
if (selection == JOptionPane.OK_OPTION) . . .
```

TIP: The message string can contain newline (`'\n'`) characters. Such a string is displayed in multiple lines.

The program in Example 9–16 lets you make these selections (see Figure 9–39). It then shows you the resulting dialog.

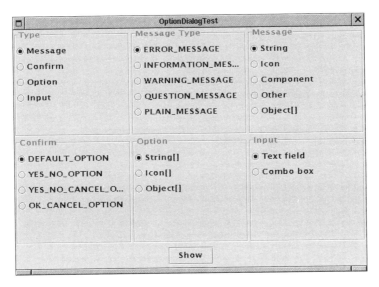

Figure 9–39: The OptionDialogTest program

Example 9–16: OptionDialogTest.java

```
1. import java.awt.*;
2. import java.awt.event.*;
3. import java.awt.geom.*;
4. import java.util.*;
5. import javax.swing.*;
6. import javax.swing.border.*;
7.
8. public class OptionDialogTest
9. {
10.    public static void main(String[] args)
11.    {
12.       OptionDialogFrame frame = new OptionDialogFrame();
13.       frame.setDefaultCloseOperation(JFrame.EXIT_ON_CLOSE);
14.       frame.show();
15.    }
16. }
17.
18. /**
19.    A panel with radio buttons inside a titled border.
20. */
21. class ButtonPanel extends JPanel
22. {
23.    /**
24.       Constructs a button panel.
25.       @param title the title shown in the border
26.       @param options an array of radio button labels
27.    */
```

```
28.    public ButtonPanel(String title, String[] options)
29.    {
30.       setBorder(BorderFactory.createTitledBorder
31.             (BorderFactory.createEtchedBorder(), title));
32.       setLayout(new BoxLayout(this,
33.          BoxLayout.Y_AXIS));
34.       group = new ButtonGroup();
35.
36.       // make one radio button for each option
37.       for (int i = 0; i < options.length; i++)
38.       {
39.          JRadioButton b = new JRadioButton(options[i]);
40.          b.setActionCommand(options[i]);
41.          add(b);
42.          group.add(b);
43.          b.setSelected(i == 0);
44.       }
45.    }
46.
47.    /**
48.       Gets the currently selected option.
49.       @return the label of the currently selected radio button.
50.    */
51.    public String getSelection()
52.    {
53.       return group.getSelection().getActionCommand();
54.    }
55.
56.    private ButtonGroup group;
57. }
58.
59. /**
60.    A frame that contains settings for selecting various option
61.    dialogs.
62. */
63. class OptionDialogFrame extends JFrame
64. {
65.    public OptionDialogFrame()
66.    {
67.       setTitle("OptionDialogTest");
68.       setSize(WIDTH, HEIGHT);
69.
70.       JPanel gridPanel = new JPanel();
71.       gridPanel.setLayout(new GridLayout(2, 3));
72.
73.       typePanel = new ButtonPanel("Type",
74.          new String[]
75.          {
76.             "Message",
77.             "Confirm",
78.             "Option",
```

```
79.            "Input"
80.        });
81.
82.    messageTypePanel = new ButtonPanel("Message Type",
83.        new String[]
84.        {
85.            "ERROR_MESSAGE",
86.            "INFORMATION_MESSAGE",
87.            "WARNING_MESSAGE",
88.            "QUESTION_MESSAGE",
89.            "PLAIN_MESSAGE"
90.        });
91.
92.    messagePanel = new ButtonPanel("Message",
93.        new String[]
94.        {
95.            "String",
96.            "Icon",
97.            "Component",
98.            "Other",
99.            "Object[]"
100.       });
101.
102.   optionTypePanel = new ButtonPanel("Confirm",
103.       new String[]
104.       {
105.           "DEFAULT_OPTION",
106.           "YES_NO_OPTION",
107.           "YES_NO_CANCEL_OPTION",
108.           "OK_CANCEL_OPTION"
109.       });
110.
111.   optionsPanel = new ButtonPanel("Option",
112.       new String[]
113.       {
114.           "String[]",
115.           "Icon[]",
116.           "Object[]"
117.       });
118.
119.   inputPanel = new ButtonPanel("Input",
120.       new String[]
121.       {
122.           "Text field",
123.           "Combo box"
124.       });
125.
126.   gridPanel.add(typePanel);
127.   gridPanel.add(messageTypePanel);
128.   gridPanel.add(messagePanel);
129.   gridPanel.add(optionTypePanel);
```

```
130.        gridPanel.add(optionsPanel);
131.        gridPanel.add(inputPanel);
132.
133.        // add a panel with a Show button
134.
135.        JPanel showPanel = new JPanel();
136.        JButton showButton = new JButton("Show");
137.        showButton.addActionListener(new ShowAction());
138.        showPanel.add(showButton);
139.
140.        Container contentPane = getContentPane();
141.        contentPane.add(gridPanel, BorderLayout.CENTER);
142.        contentPane.add(showPanel, BorderLayout.SOUTH);
143.    }
144.
145.    /**
146.        Gets the currently selected message.
147.        @return a string, icon, component or object array,
148.        depending on the Message panel selection
149.    */
150.    public Object getMessage()
151.    {
152.        String s = messagePanel.getSelection();
153.        if (s.equals("String"))
154.            return messageString;
155.        else if (s.equals("Icon"))
156.            return messageIcon;
157.        else if (s.equals("Component"))
158.            return messageComponent;
159.        else if (s.equals("Object[]"))
160.            return new Object[]
161.            {
162.                messageString,
163.                messageIcon,
164.                messageComponent,
165.                messageObject
166.            };
167.        else if (s.equals("Other"))
168.            return messageObject;
169.        else return null;
170.    }
171.
172.    /**
173.        Gets the currently selected options.
174.        @return an array of strings, icons or objects, depending
175.        on the Option panel selection
176.    */
177.    public Object[] getOptions()
178.    {
179.        String s = optionsPanel.getSelection();
180.        if (s.equals("String[]"))
```

```
181.         return new String[] { "Yellow", "Blue", "Red" };
182.      else if (s.equals("Icon[]"))
183.         return new Icon[]
184.         {
185.            new ImageIcon("yellow-ball.gif"),
186.            new ImageIcon("blue-ball.gif"),
187.            new ImageIcon("red-ball.gif")
188.         };
189.      else if (s.equals("Object[]"))
190.         return new Object[]
191.         {
192.            messageString,
193.            messageIcon,
194.            messageComponent,
195.            messageObject
196.         };
197.      else
198.         return null;
199.   }
200.
201.   /**
202.      Gets the selected message or option type
203.      @param panel the Message Type or Confirm panel
204.      @return the selected XXX_MESSAGE or XXX_OPTION constant
205.      from the JOptionPane class
206.   */
207.   public int getType(ButtonPanel panel)
208.   {
209.      String s = panel.getSelection();
210.      try
211.      {
212.         return JOptionPane.class.getField(s).getInt(null);
213.      }
214.      catch(Exception e)
215.      {
216.         return -1;
217.      }
218.   }
219.
220.   /**
221.      The action listener for the Show button shows a
222.      Confirm, Input, Message or Option dialog depending
223.      on the Type panel selection.
224.   */
225.   private class ShowAction implements ActionListener
226.   {
227.      public void actionPerformed(ActionEvent evt)
228.      {
229.         if (typePanel.getSelection().equals("Confirm"))
230.            JOptionPane.showConfirmDialog(
231.               OptionDialogFrame.this,
```

```
232.                    getMessage(),
233.                    "Title",
234.                    getType(optionTypePanel),
235.                    getType(messageTypePanel));
236.            else if (typePanel.getSelection().equals("Input"))
237.            {
238.               if (inputPanel.getSelection().equals("Text field"))
239.                  JOptionPane.showInputDialog(
240.                     OptionDialogFrame.this,
241.                     getMessage(),
242.                     "Title",
243.                     getType(messageTypePanel));
244.               else
245.                  JOptionPane.showInputDialog(
246.                     OptionDialogFrame.this,
247.                     getMessage(),
248.                     "Title",
249.                     getType(messageTypePanel),
250.                     null,
251.                     new String[] { "Yellow", "Blue", "Red" },
252.                     "Blue");
253.            }
254.            else if (typePanel.getSelection().equals("Message"))
255.               JOptionPane.showMessageDialog(
256.                  OptionDialogFrame.this,
257.                  getMessage(),
258.                  "Title",
259.                  getType(messageTypePanel));
260.            else if (typePanel.getSelection().equals("Option"))
261.               JOptionPane.showOptionDialog(
262.                  OptionDialogFrame.this,
263.                  getMessage(),
264.                  "Title",
265.                  getType(optionTypePanel),
266.                  getType(messageTypePanel),
267.                  null,
268.                  getOptions(),
269.                  getOptions()[0]);
270.         }
271.      }
272.
273.      public static final int WIDTH = 600;
274.      public static final int HEIGHT = 400;
275.
276.      private ButtonPanel typePanel;
277.      private ButtonPanel messagePanel;
278.      private ButtonPanel messageTypePanel;
279.      private ButtonPanel optionTypePanel;
280.      private ButtonPanel optionsPanel;
281.      private ButtonPanel inputPanel;
282.
```

```
283.    private String messageString = "Message";
284.    private Icon messageIcon = new ImageIcon("blue-ball.gif");
285.    private Object messageObject = new Date();
286.    private Component messageComponent = new SamplePanel();
287. }
288.
289. /**
290.    A panel with a painted surface
291. */
292.
293. class SamplePanel extends JPanel
294. {
295.    public void paintComponent(Graphics g)
296.    {
297.       super.paintComponent(g);
298.       Graphics2D g2 = (Graphics2D)g;
299.       Rectangle2D rect = new Rectangle2D.Double(0, 0,
300.          getWidth() - 1, getHeight() - 1);
301.       g2.setPaint(Color.yellow);
302.       g2.fill(rect);
303.       g2.setPaint(Color.blue);
304.       g2.draw(rect);
305.    }
306.
307.    public Dimension getMinimumSize()
308.    {
309.       return new Dimension(10, 10);
310.    }
311. }
```

---

javax.swing.JOptionPane

- static void showMessageDialog(Component parent, Object message, String title, int messageType, Icon icon)
- static void showMessageDialog(Component parent, Object message, String title, int messageType)
- static void showMessageDialog(Component parent, Object message)
- static void showInternalMessageDialog(Component parent, Object message, String title, int messageType, Icon icon)
- static void showInternalMessageDialog(Component parent, Object message, String title, int messageType)
- static void showInternalMessageDialog(Component parent, Object message)

show a message dialog or an internal message dialog. (An internal dialog is rendered entirely within its owner frame.)

Parameters: parent   The parent component (can be null)

`message`	The message to show on the dialog (can be a string, icon, component, or an array of them)	
`title`	The string in the title bar of the dialog	
`messageType`	One of `ERROR_MESSAGE`, `INFORMATION_MESSAGE`, `WARNING_MESSAGE`, `QUESTION_MESSAGE`, `PLAIN_MESSAGE`	
`icon`	An icon to show instead of one of the standard icons	

- `static int showConfirmDialog(Component parent, Object message, String title, int optionType, int messageType, Icon icon)`
- `static int showConfirmDialog(Component parent, Object message, String title, int optionType, int messageType)`
- `static int showConfirmDialog(Component parent, Object message, String title, int optionType)`
- `static int showConfirmDialog(Component parent, Object message)`
- `static int showInternalConfirmDialog(Component parent, Object message, String title, int optionType, int messageType, Icon icon)`
- `static int showInternalConfirmDialog(Component parent, Object message, String title, int optionType, int messageType)`
- `static int showInternalConfirmDialog(Component parent, Object message, String title, int optionType)`
- `static int showInternalConfirmDialog(Component parent, Object message)`

show a confirmation dialog or an internal confirmation dialog. (An internal dialog is rendered entirely within its owner frame.) Returns the option selected by the user (one of `OK_OPTION`, `CANCEL_OPTION`, `YES_OPTION`, `NO_OPTION`), or `CLOSED_OPTION` if the user closed the dialog.

Parameters:	`parent`	The parent component (can be `null`)
	`message`	The message to show on the dialog (can be a string, icon, component, or an array of them)
	`title`	The string in the title bar of the dialog
	`messageType`	One of `ERROR_MESSAGE`, `INFORMATION_MESSAGE`, `WARNING_MESSAGE`, `QUESTION_MESSAGE`, `PLAIN_MESSAGE`
	`optionType`	One of `DEFAULT_OPTION`, `YES_NO_OPTION`, `YES_NO_CANCEL_OPTION`, `OK_CANCEL_OPTION`

`icon`	An icon to show instead of one of the standard icons

- `static int showOptionDialog(Component parent, Object message, String title, int optionType, int messageType, Icon icon, Object[] options, Object default)`
- `static int showInternalOptionDialog(Component parent, Object message, String title, int optionType, int messageType, Icon icon, Object[] options, Object default)`

show an option dialog or an internal option dialog. (An internal dialog is rendered entirely within its owner frame.) Returns the index of the option selected by the user, or `CLOSED_OPTION` if the user canceled the dialog.

Parameters:	`parent`	The parent component (can be `null`)
	`message`	The message to show on the dialog (can be a string, icon, component, or an array of them)
	`title`	The string in the title bar of the dialog
	`messageType`	One of `ERROR_MESSAGE`, `INFORMATION_MESSAGE`, `WARNING_MESSAGE`, `QUESTION_MESSAGE`, `PLAIN_MESSAGE`
	`optionType`	One of `DEFAULT_OPTION`, `YES_NO_OPTION`, `YES_NO_CANCEL_OPTION`, `OK_CANCEL_OPTION`
	`icon`	An icon to show instead of one of the standard icons
	`options`	An array of options (can be strings, icons, or components)
	`default`	The default option to present to the user

- `static Object showInputDialog(Component parent, Object message, String title, int messageType, Icon icon, Object[] values, Object default)`
- `static String showInputDialog(Component parent, Object message, String title, int messageType)`
- `static String showInputDialog(Component parent, Object message)`
- `static String showInputDialog(Object message)`
- `static Object showInternalInputDialog(Component parent, Object message, String title, int messageType, Icon icon, Object[] values, Object default)`

- `static String showInternalInputDialog(Component parent, Object message, String title, int messageType)`
- `static String showInternalInputDialog(Component parent, Object message)`

show an input dialog or an internal input dialog. (An internal dialog is rendered entirely within its owner frame.) Returns the input string typed by the user, or `null` if the user canceled the dialog.

Parameters:	parent	The parent component (can be `null`)
	message	The message to show on the dialog (can be a string, icon, component, or an array of them)
	title	The string in the title bar of the dialog
	messageType	One of `ERROR_MESSAGE`, `INFORMATION_MESSAGE`, `WARNING_MESSAGE`, `QUESTION_MESSAGE`, `PLAIN_MESSAGE`
	icon	An icon to show instead of one of the standard icons
	values	An array of values to show in a combo box
	default	The default value to present to the user

Creating Dialogs

In the last section, you saw how to use the `JOptionPane` class to show a simple dialog. In this section, you will see how to create such a dialog by hand.

Figure 9–40 shows a typical modal dialog box, a program information box that is displayed when the user clicks the About button.

To implement a dialog box, you derive a class from `JDialog`. This is essentially the same process as deriving the main window for an application from `JFrame`. More precisely:

1. In the constructor of your dialog box, call the constructor of the base class `JDialog`. You will need to tell it the *owner frame* (the frame window over which the dialog pops up), the title of the dialog frame, and a Boolean flag to indicate if the dialog box is modal or modeless.

   You should supply the owner frame so that the dialog can be displayed on top of its owner, but you can also supply a `null` pointer if you don't care where the dialog is displayed. Windowing systems typically require that every pop-up window is owned by another frame. Therefore, Swing constructs a shared hidden frame that becomes the owner of all dialogs with a `null` owner.

2. Add the user interface components of the dialog box.

3. Add the event handlers.

4. Set the size for the dialog box.

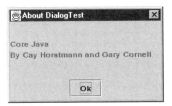

Figure 9–40: An About dialog box

Here's an example dialog box:

```
public AboutDialog(JFrame owner) extends JDialog
{
    super(owner, "About DialogTest", true);
    Container contentPane = getContentPane();

    contentPane.add(new JLabel(
        "<HTML><H1><I>Core Java</I></H1><HR>"
        + "By Cay Horstmann and Gary Cornell</HTML>"),
        BorderLayout.CENTER);

    JPanel panel = new JPanel();
    JButton ok = new JButton("Ok");

    ok.addActionListener(new
        ActionListener()
        {
            public void actionPerformed(ActionEvent evt)
            {
                setVisible(false);
            }
        });

    panel.add(ok);
    contentPane.add(panel, BorderLayout.SOUTH);

    setSize(250, 150);
}
```

As you can see, the constructor adds user interface elements: in this case, labels and a button. It adds a handler to the button and sets the size of the dialog.

To display the dialog box, you create a new dialog object and invoke the show method.

```
JDialog dialog = new AboutDialog(this);
dialog.show();
```

Actually, in the sample code below, we create the dialog box only once, and so we can reuse it whenever the user clicks the About button.

```
if (dialog == null) // first time
   dialog = new AboutDialog(this);
dialog.show();
```

When the user clicks on the OK button, the dialog box should close. This is handled in the event handler of the OK button:

```
ok.addActionListener(new
   ActionListener()
   {
      public void actionPerformed(ActionEvent evt)
      {
         setVisible(false);
      }
   });
```

When the user closes the dialog by clicking on the Close box, then the dialog is also hidden. Just as with a JFrame, you can override this behavior with the setDefaultCloseOperation method.

Example 9–17 is the code for the About dialog box test program.

Example 9–17: DialogTest.java

```
1. import java.awt.*;
2. import java.awt.event.*;
3. import javax.swing.*;
4.
5. public class DialogTest
6. {
7.    public static void main(String[] args)
8.    {
9.       DialogFrame frame = new DialogFrame();
10.       frame.setDefaultCloseOperation(JFrame.EXIT_ON_CLOSE);
11.       frame.show();
12.    }
13. }
14.
15. /**
16.    A frame with a menu whose File->About action shows a dialog.
17. */
18. class DialogFrame extends JFrame
19. {
20.    public DialogFrame()
21.    {
22.       setTitle("DialogTest");
23.       setSize(WIDTH, HEIGHT);
24.
25.       // construct a File menu
```

```
26.
27.        JMenuBar menuBar = new JMenuBar();
28.        setJMenuBar(menuBar);
29.        JMenu fileMenu = new JMenu("File");
30.        menuBar.add(fileMenu);
31.
32.        // add About and Exit menu items
33.
34.        // The About item shows the About dialog
35.
36.        JMenuItem aboutItem = new JMenuItem("About");
37.        aboutItem.addActionListener(new
38.           ActionListener()
39.           {
40.              public void actionPerformed(ActionEvent event)
41.              {
42.                 if (dialog == null) // first time
43.                    dialog = new AboutDialog(DialogFrame.this);
44.                 dialog.show(); // pop up dialog
45.              }
46.           });
47.        fileMenu.add(aboutItem);
48.
49.        // The Exit item exits the program
50.
51.        JMenuItem exitItem = new JMenuItem("Exit");
52.        exitItem.addActionListener(new
53.           ActionListener()
54.           {
55.              public void actionPerformed(ActionEvent event)
56.              {
57.                 System.exit(0);
58.              }
59.           });
60.        fileMenu.add(exitItem);
61.     }
62.
63.     public static final int WIDTH = 300;
64.     public static final int HEIGHT = 200;
65.
66.     private AboutDialog dialog;
67.  }
68.
69.  /**
70.     A sample modal dialog that displays a message and
71.     waits for the user to click the Ok button.
72.  */
73.  class AboutDialog extends JDialog
74.  {
75.     public AboutDialog(JFrame owner)
76.     {
```

```
77.          super(owner, "About DialogTest", true);
78.          Container contentPane = getContentPane();
79.
80.          // add HTML label to center
81.
82.          contentPane.add(new JLabel(
83.             "<HTML><H1><I>Core Java</I></H1><HR>"
84.             + "By Cay Horstmann and Gary Cornell</HTML>"),
85.             BorderLayout.CENTER);
86.
87.          // Ok button closes the dialog
88.
89.          JButton ok = new JButton("Ok");
90.          ok.addActionListener(new
91.             ActionListener()
92.             {
93.                public void actionPerformed(ActionEvent evt)
94.                {
95.                   setVisible(false);
96.                }
97.             });
98.
99.          // add Ok button to southern border
100.
101.         JPanel panel = new JPanel();
102.         panel.add(ok);
103.         contentPane.add(panel, BorderLayout.SOUTH);
104.
105.         setSize(250, 150);
106.      }
107. }
```

javax.swing.JDialog

- `public JDialog(JFrame parent, String title, boolean modal)`
  constructs a dialog. The dialog is not visible until it is explicitly shown.

Parameters:	`parent`	The frame that is the owner of the dialog
	`title`	The title of the dialog
	`modal`	True for modal dialogs (a modal dialog blocks input to other windows)

Data Exchange

The most common reason to put up a dialog box is to get information from the user. You have already seen how easy it is to make a dialog box object: give it initial data and then call `show()` to display the dialog box on the screen. Now let us see how to transfer data in and out of a dialog box.

Consider the dialog box in Figure 9–41 that could be used to obtain a user name and a password to connect to some on-line service.

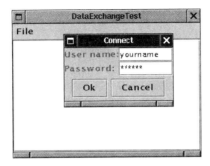

Figure 9–41: Password dialog box

Your dialog box should provide methods to set default data. For example, the `PasswordChooser` class of the example program has a method `setUser` to place default values into the next fields:

```
public void setUser(User u)
{
    username.setText(u.getName());
}
```

Once you set the defaults (if desired), you show the dialog by calling a method such as the following:

```
boolean showDialog()
{
    ok = false;
    show();
    return ok;
}
```

The user then fills in the information and clicks the OK or Cancel button. Only the event handler for the OK button sets the `ok` flag to `true`. The event handlers for both buttons call `setVisible(false)`, which terminates the `show` method. Alternatively, the user may close the dialog. If you did not install a window listener for the dialog, then the default window closing operation applies: the dialog becomes invisible, which also terminates the `show` method.

Note that the call to `show()` does not return until the dialog becomes invisible. This is a welcome change in how the AWT works. In the first version of the AWT, the call to `show` returned immediately, *even for modal dialog boxes*. That made it extremely challenging to get the data out of the dialog box.

You should test the return value of the `showDialog` method. If it is `true`, then the user accepted the dialog. In that case, call the appropriate methods to retrieve the user input. Here is a sample method:

```
public User getUser()
{
    return new User(username.getText(), password.getPassword());
}
```

In this example, we use a single class for the data that the dialog box manipulates. Some programmers simply provide methods for each user interface component (`getUsername`, `getPassword`). However, as you edit more complex objects, you want to leave it up to the dialog to find appropriate ways for displaying and editing your objects.

NOTE: Transferring data out of a modeless dialog is not as simple. When displaying a modeless dialog, the call to `show` does not block and the program continues running while the dialog is displayed. If the user selects items on a modeless dialog and then clicks OK, the dialog needs to send an event to some listener in the program. That is, another class must implement an appropriate listener interface, and an object of that class should be registered as a listener. You can implement this by sending a custom event (see Chapter 8) or by sending a property change event (see the chapter on JavaBeans in Volume 2).

The example program contains another useful improvement. When you construct a `JDialog` object, you need to specify the owner frame. However, quite often you want to show the same dialog with different owner frames. It is better if you can pick the owner frame *when you are ready to show the dialog*, not when you construct the `PasswordChooser` object.

The trick is to have the `PasswordChooser` extend `JPanel` instead of `JDialog`. Build a `JDialog` object on the fly in the `showDialog` method:

```
public boolean showDialog(Frame owner, String title)
{
    ok = false;

    if (dialog == null || dialog.getOwner() != owner)
    {
        dialog = new JDialog(owner, true);
        dialog.getContentPane().add(this);
        dialog.pack();
    }

    dialog.setTitle(title);
    dialog.show();
    return ok;
}
```

Note that it is safe to have owner equal to null.

You can do even better. Sometimes, the owner frame isn't readily available. It is easy enough to compute it from any parent component, like this:

```
Frame owner;
if (parent instanceof Frame)
   owner = (Frame) parent;
else
   owner = (Frame)SwingUtilities.getAncestorOfClass(
      Frame.class, parent);
```

We use this enhancement in our sample program. The JOptionPane class also uses this mechanism.

Example 9–18 is the complete code that illustrates the data flow into and out of a dialog box.

Example 9–18: DataExchangeTest.java

```
1. import java.awt.*;
2. import java.awt.event.*;
3. import javax.swing.*;
4.
5. public class DataExchangeTest
6. {
7.    public static void main(String[] args)
8.    {
9.       DataExchangeFrame frame = new DataExchangeFrame();
10.       frame.setDefaultCloseOperation(JFrame.EXIT_ON_CLOSE);
11.       frame.show();
12.    }
13. }
14.
15. /**
16.    A frame with a menu whose File->Connect action shows a
17.    password dialog.
18. */
19. class DataExchangeFrame extends JFrame
20. {
21.    public DataExchangeFrame()
22.    {
23.       setTitle("DataExchangeTest");
24.       setSize(WIDTH, HEIGHT);
25.
26.       // construct a File menu
27.
28.       JMenuBar mbar = new JMenuBar();
29.       setJMenuBar(mbar);
30.       JMenu fileMenu = new JMenu("File");
31.       mbar.add(fileMenu);
```

```
32.
33.        // add Connect and Exit menu items
34.
35.        JMenuItem connectItem = new JMenuItem("Connect");
36.        connectItem.addActionListener(new ConnectAction());
37.        fileMenu.add(connectItem);
38.
39.        // The Exit item exits the program
40.
41.        JMenuItem exitItem = new JMenuItem("Exit");
42.        exitItem.addActionListener(new
43.           ActionListener()
44.           {
45.              public void actionPerformed(ActionEvent event)
46.              {
47.                 System.exit(0);
48.              }
49.           });
50.        fileMenu.add(exitItem);
51.
52.        textArea = new JTextArea();
53.        getContentPane().add(new JScrollPane(textArea),
54.           BorderLayout.CENTER);
55.     }
56.
57.     public static final int WIDTH = 300;
58.     public static final int HEIGHT = 200;
59.
60.     private PasswordChooser dialog = null;
61.     private JTextArea textArea;
62.
63.     /**
64.        The Connect action pops up the password dialog.
65.     */
66.
67.     private class ConnectAction implements ActionListener
68.     {
69.        public void actionPerformed(ActionEvent event)
70.        {
71.           // if first time, construct dialog
72.
73.           if (dialog == null)
74.              dialog = new PasswordChooser();
75.
76.           // set default values
77.           dialog.setUser(new User("yourname", null));
78.
79.           // pop up dialog
80.           if (dialog.showDialog(DataExchangeFrame.this,
81.              "Connect"))
82.           {
```

```
83.                   // if accepted, retrieve user input
84.                   User u = dialog.getUser();
85.                   textArea.append(
86.                      "user name = " + u.getName()
87.                      + ", password = " + (new String(u.getPassword()))
88.                      + "\n");
89.                }
90.             }
91.       }
92. }
93.
94. /**
95.    A password chooser that is shown inside a dialog
96. */
97. class PasswordChooser extends JPanel
98. {
99.    public PasswordChooser()
100.   {
101.      setLayout(new BorderLayout());
102.
103.      // construct a panel with user name and password fields
104.
105.      JPanel panel = new JPanel();
106.      panel.setLayout(new GridLayout(2, 2));
107.      panel.add(new JLabel("User name:"));
108.      panel.add(username = new JTextField(""));
109.      panel.add(new JLabel("Password:"));
110.      panel.add(password = new JPasswordField(""));
111.      add(panel, BorderLayout.CENTER);
112.
113.      // create Ok and Cancel buttons that terminate the dialog
114.
115.      JButton okButton = new JButton("Ok");
116.      okButton.addActionListener(new
117.         ActionListener()
118.         {
119.            public void actionPerformed(ActionEvent event)
120.            {
121.               ok = true;
122.               dialog.setVisible(false);
123.            }
124.         });
125.
126.      JButton cancelButton = new JButton("Cancel");
127.      okButton.addActionListener(new
128.         ActionListener()
129.         {
130.            public void actionPerformed(ActionEvent event)
131.            {
132.               dialog.setVisible(false);
133.            }
```

```
134.            });
135.
136.        // add buttons to southern border
137.
138.        JPanel buttonPanel = new JPanel();
139.        buttonPanel.add(okButton);
140.        buttonPanel.add(cancelButton);
141.        add(buttonPanel, BorderLayout.SOUTH);
142.    }
143.
144.    /**
145.        Sets the dialog defaults.
146.        @param u the default user information
147.    */
148.    public void setUser(User u)
149.    {
150.        username.setText(u.getName());
151.    }
152.
153.    /**
154.        Gets the dialog entries.
155.        @return a User object whose state represents
156.        the dialog entries
157.    */
158.    public User getUser()
159.    {
160.        return new User(username.getText(),
161.            password.getPassword());
162.    }
163.
164.    /**
165.        Show the chooser panel in a dialog
166.        @param parent a component in the owner frame or null
167.        @param title the dialog window title
168.    */
169.    public boolean showDialog(Component parent, String title)
170.    {
171.        ok = false;
172.
173.        // locate the owner frame
174.
175.        Frame owner = null;
176.        if (parent instanceof Frame)
177.            owner = (Frame) parent;
178.        else
179.            owner = (Frame)SwingUtilities.getAncestorOfClass(
180.                Frame.class, parent);
181.
182.        // if first time, or if owner has changed, make new dialog
183.
184.        if (dialog == null || dialog.getOwner() != owner)
```

```
185.         {
186.             owner = null;
187.             dialog = new JDialog(owner, true);
188.             dialog.getContentPane().add(this);
189.             dialog.pack();
190.         }
191.
192.         // set title and show dialog
193.
194.         dialog.setTitle(title);
195.         dialog.show();
196.         return ok;
197.     }
198.
199.     private JTextField username;
200.     private JPasswordField password;
201.     private boolean ok;
202.     private JDialog dialog;
203. }
204.
205. /**
206.     A user has a name and password. For security reasons, the
207.     password is stored as a char[], not a String.
208. */
209. class User
210. {
211.     public User(String aName, char[] aPassword)
212.     {
213.         name = aName;
214.         password = aPassword;
215.     }
216.
217.     public String getName() { return name; }
218.     public char[] getPassword() { return password; }
219.
220.     public void setName(String aName) { name = aName; }
221.     public void setPassword(char[] aPassword)
222.     { password = aPassword; }
223.
224.     private String name;
225.     private char[] password;
226. }
```

File Dialogs

When you write an application, you often want to be able to open and save files. A good file dialog box that shows files and directories and lets the user navigate the file system is hard to write, and you definitely don't want to reinvent that wheel. Fortunately, Swing provides a `JFileChooser` class that allows you to display a file dialog box similar to the one that most native applications use.

`JFileChooser` dialogs are always modal. Note that the `JFileChooser` class is not a subclass of `JDialog`. Instead of calling `show`, you call `showOpenDialog` to display a dialog for opening a file or `showSaveDialog` to display a dialog for saving a file. The button for accepting a file is then automatically labeled Open or Save. You can also supply your own button label with the `showDialog` method. Figure 9–42 shows an example of the file chooser dialog box.

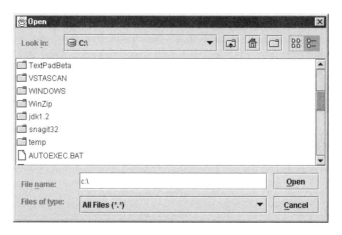

Figure 9–42: File chooser dialog box

Here are the steps needed to put up a file dialog box and recover what the user chooses from the box.

1. Make a `JFileChooser` object. Unlike the constructor for the `JDialog` class, you do not supply the parent component. This allows you to reuse a file chooser dialog with multiple frames.

    For example:

    ```
    JFileChooser chooser = new JFileChooser();
    ```

> TIP: Reusing a file chooser object is a good idea because the `JFileChooser` constructor can be quite slow, especially on Windows if the user has many mapped network drives.

2. Set the directory by calling the `setCurrentDirectory` method.

    For example, use

    ```
    chooser.setCurrentDirectory(new File("."));
    ```

    to use the current working directory. You need to supply a `File` object. `File` objects are explained in detail in Chapter 12. All you need to know for now is that there is a constructor `File(String filename)` that turns a file or directory name into a `File` object.

3. If you have a default file name that you expect the user to choose, supply it with the `setSelectedFile` method:

    ```
    chooser.setSelectedFile(new File(filename));
    ```

4. To enable the user to select multiple files in the dialog, call the `setMulti-SelectionEnabled` method. This is, of course, entirely optional and not all that common.

    ```
    chooser.setMultiSelectionEnabled(true);
    ```

5. If you want to restrict the display of files in the dialog to those of a particular type (for example, all files with extension `.gif`), then you need to set a *file filter*. We discuss file filters later in this section.

6. By default, a user can select only files with a file chooser. If you want the user to select directories, use the `setFileSelectionMode` method. Call it with `JFileChooser.FILES_ONLY` (the default), `JFileChooser.DIRECTORIES_ONLY`, or `JFileChooser.FILES_AND_DIRECTORIES`.

7. Show the dialog box by calling the `showOpenDialog` or `showSaveDialog` method. You must supply the parent component in these calls:

    ```
    int result = chooser.showOpenDialog(parent);
    ```

    or

    ```
    int result = chooser.showSaveDialog(parent);
    ```

    The only difference between these calls is the label of the "approve button," the button that the user clicks to finish the file selection. You can also call the `showDialog` method and pass an explicit text for the approve button:

    ```
    int result = chooser.showDialog(parent, "Select");
    ```

    These calls return only when the user has approved or canceled the file dialog. The return value is `JFileChooser.APPROVE_OPTION` or `JFile-Chooser.CANCEL_OPTION`.

8. You get the selected file or files with the `getSelectedFile()` or `getSe-lectedFiles()` method. These methods return either a single `File` object or an array of `File` objects. If you just need the name of the file object, call its `getPath` method. For example,

    ```
    String filename = chooser.getSelectedFile().getPath();
    ```

For the most part, these steps are simple. The major difficulty with using a file dialog is to specify a subset of files from which the user should choose. For example, suppose the user should choose a GIF image file. Then, the file chooser should only display files with extension `.gif`. It should also give the user some kind of feedback that the displayed files are of a particular category, such as "GIF Images." But the situation can be more complex. If the user should choose a JPEG image file, then the extension can be either `.jpg` or `.jpeg`. Rather than coming up with a mechanism to codify these complexities, the designers of the file chooser supply a more elegant mechanism: to restrict the displayed files, you supply an object that implements the `javax.swing.filechooser.FileFilter` interface. The file chooser passes each file to the file filter and displays only the files that the file filter accepts.

To restrict the files shown in a dialog, you need to create an object of a class that extends the `FileFilter` class. At the time of this writing, only one such subclass is supplied: the default filter that accepts all files.

It is easy to write ad hoc file filters. You simply implement the two methods of the `FileFilter` interface:

```
public boolean accept(File f);
public String getDescription();
```

NOTE: There is an unrelated `FileFilter` interface in the `java.io` package that has a single method, `boolean accept(File f)`. It is used in the `listFiles` method of the `File` class to list files in a directory. We do not know why the designers of Swing didn't extend this interface—perhaps the Java class library has now become so complex that even the programmers at Sun are no longer aware of all the standard classes and interfaces.

You will need to resolve the name conflict between these two identically named types if you import both the `java.io` and the `javax.swing.filechooser` package. The simplest remedy is to import `javax.swing.filechooser.FileFilter`, not `javax.swing.filechooser.*`.

The first method tests whether a file should be accepted. The second method returns a description of the file type that can be displayed in the file chooser dialog. For example, to filter for GIF files, you might use

```
public class GifFilter extends FileFilter
{
   public boolean accept(File f)
   {
      return f.getName().toLowerCase().endsWith(".gif")
         || f.isDirectory();
   }
   public String getDescription()
   {
      return "GIF Image";
   }
}
```

Once you have a file filter object, you use the `setFileFilter` method of the `JFileChooser` class to install it into the file chooser object:

```
chooser.setFileFilter(new GifFilter());
```

In our sample program, we supply a class `ExtensionFileFilter`, to be used as follows:

```
ExtensionFileFilter filter = new ExtensionFileFilter();
filter.addExtension("jpg");
filter.addExtension("gif");
filter.setDescription("Image files");
```

The implementation of the `ExtensionFileFilter` is a straightforward generalization of the `GifFilter` class. You may want to use that class in your own programs.

NOTE: The Java SDK contains a similar class `ExampleFileFilter` in the `demo/jfc/FileChooserDemo` directory.

You can install multiple filters to the file chooser. The user selects a filter from the combo box at the bottom of the file dialog. By default, the "All files" filter is always present in the combo box. This is a good idea, just in case a user of your program needs to select a file with a non-standard extension. However, if you want to suppress the "All files" filter, call

```
chooser.setAcceptAllFileFilterUsed(false)
```

Finally, you can customize the file chooser by providing special icons and file descriptions for each file that the file chooser displays. You do this by supplying an object of a class extending the `FileView` class in the `javax.swing.filechooser` package. This is definitely an advanced technique. Normally, you don't need to supply a file view—the pluggable look and feel supplies one for you. But if you want to show different icons for special file types, you can install your own file view. You need to extend the `FileView` class and implement five methods:

```
Icon getIcon(File f);
String getName(File f);
String getDescription(File f);
String getTypeDescription(File f);
Boolean isTraversable(File f);
```

Then you use the `setFileView` method to install your file view into the file chooser.

The file chooser calls your methods for each file or directory that it wants to display. If your method returns `null` for the icon, name, or description, the file chooser then consults the default file view of the look and feel. That is good, because it means you need to deal only with the file types for which you want to do something different.

The file chooser calls the `isTraversable` method to decide whether to open a directory when a user clicks on it. Note that this method returns a `Boolean` object, not a `boolean` value! This seems weird, but it is actually convenient—if you aren't interested in deviating from the default file view, just return `null`. The file chooser will then consult the default file view. In other words, the method returns a `Boolean` to give you the choice between three options: true (`Boolean.TRUE`), false (`Boolean.FALSE`), and don't care (`null`).

The example program contains a simple file view class. That class shows a particular icon whenever a file matches a file filter. We use it to display a palette icon for all image files.

```
class FileIconView extends FileView
{
   public FileIconView(FileFilter aFilter, Icon anIcon)
   {
      filter = aFilter;
      icon = anIcon;
   }

   public Icon getIcon(File f)
   {
      if (!f.isDirectory() && filter.accept(f))
         return icon;
      else return null;
   }

   private FileFilter filter;
   private Icon icon;
}
```

CAUTION: In J2SE version 1.2, you must define all five methods of your `FileView` subclass. Simply return `null` in the methods that you don't need. In J2SE version 1.3, the `FileView` methods are no longer abstract.

You install this file view into your file chooser with the `setFileView` method:

```
chooser.setFileView(new FileIconView(filter,
   new ImageIcon("palette.gif")));
```

The file chooser will then show the palette icon next to all files that pass the `filter`, and use the default file view to show all other files. Naturally, we use the same filter that we set in the file chooser.

> TIP: You can find a more useful `ExampleFileView` class in the `demo/jfc/`
> `FileChooserDemo` directory of the SDK. That class lets you associate icons and
> descriptions with arbitrary extensions.

Finally, you can customize a file dialog by adding an *accessory* component. For
example, Figure 9–43 shows a preview accessory next to the file list. This accessory displays a thumbnail view of the currently selected file.

An accessory can be any Swing component. In our case, we extend the `JLabel`
class and set its icon to a scaled copy of the graphics image:

```
class ImagePreviewer extends JLabel
{
   public ImagePreviewer(JFileChooser chooser)
   {
      setPreferredSize(new Dimension(100, 100));
      setBorder(BorderFactory.createEtchedBorder());
   }

   public void loadImage(File f)
   {
      ImageIcon icon = new ImageIcon(f.getPath());
      if(icon.getIconWidth() > getWidth())
         icon = new ImageIcon(icon.getImage().getScaledInstance(
            getWidth(), -1, Image.SCALE_DEFAULT));
      setIcon(icon);
      repaint();
   }
}
```

There is just one challenge. We want to update the preview image whenever the user
selects a different file. The file chooser uses the "Java Beans" mechanism of notifying
interested listeners whenever one of its properties changes. The selected file is a
property that you can monitor by installing a `PropertyChangeListener`. We
will discuss this mechanism in greater detail in Volume 2. Here is the code that you
need to trap the notifications:

```
chooser.addPropertyChangeListener(new
   PropertyChangeListener()
   {
      public void propertyChange(PropertyChangeEvent event)
      {
         if (event.getPropertyName() ==
            JFileChooser.SELECTED_FILE_CHANGED_PROPERTY)
         {
            File newFile = (File)event.getNewValue()
            // update the accessory
```

```
            }
        }
    });
```

In our example program, we add this code to the `ImagePreviewer` constructor.

Figure 9–43: A file dialog with a preview accessory

Example 9–19 contains a modification of the `ImageViewer` program from
Chapter 2, in which the file chooser has been enhanced by a custom file view and
a preview accessory.

Example 9–19: FileChooserTest.java

```
1. import java.awt.*;
2. import java.awt.event.*;
3. import java.awt.image.*;
4. import java.beans.*;
5. import java.util.*;
6. import java.io.*;
7. import javax.swing.*;
8. import javax.swing.filechooser.FileFilter;
9. import javax.swing.filechooser.FileView;
10.
11. public class FileChooserTest
12. {
13.    public static void main(String[] args)
14.    {
15.       ImageViewerFrame frame = new ImageViewerFrame();
16.       frame.setDefaultCloseOperation(JFrame.EXIT_ON_CLOSE);
17.       frame.show();
18.    }
19. }
20.
21. /**
```

```
22.    A frame that has a menu for loading an image and a display
23.    area for the loaded image.
24. */
25. class ImageViewerFrame extends JFrame
26. {
27.    public ImageViewerFrame()
28.    {
29.       setTitle("FileChooserTest");
30.       setSize(WIDTH, HEIGHT);
31.
32.       // set up menu bar
33.       JMenuBar menuBar = new JMenuBar();
34.       setJMenuBar(menuBar);
35.
36.       JMenu menu = new JMenu("File");
37.       menuBar.add(menu);
38.
39.       JMenuItem openItem = new JMenuItem("Open");
40.       menu.add(openItem);
41.       openItem.addActionListener(new FileOpenListener());
42.
43.       JMenuItem exitItem = new JMenuItem("Exit");
44.       menu.add(exitItem);
45.       exitItem.addActionListener(new
46.          ActionListener()
47.          {
48.             public void actionPerformed(ActionEvent event)
49.             {
50.                System.exit(0);
51.             }
52.          });
53.
54.       // use a label to display the images
55.       label = new JLabel();
56.       Container contentPane = getContentPane();
57.       contentPane.add(label);
58.
59.       chooser = new JFileChooser();
60.    }
61.
62.    /**
63.       This is the listener for the File->Open menu item.
64.    */
65.    private class FileOpenListener implements ActionListener
66.    {
67.       public void actionPerformed(ActionEvent evt)
68.       {
69.          // set up file chooser
70.          chooser.setCurrentDirectory(new File("."));
71.
72.          // accept all image files ending with .jpg, .jpeg, .gif
```

```
73.          final ExtensionFileFilter filter
74.             = new ExtensionFileFilter();
75.          filter.addExtension("jpg");
76.          filter.addExtension("jpeg");
77.          filter.addExtension("gif");
78.          filter.setDescription("Image files");
79.          chooser.setFileFilter(filter);
80.
81.          chooser.setAccessory(new ImagePreviewer(chooser));
82.
83.          chooser.setFileView(new FileIconView(filter,
84.             new ImageIcon("palette.gif")));
85.
86.          // show file chooser dialog
87.          int result
88.             = chooser.showOpenDialog(ImageViewerFrame.this);
89.
90.          // if image file accepted, set it as icon of the label
91.          if(result == JFileChooser.APPROVE_OPTION)
92.          {
93.             String name
94.                = chooser.getSelectedFile().getPath();
95.             label.setIcon(new ImageIcon(name));
96.          }
97.       }
98.    }
99.
100.   public static final int WIDTH = 300;
101.   public static final int HEIGHT = 400;
102.
103.   private JLabel label;
104.   private JFileChooser chooser;
105. }
106.
107. /**
108.    This file filter matches all files with a given set of
109.    extensions.
110. */
111. class ExtensionFileFilter extends FileFilter
112. {
113.    /**
114.       Adds an extension that this file filter recognizes.
115.       @param extension a file extension (such as ".txt" or "txt")
116.    */
117.    public void addExtension(String extension)
118.    {
119.       if (!extension.startsWith("."))
120.          extension = "." + extension;
121.       extensions.add(extension.toLowerCase());
122.    }
123.
```

```
124.    /**
125.        Sets a description for the file set that this file filter
126.        recognizes.
127.        @param aDescription a description for the file set
128.    */
129.    public void setDescription(String aDescription)
130.    {
131.        description = aDescription;
132.    }
133.
134.    /**
135.        Returns a description for the file set that this file
136.        filter recognizes.
137.        @return a description for the file set
138.    */
139.    public String getDescription()
140.    {
141.        return description;
142.    }
143.
144.    public boolean accept(File f)
145.    {
146.        if (f.isDirectory()) return true;
147.        String name = f.getName().toLowerCase();
148.
149.        // check if the file name ends with any of the extensions
150.        for (int i = 0; i < extensions.size(); i++)
151.            if (name.endsWith((String)extensions.get(i)))
152.                return true;
153.        return false;
154.    }
155.
156.    private String description = "";
157.    private ArrayList extensions = new ArrayList();
158. }
159.
160. /**
161.    A file view that displays an icon for all files that match
162.    a file filter.
163. */
164. class FileIconView extends FileView
165. {
166.    /**
167.        Constructs a FileIconView.
168.        @param aFilter a file filter--all files that this filter
169.        accepts will be shown with the icon.
170.        @param anIcon--the icon shown with all accepted files.
171.    */
172.    public FileIconView(FileFilter aFilter, Icon anIcon)
173.    {
174.        filter = aFilter;
```

```
175.         icon = anIcon;
176.     }
177.
178.     public Icon getIcon(File f)
179.     {
180.         if (!f.isDirectory() && filter.accept(f))
181.             return icon;
182.         else return null;
183.     }
184.
185.     private FileFilter filter;
186.     private Icon icon;
187. }
188.
189. /**
190.     A file chooser accessory that previews images.
191. */
192. class ImagePreviewer extends JLabel
193. {
194.     /**
195.         Constructs an ImagePreviewer.
196.         @param chooser the file chooser whose property changes
197.         trigger an image change in this previewer
198.     */
199.     public ImagePreviewer(JFileChooser chooser)
200.     {
201.         setPreferredSize(new Dimension(100, 100));
202.         setBorder(BorderFactory.createEtchedBorder());
203.
204.         chooser.addPropertyChangeListener(new
205.             PropertyChangeListener()
206.             {
207.                 public void propertyChange(PropertyChangeEvent
208.                     event)
209.                 {
210.                     if (event.getPropertyName() ==
211.                         JFileChooser.SELECTED_FILE_CHANGED_PROPERTY)
212.                     {
213.                         // the user has selected a new file
214.                         File f = (File)event.getNewValue();
215.
216.                         // read the image into an icon
217.                         ImageIcon icon = new ImageIcon(f.getPath());
218.
219.                         // if the icon is too large to fit, scale it
220.                         if(icon.getIconWidth() > getWidth())
221.                             icon = new ImageIcon(
222.                                 icon.getImage().getScaledInstance(
223.                                     getWidth(), -1, Image.SCALE_DEFAULT));
224.
225.                         setIcon(icon);
```

```
226.                    }
227.      }
228.           });
229.      }
230. }
```

javax.swing.JFileChooser

- `JFileChooser()`
  creates a file chooser dialog box that can be used for multiple frames.
- `void setCurrentDirectory(File dir)`
  sets the initial directory for the file dialog box.
- `void setSelectedFile(File file)`
- `void setSelectedFiles(File[] file)`
  set the default file choice for the file dialog box.
- `void setMultiSelectionEnabled(boolean b)`
  sets or clears multiple selection mode.
- `void setAcceptAllFileFilterUsed(boolean b)`
  includes or suppresses an "All files" filter in the filter combo box.
- `void setFileSelectionMode(int mode)`
  lets the user select files only (the default), directories only, or both files and directories. The mode parameter is one of `JFileChooser.FILES_ONLY`, `JFileChooser.DIRECTORIES_ONLY`, and `JFileChooser.FILES_AND_DIRECTORIES`
- `int showOpenDialog(Component parent)`
- `int showSaveDialog(Component parent)`
- `int showDialog(Component parent, String approveButtonText)`
  show a dialog in which the approve button is labeled "Open," "Save," or with the `approveButtonText` string. Returns `APPROVE_OPTION` or `CANCEL_OPTION`.
- `File getSelectedFile()`
- `File[] getSelectedFiles()`
  get the file or files that the user selected (or returns `null` if the user didn't select any file).
- `void setFileFilter(javax.swing.filechooser.FileFilter filter)`
  sets the file mask for the file dialog box. All files for which `filter.accept` returns `true` will be displayed.
- `void setFileView(FileView view)`
  sets a file view to provide information about the files that the file chooser displays.
- `void setAccessory(JComponent component)`
  sets an accessory component.

javax.swing.filechooser.FileFilter

- boolean accept(File f)

  returns true if the file chooser should display this file.

- String getDescription()

  returns a description of this file filter, for example "Image files (*.gif,*.jpeg)".

javax.swing.filechooser.FileView

- String getName(File f)

  returns the name of the file f, or null. Normally, this method simply returns f.getName().

- String getDescription(File f)

  returns a humanly readable description of the file f, or null. For example, if f is an HTML document, this method might return its title.

- String getTypeDescription(File f)

  returns a humanly readable description of the type of the file f, or null. For example, if f is an HTML document, this method might return a string "Hypertext document".

- Icon getIcon(File f)

  returns an icon for the file f, or null. For example, if f is a JPEG file, this method might return a thumbnail icon.

- Boolean isTraversable(File f)

  returns Boolean.TRUE if f is a directory that the user can open. This method might return false if a directory is conceptually a compound document. Like all FileView methods, this method can return null to indicate that the file chooser should consult the default view instead.

Color Choosers

As you saw in the preceding section, a high quality file chooser is an intricate user interface component that you definitely do not want to implement yourself. There are other common dialogs to choose a date/time, currency value, font, color, and so on that many user interface toolkits provide. The benefit is twofold. Programmers can simply use a high-quality implementation rather than rolling their own. And users have a common experience for these selections.

At this point, Swing only provides one additional chooser, the JColorChooser (see Figures 9–44 through 9–46). You use it to let users pick a color value. Like the `JFileChooser` class, the color chooser is a component, not a dialog, but it contains convenience methods to create dialogs that contain a color chooser component.

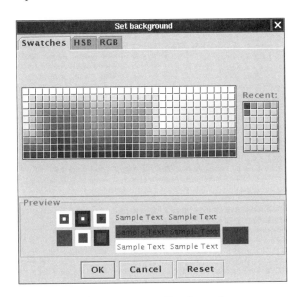

Figure 9–44: The "swatches" pane of color chooser

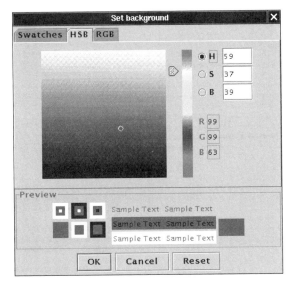

Figure 9–45: The HSB pane of a color chooser

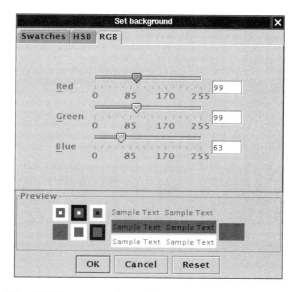

Figure 9–46: The RGB pane of a color chooser

Here is how you show a modal dialog with a color chooser

```
Color selectedColor = JColorChooser.showDialog(parent,
    title, initialColor);
```

Alternatively, you can display a modeless color chooser dialog. You supply:

- A parent component;
- The title of the dialog;
- A flag to select either a modal or a modeless dialog;
- A color chooser;
- Listeners for the OK and Cancel buttons (or `null` if you don't want a listener).

Here is how you make a modeless dialog that sets the background color when the user presses the OK button:

```
chooser = new JColorChooser();
dialog = JColorChooser.createDialog(
    parent,
    "Background Color",
    false /* not modal */,
    chooser,
    new ActionListener() // OK button listener
        {
            public void actionPerformed(ActionEvent event)
            {
                setBackground(chooser.getColor());
            }
        },
    null /* no Cancel button listener */);
```

You can do even better than that, and give the user immediate feedback of the color selection. To monitor the color selections, you need to obtain the selection model of the chooser and add a change listener:

```
chooser.getSelectionModel().addChangeListener(new
   ChangeListener()
   {
      public void stateChanged(ChangeEvent event)
      {
         do something with chooser.getColor();
      }
   });
```

In this case, there is no benefit to the OK and Cancel buttons that the color chooser dialog provides. You can just add the color chooser component directly into a modeless dialog:

```
dialog = new JDialog(parent, false /* not modal */);
dialog.getContentPane().add(chooser);
dialog.pack();
```

The program in Example 9–20 shows the three types of dialog. If you click on the Modal button, you must select a color before you can do anything else. If you click on the Modeless button, you get a modeless dialog, but the color change only happens when you click the OK button on the dialog. If you click the Immediate button, you get a modeless dialog without buttons. As soon as you pick a different color in the dialog, the background color of the panel is updated.

This ends our discussion of user interface components. The material in Chapters 7 through 9 showed you how to implement simple graphical user interfaces in Swing. Please turn to Volume 2 for more advanced Swing components and sophisticated graphics techniques.

Example 9–20: ColorChooserTest.java

```
1. import java.awlt.*;
2. import java.awt.event.*;
3. import javax.swing.*;
4. import javax.swing.event.*;
5.
6. public class ColorChooserTest
7. {
8.    public static void main(String[] args)
9.    {
10.       ColorChooserFrame frame = new ColorChooserFrame();
11.       frame.setDefaultCloseOperation(JFrame.EXIT_ON_CLOSE);
12.       frame.show();
13.    }
14. }
15.
```

```
16. /**
17.    A frame with a color chooser panel
18. */
19. class ColorChooserFrame extends JFrame
20. {
21.    public ColorChooserFrame()
22.    {
23.       setTitle("ColorChooserTest");
24.       setSize(WIDTH, HEIGHT);
25.
26.       // add color chooser panel to frame
27.
28.       ColorChooserPanel panel = new ColorChooserPanel();
29.       Container contentPane = getContentPane();
30.       contentPane.add(panel);
31.    }
32.
33.    public static final int WIDTH = 300;
34.    public static final int HEIGHT = 200;
35. }
36.
37. /**
38.    A panel with buttons to pop up three types of color choosers
39. */
40. class ColorChooserPanel extends JPanel
41. {
42.    public ColorChooserPanel()
43.    {
44.       JButton modalButton = new JButton("Modal");
45.       modalButton.addActionListener(new ModalListener());
46.       add(modalButton);
47.
48.       JButton modelessButton = new JButton("Modeless");
49.       modelessButton.addActionListener(new ModelessListener());
50.       add(modelessButton);
51.
52.       JButton immediateButton = new JButton("Immediate");
53.       immediateButton.addActionListener(new ImmediateListener());
54.       add(immediateButton);
55.    }
56.
57.    /**
58.       This listener pops up a modal color chooser
59.    */
60.    private class ModalListener implements ActionListener
61.    {
62.       public void actionPerformed(ActionEvent event)
63.       {
64.          Color defaultColor = getBackground();
65.          Color selected = JColorChooser.showDialog(
66.             ColorChooserPanel.this,
```

```
67.              "Set background",
68.              defaultColor);
69.          setBackground(selected);
70.      }
71.  }
72.
73.  /**
74.     This listener pops up a modeless color chooser.
75.     The panel color is changed when the user clicks the Ok
76.     button.
77.  */
78.  private class ModelessListener implements ActionListener
79.  {
80.      public ModelessListener()
81.      {
82.         chooser = new JColorChooser();
83.         dialog = JColorChooser.createDialog(
84.            ColorChooserPanel.this,
85.            "Background Color",
86.            false /* not modal */,
87.            chooser,
88.            new ActionListener() // OK button listener
89.                {
90.                    public void actionPerformed(ActionEvent event)
91.                    {
92.                        setBackground(chooser.getColor());
93.                    }
94.                },
95.            null /* no Cancel button listener */);
96.      }
97.
98.      public void actionPerformed(ActionEvent event)
99.      {
100.         chooser.setColor(getBackground());
101.         dialog.show();
102.      }
103.
104.      private JDialog dialog;
105.      private JColorChooser chooser;
106.  }
107.
108.  /**
109.     This listener pops up a modeless color chooser.
110.     The panel color is changed immediately when the
111.     user picks a new color.
112.  */
113.  private class ImmediateListener implements ActionListener
114.  {
115.      public ImmediateListener()
116.      {
117.         chooser = new JColorChooser();
```

```
118.            chooser.getSelectionModel().addChangeListener(new
119.               ChangeListener()
120.               {
121.                  public void stateChanged(ChangeEvent event)
122.                  {
123.                     setBackground(chooser.getColor());
124.                  }
125.               });
126.
127.            dialog = new JDialog(
128.               (Frame)null,
129.               false /* not modal */);
130.            dialog.getContentPane().add(chooser);
131.            dialog.pack();
132.         }
133.
134.      public void actionPerformed(ActionEvent event)
135.      {
136.         chooser.setColor(getBackground());
137.         dialog.show();
138.      }
139.
140.      private JDialog dialog;
141.      private JColorChooser chooser;
142.   }
143. }
```

java.swing.JColorChooser

- `JColorChooser()`

  constructs a color chooser with an initial color of white.

- `Color getColor()`
- `void setColor(Color c)`

  get and set the current color of this color chooser.

- `static Color showDialog(Component parent, String title, Color initialColor)`

  shows a modal dialog that contains a color chooser.

Parameters:	`parent`	The component over which to pop up the dialog
	`title`	The title for the dialog box frame
	`initialColor`	The initial color to show in the color chooser

- `static JDialog createDialog(Component parent, String title, boolean modal, JColorChooser chooser, ActionListener okListener, ActionListener cancelListener)`

  creates a dialog box that contains a color chooser.

Parameters:	`parent`	The component over which to pop up the dialog
	`title`	The title for the dialog box frame
	`modal`	`true` if this call should block until the dialog is closed
	`chooser`	The color chooser to add to the dialog
	`okListener,` `cancelListener`	The listeners of the OK and Cancel buttons

Chapter **10**

Applets

▼ APPLET BASICS
▼ THE APPLET HTML TAGS AND ATTRIBUTES
▼ MULTIMEDIA
▼ THE APPLET CONTEXT
▼ JAR FILES

At this point, you should be comfortable with using most of the features of the Java programming language, and you had a pretty thorough introduction to basic graphics programming in Java. We hope that you agree with us that Java is a nice (if not perfect), general-purpose OOP language, and the Swing user interface libraries are flexible and useful. That's nice, but it isn't what created the hype around Java. The unbelievable hype during the first few years of Java's life (as was mentioned in Chapter 1) stems from Java's ability to "activate the Internet." The point is that you can create a special kind of Java program (called an applet) that a Java-enabled browser can download from the Net and then run. This chapter shows you how to write basic applets. Full-featured applets depend on the programmer's mastery of Java's networking and multithreading capabilities. These advanced topics will be covered in Volume 2.

Nowadays, of course, since modern browsers support Dynamic HTML and scripting, browsers can do far more than they could when the Java platform was first released. Still, since applets are written in a full-fledged programming

577

language, they potentially have more power than any foreseeable combination of HTML, XML, and scripting will ever have.

Applet Basics

Before Java, you used HTML (the hypertext markup language) to describe the layout of a web page. HTML is simply a vehicle to indicate elements of a hypertext page. For example, `<TITLE>` indicates the title of the page, and any text that follows this tag becomes the title of the page. You indicate the end of the title with the `</TITLE>` tag. (This is one of the general rules for tags: a slash followed by the name of the element indicates the end of the element.)

The basic idea of how to use applets in a web page is simple: the HTML page must tell the browser which applets to load and then where to put each applet on the web page. As you might expect, the tag needed to use an applet must tell the browser the following:

- From where to get the class files;
- How the applet sits on the web page (size, location, and so on).

NOTE: The original way to embed a Java applet was via an `APPLET` tag with parameters that gave the information listed above. The W3 Consortium has suggested switching to the more versatile `OBJECT` tag, and the older `APPLET` tag is deprecated in the HTML 4.0 specification. The latest browsers will recognize both tags, but you should keep in mind that older browsers do not. We will cover the basics of using these tags a little later in this chapter.

The browser then retrieves the class files from the Net (or from a directory on the user's machine) and automatically runs the applet, using its Java Virtual Machine.

In addition to the applet itself, the web page can contain all the other HTML elements you have seen in use on web pages: multiple fonts, bulleted lists, graphics, links, and so on. Applets are just one part of the hypertext page. It is always worth keeping in mind that the Java programming language is *not* a tool for designing HTML pages; it is a tool for *bringing them to life*. This is not to say that the GUI design elements in a Java applet are not important, but that they must work with (and, in fact, are subservient to) the underlying HTML design of the web page.

NOTE: We do not cover general HTML tags at all; we assume that you know—or are working with someone who knows—the basics of HTML. Only a few special HTML tags are needed for Java applets. We do, of course, cover those later in this chapter. As for learning HTML, there are dozens of HTML books at your local bookstore. One that covers what you need and will not insult your intelligence is *HTML: The Definitive Guide* by Chuck Musciano and Bill Kennedy from O'Reilly & Associates.

When applets were first developed, you had to use Sun's HotJava browser to view web pages that contain applets. Naturally, few users were willing to use a separate browser just to enjoy a new web feature. Java applets became really popular when Netscape included a Java Virtual Machine in its browser. Internet Explorer soon followed suit. Unfortunately, the browser manufacturers have not kept up with Java. Both Netscape and Internet Explorer do a good job with Java 1.0 features, and their newest versions can handle most of the Java 1.1 features.

But, we can't stress enough that there have always been and will probably continue to be annoying limitations and incompatibilities. For example, Microsoft will likely never implement certain parts of Java that it feels are particularly competitive with its own technology. Netscape has basically gone out of the virtual machine business. Netscape 6 lets users plug in their own virtual machine, but Netscape 4 does not have this feature. All this makes it difficult to deploy an applet that uses modern Java features and that can still be viewed by different browsers.

To overcome this problem, Sun released a tool called the "Java Plug-In" (originally known as the "Activator"). Using the various extension mechanisms of Internet Explorer or Navigator, it seamlessly plugs into both Netscape and Internet Explorer and allows both browsers to execute Java applets by using an external Java Runtime Environment that Sun supplies. Their version of the virtual machine will presumably always be up-to-date, thus ensuring that you can always take advantage of the latest and greatest features of Java.

Once you install the Java Plug-In software, you can switch to different versions of the Java Virtual Machine. To run the applets in this book, you need to install the Java Plug-In and select the Java 1.3 virtual machine (see Figure 10–1).

Figure 10–1: Selecting the Java Virtual Machine in the Java Plug-In

Admittedly, if you are designing web pages for a wide audience, it is probably unreasonable to ask the visitors to your web page to install the Java Plug-In, which is a fairly hefty (if one-time) download. In that case, you need to design applets that can work with the Java Virtual Machines that are built into Netscape and Internet Explorer. It is then best to stick to Java 1.0 features and keep the applet as simple as possible. But frankly, if your applet is that simple, you can probably do entirely without it—use JavaScript for program logic, forms for data entry, and animated GIF files for animations. Then place the intelligence on the server, preferably with Java-based servlets and server pages.

On the other hand, if you roll out a very sophisticated Java program, you should ask yourself whether there is any benefit from using the web browser as a delivery vehicle. If not, then you can simply deliver Java applications that your users run on their local machines. You still have all benefits of Java, such as platform independence, security management, and easy database and network access. Of course, there are advantages to web deployment. For a user, it is often easier to locate an application on the Web than on the local file system. (This is particularly true for applications that aren't used every day.) For an administrator, it is easier to maintain and update an application on the Web than to push out bug fixes and improvements to lots of client desktops.

Thus, among the most successful Java programs are corporate *intranet* applications that interface with corporate information systems. For example, many companies have put expense reimbursement calculators, benefit tracking tools, schedule and vacation planners, purchase order requests, and so on, on their corporate intranet. These programs are relatively small, need to interface with databases, need more flexibility than web forms can easily handle, and need to be customized to the operations of a particular company. Applets are a perfect delivery technology for these programs. Since the user population is constrained, there is no problem with distributing the Java Plug-In.

We recommend that you choose one of the following two options for your web applications:

1. Use the Java Plug-In to deliver Java applets if you are on an intranet. This gives you maximum control over the Java platform, fewer portability headaches, and the ability to use the most advanced Java features. Of course, you must then manage the deployment of the Java Plug-In.

2. If you are not on an intranet, don't use applets. Use scripting for validation; use animated GIFs for animation; use forms and server-side processing for data entry.

A Simple Applet

For tradition's sake, let's write a `NotHelloWorld` program as an applet. Before we do that, we want to point out that, from a programming point of view, an applet isn't very strange. An applet is simply a Java class that (ultimately) extends the `java.applet.Applet` class. Note that although the `java.applet` package is not part of the `AWT` package, an applet is an AWT component, as the inheritance chain shown in Figure 10–2 illustrates. In this book, we will use the Swing set to implement applets. All of our applets will extend the `JApplet` class, the superclass for Swing applets. As you can see in Figure 10–2, `JApplet` is an immediate subclass of the ordinary `Applet` class

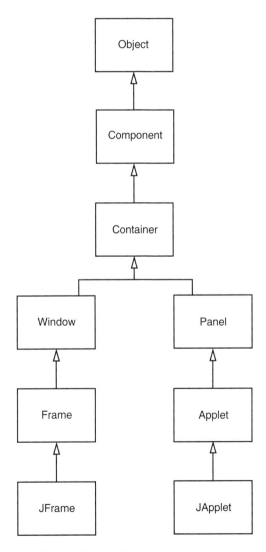

Figure 10–2: Applet inheritance hierarchy

NOTE: If your applet contains Swing components, you must extend the `JApplet` class. Swing components inside a plain `Applet` don't paint correctly.

This inheritance hierarchy has some obvious but still useful consequences. For example, since applets are AWT components, event handling in applets is done exactly as you saw in Chapter 8.

Example 10–1 shows the code for an applet version of "Not Hello World."

Notice how similar this is to the corresponding program from Chapter 7. However, because the applet lives inside a web page, there is no need to specify a method for exiting the applet.

Example 10–1: NotHelloWorldApplet.java

```
1. import java.awt.*;
2. import javax.swing.*;
3.
4. public class NotHelloWorldApplet extends JApplet
5. {
6.    public void init()
7.    {
8.       Container contentPane = getContentPane();
9.       JLabel label = new JLabel("Not a Hello, World applet",
10.          SwingConstants.CENTER);
11.       contentPane.add(label);
12.    }
13. }
```

Running the Applet Viewer

To execute the applet, you need to carry out two steps:

1.   Compile your source files into class files.

2.   Create an HTML file that tells the browser which class file to load first and how to size the applet.

It is customary (but not necessary) to give the HTML file the same name as that of the applet class inside. So, following this tradition, we will call the file `NotHelloWorldApplet.html`. Here are the contents of the file:

```
<APPLET CODE="NotHelloWorldApplet.class" WIDTH=300 HEIGHT=300>
</APPLET>
```

Before viewing the applet in a browser, it is a good idea to test it in the *applet viewer* program that is a part of the Java SDK. To use the applet viewer in our example, enter

```
appletviewer NotHelloWorldApplet.html
```

at the command line. The command line for the applet viewer program is the name of the HTML file, not the class file. Figure 10–3 shows the applet viewer, displaying this applet.

Figure 10–3: Viewing an applet in the applet viewer

TIP: You can also run applets from inside your editor or integrated environment. In Emacs, select JDE -> Run Applet from the menu. In TextPad, choose Tools -> Run Java Applet or use the CTRL+3 keyboard shortcut. You will be presented with a dialog that lists all HTML files in the current directory. If you press ESC, TextPad automatically creates a minimal HTML file for you. In Forte, you simply load the HTML page with the applet tags. Forte contains a simple browser that shows the applet running inside the web page. Alternatively, you can right-click on the source file and set the value of the "Executor" property in the Execution tab to "Applet Execution."

TIP: Here is a weird trick to avoid the additional HTML file. Add an applet tag *as a comment inside the source file:*

```
/*
  <APPLET CODE="MyApplet.class" WIDTH=300 HEIGHT=300>
  </APPLET>
*/
public class MyApplet extends JApplet
  . . .
```

Then run the applet viewer *with the source file* as its command line argument:

```
appletviewer NotHelloWorldApplet.java
```

We aren't necessarily recommending this as standard practice, but it can come in handy if you want to minimize the number of files that you need to worry about during testing.

The applet viewer is good for the first stage of testing, but at some point you need to run your applets in a browser to see them in the same way a user might use them. In particular, the applet viewer program shows you only the applet, not the surrounding HTML text. If an HTML file contains multiple applets, the applet viewer pops up multiple windows.

Viewing an Applet in a Browser

If you have a Java 2 enabled browser such as Netscape 6 or Opera, then you can simply load the HTML file into the browser. However, to run the applet in Internet Explorer or Netscape 4, you need to install the Java Plug-In into the browser and convert the HTML file so that the browser will invoke the Plug-In.

If you installed the Java 2 SDK, the Java Plug-In is automatically installed as well. However, if you want to install the Java Plug-In separately from the SDK, you can download it from `http://java.sun.com/products/plugin`.

TIP: After you install the SDK or the Java Plug-In, activate the Java Plug-In Control Panel (see Figure 10–4). In Windows, go to the Windows control panel (Start -> Settings -> Control panel) and double-click on the Java Plug-In icon. In Solaris, run the command

```
~/.netscape/java/ControlPanel
```
or visit the page

```
~/.netscape/java/ControlPanel.html
```
Then check the "Show Java Console" box. This causes a console window to appear whenever the Java Plug-In is activated (see Figure 10–5). That console window is very useful for displaying applet error messages.

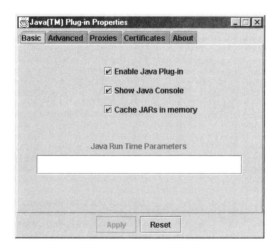

Figure 10–4: The Java Plug-In Control Panel

Figure 10–5: The Java Console

Unfortunately, the HTML tags you need to use your applet with the Java Plug-In are rather cumbersome. Rather than creating the tags by hand, it is best to run the HTML converter tool that Sun supplies for this purpose (see Figure 10–6). You can download the converter from `http://java.sun.com/products/plugin/1.3/converter.html`. Unzip the file, for example into `/usr/local/jdk/converter` or `c:\jdk\converter`.

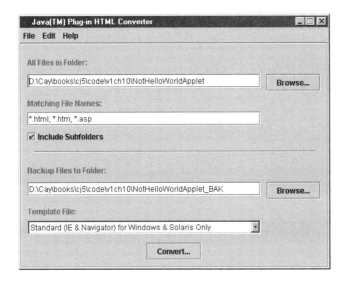

Figure 10–6: The Java Plug-In HTML converter

That converter tool translates a simple HTML file containing the traditional `APPLET` tag into the complex HTML file that is required to invoke the Java Plug-In from various browsers.

Before starting, make a directory `plugin` and copy your HTML file or files into that directory.

You can start the HTML converter as follows: Change to the `plugin` directory and issue the following command:

```
java -classpath /usr/local/jdk/converter/classes HTMLConverter
```

or

```
java -classpath c:\jdk\converter\classes HTMLConverter
```

By default, the converter shows a graphical user interface (see Figure 10–3). You can use the program to convert all files in a particular directory. If you start the program from the `plugin` directory, then all entries are set with reasonable defaults and you can just click the Convert button.

Alternatively, you can use the `HTMLConverter` shell script or batch file in the `jdk/converter/classes` directory. But then you must manually select the directory for your HTML files.

For example, for `NotHelloWorldApplet.html`, we started with the following simple HTML file:

```
<APPLET CODE="NotHelloWorldApplet.class" WIDTH=300 HEIGHT=300>
</APPLET>
```

The result of the conversion is shown in Example 10–2. We will explain these HTML tags later in this chapter.

If you prefer to use the command line, simply give a path name to the file or files that should be converted, for example

```
java -classpath /usr/local/jdk/converter/classes HTMLConverter
    *.html
```

or

```
java -classpath c:\jdk\converter\classes HTMLConverter
    MyApplet.html
```

The command-line converter converts and backs up the file in the same way as the GUI version, but it doesn't show you the GUI dialog.

By default, the converter produces HTML files that work for both Internet Explorer and Netscape Navigator. There are other conversion options—see the converter documentation for details.

The converter replaces the contents of all files in the directory and backs them up in a directory *sourcedir*_BAK. For example, if you placed your original files into a directory `plugin`, they are now replaced with the converted files, and the originals are in the directory `plugin_BAK`.

We don't like the in-place conversion, even though the converter keeps backup copies. It is often helpful to have both the original and the converted file around. We recommend the following procedure:

1. Copy the files to a temporary directory.

2. Run the converter.

3. Rename the converted files to something like `MyAppletPlugin.html`

4. Copy the renamed files back to their original location

Once you have converted the HTML files, you are ready to launch them in your browser. Simply load the converted HTML file into the browser. Provided that the Java Plug-In was installed correctly, the applet will be displayed (see Figure 10–7). If the Java Plug-In was not installed, your browser should walk you through the steps of fetching and installing it.

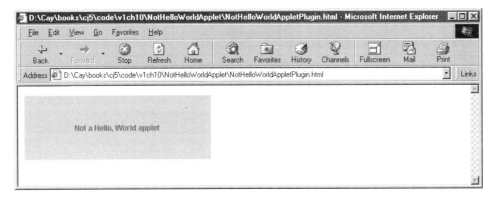

Figure 10–7: Viewing an applet in a browser

TIP: Testing applets with the Java Plug-In is a bit of a pain because you need to run your HTML files through the converter. If you use Netscape 4, you can save yourself a bit of trouble, provided that your applets don't require any Java 2 features beyond Swing. (None of the applets in this chapter do.) Grab the Swing add-on to Java 1.1 from `http://java.sun.com/products/jfc/#download-swing`. Place the file `swing.jar` into the `Netscape\Communicator\Program\Java\Classes` directory. Then, Netscape 4 is able to load applets that use the Swing set. You just need to supply a simple HTML file with an `APPLET` tag. No conversion to `EMBED` tags is necessary.

There is a similar but more complex procedure for Internet Explorer. See `http://java.sun.com/products/jfc/tsc/articles/applets/index.html` for details.

Example 10–2: NotHelloWorldAppletPlugin.html

```
1. <!--"CONVERTED_APPLET"-->
2. <!-- CONVERTER VERSION 1.3 -->
3. <OBJECT classid="clsid:8AD9C840-044E-11D1-B3E9-00805F499D93"
4. WIDTH = 300 HEIGHT = 300  codebase="http://java.sun.com/products/
   plugin/1.3/jinstall-13-win32.cab#Version=1,3,0,0">
5. <PARAM NAME = CODE VALUE = "NotHelloWorldApplet.class" >
6. PARAM NAME="type" VALUE="application/x-java-applet;version=1.3">
7. <PARAM NAME="scriptable" VALUE="false">
8. <COMMENT>
9. <EMBED type="application/x-java-applet;version=1.3"  CODE =
   "NotHelloWorldApplet.class" WIDTH = 300 HEIGHT = 300  script-
   able=false pluginspage="http://java.sun.com/products/plugin/1.3/
   plugin-install.html"><NOEMBED></COMMENT>
10. </NOEMBED></EMBED>
11. </OBJECT>
12. <!--
13. <APPLET CODE = "NotHelloWorldApplet.class" WIDTH = 300 HEIGHT = 300>
14. </APPLET>
15. -->
16. <!--"END_CONVERTED_APPLET"-->
```

Converting Applications to Applets

It is easy to convert a graphical Java application (that is, an application that uses the AWT and that you can start with the `java` command-line interpreter) into an applet that you can embed in a web page. Essentially, all of the user interface code can stay the same.

Here are the specific steps for converting an application to an applet.

1. Make an HTML page with the appropriate tag to load the applet code.

2. Supply a subclass of the `JApplet` class. Make this class `public`. Otherwise, the applet cannot be loaded.

3. Eliminate the `main` method in the application. Do not construct a frame window for the application. Your application will be displayed inside the browser.

4. Move any initialization code from the frame window constructor to the `init` method of the applet. You don't need to explicitly construct the applet object—the browser instantiates it for you and calls the `init` method.

5. Remove the call to `setSize`; for applets, sizing is done with the `WIDTH` and `HEIGHT` parameters in the actual HTML file.

6. Remove the call to `setDefaultCloseOperation`. An applet cannot be closed; it terminates when the browser exits.

7. If the application calls `setTitle`, eliminate the call to the method. Applets cannot have title bars. (You can, of course, title the web page itself, using the HTML `TITLE` tag.)

8. Don't call `show`. The applet is displayed automatically.

As an example of this transformation, we will change the calculator application from Chapter 7 into an applet. In Figure 10–8, you can see how it looks, sitting inside a web page.

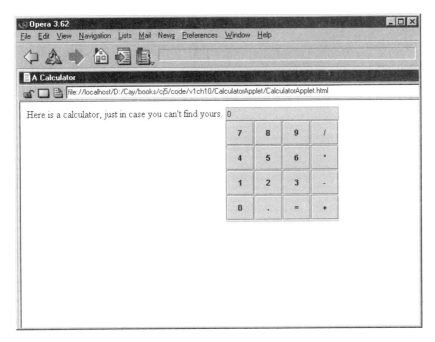

Figure 10–8: A calculator applet

Example 10–3 shows the HTML page. Note that there is some text in addition to the applet tags.

Example 10–3: Calculator.html (before processing with the HTML converter)

```
1. <HTML>
2. <TITLE>A Calculator</TITLE>
3. <BODY>
4. Here is a calculator, just in case you can't find yours.
5. <APPLET CODE="CalculatorApplet.class" WIDTH=180 HEIGHT=180>
6. </APPLET>
7. </BODY>
8. </HTML>
```

Example 10–4 is the code for the applet. We introduced a subclass of JApplet, placed the initialization code into the init method, and removed the calls to setTitle, setSize, setDefaultCloseOperation and show. The CalculatorPanel class did not change at all, and its code is omitted.

Example 10–4: CalculatorApplet.java

```
1. import java.awt.*;
2. import javax.swing.*;
3.
4. public class CalculatorApplet extends JApplet
5. {
6.    public void init()
7.    {
8.       Container contentPane = getContentPane();
9.       CalculatorPanel panel = new CalculatorPanel();
10.      contentPane.add(panel);
11.   }
12. }
```

java.applet.Applet

- void init()

  is called when the applet is first loaded. Override this method and place all initialization code here.

- void setSize(int width, int height)

  requests that the applet be resized. This would be a great method if it worked on web pages; unfortunately, it does not work in current browsers because it interferes with their page-layout mechanisms. But it does work in the applet viewer, and perhaps future browsers will support it and reflow the page when the applet size changes.

Life Cycle of an Applet

Four methods in the Applet class give you the framework on which you build any serious applet: init, start, stop, destroy. What follows is a short description of these methods, when these methods are called, and what code you should place into them.

- init

  This method is used for whatever initialization is needed for your applet. This works much like a constructor—it is automatically called by the system when Java launches the applet for the first time. Common actions in an applet include processing PARAM values and adding user interface components.

  Applets can have a default constructor, but it is customary to perform all initialization in the init method instead of the default constructor.

- start

  This method is automatically called *after* Java calls the `init` method. It is also called whenever the user returns to the page containing the applet after having gone off to other pages. This means that the `start` method can be called repeatedly, unlike the `init` method. For this reason, put the code that you want executed only once in the `init` method, rather than in the `start` method. The `start` method is where you usually restart a thread for your applet, for example, to resume an animation. If your applet does nothing that needs to be suspended when the user leaves the current web page, you do not need to implement this method (or the `stop` method).

- stop

  This method is automatically called when the user moves off the page on which the applet sits. It can, therefore, be called repeatedly in the same applet. Its purpose is to give you a chance to stop a time-consuming activity from slowing down the system when the user is not paying attention to the applet. You should not call this method directly. If your applet does not perform animation, play audio files, or perform calculations in a thread, you do not usually need this method.

- destroy

  Java guarantees to call this method when the browser shuts down normally. Since applets are meant to live on an HTML page, you do not need to worry about destroying the panel. This will happen automatically when the browser shuts down. What you *do* need to put in the `destroy` method is the code for reclaiming any non-memory-dependent resources such as graphics contexts that you may have consumed. Of course, Java calls the `stop` method before calling the `destroy` method if the applet is still active.

java.applet.Applet

- void start()
  Override this method for code that needs to be executed *every time* the user visits the browser page containing this applet. A typical action is to reactivate a thread.

- void stop()
  Override this method for code that needs to be executed *every time* the user leaves the browser page containing this applet. A typical action is to suspend a thread.

- void destroy()
  Override this method for code that needs to be executed when the user exits the browser. A typical action is to call `destroy` on system objects.

Security Basics

Because applets are designed to be loaded from a remote site and then executed locally, security becomes vital. If a user enables Java in the browser, the browser will download all the applet code on the web page and execute it immediately. The user never gets a chance to confirm or to stop individual applets from running. For this reason, applets (unlike applications) are restricted in what they can do. The *applet security manager* throws a `SecurityException` whenever an applet attempts to violate one of the access rules. (See Volume 2 for more on security managers.)

What *can* applets do on all platforms? They can show images and play sounds, get keystrokes and mouse clicks from the user, and send user input back to the host from which they were loaded. That is enough functionality to show facts and figures or to get user input for placing an order. The restricted execution environment for applets is often called the "sandbox." Applets playing in the "sandbox" cannot alter the user's system or spy on it. In this chapter, we will look only at applets that run inside the sandbox.

In particular, when running in the sandbox:

- Applets can *never* run any local executable program.

- Applets cannot communicate with any host other than the server from which they were downloaded; that server is called the *originating host*. This rule is often called "applets can only phone home." This protects applet users from applets that might try to spy on intranet resources.

- Applets cannot read from or write to the local computer's file system.

- Applets cannot find out any information about the local computer, except for the Java version used, the name and version of the operating system, and the characters used to separate files (for instance, / or \), paths (such as : or ;), and lines (such as \n or \r\n). In particular, applets cannot find out the user's name, e-mail address, and so on.

- All windows that an applet pops up carry a warning message.

All this is possible only because applets are *interpreted* by the Java Virtual Machine and not directly executed by the CPU on the user's computer. Because the interpreter checks all critical instructions and program areas, a hostile (or poorly written) applet will almost certainly not be able to crash the computer, overwrite system memory, or change the privileges granted by the operating system.

These restrictions are too strong for some situations. For example, on a corporate intranet, you can certainly imagine an applet wanting to access local files. To allow for different levels of security under different situations, you can use *signed applets.* A signed applet carries with it a certificate that indicates the identity of the signer. Cryptographic techniques ensure that such a certificate cannot be forged.

If you trust the signer, you can choose to give the applet additional rights. (We cover code signing in Volume 2.)

The point is that if you trust the signer of the applet, you can tell the browser to give the applet more privileges. You can, for example, give applets in your corporate intranet a higher level of trust than those from `www.hacker.com`. The configurable Java security model allows the continuum of privilege levels you need. You can give completely trusted applets the same privilege levels as local applications. Programs from vendors that are known to be somewhat flaky can be given access to some, but not all, privileges. Unknown applets can be restricted to the sandbox.

To sum up, Java has three separate mechanisms for enforcing security:

1. Program code is interpreted by the Java Virtual Machine, not executed directly.
2. A security manager checks all sensitive operations in the Java runtime library.
3. Applets can be signed to identify their origin.

> NOTE: In contrast, the security model of the ActiveX technology by Microsoft relies solely on the third option. If you want to run an ActiveX control at all, you must trust it completely. That model works fine when you deal with a small number of trusted suppliers, but it simply does not scale up to the World Wide Web. If you use Internet Explorer, you will see the ActiveX mechanism at work. You'll need to accept Sun's certificate to install the Java Plug-In on Internet Explorer. The certificate tells you that the code came from Sun. It doesn't tell you anything about the quality of the code. Once you accept the installation, the program runs without any further security checks.

Pop-Up Windows in Applets

An applet sits embedded in a web page, in a frame of a size that is fixed by the `WIDTH` and `HEIGHT` values in the applet tags of the HTML page. This can be quite limiting. Many programmers wonder whether they can have a pop-up window to make better use of the available space. It is indeed possible to create a pop-up frame. Here is a simple applet with a single button labeled Calculator. When you click on the button, a calculator pops up in a separate window.

The pop-up is easy to do. Simply use a `JFrame`, but don't call `setDefault-CloseOperation`.

```
frame = new CalculatorFrame();
frame.setTitle("Calculator");
frame.setSize(200, 200);
```

When the user clicks the button, toggle the frame so that it is shown if it isn't visible and hidden if it is. When you click on the calculator button, the dialog box pops up and floats over the web page. When you click on the button again, the calculator goes away.

```java
JButton calcButton = new JButton("Calculator");
calcButton.addActionListener(new
   ActionListener()
   {
      public void actionPerformed(ActionEvent evt)
      {
         if (frame.isVisible()) frame.setVisible(false);
         else frame.show();
      }
   });
```

There is, however, a catch that you need to know about before you put this applet on your web page. To see how the calculator looks to a potential user, load the web page from a browser, not the applet viewer. The calculator will be surrounded by a border with a warning message (see Figure 10–9).

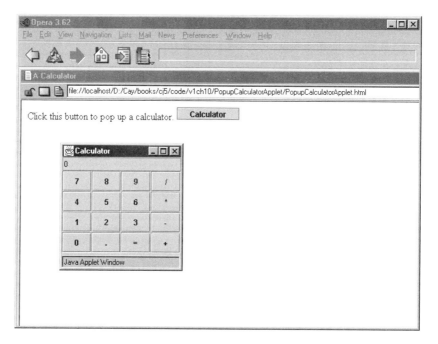

Figure 10–9: A pop-up window inside a browser

In early browser versions, that message was very ominous: "Untrusted Java Applet Window." Every successive version of the SDK watered down the warning a bit—"Unauthenticated Java Applet Window," or "Warning: Java Applet Window." Now it is simply "Java Applet Window."

This message is a security feature of all web browsers. The browser wants to make sure that your applet does not launch a window that the user might mistake for a local application. The fear is that an unsuspecting user could visit a web page, which automatically launches the applets on it, and mistakenly type in a password or credit card number, which the applet would send back to its host.

To avoid any possibility of shenanigans like this, all pop-up windows launched by an applet bear a warning label. If your browser supports signed applets, you can configure it to omit the warning message for pop-up windows that are spawned by signed applets.

Example 10–5 shows the code for the PopupCalculatorApplet class. The code for the CalculatorPanel is unchanged from Chapter 9 and is not shown.

Example 10–5: PopupCalculatorApplet.java

```
1. import java.awt.*;
2. import java.awt.event.*;
3. import javax.swing.*;
4.
5. public class PopupCalculatorApplet extends JApplet
6. {
7.    public void init()
8.    {
9.       // create a frame with a calculator panel
10.
11.      frame = new JFrame();
12.      frame.setTitle("Calculator");
13.      frame.setSize(200, 200);
14.      frame.getContentPane().add(new CalculatorPanel());
15.
16.      // add a button that pops up or hides the calculator
17.
18.      JButton calcButton = new JButton("Calculator");
19.      getContentPane().add(calcButton);
20.
21.      calcButton.addActionListener(new
22.         ActionListener()
23.         {
24.            public void actionPerformed(ActionEvent evt)
25.            {
26.               if (frame.isVisible()) frame.setVisible(false);
27.               else frame.show();
28.            }
29.         });
30.   }
31.
32.   private JFrame frame;
33. }
```

The Applet HTML Tags and Attributes

We'll first focus on the APPLET tag, although it is deprecated in the latest versions of the W3 HTML specification. This is because Sun's applet viewer and the Java Plug-In HTML translator don't yet understand the newer OBJECT tag.

In its most basic form, an example for using the `APPLET` tag looks like this:

```
<APPLET CODE="NotHelloWorldApplet.class" WIDTH=100 HEIGHT=100>
```

As you have seen, the `CODE` attribute gives the name of the class file and must include the `.class` extension; the `WIDTH` and `HEIGHT` attributes size the window that will hold the applet. Both are measured in pixels. You also need a matching `<APPLET>` tag that marks the end of the HTML tagging needed for an applet. The text between the `<APPLET>` and `</APPLET>` tags is displayed only if the browser cannot show applets. These tags are required. If any are missing, the browser cannot load your applet.

All of this information would usually be embedded in an HTML page that, at the very least, might look like this:

```
<HTML>
<HEAD>
<TITLE>NotHelloWorldApplet</TITLE>
</HEAD>
<BODY>
The next line of text is displayed under
the auspices of Java:
<APPLET CODE="NotHelloWorldApplet.class" WIDTH=100 HEIGHT=100>
If your browser could show Java, you would see
an applet here
</APPLET>
</BODY>
</HTML>
```

> NOTE: According to the HTML specification, the HTML tags and attributes such as `APPLET` can be in upper- or lowercase. Case is relevant in identifying the name of the applet class. The letter case may be significant in other items enclosed in quotes, such as names of JAR files, if the web server file system is case sensitive.

Applet Attributes for Positioning

What follows are short discussions of the various attributes that you can (or must) use within the `APPLET` tag to position your applet. For those familiar with HTML, many of these attributes are similar to those used with the `IMG` tag for image placement on a web page.

*   `WIDTH, HEIGHT`

    These attributes are required and give the width and height of the applet, measured in pixels. In the applet viewer, this is the initial size of the applet. You can resize any window that the applet viewer creates. In a browser, you *cannot* resize the applet. You will need to make a good guess about how much space your applet requires to show up well for all users.

- ALIGN

  This attribute specifies the alignment of the applet. There are two basic choices. The applet can be a block with text flowing around it, or the applet can be *inline,* floating inside a line of text as if it were an oversized text character. The first two values (LEFT and RIGHT) make the text flow around the applet. The others make the applet flow with the text.

  The choices are described in Table 10–1.

Table 10–1: Applet positioning attributes

Attribute	What It Does
LEFT	Places the applet at the left margin of the page. Text that follows on the page goes in the space to the right of the applet.
RIGHT	Places the applet at the right margin of the page. Text that follows on the page goes in the space to the left of the applet.
BOTTOM	Places the bottom of the applet at the bottom of the text in the current line.
TOP	Places the top of the applet with the top of the current line.
TEXTTOP	Places the top of the applet with the top of the text in the current line.
MIDDLE	Places the middle of the applet with the baseline of the current line.
ABSMIDDLE	Places the middle of the applet with the middle of the current line.
BASELINE	Places the bottom of the applet with the baseline of the current line.
ABSBOTTOM	Places the bottom of the applet with the bottom of the current line.
VSPACE, HSPACE	These optional attributes specify the number of pixels above and below the applet (VSPACE) and on each side of the applet (HSPACE).

Figure 10–10 shows all alignment options for an applet that floats with the surrounding text. The vertical bar at the beginning of each line is an image. Since the image is taller than the text, you can see the difference between alignment with the top or bottom of the line and the top or bottom of the text.

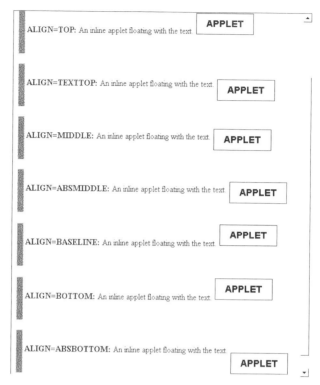

Figure 10–10: Applet alignment

Applet Attributes for Code

The following applet attributes tell the browser how to locate the applet code; here are short descriptions.

- CODE

    This attribute gives the name of the applet's class file. This name is taken relative to the codebase (see below) or relative to the current page.

    If you use a relative path name, then the path name must match the package of the applet class. For example, if the applet class is in the package com.mycompany, then the attribute is CODE="com/mycompany/MyApplet.class". The alternative CODE="com.mycompany.MyApplet.class" is also permitted. But you cannot use absolute path names here. Use the CODEBASE attribute if your class file is located elsewhere.

    The CODE attribute specifies only the name of the class that contains the applet class. Of course, your applet may contain other class files. Once the browser's class loader loads the class containing the applet, it will realize that it needs more class files, and will load them.

Either the `CODE` or the `OBJECT` attribute (see below) is required.

- CODEBASE

  This optional attribute tells the browser that your class files are found below the directory indicated in the `CODEBASE` attribute. For example, if an applet called `CalculatorApplet` is in the directory `MyApplets`, and the `MyApplets` directory is *below* the location of the web page, you would use:

  ```
  <APPLET CODE="CalculatorApplet.class" CODEBASE="MyApplets"
      WIDTH=100 HEIGHT=150>
  ```

  In other words, the file layout looks like this:

  ```
  aDirectory/
      CalculatorApplet.html
      MyApplets/
          CalculatorApplet.class
  ```

- ARCHIVE

  This optional attribute lists the Java archive file or files containing classes and other resources for the applet. (See the section on JAR files later in this chapter for more on Java archive files.) These files are fetched from the web server before the applet is loaded. This technique speeds up the loading process significantly since only one HTTP request is necessary to load a JAR file that contains many smaller files. The JAR files are separated by commas. For example:

  ```
  <APPLET CODE="CalculatorApplet.class" ARCHIVE=
      "CalculatorClasses.jar,corejava/CoreJavaClasses.jar"
      WIDTH=100 HEIGHT=150>
  ```

TIP: This attribute has one very important application. If you have an applet that uses the Swing set but does not otherwise require any Java 2 features, you can deploy it in browsers compatible with Java 1.1 browsers (such as Netscape 4 and Internet Explorer) by supplying a JAR file that contains all Swing classes. You can obtain the appropriate JAR file by downloading the Swing supplement to Java 1.1 from `http://java.sun.com/products/jfc/#download-swing`. You must then package your applet inside a JAR file and load it together with the Swing JAR file. Then, supply an `ARCHIVE` parameter that looks like this:

```
    <APPLET CODE="CalculatorApplet.class"
        ARCHIVE="CalculatorAppletClasses.jar,swing.jar"
        WIDTH=100 HEIGHT=150>
```

The file `swing.jar` is about one Mbyte, which is a pretty hefty download. So, you may not want to do this in a situation where some users might use a dial-up line to access your web page. Of course, the Java Plug-In download is even larger, but it only needs to be done once. The JAR file is downloaded every time.

- OBJECT

  As another way to specify the applet class file, you can specify the name of a file that contains the serialized applet object, but browsers vary in support of this attribute. You will definitely need to use the Java Plug-In if you want to use this feature. (An object is *serialized* when you write all its data fields to a file. We will discuss serialization in Chapter 12.) The object is deserialized from the file to return it to its previous state. When you use this attribute, the init method is *not* called, but the applet's start method is called. Before serializing an applet object, you should call its stop method. This feature is useful for implementing a persistent browser that automatically reloads its applets and has them return to the same state that they were in when the browser was closed. This is a specialized feature, not normally encountered by web page designers.

  Either CODE or OBJECT must be present in every APPLET tag. For example,

  ```
  <APPLET OBJECT="CalculatorApplet.ser" WIDTH=100 HEIGHT=150>
  ```

- NAME

  Scripters will want to give the applet a NAME attribute that they can use to refer to the applet when scripting. Both Netscape and Internet Explorer let you call methods of an applet on a page through JavaScript. This is not a book on JavaScript, so we only give you a brief idea of the code that is required to call Java code from JavaScript.

NOTE: JavaScript is a scripting language that can be used inside web pages, invented by Netscape and originally called LiveScript. It has little to do with Java, except for some similarity in syntax. It was a marketing move to call it JavaScript. A subset (with the catchy name of ECMAScript) is standardized as ECMA-262. But, to nobody's surprise, Netscape and Microsoft support incompatible extensions of that standard in their browsers. For more information on JavaScript, we recommend the book *JavaScript: The Definitive Guide* by David Flanagan, published by O'Reilly & Associates.

To access an applet from JavaScript, you first have to give it a name.

```
<APPLET CODE="CalculatorApplet.class"
   WIDTH=100 HEIGHT=150
   NAME="calc">
</APPLET>
```

You can then refer to the object as document.applets.*appletname*. For example,

```
var calcApplet = document.applets.calc;
```

Through the magic of the integration between Java and JavaScript that both Netscape and Internet Explorer provide, you can call applet methods:

```
calcApplet.clear();
```

(Our calculator applet doesn't have a `clear` method; we just want to show you the syntax.)

TIP: In `http://www.javaworld.com/javatips/jw-javatip80.html`, Francis Lu uses JavaScript-to-Java communication to solve an age-old problem: to resize an applet so that it isn't bound by hardcoded `WIDTH` and `HEIGHT` attributes. This is a good example of the integration between Java and JavaScript. It also shows how messy it is to write JavaScript that works on multiple browsers.

The `NAME` attribute is also essential when you want two applets on the same page to communicate with each other directly. You specify a name for each current applet instance. You pass this string to the `getApplet` method of the `AppletContext` class. We will discuss this mechanism, called *inter-applet communication*, later in this chapter.

Applet Attributes for Java-Challenged Viewers

If a web page containing an `APPLET` tag is viewed by a browser that is not aware of Java applets, then the browser ignores the unknown `APPLET` and `PARAM` tags. All text between the `<APPLET>` and `</APPLET>` tags is displayed by the browser. Conversely, Java-aware browsers do not display any text between the `<APPLET>` and `</APPLET>` tags. You can display messages inside these tags for those poor folks that use a prehistoric browser. For example,

```
<APPLET CODE="CalculatorApplet.class" WIDTH=100 HEIGHT=150>
If your browser could show Java, you would see
a calculator here
</APPLET>
```

Of course, nowadays most browsers know about Java, but Java may be deactivated, perhaps by the user or by a paranoid system administrator. You can then use the `ALT` attribute to display a message to these unfortunate souls.

```
<APPLET CODE="CalculatorApplet.class" WIDTH=100 HEIGHT=150
ALT="If your browser could show Java, you would see
a calculator here">
```

The OBJECT Tag

The `OBJECT` tag is part of the HTML 4.0 standard, and the W3 consortium suggests that people use it instead of the `APPLET` tag. There are 35 different attributes to the `OBJECT` tag, most of which (such as `ONKEYDOWN`) are relevant only to people writing Dynamic HTML. The various positioning attributes such as `ALIGN` and `HEIGHT` work exactly as they did for the `APPLET` tag. The key attribute in the `OBJECT` tag for your Java applets is the `CLASSID` attribute. This attribute specifies the location of the object. Of course, `OBJECT` tags can load different kinds of objects, such as Java applets or ActiveX components like the Java Plug-In itself. In the `CODETYPE` attribute, you specify the nature of the object. For example, Java applets have a code type of `application/java`. Here is an `OBJECT` tag to load a Java applet:

```
<OBJECT
   CODETYPE="application/java"
   CLASSID="java:CalculatorApplet.class"
   WIDTH=100 HEIGHT=150>
```

Note that the `CLASSID` attribute can be followed by a `CODEBASE` attribute that works exactly as it did with the `APPLET` tag.

You can use the `OBJECT` tag to load applets into the current versions of Netscape and Internet Explorer, but the applet viewer and the Java Plug-In HTML converter do not understand the `OBJECT` tag for applets.

Java Plug-In Tags

The Java Plug-In is loaded as a Netscape plug-in or an ActiveX control, via the `EMBED` or `OBJECT` tag. For example, the equivalent of the tag

```
<APPLET
   CODE="CalculatorApplet.class"
   CODEBASE="MyApplets"
   WIDTH=100
   HEIGHT=150>
<PARAM NAME="Font" VALUE="Helvetica">
</APPLET>
```

in Netscape Navigator is

```
<EMBED TYPE="application/x-java-applet;version=1.3"
   PLUGINSPAGE="http://java.sun.com/products/plugin/1.3
      /plugin-install.html"
   CODE="CalculatorApplet.class"
   CODEBASE="MyApplets"
   WIDTH=100
   HEIGHT=150>
<PARAM NAME="Font" VALUE="Helvetica">
</EMBED>
```

The equivalent tag in Internet Explorer is

```
<OBJECT CLASSID="clsid:8AD9C840-044E-11D1-B3E9-00805F499D93"
   CODEBASE="http://java.sun.com/products/plugin/1.1
      /jinstall-11-win32.cab#Version=1,3,0,0"
   WIDTH=100
```

```
    HEIGHT=150>
  <PARAM NAME="TYPE" VALUE="application/x-java-applet;
    version=1.3">
  <PARAM NAME="CODE" VALUE="CalculatorApplet.class">
  <PARAM NAME="CODEBASE" VALUE="MyApplets">
  <PARAM NAME="Font" VALUE="Helvetica">
  </OBJECT>
```

Here are the details of the tag conversions if you insist on doing them by hand.

It is easy to convert from the APPLET tag to the EMBED tag: just change APPLET to EMBED and add the TYPE and PLUGINSPAGE attributes.

Converting from the APPLET tag to the OBJECT tag is more complex. You need to add the CLASSID and CODEBASE attributes, and add a PARAM tag with name TYPE. (The CLASSID is always the same number; it is the globally unique ActiveX ID of the Java Plug-In.) Keep all attributes, except the ones listed in Table 10–2 that need to be converted to PARAM tags. If they conflict with existing PARAM tags, you can optionally use the prefix JAVA_ for the parameter names; for example,

```
  <PARAM NAME="JAVA_CODE" VALUE="CalculatorApplet.class">
```

As you can see, the differences between these tags are purely cosmetic. In practice, it is best to use the Java Plug-In HTML converter or some other script to produce the HTML code automatically.

The Java Plug-In HTML converter also adds glue code that automatically selects the tags that match the browser. It either uses JavaScript or an incredibly convoluted sequence of tags that are selectively ignored by different browsers. For more information on this sordid topic, have a look at the HTML converter documentation or the article at http://java.sun.com/products/jfc/tsc/articles/plugin/index.html.

Table 10–2: Translating between APPLET and OBJECT attributes

APPLET	OBJECT
ALT=...	N/A
ARCHIVE=...	<PARAM NAME="ARCHIVE" VALUE=...>
CODE=...	<PARAM NAME="CODE" VALUE=...>
CODEBASE=...	<PARAM NAME="CODEBASE" VALUE=...>
OBJECT=...	<PARAM NAME="OBJECT" VALUE=...>

Passing Information to Applets

Just as applications can use command-line information, applets can use parameters that are embedded in the HTML file. This is done via the HTML tag called PARAM along with attributes that you define. For example, suppose you want to let the web page determine the style of the font to use in your applet. You could use the following HTML tags:

```
<APPLET CODE="FontParamApplet.class" WIDTH=200, HEIGHT=200>
<PARAM NAME="font" VALUE="Helvetica">
</APPLET>
```

You then pick up the value of the parameter, using the `getParameter` method of the `Applet` class, as in the following example:

```
public class FontParamApplet extends JApplet
{
    public void init()
    {
        String fontName = getParameter("font");
        . . .
    }
    . . .
}
```

> NOTE: You can call the `getParameter` method only in the `init` method of the applet, not in the constructor. When the applet constructor is executed, the parameters are not yet prepared. Since the layout of most nontrivial applets is determined by parameters, we recommend that you don't supply constructors to applets. Simply place all initialization code into the `init` method.

Parameters are always returned as strings. You need to convert the string to a numeric type if that is what is called for. You do this in the standard way by using the appropriate method, such as `parseInt` of the `Integer` class.

For example, if we wanted to add a size parameter for the font, then the HTML code might look like this:

```
<APPLET CODE="FontParamApplet.class" WIDTH=200 HEIGHT=200>
<PARAM NAME="font" VALUE="Helvetica">
<PARAM NAME="size" VALUE="24">
</APPLET>
```

The following source code shows how to read the integer parameter.

```
public class FontParamApplet extends JApplet
{
    public void init()
    {
        String fontName = getParameter("font");
        int fontSize = Integer.parseInt(getParameter("size"));
        . . .
    }
}
```

> NOTE: The strings used when you define the parameters via the PARAM tag and those used in the getParameter method must match exactly. In particular, both are case sensitive.

In addition to ensuring that the parameters match in your code, you should find out whether or not the `size` parameter was left out. You do this with a simple test for `null`. For example:

```
int fontsize;
String sizeString = getParameter("size");
if (sizeString == null) fontSize = 12;
else fontSize = Integer.parseInt(sizeString);
```

Here is a useful applet that uses parameters extensively. The applet draws a bar chart, shown in Figure 10–11.

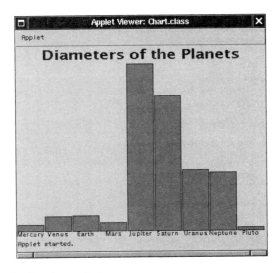

Figure 10–11: A chart applet

The applet takes the labels and the heights of the bars from the PARAM values in the HTML file. Here is what the HTML file for Figure 10–11 looks like:

```
<APPLET CODE="Chart.class" WIDTH=400 HEIGHT=300>
<PARAM NAME="title" VALUE="Diameters of the Planets">
<PARAM NAME="values" VALUE="9">
<PARAM NAME="name_1" VALUE="Mercury">
<PARAM NAME="name_2" VALUE="Venus">
<PARAM NAME="name_3" VALUE="Earth">
<PARAM NAME="name_4" VALUE="Mars">
<PARAM NAME="name_5" VALUE="Jupiter">
<PARAM NAME="name_6" VALUE="Saturn">
<PARAM NAME="name_7" VALUE="Uranus">
```

```
<PARAM NAME="name_8" VALUE="Neptune">
<PARAM NAME="name_9" VALUE="Pluto">
<PARAM NAME="value_1" VALUE="3100">
<PARAM NAME="value_2" VALUE="7500">
<PARAM NAME="value_3" VALUE="8000">
<PARAM NAME="value_4" VALUE="4200">
<PARAM NAME="value_5" VALUE="88000">
<PARAM NAME="value_6" VALUE="71000">
<PARAM NAME="value_7" VALUE="32000">
<PARAM NAME="value_8" VALUE="30600">
<PARAM NAME="value_9" VALUE="1430">
</APPLET>
```

You could have set up an array of strings and an array of numbers in the applet, but there are two advantages to using the PARAM mechanism instead. You can have multiple copies of the same applet on your web page, showing different graphs: just put two APPLET tags with different sets of parameters on the page. And you can change the data that you want to chart. Admittedly, the diameters of the planets will stay the same for quite some time, but suppose your web page contains a chart of weekly sales data. It is easy to update the web page because it is plain text. Editing and recompiling a Java file on a weekly basis is more tedious.

In fact, there are commercial Java beans that make much fancier graphs than the one in our chart applet. If you buy one, you can drop it into your web page and feed it parameters without ever needing to know how the applet renders the graphs.

Example 10–6 is the source code of our chart applet. Note that the init method reads the parameters, and the paintComponent method draws the chart.

Example 10–6: Chart.java

```
1. import java.awt.*;
2. import java.awt.font.*;
3. import java.awt.geom.*;
4. import javax.swing.*;
5.
6. public class Chart extends JApplet
7. {
8.    public void init()
9.    {
10.       String v = getParameter("values");
11.       if (v == null) return;
12.       int n = Integer.parseInt(v);
13.       double[] values = new double[n];
14.       String[] names = new String[n];
15.       int i;
16.       for (i = 0; i < n; i++)
17.       {
18.          values[i] = Double.parseDouble
```

```
19.             (getParameter("value_" + (i + 1)));
20.          names[i] = getParameter("name_" + (i + 1));
21.       }
22.
23.       Container contentPane = getContentPane();
24.       contentPane.add(new ChartPanel(values, names,
25.          getParameter("title")));
26.    }
27. }
28.
29. /**
30.    A panel that draws a bar chart.
31. */
32. class ChartPanel extends JPanel
33. {
34.    /**
35.       Constructs a ChartPanel.
36.       @param v the array of values for the chart
37.       @param n the array of names for the values
38.       @param t the title of the chart
39.    */
40.    public ChartPanel(double[] v, String[] n, String t)
41.    {
42.       names = n;
43.       values = v;
44.       title = t;
45.    }
46.
47.    public void paintComponent(Graphics g)
48.    {
49.       super.paintComponent(g);
50.       Graphics2D g2 = (Graphics2D)g;
51.
52.       // compute the minimum and maximum values
53.       if (values == null) return;
54.       double minValue = 0;
55.       double maxValue = 0;
56.       for (int i = 0; i < values.length; i++)
57.       {
58.          if (minValue > values[i]) minValue = values[i];
59.          if (maxValue < values[i]) maxValue = values[i];
60.       }
61.       if (maxValue == minValue) return;
62.
63.       int panelWidth = getWidth();
64.       int panelHeight = getHeight();
65.
66.       Font titleFont = new Font("SansSerif", Font.BOLD, 20);
67.       Font labelFont = new Font("SansSerif", Font.PLAIN, 10);
```

```
68.
69.         // compute the extent of the title
70.         FontRenderContext context = g2.getFontRenderContext();
71.         Rectangle2D titleBounds
72.            = titleFont.getStringBounds(title, context);
73.         double titleWidth = titleBounds.getWidth();
74.         double top = titleBounds.getHeight();
75.
76.         // draw the title
77.         double y = -titleBounds.getY(); // ascent
78.         double x = (panelWidth - titleWidth) / 2;
79.         g2.setFont(titleFont);
80.         g2.drawString(title, (float)x, (float)y);
81.
82.         // compute the extent of the bar labels
83.         LineMetrics labelMetrics
84.            = labelFont.getLineMetrics("", context);
85.         double bottom = labelMetrics.getHeight();
86.
87.         y = panelHeight - labelMetrics.getDescent();
88.         g2.setFont(labelFont);
89.
90.         // get the scale factor and width for the bars
91.         double scale = (panelHeight - top - bottom)
92.            / (maxValue - minValue);
93.         int barWidth = panelWidth / values.length;
94.
95.         // draw the bars
96.         for (int i = 0; i < values.length; i++)
97.         {
98.            // get the coordinates of the bar rectangle
99.            double x1 = i * barWidth + 1;
100.           double y1 = top;
101.           double height = values[i] * scale;
102.           if (values[i] >= 0)
103.              y1 += (maxValue - values[i]) * scale;
104.           else
105.           {
106.              y1 += maxValue * scale;
107.              height = -height;
108.           }
109.
110.           // fill the bar and draw the bar outline
111.           Rectangle2D rect = new Rectangle2D.Double(x1, y1,
112.              barWidth - 2, height);
113.           g2.setPaint(Color.red);
114.           g2.fill(rect);
115.           g2.setPaint(Color.black);
```

```
116.            g2.draw(rect);
117.
118.            // draw the centered label below the bar
119.            Rectangle2D labelBounds
120.                = labelFont.getStringBounds(names[i], context);
121.
122.            double labelWidth = labelBounds.getWidth();
123.            x = i * barWidth + (barWidth - labelWidth) / 2;
124.            g2.drawString(names[i], (float)x, (float)y);
125.        }
126.    }
127.
128.    private double[] values;
129.    private String[] names;
130.    private String title;
131.}
```

`java.applet.Applet`

- `public String getParameter(String name)`
  gets a parameter defined with a PARAM directive in the web page loading the applet. The string is case sensitive.

- `public String getAppletInfo()`
  is a method that many applet authors override to return a string that contains information about the author, version, and copyright of the current applet. You need to create this information by overriding this method in your applet class.

- `public String[][] getParameterInfo()`
  is a method that many applet authors override to return an array of PARAM tag options that this applet supports. Each row contains three entries: the name, the type, and a description of the parameter. Here is an example:

  ```
  "fps", "1-10", "frames per second"
  "repeat", "boolean", "repeat image loop?"
  "images", "url", "directory containing images"
  ```

Multimedia

Applets can handle both images and audio. As we write this, images must be in GIF or JPEG form, audio files in AU, AIFF, WAV, or MIDI. Animated GIFs are ok, and the animation is displayed. Usually the files containing this information are specified as a URL, so we take URLs up first.

URLs

A URL is really nothing more than a description of a resource on the Internet. For example, `"http://java.sun.com/index.html"` tells the browser to use the hypertext transfer protocol on the file `index.html` located at `java.sun.com`.

Java has the class `URL` that encapsulates URLs. The simplest way to make a URL is to give a string to the `URL` constructor:

```
URL u = new URL("http://java.sun.com/index.html");
```

This is called an *absolute* URL because we specify the entire resource name. Another useful URL constructor is a *relative* URL.

```
URL data = new URL(u, "data/planets.dat");
```

This specifies the file `planets.dat`, located in the `data` subdirectory of the URL `u`.

Both constructors make sure that you have used the correct syntax for a URL. If you haven't, they cause a `MalformedURLException`. This is one of the exceptions that the compiler will not let you ignore. The relevant code is as follows:

```
try
{
    String s = "http://java.sun.com/index.html";
    URL u = new URL(s);
    . . .
}
catch(MalformedURLException exception)
{
    // deal with error
    exception.printStackTrace();
}
```

We will discuss this syntax for dealing with exceptions in detail in Chapter 12. Until then, if you see code like this in one of our code samples, just gloss over the `try` and `catch` keywords.

A common way of obtaining a URL is to ask an applet where it came from, in particular:

- What is the URL of the page that is calling it?
- What is the URL of the applet itself?

To find the former, use the `getDocumentBase` method; to find the latter, use `getCodeBase`. You do not need to place these calls in a `try` block.

> NOTE: You can access secure web pages (`https` URLs) from applets and through the Java Plug-In—see `http://java.sun.com/products/plugin/1.3/docs/https.html`. This uses the SSL capabilities of the underlying browser.

Obtaining Multimedia Files

You can retrieve images and audio files with the `getImage` and `getAudioClip` methods. For example:

```
Image cat = getImage(getDocumentBase(), "images/cat.gif");
AudioClip meow = getAudioClip(getDocumentBase(),
    "audio/meow.au");
```

Here, we use the `getDocumentBase` method that returns the URL from which your applet is loaded. The second argument to the `URL` constructor specifies where the image or audio clip is located, relative to the base document. (Applets do not need to go through a `Toolkit` object to get an image.)

> NOTE: The images and audio clips must be located on the same server that hosts the applet code. For security reasons, applets cannot access files on another server ("applets can only phone home").

Once you have the images and audio clips, what can you do with them? You saw in Chapter 7 how to display a single image. In the multithreading chapter of Volume 2, you will see how to play an animation sequence composed of multiple images. To play an audio clip, simply invoke its `play` method.

You can also call `play` without first loading the audio clip.

```
play(getDocumentBase(), "audio/meow.au");
```

However, to show an image, you must first load it.

For faster downloading, multimedia objects can be stored in JAR files (see the section below). The `getImage` and `getAudioClip/play` methods automatically search the JAR files of the applet. If the image or audio file is contained in a JAR file, it is loaded immediately. Otherwise, the browser requests it from the web server.

`java.net.URL`

- `URL(String name)`
  creates a URL object from a string describing an absolute URL.

- `URL(URL base, String name)`
  creates a relative URL object. If the string `name` describes an absolute URL, then the `base` URL is ignored. Otherwise, it is interpreted as a relative directory from the `base` URL.

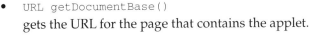

`java.applet.Applet`

- `URL getDocumentBase()`
  gets the URL for the page that contains the applet.

- `URL getCodeBase()`
  gets the URL of the applet code itself.

- `void play(URL url)`
- `void play(URL url, String name)`
  The first form plays an audio file specified by the URL. The second form uses the string to provide a path relative to the URL in the first argument. Nothing happens if the audio clip cannot be found.

- `AudioClip getAudioClip(URL url)`
- `AudioClip getAudioClip(URL url, String name)`

  The first form gets an audio clip, given a URL. The second form uses the string to provide a path relative to the URL in the first argument. The methods return `null` if the audio clip cannot be found.

- `Image getImage(URL url)`
- `Image getImage(URL url, String name)`

  return an image object that encapsulates the image specified by the URL. If the image does not exist, this method immediately returns `null`. Otherwise, a separate thread is launched to load the image. See Chapter 7 for details on image acquisition.

The Applet Context

An applet runs inside a browser or the applet viewer. An applet can ask the browser to do things for it, for example, fetch an audio clip, show a short message in the status line, or show a different web page. The ambient browser can carry out these requests, or it can ignore them. For example, if an applet running inside the applet viewer asks the applet viewer program to show a web page, nothing happens.

To communicate with the browser, an applet calls the `getAppletContext` method. That method returns an object that implements an interface of type `Applet-Context`. You can think of the concrete implementation of the `AppletContext` interface as a communication path between the applet and the ambient browser. In addition to `getAudioClip` and `getImage`, the `AppletContext` interface contains several useful methods, which we discuss in the next few sections.

Inter-Applet Communication

A web page can contain more than one applet. If a web page contains multiple applets from the same `CODEBASE`, they can communicate with each other. Naturally, this is an advanced technique that you probably will not need very often.

If you give `NAME` attributes to each applet in the HTML file, you can use the `getApplet(String)` method of the `AppletContext` interface to get a reference to the applet. For example, if your HTML file contains the tag

```
<APPLET CODE="Chart.class" WIDTH=100 HEIGHT=100 NAME="Chart1">
```

then the call

```
Applet chart1 = getAppletContext().getApplet("Chart1");
```

gives you a reference to the applet. What can you do with the reference? Provided you give the `Chart` class a method to accept new data and redraw the chart, you can call this method by making the appropriate cast.

```
((Chart)chart1).setData(3, "Earth", 9000);
```

You can also list all applets on a web page, whether or not they have a `NAME` attribute. The `getApplets` method returns a so-called *enumeration object*. (You will learn more about enumeration objects in Volume 2.) Here is a loop that prints the class names of all applets on the current page.

```
Enumeration e = getAppletContext().getApplets();
while (e.hasMoreElements())
{
   Object a = e.nextElement();
   System.out.println(a.getClass().getName());
}
```

An applet cannot communicate with an applet on a different web page.

Displaying Items in the Browser

You have access to two areas of the ambient browsers: the status line and the web page display area. Both use methods of the `AppletContext` class.

You can display a string in the status line at the bottom of the browser with the `showStatus` message, for example,

```
showStatus("Loading data . . . please wait");
```

> TIP: In our experience, `showStatus` is of limited use. The browser is also using the status line, and, more often than not, it will overwrite your precious message with chatter like "`Applet running`". Use the status line for fluff messages like "Loading data . . . please wait," but not for something that the user cannot afford to miss.

You can tell the browser to show a different web page with the `showDocument` method. There are several ways to do this. The simplest is with a call to `show-Document` with one argument, the URL you want to show.

```
URL u = new URL("http://java.sun.com/index.html");
getAppletContext().showDocument(u);
```

The problem with this call is that it opens the new web page in the same window as your current page, thereby displacing your applet. To return to your applet, the user must click the Back button of the browser.

You can tell the browser to show the applet in another window by giving a second parameter in the call to `showDocument`. The second argument is a string. If it is the special string "`_blank`", the browser opens a new window with the document, instead of displacing the current document. More importantly, if you take advantage of the frame feature in HTML, you can split a browser window into multiple frames, each of which has a name. You can put your applet into one frame and have it show documents in other frames. We will show you an example of how to do this in the next section.

Table 10–3 shows all possible arguments to `showDocument`.

Table 10–3: `showDocument` **arguments**

Second Argument to showDocument	Location
`"_self"` or none	Show the document in the current frame.
`"_parent"`	Show the document in the parent frame.
`"_top"`	Show the document in the topmost frame.
`"_blank"`	Show in new, unnamed, top-level window.
Any other string	Show in the frame with that name. If no frame with that name exists, open a new window and give it that name.

java.applet.Applet

- `public AppletContext getAppletContext()`

  gives you a handle to the applet's browser environment. On most browsers, you can use this information to control the browser in which the applet is running.

- `void showStatus(String msg)`

  shows the string specified in the status line of the browser.

- `AudioClip getAudioClip(URL url)`

  returns an `AudioClip` object, which stores the sound file specified by the URL. Use the `play` method to actually play the file.

java.applet.AppletContext

- `Enumeration getApplets()`

  returns an enumeration (see Volume 2) of all the applets in the same context, that is, the same web page.

- `Applet getApplet(String name)`

  returns the applet in the current context with the given name; returns `null` if none exists. Only the current web page is searched.

- `void showDocument(URL url)`
- `void showDocument(URL url, String target)`

  show a new web page in a frame in the browser. In the first form, the new page displaces the current page. The second form uses the string to identify the target frame. The target string can be one of the following: `"_self"` (show in current frame, equivalent to the first form of the method), `"_parent"` (show in parent frame), `"_top"` (show in topmost frame), and `"_blank"` (show in new, unnamed, top-level window). Or, the target string can be the name of a frame.

> NOTE: Sun's applet viewer does not show web pages. The `showDocument` command is ignored in the applet viewer.

A Bookmark Applet

This applet takes advantage of the frame feature in HTML 3.2 or later. We divide the screen vertically into two frames. The left frame contains a Java applet that shows a list of bookmarks. When you select any of the bookmarks, the applet then goes to the corresponding web page and displays it on the right (see Figure 10–12).

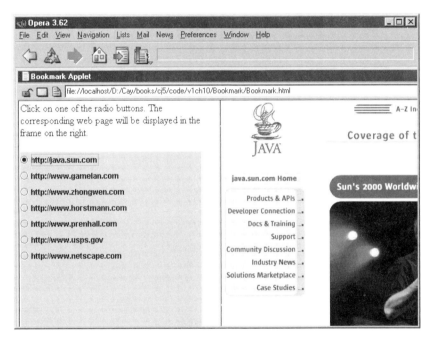

Figure 10–12: A bookmark applet

Example 10–7 shows the HTML file that defines the frames.

Example 10–7: Bookmark.html

```
1. <HTML>
2. <HEAD>
3. <TITLE>Bookmark Applet</TITLE>
4. </HEAD>
5. <FRAMESET COLS="320,*">
6. <FRAME NAME="left" SRC="Left.html"
7.    MARGINHEIGHT=2 MARGINWIDTH=2
8.    SCROLLING = "no" NORESIZE>
```

```
 9. <FRAME NAME="right" SRC="Right.html"
10.    MARGINHEIGHT=2 MARGINWIDTH=2
11.    SCROLLING = "yes" NORESIZE>
12. </FRAMESET>
13. </HTML>
```

We will not go over the exact syntax elements. What is important is that each frame has two essential features: a name (given by the NAME attribute) and a URL (given by the SRC attribute). We could not think of any good names for the frames, so we simply named them "left" and "right".

The left frame (Example 10–8) loads a file that we called Left.html, which loads the applet into the left frame. It simply specifies the applet and the bookmarks. You can customize this file for your own web page by changing the bookmarks.

Example 10–8: Left.html (before processing with the HTML converter)

```
 1. <HTML>
 2. <TITLE>A Bookmark Applet</TITLE>
 3. <BODY>
 4. Click on one of the radio buttons.
 5. The corresponding web page
 6. will be displayed in the frame on the right.
 7. <P>
 8. <APPLET CODE="Bookmark.class" WIDTH=290 HEIGHT=300>
 9. <PARAM NAME=link_1 VALUE="http://java.sun.com">
10. <PARAM NAME=link_2 VALUE="http://www.gamelan.com">
11. <PARAM NAME=link_3 VALUE="http://www.zhongwen.com">
12. <PARAM NAME=link_4 VALUE="http://www.horstmann.com">
13. <PARAM NAME=link_5 VALUE="http://www.prenhall.com">
14. <PARAM NAME=link_6 VALUE="http://usps.com">
15. <PARAM NAME=link_7 VALUE="http://www.netscape.com">
16. </APPLET>
17. </BODY>
18. </HTML>
```

The right frame (Example 10–9) loads a dummy file that we called Right.html. (Netscape did not approve when we left the right frame blank, so we gave it a dummy file for starters.)

Example 10–9: Right.html

```
1. <HTML>
2. <TITLE>
3. Web pages will be displayed here.
4. </TITLE>
5. <BODY>
6. Click on one of the radio buttons to the left.
7. The corresponding web page will be displayed here.
```

8. `</BODY>`
9. `</HTML>`

The code for the bookmark applet that is given in Example 10–10 is simple. It reads the values of the parameters link_1, link_2, and so on, and turns each of them into a radio button. When you select one of the radio buttons, the showDocument method displays the corresponding page in the right frame.

Example 10–10: Bookmark.java

```
1. import java.awt.*;
2. import java.awt.event.*;
3. import java.applet.*;
4. import java.util.*;
5. import java.net.*;
6. import javax.swing.*;
7.
8. public class Bookmark extends JApplet
9. {
10.    public void init()
11.    {
12.        Box box = Box.createVerticalBox();
13.        ButtonGroup group = new ButtonGroup();
14.
15.        int i = 1;
16.        String urlString;
17.
18.        // read all link_n parameters
19.        while ((urlString = getParameter("link_" + i)) != null)
20.        {
21.
22.            try
23.            {
24.                final URL url = new URL(urlString);
25.
26.                // make a radio button for each link
27.                JRadioButton button = new JRadioButton(urlString);
28.                box.add(button);
29.                group.add(button);
30.
31.                // selecting the radio button shows the URL in
32.                // the "right" frame
33.                button.addActionListener(new
34.                    ActionListener()
35.                    {
36.                        public void actionPerformed(ActionEvent event)
37.                        {
38.                            AppletContext context = getAppletContext();
```

```
39.                        context.showDocument(url, "right");
40.                     }
41.                  });
42.              }
43.              catch(MalformedURLException exception)
44.              {
45.                  exception.printStackTrace();
46.              }
47.
48.              i++;
49.          }
50.
51.          Container contentPane = getContentPane();
52.          contentPane.add(box);
53.      }
54. }
```

It's an Applet. It's an Application. It's Both!

Quite a few years ago, a "Saturday Night Live" skit poking fun at a television commercial showed a couple arguing about a white, gelatinous substance. The husband said, "It's a dessert topping." The wife said, "It's a floor wax." And the announcer concluded triumphantly, "It's both!"

Well, in this section, we will show you how to write a Java program that is *both* an applet and an application. That is, you can load the program with the applet viewer or a browser, or you can start it from the command line with the java interpreter. We are not sure how often this comes up—we found it interesting that this could be done at all and thought you would, too.

The screen shots in Figures 10–13 and 10–14 show the *same* program, launched from the command line as an application and viewed inside the applet viewer as an applet.

Figure 10–13: The calculator as an application

Figure 10–14: The calculator as an applet

Let us see how this can be done. Every class file has exactly one public class. In order for the applet viewer to launch it, that class must derive from `Applet`. In order for Java to start the application, it must have a static `main` method. So far, we have

```
class MyAppletApplication extends JApplet
{
   public void init() { . . . }
   . . .
   static public void main(String[] args) { . . . }
}
```

What can we put into `main`? Normally, we make an object of the class and invoke `show` on it. But this case is not so simple. You cannot show a naked applet. The applet must be placed inside a frame. And once it is inside the frame, its `init` method needs to be called.

To provide a frame, we create the class `AppletFrame`, like this:

```
public class AppletFrame extends JFrame
{
   public AppletFrame(Applet anApplet)
   {
      applet = anApplet;
      Container contentPane = getContentPane();
      contentPane.add(applet);
      . . .
   }
   . . .
}
```

The constructor of the frame puts the applet (which derives from `Component`) inside the frame.

In the `main` method of the applet/application, we make a new frame of this kind.

```
class MyAppletApplication extends JApplet
{
   public void init() { . . . }
   . . .
   public static void main(String args[])
   {
      AppletFrame frame
         = new AppletFrame(new MyAppletApplication());
      frame.setTitle("MyAppletApplication");
      frame.setSize(WIDTH, HEIGHT);
      frame.setDefaultCloseOperation(JFrame.EXIT_ON_CLOSE);
      frame.show();
   }
}
```

There is one catch. If the program is started with the Java interpreter and not the applet viewer, and it calls `getAppletContext`, it gets a `null` pointer because it has not been launched inside a browser. This causes a runtime crash whenever we have code like

```
getAppletContext().showStatus(message);
```

While we do not want to write a full-fledged browser, we do need to supply the bare minimum to make calls like this work. The call displays no message, but at least it will not crash the program. It turns out that all we need to do is implement two interfaces: `AppletStub` and `AppletContext`.

You have already seen applet contexts in action. They are responsible for fetching images and audio files and for displaying web pages. They can, however, politely refuse, and this is what our applet context will do. The major purpose of the `AppletStub` interface is to locate the applet context. Every applet has an applet stub (set with the `setStub` method of the `Applet` class).

In our case, `AppletFrame` implements both `AppletStub` and `AppletContext`. We supply the bare minimum functionality that is necessary to implement these two interfaces.

```
public class AppletFrame extends JFrame
   implements AppletStub, AppletContext
{
   . . .
   // AppletStub methods
   public boolean isActive() { return true; }
   public URL getDocumentBase() { return null; }
   public URL getCodeBase() { return null; }
   public String getParameter(String name) { return ""; }
```

```
    public AppletContext getAppletContext() { return this; }
    public void appletResize(int width, int height) {}

    // AppletContext methods
    public AudioClip getAudioClip(URL url) { return null; }
    public Image getImage(URL url) { return null; }
    public Applet getApplet(String name) { return null; }
    public Enumeration getApplets() { return null; }
    public void showDocument(URL url) {}
    public void showDocument(URL url, String target) {}
    public void showStatus(String status) {}
}
```

NOTE: When you compile this file, you will get a warning that `java.awt.Window` also has a method called `isActive` that has package visibility. Since this class is not in the same package as the `Window` class, it cannot override the `Window.isActive` method. That is fine with us—we want to supply a new `isActive` method for the `AppletStub` interface. And, interestingly enough, it is entirely legal to add a new method with the same signature to the subclass. Whenever the object is accessed through a `Window` reference inside the `java.awt` package, the package-visible `Window.isActive` method is called. But whenever the object is accessed through an `AppletFrame` or `AppletStub` reference, the `AppletFrame.isActive` method is called.

Next, the constructor of the frame class calls `setStub` on the applet to make itself its stub.

```
    public AppletFrame(Applet anApplet)
    {
        applet = anApplet
        Container contentPane = getContentPane();
        contentPane.add(applet);
        applet.setStub(this);
    }
```

One final twist is possible. Suppose we want to use the calculator as an applet and application simultaneously. Rather than moving the methods of the `CalculatorApplet` class into the `CalculatorAppletApplication` class, we will just use inheritance. Here is the code for the class that does this.

```
    public class CalculatorAppletApplication extends CalculatorApplet
    {
        public static void main(String args[])
        {
            AppletFrame frame
                = new AppletFrame(new CalculatorApplet());
            . . .
        }
    }
```

You can do this with any applet, not just with the calculator applet. All you need to do is derive a class `MyAppletApplication` from your applet class and pass a `new MyApplet()` object to the `AppletFrame` in the `main` method. The result is a class that is both an applet and an application.

Just for fun, we use the previously mentioned trick of adding the `APPLET` tag as a comment to the source file. Then you can invoke the applet viewer with the source (!) file without requiring an additional HTML file.

Examples 10–11 and 10–12 list the code. You need to copy the `Calculator-Applet.java` file into the same directory to compile the program. Try running both the applet and the application:

```
appletviewer CalculatorAppletApplication.java
java CalculatorAppletApplication
```

Example 10–11: AppletFrame.java

```
1. import java.awt.*;
2. import java.awt.event.*;
3. import java.applet.*;
4. import java.net.*;
5. import java.util.*;
6. import javax.swing.*;
7.
8. public class AppletFrame extends JFrame
9.    implements AppletStub, AppletContext
10. {
11.    public AppletFrame(Applet anApplet)
12.    {
13.       applet = anApplet;
14.       Container contentPane = getContentPane();
15.       contentPane.add(applet);
16.       applet.setStub(this);
17.    }
18.
19.    public void show()
20.    {
21.       applet.init();
22.       super.show();
23.       applet.start();
24.    }
25.
26.    // AppletStub methods
27.    public boolean isActive() { return true; }
28.    public URL getDocumentBase() { return null; }
29.    public URL getCodeBase() { return null; }
30.    public String getParameter(String name) { return ""; }
31.    public AppletContext getAppletContext() { return this; }
32.    public void appletResize(int width, int height) {}
33.
```

```
34.   // AppletContext methods
35.   public AudioClip getAudioClip(URL url) { return null; }
36.   public Image getImage(URL url) { return null; }
37.   public Applet getApplet(String name) { return null; }
38.   public Enumeration getApplets() { return null; }
39.   public void showDocument(URL url) {}
40.   public void showDocument(URL url, String target) {}
41.   public void showStatus(String status) {}
42.
43.   private Applet applet;
44. }
```

Example 10–12: CalculatorAppletApplication.java

```
1. /*
2.   The applet viewer reads the tags below if you call it with
3.       appletviewer CalculatorAppletApplication.java (!)
4.   No separate HTML file is required.
5.   <APPLET CODE="CalculatorAppletApplication.class"
6.      WIDTH=200 HEIGHT=200>
7.   </APPLET>
8. */
9.
10. import javax.swing.*;
11.
12. public class CalculatorAppletApplication
13.    extends CalculatorApplet
14. // It's an applet. It's an application. It's BOTH!
15. {
16.    public static void main(String[] args)
17.    {
18.       AppletFrame frame
19.          = new AppletFrame(new CalculatorApplet());
20.       frame.setTitle("CalculatorAppletApplication");
21.       frame.setSize(WIDTH, HEIGHT);
22.       frame.setDefaultCloseOperation(JFrame.EXIT_ON_CLOSE);
23.       frame.show();
24.    }
25.
26.    public static final int WIDTH = 200;
27.    public static final int HEIGHT = 200;
28. }
```

JAR Files

The calculator applet from this chapter uses four classes: CalculatorApplet, CalculatorPanel and two inner classes. You know that the applet tag references the class file that contains the class derived from JApplet:

```
<APPLET CODE="CalculatorApplet.class" WIDTH=100 HEIGHT=150>
```

When the browser reads this line, it makes a connection to the web server and fetches the file `CalculatorApplet.class`. The *class loader* of the Java interpreter that is built into the browser then loads the `CalculatorApplet` class from that file. During the loading process, the class loader must *resolve* the other classes used in this class. After doing so, it then knows it needs more classes to run the applet. The browser, therefore, makes additional connections to the web server. Most applets consist of multiple classes, and the web browser must make many connections, one for each class file. Loading such an applet over a slow network connection can take many minutes.

 NOTE: It is important to remember that the reason for this long loading time is not the size of the class files—they are quite small. Rather it is because of the considerable overhead involved in establishing a connection to the web server.

Java supports an improved method for loading class files, which allows you to package all the needed class files into a single file. This file can then be downloaded with a *single* HTTP request to the server. Files that archive Java class files are called Java Archive (JAR) files. JAR files can contain both class files and other file types such as image and sound files. JAR files are compressed, using the familiar ZIP compression format, which further reduces the download time.

You use the `jar` tool to make JAR files. (In the default installation, it's in the `jdk/bin` directory.) The most common command to make a new JAR file uses the following syntax:

```
jar cvf JARFileName File1 File2 . . .
```

For example,

```
jar cvf CalculatorClasses.jar *.java icon.gif
```

In general, the `jar` command has the format

```
jar options File1 File2 . . .
```

Table 10–4 lists all the options for the `jar` program. They are similar to the options of the UNIX `tar` command.

Table 10–4: `jar` program options

Option	Description
c	Creates a new or empty archive and adds files to it. If any of the specified file names are directories, then the `jar` program processes them recursively.
t	Displays the table of contents.
u	Updates an existing JAR file.

Table 10–4: `jar` program options (continued)

Option	Description
x	Extracts files. If you supply one or more file names, only those files are extracted. Otherwise, all files are extracted.
f	Specifies the JAR file name as the second command-line argument. If this parameter is missing, then `jar` will write the result to standard output (when creating a JAR file) or read it from standard input (when extracting or tabulating a JAR file).
v	Generates verbose output.
m	Adds a *manifest* to the JAR file. A manifest is a description of the archive contents and origin. Every archive has a default manifest, but you can supply your own if you want to authenticate the contents of the archive. We will discuss this in the security chapter of Volume 2.
0	Stores without ZIP compression.
M	Does not create a manifest file for the entries.
i	Creates an index file (see below for more information).
C	Temporarily change the directory. For example, `jar cvf JARFileName.jar -C classes *.class` changes to the `classes` subdirectory to add class files.

Once you have a JAR file, you need to reference it in the `APPLET` tag, as in the following example.

```
<APPLET CODE="CalculatorApplet.class"
    ARCHIVE="CalculatorClasses.jar"
    WIDTH=100 HEIGHT=150>
```

Note that the `CODE` attribute must still be present. The `CODE` attribute tells the browser the name of the applet. The `ARCHIVE` is merely a source where the applet class and other files may be located. Whenever a class, image, or sound file is needed, the browser searches the JAR files in the `ARCHIVE` list first. Only if the file is not contained in the archive will it be fetched from the web server.

The Manifest

JAR files are not just used for applets. You can package application programs, program components (sometimes called "Java beans"—see Chapter 8 of Volume 2) and code libraries into JAR files. For example, the runtime library of the SDK is contained in a very large file `rt.jar`.

A JAR file is simply a ZIP file that contains classes, other files that a program may need (such as icon images), and a *manifest* file that describes special features of the archive.

The manifest file is called `MANIFEST.MF` and is located in a special `META-INF` subdirectory of the JAR file. The minimum legal manifest is quite boring: just

```
Manifest-Version: 1.0
```

Complex manifests can have many more entries. The manifest entries are grouped into sections. The first section in the manifest is called the *main section*. It applies to the whole JAR file. Subsequent entries can specify properties of named entities such as individual files, packages, or URLs. Those entries must begin with a `Name` entry. Sections are separated by blank lines. For example,

```
Manifest-Version: 1.0
lines describing this archive

Name: Woozle.class
lines describing this file

Name: foo/bar/
lines describing this package
```

To edit the manifest, place the lines that you want to add to the manifest into a text file. Then run

```
jar cfm JARFileName ManifestFileName . . .
```

For example, to make a new JAR file with a manifest, run:

```
jar cfm MyArchive.jar manifest.mf com/mycompany/mypkg/*.class
```

To add items to the manifest of an existing JAR file, place the additions into a text file and use a command such as

```
jar cfm MyArchive.jar manifest-additions.mf
```

For more information on the JAR and manifest file formats, see `http://java.sun.com/j2se/1.3/docs/guide/jar/jar.html`.

TIP: If you have a large applet, chances are that not all users require all of its functionality. To reduce the download time, you can break up the applet code into multiple JAR files and add an *index* to the main JAR file. Then the class loader knows which JAR files contain a particular package or resource. To generate an index, you need to set the `Class-Path` attribute to the manifest of the main JAR file. Then run

```
jar -i MyAppletMain.jar
```

This command adds a file `INDEX.LIST` to the `META-INF` directory of the JAR file.

JAR Caching

By default, browsers use the browser cache to cache applet code. That is, if you revisit a site that uses an applet, and if the browser cache still contains the JAR file, and the file hasn't changed, then it is not downloaded again. That is a good scheme, but the browser cache isn't as long-lived as one would like for applets. For example, if you visit an expense reporting applet once a month, then it is likely that it is flushed from the cache every time you visit it.

The Java Plug-In supports a mechanism for making applets "stickier." If you want an applet to stay at the end-user site for a longer period of time, use the CACHE_OPTION, CACHE_ARCHIVE, and CACHE_VERSION keys.

You need to specify these keys as parameters or attributes, depending on the OBJECT or EMBED tag, in the following way:

```
<OBJECT ....>
    <PARAM NAME="ARCHIVE" VALUE="...">
    . . .
    ^ARAM NAME="CACHE_OPTION" VALUE="...">
    <PARAM NAME="CACHE_ARCHIVE" VALUE="...">
    <PARAM NAME="CACHE_VERSION" VALUE="...">
</OBJECT>
```

or

```
<EMBED ...
    ARCHIVE="..."
    CACHE_OPTION="..."
    CACHE_ARCHIVE="..."
    CACHE_VERSION="..."
    . . .
    >
```

The CACHE_OPTION key has one of three values:

- No: Do not cache the applet at all.
- Browser: Let the browser cache the applet (the default).
- Plugin: Let the Plug-In cache the applet.

The CACHE_ARCHIVE value specifies the files to be cached, for example "MyApplet.jar,MyLibrary.jar".

NOTE: A JAR file should be listed in either the ARCHIVE or the CACHE_ARCHIVE but not in both.

The CACHE_VERSION key/value pair is optional. The value is a list of version numbers, matching the JAR files in the CACHE_ARCHIVE list, that represent the required versions of the JAR files. If these versions already exist on the client, then they don't have to be downloaded. If no versions are specified, then the dates of the JAR files are used for comparison. You need to use version numbers for caching when you retrieve JAR files with SSL because the last-modified date is not available to the Java Plug-In in that situation.

For more information on applet caching, see `http://java.sun.com/products/plugin/1.3/docs/appletcaching.html`.

Self-Running JAR files

So far you have seen how to package applets in a JAR file. For applets, the appeal of the JAR format is to reduce the number of files that the browser has to download in separate HTTP requests. But JAR files are also useful to distribute application programs, to reduce file clutter on your users' computers. Simply place all files that your application needs into a JAR file and then add a manifest entry that specifies the *main class* of your program—the class that you would normally specify when invoking the `java` interpreter.

Make a file, say, `mainclass.mf`, containing a line such as

```
Main-Class: com/mypackage/MainFrame
```

Do not add a `.class` extension to the main class name. Then run the `jar` command:

```
jar cvfm MyProgram.jar mainclass.mf files to add
```

Users can now simply start the program as

```
java -jar MyProgram.jar
```

Resources

Classes that are used in both applets and applications often use associated data files, such as:

*   Image and sound files
*   Text files with message strings and button labels
*   Files with binary data, for example, to describe the layout of a map

In Java, such an associated file is called a *resource*.

> NOTE: In Windows, the term "resource" has a more specialized meaning. Windows resources also consist of images, button labels, and so on, but they are attached to the executable file and accessed by a standard programming interface. In contrast, Java resources are stored as separate files, not as part of class files. And it is up to each class to access and interpret the resource data.

For example, consider a class `AboutPanel` that displays a message such as the one in Figure 10–15.

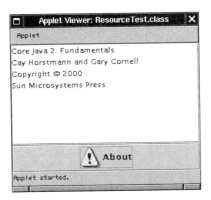

Figure 10–15: Displaying a resource from a JAR file

Of course, the book title and copyright year in the panel will change for the next edition of the book. To make it easy to track this change, we want to put the text inside a file and not hardcode it as a string.

But where should you put a file such as about.txt? Of course, it would be convenient if you simply placed it with the rest of the program files, for example in a JAR file.

The class loader knows how to search for class files until it has located them somewhere on the class path, or in an archive, or on a web server. The resource mechanism gives you the same convenience for files that aren't class files. Here are the necessary steps:

1.   Get the Class object of the class that has a resource, for example, AboutPanel.class.

2.   Call getResource(filename) to get the resource location as a URL.

3.   If the resource is an image or audio file, read it directly with the getImage or getAudioClip method.

4.   Otherwise, use the openStream method on the URL to read in the data in the file. (See Chapter 12 for more on streams.)

The point is that the class loader remembers how to locate the class, and then it can search for the associated resource in the same location.

For example, to make an icon with the image file about.gif, do the following:

```
URL url = AboutPanel.class.getResource("about.gif");
ImageIcon icon = new ImageIcon(url);
```

That means "locate the about.gif file at the same place where you find AboutPanel.class".

To read in the file `about.txt`, you can use similar commands:

```
URL url = AboutPanel.class.getResource("about.txt");
InputStream in = url.openStream();
```

Because this combination is so common, there is a convenient shortcut method: `getResourceAsStream` returns an `InputStream`, not a `URL`.

```
InputStream in
    = AboutPanel.class.getResourceAsStream("about.txt");
```

To read from this stream, you will need to know how to process input (see Chapter 12 for details). In the sample program, we read the stream a line at a time with the following instructions:

```
InputStream in = AboutPanel.class.
    getResourceAsStream("about.txt");
BufferedReader reader = new BufferedReader(new
    InputStreamReader(in));
String line;
while ((line = reader.readLine()) != null)
    textArea.append(line + "\n");
```

On the CD-ROM, you will find a JAR file that contains all class files for this example and the resource files `about.gif` and `about.txt`. This demonstrates that the applet locates the resource file in the same location as the class file, namely, inside the JAR file.

TIP: As you saw in the preceding section, you can place image and audio files inside a JAR file and simply access them with the `getImage` and `getAudioClip` methods—these methods automatically search JAR files. But, to load other files from a JAR file, you need the `getResourceAsStream` method.

Instead of placing a resource file inside the same directory as the class file, you can place it in a subdirectory. You can use a hierarchical resource name such as

```
data/text/about.txt
```

This is a relative resource name, and it is interpreted relative to the package of the class that is loading the resource. Note that you must always use the / separator, regardless of the directory separator on the system that actually stores the resource files. For example, on the Windows file system, the resource loader automatically translates / to \ separators.

A resource name starting with a / is called an absolute resource name. It is located in the same way that a class inside a package would be located. For example, a resource

```
/corejava/title.txt
```

is located in the `corejava` directory (which may be a subdirectory of the class path, inside a JAR file, or on a web server).

Automating the loading of files is all that the resource loading feature does. There are no standard methods for interpreting the contents of a resource file. Each applet must have its own way of interpreting the contents of its resource files.

Another common application of resources is the internationalization of applets and applications. Language-dependent strings, such as messages and user interface labels, are stored in resource files, with one file for each language. The *internationalization API*, which is discussed in Chapter 10 of Volume 2, supports a standard method for organizing and accessing these localization files.

Example 10–13 is the HTML source for testing a resource; Example 10–14 is the Java code.

Example 10–13: ResourceTest.html

```
1. <APPLET CODE="ResourceTest.class"
2.    WIDTH=300 HEIGHT=200
3.    ARCHIVE="ResourceTest.jar">
4. </APPLET>
5.
```

Example 10–14: ResourceTest.java

```
1. import java.awt.*;
2. import java.awt.event.*;
3. import java.io.*;
4. import java.net.*;
5. import javax.swing.*;
6.
7. public class ResourceTest extends JApplet
8. {
9.    public void init()
10.    {
11.       Container contentPane = getContentPane();
12.       contentPane.add(new AboutPanel());
13.    }
14. }
15.
16. /**
17.    A panel with a text area and an "About" button. Pressing
18.    the button fills the text area with text from a resource.
19. */
20. class AboutPanel extends JTextArea
21. {
22.    public AboutPanel()
23.    {
24.       setLayout(new BorderLayout());
```

```
25.
26.         // add text area
27.         textArea = new JTextArea();
28.         add(new JScrollPane(textArea), BorderLayout.CENTER);
29.
30.         // add About button
31.         URL aboutURL = AboutPanel.class.getResource("about.gif");
32.         JButton aboutButton = new JButton("About",
33.            new ImageIcon(aboutURL));
34.         aboutButton.addActionListener(new AboutAction());
35.         add(aboutButton, BorderLayout.SOUTH);
36.      }
37.
38.      private JTextArea textArea;
39.
40.      private class AboutAction implements ActionListener
41.      {
42.         public void actionPerformed(ActionEvent event)
43.         {
44.            try
45.            {
46.               // read text from resource into text area
47.               InputStream in = AboutPanel.class.
48.                  getResourceAsStream("about.txt");
49.               BufferedReader reader = new BufferedReader(new
50.                  InputStreamReader(in));
51.               String line;
52.               while ((line = reader.readLine()) != null)
53.                  textArea.append(line + "\n");
54.            }
55.            catch(IOException exception)
56.            {
57.               exception.printStackTrace();
58.            }
59.         }
60.      }
61. }
```

 java.lang.Class

- URL getResource(String name)
- InputStream getResourceAsStream(String name)

  find the resource in the same place as the class and then return a URL or input stream you can use for loading the resource. The methods return null if the resource isn't found, and so do not throw an exception for an I/O error.

  Parameters: name   The resource name

Optional Packages

As you saw, JAR files are useful to package both applets and applications. They are also commonly used to package code libraries. You can add any set of classes into a JAR file and make the classes available by adding the JAR file to the class path. For commonly used code libraries, you can bypass that step by turning a JAR file into an *optional package.*

NOTE: In prior versions of J2SE, optional packages were called *extensions.* The "package" term is a bit misleading—an optional package can contain classes from multiple Java programming language packages.

The main section of the manifest of an optional package describes the contents. Here is an example.

```
Extension-Name: com.mycompany.myextension
Specification-Vendor: My Company, Inc
Specification-Version: 1.0
Implementation-Vendor-Id: com.mycompany
Implementation-Vendor: My Company, Inc
Implementation-Version: 1.0.3
```

The extension name can be completely arbitrary. Just like with Java language packages, you can ensure uniqueness by using reversed domain names.

A program that requires extensions specifies them in the main section of its manifest:

```
Extension-List: myext otherext
myext-Extension-Name: com.mycompany.myextension
myext-Specification-Version: 1.0
myext-Implementation-Version: 1.0.1
myext-Implementation-Vendor-Id: com.mycompany
otherext-Extension-Name: com.hal.util
otherext-Specification-Version: 2.0
```

This particular application needs two optional packages, with *aliases* myext and anotherext. The *alias*-Extension-Name line yields the actual extension name. The application states that it requires a myext package that conforms to specification 1.0 or higher and implementation 1.0.1 or higher, and it insists that the package be implemented by a specific vendor. For the other extension, the program only requires that it conforms to specification 2.0 or higher. Any implementation and vendor are acceptable.

When the program starts, it needs to locate the optional packages. An optional package JAR can simply be dropped into the jre/lib/ext directory. Alternatively, the program can specify a URL where the optional package can be downloaded, such as

```
alias-Implementation-URL: http://www.mycompany.com/pack-
ages/myextension.jar
```

For more information on optional packages, see `http://java.sun.com/`
`j2se/1.3/docs/guide/extensions/index.html`.

Sealing

We mentioned in Chapter 4 that you can *seal* a Java language package to ensure
that no further classes can add themselves to it. Sealing protects the features with
package visibility. To achieve this, you put all classes of the package into a JAR
file. By default, packages in a JAR file are not sealed. You can change that global
default by placing the line

```
Sealed: true
```

into the main section of the manifest. For each individual package, you can specify whether you want the package sealed or not, by adding another section to the
JAR file, like this:

```
Name: com/mycompany/mypackage/
Sealed: true

Name: com/hal/util/
Sealed: false
```

To seal a package, make a text file with the manifest instructions. Then run the
`jar` command:

```
jar cvfm MyPackage.jar sealed.mf files to add
```

This concludes our discussion of applets. In the next chapter, you will learn
how to use exceptions to tell your programs what to do when problems arise at
runtime. We'll also give you tips and techniques for testing and debugging, so
that hopefully not too many things will go wrong when your programs run.

Chapter **11**

Exceptions and Debugging

▼ DEALING WITH ERRORS

▼ CATCHING EXCEPTIONS

▼ SOME TIPS ON USING EXCEPTIONS

▼ DEBUGGING TECHNIQUES

▼ USING A DEBUGGER

In a perfect world, users would never enter data in the wrong form, files they choose to open would always exist, and code would never have bugs. So far, we have mostly presented code as though we lived in this kind of perfect world. It is now time to turn to the mechanisms Java has for dealing with the real world of bad data and buggy code.

Encountering errors is unpleasant. If a user loses all the work he or she did during a program session because of a programming mistake or some external circumstance, that user may forever turn away from your program. At the very least, you must:

- Notify the user of an error;
- Save all work;
- Allow users to gracefully exit the program.

For exceptional situations, such as bad input data with the potential to bomb the program, Java uses a form of error-trapping called, naturally enough, *exception handling*. Exception handling in Java is similar to that in C++ or Delphi. The first part of this chapter covers Java's exceptions.

The second part of this chapter concerns finding bugs in your code before they cause exceptions at run time. Unfortunately, if you use just the SDK, then bug detection is the same as it was back in the Dark Ages. We give you some tips and a few tools to ease the pain. Then, we explain how to use the command-line debugger as a tool of last resort. For the serious Java developer, products such as Sun's Forte, Symantec's Café, and Inprise's JBuilder have quite useful debuggers. We give you an introduction to the Forte debugger.

Dealing with Errors

Suppose an error occurs while a Java program is running. The error might be caused by a file containing wrong information, a flaky network connection, or (we hate to mention it) use of an invalid array index or an attempt to use an object reference that hasn't yet been assigned to an object. Users expect that programs will act sensibly when errors happen. If an operation cannot be completed because of an error, the program ought to either:

• Return to a safe state and enable the user to execute other commands;

or

• Allow the user to save all his or her work and terminate the program gracefully.

This may not be easy to do: the code that detects (or even causes) the error condition is usually far removed from the code that can roll back the data to a safe state, or the code that can save the user's work and exit cheerfully. The mission of exception handling is to transfer control from where the error occurred to an error-handler that can deal with the situation. To handle exceptional situations in your program, you must take into account the errors and problems that may occur. What sorts of problems do you need to consider?

User input errors. In addition to the inevitable typos, some users like to blaze their own trail instead of following directions. Suppose, for example, that a user asks to connect to a URL that is syntactically wrong. Your code should check the syntax, but suppose it does not. Then the network package will complain.

Device errors. Hardware does not always do what you want it to. The printer may be turned off. A web page may be temporarily unavailable. Devices will often fail in the middle of a task. For example, a printer may run out of paper in the middle of a printout.

Physical limitations. Disks can fill up; you can run out of available memory.

Code errors. A method may not perform correctly. For example, it could deliver wrong answers or use other methods incorrectly. Computing an invalid array index, trying to find a nonexistent entry in a hash table, and trying to pop an empty stack are all examples of a code error.

The traditional reaction to an error in a method is to return a special error code that the calling method analyzes. For example, methods that read information back from files often return a –1 end-of-file value marker rather than a standard character. This can be an efficient method for dealing with many exceptional conditions. Another common return value to denote an error condition is the `null` reference. In Chapter 10, you saw an example of this with the `get-Parameter` method of the `Applet` class that returns `null` if the queried parameter is not present.

Unfortunately, it is not always possible to return an error code. There may be no obvious way of distinguishing valid and invalid data. A method returning an integer cannot simply return –1 to denote the error—the value –1 might be a perfectly valid result.

Instead, as we mentioned back in Chapter 5, Java allows every method an alternate exit path if it is unable to complete its task in the normal way. In this situation, the method does not return a value. Instead, it *throws* an object that encapsulates the error information. Note that the method exits immediately; it does not return its normal (or any) value. Moreover, execution does not resume at the code that called the method; instead, the exception-handling mechanism begins its search for an *exception handler* that can deal with this particular error condition.

Exceptions have their own syntax and are part of a special inheritance hierarchy. We take up the syntax first and then give a few hints on how to use this language feature effectively.

The Classification of Exceptions

In Java, an exception object is always an instance of a class derived from `Throwable`. As you will soon see, you can create your own exception classes, if the ones built into Java do not suit your needs.

Figure 11–1 is a simplified diagram of the exception hierarchy in Java.

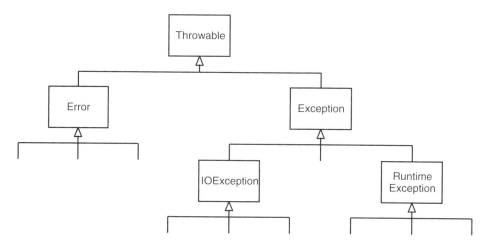

Figure 11–1: Exception hierarchy in Java

Notice that all exceptions descend from `Throwable`, but the hierarchy immediately splits into two branches: `Error` and `Exception`.

The `Error` hierarchy describes internal errors and resource exhaustion inside the Java runtime system. You should not throw an object of this type. There is little you can do if such an internal error occurs, beyond notifying the user and trying to terminate the program gracefully. These situations are quite rare.

When doing Java programming, you focus on the `Exception` hierarchy. The `Exception` hierarchy also splits into two branches: exceptions that derive from `RuntimeException` and those that do not. The general rule is this:

- A `RuntimeException` happens because you made a programming error. Any other exception occurs because a bad thing, such as an I/O error, happened to your otherwise good program.

Exceptions that inherit from `RuntimeException` include such problems as:

- A bad cast;
- An out-of-bounds array access;
- A null pointer access.

Exceptions that do not inherit from `RuntimeException` include:

- Trying to read past the end of a file;
- Trying to open a malformed URL;
- Trying to find a `Class` object for a string that does not denote an existing class.

The rule "If it is a `RuntimeException`, it was your fault" works pretty well. You could have avoided that `ArrayIndexOutOfBoundsException` by testing the array index against the array bounds. The `NullPointerException` would not have happened had you checked whether or not the variable was `null` before using it.

How about a malformed URL? Isn't it also possible to find out whether it is "malformed" before using it? Well, different browsers can handle different kinds of URLs. For example, Netscape can deal with a `mailto:` URL, whereas the applet viewer cannot. Thus, the notion of "malformed" depends on the environment, not just on your code.

The Java Language Specification calls any exception that derives from the class `Error` or the class `RuntimeException` an *unchecked* exception. All other exceptions are called *checked* exceptions. This is useful terminology that we will also adopt.

NOTE: The name `RuntimeException` is somewhat confusing. Of course, all of the errors we are discussing occur at run time.

C++ NOTE: If you are familiar with the (much more limited) exception hierarchy of the standard C++ library, you will be really confused at this point. C++ has two fundamental exception classes, `runtime_error` and `logic_error`. The `logic_error` class is the equivalent of Java's `RuntimeException` and also denotes logical errors in the program. The `runtime_error` class is the base class for exceptions caused by unpredictable problems. It is equivalent to exceptions in Java that are not of type `RuntimeException`.

Advertising the Exceptions That a Method Throws

A Java method can throw an exception if it encounters a situation it cannot handle. The idea is simple: a method will not only tell the Java compiler what values it can return, *it is also going to tell the compiler what can go wrong*. For example, code that attempts to read from a file knows that the file might not exist or that it might be empty. The code that tries to process the information in a file therefore will need to notify the compiler that it can throw some sort of `IOException`.

The place where you advertise that your method can throw an exception is in the header of the method; the header changes to reflect the checked exceptions the method can throw. For example, here is the header for a method in the `BufferedReader` class from the standard library. The method reads a line of text from a stream, such as a file or network connection. (See Chapter 12 for more on streams.)

```
public String readLine() throws IOException
```

The header indicates this method returns a string, but it *also* has the capacity to go wrong in a special way—by throwing an IOException. If this sad state should come to pass, the method will not return a string but instead will throw an object of the IOException class. If it does, then the runtime system will begin to search for an exception handler that knows how to deal with IOException objects.

When you write your own methods, you don't have to advertise every possible throwable object that your method might actually throw. To understand when (and what) you have to advertise in the throws clause of the methods you write, keep in mind that an exception is thrown in any of the following four situations:

1.   You call a method that throws a checked exception, for example, the read-Line method of the BufferedReader class.

2.   You detect an error and throw a checked exception with the throw statement (we cover the throw statement in the next section).

3.   You make a programming error, such as a[-1] = 0 that gives rise to an unchecked exception such as an ArrayIndexOutOfBoundsException.

4.   An internal error occurs in the virtual machine or runtime library.

If either of the first two scenarios occurs, you must tell the programmers who will use your method that there is the possibility of an exception. Why? Any method that throws an exception is a potential death trap. If no handler catches the exception, the current thread of execution terminates.

As with Java methods that are part of the supplied classes, you declare that your method may throw an exception with an *exception specification* in the method header.

```
class MyAnimation
{
    . . .

    public Image loadImage(String s) throws IOException
    {
        . . .
    }
}
```

If a method might throw more than one checked exception, you must indicate all exceptions in the header. Separate them by a comma as in the following example:

```
class MyAnimation
{
    . . .
    public Image loadImage(String s)
        throws EOFException, MalformedURLException
    {
        . . .
    }
}
```

However, you do not need to advertise internal Java errors, that is, exceptions inheriting from `Error`. Any code could potentially throw those exceptions, and they are entirely beyond your control.

Similarly, you should not advertise unchecked exceptions inheriting from `RuntimeException`.

```
class MyAnimation
{
    . . .
    void drawImage(int i)
        throws ArrayIndexOutOfBoundsException // NO!!!
    {
        . . .
    }
}
```

These runtime errors are completely under your control. If you are so concerned about array index errors, you should spend the time needed to fix them instead of advertising the possibility that they can happen.

In summary, a method must declare all the *checked* exceptions that it might throw. Unchecked exceptions are either beyond your control (`Error`) or result from conditions that you should not have allowed in the first place (`RuntimeException`). If your method fails to faithfully declare all checked exceptions, the compiler will issue an error message.

Of course, as you have already seen in quite a few examples, instead of declaring the exception, you can also catch it. Then the exception won't be thrown out of the method, and no `throws` specification is necessary. You will see later in this chapter how to decide whether to catch an exception or to enable someone else to catch it.

CAUTION: If you override a method from a superclass in your subclass, the subclass method cannot throw more checked exceptions than the superclass method that you replace. (It can throw fewer, if it likes.) In particular, if the superclass method throws no checked exception at all, neither can the subclass. For example, if you override `JCompo-nent.paintComponent`, your `paintComponent` method must not throw any checked exceptions, since the superclass method doesn't throw any.

When a method in a class declares that it throws an exception that is an instance of a particular class, then it may throw an exception of that class or of any of its subclasses. For example, the `readLine` method of the `BufferedReader` class says that it throws an `IOException`. We do not know what kind of `IOException`. It could be a plain `IOException` or an object of one of the various child classes, such as `EOFException`.

> C++ NOTE: The `throws` specifier is the same as the `throw` specifier in C++, with one important difference. In C++, `throw` specifiers are enforced at run time, not at compile time. That is, the C++ compiler pays no attention to exception specifications. But if an exception is thrown in a function that is not part of the `throw` list, then the `unexpected` function is called, and, by default, the program terminates.
>
> Also, in C++, a function may throw any exception if no `throw` specification is given. In Java, a method without a `throws` specifier may not throw any checked exception at all.

How to Throw an Exception

Let us suppose something terrible has happened in your code. You have a method, `readData`, that is reading in a file whose header promised

```
Content-length: 1024
```

But, you get an end of file after 733 characters. You decide this situation is so abnormal that you want to throw an exception.

You need to decide what exception type to throw. Some kind of `IOException` would be a good choice. Perusing the Java API documentation, you find an `EOFException` with the description "Signals that an EOF has been reached unexpectedly during input." Perfect. Here is how you throw it:

```
throw new EOFException();
```

or, if you prefer,

```
EOFException e = new EOFException();
throw e;
```

Here is how it all fits together:

```
String readData(BufferedReader in) throws EOFException
{
   . . .
   while (. . .)
   {
      if (ch == -1) // EOF encountered
      {
         if (n < len)
            throw new EOFException();
```

```
      }
         . . .
    }
    return s;
}
```

The `EOFException` has a second constructor that takes a string argument. You can put this to good use by describing the exceptional condition more carefully.

```
String gripe = "Content-length: " + len + ", Received: " + n;
throw new EOFException(gripe);
```

As you can see, throwing an exception is easy if one of the existing exception classes works for you. In this case:

1. Find an appropriate exception class;

2. Make an object of that class;

3. Throw it.

Once a method throws an exception, the method does not return to its caller. This means that you do not have to worry about cooking up a default return value or an error code.

C++ NOTE: Throwing an exception is the same in C++ and in Java, with one small exception. In Java, you can throw only objects of child classes of `Throwable`. In C++, you can throw values of any type.

Creating Exception Classes

Your code may run into a problem that is not adequately described by any of the standard exception classes. In this case, it is easy enough to create your own exception class. Just derive it from `Exception` or from a child class of `Exception` such as `IOException`. It is customary to give both a default constructor and a constructor that contains a detailed message. (The `toString` method of the `Throwable` base class prints out that detailed message, which is handy for debugging.)

```
class FileFormatException extends IOException
{
   public FileFormatException() {}
   public FileFormatException(String gripe)
   {
      super(gripe);
   }
}
```

Now you are ready to throw your very own exception type.

```
String readData(BufferedReader in) throws FileFormatException
{
```

```
    . . .
    while (. . .)
    {
       if (ch == -1) // EOF encountered
       {
          if (n < len)
             throw new FileFormatException();
       }
          . . .
    }
    return s;
}
```

java.lang.Throwable

- `Throwable()`

  constructs a new Throwable object with no detailed message.

- `Throwable(String message)`

  constructs a new Throwable object with the specified detailed message. By convention, all derived exception classes support both a default constructor and a constructor with a detailed message.

- `String getMessage()`

  gets the detailed message of the Throwable object.

Catching Exceptions

You now know how to throw an exception. It is pretty easy. You throw it and you forget it. Of course, some code has to catch the exception. Catching exceptions requires more planning.

If an exception occurs that is not caught anywhere in a nongraphical application, the program will terminate and print a message to the console giving the type of the exception and a stack trace. A graphics program (both an applet and an application) prints the same error message, but the program goes back to its user interface processing loop. (When you are debugging a graphically based program, it is a good idea to keep the console available on the screen and not minimized.)

To catch an exception, you set up a `try/catch` block. The simplest form of the `try` block is as follows:

```
try
{
   code
   more code
   more code
}
```

```
catch (ExceptionType e)
{
    handler for this type
}
```

If any of the code inside the `try` block throws an exception of the class specified in the `catch` clause, then,

1. The program skips the remainder of the code in the `try` block;

2. The program executes the handler code inside the `catch` clause.

If none of the code inside the `try` block throws an exception, then the program skips the `catch` clause.

If any of the code in a method throws an exception of a type other than the one named in the `catch` clause, this method exits immediately. (Hopefully, one of its callers has already coded a `catch` clause for that type.)

To show this at work, here is some fairly typical code for reading in text:

```
public void read(BufferedReader reader)
{
    try
    {
        boolean done = false;
        while (!done)
        {
            String line = reader.readLine();
            if (line == null) // end of file
                done = true;
            else
            {
                process line;
            }
        }
    }
    catch (IOException exception)
    {
        exception.printStackTrace();
    }
}
```

Notice that most of the code in the `try` clause is straightforward: it reads and processes lines until we encounter the end of the file. As you can see by looking at the Java API, there is the possibility that the `readLine` method will throw an `IOException`. In that case, we skip out of the entire `while` loop, enter the `catch` clause and generate a stack trace. For a toy program, that seems like a reasonable way to deal with this exception. What other choice do you have?

Often, the best choice is to do nothing at all. If an error occurs in the readLine method, let the caller of the read method worry about it! If we take that approach, then we have to advertise the fact that the method may throw an IOException.

```
public void read(BufferedReader reader) throws IOException
{
    boolean done = false;
    while (!done)
    {
        String line = reader.readLine();
        if (line == null) // end of file
            done = true;
        else
        {
            process line;
        }
    }
}
```

Remember, the compiler strictly enforces the throws specifiers. If you call a method that throws a checked exception, you must either handle it or pass it on.

Which of the two is better? As a general rule, you should catch those exceptions that you know how to handle, and propagate those that you do not know how to handle. When you propagate an exception, you must add a throws specifier to alert the caller that an exception may be thrown.

Look at the Java API documentation to see what methods throw which exceptions. Then, decide whether you should handle them or add them to the throws list. There is nothing embarrassing about the latter choice. It is better to direct an exception to a competent handler than to squelch it.

Please keep in mind that there is one exception to this rule, as we mentioned earlier. If you are writing a method that overrides a superclass method that throws no exceptions (such as paintComponent in JComponent), then you *must* catch each checked exception in the method's code. You are not allowed to add more throws specifiers to a subclass method than are present in the superclass method.

TIP: Don't be shy about throwing or propagating exceptions to signal problems that you can't handle properly. On the other hand, your fellow programmers will hate you if you write methods that throw exceptions unnecessarily and that they must handle or pass on. If you can do something intelligent about an exceptional condition, then you should not use the sledgehammer of an exception.

C++ NOTE: Catching exceptions is almost the same in Java and in C++. Strictly speaking, the analog of

```
catch (Exception e) // Java
```

is

```
catch (Exception& e) // C++
```

There is no analog to the C++ `catch (...)`. This is not needed in Java because all exceptions derive from a common superclass.

Catching Multiple Exceptions

You can catch multiple exception types in a `try` block and handle each type differently. You use a separate `catch` clause for each type as in the following example:

```
try
{
    code that might
    throw exceptions
}
catch (MalformedURLException e1)
{
    // emergency action for malformed URLs
}
catch (UnknownHostException e2)
{
    // emergency action for unknown hosts
}
catch (IOException e3)
{
    // emergency action for all other I/O problems
}
```

The exception object (`e1`, `e2`, `e3`) may contain information about the nature of the exception. To find out more about the object, try

```
e3.getMessage()
```

to get the detailed error message (if there is one), or

```
e3.getClass().getName()
```

to get the actual type of the exception object.

Rethrowing Exceptions

Occasionally, you need to catch an exception without addressing the root cause of it. This need typically occurs when you have to do some local cleanup but can't fully resolve the problem. You then want to take your emergency action and again call `throw` to send the exception back up the calling chain. You can see a typical example of this in the following code.

```
Graphics g = image.getGraphics();
try
{
   code that might
   throw exceptions
}
catch (MalformedURLException e)
{
   g.dispose();
   throw e;
}
```

The above code shows one of the most common reasons for having to rethrow an exception that you have caught. If you do not dispose of the graphics context object in the `catch` clause, it will *never* be disposed of. (Of course, its `finalize` method might dispose of it, but that can take a long time.)

On the other hand, the underlying cause, the malformed URL exception, *has not disappeared*. You still want to report it to the authorities, who presumably know how to deal with such an exception. (See the next section for a more elegant way to achieve the same result.)

You can also throw a different exception than the one you catch.

```
try
{
   acme.util.Widget a = new acme.util.Widget();
   a.load(s);
   a.paint(g);
}
catch (RuntimeException e)
{
   // sheesh—another ACME error
   throw new Exception("ACME error");
}
```

The `finally` Clause

When your code throws an exception, it stops processing the remaining code in your method and exits the method. This is a problem if the method has acquired some local resource that only it knows about and if that resource must be cleaned up. One solution is to catch and rethrow all exceptions. But this solution is tedious because you need to clean up the resource allocation in two places, in the normal code and in the exception code.

Java has a better solution, the `finally` clause:

```
Graphics g = image.getGraphics();
```

```
try
{
   code that might
   throw exceptions
}
catch (IOException e)
{
   show error dialog
}
finally
{
   g.dispose();
}
```

This program executes the code in the `finally` clause whether or not an exception was caught. This means, in the example code above, the program will dispose of the graphics context *under all circumstances.*

Let us look at the three possible situations where the program will execute the `finally` clause.

1. The code throws no exceptions. In this event, the program first executes all the code in the `try` block. Then, it executes the code in the `finally` clause. Afterwards, execution continues with the first line after the `try` block.

2. The code throws an exception that is caught in a `catch` clause, in our case, an `IOException`. For this, the program executes all code in the `try` block, up to the point at which the exception was thrown. The remaining code in the `try` block is skipped. Then, the program executes the code in the matching `catch` clause, then the code in the `finally` clause.

    If the `catch` clause does not throw an exception, then the program executes the first line after the `try` block. If it does, then the exception is thrown back to the caller of this method.

3. The code throws an exception that is not caught in any `catch` clause. For this, the program executes all code in the `try` block until the exception is thrown. The remaining code in the `try` block is skipped. Then, the code in the `finally` clause is executed, and the exception is thrown back to the caller of this method.

You can use the `finally` clause without a `catch` clause. For example, consider the following `try` statement:

```
Graphics g = image.getGraphics();
try
{
   code that might
   throw exceptions
```

```
   }
   finally
   {
      g.dispose();
   }
```

The `g.dispose()` command in the `finally` clause is executed whether or not an exception is encountered in the `try` block. Of course, if an exception is encountered, it is rethrown and must be caught in another `catch` clause.

CAUTION: The `finally` clause leads to unexpected control flow when you exit the middle of a `try` block with a `return` statement. Before the method returns, the contents of the `finally` block is executed. If it also contains a `return` statement, then it masks the original return value. Consider this contrived example:

```
   public static int f(int n)
   {
      try
      {
         int r = n * n;
         return r;
      }
      finally
      {
         if (n == 2) return 0;
      }
   }
```

If you call `f(2)`, then the `try` block computes `r = 4` and executes the `return` statement. However, the `finally` clause is executed before the method actually returns. The `finally` clause causes the method to return 0, ignoring the original return value of 4.

Sometimes the `finally` clause gives you grief, namely if the cleanup method can also throw an exception. A typical case is closing a stream. (See Chapter 12 for more information on streams.) Suppose you want to make sure that you close a stream when an exception hits in the stream processing code.

```
   InputStream in;
   try
   {
      code that might
      throw exceptions
   }
   catch (IOException e)
   {
      show error dialog
   }
   finally
```

```
    {
        in.close();
    }
```

Now suppose that the code in the `try` block throws some exception *other than an* `IOException` that is of interest to the caller of the code. The `finally` block executes, and the `close` method is called. That method can itself throw an `IOException`! When it does, then the original exception is lost and the `IOException` is thrown instead. That is very much against the spirit of exception handling.

It is always a good idea—unfortunately not one that the designers of the `InputStream` class chose to follow—to throw no exceptions in cleanup operations such as `dispose`, `close`, and so on, that you expect users to call in `finally` blocks.

C++ NOTE: There is one fundamental difference between C++ and Java with regard to exception handling. Java has no destructors; thus, there is no stack unwinding as in C++. This means that the Java programmer must manually place code to reclaim resources in `finally` blocks. Of course, since Java does garbage collection, there are far fewer resources that require manual deallocation.

A Final Look at Java Error- and Exception-Handling

Example 11–1 deliberately generates a number of different errors and catches various exceptions (see Figure 11–2).

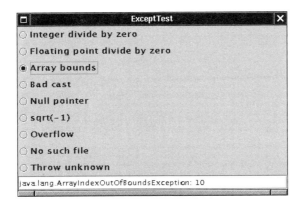

Figure 11–2: A program that generates exceptions

Try it out. Click on the buttons and see what exceptions are thrown.

As you know, a programmer error such as a bad array index throws a `RuntimeException`. An attempt to open a nonexistent file triggers an

IOException. Perhaps surprisingly, floating-point errors such as dividing by 0.0 or taking the square root of -1 do not generate exceptions. (Integer division by 0 throws an ArithmeticException.)

We trap the exceptions that the actionPerformed methods throw in the fireActionPerformed method of the radio buttons and display them in the text field. However, the actionPerformed method is declared to throw no checked exceptions. Thus, the handler for the "No such file" button must catch the IOException.

If you click on the "Throw unknown" button, an UnknownError object is thrown. This is not a subclass of Exception, so our program does not catch it. Instead, the user interface code prints an error message and a stack trace to the console.

Example 11–1: ExceptTest.java

```
1. import java.awt.*;
2. import java.awt.event.*;
3. import javax.swing.*;
4. import java.io.*;
5.
6. public class ExceptTest
7. {
8.    public static void main(String[] args)
9.    {
10.       ExceptTestFrame frame = new ExceptTestFrame();
11.       frame.setDefaultCloseOperation(JFrame.EXIT_ON_CLOSE);
12.       frame.show();
13.    }
14. }
15.
16. /**
17.    A frame with a panel for testing various exceptions
18. */
19. class ExceptTestFrame extends JFrame
20. {
21.    public ExceptTestFrame()
22.    {
23.       setTitle("ExceptTest");
24.       Container contentPane = getContentPane();
25.       ExceptTestPanel panel = new ExceptTestPanel();
26.       contentPane.add(panel);
27.       pack();
28.    }
29. }
30.
31. /**
32.    A panel with radio buttons for running code snippets
33.    and studying their exception behavior
```

```
34.  */
35.  class ExceptTestPanel extends Box
36.  {
37.     public ExceptTestPanel()
38.     {
39.        super(BoxLayout.Y_AXIS);
40.        group = new ButtonGroup();
41.
42.        // add radio buttons for code snippets
43.
44.        addRadioButton("Integer divide by zero", new
45.           ActionListener()
46.           {
47.              public void actionPerformed(ActionEvent event)
48.              {
49.                 a[1] = 1 / (a.length - a.length);
50.              }
51.           });
52.
53.        addRadioButton("Floating point divide by zero", new
54.           ActionListener()
55.           {
56.              public void actionPerformed(ActionEvent event)
57.              {
58.                 a[1] = a[2] / (a[3] - a[3]);
59.              }
60.           });
61.
62.        addRadioButton("Array bounds", new
63.           ActionListener()
64.           {
65.              public void actionPerformed(ActionEvent event)
66.              {
67.                 a[1] = a[10];
68.              }
69.           });
70.
71.        addRadioButton("Bad cast", new
72.           ActionListener()
73.           {
74.              public void actionPerformed(ActionEvent event)
75.              {
76.                 a = (double[])event.getSource();
77.              }
78.           });
79.
80.        addRadioButton("Null pointer", new
81.           ActionListener()
82.           {
83.              public void actionPerformed(ActionEvent event)
84.              {
```

```
85.                    event = null;
86.                    System.out.println(event.getSource());
87.                }
88.          });
89.
90.      addRadioButton("sqrt(-1)", new
91.          ActionListener()
92.          {
93.             public void actionPerformed(ActionEvent event)
94.             {
95.                a[1] = Math.sqrt(-1);
96.             }
97.          });
98.
99.      addRadioButton("Overflow", new
100.         ActionListener()
101.         {
102.            public void actionPerformed(ActionEvent event)
103.            {
104.               a[1] = 1000 * 1000 * 1000 * 1000;
105.               int n = (int)a[1];
106.            }
107.         });
108.
109.     addRadioButton("No such file", new
110.         ActionListener()
111.         {
112.            public void actionPerformed(ActionEvent event)
113.            {
114.               try
115.               {
116.                  FileInputStream is
117.                     = new FileInputStream("No such file");
118.               }
119.               catch (IOException exception)
120.               {
121.                  textField.setText(exception.toString());
122.               }
123.            }
124.         });
125.
126.     addRadioButton("Throw unknown", new
127.         ActionListener()
128.         {
129.            public void actionPerformed(ActionEvent event)
130.            {
131.               throw new UnknownError();
132.            }
133.         });
134.
135.     // add the text field for exception display
```

```
136.        textField = new JTextField(30);
137.        add(textField);
138.     }
139.
140.     /**
141.        Adds a radio button with a given listener to the
142.        panel. Traps any exceptions in the actionPerformed
143.        method of the listener.
144.        @param s the label of the radio button
145.        @param listener the action listener for the radio button
146.     */
147.     private void addRadioButton(String s, ActionListener listener)
148.     {
149.        JRadioButton button = new JRadioButton(s, false)
150.           {
151.              // the button calls this method to fire an
152.              // action event. We override it to trap exceptions
153.              protected void fireActionPerformed(ActionEvent event)
154.              {
155.                 try
156.                 {
157.                    super.fireActionPerformed(event);
158.                    textField.setText("No exception");
159.                 }
160.                 catch (Exception exception)
161.                 {
162.                    textField.setText(exception.toString());
163.                 }
164.              }
165.           };
166.
167.        button.addActionListener(listener);
168.        add(button);
169.        group.add(button);
170.     }
171.
172.     private ButtonGroup group;
173.     private JTextField textField;
174.     private double[] a = new double[10];
175. }
```

Some Tips on Using Exceptions

There is a tendency to overuse exceptions. After all, who wants to go to the trouble to write methods that parse input when exception-handling makes it so easy? Instead of parsing a URL when the user enters it, just send it off to a method that catches a `MalformedURLException`. Saves time, saves trouble. Wrong! While having an exception handler costs nothing, the actual handling of an exception will almost always cost a lot of time. Misusing exceptions can therefore slow your code down dramatically. Here are four tips on using exceptions.

1. *Exception-handling is not supposed to replace a simple test.*

    As an example of this, we wrote some code that uses the built-in `Stack` class. The code in Example 11–2 tries 1,000,000 times to pop an empty stack. It first does this by finding out whether or not the stack is empty.

    ```
    if (!s.empty()) s.pop();
    ```

    Next, we tell it to pop the stack no matter what. Then, we catch the `EmptyStackException` that tells us that we should not have done that.

    ```
    try()
    {
        s.pop();
    }
    catch (EmptyStackException e)
    {
    }
    ```

    On our test machine, we got the timing data in Table 11–1.

    Table 11–1: Timing data

Test	Throw/Catch
110 milliseconds	24550 milliseconds

    As you can see, it took far longer to catch an exception than it does to perform a simple test. The moral is: Use exceptions for exceptional circumstances only.

2. *Do not micromanage exceptions.*

    Many programmers wrap every statement in a separate `try` block.

    ```
    InputStream is;
    Stack s;

    for (i = 0; i < 100; i++)
    {
        try
        {
            n = s.pop();
        }
        catch (EmptyStackException s)
        {
            // stack was empty
        }
        try
        {
    ```

```
          out.writeInt(n);
      }
      catch (IOException e)
      {
          // problem writing to file
      }
  }
```

This approach blows up your code dramatically. Think about the task that you want the code to accomplish. Here we want to pop 100 numbers off a stack and save them to a file. (Never mind why—it is just a toy example.) There is nothing we can do if a problem rears its ugly head. If the stack is empty, it will not become occupied. If there is an error in the file, the error will not magically go away. It therefore makes sense to wrap the *entire task* in a `try` block. If any one operation fails, you can then abandon the task.

```
  try
  {
      for (i = 0; i < 100; i++)
      {
          n = s.pop();
          out.writeInt(n);
      }
  }
  catch (IOException e)
  {
      // problem writing to file
  }
  catch (EmptyStackException s)
  {
      // stack was empty
  }
```

This code looks much cleaner. It fulfills one of the promises of exception-handling, to *separate* normal processing from error-handling.

3. *Do not squelch exceptions.*

In Java, there is the tremendous temptation to shut up exceptions. You write a method that calls a method that might throw an exception once a century. The compiler whines because you have not declared the exception in the `throws` list of your method. You do not want to put it in the `throws` list because then the compiler will whine about all the methods that call your method. So you just shut it up:

```
  public Image loadImage(String s)
  {
      try
      {
          lots of code
      }
```

```
        catch (Exception e)
        {} // so there
    }
```

Now your code will compile without a hitch. It will run fine, except when an exception occurs. Then, the exception will be silently ignored. If you believe that exceptions are at all important, you need to make some effort to handle them right.

4. *Propagating exceptions is not a sign of shame.*

Many programmers feel compelled to catch all exceptions that are thrown. If they call a method that throws an exception, such as the FileInputStream constructor or the readLine method, they instinctively catch the exception that may be generated. Often, it is actually better to *propagate* the exception instead of catching it:

```
public void readStuff(String name) throws IOException
{
    FileInputStream in = new FileInputStream(name);
    . . .
}
```

Higher-level methods are often better equipped to inform the user of errors or to abandon unsuccessful commands.

Example 11–2: ExceptionalTest.java

```
1. import java.util.*;
2.
3. public class ExceptionalTest
4. {
5.    public static void main(String[] args)
6.    {
7.        int i = 0;
8.        int ntry = 1000000;
9.        Stack s = new Stack();
10.       long s1;
11.       long s2;
12.
13.       // test a stack for emptiness ntry times
14.       System.out.println("Testing for empty stack");
15.       s1 = new Date().getTime();
16.       for (i = 0; i <= ntry; i++)
17.           if (!s.empty()) s.pop();
18.       s2 = new Date().getTime();
19.       System.out.println((s2 - s1) + " milliseconds");
20.
21.       // pop an empty stack ntry times and catch the
22.       // resulting exception
```

```
23.       System.out.println("Catching EmptyStackException");
24.       s1 = new Date().getTime();
25.       for (i = 0; i <= ntry; i++)
26.       {
27.          try
28.          {
29.             s.pop();
30.          }
31.          catch(EmptyStackException e)
32.          {
33.          }
34.       }
35.       s2 = new Date().getTime();
36.       System.out.println((s2 - s1) + " milliseconds");
37.    }
38. }
```

Debugging Techniques

Suppose you wrote your program and made it bulletproof by catching and properly handling all exceptions. Then you run it, and it does not work right. Now what? (If you never have this problem, you can skip the remainder of this chapter.)

Of course, it is best if you have a convenient and powerful debugger. Debuggers are available as a part of professional development environments such as Inprise JBuilder, Symantec Café, or Sun's Forte. However, if you use a new version of Java that is not yet supported by development environments, or if you are on a budget or work on an unusual platform, you will need to do a great deal of debugging by the time-honored method of inserting print statements into your code.

Useful Tricks for Debugging

Here are some tips for efficient debugging if you have to do it all yourself.

1. You can print the value of any variable with code like this:

    ```
    System.out.println("x = " + x);
    ```

    If x is a number, it is converted to its string equivalent. If x is an object, then Java calls its toString method. Most of the classes in the Java library are very conscientious about overriding the toString method to give you useful information about the class. This is a real boon for debugging. You should make the same effort in your classes.

2. To get the state of the current object, print the state of the this object.

    ```
    System.out.println("Entering loadImage. this = " + this);
    ```

This code calls the toString method of the current class, and you get a printout of all instance fields. Of course, this approach works best when the toString method does a conscientious job and reports the values of all data fields.

3. Recall that we gave you the code for a generic toString method in Chapter 5—we used the reflection feature to enumerate and print all data fields. Here is an even shorter version of that code.

```java
public String toString()
{
    java.util.HashMap h = new java.util.HashMap();
    Class cls = getClass();
    java.lang.reflect.Field[] f = cls.getDeclaredFields();
    try
    {
        java.lang.reflect.AccessibleObject.setAccessible(f,
            true);
        for (int i = 0; i < f.length; i++)
            h.put(f[i].getName(), f[i].get(this));
    }
    catch (Exception e) {}

    if (cls.getSuperclass() != Object.class)
        h.put("super", super.toString());
    return cls.getName() + h;
}
```

The code uses the reflection mechanism to enumerate all fields. It puts the pairs (field name, field value) into a hash table. It then uses the toString method of the Hashtable class to print out the names and values. The only drawback is that the (name, value) pairs are listed in random order.

Here is a typical printout:

```
Employee{hireDay=Sun Oct 01 00:00:00 PDT 1989, name=Harry
Hacker, salary=52500.0}
```

4. One seemingly little-known but very useful trick is that you can put a separate main method in each class. Inside it, you can put a unit test stub that lets you test the class in isolation.

```java
public class MyClass
{
    methods and fields
    . . .
    public static void main(String[] args)
    {
        test code
    }
}
```

Make a few objects, call all methods, and check that each of them does the right thing. You can leave all these `main` methods in place and call the Java interpreter separately on each of the files to run the tests. When you run an applet, none of these `main` methods are ever called. When you run an application, the Java interpreter calls only the `main` method of the startup class.

5. You can get a stack trace from any exception object with the `print-StackTrace` method in the `Throwable` class. The following code catches any exception, prints the exception object and the stack trace, and rethrows the exception so it can find its intended handler.

```
try
{
    . . .
}
catch (Throwable t)
{
    t.printStackTrace();
    throw t;
}
```

You don't even need to catch an exception to generate a stack trace. Simply insert the statement

```
Thread.dumpStack();
```

anywhere into your code to get a stack trace.

6. Normally, the stack trace is displayed on `System.out`. You can send it to a file with the `void printStackTrace(PrintWriter s)` method. Or, if you want to display the stack trace in a window, here is how you can capture it into a string:

```
StringWriter out = new StringWriter();
new Throwable().printStackTrace(new PrintWriter(out));
String trace = out.toString();
```

(See Chapter 12 for the `PrintWriter` and `StringWriter` classes.)

7. It is often handy to trap program errors in a file. However, errors are sent to `System.err`, not `System.out`. Therefore, you cannot simply trap them by running

```
java MyProgram > errors.txt
```

In UNIX, this is not a problem. For example, if you use `bash` as your shell, simply capture the error stream as

```
java MyProgram 2> errors.txt
```

To capture both `System.err` and `System.out` in the same file, use

```
java MyProgram 2>&1 errors.txt
```

Some operating systems (such as Windows 95 or 98) do not have such a convenient method. Here is a remedy. Use the following Java program:

```java
import java.io.*;
public class Errout
{
    public static void main(String[] args) throws IOException
    {
        Process p = Runtime.getRuntime().exec(args);
        BufferedReader err = new BufferedReader(new
            InputStreamReader(p.getErrorStream()));
        String line;
        while ((line = err.readLine()) != null)
            System.out.println(line);
    }
}
```

Then run your program as

```
java Errout java MyProgram.java > errors.txt
```

C++ NOTE: A more efficient way of getting the same result in Windows is to compile this C program into a file `errout.exe`:

```c
#include <io.h>
#include <stdio.h>
#include <process.h>
int main(int argc, char* argv[])
{
    dup2(1, 2); /* make stderr go to stdout */
    execvp(argv[1], argv + 1);
    return 0;
}
```

Then you can run:

```
errout java MyProgram.java > errors.txt
```

8. To watch class loading, run the `java` interpreter with the `-verbose` flag. You get a printout such as:

```
[Opened C:\PROGRAM FILES\JAVASOFT\JRE\1.3\lib\rt.jar]
[Opened C:\PROGRAM FILES\JAVASOFT\JRE\1.3\lib\i18n.jar]
[Opened C:\PROGRAM FILES\JAVASOFT\JRE\1.3\lib\sunrsasign.jar]
[Loaded java.lang.Object from C:\PROGRAM FILES\JAVASOFT\JRE\1.3\lib\rt.jar]
[Loaded java.io.Serializable from C:\PROGRAM FILES\JAVASOFT\JRE\1.3\lib\rt.jar]
[Loaded java.lang.Comparable from C:\PROGRAM FILES\JAVASOFT\JRE\1.3\lib\rt.jar]
[Loaded java.lang.String from C:\PROGRAM FILES\JAVASOFT\JRE\1.3\lib\rt.jar]
[Loaded java.lang.Class from C:\PROGRAM FILES\JAVASOFT\JRE\1.3\lib\rt.jar]
[Loaded java.lang.Cloneable from C:\PROGRAM FILES\JAVASOFT\JRE\1.3\lib\rt.jar]
[Loaded java.lang.ClassLoader from C:\PROGRAM FILES\JAVASOFT\JRE\1.3\lib\rt.jar]
...
```

This can occasionally be helpful to diagnose class path problems.

9. If you ever looked at a Swing window and wondered how its designer managed to get all the components to line up so nicely, you can spy on the contents. Press CTRL+SHIFT+F1, and you get a printout of all components in the hierarchy:

```
FontDialog[frame0,0,0,300x200,layout=java.awt.BorderLayout,...
  javax.swing.JRootPane[,4,23,292x173,layout=javax.swing.JRootPane$RootLayout,...
    javax.swing.JPanel[null.glassPane,0,0,292x173,hidden,layout=java.awt.FlowLayout,...
    javax.swing.JLayeredPane[null.layeredPane,0,0,292x173,...
      javax.swing.JPanel[null.contentPane,0,0,292x173,layout=java.awt.GridBagLayout,...
        javax.swing.JList[,0,0,73x152,alignmentX=null,alignmentY=null,...
          javax.swing.CellRendererPane[,0,0,0x0,hidden]
            javax.swing.DefaultListCellRenderer$UIResource[,-73,-19,0x0,...
        javax.swing.JCheckBox[,157,13,50x25,layout=javax.swing.OverlayLayout,...
        javax.swing.JCheckBox[,156,65,52x25,layout=javax.swing.OverlayLayout,...
        javax.swing.JLabel[,114,119,30x17,alignmentX=0.0,alignmentY=null,...
        javax.swing.JTextField[,186,117,105x21,alignmentX=null,alignmentY=null,...
        javax.swing.JTextField[,0,152,291x21,alignmentX=null,alignmentY=null,...
```

10. If you design your own custom Swing component, and it doesn't seem to be displayed correctly, you'll really love the *Swing graphics debugger*. And even if you don't write your own component classes, it is instructive and fun to see exactly how the contents of a component are drawn. To turn on debugging for a Swing component, use the `setDebugGraphicsOptions` method of the `JComponent` class. The following options are available:

`DebugGraphics.FLASH_OPTION`	Flashes each line, rectangle, and text in red before drawing it
`DebugGraphics.LOG_OPTION`	Prints a message for each drawing operation
`DebugGraphics.BUFFERED_OPTION`	Displays the operations that are performed on the offscreen buffer
`DebugGraphics.NONE_OPTION`	Turns graphics debugging off

We have found that for the flash option to work, you must disable "double buffering," the strategy used by Swing to reduce flicker when updating a window. The magic incantation for turning on the flash option is:

```
RepaintManager.currentManager(getRootPane())
  .setDoubleBufferingEnabled(false);

((JComponent)getContentPane())
  .setDebugGraphicsOptions(DebugGraphics.FLASH_OPTION);
```

Simply place these lines at the end of your frame constructor. When the program runs, you will see the content pane filled in slow motion. Or, for more localized debugging, just call `setDebugGraphicsOptions` for a single component. Control freaks can set the duration, count, and color of the flashes—see the online documentation of the `DebugGraphics` class for details.

Assertions

It often happens that your code relies on the fact that some of your variables have certain values. For example, object references are supposed to be initialized, and integer indexes are supposed to be within certain limits. It is a good idea to occasionally check these assumptions. If the assumptions turn out to be incorrect, you can throw an exception. Here is a typical example:

```
public void f(int[] a, int i)
{
   if (!(a != null && i >= 0 && i < a.length))
      throw new IllegalArgumentError("Assertion failed");
   . . .
}
```

Such checks are usually called *assertions*. We want to assert that some condition is true before continuing.

The C programming language has a useful `assert` macro that we will imitate with an `Assertion` class.

To check an assertion, call the static method `check`:

```
public void f(int[] a, int i)
{
   Assertion.check(a != null && i >= 0 && i < a.length,
      "X.f: invalid parameter a");
   . . .
}
```

If the condition is violated, you get a stack trace:

```
Assertion failed. X.f: invalid parameter a
java.lang.Exception: Stack trace
        at java.lang.Thread.dumpStack(Unknown Source)
        at Assertion.check(Assertion.java:23)
        at X.f(X.java:49)
        at X.main(X.java:121)
```

If you are finished debugging, call the static method:

```
Assertion.setNdebug(true);
```

Then the `check` method no longer checks assertions.

Here is the implementation of the `check` method:

```
public class Assertion
{
   public static void check(boolean b, String s)
   {
      if (!ndebug && !b)
      {
         System.err.print("Assertion failed. ");
```

```
        if (s != null) System.err.print(s);
        System.err.println();
        Thread.dumpStack();
        System.exit(1);
     }
   }
   . . .
 }
```

This imitates the C behavior as closely as possible. If you would prefer another behavior, you can easily modify the assertion class.

Assertions are strictly a debugging tool. We don't ever expect the condition to be false, and if it is, we are happy to be notified and to have the program terminate. Once the program has been debugged and is deployed, all assertions should go away, since checking the conditions increases the running time and code size.

The question is how to remove the assertion code. Of course, you can manually remove all assertions, but that is tedious. Furthermore, if the release version did not turn out to be quite as perfect as you thought, you might have to stick them all back in to help in the next round of debugging. The "official" solution to this problem is to use a static final variable that is set to `true` during debugging and to `false` when the program is deployed:

```
public void f(int[] a, int i)
{
   if (debug) // a static final variable
      Assertion.check(a != null && i >= 0 && i < a.length,
         "X.f: invalid parameter a");
   . . .
}
```

If `debug` is `false`, then the compiler realizes that the call to `Assertion.check` can never happen and no code is generated. Of course, you have to recompile whenever you switch between the debug and release versions. This is still somewhat tedious, and there is an even better way.

We simply put the test into a separate class and then *fail to ship the code for that class with the release version!* Of course, the easiest way to generate a simple new class is as an anonymous inner class:

```
public void f(final int[] a, final int i)
{
   if (debug) // a boolean variable, not necessarily static final
      new Assertion()
      {
         {
```

```
        check(a != null && i >= 0 && i < a.length
           "X.f: invalid parameter a");
      }
   };
      . . .
 }
```

As so often is the case with inner class code, this code snippet looks exceedingly mysterious. The statement

```
new Assertion() { . . . };
```

creates an object of an anonymous class that inherits from `Assertion`. That anonymous class has no methods, just a single constructor. The constructor is written as an initialization block (see Chapter 4) since we cannot give names to constructors of anonymous classes.

When the `debug` variable is `true`, then the compiler loads the inner class and constructs an assertion object. The constructor calls the static `check` method of the `Assertion` class and tests the condition. (Because local class code can only refer to `final` variables of the ambient block, the parameters of `f` had to be declared `final`.) However, if `debug` is `false`, then the inner class is not even loaded. That means the inner class code need not be shipped with the release version of the program!

 C++ NOTE: This assertion facility is not as convenient as the one offered by C and C++. The C `assert` macro causes the tested expression to be printed out when the assertion fails. And by defining the `NDEBUG` macro and recompiling, you not only turn off assertions, they do not generate any code. Both of these capabilities are possible because `assert` is a feature of the preprocessor. Java has no preprocessor, and hence it is not possible to play tricks with macros. However, in Java you can use dynamic linking to conditionally activate code, which is ultimately a more elegant mechanism.

Using a Console Window

If you run an applet inside a browser, you may not be able to see any messages that are sent to `System.out`. Most browsers will have some sort of Java Console window. (Check the help system for your browser.) For example, Netscape Navigator has one, as does Internet Explorer 4 and above. If you use the Java Plug-In, check the Show Java Console box in the configuration panel (see Chapter 10).

Moreover, the Java Console window has a set of scroll bars, so you can retrieve messages that have scrolled off the window. Windows users will find this a definite advantage over the DOS shell window in which the `System.out` output normally appears.

We give you a similar window class so you can enjoy the same benefit of seeing your debugging messages in a window when debugging a program. Figure 11–3 shows our `ConsoleWindow` class in action.

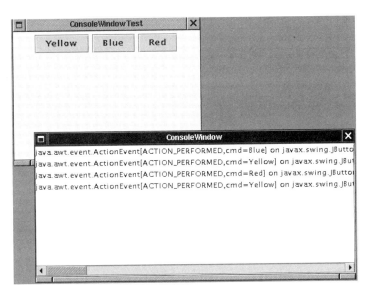

Figure 11–3: The console window

The class is easy to use. Simply call:

```
ConsoleWindow.init()
```

Then print to `System.out` or `System.err` in the normal way.

Example 11–3 lists the code for the `ConsoleWindow` class. As you can see, the class is very simple. Messages are displayed in a `JTextArea` inside a `JScrollPane`. We call the `System.setOut` and `System.setErr` methods to set the output and error streams to a special stream that adds all messages to the text area. (See Chapter 12 for more information on streams.)

Example 11–3: ConsoleWindow.java

```
1. import java.awt.*;
2. import java.awt.event.*;
3. import javax.swing.*;
4. import java.io.*;
5.
6. /**
7.    A window that displays the bytes sent to System.out
```

```
8.    and System.err
9. */
10. public class ConsoleWindow
11. {
12.    public static void init()
13.    {
14.        JFrame frame = new JFrame();
15.        frame.setTitle("ConsoleWindow");
16.        final JTextArea output = new JTextArea();
17.        output.setEditable(false);
18.        frame.getContentPane().add(new JScrollPane(output));
19.        frame.setSize(300, 200);
20.        frame.setLocation(200, 200);
21.        frame.show();
22.
23.        // define a PrintStream that sends its bytes to the
24.        // output text area
25.        PrintStream consoleStream = new PrintStream(new
26.            OutputStream()
27.            {
28.                public void write(int b) {} // never called
29.                public void write(byte[] b, int off, int len)
30.                {
31.                    output.append(new String(b, off, len));
32.                }
33.            });
34.
35.        // set both System.out and System.err to that stream
36.        System.setOut(consoleStream);
37.        System.setErr(consoleStream);
38.    }
39. }
```

Tracing AWT Events

When you write a fancy user interface in Java, you need to know what events AWT sends to what components. Unfortunately, the AWT documentation is somewhat sketchy in this regard. For example, suppose you want to show hints in the status line when the user moves the mouse over different parts of the screen. The AWT generates mouse and focus events that you may be able to trap.

We give you a useful EventTrace class to spy on these events. It prints out all event handling methods and their parameters. See Figure 11–4 for a display of the traced events.

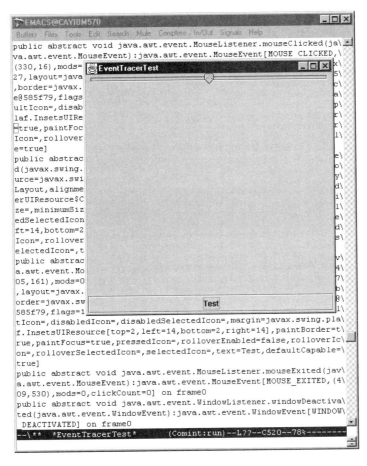

Figure 11–4: The EventTracer class at work

To spy on messages, add the component whose events you want to trace to an event tracer:

```
EventTracer tracer = new EventTracer();
tracer.add(frame);
```

This prints out a textual description of all events, like this:

```
. . .
public abstract void java.awt.event.ComponentListener
.componentShown(java.awt.event.ComponentEvent):java.awt.event
.ComponentEvent[COMPONENT_SHOWN] on frame0
public abstract void java.awt.event.WindowListener
.windowOpened(java.awt.event.WindowEvent):java.awt.event
.WindowEvent[WINDOW_OPENED] on frame0
. . .
```

You may want to capture this output in a file or a console window, as explained in the preceding sections.

Example 11–4 is the `EventTracer` class. The idea behind the class is easy even if the implementation is a bit mysterious.

1. When you add a component to the event tracer in the `add` method, the JavaBeans introspection class analyzes the component for methods of the form `void addXxxListener(XxxEvent)`. (See Chapter 7 of Volume 2 for more information on JavaBeans.) For each matching method, an `EventSetDescriptor` is generated. We pass each descriptor to the `addListener` method.

2. If the component is a container, we enumerate its components and recursively call `add` for each of them.

3. The `addListener` method is called with two parameters: the component on whose events we want to spy, and the event set descriptor. The `getListenerType` method of the `EventSetDescriptor` class returns a `Class` object that describes the event listener interface such as `Action-Listener` or `ChangeListener`. We create a proxy object for that interface. The proxy handler simply prints the name and event parameter of the invoked event method. The `getAddListenerMethod` method of the `EventSetDescriptor` class returns a `Method` object that we use to add the proxy object as the event listener to the component.

    This program is a good example of the power of the reflection mechanism. We don't have to hardwire the fact that the `JButton` class has a method `addActionListener` whereas a `JSlider` has a method `addChangeListener`. The reflection mechanism discovers these facts for us.

NOTE: The proxy mechanism makes this program dramatically easier. In prior editions of this book, we needed to define a listener that simultaneously implements the `MouseListener`, `ComponentListener`, `FocusListener`, `KeyListener`, `ContainerListener`, `WindowListener`, `TextListener`, `Adjustment-Listener`, `ActionListener` and `ItemListener` interfaces, and a couple of dozen methods that print the event parameter. The proxy mechanism is explained at the end of Chapter 5.

Example 11–5 tests the event tracer. The program displays a frame with a button and a slider and traces the events that these components generate.

Example 11–4: EventTracer.java

```
1. import java.awt.*;
2. import java.awt.event.*;
3. import java.beans.*;
4. import java.lang.reflect.*;
5.
6. public class EventTracer
7. {
8.    public EventTracer()
9.    {
10.       // the handler for all event proxies
11.       handler = new
12.          InvocationHandler()
13.          {
14.             public Object invoke(Object proxy,
15.                Method method, Object[] args)
16.             {
17.                System.out.println(method + ":" + args[0]);
18.                return null;
19.             }
20.          };
21.    }
22.
23.    /**
24.       Adds event tracers for all events to which this component
25.       and its children can listen
26.       @param c a component
27.    */
28.    public void add(Component c)
29.    {
30.       try
31.       {
32.          // get all events to which this component can listen
33.          BeanInfo info = Introspector.getBeanInfo(c.getClass());
34.
35.          EventSetDescriptor[] eventSets
36.             = info.getEventSetDescriptors();
37.          for (int i = 0; i < eventSets.length; i++)
38.             addListener(c, eventSets[i]);
39.       }
40.       catch (IntrospectionException exception) {}
41.       // ok not to add listeners if exception is thrown
42.
43.       if (c instanceof Container)
44.       {
45.          // get all children and call add recursively
46.          Component[] a = ((Container)c).getComponents();
47.          for (int i = 0; i < a.length; i++)
```

```
48.              add(a[i]);
49.          }
50.      }
51.
52.      /**
53.          Add a listener to the given event set
54.          @param c a component
55.          @param eventSet a descriptor of a listener interface
56.      */
57.      public void addListener(Component c,
58.          EventSetDescriptor eventSet)
59.      {
60.          // make proxy object for this listener type and route
61.          // all calls to the handler
62.          Object proxy = Proxy.newProxyInstance(null,
63.              new Class[] { eventSet.getListenerType() }, handler);
64.
65.          // add the proxy as a listener to the component
66.          Method addListenerMethod
67.              = eventSet.getAddListenerMethod();
68.          try
69.          {
70.              addListenerMethod.invoke(c, new Object[] { proxy });
71.          }
72.          catch(InvocationTargetException e) {}
73.          catch(IllegalAccessException e) {}
74.          // ok not to add listener if exception is thrown
75.      }
76.
77.      private InvocationHandler handler;
78. }
```

Example 11–5: EventTracerTest.java

```
1. import java.awt.*;
2. import java.awt.event.*;
3. import javax.swing.*;
4.
5. public class EventTracerTest
6. {
7.      public static void main(String[] args)
8.      {
9.          JFrame frame = new JFrame();
10.         frame.setDefaultCloseOperation(JFrame.EXIT_ON_CLOSE);
11.         frame.show();
12.     }
13. }
14.
15. class EventTracerFrame extends JFrame
```

```
16.  {
17.     public EventTracerFrame()
18.     {
19.        setTitle("EventTracerTest");
20.        setSize(WIDTH, HEIGHT);
21.
22.        // add a slider and a button
23.        Container contentPane = getContentPane();
24.
25.        contentPane.add(new JSlider(), BorderLayout.NORTH);
26.        contentPane.add(new JButton("Test"), BorderLayout.SOUTH);
27.
28.        // trap all events of components inside the frame
29.        EventTracer tracer = new EventTracer();
30.        tracer.add(this);
31.     }
32.
33.     public static final int WIDTH = 400;
34.     public static final int HEIGHT = 400;
35.  }
```

The AWT Robot

Version 1.3 of Java 2 adds a `Robot` class that you can use to send keystrokes and mouse clicks to any AWT program. This class is intended for automatic testing of user interfaces.

To get a robot, you need to first get a `GraphicsDevice` object. You get the default screen device through the sequence of calls:

```
GraphicsEnvironment environment
   = GraphicsEnvironment.getLocalGraphicsEnvironment();
GraphicsDevice screen
   = environment.getDefaultScreenDevice();
```

Then you construct a robot as:

```
Robot robot = new Robot(screen);
```

To send a keystroke, tell the robot to simulate a key press and a key release:

```
robot.keyPress(KeyEvent.VK_TAB);
robot.keyRelease(KeyEvent.VK_TAB);
```

For a mouse click, you first need to move the mouse and then press and release a button:

```
robot.mouseMove(x, y);
robot.mousePress(InputEvent.BUTTON1_MASK);
robot.mouseRelease(InputEvent.BUTTON1_MASK);
```

Here `x` and `y` are absolute screen pixel coordinates.

The idea is that you simulate key and mouse input, and afterwards take a screen snapshot to see whether the application did what it was supposed to. You capture the screen with the `createScreenCapture` method:

```
Rectangle rect = new Rectangle(x, y, width, height);
BufferedImage image = robot.createScreenCapture(rect);
```

The rectangle coordinates also refer to absolute screen pixels.

Finally, you usually want to add a small delay between robot instructions so that the application can catch up. Use the `delay` method and give it the number of milliseconds to delay. For example:

```
robot.delay(1000); // delay by 1000 milliseconds
```

The program in Example 11–6 shows how you can use the robot. A robot tests the button test program that you saw in Chapter 8. First, pressing the space bar activates the left most button. Then the robot waits for two seconds so that you can see what it has done. After the delay, the robot simulates the tab key and another space bar press to click on the next button. Finally, we simulate a mouse click on the third button. (You may need to adjust the x and y coordinates of the program to actually press the button.) The program ends by taking a screen capture and displaying it in another frame.

As you can see from this example, the `Robot` class is not by itself suitable for convenient user interface testing. Instead, it is a basic building block that can be a foundational part of a testing tool. A professional testing tool can capture, store, and replay user interaction scenarios and find out the screen locations of the components so that mouse clicks aren't guesswork. At the time of this writing, the robot is brand new and we are not aware of any sophisticated testing tools for Java user interfaces. We expect these tools to materialize in the future.

Example 11–6: RobotTest.java

```
1. import java.awt.*;
2. import java.awt.event.*;
3. import java.awt.image.*;
4. import javax.swing.*;
5.
6. public class RobotTest
7. {
8.    public static void main(String[] args)
9.    {
10.       // make frame with a button panel
11.
12.       ButtonFrame frame = new ButtonFrame();
13.       frame.setDefaultCloseOperation(JFrame.EXIT_ON_CLOSE);
14.       frame.show();
```

```
15.
16.        // attach a robot to the screen device
17.
18.        GraphicsEnvironment environment
19.            = GraphicsEnvironment.getLocalGraphicsEnvironment();
20.        GraphicsDevice screen
21.            = environment.getDefaultScreenDevice();
22.
23.        try
24.        {
25.            Robot robot = new Robot(screen);
26.            run(robot);
27.        }
28.        catch (AWTException exception)
29.        {
30.            System.err.println("Can't construct robot.");
31.        }
32.    }
33.
34.    /**
35.        Runs a sample test procedure
36.        @param robot the robot attached to the screen device
37.    */
38.    public static void run(Robot robot)
39.    {
40.        // simulate a space bar press
41.        robot.keyPress(' ');
42.        robot.keyRelease(' ');
43.
44.        // simulate a tab key followed by a space
45.        robot.delay(2000);
46.        robot.keyPress(KeyEvent.VK_TAB);
47.        robot.keyRelease(KeyEvent.VK_TAB);
48.        robot.keyPress(' ');
49.        robot.keyRelease(' ');
50.
51.        // simulate a mouse click over the rightmost button
52.        robot.delay(2000);
53.        robot.mouseMove(200, 50);
54.        robot.mousePress(InputEvent.BUTTON1_MASK);
55.        robot.mouseRelease(InputEvent.BUTTON1_MASK);
56.
57.        // capture the screen and show the resulting image
58.        robot.delay(2000);
59.        BufferedImage image = robot.createScreenCapture(
60.            new Rectangle(0, 0, 400, 300));
61.
```

```
62.        ImageFrame frame = new ImageFrame(image);
63.        frame.show();
64.     }
65.  }
66.
67.  /**
68.     A frame to display a captured image
69.  */
70.  class ImageFrame extends JFrame
71.  {
72.     /**
73.        @param image the image to display
74.     */
75.     public ImageFrame(Image image)
76.     {
77.        setTitle("Capture");
78.        setSize(WIDTH, HEIGHT);
79.
80.        Container contentPane = getContentPane();
81.        JLabel label = new JLabel(new ImageIcon(image));
82.        contentPane.add(label);
83.     }
84.
85.     public static final int WIDTH = 450;
86.     public static final int HEIGHT = 350;
87.  }
```

 java.awt.GraphicsEnvironment

- `static GraphicsEnvironment getLocalGraphicsEnvironment()`
  returns the local graphics environment.

- `GraphicsDevice getDefaultScreenDevice()`
  returns the default screen device. Note that computers with multiple monitors have one graphics device per screen—use the `getScreenDevices` method to obtain an array of all screen devices.

 java.awt.Robot

- `Robot(GraphicsDevice device)`
  constructs a robot that can interact with the given device.

- `void keyPress(int key)`
- `void keyRelease(int key)`
  simulate a key press or release.

  Parameters: key   The key code. See the `KeyStroke` class for
                                more information on key codes.

- ```
  void mouseMove(int x, int y)
  ```
  simulates a mouse move.

  Parameters: `x, y`   The mouse position in absolute pixel
                                  coordinates

- ```
  void mousePress(int eventMask)
  ```
- ```
  void mouseRelease(int eventMask)
  ```
  simulate a mouse button press or release.

  Parameters: `eventMask`   The event mask describing the mouse
                                  buttons. See the `InputEvent` class for
                                  more information on event masks.

- ```
  void delay(int milliseconds)
  ```
  delays the robot for the given number of milliseconds.

- ```
  BufferedImage createScreenCapture(Rectangle rect)
  ```
  captures a portion of the screen.

  Parameters: `rect`   The rectangle to be captured, in absolute
                                  pixel coordinates

Profiling

You may have a program that works correctly but is too slow to be useful. Of
course, before you rewrite the program, you want to know why it is too slow.
This is not something that you should leave to guesswork. It is not uncommon
for even experienced programmers to guess wrong, spend time optimizing a
part of the code that doesn't get executed all that often, and still have a poorly
performing program. Instead, you should turn to a profiler.

The Java 2 SDK includes a very rudimentary profiling tool called HPROF
that is really just a proof of concept, not a serious tool. More importantly,
the JVM includes a *profiler interface* that tool vendors can use to build sophisticated profiling tools. For more information on the JVM profiler interface,
see `http://java.sun.com/products/jdk/1.3/docs/guide/jvmpi/`
`jvmpi.html`. HPROF is an example of a program that utilizes the JVM
profiler interface. Other, more powerful profiling tools are available
commercially.

To run the profiler on a program, use the following command line:

```
java -Xrunhprof:option1=value1,option2=value2,... MyProg
```

Table 11–2 shows the profiler options.
```

Table 11–2: HPROF options

Option Name and Value	Description	Default
cpu=samples|times	CPU usage	None
heap=dump|sites|all	Heap profiling	all
monitor=y|n	Monitor contention	n
format=a|b	Text (ASCII) or binary	a
file=name	Write data to file	java.hprof.txt for text, java.hprof for binary
net=host:port	Send data to socket	Write to file
depth=size	Stack trace depth	4
cutoff=value	Output cutoff point	0.0001
lineno=y|n	Line number in traces?	y
thread=y|n	Thread in traces?	n
doe=y|n	Dump on exit?	y

The cpu and heap options are the most useful ones. The cpu=samples option periodically samples the runtime stacks of all threads, and tracks how often a particular stack frame was captured. You'll see an example later in this section. The cpu=times option tracks when each method was entered and exited. The heap=sites option tracks object allocations and deallocations.

Let us look at an example. The program in Example 11–7 is a simple word count program, just like the UNIX wc utility. It counts the number of lines, words, and characters in System.in. For example, to count words in jdk1.3/README.txt, you would execute

```
java WordCount < jdk1.3/README.txt
```

The WordCount program is very simple. It reads input a line at a time, using the BufferedReader.readLine method. To count the characters, we simply print the length of the input string. To count the words, we use the countTokens method of the StringTokenizer class. (See Chapter 12 for more information on the BufferedReader and StringTokenizer classes.)

The program works correctly, but it is extremely slow on larger files. Counting the words in the full text of "Alice in Wonderland" (28195 words in about 150K bytes) takes 80 seconds on our test machine, whereas the wc program does the same job in less than a second.

Of course, with a simple program like this, it is not difficult to spot the reason for the poor performance. But let us nevertheless run the profiler to see our suspicions verified. You may want to have a guess before looking at the numbers.

Clearly, concatenating the input to a long string is wasteful and unnecessary. How about the string tokenizer? Is it inefficient to count tokens?

Run the profiler as

```
java -Xrunhprof:cpu=samples WordCount < gutenberg/alice30.txt
```

By default, the profiler sends its output to the file `java.hprof.txt`. You can change the output file with the `file` option.

Open the file and look at the very end, in the `CPU SAMPLES` section. The section starts out like this:

```
rank   self    accum    count    trace method
  1   37.23%  37.23%    1246      3 java.lang.StringBuffer.expandCapacity
  2   32.24%  69.47%    1079     10 java.lang.StringBuffer.expandCapacity
  3   28.56%  98.03%     956      6 java.lang.String.getChars
  4    0.30%  98.33%      10     17 WordCount.main
  5    0.21%  98.54%       7      7 java.lang.StringBuffer.toString
  6    0.18%  98.72%       6     20 WordCount.main
  7    0.15%  98.86%       5      4 java.io.BufferedReader.readLine
  8    0.15%  99.01%       5     16 java.lang.String.<init>
  9    0.12%  99.13%       4     11 java.lang.StringBuffer.append
 10    0.12%  99.25%       4     13 WordCount.main
   . . .
```

To interpret this table, you need to match up the entries in the trace column with the TRACE listings earlier in the output. The listings appear in seemingly random order. Here are the ones that match up the three top-ranked entries in the CPU samples:

```
TRACE 3:
java.lang.StringBuffer.expandCapacity(StringBuffer.java:202)
java.lang.StringBuffer.append(StringBuffer.java:401)
WordCount.main(WordCount.java:18)

TRACE 10:
java.lang.StringBuffer.expandCapacity(StringBuffer.java:Unknown line)
java.lang.StringBuffer.append(StringBuffer.java:401)
WordCount.main(WordCount.java:18)

TRACE 6:
java.lang.String.getChars(String.java:Unknown line)
java.lang.StringBuffer.append(StringBuffer.java:402)
WordCount.main(WordCount.java:18)
```

As you can see, they all happen to point to the same line of source code, namely line 18:

```
input += line;
```

You may wonder why there are two identical-looking stack traces. To solve this mystery, run the `javap` decompiler:

```
javap -c -l WordCount
```

The code for line 18 is:

```
48 new #8 <Class java.lang.StringBuffer>
51 dup
52 invokespecial #9 <Method java.lang.StringBuffer()>
55 aload_1
56 invokevirtual #10 <Method java.lang.StringBufferappend-
   (java.lang.String)>
59 aload 4
61 invokevirtual #10 <Method java.lang.StringBufferappend-
   (java.lang.String)>
64 invokevirtual #12 <Method java.lang.String toString()>
67 astore_1
```

In other words, the compiler translates

```
input += line;
```

into

```
StringBuffer temp = new StringBuffer();
temp.append(input);
temp.append(line);
input = temp.toString();
```

As you can see, there are two calls to the append method, and apparently each of them is time-consuming. Of course, this problem is easy to fix. There is no need to concatenate all input. Simply count the number of characters and words separately for each input line, and the program will run about as fast as the native UNIX program.

In addition to timing data, the HPROF program can also show you heap allocations. For example, run the command

```
java -Xrunhprof:heap=sites WordCount < alice30.txt
```

The output starts with

```
rank   self   accum     bytes objs   bytes    objs trace name
   1 65.49% 65.49%    398250    3 477753252 7703    468 [C
   2 24.59% 90.08%    149524  157  149524    157      1 [I
   3  3.17% 93.25%     19282  739   19478    755      1 [C
   .  .  .
```

This means that stack trace 468 allocated a huge number of character arrays ([C). The stack trace is

```
TRACE 468:
java.lang.StringBuffer.expandCapacity(StringBuffer.java:202)
java.lang.StringBuffer.append(StringBuffer.java:401)
WordCount.main(WordCount.java:18)
```

It again points to the infamous line 18.

This section showed you how you can use the information that the HPROF program generates to find trouble spots in your program. However, in a larger program, the HPROF output is going to be unwieldy, and you should use a professional profiling tool.

Example 11–7: WordCount.java

```java
1. import java.io.*;
2. import java.util.*;
3.
4. /**
5.    A program for counting the count of lines, words,
6.    and sentences in System.in
7. */
8. public class WordCount
9. {
10.    public static void main(String[] args)
11.    {
12.       String input = "";
13.       int lines = 0;
14.       try
15.       {
16.          BufferedReader reader = new BufferedReader(new
17.             InputStreamReader(System.in));
18.          String line;
19.          // read input lines until the end of file is reached
20.          while ((line = reader.readLine()) != null)
21.          {
22.             line += "\n";
23.             input += line; // add line to input string
24.             lines++; // increment line count
25.          }
26.       }
27.       catch (IOException exception)
28.       {
29.          exception.printStackTrace();
30.       }
31.
32.       // split the input into tokens to count all words
33.       StringTokenizer tokenizer = new StringTokenizer(input);
34.       int words = tokenizer.countTokens();
35.
36.       // print count of lines, words, and characters in input
37.       System.out.println(lines + " " + words
38.          + " " + input.length());
39.    }
40. }
```

Coverage Testing

The J2SE SDK contains a *coverage testing* tool called JCOV. During coverage testing, you measure which code in your program has been executed during test runs. After all, if your test cases never execute a particular code branch, it is entirely possible that undetected errors are lurking there.

JCOV is even more primitive than HPROF, and we will describe it only briefly. For example, to track which methods are used in a particular run of the `OptionPaneTest` program of Chapter 9, run

```
java -Xrunjcov:type=M OptionDialogTest
```

The JCOV tool stores the coverage analysis in a file named `java.jcov`. Here is a typical output:

```
JCOV-DATA-FILE-VERSION: 2.0
CLASS: ButtonPanel []
SRCFILE: OptionDialogTest.java
TIMESTAMP: 0
DATA: M
#kind line  position count
METHOD: getSelection()Ljava/lang/String; []
1  60 0     8
METHOD: <init>(Ljava/lang/String;[Ljava/lang/String;)V [public]
1  36 0     6
CLASS: OptionDialogFrame$ShowAction []
SRCFILE: OptionDialogTest.java
TIMESTAMP: 0
DATA: M
#kind line  position count
METHOD: actionPerformed(Ljava/awt/event/ActionEvent;)V [public]
1  233   0     2
METHOD: <init>(LOptionDialogFrame;)V [private]
1  229   0     1
METHOD: <init>(LOptionDialogFrame;LOptionDialogFrame$1;)V []
1  229   0     1
CLASS: OptionDialogTest [public]
SRCFILE: OptionDialogTest.java
TIMESTAMP: 0
DATA: M
#kind line  position count
METHOD: main([Ljava/lang/String;)V [public static]
1  17 0     1
METHOD: <init>()V [public]
1  13 0     0
```

For example, the `<init>` method of the `ButtonPanel` was executed six times, to construct six panels. The default constructor of the `OptionDialogTest` class was not executed at all—that makes sense since we never instantiated the class and called only the static `main` method.

For more help on JCOV, run

```
java -Xrunjcov:help
```

and look at the file `jvm.jcov.txt` in the `jre/lib` directory.

The JCOV tool, just like HPROF, is more a proof of concept than a usable tool. Professional profiling tools give you coverage analysis in a format that is easier to interpret.

Using a Debugger

Debugging with print statements is not one of life's more joyful experiences. You constantly find yourself adding and removing the statements, then recompiling the program. Using a debugger is better because a debugger runs your program in full motion until it reaches a breakpoint, and then you can look at everything that interests you.

The JDB Debugger

The SDK includes JDB, an extremely rudimentary command-line debugger. Its user interface is so minimal that you will not want to use it except as a last resort. It really is more a proof of concept than a usable tool. We nevertheless give a brief introduction because there are situations in which it is better than no debugger at all. Of course, many Java programming environments have far more convenient debuggers. The main principles of all debuggers are the same, and you may want to use the example in this section to learn to use the debugger in your environment instead of JDB.

Examples 11–8 through 11–10 show a deliberately corrupted version of the `ButtonTest` program from Chapter 8. (We had to break up the program and place each class into a separate file to overcome a limitation of the Forte debugger.)

When you click on any of the buttons, nothing happened. Look at the source code—button clicks are supposed to set the background color to the color specified by the button name.

Example 11–8: BuggyButtonTest.java

```
1. import javax.swing.*;
2.
3. public class BuggyButtonTest
4. {
5.   public static void main(String[] args)
6.   {
7.     BuggyButtonFrame frame = new BuggyButtonFrame();
8.     frame.setDefaultCloseOperation(JFrame.EXIT_ON_CLOSE);
9.     frame.show();
10.   }
11. }
```

Example 11–9: BuggyButtonFrame.java

```
1. import java.awt.*;
2. import javax.swing.*;
3.
4. public class BuggyButtonFrame extends JFrame
5. {
```

```
6.    public BuggyButtonFrame()
7.    {
8.       setTitle("BuggyButtonTest");
9.       setSize(WIDTH, HEIGHT);
10.
11.      // add panel to frame
12.
13.      BuggyButtonPanel panel = new BuggyButtonPanel();
14.      Container contentPane = getContentPane();
15.      contentPane.add(panel);
16.   }
17.
18.   public static final int WIDTH = 300;
19.   public static final int HEIGHT = 200;
20. }
```

Example 11–10: BuggyButtonPanel.java

```
1. import java.awt.*;
2. import java.awt.event.*;
3. import javax.swing.*;
4.
5. class BuggyButtonPanel extends JPanel
6. {
7.    public BuggyButtonPanel()
8.    {
9.       ActionListener listener = new ButtonListener();
10.
11.      JButton yellowButton = new JButton("Yellow");
12.      add(yellowButton);
13.      yellowButton.addActionListener(listener);
14.
15.      JButton blueButton = new JButton("Blue");
16.      add(blueButton);
17.      blueButton.addActionListener(listener);
18.
19.      JButton redButton = new JButton("Red");
20.      add(redButton);
21.      redButton.addActionListener(listener);
22.   }
23.
24.   private class ButtonListener implements ActionListener
25.   {
26.      public void actionPerformed(ActionEvent event)
27.      {
28.         String arg = event.getActionCommand();
29.         if (arg.equals("yellow"))
30.            setBackground(Color.yellow);
31.         else if (arg.equals("blue"))
32.            setBackground(Color.blue);
33.         else if (arg.equals("red"))
```

```
34.              setBackground(Color.red);
35.          repaint();
36.      }
37.  }
38. }
```

In a program this short, you may be able to find the bug just by reading the source code. Let us pretend that this was so complicated a program that reading the source code is not practical. Here is how you can run the debugger to locate the error.

To use JDB, you must first compile your program with the -g option, for example:

```
javac -g BuggyButtonTest.java BuggyButtonFrame.java
   BuggyButtonPanel.java
```

When you compile with this option, the compiler adds the names of local variables and other debugging information into the class files. Then you launch the debugger:

```
jdb BuggyButtonTest
```

Once you launch the debugger, you will see a display that looks something like this:

```
Initializing jdb...
>
```

The > prompt indicates the debugger is waiting for a command. Table 11–3 shows all the debugger commands. Items enclosed in [...] are optional, and the suffix (s) means that you can supply one or more arguments separated by spaces.

Table 11–3: Debugging commands

`threads [`*`threadgroup`*`]`	Lists threads
`thread `*`thread_id`*	Sets default thread
`suspend [`*`thread_id(s)`*`]`	Suspends threads (default: `all`)
`resume [`*`thread_id(s)`*`]`	Resumes threads (default: `all`)
`where [`*`thread_id`*`]` **or** `all`	Dumps a thread's stack
`wherei [`*`thread_id`*`]` **or** `all`	Dumps a thread's stack and program counter info
`threadgroups`	Lists threadgroups
`threadgroup `*`name`*	Sets current threadgroup
`print `*`name(s)`*	Prints object or field
`dump `*`name(s)`*	Prints all object information
`locals`	Prints all current local variables
`classes`	Lists currently known classes

Table 11–3: Debugging commands (continued)

methods *class*	Lists a class's methods
stop in *class.method*	Sets a breakpoint in a method
stop at *class:line*	Sets a breakpoint at a line
up [*n*]	Moves up a thread's stack
down [*n*]	Moves down a thread's stack
clear *class:line*	Clears a breakpoint
step	Executes the current line, stepping inside calls
stepi	Executes the current instruction
step up	Executes until the end of the current method
next	Executes the current line, stepping over calls
cont	Continues execution from breakpoint
catch *class*	Breaks for the specified exception
ignore *class*	Ignores the specified exception
list [*line*]	Prints source code
use [*path*]	Displays or changes the source path
memory	Reports memory usage
gc	Frees unused objects
load *class*	Loads Java class to be debugged
run [*class* [*args*]]	Starts execution of a loaded Java class
!!	Repeats last command
help (or ?)	Lists commands
exit (or quit)	Exits debugger

We will cover only the most useful JDB commands in this section. The basic idea, though, is simple: you set one or more breakpoints, then run the program. When the program reaches one of the breakpoints you set, it stops. Then, you can inspect the values of the local variables to see if they are what they are supposed to be.

To set a breakpoint, use the

    stop in *class.method*

or

    stop at *class:line*

command.

For example, let us set a breakpoint in the `actionPerformed` method of `BuggyButtonTest`. To do this, enter:

```
stop in BuggyButtonPanel$ButtonListener.actionPerformed
```

Now we want to run the program up to the breakpoint, so enter:

```
run
```

The program will run, but the breakpoint won't be hit until Java starts processing code in the `actionPerformed` method. For this, click on the Yellow button. The debugger breaks at the *start* of the `actionPerformed` method. You'll see:

```
Breakpoint hit: thread="AWT-EventQueue-0", BuggyButtonPanel$But-
tonListener.actionPerformed(), line=28, bci=0
  28            String arg = event.getActionCommand();
```

Because the debugger does not give you a window with the current source line showing, it is easy to lose track of where you are; the `list` command lets you find out where you are. While the program is stopped after you enter `list`, the debugger will show you the current line and a couple of the lines above and below. You also see the line numbers. For example:

```
24        private class ButtonListener implements ActionListener
25        {
26            public void actionPerformed(ActionEvent event)
27            {
28=>            String arg = event.getActionCommand();
29              if (arg.equals("yellow"))
30                  setBackground(Color.yellow);
31              else if (arg.equals("blue"))
32                  setBackground(Color.blue);
33              else if (arg.equals("red"))
```

Type `locals` to see all local variables. For example:

```
Method arguments:
  event = instance of java.awt.event.ActionEvent(id=698)
Local variables:
```

For more detail, use:

```
dump variable
```

For example,

```
dump event
```

displays all instance fields of the `evt` variable.

```
event = instance of java.awt.event.ActionEvent(id=698) {
    SHIFT_MASK: 1
    CTRL_MASK: 2
    META_MASK: 4
    ALT_MASK: 8
```

```
ACTION_FIRST: 1001
ACTION_LAST: 1001
ACTION_PERFORMED: 1001
actionCommand: "Yellow"
modifiers: 0
serialVersionUID: -7671078796273832149
. . .
```

There are two basic commands to single-step through a program. The `step` command steps into every method call. The `next` command goes to the next line without stepping inside any further method calls. Type `next` twice and then type `list` to see where you are.

The program stops in line 31.

```
27            {
28                String arg = event.getActionCommand();
29                if (arg.equals("yellow"))
30                    setBackground(Color.yellow);
31=>              else if (arg.equals("blue"))
32                    setBackground(Color.blue);
33                else if (arg.equals("red"))
34                    setBackground(Color.red);
35                repaint();
36            }
```

That is not what should have happened. It was supposed to call `setColor(Color.yellow)` and then go to the `repaint` command.

Dump the `arg` variable.

```
arg = "Yellow"
```

Now you can see what happened. The value of `arg` was `"Yellow"`, with an uppercase Y, but the comparison tested

```
if (arg.equals("yellow"))
```

with a lowercase `y`. Mystery solved.

To quit the debugger, type:

```
quit
```

As you can see from this example, the debugger can be used to find an error, but the command-line interface is very inconvenient. Remember to use `list` and `locals` whenever you are confused about where you are. But if you have any choice at all, use a better debugger for serious debugging work.

The Forte Debugger

Forte has a modern and convenient debugger that has many of the amenities that you would expect. In particular, you can set breakpoints, inspect variables, and single-step through a program.

To set a breakpoint, move the cursor to the desired line and select Debug -> Add/
Remove Breakpoint from the menu, or press the CTRL+F8 keyboard shortcut. The
breakpoint line is highlighted (see Figure 11–5).

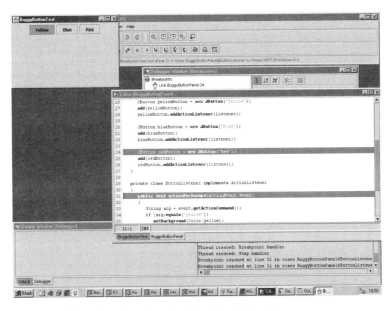

Figure 11–5: A breakpoint in the Forte debugger

You can see all currently set breakpoints in the breakpoints tab of the debugger
window (see Figure 11–6).

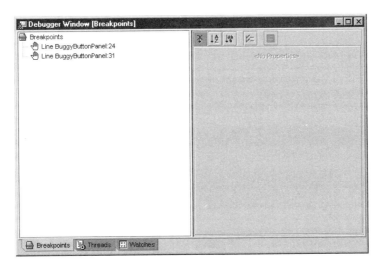

Figure 11–6: The breakpoint list

To start debugging, select Debug -> Start debugging or press the F5 key. The program starts running. Set a breakpoint in the first line of the `actionPerformed` method.

 CAUTION: In Forte 1.0, you must break the program into multiple source files, one for each outer class. Otherwise the debugger gets confused when you try to set breakpoints.

To see the value of a variable, select Debug -> Add watch or press the SHIFT+F8 keyboard shortcut. Then type the name of the variable you want to see. The variable shows up in the watch window. You can expand the items in the window by clicking on the tree handles (see Figure 11–7).

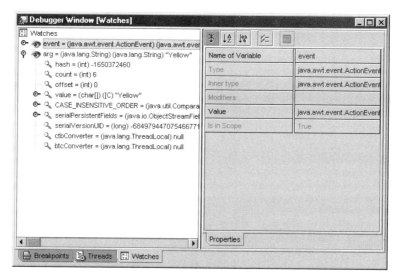

Figure 11–7: The Forte watch window

To single-step through the application, use the Debug -> Trace over (F8) or Debug -> Trace into (F7) commands. In our example, press the F8 key twice to see how the program skips over the `setBackground(Color.yellow)` command. Then watch the value of `args` to see the reason.

 CAUTION: In Forte 1.0, single-stepping is quite slow. Be patient after pressing the F8 or F7 key and wait until the cursor has moved to the next line before pressing another key.

As you can see, the Forte debugger is much easier to use than JDB because you have visual feedback to indicate where you are in the program. Setting break-points and inspecting variables is also much easier. This is typical of debuggers that are a part of an integrated development environment.

This chapter introduced you to exception handling and gave you some useful hints for testing and debugging. The final chapter of this book covers the stream, reader, writer, and file classes that you need to program input and output.

Chapter 12

Streams and Files

▼ STREAMS
▼ THE COMPLETE STREAM ZOO
▼ ZIP FILE STREAMS
▼ PUTTING STREAMS TO USE
▼ OBJECT STREAMS
▼ FILE MANAGEMENT

Applets are not normally allowed to work with files on the user's system. Applications, of course, need to do this a lot. In this chapter, we cover the methods for handling files and directories as well as the methods for actually writing and reading back information to and from files. This chapter also shows you the object serialization mechanism that lets you store objects as easily as you can store text or numeric data.

Streams

Input/output techniques are not particularly exciting, but without the ability to read and write data, your programs are severely limited. This chapter is about how to get input from any source of data that can send out a sequence of bytes and how to send output to any destination that can receive a sequence of bytes. These sources and destinations of byte sequences can be—and often are—files, but they can also be network connections and even blocks of memory. There is a nice payback to keeping this generality in mind: for example, information stored in files and information retrieved from a network connection is handled in *essentially the same way*. (See Volume 2 for more information about programming with networks.) Of course, while data is always *ultimately* stored as a sequence of bytes, it is often more convenient to think of it as having some higher-level structure such as being a sequence of characters or objects. For that reason, we dispense with low-level input/output quickly and focus on higher level facilities for the majority of the chapter.

In Java, an object from which we can read a sequence of bytes is called an *input stream*. An object to which we can write a sequence of bytes is called an *output stream*. These are specified in the abstract classes InputStream and OutputStream. Since byte-oriented streams are inconvenient for processing information stored in Unicode (recall that Unicode uses two bytes per character), there is a separate hierarchy of classes for processing Unicode characters that inherit from the abstract Reader and Writer classes. These classes have read and write operations that are based on 2-byte Unicode characters rather than on single-byte characters.

You saw abstract classes in Chapter 5. Recall that the point of an abstract class is to provide a mechanism for factoring out the common behavior of classes to a higher level. This leads to cleaner code and makes the inheritance tree easier to understand. The same game is at work with input and output in the Java programming language.

As you will soon see, Java derives from these four abstract classes a zoo of concrete classes: you can visit almost any conceivable input/output creature in this zoo.

Reading and Writing Bytes

The InputStream class has an abstract method:

```
abstract int read()
```

This method reads one byte and returns the byte that was read, or –1 if it encounters the end of the input source. The designer of a concrete input stream class overrides this method to provide useful functionality. For example, in the FileInputStream class, this method reads one byte from a file. System.in is a predefined object of a subclass of InputStream that allows you to read information from the keyboard.

The InputStream class also has nonabstract methods to read an array of bytes or to skip a number of bytes. These methods call the abstract read method, so that subclasses need to override only one method.

Similarly, the OutputStream class defines the abstract method

```
abstract void write(int b)
```

which writes one byte to an output location.

Both the read and write methods can *block* a thread until the byte is actually read or written. This means that if the stream cannot immediately be read from or written to (usually because of a busy network connection), Java suspends the thread containing this call. This gives other threads the chance to do useful work while the method is waiting for the stream to again become available. (We discuss threads in depth in Volume 2.)

The `available` method lets you check the number of bytes that are currently available for reading. This means a fragment like the following is unlikely to ever block:

```
int bytesAvailable = System.in.available();
if (bytesAvailable > 0)
{
    byte[] data = new byte[bytesAvailable];
    System.in.read(data);
}
```

When you have finished reading or writing to a stream, close it by calling the `close` method. This call frees up operating system resources that are in limited supply. If an application opens too many streams without closing them, system resources may become depleted. Closing an output stream also *flushes* the buffer used for the output stream: any characters that were temporarily placed in a buffer so that they could be delivered as a larger packet are sent off. In particular, if you do not close a file, the last packet of bytes may never be delivered. You can also manually flush the output with the `flush` method.

Even if a stream class provides concrete methods to work with the raw `read` and `write` functions, Java programmers rarely use them because programs rarely need to read and write streams of bytes. The data that you are interested in probably contain numbers, strings, and objects.

Java gives you many stream classes derived from the basic `InputStream` and `OutputStream` classes that let you work with data in the forms that you usually use rather than at the low, byte level.

java.io.InputStream

- `abstract int read()`
  reads a byte of data and returns the byte read. The `read` method returns a –1 at the end of the stream.

- `int read(byte[] b)`
  reads into an array of bytes and returns the actual number of bytes read, or –1 at the end of the stream. The `read` method reads at most `b.length` bytes.

- `int read(byte[] b, int off, int len)`
  reads into an array of bytes. The `read` method returns the actual number of bytes read, or –1 at the end of the stream.

Parameters: b   The array into which the data is read

off The offset into b where the first bytes should be placed

len The maximum number of bytes to read

- `long skip(long n)`

skips n bytes in the input stream. It returns the actual number of bytes skipped (which may be less than n if the end of the stream was encountered).

- `int available()`

returns the number of bytes available without blocking. (Recall that blocking means that the current thread loses its turn.)

- `void close()`

closes the input stream.

- `void mark(int readlimit)`

puts a marker at the current position in the input stream. (Not all streams support this feature.) If more than readlimit bytes have been read from the input stream, then the stream is allowed to forget the marker.

- `void reset()`

returns to the last marker. Subsequent calls to read reread the bytes. If there is no current marker, then the stream is not reset.

- `boolean markSupported()`

returns true if the stream supports marking.

java.io.OutputStream

- `abstract void write(int n)`

writes a byte of data.

- `void write(byte[] b)`

writes all bytes in the array b.

- `void write(byte[] b, int off, int len)`

Parameters: b   The array from which to write the data

off   The offset into b to the first byte that will be written

len   The number of bytes to write

- `void close()`

flushes and closes the output stream.

- `void flush()`

flushes the output stream, that is, sends any buffered data to its destination.

The Complete Stream Zoo

Unlike C, which gets by just fine with a single type FILE*, Java has a whole zoo of more than 60 (!) different stream types (see Figures 12–1 and 12–2). Library designers claim that there is a good reason to give users a wide choice of stream types: it is supposed to reduce programming errors. For example, in C, some people think it is a common mistake to send output to a file that was open only for reading. (Well, it is not that common, actually.) Naturally, if you do this, the output is ignored at run time. In Java and C++, the compiler catches that kind of mistake because an InputStream (Java) or istream (C++) has no methods for output.

(We would argue that, in C++ and even more so in Java, the main tool that the stream interface designers have against programming errors is intimidation. The sheer complexity of the stream libraries keeps programmers on their toes.)

C++ NOTE: ANSI C++ gives you more stream types than you want, such as istream, ostream, iostream, ifstream, ofstream, fstream, wistream, wifstream, istrstream, and so on (18 classes in all). But Java really goes overboard with streams and gives you the separate classes for selecting buffering, lookahead, random access, text formatting, or binary data.

Let us divide the animals in the stream class zoo by how they are used. Four abstract classes are at the base of the zoo: InputStream, OutputStream, Reader, and Writer. You do not make objects of these types, but other methods can return them. For example, as you saw in Chapter 10, the URL class has the method openStream that returns an InputStream. You then use this InputStream object to read from the URL. As we mentioned before, the InputStream and OutputStream classes let you read and write only individual bytes and arrays of bytes; they have no methods to read and write strings and numbers. You need more-capable child classes for this. For example, DataInputStream and DataOutputStream let you read and write all the basic Java types.

For Unicode text, on the other hand, as we mentioned before, you use classes that descend from Reader and Writer. The basic methods of the Reader and Writer classes are similar to the ones for InputStream and OutputStream.

```
abstract int read()
abstract void write(int b)
```

They work just as the comparable methods do in the InputStream and OutputStream classes except, of course, the read method returns either a Unicode character (as an integer between 0 and 65535) or –1 when you have reached the end of the file.

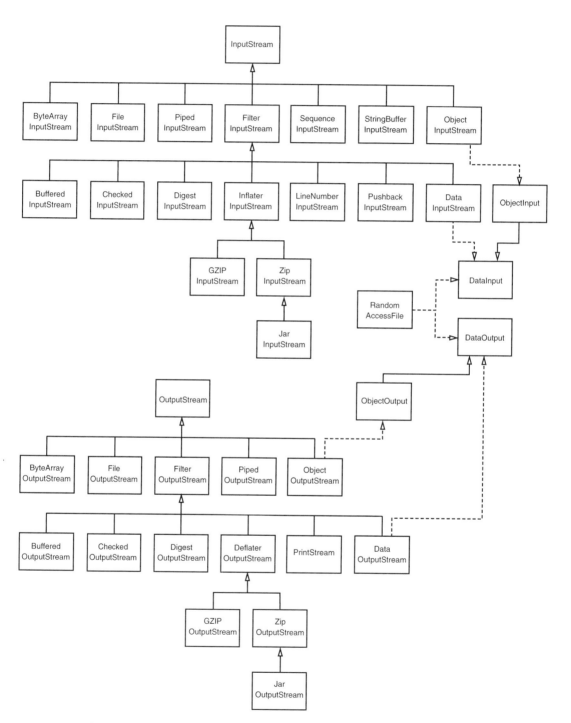

Figure 12–1: Input and Output stream hierarchy

Finally, there are streams that do useful stuff, for example, the `ZipInputStream` and `ZipOutputStream` that let you read and write files in the familiar ZIP compression format.

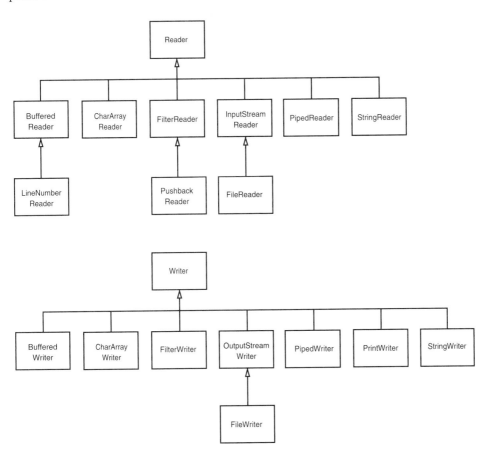

Figure 12–2: Reader and Writer hierarchy

Layering Stream Filters

`FileInputStream` and `FileOutputStream` give you input and output streams attached to a disk file. You give the file name or full path name of the file in the constructor. For example,

```
FileInputStream fin = new FileInputStream("employee.dat");
```

looks in the current directory for a file named `"employee.dat"`.

> CAUTION: Since the backslash character is the escape character in Java strings, be sure to use `\\` for Windows-style path names (`"C:\\Windows\\win.ini"`). In Windows, you can also use a single forward slash (`"C:/Windows/win.ini"`) since most Windows file handling system calls will interpret forward slashes as file separators. However, this is not recommended—the behavior of the Windows system functions is subject to change, and on other operating systems, the file separator may yet be different. Instead, for portable programs, you should use the correct file separator character. It is stored in the constant string `File.separator`.

You can also use a `File` object (see the end of the chapter for more on file objects):

```
File f = new File("employee.dat");
FileInputStream fin = new FileInputStream(f);
```

Like the abstract `InputStream` and `OutputStream` classes, these classes only support reading and writing on the byte level. That is, we can only read bytes and byte arrays from the object `fin`.

```
byte b = (byte)fin.read();
```

> TIP: Since all the classes in `java.io` interpret relative path names as starting with the user's current working directory, you may want to know this directory. You can get at this information via a call to `System.getProperty("user.dir")`.

As you will see in the next section, if we just had a `DataInputStream`, then we could read numeric types:

```
DataInputStream din = . . .;
double s = din.readDouble();
```

But just as the `FileInputStream` has no methods to read numeric types, the `DataInputStream` has no method to get data from a file.

Java uses a clever mechanism to separate two kinds of responsibilities. Some streams (such as the `FileInputStream` and the input stream returned by the `openStream` method of the URL class) can retrieve bytes from files and other more exotic locations. Other streams (such as the `DataInputStream` and the `PrintWriter`) can assemble bytes into more useful data types. The Java programmer has to combine the two into what are often called *filtered streams* by feeding an existing stream to the constructor of another stream. For example, to be able to read numbers from a file, first create a `FileInputStream` and then pass it to the constructor of a `DataInputStream`.

```
FileInputStream fin = new FileInputStream("employee.dat");
DataInputStream din = new DataInputStream(fin);
double s = din.readDouble();
```

It is important to keep in mind that the data input stream that we created with the above code does not correspond to a new disk file. The newly created stream *still* accesses the data from the file attached to the file input stream, but the point is that it now has a more capable interface.

If you look at Figure 12–1 again, you can see the classes `FilterInputStream` and `FilterOutputStream`. You combine their child classes into a new filtered stream to construct the streams you want. For example, by default, streams are not buffered. That is, every call to read contacts the operating system to ask it to dole out yet another byte. If you want buffering *and* data input for a file named `employee.dat` in the current directory, you need to use the following rather monstrous sequence of constructors:

```
DataInputStream din = new DataInputStream
    (new BufferedInputStream
        (new FileInputStream("employee.dat")));
```

Notice that we put the `DataInputStream` *last* in the chain of constructors because we want to use the `DataInputStream` methods, and we want *them* to use the buffered `read` method. Regardless of the ugliness of the above code, it is necessary: you must be prepared to continue layering stream constructors until you have access to the functionality you want.

Sometimes you'll need to keep track of the intermediate streams when chaining them together. For example, when reading input, you often need to peek at the next byte to see if it is the value that you expect. Java provides the `Pushback-InputStream` for this purpose.

```
PushbackInputStream pbin = new PushbackInputStream
    (new BufferedInputStream
        (new FileInputStream("employee.dat")));
```

Now you can speculatively read the next byte

```
int b = pbin.read();
```

and throw it back if it isn't what you wanted.

```
if (b != '<') pbin.unread(b);
```

But reading and unreading are the *only* methods that apply to the pushback input stream. If you want to look ahead and also read numbers, then you need both a pushback input stream and a data input stream reference.

```
DataInputStream din = new DataInputStream
    (pbin = new PushbackInputStream
        (new BufferedInputStream
        (new FileInputStream("employee.dat"))));
```

Of course, in the stream libraries of other programming languages, niceties such as buffering and lookahead are automatically taken care of, so it is a bit of a hassle in Java that one has to resort to layering stream filters in these cases. But the ability to mix and match filter classes to construct truly useful sequences of streams does give you an immense amount of flexibility. For example, you can read numbers from a compressed ZIP file by using the following sequence of streams (see Figure 12–3).

```
ZipInputStream zin
    = new ZipInputStream(new FileInputStream("employee.zip"));
DataInputStream din = new DataInputStream(zin);
```

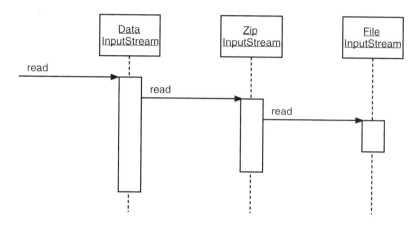

Figure 12–3: A sequence of filtered stream

(See the section on ZIP file streams later in this chapter for more on Java's ability to handle ZIP files.)

All in all, apart from the rather monstrous constructors that are needed to layer streams, the ability to mix and match streams is a very useful feature of Java!

 java.io.FileInputStream

- `FileInputStream(String name)`
  creates a new file input stream, using the file whose path name is specified by the `name` string.

- `FileInputStream(File f)`
  creates a new file input stream, using the information encapsulated in the `File` object. (The `File` class is described at the end of this chapter.)

 java.io.FileOutputStream

- `FileOutputStream(String name)`
  creates a new file output stream specified by the `name` string. Path names that are not absolute are resolved relative to the current working directory. *Caution:* This method automatically deletes any existing file with the same name.

- `FileOutputStream(String name, boolean append)`
  creates a new file output stream specified by the `name` string. Path names that are not absolute are resolved relative to the current working directory. If the `append` parameter is `true`, then data is added at the end of the file. An existing file with the same name will not be deleted.

- `FileOutputStream(File f)`
  creates a new file output stream using the information encapsulated in the `File` object. (The `File` class is described at the end of this chapter.) *Caution:* This method automatically deletes any existing file with the same name as the name of `f`.

java.io.BufferedInputStream

- `BufferedInputStream(InputStream in)`
  creates a new buffered stream with a default buffer size. A buffered input stream reads characters from a stream without causing a device access every time. When the buffer is empty, a new block of data is read into the buffer.

- `BufferedInputStream(InputStream in, int n)`
  creates a new buffered stream with a user-defined buffer size.

java.io.BufferedOutputStream

- `BufferedOutputStream(OutputStream out)`
  creates a new buffered stream with a default buffer size. A buffered output stream collects characters to be written without causing a device access every time. When the buffer fills up, or when the stream is flushed, the data is written.

- `BufferedOutputStream(OutputStream out, int n)`
  creates a new buffered stream with a user-defined buffer size.

java.io.PushbackInputStream

- `PushbackInputStream(InputStream in)`
  constructs a stream with one-byte lookahead.

- `PushbackInputStream(InputStream in, int size)`
  constructs a stream with a pushback buffer of specified size.

- `void unread(int b)`
  pushes back a byte, which is retrieved again by the next call to read. You can push back only one character at a time.

  Parameters: b   The byte to be read again

Data Streams

You often need to write the result of a computation or read one back. The data streams support methods for reading back all of the basic Java types. To write a number, character, Boolean value, or string, use one of the following methods of the `DataOutput` interface:

```
writeChars
writeByte
writeInt
writeShort
writeLong
writeFloat
writeDouble
writeChar
writeBoolean
writeUTF
```

For example, `writeInt` always writes an integer as a 4-byte binary quantity regardless of the number of digits, and `writeDouble` always writes a `double` as an 8-byte binary quantity. The resulting output is not humanly readable but the space needed will be the same for each data type, and reading it back in will be faster. (See the section on the `PrintWriter` class later in this chapter for how to output numbers as human readable text.)

> NOTE: There are two different methods of storing integers and floating-point numbers in memory, depending on the platform you are using. Suppose, for example, you are working with a 4-byte quantity, like an `int` or a `float`. This can be stored in such a way that the first of the 4 bytes in memory holds the most significant byte (MSB) of the value, the so-called big-endian method, or it can hold the least significant byte (LSB) first, which is called, naturally enough, the little-endian method. For example, the SPARC uses big-endian; the Pentium, little-endian. This can lead to problems. For example, when saving a file using C or C++, the data is saved exactly as the processor stores it. That makes it challenging to move even the simplest data files from one platform to another. In Java, all values are written in the big-endian fashion, regardless of the processor. That makes Java data files platform independent.

The `writeUTF` method writes string data using Unicode Text Format (UTF). UTF format is as follows. A 7-bit ASCII value (that is, a 16-bit Unicode character with the top 9 bits zero) is written as one byte:

$$0a_6a_5a_4a_3a_2a_1a_0$$

A 16-bit Unicode character with the top 5 bits zero is written as a 2-byte sequence:

$$110a_{10}a_9a_8a_7a_6 \quad 10a_5a_4a_3a_2a_1a_0$$

(The top zero bits are not stored.)

All other Unicode characters are written as 3-byte sequences:

$$1110a_{15}a_{14}a_{13}a_{12} \quad 10a_{11}a_{10}a_9a_8a_7a_6 \quad 10a_5a_4a_3a_2a_1a_0$$

This is a useful format for text consisting mostly of ASCII characters because ASCII characters still take only a single byte. On the other hand, it is not a good format for Asiatic languages, for which you are better off directly writing sequences of double-byte Unicode characters. Use the `writeChars` method for that purpose.

Note that the top bits of a UTF byte determine the nature of the byte in the encoding scheme.

`0xxxxxxx`	:	ASCII
`10xxxxxx`	:	Second or third byte
`110xxxxx`	:	First byte of 2-byte sequence
`1110xxxx`	:	First byte of 3-byte sequence

To read the data back in, use the following methods:

`readInt`	`readDouble`
`readShort`	`readChar`
`readLong`	`readBoolean`
`readFloat`	`readUTF`

NOTE: The binary data format is compact and platform independent. Except for the UTF strings, it is also suited to random access. The major drawback is that binary files are not readable by humans.

`java.io.DataInput`

- `boolean readBoolean()`
  reads in a Boolean value.
- `byte readByte()`
  reads an 8-bit byte.
- `char readChar()`
  reads a 16-bit Unicode character.
- `double readDouble()`
  reads a 64-bit double.
- `float readFloat()`
  reads a 32-bit float.
- `void readFully(byte[] b)`
  reads bytes into the array b , blocking until all bytes are read.
  Parameters: b   The buffer into which the data is read

- `void readFully(byte[] b, int off, int len)`
  reads bytes into the array b, blocking until all bytes are read.

  Parameters: b   The buffer into which the data is read

                            off   The start offset of the data

                            len   The maximum number of bytes read

- `int readInt()`
  reads a 32-bit integer.

- `String readLine()`
  reads in a line that has been terminated by a `\n`, `\r`, `\r\n`, or EOF. Returns a string containing all bytes in the line converted to Unicode characters.

- `long readLong()`
  reads a 64-bit long integer.

- `short readShort()`
  reads a 16-bit short integer.

- `String readUTF()`
  reads a string of characters in UTF format.

- `int skipBytes(int n)`
  skips n bytes, blocking until all bytes are skipped.

  Parameters: n   The number of bytes to be skipped

`java.io.DataOutput`

- `void writeBoolean(boolean b)`
  writes a Boolean value.

- `void writeByte(byte b)`
  writes an 8-bit byte.

- `void writeChar(char c)`
  writes a 16-bit Unicode character.

- `void writeChars(String s)`
  writes all characters in the string.

- `void writeDouble(double d)`
  writes a 64-bit double.

- `void writeFloat(float f)`
  writes a 32-bit float.

- `void writeInt(int i)`
  writes a 32-bit integer.

- `void writeLong(long l)`
  writes a 64-bit long integer.
- `void writeShort(short s)`
  writes a 16-bit short integer.
- `void writeUTF(String s)`
  writes a string of characters in UTF format.

Random-Access File Streams

The `RandomAccessFile` stream class lets you find or write data anywhere in a file. It implements both the `DataInput` and `DataOutput` interfaces. Disk files are random access, but streams of data from a network are not. You open a random-access file either for reading only or for both reading and writing. You specify the option by using the string `"r"` (for read access) or `"rw"` (for read/write access) as the second argument in the constructor.

```
RandomAccessFile in = new RandomAccessFile("employee.dat", "r");
RandomAccessFile inOut
   = new RandomAccessFile("employee.dat", "rw");
```

When you open an existing file as a `RandomAccessFile`, it does not get deleted.

A random-access file also has a *file pointer* setting that comes with it. The file pointer always indicates the position of the next record that will be read or written. The `seek` method sets the file pointer to an arbitrary byte position within the file. The argument to `seek` is a `long` integer between zero and the length of the file in bytes.

The `getFilePointer` method returns the current position of the file pointer.

To read from a random-access file, you use the same methods—such as `readInt` and `readUTF`—as for `DataInputStream` objects. That is no accident. These methods are actually defined in the `DataInput` interface that both `DataInput-Stream` and `RandomAccessFile` implement.

Similarly, to write a random-access file, you use the same `writeInt` and `writeUTF` methods as in the `DataOutputStream` class. These methods are defined in the `DataOutput` interface that is common to both classes.

The advantage of having the `RandomAccessFile` class implement both `DataInput` and `DataOutput` is that this lets you use or write methods whose argument types are the `DataInput` and `DataOutput` *interfaces*.

```
class Employee
{  . . .
   read(DataInput in) { . . . }
   write(DataOutput out) { . . . }
}
```

Note that the `read` method can handle either a `DataInputStream` or a `RandomAccessFile` object because both of these classes implement the `DataInput` interface. The same is true for the `write` method.

java.io.RandomAccessFile

- `RandomAccessFile(String name, String mode)`

Parameters:	name	System-dependent file name
	mode	`"r"` for reading only, or `"rw"` for reading and writing

- `RandomAccessFile(File file, String mode)`

Parameters:	file	A `File` object encapsulating a system-dependent file name. (The `File` class is described at the end of this chapter.)
	mode	`"r"` for reading only, or `"rw"` for reading and writing

- `long getFilePointer()`

  returns the current location of the file pointer.

- `void seek(long pos)`

  sets the file pointer to `pos` bytes from the beginning of the file.

- `long length()`

  returns the length of the file in bytes.

Text Streams

In the last section, we discussed *binary* input and output. While binary I/O is fast and efficient, it is not easily readable by humans. In this section, we will focus on *text* I/O. For example, if the integer 1234 is saved in binary, it is written as the sequence of bytes `00 00 04 D2` (in hexadecimal notation). In text format, it is saved as the string `"1234"`.

Unfortunately, doing this in Java requires a bit of work, because, as you know, Java uses Unicode characters. That is, the character encoding for the string `"1234"` really is `00 31 00 32 00 33 00 34` (in hex). However, at the present time most environments where your Java programs will run use their own character encoding. This may be a single-byte, double-byte, or variable-byte scheme. For example, under Windows, the string would need to be written in ASCII, as `31 32 33 34`, without the extra zero bytes. If the Unicode encoding were written into a text file, then it would be quite unlikely that the resulting file will be humanly readable with the tools of the host environment. To overcome this problem, as we mentioned before, Java now has a set of stream filters that bridges the gap between Unicode-encoded text and the character encoding used by the local operating system. All of these classes descend from the abstract `Reader` and `Writer` classes, and the names are reminiscent of the ones used for binary data. For example, the `InputStreamReader` class turns an input stream that contains bytes in a particular character encoding into a reader that emits Unicode characters. Similarly, the `OutputStreamWriter` class turns a stream of Unicode characters into a stream of bytes in a particular character encoding.

For example, here is how you make an input reader that reads keystrokes from the console and automatically converts them to Unicode.

```
InputStreamReader in = new InputStreamReader(System.in);
```

This input stream reader assumes the normal character encoding used by the host system. For example, under Windows, it uses the ISO 8859-1 encoding (also known as ISO Latin-1 or, among Windows programmers, as "ANSI code"). You can choose a different encoding by specifying it in the constructor for the `InputStreamReader`. This takes the form

```
InputStreamReader(InputStream, String)
```

where the string describes the encoding scheme that you want to use. For example,

```
InputStreamReader in = new InputStreamReader(new
    FileInputStream("kremlin.dat"), "8859_5");
```

Tables 12–1 and 12–2 list the currently supported encoding schemes.

Local encoding schemes cannot represent all Unicode characters. If a character cannot be represented, it is transformed to a ?

Table 12–1: Basic character encodings (in `rt.jar`)

Name	Description
ASCII	American Standard Code for Information Exchange
Cp1252	Windows Latin-1
ISO8859_1	ISO 8859-1, Latin alphabet No. 1
UnicodeBig	Sixteen-bit Unicode Transformation Format, big-endian byte order, with byte-order mark
UnicodeBigUnmarked	Sixteen-bit Unicode Transformation Format, big-endian byte order
UnicodeLittle	Sixteen-bit Unicode Transformation Format, little-endian byte order, with byte-order mark
UnicodeLittle Unmarked	Sixteen-bit Unicode Transformation Format, little-endian byte order
UTF8	Eight-bit Unicode Transformation Format
UTF-16	Sixteen-bit Unicode Transformation Format, byte order specified by a mandatory initial byte-order mark

Table 12–2: Extended Character Encodings (in `i18n.jar`**)**

Name	Description
Big5	Big5, Traditional Chinese
Cp037	USA, Canada (Bilingual, French), Netherlands, Portugal, Brazil, Australia
Cp273	IBM Austria, Germany
Cp277	IBM Denmark, Norway
Cp278	IBM Finland, Sweden
Cp280	IBM Italy
Cp284	IBM Catalan/Spain, Spanish Latin America
Cp285	IBM United Kingdom, Ireland
Cp297	IBM France
Cp420	IBM Arabic
Cp424	IBM Hebrew
Cp437	MS-DOS United States, Australia, New Zealand, South Africa
Cp500	EBCDIC 500V1
Cp737	PC Greek
Cp775	PC Baltic
Cp838	IBM Thailand extended SBCS
Cp850	MS-DOS Latin-1
Cp852	MS-DOS Latin-2
Cp855	IBM Cyrillic
Cp856	IBM Hebrew
Cp857	IBM Turkish
Cp858	Variant of Cp850 with Euro character
Cp860	MS-DOS Portuguese
Cp861	MS-DOS Icelandic
Cp862	PC Hebrew
Cp863	MS-DOS Canadian French
Cp864	PC Arabic
Cp865	MS-DOS Nordic
Cp866	MS-DOS Russian
Cp868	MS-DOS Pakistan
Cp869	IBM Modern Greek
Cp870	IBM Multilingual Latin-2
Cp871	IBM Iceland
Cp874	IBM Thai

Table 12–2: Extended Character Encodings (in `i18n.jar`**) (continued)**

Name	Description
Cp875	IBM Greek
Cp918	IBM Pakistan (Urdu)
Cp921	IBM Latvia, Lithuania (AIX, DOS)
Cp922	IBM Estonia (AIX, DOS)
Cp930	Japanese Katakana-Kanji mixed with 4370 UDC, superset of 5026
Cp933	Korean Mixed with 1880 UDC, superset of 5029
Cp935	Simplified Chinese Host mixed with 1880 UDC, superset of 5031
Cp937	Traditional Chinese Host mixed with 6204 UDC, superset of 5033
Cp939	Japanese Latin Kanji mixed with 4370 UDC, superset of 5035
Cp942	IBM OS/2 Japanese, superset of Cp932
Cp942C	Variant of Cp942
Cp943	IBM OS/2 Japanese, superset of Cp932 and `Shift-JIS`
Cp943C	Variant of Cp943
Cp948	OS/2 Chinese (Taiwan) superset of 938
Cp949	PC Korean
Cp949C	Variant of Cp949
Cp950	PC Chinese (Hong Kong, Taiwan)
Cp964	AIX Chinese (Taiwan)
Cp970	AIX Korean
Cp1006	IBM AIX Pakistan (Urdu)
Cp1025	IBM Multilingual Cyrillic: Bulgaria, Bosnia, Herzegovinia, Macedonia (FYR)
Cp1026	IBM Latin-5, Turkey
Cp1046	IBM Arabic - Windows
Cp1097	IBM Iran (Farsi)/Persian
Cp1098	IBM Iran (Farsi)/Persian (PC)
Cp1112	IBM Latvia, Lithuania
Cp1122	IBM Estonia
Cp1123	IBM Ukraine
Cp1124	IBM AIX Ukraine
Cp1140	Variant of Cp037 with Euro character
Cp1141	Variant of Cp273 with Euro character

Table 12–2: Extended Character Encodings (in `i18n.jar`**) (continued)**

Name	Description
Cp1142	Variant of Cp277 with Euro character
Cp1143	Variant of Cp278 with Euro character
Cp1144	Variant of Cp280 with Euro character
Cp1145	Variant of Cp284 with Euro character
Cp1146	Variant of Cp285 with Euro character
Cp1147	Variant of Cp297 with Euro character
Cp1148	Variant of Cp500 with Euro character
Cp1149	Variant of Cp871 with Euro character
Cp1250	Windows Eastern European
Cp1251	Windows Cyrillic
Cp1253	Windows Greek
Cp1254	Windows Turkish
Cp1255	Windows Hebrew
Cp1256	Windows Arabic
Cp1257	Windows Baltic
Cp1258	Windows Vietnamese
Cp1381	IBM OS/2, DOS People's Republic of China (PRC)
Cp1383	IBM AIX People's Republic of China (PRC)
Cp33722	IBM-eucJP - Japanese (superset of 5050)
EUC_CN	GB2312, EUC encoding, Simplified Chinese
EUC_JP	JIS X 0201, 0208, 0212, EUC encoding, Japanese
EUC_KR	KS C 5601, EUC encoding, Korean
EUC_TW	CNS11643 (Plane 1-3), EUC encoding, Traditional Chinese
GBK	GBK, Simplified Chinese
ISO2022CN	ISO 2022 CN, Chinese (conversion to Unicode only)
ISO2022CN_CNS	CNS 11643 in ISO 2022 CN form, Traditional Chinese (conversion from Unicode only)
ISO2022CN_GB	GB 2312 in ISO 2022 CN form, Simplified Chinese (conversion from Unicode only)
ISO2022JP	JIS X 0201, 0208 in ISO 2022 form, Japanese
ISO2022KR	ISO 2022 KR, Korean
ISO8859_2	ISO 8859-2, Latin alphabet No. 2
ISO8859_3	ISO 8859-3, Latin alphabet No. 3
ISO8859_4	ISO 8859-4, Latin alphabet No. 4
ISO8859_5	ISO 8859-5, Latin/Cyrillic alphabet

Table 12–2: Extended Character Encodings (in `i18n.jar`**) (continued)**

Name	Description
ISO8859_6	ISO 8859-6, Latin/Arabic alphabet
ISO8859_7	ISO 8859-7, Latin/Greek alphabet
ISO8859_8	ISO 8859-8, Latin/Hebrew alphabet
ISO8859_9	ISO 8859-9, Latin alphabet No. 5
ISO8859_13	ISO 8859-13, Latin alphabet No. 7
ISO8859_15_FDIS	ISO 8859-15, Latin alphabet No. 9
JIS0201	JIS X 0201, Japanese
JIS0208	JIS X 0208, Japanese
JIS0212	JIS X 0212, Japanese
JISAutoDetect	Detects and converts from Shift-JIS, EUC-JP, ISO 2022 JP (conversion to Unicode only)
Johab	Johab, Korean
KOI8_R	KOI8-R, Russian
MS874	Windows Thai
MS932	Windows Japanese
MS936	Windows Simplified Chinese
MS949	Windows Korean
MS950	Windows Traditional Chinese
MacArabic	Macintosh Arabic
MacCentralEurope	Macintosh Latin-2
MacCroatian	Macintosh Croatian
MacCyrillic	Macintosh Cyrillic
MacDingbat	Macintosh Dingbat
MacGreek	Macintosh Greek
MacHebrew	Macintosh Hebrew
MacIceland	Macintosh Iceland
MacRoman	Macintosh Roman
MacRomania	Macintosh Romania
MacSymbol	Macintosh Symbol
MacThai	Macintosh Thai
MacTurkish	Macintosh Turkish
MacUkraine	Macintosh Ukraine
SJIS	Shift-JIS, Japanese
TIS620	TIS620, Thai

Because it is so common to want to attach a reader or writer to a file, there is a pair of convenience classes, `FileReader` and `FileWriter`, for this purpose. For example, the writer definition

```
FileWriter out = new FileWriter("output.txt");
```

is equivalent to

```
OutputStreamWriter out = new OutputStreamWriter(new
    FileOutputStream("output.txt"));
```

Writing Text Output

For text output, you want to use a `PrintWriter`. A print writer can print strings and numbers in text format. Just as a `DataOutputStream` has useful output methods but no destination, a `PrintWriter` must be combined with a destination writer.

```
PrintWriter out = new PrintWriter(new
    FileWriter("employee.txt"));
```

You can also combine a print writer with a destination (output) stream.

```
PrintWriter out = new PrintWriter(new
    FileOutputStream("employee.txt"));
```

The `PrintWriter(OutputStream)` constructor automatically adds an `OutputStreamWriter` to convert Unicode characters to bytes in the stream.

To write to a print writer, you use the same `print` and `println` methods that you used with `System.out`. You can use these methods to print numbers (`int`, `short`, `long`, `float`, `double`), characters, Boolean values, strings, and objects.

NOTE: Java veterans probably wonder whatever happened to the `PrintStream` class and to `System.out`. In Java 1.0, the `PrintStream` class simply truncated all Unicode characters to ASCII characters by dropping the top byte. Conversely, the `readLine` method of the `DataInputStream` turned ASCII to Unicode by setting the top byte to 0. Clearly, that was not a clean or portable approach, and it was fixed with the introduction of readers and writers in Java 1.1. For compatibility with existing code, `System.in`, `System.out`, and `System.err` are still streams, not readers and writers. But now the `PrintStream` class internally converts Unicode characters to the default host encoding in the same way as the `PrintWriter`. Objects of type `PrintStream` act exactly like print writers when you use the `print` and `println` methods, but unlike print writers, they allow you to send raw bytes to them with the `write(int)` and `write(byte[])` methods.

For example, consider this code:

```
String name = "Harry Hacker";
double salary = 75000;
out.print(name);
out.print(' ');
out.println(salary);
```

This writes the characters

```
Harry Hacker 75000
```

to the stream `out`. The characters are then converted to bytes and end up in the file `employee.txt`.

The `println` method automatically adds the correct end-of-line character for the target system (`"\r\n"` on Windows, `"\n"` on UNIX, `"\r"` on Macs) to the line. This is the string obtained by the call `System.getProperty("line.separator")`.

If the writer is set to *autoflush mode*, then all characters in the buffer are sent to their destination whenever `println` is called. (Print writers are always buffered.) By default, autoflushing is *not* enabled. You can enable or disable autoflushing by using the `PrintWriter(Writer, boolean)` constructor and passing the appropriate Boolean as the second argument.

```
PrintWriter out = new PrintWriter(new
    FileWriter("employee.txt"), true); // autoflush
```

The `print` methods don't throw exceptions. You can call the `checkError` method to see if something went wrong with the stream.

NOTE: You cannot write raw bytes to a `PrintWriter`. Print writers are designed for text output only.

---

java.io.PrintWriter

- `PrintWriter(Writer out)`
  creates a new `PrintWriter`, without automatic line flushing.

  Parameters: out   A character-output writer

- `PrintWriter(Writer out, boolean autoFlush)`
  creates a new `PrintWriter`.

  Parameters: out   A character-output writer

                    autoFlush   If `true`, the `println` methods will flush
                                the output buffer

- `PrintWriter(OutputStream out)`
  creates a new `PrintWriter`, without automatic line flushing, from an existing `OutputStream` by automatically creating the necessary intermediate `OutputStreamWriter`.

  Parameters: out   An output stream

- `PrintWriter(OutputStream out, boolean autoFlush)`
  creates a new `PrintWriter` from an existing `OutputStream` but allows you to determine whether the writer autoflushes or not.

  Parameters: `out`   An output stream

                        `autoFlush` If `true`, the `println` methods will flush the output buffer

- `void print(Object obj)`
  prints an object by printing the string resulting from `toString`.

  Parameters: `obj`   The object to be printed

- `void print(String s)`
  prints a Unicode string.

- `void println(String s)`
  prints a string followed by a line terminator. Flushes the stream if the stream is in autoflush mode.

- `void print(char[] s)`
  prints an array of Unicode characters.

- `void print(char c)`
  prints a Unicode character.

- `void print(int i)`
  prints an integer in text format.

- `void print(long l)`
  prints a long integer in text format.

- `void print(float f)`
  prints a floating-point number in text format.

- `void print(double d)`
  prints a double-precision floating-point number in text format.

- `void print(boolean b)`
  prints a Boolean value in text format.

- `boolean checkError()`
  returns `true` if a formatting or output error occurred. Once the stream has encountered an error, it is tainted and all calls to `checkError` return `true`.

Reading Text Input

As you know:

- To write data in binary format, you use a `DataOutputStream`.
- To write in text format, you use a `PrintWriter`.

Therefore, you might expect that there is an analog to the `DataInputStream` that lets you read data in text format. Unfortunately, Java does not provide such a class. (That is why we wrote our own `Console` class for use in the beginning chapters.) The only game in town for processing text input is the `Buffered-Reader` method—it has a method, `readLine`, that lets you read a line of text. You need to combine a buffered reader with an input source.

```
BufferedReader in = new BufferedReader(new
    FileReader("employee.txt"));
```

The `readLine` method returns `null` when no more input is available. A typical input loop, therefore, looks like this:

```
String line;
while ((line = in.readLine()) != null)
{
    do something with line
}
```

The `FileReader` class already converts bytes to Unicode characters. For other input sources, you need to use the `InputStreamReader`—unlike the `Print-Writer`, the `InputStreamReader` has no automatic convenience method to bridge the gap between bytes and Unicode characters.

```
BufferedReader in2 = new BufferedReader(new
    InputStreamReader(System.in));
BufferedReader in3 = new BufferedReader(new
    InputStreamReader(url.openStream()));
```

To read numbers from text input, you need to read a string first and then convert it.

```
String s = in.readLine();
double x = Double.parseDouble(s);
```

That works if there is a single number on each line. Otherwise, you must work harder and break up the input string, for example, by using the `StringToken-izer` utility class. We will see an example of this later in this chapter.

TIP: Java has `StringReader` and `StringWriter` classes that allow you to treat a string as if it were a data stream. This can be quite convenient if you want to use the same code to parse both strings and data from a stream.

ZIP File Streams

ZIP files are archives that store one or more files in (usually) compressed format. Java 1.1 can handle both GZIP and ZIP format. (See RFC 1950, RFC 1951, and RFC 1952, for example, at `http://www.faqs.org/rfcs`.) In this section we concentrate on the more familiar (but somewhat more complicated) ZIP format and leave the GZIP classes to you if you need them. (They work in much the same way.)

NOTE: The classes for handling ZIP files are in `java.util.zip` and not in `java.io`, so remember to add the necessary `import` statement. Although not part of `java.io`, the `GZIP` and `ZIP` classes subclass `java.io.FilterInputStream` and `java.io.FilterOutputStream`. The `java.util.zip` packages also contain classes for computing cyclic redundancy check (CRC) checksums. (CRC is a method to generate a hashlike code that the receiver of a file can use to check the integrity of the data.)

Each ZIP file has a header with information such as the name of the file and the compression method that was used. In Java, you use a `ZipInputStream` to read a ZIP file by layering the `ZipInputStream` constructor onto a `FileInputStream`. You then need to look at the individual entries in the archive. The `getNextEntry` method returns an object of type `ZipEntry` that describes the entry. The `read` method of the `ZipInputStream` is modified to return –1 at the end of the current entry (instead of just at the end of the ZIP file). You must then call `closeEntry` to read the next entry. Here is a typical code sequence to read through a ZIP file:

```
ZipInputStream zin = new ZipInputStream
   (new FileInputStream(zipname));
ZipEntry entry;
while ((entry = zin.getNextEntry()) != null)
{
   analyze entry;
   read the contents of zin;
   zin.closeEntry();
}
zin.close();
```

To read the contents of a ZIP entry, you will probably not want to use the raw `read` method; usually, you will use the methods of a more competent stream filter. For example, to read a text file inside a ZIP file, you can use the following loop:

```
BufferedReader in = new BufferedReader
   (new InputStreamReader(zin));
String s;
while ((s = in.readLine()) != null)
   do something with s;
```

The program in Example 12–1 lets you open a ZIP file. It then displays the files stored in the ZIP archive in the list box at the top of the screen. If you double-click on one of the files, the contents of the file are displayed in the text area, as shown in Figure 12–4.

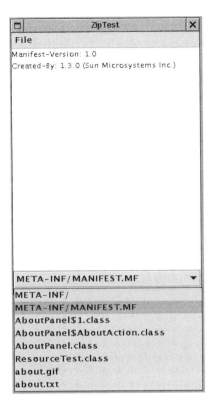

Figure 12–4: The ZipTest program

Example 12–1: **ZipTest.java**

```
1. import java.awt.*;
2. import java.awt.event.*;
3. import java.io.*;
4. import java.util.*;
5. import java.util.zip.*;
6. import javax.swing.*;
7. import javax.swing.filechooser.FileFilter;
8.
9. public class ZipTest
10. {
11.    public static void main(String[] args)
12.    {
13.       ZipTestFrame frame = new ZipTestFrame();
14.       frame.setTitle("ZipTest");
15.       frame.setSize(300, 400);
16.       frame.setDefaultCloseOperation(JFrame.EXIT_ON_CLOSE);
17.       frame.show();
18.    }
19. }
20.
```

```
21. /**
22.    A frame with a text area to show the contents of a file inside
23.    a zip archive, a combo box to select different files in the
24.    archive, and a menu to load a new archive.
25. */
26. class ZipTestFrame extends JFrame
27. {
28.    public ZipTestFrame()
29.    {
30.       // add the menu and the Open and Exit menu items
31.       JMenuBar menuBar = new JMenuBar();
32.       JMenu menu = new JMenu("File");
33.
34.       JMenuItem openItem = new JMenuItem("Open");
35.       menu.add(openItem);
36.       openItem.addActionListener(new OpenAction());
37.
38.       JMenuItem exitItem = new JMenuItem("Exit");
39.       menu.add(exitItem);
40.       exitItem.addActionListener(new
41.          ActionListener()
42.          {
43.             public void actionPerformed(ActionEvent event)
44.             {
45.                System.exit(0);
46.             }
47.          });
48.
49.       menuBar.add(menu);
50.       setJMenuBar(menuBar);
51.
52.       // add the text area and combo box
53.       fileText = new JTextArea();
54.       fileCombo = new JComboBox();
55.       fileCombo.addActionListener(new
56.          ActionListener()
57.          {
58.             public void actionPerformed(ActionEvent event)
59.             {
60.                loadZipFile((String)fileCombo.getSelectedItem());
61.             }
62.          });
63.
64.       Container contentPane = getContentPane();
65.       contentPane.add(fileCombo, BorderLayout.SOUTH);
66.       contentPane.add(fileText, BorderLayout.CENTER);
67.    }
68.
69.    /**
70.       This is the listener for the File->Open menu item.
71.    */
72.    private class OpenAction implements ActionListener
73.    {
```

```
74.     public void actionPerformed(ActionEvent evt)
75.     {
76.        // prompt the user for a zip file
77.        JFileChooser chooser = new JFileChooser();
78.        chooser.setCurrentDirectory(new File("."));
79.        ExtensionFileFilter filter = new ExtensionFileFilter();
80.        filter.addExtension(".zip");
81.        filter.addExtension(".jar");
82.        filter.setDescription("ZIP archives");
83.        chooser.setFileFilter(filter);
84.        int r = chooser.showOpenDialog(ZipTestFrame.this);
85.        if (r == JFileChooser.APPROVE_OPTION)
86.        {
87.           zipname = chooser.getSelectedFile().getPath();
88.           scanZipFile();
89.        }
90.     }
91.  }
92.
93.  /**
94.     Scans the contents of the zip archive and populates
95.     the combo box.
96.  */
97.  public void scanZipFile()
98.  {
99.     fileCombo.removeAllItems();
100.    try
101.    {
102.       ZipInputStream zin = new ZipInputStream(new
103.          FileInputStream(zipname));
104.       ZipEntry entry;
105.       while ((entry = zin.getNextEntry()) != null)
106.       {
107.          fileCombo.addItem(entry.getName());
108.          zin.closeEntry();
109.       }
110.       zin.close();
111.    }
112.    catch (IOException e)
113.    {
114.       e.printStackTrace();
115.    }
116.  }
117.
118.  /**
119.     Loads a file from the zip archive into the text area
120.     @param name the name of the file in the archive
121.  */
122.  public void loadZipFile(String name)
123.  {
124.     try
125.     {
126.        ZipInputStream zin = new ZipInputStream(new
```

```
127.               FileInputStream(zipname));
128.          ZipEntry entry;
129.          fileText.setText("");
130.
131.          // find entry with matching name in archive
132.          while ((entry = zin.getNextEntry()) != null)
133.          {
134.             if (entry.getName().equals(name))
135.             {
136.                // read entry into text area
137.                BufferedReader in = new BufferedReader(new
138.                   InputStreamReader(zin));
139.                String line;
140.                while ((line = in.readLine()) != null)
141.                {
142.                   fileText.append(line);
143.                   fileText.append("\n");
144.                }
145.             }
146.             zin.closeEntry();
147.          }
148.          zin.close();
149.       }
150.       catch (IOException e)
151.       {
152.          e.printStackTrace();
153.       }
154.    }
155.
156.    private JComboBox fileCombo;
157.    private JTextArea fileText;
158.    private String zipname;
159. }
160.
161. /**
162.    This file filter matches all files with a given set of
163.    extensions. From FileChooserTest in chapter 9
164. */
165. class ExtensionFileFilter extends FileFilter
166. {
167.    /**
168.       Adds an extension that this file filter recognizes.
169.       @param extension a file extension (such as ".txt" or "txt")
170.    */
171.    public void addExtension(String extension)
172.    {
173.       if (!extension.startsWith("."))
174.          extension = "." + extension;
175.       extensions.add(extension.toLowerCase());
176.    }
177.
178.    /**
179.       Sets a description for the file set that this file filter
```

```
180.        recognizes.
181.        @param aDescription a description for the file set
182.     */
183.     public void setDescription(String aDescription)
184.     {
185.        description = aDescription;
186.     }
187.
188.     /**
189.        Returns a description for the file set that this file
190.        filter recognizes.
191.        @return a description for the file set
192.     */
193.     public String getDescription()
194.     {
195.        return description;
196.     }
197.
198.     public boolean accept(File f)
199.     {
200.        if (f.isDirectory()) return true;
201.        String name = f.getName().toLowerCase();
202.
203.        // check if the file name ends with any of the extensions
204.        for (int i = 0; i < extensions.size(); i++)
205.           if (name.endsWith((String)extensions.get(i)))
206.              return true;
207.        return false;
208.     }
209.
210.     private String description = "";
211.     private ArrayList extensions = new ArrayList();
212. }
```

NOTE: The ZIP input stream throws a `ZipException` when there is an error in read-ing a ZIP file. Normally this error occurs when the ZIP file is corrupted.

To write a ZIP file, you open a `ZipOutputStream` by layering it onto a `File-OutputStream`. For each entry that you want to place into the ZIP file, you create a `ZipEntry` object. You pass the file name to the `ZipEntry` constructor; it sets the other parameters such as file date and decompression method automatically. You can override these settings if you like. Then, you call the `putNextEntry` method of the `ZipOutputStream` to begin writing a new file. Send the file data to the ZIP stream. When you are done, call `closeEntry`. Repeat for all the files you want to store. Here is a code skeleton:

```
FileOutputStream fout = new FileOutputStream("test.zip");
ZipOutputStream zout = new ZipOutputStream(fout);
for all files
{
```

```
        ZipEntry ze = new ZipEntry(file name);
        zout.putNextEntry(ze);
        send data to zout;
        zout.closeEntry();
    }
    zout.close();
```

NOTE: JAR files (which were discussed in Chapter 10) are simply ZIP files with another entry, the so-called manifest. You use the `JarInputStream` and `JarOutputStream` classes to read and write the manifest entry.

ZIP streams are a good example of the power of the stream abstraction. Both the source and the destination of the ZIP data are completely flexible. You layer the most convenient reader stream onto the ZIP file stream to read the data that is stored in compressed form, and that reader doesn't even realize that the data is being decompressed as it is being requested. And the source of the bytes in ZIP formats need not be a file—the ZIP data can come from a network connection. In fact, the JAR files that we discussed in Chapter 10 are ZIP-formatted files. Whenever the class loader of an applet reads a JAR file, it reads and decompresses data from the network.

java.util.zip.ZipInputStream

- `ZipInputStream(InputStream in)`
  This constructor creates a `ZipInputStream` that allows you to inflate data from the given `InputStream`.

  Parameters: in   The underlying input stream

- `ZipEntry getNextEntry()`
  returns a `ZipEntry` object for the next entry or `null` if there are no more entries.

- `void closeEntry()`
  closes the current open entry in the ZIP file. You can then read the next entry by using `getNextEntry()`.

java.util.zip.ZipOutputStream

- `ZipOutputStream(OutputStream out)`
  This constructor creates a `ZipOutputStream` that you use to write compressed data to the specified `OutputStream`.

  Parameters: out   The underlying output stream

- `void putNextEntry(ZipEntry ze)`
  writes the information in the given `ZipEntry` to the stream and positions the stream for the data. The data can then be written to the stream by `write()`.

  Parameters: ze   The new entry

- `void closeEntry()`
  closes the currently open entry in the ZIP file. Use the `putNextEntry` method to start the next entry.

- `void setLevel(int level)`
  sets the default compression level of subsequent `DEFLATED` entries. The default value is `Deflater.DEFAULT_COMPRESSION`. Throws an `IllegalArgumentException` if the level is not valid.

Parameters:	level	A compression level, from 0 (`NO_COMPRESSION`) to 9 (`BEST_COMPRESSION`)

- `void setMethod(int method)`
  sets the default compression method for this `ZipOutputStream` for any entries that do not specify a method.

Parameters:	method	The compression method, either `DEFLATED` or `STORED`

java.util.zip.ZipEntry

- `ZipEntry(String name)`

Parameters:	name	The name of the entry

- `long getCrc()`
  returns the CRC32 checksum value for this `ZipEntry`.

- `String getName()`
  returns the name of this entry.

- `long getSize()`
  returns the uncompressed size of this entry, or –1 if the uncompressed size is not known.

- `boolean isDirectory()`
  returns a Boolean that indicates whether or not this entry is a directory.

- `void setMethod(int method)`

Parameters:	method	The compression method for the entry; must be either `DEFLATED` or `STORED`

- `void setSize(long size)`
  sets the size of this entry. Only required if the compression method is `STORED`.

Parameters:	size	The uncompressed size of this entry

- `void setCrc(long crc)`
  sets the CRC32 checksum of this entry. Use the `CRC32` class to compute this checksum. Only required if the compression method is `STORED`.

Parameters:	crc	The checksum of this entry

java.util.zip.ZipFile

- ZipFile(String name)

  this constructor creates a ZipFile for reading from the given string.

  Parameters: name   A string that contains the path name of the file

- ZipFile(File file)

  this constructor creates a ZipFile for reading from the given File object.

  Parameters: file   The file to read; the File class is described at the end of this chapter

- Enumeration entries()

  returns an Enumeration object that enumerates the ZipEntry objects that describe the entries of the ZipFile.

- ZipEntry getEntry(String name)

  returns the entry corresponding to the given name, or null if there is no such entry.

  Parameters: name   The entry name

- InputStream getInputStream(ZipEntry ze)

  returns an InputStream for the given entry.

  Parameters: ze   A ZipEntry in the ZIP file

- String getName()

  returns the path of this ZIP file.

Putting Streams to Use

In the next four sections, we will show you how to put some of the creatures in the stream zoo to good use. For these examples, we will assume you are working with the Employee class and some of its derived classes, such as Manager. (See Chapters 4 and 5 for more on these example classes.) We will consider four separate scenarios for saving an array of employee records to a file and then reading them back into memory.

1.   Saving data of the same type (Employee) in text format;
2.   Saving data of the same type in binary format;
3.   Saving and restoring polymorphic data (a mixture of Employee and Manager objects);
4.   Saving and restoring data containing embedded references (managers with pointers to other employees).

Writing Delimited Output

In this section, you will learn how to store an array of `Employee` records in the time-honored *delimited* format. This means that each record is stored in a separate line. Instance fields are separated from each other by delimiters. We use a vertical bar (|) as our delimiter. (A colon (:) is another popular choice. Part of the fun is that everyone uses a different delimiter.) Naturally, we punt on the issue of what might happen if a | actually occurred in one of the strings we save.

NOTE: Especially on UNIX systems, an amazing number of files are stored in exactly this format. We have seen entire employee databases with thousands of records in this format, queried with nothing more than the UNIX `awk`, `sort`, and `join` utilities. (In the PC world, where desktop database programs are available at low cost, this kind of ad hoc storage is much less common.)

Here is a sample set of records:

```
Harry Hacker|35500|1989|10|1
Carl Cracker|75000|1987|12|15
Tony Tester|38000|1990|3|15
```

Writing records is simple. Since we write to a text file, we use the `PrintWriter` class. We simply write all fields, followed by either a | or, for the last field, a `\n`. Finally, in keeping with the idea that we want the *class* to be responsible for responding to messages, we add a method, `writeData`, to our `Employee` class.

```java
public void writeData(PrintWriter out) throws IOException
{
   GregorianCalendar calendar = new GregorianCalendar();
   calendar.setTime(hireDay);
   out.println(name + "|"
      + salary + "|"
      + calendar.get(Calendar.YEAR) + "|"
      + (calendar.get(Calendar.MONTH) + 1) + "|"
      + calendar.get(Calendar.DAY_OF_MONTH));
}
```

To read records, we read in a line at a time and separate the fields. This is the topic of the next section, in which we use a utility class supplied with Java to make our job easier.

String Tokenizers and Delimited Text

When reading a line of input, we get a single long string. We want to split it into individual strings. This means finding the | delimiters and then separating out the individual pieces, that is, the sequence of characters up to the next delimiter.

(These are usually called *tokens*.) The `StringTokenizer` class in `java.util` is designed for exactly this purpose. It gives you an easy way to break up a large string that contains delimited text. The idea is that a string tokenizer object attaches to a string. When you construct the tokenizer object, you specify which characters are the delimiters. For example, we need to use

```
StringTokenizer t = new StringTokenizer(line, "|");
```

You can specify multiple delimiters in the string. For example, to set up a string tokenizer that would let you search for any delimiter in the set

```
" \t\n\r"
```

use the following:

```
StringTokenizer t = new StringTokenizer(line, " \t\n\r");
```

(Notice that this means that any white space marks off the tokens.)

> NOTE: These four delimiters are used as the defaults if you construct a string token-
> izer like this:
> ```
> StringTokenizer t = new StringTokenizer(line);
> ```

Once you have constructed a string tokenizer, you can use its methods to quickly extract the tokens from the string. The `nextToken` method returns the next unread token. The `hasMoreTokens` method returns `true` if more tokens are available.

> NOTE: In our case, we know how many tokens we have in every line of input. In gen-
> eral, you have to be a bit more careful: call `hasMoreTokens` before calling `next-`
> `Token` because the `nextToken` method throws an exception when no more tokens
> are available.

java.util.StringTokenizer

- `StringTokenizer(String str, String delim)`

Parameters:	str	The input string from which tokens are read
	delim	A string containing delimiter characters (every character in this string is a delimiter)

- `StringTokenizer(String str)`

  constructs a string tokenizer with the default delimiter set `" \t\n\r"`.

- `boolean hasMoreTokens()`

  returns `true` if more tokens exist.

- `String nextToken()`

  returns the next token; throws a `NoSuchElementException` if there are no more tokens.

- `String nextToken(String delim)`

  returns the next token after switching to the new delimiter set. The new delimiter set is subsequently used.

- `int countTokens()`

  returns the number of tokens still in the string.

Reading Delimited Input

Reading in an `Employee` record is simple. We simply read in a line of input with the `readLine` method of the `BufferedReader` class. Here is the code needed to read one record into a string.

```
BufferedReader in
    = new BufferedReader(new FileReader("employee.dat"));
. . .
String line = in.readLine();
```

Next, we need to extract the individual tokens. When we do this, we end up with *strings*, so we need to convert them to numbers.

Just as with the `writeData` method, we add a `readData` method of the `Employee` class. When you call

```
e.readData(in);
```

this method overwrites the previous contents of `e`. Note that the method may throw an `IOException` if the `readLine` method throws that exception. There is nothing this method can do if an `IOException` occurs, so we just let it propagate up the call chain.

Here is the code for this method:

```
public void readData(BufferedReader in) throws IOException
{
    String s = in.readLine();
    StringTokenizer t = new StringTokenizer(s, "|");
    name = t.nextToken();
    salary = Double.parseDouble(t.nextToken());
    int y = Integer.parseInt(t.nextToken());
    int m = Integer.parseInt(t.nextToken());
    int d = Integer.parseInt(t.nextToken());
    GregorianCalendar calendar
        = new GregorianCalendar(y, m - 1, d);
        // GregorianCalendar uses 0 = January
    hireDay = calendar.getTime();
}
```

Finally, in the code for a program that tests these methods, the static method

```
void writeData(Employee[] e, PrintWriter out)
```

first writes the length of the array, then writes each record. The static method

```
Employee[] readData(BufferedReader in)
```

first reads in the length of the array, then reads in each record, as illustrated in Example 12–2.

Example 12–2: DataFileTest.java

```
1. import java.io.*;
2. import java.util.*;
3.
4. public class DataFileTest
5. {
6.    public static void main(String[] args)
7.    {
8.       Employee[] staff = new Employee[3];
9.
10.       staff[0] = new Employee("Carl Cracker", 75000,
11.          1987, 12, 15);
12.       staff[1] = new Employee("Harry Hacker", 50000,
13.          1989, 10, 1);
14.       staff[2] = new Employee("Tony Tester", 40000,
15.          1990, 3, 15);
16.
17.       try
18.       {
19.          // save all employee records to the file employee.dat
20.          PrintWriter out = new PrintWriter(new
21.             FileWriter("employee.dat"));
22.          writeData(staff, out);
23.          out.close();
24.
25.          // retrieve all records into a new array
26.          BufferedReader in = new BufferedReader(new
27.             FileReader("employee.dat"));
28.          Employee[] newStaff = readData(in);
29.          in.close();
30.
31.          // print the newly read employee records
32.          for (int i = 0; i < newStaff.length; i++)
33.             System.out.println(newStaff[i]);
34.       }
35.       catch(IOException exception)
36.       {
37.          exception.printStackTrace();
38.       }
39.    }
40.
41.    /**
```

```
42.        Writes all employees in an array to a print writer
43.        @param e an array of employees
44.        @param out a print writer
45.     */
46.     static void writeData(Employee[] e, PrintWriter out)
47.        throws IOException
48.     {
49.        // write number of employees
50.        out.println(e.length);
51.
52.        for (int i = 0; i < e.length; i++)
53.           e[i].writeData(out);
54.     }
55.
56.     /**
57.        Reads an array of employees from a buffered reader
58.        @param in the buffered reader
59.        @return the array of employees
60.     */
61.     static Employee[] readData(BufferedReader in)
62.        throws IOException
63.     {
64.        // retrieve the array size
65.        int n = Integer.parseInt(in.readLine());
66.
67.        Employee[] e = new Employee[n];
68.        for (int i = 0; i < n; i++)
69.        {
70.           e[i] = new Employee();
71.           e[i].readData(in);
72.        }
73.        return e;
74.     }
75. }
76.
77. class Employee
78. {
79.     public Employee() {}
80.
81.     public Employee(String n, double s,
82.        int year, int month, int day)
83.     {
84.        name = n;
85.        salary = s;
86.        GregorianCalendar calendar
87.           = new GregorianCalendar(year, month - 1, day);
88.           // GregorianCalendar uses 0 = January
89.        hireDay = calendar.getTime();
90.     }
91.
92.     public String getName()
93.     {
```

```
94.        return name;
95.     }
96.
97.     public double getSalary()
98.     {
99.        return salary;
100.    }
101.
102.    public Date getHireDay()
103.    {
104.       return hireDay;
105.    }
106.
107.    public void raiseSalary(double byPercent)
108.    {
109.       double raise = salary * byPercent / 100;
110.       salary += raise;
111.    }
112.
113.    public String toString()
114.    {
115.       return getClass().getName()
116.          + "[name=" + name
117.          + ",salary=" + salary
118.          + ",hireDay=" + hireDay
119.          + "]";
120.    }
121.
122.    /**
123.       Writes employee data to a print writer
124.       @param out the print writer
125.    */
126.    public void writeData(PrintWriter out) throws IOException
127.    {
128.       GregorianCalendar calendar = new GregorianCalendar();
129.       calendar.setTime(hireDay);
130.       out.println(name + "|"
131.          + salary + "|"
132.          + calendar.get(Calendar.YEAR) + "|"
133.          + (calendar.get(Calendar.MONTH) + 1) + "|"
134.          + calendar.get(Calendar.DAY_OF_MONTH));
135.    }
136.
137.    /**
138.       Reads employee data from a buffered reader
139.       @param in the buffered reader
140.    */
141.    public void readData(BufferedReader in) throws IOException
142.    {
143.       String s = in.readLine();
144.       StringTokenizer t = new StringTokenizer(s, "|");
145.       name = t.nextToken();
```

```
146.        salary = Double.parseDouble(t.nextToken());
147.        int y = Integer.parseInt(t.nextToken());
148.        int m = Integer.parseInt(t.nextToken());
149.        int d = Integer.parseInt(t.nextToken());
150.        GregorianCalendar calendar
151.           = new GregorianCalendar(y, m - 1, d);
152.           // GregorianCalendar uses 0 = January
153.        hireDay = calendar.getTime();
154.     }
155.
156.     private String name;
157.     private double salary;
158.     private Date hireDay;
159. }
```

Random-Access Streams

If you have a large number of employee records of variable length, the storage technique used in the preceding section suffers from one limitation: it is not possible to read a record in the middle of the file without first reading all records that come before it. In this section, we will make all records the same length. This lets us implement a random-access method for reading back the information using the `RandomAccessFile` class that you saw earlier—we can use this to get at any record in the same amount of time.

We will store the numbers in the instance fields in our classes in a binary format. This is done with the `writeInt` and `writeDouble` methods of the `DataOutput` interface. (As we mentioned earlier, this is the common interface of the `DataOutputStream` and the `RandomAccessFile` classes.)

However, since the size of each record must remain constant, we need to make all the strings the same size when we save them. The variable-size UTF format does not do this, and the rest of the Java library provides no convenient means of accomplishing this. We need to write a bit of code to implement two helper methods to make the strings the same size. We will call the methods `writeFixedString` and `readFixedString`. These methods read and write Unicode strings that always have the same length.

The `writeFixedString` method takes the parameter `size`. Then, it writes the specified number of characters, starting at the beginning of the string. (If there are too few characters the method pads the string, using characters whose Unicode values are zero.) Here is the code for the `writeFixedString` method:

```
static void writeFixedString(String s, int size, DataOutput out)
   throws IOException
{
   int i;
   for (i = 0; i < size; i++)
   {
```

```
      char ch = 0;
      if (i < s.length()) ch = s.charAt(i);
      out.writeChar(ch);
   }
}
```

The `readFixedString` method reads characters from the input stream until it has consumed `size` characters or until it encounters a character with Unicode 0. Then, it should skip past the remaining zero characters in the input field.

For added efficiency, this method uses the `StringBuffer` class to read in a string. A `StringBuffer` is an auxiliary class that lets you preallocate a memory block of a given length. In our case, we know that the string is, at most, `size` bytes long. We make a string buffer in which we reserve `size` characters. Then we append the characters as we read them in.

> NOTE: Using the `StringBuffer` class in this way is more efficient than reading in characters and appending them to an existing string. Every time you append characters to a string, the string object needs to find new memory to hold the larger string: this is time-consuming. Appending even more characters means the string needs to be relocated again and again. Using the `StringBuffer` class avoids this problem.

Once the string buffer holds the desired string, we need to convert it to an actual `String` object. This is done with the `String(StringBuffer b)` constructor or the `StringBuffer.toString()` method. These methods do not copy the characters from the string buffer to the string. Instead, they *freeze* the buffer contents. If you later call a method that makes a modification to the `StringBuffer` object, the buffer object first gets a new copy of the characters and then modifies that copy. The string object keeps the frozen contents.

```
static String readFixedString(int size, DataInput in)
   throws IOException
{
   StringBuffer b = new StringBuffer(size);
   int i = 0;
   boolean more = true;
   while (more && i < size)
   {
      char ch = in.readChar();
      i++;
      if (ch == 0) more = false;
      else b.append(ch);
   }
   in.skipBytes(2 * (size - i));
   return b.toString();
}
```

> NOTE: These two functions are packaged inside the `DataIO` helper class.

To write a fixed-size record, we simply write all fields in binary.

```
public void writeData(DataOutput out) throws IOException
{
    DataIO.writeFixedString(name, NAME_SIZE, out);
    out.writeDouble(salary);

    GregorianCalendar calendar = new GregorianCalendar();
    calendar.setTime(hireDay);
    out.writeInt(calendar.get(Calendar.YEAR));
    out.writeInt(calendar.get(Calendar.MONTH) + 1);
    out.writeInt(calendar.get(Calendar.DAY_OF_MONTH));
}
```

Reading the data back is just as simple.

```
public void readData(DataInput in) throws IOException
{
    name = DataIO.readFixedString(NAME_SIZE, in);
    salary = in.readDouble();
    int y = in.readInt();
    int m = in.readInt();
    int d = in.readInt();
    GregorianCalendar calendar
        = new GregorianCalendar(y, m - 1, d);
        // GregorianCalendar uses 0 = January
    hireDay = calendar.getTime();
}
```

In our example, each employee record is 100 bytes long because we specified that the name field would always be written using 40 characters. This gives us a breakdown as indicated in the following:

40 characters = 80 bytes for the name

1 `double` = 8 bytes

3 `int` = 12 bytes

As an example, suppose you want to position the file pointer to the third record. You can use the following version of the `seek` method:

```
long n = 3;
int RECORD_SIZE = 100;
in.seek((n - 1) * RECORD_SIZE);
```

Then you can read a record:

```
Employee e = new Employee();
e.readData(in);
```

If you want to modify the record and then save it back into the same location, remember to set the file pointer back to the beginning of the record:

```
in.seek((n - 1) * RECORD.SIZE);
e.writeData(in);
```

To determine the total number of bytes in a file, use the `length` method. The total number of records is the length divided by the size of each record.

```
long int nbytes = in.length(); // length in bytes
int nrecords = (int)(nbytes / RECORD_SIZE);
```

The test program shown in Example 12–3 writes three records into a data file and then reads them from the file in reverse order. To do this efficiently requires random access—we need to get at the third record first.

Example 12–3: RandomFileTest.java

```
1. import java.io.*;
2. import java.util.*;
3.
4. public class RandomFileTest
5. {
6.    public static void main(String[] args)
7.    {
8.       Employee[] staff = new Employee[3];
9.
10.      staff[0] = new Employee("Carl Cracker", 75000,
11.         1987, 12, 15);
12.      staff[1] = new Employee("Harry Hacker", 50000,
13.         1989, 10, 1);
14.      staff[2] = new Employee("Tony Tester", 40000,
15.         1990, 3, 15);
16.
17.      try
18.      {
19.         // save all employee records to the file employee.dat
20.         DataOutputStream out = new DataOutputStream(new
21.            FileOutputStream("employee.dat"));
22.         for (int i = 0; i < staff.length; i++)
23.            staff[i].writeData(out);
24.         out.close();
25.
26.         // retrieve all records into a new array
27.         RandomAccessFile in
28.            = new RandomAccessFile("employee.dat", "r");
29.         // compute the array size
30.         int n = (int)(in.length() / Employee.RECORD_SIZE);
31.         Employee[] newStaff = new Employee[n];
32.
33.         // read employees in reverse order
34.         for (int i = n - 1; i >= 0; i--)
35.         {
```

```
36.                newStaff[i] = new Employee();
37.                in.seek(i * Employee.RECORD_SIZE);
38.                newStaff[i].readData(in);
39.            }
40.            in.close();
41.
42.            // print the newly read employee records
43.            for (int i = 0; i < newStaff.length; i++)
44.                System.out.println(newStaff[i]);
45.        }
46.        catch(IOException e)
47.        {
48.            e.printStackTrace();
49.        }
50.
51.    }
52. }
53.
54. class Employee
55. {
56.    public Employee() {}
57.
58.    public Employee(String n, double s,
59.        int year, int month, int day)
60.    {
61.        name = n;
62.        salary = s;
63.        GregorianCalendar calendar
64.            = new GregorianCalendar(year, month - 1, day);
65.            // GregorianCalendar uses 0 = January
66.        hireDay = calendar.getTime();
67.    }
68.
69.    public String getName()
70.    {
71.        return name;
72.    }
73.
74.    public double getSalary()
75.    {
76.        return salary;
77.    }
78.
79.    public Date getHireDay()
80.    {
81.        return hireDay;
82.    }
83.
84.    public void raiseSalary(double byPercent)
85.    {
86.        double raise = salary * byPercent / 100;
87.        salary += raise;
```

```
88.     }
89.
90.     public String toString()
91.     {
92.        return getClass().getName()
93.           + "[name=" + name
94.           + ",salary=" + salary
95.           + ",hireDay=" + hireDay
96.           + "]";
97.     }
98.
99.     /**
100.       Writes employee data to a data output
101.       @param out the data output
102.     */
103.     public void writeData(DataOutput out) throws IOException
104.     {
105.        DataIO.writeFixedString(name, NAME_SIZE, out);
106.        out.writeDouble(salary);
107.
108.        GregorianCalendar calendar = new GregorianCalendar();
109.        calendar.setTime(hireDay);
110.        out.writeInt(calendar.get(Calendar.YEAR));
111.        out.writeInt(calendar.get(Calendar.MONTH) + 1);
112.        out.writeInt(calendar.get(Calendar.DAY_OF_MONTH));
113.     }
114.
115.     /**
116.       Reads employee data from a data input
117.       @param in the data input
118.     */
119.     public void readData(DataInput in) throws IOException
120.     {
121.        name = DataIO.readFixedString(NAME_SIZE, in);
122.        salary = in.readDouble();
123.        int y = in.readInt();
124.        int m = in.readInt();
125.        int d = in.readInt();
126.        GregorianCalendar calendar
127.           = new GregorianCalendar(y, m - 1, d);
128.           // GregorianCalendar uses 0 = January
129.        hireDay = calendar.getTime();
130.     }
131.
132.     public static final int NAME_SIZE = 40;
133.     public static final int RECORD_SIZE
134.        = 2 * NAME_SIZE + 8 + 4 + 4 + 4;
135.
136.     private String name;
137.     private double salary;
138.     private Date hireDay;
139. }
```

```
140.
141. class DataIO
142. {  public static String readFixedString(int size,
143.       DataInput in) throws IOException
144.    {
145.       StringBuffer b = new StringBuffer(size);
146.       int i = 0;
147.       boolean more = true;
148.       while (more && i < size)
149.       {
150.          char ch = in.readChar();
151.          i++;
152.          if (ch == 0) more = false;
153.          else b.append(ch);
154.       }
155.       in.skipBytes(2 * (size - i));
156.       return b.toString();
157.    }
158.
159.    public static void writeFixedString(String s, int size,
160.       DataOutput out) throws IOException
161.    {
162.       int i;
163.       for (i = 0; i < size; i++)
164.       {
165.          char ch = 0;
166.          if (i < s.length()) ch = s.charAt(i);
167.          out.writeChar(ch);
168.       }
169.    }
170. }
```

java.lang.StringBuffer

- `StringBuffer()`
  constructs an empty string buffer.

- `StringBuffer(int length)`
  constructs an empty string buffer with the initial capacity `length`.

- `StringBuffer(String str)`
  constructs a string buffer with the initial contents `str`.

- `int length()`
  returns the number of characters of the buffer.

- `int capacity()`
  returns the current capacity, that is, the number of characters that can be contained in the buffer before it must be relocated.

- `void ensureCapacity(int m)`
  enlarges the buffer if the capacity is fewer than m characters.

- void setLength(int n)

  If n is less than the current length, characters at the end of the string are discarded. If n is larger than the current length, the buffer is padded with '\0' characters.

- char charAt(int i)

  returns the ith character (i is between 0 and length()-1); throws a StringIndexOutOfBoundsException if the index is invalid.

- void getChars(int from, int to, char[] a, int offset)

  copies characters from the string buffer into an array.

Parameters:	from	The first character to copy
	to	The first character not to copy
	a	The array to copy into
	offset	The first position in a to copy into

- void setCharAt(int i, char ch)

  sets the ith character to ch.

- StringBuffer append(String str)

  appends a string to the end of this buffer (the buffer may be relocated as a result); returns this.

- StringBuffer append(char c)

  appends a character to the end of this buffer (the buffer may be relocated as a result); returns this.

- StringBuffer insert(int offset, String str)

  inserts a string at position offset into this buffer (the buffer may be relocated as a result); returns this.

- StringBuffer insert(int offset, char c)

  inserts a character at position offset into this buffer (the buffer may be relocated as a result); returns this.

- String toString()

  returns a string pointing to the same data as the buffer contents. (No copy is made.)

java.lang.String

- String(StringBuffer buffer)

  makes a string pointing to the same data as the buffer contents. (No copy is made.)

Object Streams

Using a fixed-length record format is a good choice if you need to store data of the same type. However, objects that you create in an object-oriented program are rarely all of the same type. For example, you may have an array called `staff` that is nominally an array of `Employee` records but contains objects that are actually instances of a child class such as `Manager`.

If we want to save files that contain this kind of information, we must first save the type of each object and then the data that defines the current state of the object. When we read this information back from a file, we must:

- Read the object type;
- Create a blank object of that type;
- Fill it with the data that we stored in the file.

It is entirely possible (if very tedious) to do this by hand, and in the first edition of this book we did exactly this. However, Sun Microsystems developed a powerful mechanism that allows this to be done with much less effort. As you will soon see, this mechanism, called *object serialization*, almost completely automates what was previously a very tedious process. (You will see later in this chapter where the term "serialization" comes from.)

Storing Objects of Variable Type

To save object data, you first need to open an `ObjectOutputStream` object:

```
ObjectOutputStream out = new ObjectOutputStream(new
    FileOutputStream("employee.dat"));
```

Now, to save an object, you simply use the `writeObject` method of the `ObjectOutputStream` class as in the following fragment:

```
Employee harry = new Employee("Harry Hacker", 50000,
    1989, 10, 1);
Manager boss = new Manager("Carl Cracker", 80000,
    1987, 12, 15);
out.writeObject(harry);
out.writeObject(boss);
```

To read the objects back in, first get an `ObjectInputStream` object:

```
ObjectInputStream in = new ObjectInputStream(new
    FileInputStream("employee.dat"));
```

Then, retrieve the objects in the same order in which they were written, using the `readObject` method.

```
Employee e1 = (Employee)in.readObject();
Employee e2 = (Employee)in.readObject();
```

When reading back objects, you must carefully keep track of the number of objects that were saved, their order, and their types. Each call to `readObject` reads in another object of the type `Object`. You, therefore, will need to cast it to its correct type.

If you don't need the exact type or you don't remember it, then you can cast it to any superclass or even leave it as type `Object`. For example, e2 is an `Employee` object variable even though it actually refers to a `Manager` object. If you need to dynamically query the type of the object, you can use the `getClass` method that we described in Chapter 5.

You can write and read only *objects* with the `writeObject`/`readObject` methods, not numbers. To write and read numbers, you use methods such as `writeInt`/`readInt` or `writeDouble`/`readDouble`. (The object stream classes implement the `DataInput`/`DataOutput` interfaces.) Of course, numbers inside objects (such as the salary field of an `Employee` object) are saved and restored automatically. Recall that, in Java, strings and arrays are objects and can, therefore, be restored with the `writeObject`/`readObject` methods.

There is, however, one change you need to make to any class that you want to save and restore in an object stream. The class must implement the `Serializable` interface:

```
class Employee implements Serializable { . . . }
```

The `Serializable` interface has no methods, so you don't need to change your classes in any way. In this regard, it is similar to the `Cloneable` interface that we also discussed in Chapter 5. However, to make a class cloneable, you still had to override the `clone` method of the `Object` class. To make a class serializable, you do not need to do *anything* else. Why aren't all classes serializable by default? We will discuss this in the section "Security."

Example 12–4 is a test program that writes an array containing two employees and one manager to disk and then restores it. Writing an array is done with a single operation:

```
Employee[] staff = new Employee[3];
. . .
out.writeObject(staff);
```

Similarly, reading in the result is done with a single operation. However, we must apply a cast to the return value of the `readObject` method:

```
Employee[] newStaff = (Employee[])in.readObject();
```

Once the information is restored, we give each employee a 100% raise, not because we are feeling generous, but because you can then easily distinguish employee and manager objects by their different `raiseSalary` actions. This should convince you that we did restore the correct types.

Example 12–4: ObjectFileTest.java

```
1. import java.io.*;
2. import java.util.*;
3.
4. class ObjectFileTest
```

```
 5. {
 6.    public static void main(String[] args)
 7.    {
 8.       Manager boss = new Manager("Carl Cracker", 80000,
 9.          1987, 12, 15);
10.       boss.setBonus(5000);
11.
12.       Employee[] staff = new Employee[3];
13.
14.       staff[0] = boss;
15.       staff[1] = new Employee("Harry Hacker", 50000,
16.          1989, 10, 1);
17.       staff[2] = new Employee("Tony Tester", 40000,
18.          1990, 3, 15);
19.
20.       try
21.       {
22.          // save all employee records to the file employee.dat
23.          ObjectOutputStream out = new ObjectOutputStream(new
24.             FileOutputStream("employee.dat"));
25.          out.writeObject(staff);
26.          out.close();
27.
28.          // retrieve all records into a new array
29.          ObjectInputStream in =  new ObjectInputStream(new
30.             FileInputStream("employee.dat"));
31.          Employee[] newStaff = (Employee[])in.readObject();
32.          in.close();
33.
34.          // print the newly read employee records
35.          for (int i = 0; i < newStaff.length; i++)
36.             System.out.println(newStaff[i]);
37.       }
38.       catch (Exception e)
39.       {
40.          e.printStackTrace();
41.       }
42.    }
43. }
44.
45. class Employee implements Serializable
46. {
47.    public Employee() {}
48.
49.    public Employee(String n, double s,
50.       int year, int month, int day)
51.    {
52.       name = n;
53.       salary = s;
54.       GregorianCalendar calendar
55.          = new GregorianCalendar(year, month - 1, day);
56.          // GregorianCalendar uses 0 = January
57.       hireDay = calendar.getTime();
```

```
58.     }
59.
60.     public String getName()
61.     {
62.         return name;
63.     }
64.
65.     public double getSalary()
66.     {
67.         return salary;
68.     }
69.
70.     public Date getHireDay()
71.     {
72.         return hireDay;
73.     }
74.
75.     public void raiseSalary(double byPercent)
76.     {
77.         double raise = salary * byPercent / 100;
78.         salary += raise;
79.     }
80.
81.     public String toString()
82.     {
83.         return getClass().getName()
84.             + "[name=" + name
85.             + ",salary=" + salary
86.             + ",hireDay=" + hireDay
87.             + "]";
88.     }
89.
90.     private String name;
91.     private double salary;
92.     private Date hireDay;
93. }
94.
95. class Manager extends Employee
96. {
97.     /**
98.         @param n the employee's name
99.         @param s the salary
100.        @param year the hire year
101.        @param year the hire month
102.        @param year the hire day
103.     */
104.     public Manager(String n, double s,
105.         int year, int month, int day)
106.     {
107.         super(n, s, year, month, day);
108.         bonus = 0;
109.     }
110.
```

```
111.    public double getSalary()
112.    {
113.       double baseSalary = super.getSalary();
114.       return baseSalary + bonus;
115.    }
116.
117.    public void setBonus(double b)
118.    {
119.       bonus = b;
120.    }
121.
122.    public String toString()
123.    {
124.       return super.toString()
125.          + "[bonus=" + bonus
126.          + "]";
127.    }
128.
129.    private double bonus;
130. }
```

`java.io.ObjectOutputStream`

- `ObjectOutputStream(OutputStream out)`
  creates an `ObjectOutputStream` so that you can write objects to the
  specified `OutputStream`.

- `void writeObject(Object obj)`
  writes the specified object to the `ObjectOutputStream`. This method
  saves the class of the object, the signature of the class, and the values of
  any non-static, non-transient field of the class and its superclasses.

`java.io.ObjectInputStream`

- `ObjectInputStream(InputStream is)`
  creates an `ObjectInputStream` to read back object information from the
  specified `InputStream`.

- `Object readObject()`
  reads an object from the `ObjectInputStream`. In particular, this reads back
  the class of the object, the signature of the class, and the values of the
  nontransient and nonstatic fields of the class and all of its superclasses. It does
  deserializing to allow multiple object references to be recovered.

Object Serialization File Format

Object serialization saves object data in a particular file format. Of course, you can
use the `writeObject`/`readObject` methods without having to know the exact
sequence of bytes that represents objects in a file. Nonetheless, we found studying
the data format to be extremely helpful for gaining insight into the object streaming

process. We did this by looking at hex dumps of various saved object files. However, the details are somewhat technical, so feel free to skip this section if you are not interested in the implementation.

Every file begins with the 2-byte "magic number"

```
AC ED
```

followed by the version number of the object serialization format, which is currently

```
00 05
```

(We will be using hexadecimal numbers throughout this section to denote bytes.) Then, it contains a sequence of objects, in the order that they were saved.

String objects are saved as

```
74                     2-byte length           characters
```

For example, the string "Harry" is saved as

```
74 00 05 Harry
```

The Unicode characters of the string are saved in UTF format.

When an object is saved, the class of that object must be saved as well. The class description contains

1. The name of the class;
2. The *serial version unique ID,* which is a fingerprint of the data field types and method signatures;
3. A set of flags describing the serialization method;
4. A description of the data fields.

Java gets the fingerprint by:

1. Ordering descriptions of the class, superclass, interfaces, field types, and method signatures in a canonical way;
2. Then applying the so-called Secure Hash Algorithm (SHA) to that data.

SHA is a very fast algorithm that gives a "fingerprint" to a larger block of information. This fingerprint is always a 20-byte data packet, regardless of the size of the original data. It is created by a clever sequence of bit operations on the data that makes it essentially 100 percent certain that the fingerprint will change if the information is altered in any way. SHA is a U.S. standard, recommended by the National Institute for Science and Technology (NIST). (For more details on SHA, see, for example, *Cryptography and Network Security: Principles and Practice*, by William Stallings [Prentice Hall].) However, Java uses only the first 8 bytes of the SHA code as a class fingerprint. It is still very likely that the class fingerprint will change if the data fields or methods change in any way.

Java can then check the class fingerprint to protect us from the following scenario: An object is saved to a disk file. Later, the designer of the class makes a change, for example, by removing a data field. Then, the old disk file is read in again. Now the data layout on the disk no longer matches the data layout in memory. If the data were read back in its old form, it could corrupt memory. Java takes great care to make such memory corruption close to impossible. Hence, it checks, using the fingerprint, that the class definition has not changed when restoring an object. It does this by comparing the fingerprint on disk with the fingerprint of the current class.

NOTE: Technically, as long as the data layout of a class has not changed, it ought to be safe to read objects back in. But Java is conservative and checks that the methods have not changed either. (After all, the methods describe the meaning of the stored data.) Of course, in practice, classes do evolve, and it may be necessary for a program to read in older versions of objects. We will discuss this in the section entitled "Versioning."

Here is how a class identifier is stored:

> 72
>
> 2-byte length of class name
>
> class name
>
> 8-byte fingerprint
>
> 1-byte flag
>
> 2-byte count of data field descriptors
>
> data field descriptors
>
> 78 (end marker)
>
> superclass type (70 if none)

The flag byte is composed of 3 bit masks, defined in

```
java.io.ObjectStreamConstants:
static final byte SC_WRITE_METHOD = 1;
   // class has writeObject method that writes additional data
static final byte SC_SERIALIZABLE = 2;
   // class implements Serializable interface
static final byte SC_EXTERNALIZABLE = 4;
   // class implements Externalizable interface
```

We will discuss the Externalizable interface later in this chapter. Externalizable classes supply custom read and write methods that take over the output of their instance fields. The classes that we write implement the Serializable interface and will have a flag value of 02. However, the java.util.Date class is externalizable and has a flag of 03.

Each data field descriptor has the format:

> 1-byte type code

2-byte length of field name

field name

class name (if field is an object)

The type code is one of the following:

B	byte
C	char
D	double
F	float
I	int
J	long
L	**object**
S	short
Z	boolean
[	**array**

When the type code is `L`, the field name is followed by the field type. Class and field name strings do not start with the string code `74`, but field types do. Field types use a slightly different encoding of their names, namely, the format used by native methods. (See Volume 2 for native methods.)

For example, the salary field of the `Employee` class is encoded as:

```
D 00 06 salary
```

Here is the complete class descriptor of the `Employee` class:

`72 00 08 Employee`	
`E6 D2 86 7D AE AC 18 1B 02`	Fingerprint and flags
`00 03`	Number of instance fields
`D 00 06 salary`	Instance field type and name
`L 00 07 hireDay`	Instance field type and name
`74 00 10 Ljava/util/Date;`	Instance field class name—`String`
`L 00 04 name`	Instance field type and name
`74 00 12 Ljava/lang/String;`	Instance field class name—`String`
`78`	End marker
`70`	No superclass

These descriptors are fairly long. If the *same* class descriptor is needed again in the file, then an abbreviated form is used:

```
71        4-byte serial number
```

The serial number refers to the previous explicit class descriptor. We will discuss the numbering scheme later.

An object is stored as

| 73 | class descriptor | object data |

For example, here is how an `Employee` object is stored:

40 E8 6A 00 00 00 00 00	`salary` field value—`double`
73	`hireDay` field value—new object
71 00 7E 00 08	Existing class `java.util.Date`
77 08 00 00 00 91 1B 4E B1 80 78	External storage—details later
74 00 0C Harry Hacker	`name` field value—`String`

As you can see, the data file contains enough information to restore the `Employee` object.

Arrays are saved in the following format:

| 75 | class descriptor | 4-byte number of entries | entries |

The array class name in the class descriptor is in the same format as that used by native methods (which is slightly different from the class name used by class names in other class descriptors). In this format, class names start with an `L` and end with a semicolon.

For example, an array of three `Employee` objects starts out like this:

75	Array
72 00 0B [LEmployee;	New class, string length, class name `Employee[]`
FC BF 36 11 C5 91 11 C7 02	Fingerprint and flags
00 00	Number of instance fields
78	End marker
70	No superclass
00 00 00 03	Number of array entries

Note that the fingerprint for an array of `Employee` objects is different from a fingerprint of the `Employee` class itself.

Of course, studying these codes can be about as exciting as reading the average phone book. But it is still instructive to know that the object stream contains a detailed description of all the objects that it contains, with sufficient detail to allow reconstruction of both objects and arrays of objects.

The Problem of Saving Object References

We now know how to save objects that contain numbers, strings, or other simple objects. However, there is one important situation that we still need to consider. What happens when one object is shared by several objects as part of its state?

To illustrate the problem, let us make a slight modification to the `Manager` class. Let's assume that each manager has a secretary, implemented as an instance variable secretary of type `Employee`. (It would make sense to derive a class `Secretary` from `Employee` for this purpose, but we will not do that here.)

```
class Manager extends Employee
{
   . . .
   private Employee secretary;
}
```

Having done this, you must keep in mind that the `Manager` object now contains a *reference* to the `Employee` object that describes the secretary, *not* a separate copy of the object.

In particular, two managers can share the same secretary, as is the case in Figure 12–5 and the following code:

```
harry = new Employee("Harry Hacker", . . .);
Manager carl = new Manager("Carl Cracker", . . .);
carl.setSecretary(harry);
Manager tony = new Manager("Tony Tester", . . .);
tony.setSecretary(harry);
```

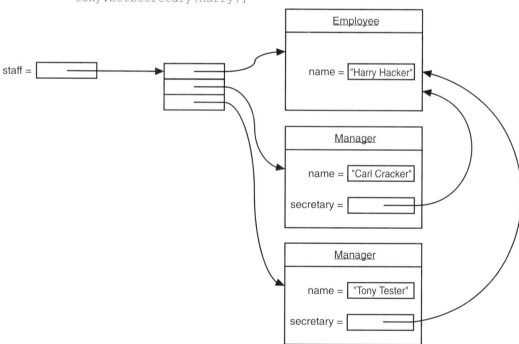

Figure 12–5: Two managers can share a mutual employee

Now, suppose we write the employee data to disk. What we *don't* want is for the `Manager` to save its information according to the following logic:

- Save employee data;
- Save secretary data.

Then, the data for `harry` would be saved *three times*. When reloaded, the objects would have the configuration shown in Figure 12–6.

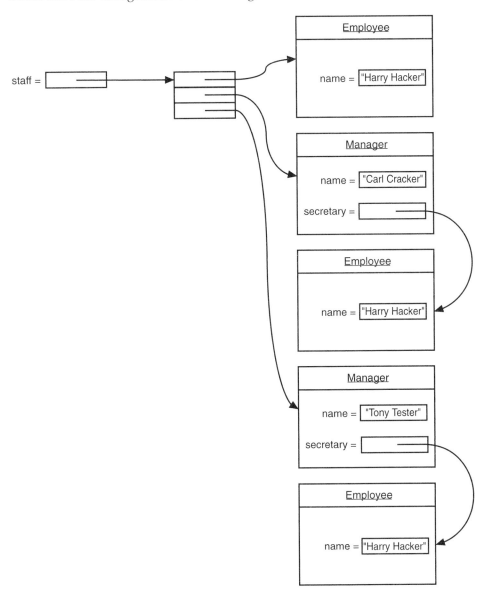

Figure 12–6: Here, Harry is saved three times

This is not what we want. Suppose the secretary gets a raise. We would not want to hunt for all other copies of that object and apply the raise as well. We want to save and restore only *one copy* of the secretary. To do this, we must copy and restore the original references to the objects. In other words, we want the object layout on disk to be exactly like the object layout in memory. This is called *persistence* in object-oriented circles.

Of course, we cannot save and restore the memory addresses for the secretary objects. When an object is reloaded, it will likely occupy a completely different memory address than it originally did.

Instead, Java uses a *serialization* approach. Hence, the name *object serialization* for this mechanism. Here is the algorithm:

- All objects that are saved to disk are given a serial number (1, 2, 3, and so on, as shown in Figure 12–7).
- When saving an object to disk, find out if the same object has already been stored.
- If it has been stored previously, just write "same as previously saved object with serial number *x*". If not, store all its data.

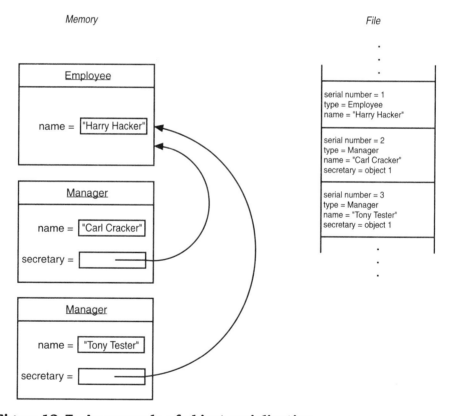

Figure 12–7: An example of object serialization

When reading back the objects, simply reverse the procedure. For each object that you load, note its sequence number and remember where you put it in memory. When you encounter the tag "same as previously saved object with serial number

x'', you look up where you put the object with serial number x and set the object reference to that memory address.

Note that the objects need not be saved in any particular order. Figure 12–8 shows what happens when a manager occurs first in the staff array.

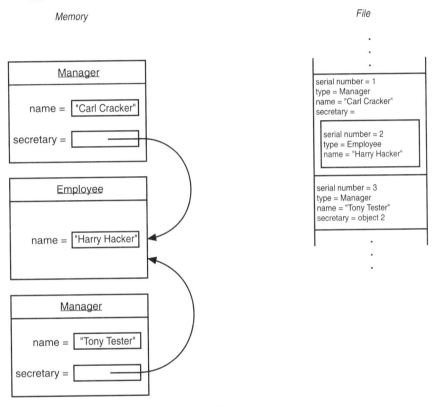

Figure 12–8: Objects saved in random order

All of this sounds confusing, and it is. Fortunately, when object streams are used, the process is also *completely automatic*. Object streams assign the serial numbers and keep track of duplicate objects. The exact numbering scheme is slightly different from that used in the figures—see the next section.

NOTE: In this chapter, we use serialization to save a collection of objects to a disk file and retrieve it exactly as we stored it. Another very important application is the transmittal of a collection of objects across a network connection to another computer. Just as raw memory addresses are meaningless in a file, they are also meaningless when communicating with a different processor. Since serialization replaces memory addresses with serial numbers, it permits the transport of object collections from one machine to another. We will study that use of serialization when discussing remote method invocation in Volume 2.

Example 12–5 is a program that saves and reloads a network of employee and manager objects (some of which share the same employee as a secretary). Note that the secretary object is unique after reloading—when `newStaff[1]` gets a raise, that is reflected in the secretary fields of the managers.

Example 12–5: ObjectRefTest.java

```
1. import java.io.*;
2. import java.util.*;
3.
4. class ObjectRefTest
5. {
6.    public static void main(String[] args)
7.    {
8.       Employee harry = new Employee("Harry Hacker", 50000,
9.          1989, 10, 1);
10.      Manager boss = new Manager("Carl Cracker", 80000,
11.         1987, 12, 15);
12.      boss.setSecretary(harry);
13.
14.      Employee[] staff = new Employee[3];
15.
16.      staff[0] = boss;
17.      staff[1] = harry;
18.      staff[2] = new Employee("Tony Tester", 40000,
19.         1990, 3, 15);
20.
21.      try
22.      {
23.         // save all employee records to the file employee.dat
24.         ObjectOutputStream out = new ObjectOutputStream(new
25.            FileOutputStream("employee.dat"));
26.         out.writeObject(staff);
27.         out.close();
28.
29.         // retrieve all records into a new array
30.         ObjectInputStream in =  new ObjectInputStream(new
31.            FileInputStream("employee.dat"));
32.         Employee[] newStaff = (Employee[])in.readObject();
33.         in.close();
34.
35.         // raise secretary's salary
36.         newStaff[1].raiseSalary(10);
37.
38.         // print the newly read employee records
39.         for (int i = 0; i < newStaff.length; i++)
40.            System.out.println(newStaff[i]);
41.      }
42.      catch (Exception e)
43.      {
44.         e.printStackTrace();
```

```
45.            }
46.        }
47. }
48.
49. class Employee implements Serializable
50. {
51.     public Employee() {}
52.
53.     public Employee(String n, double s,
54.         int year, int month, int day)
55.     {
56.         name = n;
57.         salary = s;
58.         GregorianCalendar calendar
59.             = new GregorianCalendar(year, month - 1, day);
60.             // GregorianCalendar uses 0 = January
61.         hireDay = calendar.getTime();
62.     }
63.
64.     public String getName()
65.     {
66.         return name;
67.     }
68.
69.     public double getSalary()
70.     {
71.         return salary;
72.     }
73.
74.     public Date getHireDay()
75.     {
76.         return hireDay;
77.     }
78.
79.     public void raiseSalary(double byPercent)
80.     {
81.         double raise = salary * byPercent / 100;
82.         salary += raise;
83.     }
84.
85.     public String toString()
86.     {
87.         return getClass().getName()
88.             + "[name=" + name
89.             + ",salary=" + salary
90.             + ",hireDay=" + hireDay
91.             + "]";
92.     }
93.
94.     private String name;
95.     private double salary;
96.     private Date hireDay;
```

```
97.  }
98.
99.  class Manager extends Employee
100. {
101.     /**
102.         Constructs a Manager without a secretary
103.         @param n the employee's name
104.         @param s the salary
105.         @param year the hire year
106.         @param year the hire month
107.         @param year the hire day
108.     */
109.     public Manager(String n, double s,
110.         int year, int month, int day)
111.     {
112.         super(n, s, year, month, day);
113.         secretary = null;
114.     }
115.
116.     /**
117.         Assigns a secretary to the manager.
118.         @param s the secretary
119.     */
120.     public void setSecretary(Employee s)
121.     {
122.         secretary = s;
123.     }
124.
125.     public String toString()
126.     {
127.         return super.toString()
128.             + "[secretary=" + secretary
129.             + "]";
130.     }
131.
132.     private Employee secretary;
133. }
```

Output Format for Object References

This section continues the discussion of the output format of object streams. If you skipped the previous discussion, you should skip this section as well.

All objects (including arrays and strings) and all class descriptors are given serial numbers as they are saved in the output file. This process is referred to as *serialization* because every saved object is assigned a serial number. (The count starts at 00 7E 00 00.)

We already saw that a full class descriptor for any given class occurs only once. Subsequent descriptors refer to it. For example, in our previous example, the second reference to the Day class in the array of days was coded as

71 00 7E 00 02

The same mechanism is used for objects. If a reference to a previously saved object is written, it is saved in exactly the same way, that is, `71` followed by the serial number. It is always clear from the context whether the particular serial reference denotes a class descriptor or an object.

Finally, a null reference is stored as

```
70
```

Here is the commented output of the `ObjectRefTest` program of the preceding section. If you like, run the program, look at a hex dump of its data file `employee.dat`, and compare it with the commented listing. The important lines toward the end of the output show the reference to a previously saved object.

`AC ED 00 05`	File header
`75`	Array `staff` (serial #1)
`72 00 0B [LEmployee;`	New class, string length, class name `Employee[]` (serial #0)
`FC BF 36 11 C5 91 11 C7 02`	Fingerprint and flags
`00 00`	Number of instance fields
`78`	End marker
`70`	No superclass
`00 00 00 03`	Number of array entries
`73`	`staff[0]`—new object (serial #7)
`72 00 07 Manager`	New class, string length, class name (serial #2)
`36 06 AE 13 63 8F 59 B7 02`	Fingerprint and flags
`00 01`	Number of data fields
`L 00 09 secretary`	Instance field type and name
`74 00 0A LEmployee;`	Instance field class name—`String` (serial #3)
`78`	End marker
`72 00 08 Employee`	Superclass—new class, string length, class name (serial #4)
`E6 D2 86 7D AE AC 18 1B 02`	Fingerprint and flags
`00 03`	Number of instance fields
`D 00 06 salary`	Instance field type and name
`L 00 07 hireDay`	Instance field type and name
`74 00 10 Ljava/util/Date;`	Instance field class name—`String` (serial #5)
`L 00 04 name`	Instance field type and name
`74 00 12 Ljava/lang/String;`	Instance field class name—`String` (serial #6)

78	End marker
70	No superclass
40 F3 88 00 00 00 00 00	`salary` field value—`double`
73	`hireDay` field value—new object (serial #9)
72 00 0E java.util.Date	New class, string length, class name (serial #8)
68 6A 81 01 4B 59 74 19 03	Fingerprint and flags
00 00	No instance variables
78	End marker
70	No superclass
77 08	External storage, number of bytes
00 00 00 83 E9 39 E0 00	Date
78	End marker
74 00 0C Carl Cracker	`name` field value—`String` (serial #10)
73	`secretary` field value—new object (serial #11)
71 00 7E 00 04	existing class (use serial #4)
40 E8 6A 00 00 00 00 00	`salary` field value—`double`
73	`hireDay` field value—new object (serial #12)
71 00 7E 00 08	Existing class (use serial #8)
77 08	External storage, number of bytes
00 00 00 91 1B 4E B1 80	Date
78	End marker
74 00 0C Harry Hacker	`name` field value—`String` (serial #13)
71 00 7E 00 0B	`staff[1]`—existing object (use serial #11)
73	`staff[2]`—new object (serial #14)
71 00 7E 00 04	Existing class (use serial #4)
40 E3 88 00 00 00 00 00	`salary` field value—`double`
73	`hireDay` field value—new object (serial #15)
71 00 7E 00 08	Existing class (use serial #8)
77 08	External storage, number of bytes
00 00 00 94 6D 3E EC 00 00	Date
78	End marker
74 00 0B Tony Tester	`name` field value—`String` (serial # 16)

It is usually not important to know the exact file format (unless you are trying to create an evil effect by modifying the data—see the next section). What you should remember is this:

- The object stream output contains the types and data fields of all objects.
- Each object is assigned a serial number.
- Repeated occurrences of the same object are stored as references to that serial number.

Security

Even if you only glanced at the file format description of the preceding section, it should become obvious that a knowledgeable hacker can exploit this information and modify an object file so that invalid objects will be read in when you reload the file.

Suppose, for example, that the `Employee` constructor checks that the salary is within a reasonable range, say between $1 and $199,999. For example, if you try to build a `new Employee("Eddy Embezzler", 500000.0, . . .)`, no object is created and an `IllegalArgumentException` is thrown instead.

However, this safety guarantee can be subverted through serialization. When an `Employee` object is read in from an object stream, it is possible—either through a device error or through malice—that the stream contains an invalid salary. There is nothing that the serialization mechanism can do in this case—it has no understanding of the constraints that define a legal salary.

For that reason, Java's serialization mechanism provides a way for individual classes to add validation or any other desired action instead of the default behavior. A serializable class can define methods with the signature

```
private void readObject(ObjectInputStream in)
    throws IOException, ClassNotFoundException;
private void writeObject(ObjectOutputStream out)
    throws IOException;
```

Then, the data fields are no longer automatically serialized, and these methods are called instead.

For example, let us add validation to the `Employee` class. We don't need to change the writing of `Employee` objects, so we won't implement the `writeObject` method.

In the `readObject` method, we first need to read the object state that was written by the default `write` method, by calling the `defaultReadObject` method. This is a special method of the `ObjectInputStream` class that can only be called from within a `readObject` method of a serializable class.

```
class Employee
{  . . .
   private void readObject(ObjectInputStream in)
```

```
                     throws IOException, ClassNotFoundException
         {
             in.defaultReadObject();
             if (!isValid()) throw new IOException("Invalid object");
         }
     }
```

The `isValid` method checks whether the object is in a valid state. That is the same method that you should use in every constructor to check the constructor arguments. If the object state is not valid (for example, because someone modified the data file), then throw an exception.

> NOTE: Another way of protecting serialized data from tampering is authentication. As you will see in Volume 2, a stream can save a message digest (such as the SHA finger-print) to detect any corruption of the stream data.

Classes can also write additional information to the output stream by defining a `writeObject` method that first calls `defaultWriteObject` and then writes other data. Of course, the `readObject` method must then read the saved data—otherwise, the stream state will be out of sync with the object. Also, the `writeObject` and `readObject` can completely bypass the default storage of the object data by simply *not* calling the `defaultWriteObject` and `defaultReadObject` methods.

For example, the `java.util.Date` class supplies its own `readObject` and `writeObject` methods that write the date as a number of milliseconds from the epoch (January 1, 1970, midnight UTC). The `Date` class has a complex internal representation that stores both a `Calendar` object and a millisecond count, to optimize lookups. The state of the `Calendar` is redundant and does not have to be saved.

The `readObject` and `writeObject` methods only need to save and load their data fields. They should not concern themselves with superclass data or any other class information.

Rather than letting the serialization mechanism save and restore object data, a class can define its own mechanism. To do this, a class must implement the `Externalizable` interface. This in turn requires it to define two methods:

```
    public void readExternal(ObjectInputStream in)
       throws IOException, ClassNotFoundException;
    public void writeExternal(ObjectOutputStream out)
       throws IOException;
```

Unlike the `readObject` and `writeObject` methods that were described in the preceding section, these methods are fully responsible for saving and restoring the entire object, *including the superclass data*. The serialization mechanism merely records the class of the object in the stream. When reading an externalizable object, the object stream creates an object with the default constructor and then calls the `readExternal` method. Here is how you can implement these methods for the `Employee` class:

```
public void readExternal(java.io.ObjectInput s)
    throws ClassNotFoundException, IOException
{
    name = s.readUTF();
    salary = s.readUTF();
    hireDay = new Date(s.readLong());
}

public void writeExternal(java.io.ObjectOutput s)
    throws IOException
{
    s.writeUTF(name);
    s.writeDouble(salary);
    s.writeLong(hireDay.getTime());
}
```

TIP: Serialization is somewhat slow because the virtual machine must discover the structure of each object. If you are very concerned about performance and if you read and write a large number of objects of a particular class, you should investigate the use of the `Externalizable` interface. The tech tip `http://devel-oper.java.sun.com/developer/TechTips/txtarchive/Apr00_Stu.txt` demonstrates that in the case of an employee class, using external reading and writing was about 35-40% faster than the default serialization.

CAUTION: Unlike the `readObject` and `writeObject` methods, which are private and can only be called by the serialization mechanism, the `readExternal` and `writeExternal` methods are public. In particular, `readExternal` potentially permits modification of the state of an existing object.

Finally, certain data members should never be serialized, for example, integer values that store file handles or handles of windows that are only meaningful to native methods. Such information is guaranteed to be useless when you reload an object at a later time or transport it to a different machine. In fact, improper values for such fields can actually cause native methods to crash. Java has an easy mechanism to prevent such fields from ever being serialized. Mark them with the keyword `transient`. Transient fields are always skipped when objects are serialized.

As you saw, by default all non-`static`, non-`transient` fields of an object are serialized. If for whatever reason you aren't happy about this mechanism, you can turn off this default selection of serialized fields and instead nominate any other values for serialization. You do this by specifying an array of `ObjectStreamField` objects, each of which gives the name and type of a value. You must define a `private static final` array and call it `serialPersistentFields`. This is not a common thing to do, and we don't want to dwell on the details. We'll walk through a simple example, but you need to refer to the API documentation for more information.

Suppose you want to save the state of the `hireDay` object not by streaming out the `Date` value, but instead by saving the single number

```
10000 * year + 100 * month + day
```

For example, February 28, 1996 would be saved as the number `19960228`. We'll call this value `date`. You tell the `Employee` class that its serialized form consists of three fields, like this:

```
class Employee
{  . . .
   private static final ObjectStreamField[]
      serialPersistentFields =
   {
      new ObjectStreamField("name", String.class),
      new ObjectStreamField("salary", double.class),
      new ObjectStreamField("date", long.class)
   };
}
```

Now you need to take over the streaming of this class. In the `writeObject` method, you retrieve the set of fields for the object with the `putFields` method. (This method returns an object that encapsulates the field set—it's type is the inner class `ObjectOutputStream.PutField`). You then set the value of the fields, and finally you write the field set to the stream:

```
private void writeObject(ObjectOutputStream out)
   throws IOException
{
   ObjectOutputStream.PutField fields = out.putFields();
   fields.put("name", name);
   fields.put("salary", salary);
   GregorianCalendar calendar = new GregorianCalendar();
   calendar.setTime(hireDay);
   fields.put("date", calendar.get(Calendar.YEAR) * 10000L
      + (calendar.get(Calendar.MONTH) + 1) * 100
      + calendar.get(Calendar.DAY_OF_MONTH));
   out.writeFields();
}
```

To read the object back, you override the `readObject` method. First, read in all the fields with the `readFields` method. Then, retrieve the value of each field with one of the overloaded `get` methods of the inner class `ObjectInputStream.GetField`. The first argument of the `get` method is the name of the field. The second value is the default, to be used when the field is not present.

(This could happen if the version of the object on the stream is different than the current version of the class.) You have to be careful about the *type* of the default value—the type is used to pick between overloaded methods:

```
int get(String name, int defval);
long get(String name, long defval);
float get(String name, float defval);
double get(String name, double defval);
char get(String name, char defval);
short get(String name, short defval);
. . .
```

If the default value is zero, you must supply a zero of the appropriate type:

```
0
0L
0.0F
0.0
'\0'
(short)0
. . .
```

Here is the readObject method for our modified Day class. It reads the date value and splits it up into day, month, and year.

```
private void readObject(ObjectInputStream in)
    throws IOException, ClassNotFoundException
{
    ObjectInputStream.GetField fields = in.readFields();
    name = fields.get("name", "");
    salary = fields.get("salary", 0.0);
    long date = fields.get("date", 0L);
    d = (int)(date % 100);
    m = (int)((date / 100) % 100);
    y = (int)(date / 10000);
    GregorianCalendar calendar
        = new GregorianCalendar(y, m - 1, d);
    hireDay = calendar.getTime();
}
```

Couldn't we just have used the writeExternal/readExternal mechanism instead? There is a slight difference—by using serial fields, the stream contains the name and type of the date value, not just raw bytes. Thus, the stream can still do type checking and versioning when reading the object back in.

Beyond the possibility of data corruption, there is another potentially worrisome security aspect to serialization. Any code that can access a reference to a serializable object can

- Write that object to a stream;
- Then study the stream contents.

Thereby it is possible to know the values of all the data fields in the objects, *even the private ones*. After all, the serialization mechanism automatically saves all private data. Fortunately, this knowledge cannot be used to *modify* data. The `readObject` method does not overwrite an existing object but always creates a new object. Nevertheless, if you need to keep certain information safe from inspection via the serialization mechanism, you should take one of the following three steps:

1. Don't make the class serializable.
2. Mark the sensitive data fields as `transient`.
3. Do not use the default mechanism for saving and restoring objects. Instead, define `readObject`/`writeObject` or `readExternal`/`writeExternal` to encrypt the data.

Versioning

In the past sections, we showed you how to save relatively small collections of objects via an object stream. But those were just demonstration programs. With object streams, it helps to think big. Suppose you write a program that lets the user produce a document. This document contains paragraphs of text, tables, graphs, and so on. You can stream out the entire document object with a single call to `writeObject`:

```
out.writeObject(doc);
```

The paragraph, table, and graph objects are automatically streamed out as well. One user of your program can then give the output file to another user who also has a copy of your program, and that program loads the entire document with a single call to `readObject`:

```
doc = (Document)in.readObject();
```

This is very useful, but your program will inevitably change, and you will release a version 1.1. Can version 1.1 read the old files? Can the users who still use 1.0 read the files that the new version is now producing? Clearly, it would be desirable if object files could cope with the evolution of classes.

At first glance it seems that this would not be possible. When a class definition changes in any way, then its SHA fingerprint also changes, and you know that object streams will refuse to read in objects with different fingerprints. However, a class can indicate that it is *compatible* with an earlier version of itself. To do this, you must first obtain the fingerprint of the *earlier* version of the class. You use the stand-alone `serialver` program that is part of the SDK to obtain this number. For example, running

```
serialver Employee
```

prints out

```
Employee:    static final long serialVersionUID =
-1814239825517340645L;
```

If you start the `serialver` program with the `-show` option, then the program brings up a graphical dialog box (see Figure 12–9).

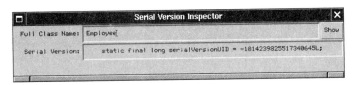

Figure 12–9: The graphical version of the `serialver` program

All *later* versions of the class must define the `serialVersionUID` constant to the same fingerprint as the original.

```
class Employee // version 1.1
{   . . .
    public static final long serialVersionUID
        = -1814239825517340645L;
}
```

When a class has a static data member named `serialVersionUID`, it will not compute the fingerprint manually but instead will use that value.

Once that static data member has been placed inside a class, the serialization system is now willing to read in different versions of objects of that class.

If only the methods of the class change, then there is no problem with reading the new object data. However, if data fields change, then you may have problems. For example, the old file object may have more or fewer data fields than the one in the program, or the types of the data fields may be different. In that case, the object stream makes an effort to convert the stream object to the current version of the class.

The object stream compares the data fields of the current version of the class with the data fields of the version in the stream. Of course, the object stream considers only the nontransient and nonstatic data fields. If two fields have matching names but different types, then the object stream makes no effort to convert one type to the other—the objects are incompatible. If the object in the stream has data fields that are not present in the current version, then the object stream ignores the additional data. If the current version has data fields that are not present in the streamed object, the added fields are set to their default (`null` for objects, zero for numbers and `false` for Boolean values).

Here is an example. Suppose we have saved a number of employee records on disk, using the original version (1.0) of the class. Now we change the `Employee` class to version 2.0 by adding a data field called `department`. Figure 12–10 shows what happens when a 1.0 object is read into a program that uses 2.0 objects. The department field is set to `null`. Figure 12–11 shows the opposite scenario: a program using 1.0 objects reads a 2.0 object. The additional `department` field is ignored.

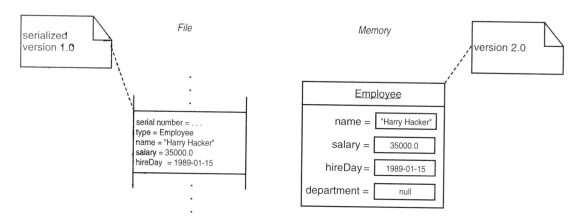

Figure 12–10: Reading an object with fewer data fields

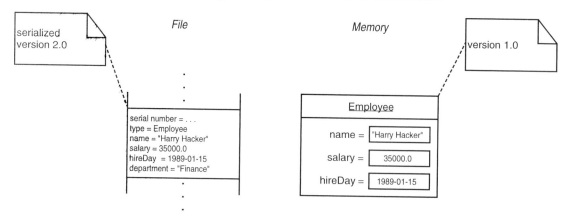

Figure 12–11: Reading an object with more data fields

Is this process safe? It depends. Dropping a data field seems harmless—the recipient still has all the data that it knew how to manipulate. Setting a data field to null may not be so safe. Many classes work hard to initialize all data fields in all constructors to non-null values, so that the methods don't have to be prepared to handle null data. It is up to the class designer to implement additional code in the readObject method to fix version incompatibilities or to make sure the methods are robust enough to handle null data.

Using Serialization for Cloning

There is an amusing (and, occasionally, very useful) use for the serialization mechanism: it gives you an easy way to clone an object provided the class is serializable. (Recall from Chapter 6 that you need to do a bit of work to allow an object to be cloned.)

To clone a serializable object, simply serialize it to an output stream, and then read it back in. The result is a new object that is a deep copy of the existing object. You don't have to write the object to a file—you can use a `ByteArrayOutputStream` to save the data into a byte array.

As Example 12–6 shows, to get `clone` for free, simply derive from the `SerialClo-neable` class, and you are done.

You should be aware that this method, although clever, will usually be much slower than a clone method that explicitly constructs a new object and copies or clones the data fields (as you saw in Chapter 6).

Example 12–6: SerialCloneTest.java

```
 1. import java.io.*;
 2. import java.util.*;
 3.
 4. public class SerialCloneTest
 5. {
 6.    public static void main(String[] args)
 7.    {
 8.       Employee harry = new Employee("Harry Hacker", 35000,
 9.          1989, 10, 1);
10.       // clone harry
11.       Employee harry2 = (Employee)harry.clone();
12.
13.       // mutate harry
14.       harry.raiseSalary(10);
15.
16.       // now harry and the clone are different
17.       System.out.println(harry);
18.       System.out.println(harry2);
19.    }
20. }
21.
22. /**
23.    A class whose clone method uses serialization.
24. */
25. class SerialCloneable implements Cloneable, Serializable
26. {
27.    public Object clone()
28.    {
29.       try
30.       {
31.          // save the object to a byte array
32.          ByteArrayOutputStream bout = new
33.             ByteArrayOutputStream();
34.          ObjectOutputStream out
35.             = new ObjectOutputStream(bout);
36.          out.writeObject(this);
```

```
37.          out.close();
38.
39.          // read a clone of the object from the byte array
40.          ByteArrayInputStream bin = new
41.             ByteArrayInputStream(bout.toByteArray());
42.          ObjectInputStream in = new ObjectInputStream(bin);
43.          Object ret = in.readObject();
44.          in.close();
45.
46.          return ret;
47.       }
48.       catch (Exception e)
49.       {
50.          return null;
51.       }
52.    }
53. }
54.
55. /**
56.    The familiar Employee class, redefined to extend the
57.    SerialCloneable class.
58. */
59. class Employee extends SerialCloneable
60. {
61.    public Employee(String n, double s,
62.       int year, int month, int day)
63.    {
64.       name = n;
65.       salary = s;
66.       GregorianCalendar calendar
67.          = new GregorianCalendar(year, month - 1, day);
68.          // GregorianCalendar uses 0 = January
69.       hireDay = calendar.getTime();
70.    }
71.
72.    public String getName()
73.    {
74.       return name;
75.    }
76.
77.    public double getSalary()
78.    {
79.       return salary;
80.    }
81.
82.    public Date getHireDay()
83.    {
84.       return hireDay;
85.    }
86.
87.    public void raiseSalary(double byPercent)
```

```
88.    {
89.       double raise = salary * byPercent / 100;
90.       salary += raise;
91.    }
92.
93.    public String toString()
94.    {
95.       return getClass().getName()
96.          + "[name=" + name
97.          + ",salary=" + salary
98.          + ",hireDay=" + hireDay
99.          + "]";
100.   }
101.
102.   private String name;
103.   private double salary;
104.   private Date hireDay;
105. }
```

File Management

You have learned how to read and write data from a file. However, there is more to file management than reading and writing. The `File` class encapsulates the functionality that you will need to work with the file system on the user's machine. For example, you use the `File` class to find out when a file was last modified or to remove or rename the file. In other words, the stream classes are concerned with the contents of the file, whereas the `File` class is concerned with the storage of the file on a disk.

NOTE: As is so often the case in Java, the `File` class takes the least common denominator approach. For example, under Windows, you can find out (or set) the read-only flag for a file, but while you can find out if it is a hidden file, you can't hide it without using a native method (see Volume 2).

The simplest constructor for a `File` object takes a (full) file name. If you don't supply a path name, then Java uses the current directory. For example:

```
File f = new File("test.txt");
```

gives you a file object with this name in the current directory. (The current directory is the directory in which the program is running.) A call to this constructor *does not create a file with this name if it doesn't exist.* Actually, creating a file from a `File` object is done with one of the stream class constructors or the `createNewFile` method in the `File` class. The `createNewFile` method only creates a file if no file with that name exists, and it returns a `boolean` to tell you whether it was successful.

On the other hand, once you have a `File` object, the `exists` method in the `File` class tells you whether a file exists with that name. For example, the following trial program would almost certainly print "false" on anyone's machine, and yet it can print out a path name to this nonexistent file.

```
import java.io.*;

public class Test
{
   public static void main(String args[])
   {
      File f = new File("afilethatprobablydoesntexist");
      System.out.println(f.getAbsolutePath());
      System.out.println(f.exists());
   }
}
```

There are two other constructors for `File` objects:

```
File(String path, String name)
```

which creates a `File` object with the given name in the directory specified by the `path` parameter. (If the `path` parameter is `null`, this constructor creates a `File` object using the current directory.)

Finally, you can use an existing `File` object in the constructor:

```
File(File dir, String name)
```

where the `File` object represents a directory and, as before, if `dir` is `null`, the constructor creates a `File` object in the current directory.

Somewhat confusingly, a `File` object can represent either a file or a directory (perhaps because the operating system that the Java designers were most familiar with happens to implement directories as files). You use the `isDirectory` and `isFile` methods to tell whether the file object represents a file or a directory. This is surprising—in an object-oriented system, one might have expected a separate `Directory` class, perhaps extending the `File` class.

To make an object representing a directory, you simply supply the directory name in the `File` constructor:

```
File tempDir = new File(File.separator + "temp");
```

If this directory does not yet exist, you can create it with the `mkdir` method:

```
tempDir.mkdir();
```

If a file object represents a directory, use `list()` to get an array of the file names in that directory. The program in Example 12–7 uses all these methods to print out the directory substructure of whatever path is entered on the command line. (It would be easy enough to change this program into a utility class that returns a vector of the subdirectories for further processing.)

Example 12–7: FindDirectories.java

```
1. import java.io.*;
2.
3. public class FindDirectories
4. {
5.    public static void main(String[] args)
6.    {
7.       // if no arguments provided, start at the parent directory
8.       if (args.length == 0) args = new String[] { ".." };
9.
10.      try
11.      {
12.         File pathName = new File(args[0]);
13.         String[] fileNames = pathName.list();
14.
15.         // enumerate all files in the directory
16.         for (int i = 0; i < fileNames.length; i++)
17.         {
18.            File f = new File(pathName.getPath(),
19.               fileNames[i]);
20.
21.            // if the file is again a directory, call
22.            // the main method recursively
23.            if (f.isDirectory())
24.            {
25.               System.out.println(f.getCanonicalPath());
26.               main(new String [] { f.getPath() });
27.            }
28.         }
29.      }
30.      catch(IOException e)
31.      {
32.         e.printStackTrace();
33.      }
34.   }
35. }
```

Rather than listing all files in a directory, you can use a `FileNameFilter` object as a parameter to the `list` method to narrow down the list. These objects are simply instances of a class that satisfies the `FilenameFilter` interface.

All a class needs to do to implement the `FilenameFilter` interface is define a method called `accept`. Here is an example of a simple `FilenameFilter` class that allows only files with a specified extension:

```
public class ExtensionFilter implements FilenameFilter
```

```
{
    public ExtensionFilter(String ext)
    {
        extension = "." + ext;
    }

    public boolean accept(File dir, String name)
    {
        return name.endsWith(extension);
    }

    private String extension;
}
```

When writing portable programs, it is a challenge to specify file names with subdirectories. As we mentioned earlier, it turns out that you can use a forward slash (the UNIX separator) as the directory separator in Windows as well, but other operating systems might not permit this, so we don't recommend using a forward slash.

 CAUTION: If you do use forward slashes as directory separators in Windows when constructing a `File` object, the `getAbsolutePath` method returns a file name that contains forward slashes, which will look strange to Windows users. Instead, use the `getCanonicalPath` method—it replaces the forward slashes with backslashes.

It is much better to use the information about the current directory separator that the `File` class stores in a static instance field called `separator`. (In a Windows environment, this is a backslash (\\); in a UNIX environment, it is a forward slash (/). For example:

```
File foo = new File("Documents" + File.separator + "data.txt")
```

Of course, if you use the second alternate version of the `File` constructor,

```
File foo = new File("Documents", "data.txt")
```

then Java will supply the correct separator.

The API notes that follow give you what we think are the most important remaining methods of the `File` class; their use should be straightforward.

You have now reached the end of the first volume of Core Java. This volume covered the fundamentals of the Java programming language and the parts of the standard library that you need for most programming projects. We hope that you enjoyed your tour through the Java fundamentals and that you found useful information along the way. For advanced topics, such as networking, multithreading, security, and internationalization, please turn to the second volume.

`java.io.File`

- `boolean canRead()`
  indicates whether the file can be read by the current application.

- `boolean canWrite()`
  indicates whether the file is writable or read-only.

- `static boolean createTempFile(String prefix, String suffix)`
  `static boolean createTempFile(String prefix, String suffix,`
  `File directory)`
  creates a temporary file in the system's default temp directory or the given directory, using the given prefix and suffix to generate the temporary name.

Parameters:	`prefix`	A prefix string that is at least three characters long
	`suffix`	An optional suffix. If `null`, `.tmp` is used
	`directory`	The directory in which the file is created. If it is `null`, the file is created in the current working directory

- `boolean delete()`
  tries to delete the file; returns `true` if the file was deleted; `false` otherwise.

- `void deleteOnExit()`
  requests that the file be deleted when the VM shuts down.

- `boolean exists()`
  `true` if the file or directory exists; `false` otherwise.

- `String getAbsolutePath()`
  returns a string that contains the absolute path name. Tip: Use `getCanonicalPath` instead.

- `File getCanonicalFile()`
  returns a `File` object that contains the canonical path name for the file. In particular, redundant " . " directories are removed, the correct directory separator is used, and the capitalization preferred by the underlying file system is obtained.

- `String getCanonicalPath()`
  returns a string that contains the canonical path name. In particular, redundant " . " directories are removed, the correct directory separator is used, and the capitalization preferred by the underlying file system is obtained.

- `String getName()`

  returns a string that contains the file name of the `File` object (does not include path information).

- `String getParent()`

  returns a string that contains the name of the parent of this `File` object. If this `File` object is a file, then the parent is the directory containing it. If it is a directory, then the parent is the parent directory or `null` if there is no parent directory.

- `File getParentFile()`

  returns a `File` object for the parent of this `File` directory. See `getParent` for a definition of "parent".

- `String getPath()`

  returns a string that contains the path name of the file.

- `boolean isDirectory()`

  returns `true` if the `File` represents a directory; `false` otherwise.

- `boolean isFile()`

  returns `true` if the `File` object represents a file as opposed to a directory or a device.

- `boolean isHidden()`

  returns `true` if the `File` object represents a hidden file or directory.

- `long lastModified()`

  returns the time the file was last modified (counted in milliseconds since Midnight January 1, 1970 GMT), or 0 if the file does not exist. Use the `Date(long)` constructor to convert this value to a date.

- `long length()`

  returns the length of the file in bytes, or 0 if the file does not exist.

- `String[] list()`

  returns an array of strings that contain the names of the files and directories contained by this `File` object, or `null` if this `File` was not representing a directory.

- `String[] list(FilenameFilter filter)`

  returns an array of the names of the files and directories contained by this `File` that satisfy the filter, or `null` if none exist.

  Parameters: filter   The `FilenameFilter` object to use

- `File[] listFiles()`

  returns an array of `File` objects corresponding to the files and directories contained by this `File` object, or `null` if this `File` was not representing a directory.

- `File[] listFiles(FilenameFilter filter)`

  returns an array of `File` objects for the files and directories contained by this `File` that satisfy the filter, or `null` if none exist.

  Parameters: `filter`   The `FilenameFilter` object to use

- `static File[] listRoots()`

  returns an array of `File` objects corresponding to all the available file roots. (For example, on a Windows system, you get the `File` objects representing the installed drives (both local drives and mapped network drives). On a UNIX system, you simply get "`/`".)

- `boolean createNewFile()`

  automatically makes a new file whose name is given by the `File` object, if no file with that name exists. That is, the checking for the file name and the creation are not interrupted by other file system activity. Returns `true` if the method created the file.

- `boolean mkdir()`

  makes a subdirectory whose name is given by the `File` object. Returns `true` if the directory was successfully created; `false` otherwise.

- `boolean mkdirs()`

  unlike `mkdir`, creates the parent directories if necessary. Returns `false` if any of the necessary directories could not be created.

- `boolean renameTo(File dest)`

  returns `true` if the name was changed; `false` otherwise.

  Parameters: `dest`   A `File` object that specifies the new name

- `boolean setLastModified(long time)`

  sets the last modified time of the file. Returns `true` if successful, `false` otherwise.

  Parameters: `time`   A long integer representing the number of milliseconds since Midnight January 1, 1970, GMT. Use the `getTime` method of the `Date` class to calculate this value.

- `boolean setReadOnly()`

  sets the file to be read-only. Returns `true` if successful, `false` otherwise.

- `URL toURL()`

  converts the `File` object to a file `URL`.

java.io.FilenameFilter

- `boolean accept(File dir, String name)`

  should be defined to return `true` if the file matches the filter criterion.

  Parameters: dir   A `File` object representing the directory that contains the file

                          name   The name of the file

Java Keywords

Keyword	Meaning	See Chapter
abstract	an abstract class or method	5
boolean	the Boolean type	3
break	breaks out of a switch or loop	3
byte	the 8-bit integer type	3
case	a case of a switch	3
catch	the clause of a try block catching an exception	11
char	the Unicode character type	3
class	defines a class type	4
const	not used	
continue	continues at the end of a loop	3
default	the default clause of a switch	3
do	the top of a do/while loop	3
double	the double-precision floating-number type	3
else	the else clause of an if statement	3
extends	defines the parent class of a class	4
final	a constant, or a class or method that cannot be overridden	5
finally	the part of a try block that is always executed	11
float	the single-precision floating-point type	3
for	a loop type	3
goto	not used	
if	a conditional statement	3
implements	defines the interface(s) that a class implements	6
import	imports a package	4
instanceof	tests if an object is an instance of a class	5

`int`	the 32-bit integer type	3
`interface`	an abstract type with methods that a class can implement	6
`long`	the 64-bit long integer type	3
`native`	a method implemented by the host system (see Volume 2)	
`new`	allocates a new object or array	3
`null`	a null reference	3
`package`	a package of classes	4
`private`	a feature that is accessible only by methods of this class	4
`protected`	a feature that is accessible only by methods of this class, its children, and other classes in the same package	5
`public`	a feature that is accessible by methods of all classes	4
`return`	returns from a method	3
`short`	the 16-bit integer type	3
`static`	a feature that is unique to its class, not to objects of its class	3
`super`	the superclass object or constructor	5
`switch`	a selection statement	3
`synchronized`	a method that is atomic to a thread (see Volume 2)	
`this`	the implicit argument of a method, or a constructor of this class	4
`throw`	throws an exception	11
`throws`	the exceptions that a method can throw	11
`transient`	marks data that should not be persistent	12
`try`	a block of code that traps exceptions	11
`void`	denotes a method that returns no value	3
`volatile`	not used	
`while`	a loop	3

Index

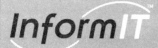

End User License Agreement
Sun Microsystems, Inc. Binary Code License Agreement

READ THE TERMS OF THIS AGREEMENT AND ANY PROVIDED SUPPLEMENTAL LICENSE TERMS (COLLECTIVELY "AGREEMENT") CAREFULLY BEFORE OPENING THE SOFTWARE MEDIA PACKAGE. BY OPENING THE SOFTWARE MEDIA PACKAGE, YOU AGREE TO THE TERMS OF THIS AGREEMENT. IF YOU ARE ACCESSING THE SOFTWARE ELECTRONICALLY, INDICATE YOUR ACCEPTANCE OF THESE TERMS BY SELECTING THE "ACCEPT" BUTTON AT THE END OF THIS AGREEMENT. IF YOU DO NOT AGREE TO ALL THESE TERMS, PROMPTLY RETURN THE UNUSED SOFTWARE TO YOUR PLACE OF PURCHASE FOR A REFUND OR, IF THE SOFTWARE IS ACCESSED ELECTRONICALLY, SELECT THE "DECLINE" BUTTON AT THE END OF THIS AGREEMENT.

1. **License to Use.** Sun grants you a non-exclusive and non-transferable license for the internal use only of the accompanying software and documentation and any error corrections provided by Sun (collectively "Software"), by the number of users and the class of computer hardware for which the corresponding fee has been paid.

2. **Restrictions** Software is confidential and copyrighted. Title to Software and all associated intellectual property rights is retained by Sun and/or its licensors. Except as specifically authorized in any Supplemental License Terms, you may not make copies of Software, other than a single copy of Software for archival purposes. Unless enforcement is prohibited by applicable law, you may not modify, decompile, or reverse engineer Software. You acknowledge that Software is not designed, licensed or intended for use in the design, construction, operation or maintenance of any nuclear facility. Sun disclaims any express or implied warranty of fitness for such uses. No right, title or interest in or to any trademark, service mark, logo or trade name of Sun or its licensors is granted under this Agreement.

3. **Limited Warranty.** Sun warrants to you that for a period of ninety (90) days from the date of purchase, as evidenced by a copy of the receipt, the media on which Software is furnished (if any) will be free of defects in materials and workmanship under normal use. Except for the foregoing, Software is provided "AS IS". Your exclusive remedy and Sun's entire liability under this limited warranty will be at Sun's option to replace Software media or refund the fee paid for Software.

4. **Disclaimer of Warranty.** UNLESS SPECIFIED IN THIS AGREEMENT, ALL EXPRESS OR IMPLIED CONDITIONS, REPRESENTATIONS AND WARRANTIES, INCLUDING ANY IMPLIED WARRANTY OF MERCHANTABILITY, FITNESS FOR A PARTICULAR PURPOSE OR NON-INFRINGEMENT ARE DISCLAIMED, EXCEPT TO THE EXTENT THAT THESE DISCLAIMERS ARE HELD TO BE LEGALLY INVALID.

5. **Limitation of Liability.** TO THE EXTENT NOT PROHIBITED BY LAW, IN NO EVENT WILL SUN OR ITS LICENSORS BE LIABLE FOR ANY LOST REVENUE, PROFIT OR DATA, OR FOR SPECIAL, INDIRECT, CONSEQUENTIAL, INCIDENTAL OR PUNITIVE DAMAGES, HOWEVER CAUSED REGARDLESS OF THE THEORY OF LIABILITY, ARISING OUT OF OR RELATED TO THE USE OF OR INABILITY TO USE SOFTWARE, EVEN IF SUN HAS BEEN ADVISED OF THE POSSIBILITY OF SUCH DAMAGES. In no event will Sun's liability to you, whether in contract, tort (including negligence), or otherwise, exceed the amount paid by you for Software under this Agreement. The foregoing limitations will apply even if the above stated warranty fails of its essential purpose.

6. **Termination.** This Agreement is effective until terminated. You may terminate this Agreement at any time by destroying all copies of Software. This Agreement will terminate

immediately without notice from Sun if you fail to comply with any provision of this Agreement. Upon Termination, you must destroy all copies of Software.

7. **Export Regulations.** All Software and technical data delivered under this Agreement are subject to US export control laws and may be subject to export or import regulations in other countries. You agree to comply strictly with all such laws and regulations and acknowledge that you have the responsibility to obtain such licenses to export, re-export, or import as may be required after delivery to you.

8. **U.S. Government Restricted Rights.** If Software is being acquired by or on behalf of the U.S. Government or by a U.S. Government prime contractor or subcontractor (at any tier), then the Government's rights in Software and accompanying documentation will be only as set forth in this Agreement; this is in accordance with 48 CFR 227.7201 through 227.7202-4 (for Department of Defense (DOD) acquisitions) and with 48 CFR 2.101 and 12.212 (for non-DOD acquisitions).

9. **Governing Law.** Any action related to this Agreement will be governed by California law and controlling U.S. federal law. No choice

10. **Severability.** If any provision of this Agreement is held to be unenforceable, this Agreement will remain in effect with the provision omitted, unless omission would frustrate the intent of the parties, in which case this Agreement will immediately terminate.

11. **Integration.** This Agreement is the entire agreement between you and Sun relating to its subject matter. It supersedes all prior or contemporaneous oral or written communications, proposals, representations and warranties and prevails over any conflicting or additional terms of any quote, order, acknowledgment, or other communication between the parties relating to its subject matter during the term of this Agreement. No modification of this Agreement will be binding, unless in writing and signed by an authorized representative of each party.

For inquiries please contact: Sun Microsystems, Inc. 901 San Antonio Road, Palo Alto, California 94303

JAVA™ 2 SOFTWARE DEVELOPMENT KIT STANDARD EDITION VERSION 1.3 SUPPLEMENTAL LICENSE TERMS

These supplemental license terms ("Supplemental Terms") add to or modify the terms of the Binary Code License Agreement (collectively, the "Agreement"). Capitalized terms not defined in these Supplemental Terms shall have the same meanings ascribed to them in the Agreement. These Supplemental Terms shall supersede any inconsistent or conflicting terms in the Agreement, or in any license contained within the Software.

1. **Internal Use and Development License Grant.** Subject to the terms and conditions of this Agreement, including, but not limited to, Section 2 (Redistributables) and Section 4 (Java Technology Restrictions) of these Supplemental Terms, Sun grants you a non-exclusive, non-transferable, limited license to reproduce the Software for internal use only for the sole purpose of development of your Java™ applet and application ("Program"), provided that you do not redistribute the Software in whole or in part, either separately or included with any Program.

2. **Redistributables.** In addition to the license granted in Paragraph 1 above, Sun grants you a non-exclusive, non-transferable, limited license to reproduce and distribute, only as part of your separate copy of JAVA(TM) 2 RUNTIME ENVIRONMENT STANDARD EDITION VERSION 1.3 software, those files specifically identified as redistributable in the JAVA(TM) 2 RUNTIME ENVIRONMENT STANDARD EDITION VERSION 1.3 "README" file (the "Redistributables") provided that: (a) you distribute the Redistributables complete and

unmodified (unless otherwise specified in the applicable README file), and only bundled as part of the Java^{TM} applets and applications that you develop (the "Programs"); (b) you do not distribute additional software intended to supersede any component(s) of the Redistributables; (c) you do not remove or alter any proprietary legends or notices contained in or on the Redistributables; (d) you only distribute the Redistributables pursuant to a license agreement that protects Sun's interests consistent with the terms contained in the Agreement, and (e) you agree to defend and indemnify Sun and its licensors from and against any damages, costs, liabilities, settlement amounts and/or expenses (including attorneys' fees) incurred in connection with any claim, lawsuit or action by any third party that arises or results from the use or distribution of any and all Programs and/or Software.

3.   **Separate Distribution License Required.** You understand and agree that you must first obtain a separate license from Sun prior to reproducing or modifying any portion of the Software other than as provided with respect to Redistributables in Paragraph 2 above.

4.   **Java Technology Restrictions.** You may not modify the Java Platform Interface ("JPI", identified as classes contained within the "java" package or any subpackages of the "java" package), by creating additional classes within the JPI or otherwise causing the addition to or modification of the classes in the JPI. In the event that you create an additional class and associated API(s) which (i) extends the functionality of a Java environment, and (ii) is exposed to third party software developers for the purpose of developing additional software which invokes such additional API, you must promptly publish broadly an accurate specification for such API for free use by all developers. You may not create, or authorize your licensees to create additional classes, interfaces, or subpackages that are in any way identified as "java", "javax", "sun" or similar convention as specified by Sun in any class file naming convention. Refer to the appropriate version of the Java Runtime Environment binary code license (currently located at http://www.java.sun.com/jdk/index.html) for the availability of runtime code which may be distributed with Java applets and applications.

5.   **Trademarks and Logos.** You acknowledge and agree as between you and Sun that Sun owns the Java trademark and all Java-related trademarks, service marks, logos and other brand designations including the Coffee Cup logo and Duke logo ("Java Marks"), and you agree to comply with the Sun Trademark and Logo Usage Requirements currently located at http://www.sun.com/policies/trademarks. Any use you make of the Java Marks inures to Sun's benefit.

6.   **Source Code.** Software may contain source code that is provided solely for reference purposes pursuant to the terms of this Agreement.

7.   **Termination.** Sun may terminate this Agreement immediately should any Software become, or in Sun's opinion be likely to become, the subject of a claim of infringement of a patent, trade secret, copyright or other intellectual property right.

JAVA(TM) DEVELOPMENT TOOLS
FORTE(TM) FOR JAVA(TM), COMMUNITY EDITION, VERSION 1.0
SUPPLEMENTAL LICENSE TERMS

These supplemental license terms ("Supplement") add to or modify the terms of the Binary Code License Agreement (collectively, the "Agreement"). Capitalized terms not defined in this Supplement shall have the same meanings ascribed to them in the Agreement. These Supplemental terms shall supersede any inconsistent or conflicting terms in the Agreement, or in any license contained within the Software.

1.   **Internal Use and Development License Grant.** Subject to the terms and conditions of this Agreement, including but not limited to Section 3 (Java Technology Restrictions) of this Supplement, Sun grants you a non-exclusive, non-transferable, limited license to reproduce internally and use internally the binary form of the Software for the sole purpose of designing, developing and testing your Java(TM) applets and applications intended to run on a compatible Java environment (the "Programs").

2.   **License to Distribute.** Subject to the terms and conditions of this Agreement, including but not limited to Section 3 (Java Technology Restrictions) of this Supplement, Sun grants you a non-exclusive, non-transferable, limited license to reproduce and distribute the binary form of the Software, to third party end users, either separately or bundled with Programs provided that you: (i) distribute the Software complete and unmodified; (ii) do not distribute additional software intended to supersede any component(s) of the Software; (iii) do not remove or alter any proprietary legends or notices contained in or on the Software; and (iv) only distribute the Software pursuant to a license agreement that protects Sun's interests consistent with the terms contained in this Agreement, and (v) agree to defend and indemnify Sun and its licensors from and against any damages, costs, liabilities, settlement amounts and/or expenses (including attorneys' fees) incurred in connection with any claim, lawsuit or action by any third party that arises or results from the use or distribution of any and all Programs and/or Software.

3.   **Java Technology Restrictions.** (i) You may not modify the Java Platform Interface ("JPI", identified as classes contained within the "java" package or any subpackages of the "java" package), by creating additional classes within the JPI or otherwise causing the addition to or modification of the classes in the JPI. (ii) In the event that you create an additional class and associated API(s) which (a) extends the functionality of a Java Platform; and, (b) is exposed to third party software developers for the purpose of developing additional software which invokes such additional API, you must promptly publish broadly an accurate specification for such API for free use by all developers. (iii) You may not create, or authorize your licensees to create additional classes, interfaces, or subpackages that are in any way identified as "java", "Javax" or "sun" or similar as specified by Sun in any class file naming convention designation. Refer to the Java Runtime Environment Version 1.3 binary code license (http://java.sun.com/products/jdk/1.3/jre/index.html) for the availability of runtime code that may be distributed with Java applets and applications.

5.   **Trademarks and Logos.** You acknowledge and agree as between you and Sun that Sun owns the Java trademark and all Java-related trademarks, service marks, logos and other brand designations including the Coffee Cup logo and Duke logo ("Java Marks"), and you agree to comply with the Sun Trademark and Logo Usage Requirements currently located at http://www.sun.com/policies/trademarks. Any use you make of the Java Marks inures to Sun's benefit.

6.   **Source Code.** Software may contain source code that is provided solely for reference purposes pursuant to the terms of this Agreement. Source code may not be redistributed.

(continued from page 806)

- Copy the `corejava.zip` file to that directory.
- Change to that directory.
- Execute the command

  `jar xvf corejava.zip`

Updates and Bug Fixes

The CD-ROM contains well over a hundred sample programs, and some of them are bound to have minor glitches and inconsistencies. We keep a list of frequently asked questions, a list of typographical errors, and bug fixes on the Core Java Web page at `http://www.horstmann.com/corejava.html`. We very much welcome any reports of typographical errors, example program bugs, and suggestions for improvement.

Before contacting us, please consider the following:

1. Please check the FAQ and list of bug reports on the *Core Java* Web page before mailing us. We get many duplicate queries and bug reports.

2. Please, no requests for handholding. Many readers have successfully compiled and executed the programs on the CD-ROM. If you have problems, there is an overwhelming likelihood that the problem is on your end, not because of a flaw with the CD-ROM contents. On the other hand, if we goofed and there is a serious problem with the CD-ROM, then there is an overwhelming chance that hundreds of readers complained to us already and that you will find a resolution on the FAQ.

3. We want to support and improve the *Core Java* book and example files, but we cannot help you with problems with your development environment or the free programs on the CD-ROM. Please contact the product vendor for assistance in those cases.

4. Finally, when contacting us, please use e-mail only. Please don't be disappointed if we don't answer every query or if we don't get back to you immediately. We do read all e-mail and consider your input to make future editions of this book clearer and more informative.

Technical Support

Prentice Hall does not offer technical support for the software on this CD-ROM. However, if there is a problem with the media, you may obtain a replacement copy by e-mailing us with your problem at: `disc_exchange@prenhall.com`.

About the CD-ROM

Use of this software is subject to the Sun Microsystems, Inc. Binary Code License Agreement contained on page 801. Read this agreement carefully. By opening this package, you are agreeing to be bound by the terms and conditions of this agreement.

Contents of the CD-ROM

The `corejava` directory contains the example files for this volume of *Core Java*. The `forte` directory contains Forte for Java Community Edition (an open source integrated development environment) for Windows and Solaris. The `htmlconverter` directory contains the Java Plug-in Software HTML Converter for Windows and Solaris. The `jdk` directory contains the Java™2 SDK Standard Edition, v. 1.3, for Windows and Solaris. The `textpad` directory contains an evaluation version of the TextPad 4.4 for Windows text editor. The `winzip` directory contains an evaluation version of the WinZip 8.0 for Windows archive utility.

NOTE: If you do not have a CD-ROM drive, you can download the materials from the Internet. Look for them at the following URLs:

Core Java files	www.phptr.com/corejava
Java 2 SDK	java.sun.com/j2se/1.3/
Forte for Java	www.sun.com/forte/ffj/ce/
HTML Converter	java.sun.com/products/plugin
TextPad	www.textpad.com
Winzip	www.winzip.com

TIP: Sun Microsystems frequently releases updates to the Java 2 SDK. You should check the Java web site `http://java.sun.com/j2se/` to see whether a newer version is available. In that case, we recommend that you download and install the SDK from the Web instead of the CD.

Installing the Core Java Example Files

The CD-ROM contains the source code for all example programs in the book. All files are packed inside a single ZIP archive, `corejava.zip`.

If you have a ZIP utility such as WinZip (which is supplied on the CD-ROM), you can use it to unzip the files. Otherwise, you need to first install the Java 2 SDK. Then use the `jar` program to unzip the file:

* Make sure the SDK is installed.
* Make a directory `CoreJavaBook`.

(continued on previous page)